D1616828

PRINCIPLES & METHODS OF
STATISTICAL ANALYSIS

Sara Miller McCune founded SAGE Publishing in 1965 to support the dissemination of usable knowledge and educate a global community. SAGE publishes more than 1000 journals and over 800 new books each year, spanning a wide range of subject areas. Our growing selection of library products includes archives, data, case studies and video. SAGE remains majority owned by our founder and after her lifetime will become owned by a charitable trust that secures the company's continued independence.

Los Angeles | London | New Delhi | Singapore | Washington DC | Melbourne

PRINCIPLES & METHODS OF
STATISTICAL ANALYSIS

Jerome Frieman
Donald A. Saucier
Stuart S. Miller

Kansas State University

Los Angeles | London | New Delhi
Singapore | Washington DC | Melbourne

FOR INFORMATION:

SAGE Publications, Inc.
2455 Teller Road
Thousand Oaks, California 91320
E-mail: order@sagepub.com

SAGE Publications Ltd.
1 Oliver's Yard
55 City Road
London EC1Y 1SP
United Kingdom

SAGE Publications India Pvt. Ltd.
B 1/I 1 Mohan Cooperative Industrial Area
Mathura Road, New Delhi 110 044
India

SAGE Publications Asia-Pacific Pte. Ltd.
3 Church Street
#10-04 Samsung Hub
Singapore 049483

Acquisitions Editor: Leah Fargotstein
Editorial Assistant: Yvonne McDuffee
Production Editor: Jane Haenel
Copy Editor: Paula L. Fleming
Typesetter: Hurix Systems Pvt. Ltd.
Proofreader: Jennifer Grubba
Indexer: Jeanne Busemeyer
Cover Designer: Anupama Krishnan
Marketing Manager: Susannah Goldes

Cover credit: Renoir, Auguste. *Bal du moulin de la Galette*. 1876. Oil on canvas. Private collection.

Printed in the United States of America

Library of Congress Cataloging-in-Publication Data

Names: Frieman, Jerome, author. | Saucier, Donald A., author.

Title: Principles & methods of statistical analysis / Jerome Frieman, Donald A. Saucier, Stuart Miller, Kansas State University.

Other titles: Principles and methods of statistical analysis

Description: First Edition. | Thousand Oaks : SAGE Publications, [2017] | Includes bibliographical references and index.

Identifiers: LCCN 2016048460 | ISBN 9781483358598 (hardcover : alk. paper)

Subjects: LCSH: Statistics—Methodology.

Classification: LCC HA29 .F76812 2017 | DDC 001.4/22—dc23

LC record available at https://lccn.loc.gov/2016048460

This book is printed on acid-free paper.

17 18 19 20 21 10 9 8 7 6 5 4 3 2 1

BRIEF CONTENTS

DETAILED CONTENTS

PART II • THE BEHAVIOR OF DATA

PART III • THE BASICS OF STATISTICAL INFERENCE: DRAWING CONCLUSIONS FROM OUR DATA   91

PART IV • SPECIFIC TECHNIQUES TO ANSWER SPECIFIC QUESTIONS

PREFACE

With the availability of computer programs that can be accessed from our desks, the teaching of quantitative methods is moving toward teaching our students how to use those programs and away from teaching them the foundations of those methods we use in psychology. One result of this trend is that students have less understanding of the statistical theory that underlies the procedures they use on a regular basis. They are thus more tied to the programs they are familiar with and may have difficulty understanding the great advances in statistical theory and methods that have occurred in the past 50 or so years, especially those that address the problems that occur when our data do not meet the assumptions of the classical statistical model. As a result, many of our students are not prepared to deal with these situations or to read articles and books that explore new techniques to address them.

Our intention in this book is twofold: One is to provide our students with the necessary background in statistical theory so that they can understand the basic logic behind the statistical methods they use and use those methods properly. They will also have the knowledge necessary to read and understand the more advanced presentations of statistical methods and results that appear in journals such as *Psychological Methods, Sociological Methods & Research,* and *Journal of Educational and Behavioral Statistics.*

The other is to introduce students (and in many cases their instructors) to a number of relatively new techniques for data analysis that are not widely known. Although these techniques are quite useful for data analysis in the behavioral and social sciences, most of them are not included in the current textbooks on the market at the introductory and intermediate level.

WHAT MAKES THIS BOOK DIFFERENT

This book is intended for advanced undergraduate students and first-year graduate students in the behavioral sciences who are taking a one-semester course in quantitative methods or statistics. These students have already completed a course in basic statistics and possess some knowledge of the standard basic statistical methods (e.g., means, variances, *z*-scores, normal distributions, correlation, Student's *t*-test, and perhaps one-way analysis of variance). However, they have not been taught the statistical principles that underlie the proper use of these methods and do not know what to do when confronted with data that do not meet the assumptions of the classical statistical model. To provide such information, we give extended treatment to the following issues:

- The importance of engaging in exploratory data analysis before conducting inferential statistical analyses
- The foundations upon which statistical methods are based
- Estimation of parameters and how to deal with "messy data" when both estimating parameters and conducting hypothesis tests
- The appropriateness of various statistical models for our research problems
- Correct and incorrect inferences from data to hypotheses
- The relationship between hypothesis tests on means and correlations between the independent and dependent variables in experiments to estimate treatment effects

We present statistical topics in the context of research on specific antisocial behaviors—cyberbullying, stereotyping, prejudice, and discrimination—using real data from ongoing research programs on these behaviors. We introduce the statistical topics in the context of those research programs.

PRESENTATION STYLE

Our presentation style is primarily narrative. Given that the focus of the book is directed toward an intuitive understanding of the principles of statistical theory as they apply to research in psychology and other social sciences, we present mathematical proofs and derivations, where appropriate, in boxes. We include these derivations and proofs to convince the skeptical reader of the validity of the conclusions.

To avoid getting sidetracked, however, we have omitted derivations and proofs that require unusual solutions or more advanced techniques. When we use algebra, we clearly label each step. Since most of the derivations and proofs that a typical student is likely to encounter can be constructed from a small set of operations and strategies, the derivations and proofs in this book are designed to help students identify these strategies. We include an appendix that details the rules of algebra most commonly encountered in statistical work. However, because the derivations and proofs are supplemental to the text, they can be omitted by the reader who wishes to learn the conclusion but not how that conclusion was reached mathematically.

Likewise, we present methods, rules, and examples for computing the values of the statistics and tests and constructing graphical presentations in boxes. We provide data sets for these examples on the website for this book.

OUTSTANDING FEATURES

Another major distinction between this textbook and others currently on the market is our inclusion of the following topics, many of which do not appear in the current books intended for this audience:

Methods for exploratory data analysis:
- Methods for identifying outliers
- Quantile plots
- Quantile–quantile plots
- Normal quantile plots
- Analysis of residuals in scatterplots

Methods for estimating parameters
- Bootstrap methods
- Robust estimators (L-estimators, M-estimators, MAD)
- Robust regression

Models and methods for hypothesis testing:
- Randomization (resampling, permutation) models and randomization (permutation) tests for experiments and correlation

A second distinctive feature is our use of research on cyberbullying, stereotyping, prejudice, and discrimination as examples in the book. We believe that research on these topics can provide examples of the research questions under discussion. Focusing on these research areas provides further integration among the various chapters and topics.

A third distinctive feature of this book is our extended presentations of a number of important traditional concepts in statistics that students will continue to encounter when they read more advanced papers and books on statistical methods and procedures. These include the following:

Expected value operators

Likelihood functions

Maximum likelihood estimation

Least squares estimation

Our intent is to provide students with a basic understanding of these concepts so that they will recognize and be comfortable with them when they encounter them in the future.

ORGANIZATION OF THE BOOK

We arranged the 15 chapters of the proposed book into four parts or sections. In addition, there are a prologue, an epilogue, and a set of appendices.

Part I (Getting Started) sets the stage by focusing on an example experiment designed to assess how individuals react to being cyberbullied. We use this example to introduce the classical statistical model and how this model is used when we do not obtain our participants through random sampling. We address the statistical issues raised in Chapter 1 later in the book where appropriate. The second chapter in this section introduces a number of exploratory data analysis techniques.

Part II (The Behavior of Data) consists of a single chapter that provides the theoretical foundation for the remainder of the book. Students who master these principles understand a lot about why we do what we do when using statistical methods to analyze data.

Part III (The Basics of Statistical Inference: Drawing Conclusions From Our Data) focuses in its three chapters on the basic principles of estimating parameters, robust estimators, and the general principles of hypothesis testing with the classical statistical model. The presentation builds on the foundation laid in Part II and provides the basic principles used in Part IV.

Part IV (Specific Techniques to Answer Specific Questions) presents in nine chapters the application of the principles in Parts II and III to a variety of situations, including Student's *t*-test, binomial distribution tests, randomization/permutation tests for experiments and correlation, correlation and regression (including nonlinear regression), estimating effect sizes, chi square tests for goodness of fit and contingency tables, analysis of variance, and the general linear model approach to analyzing data from experiments.

In our short epilogue, we provide closure by going back to the questions raised in Chapter 1 and reviewing how the various statistical techniques described in this book help us reach conclusions about the effects of cyberbullying, stereotyping, prejudice, and discrimination.

The appendixes include the following information:

Rules of algebra

Rules for the summation operator

Statistical tables

LEVEL

This book is conceived as an intermediate-level text. The adjective *intermediate* is used because it is anticipated that the primary intended audience has completed an introductory course in statistics. The only assumption made about the intended audience is that they have some knowledge of college algebra (a prerequisite for most introductory statistics courses). However, the level of mathematical sophistication required is no higher than high school algebra and some knowledge of the rules of the summation operator, for example, $\sum(X + Y) = \sum X + \sum Y$. We include appendices to bring all students to that level of mastery. It has been our experience that after completing an introductory statistics course, most students know how to compute some of the commonly used statistics and how to use some of the commonly used hypothesis tests. But these students often have little understanding of the underlying principles of these methods and how to use them to analyze data. Our overall intent is to provide them with this knowledge so that they become more effective and productive in their research programs.

Most, if not all, graduate programs in psychology, sociology, political science, and education require their students to take a quantitative course taught in their own department. These courses are typically called quantitative methods, research methods, statistical methods, intermediate statistics, or psychological or sociological statistics. Since most graduate programs require their students to have had basic statistics as undergraduates, these courses are typically taught at the intermediate level, that is, requiring more than an introductory text but one that is not as rigorous as the texts used in a statistics department. This book should appeal more to instructors in psychology and education because the second part of the book so heavily emphasizes experimental rather than field research.

DIGITAL RESOURCES

study.sagepub.com/friemanstats

Calling all instructors!

It's easy to log on to SAGE's password-protected Instructor Teaching Site for complete and protected access to all text-specific Instructor Resources. Simply provide your institutional information for verification and within 72 hours you'll be able to use your login information for any SAGE title!

Password-protected **Instructor Resources** include the following:

- A **Microsoft® Word test bank** is available containing multiple choice, true/false, short answer, and essay questions for each chapter. The test bank provides you with a diverse range of pre-written options as well as the opportunity for editing any question and/or inserting your own personalized questions to effectively assess students' progress and understanding.

- Editable, chapter-specific Microsoft® **PowerPoint® slides** offer you complete flexibility in easily creating a multimedia presentation for your course. Highlight essential content and features.
- **Discussion questions** help launch classroom interaction by prompting students to engage with the material and by reinforcing important content.
- Lively and stimulating **class activities** can be used in class to reinforce active learning. The activities apply to individual or group projects.
- EXCLUSIVE! Access to certain full-text **SAGE journal articles** that have been carefully selected for each chapter. Each article supports and expands on the concepts presented in the chapter. This feature also provides questions to focus and guide student interpretation. Combine cutting-edge academic journal scholarship with the topics in your course for a robust classroom experience.
- **Web resources** include links to multimedia that appeal to students with different learning styles.

Use the Student Study Site to get the most out of your course!

Our **Student Study Site** is completely open-access and offers a wide range of additional features.

The open-access **Student Study Site** includes the following:

- Mobile-friendly **web quizzes** allow for independent assessment of progress made in learning course material.
- EXCLUSIVE! Access to certain full-text **SAGE journal articles** that have been carefully selected for each chapter. Each article supports and expands on the concepts presented in the chapter. This feature also provides questions to focus and guide student interpretation. Combine cutting-edge academic journal scholarship with the topics in your course for a robust classroom experience.
- **Web resources** include links to multimedia that appeal to students with different learning styles.

ACKNOWLEDGMENTS

We would like to thank Vicki Knight for her encouragement, advice, and guidance in the early stages of this project. After Vicki retired, Leah Fargotstein took over as editor for our book and, along with Reid Hester, helped, guided, and encouraged us to improve our manuscript. We are indebted to other SAGE personnel, including Paula Fleming, Jane Haenel, Yvonne McDuffey, and Jessica Miller, who helped bring this book to completion.

We would also like to thank the following reviewers who, from the beginning of the project, provided invaluable input about the content of the book:

Robert J. Eger III, *Naval Postgraduate School*

Thomas W. Hancock, *University of Central Oklahoma*

Patrick R. Harrison, *University of North Carolina at Chapel Hill*

Julie Hicks Patrick, *West Virginia University*

George S. Robinson Jr., *North Carolina A&T State University*

Amy Lynne Shelton, *The Johns Hopkins University*

Zhigang Wang, *Carleton University*

Keith F. Widaman, *University of California at Riverside*

John L. Woodard, *Wayne State University*

We would also like to thank our friend and colleague Chris Barlett. Not only did he graciously provide fascinating data for us to use as examples throughout the book, but he also provided keen insight into what the book could be.

Finally, we each wish to thank our students. We would like to thank both the graduate students in our classes who, over the years, have helped refine the material and its presentation and the graduate and undergraduate student research collaborators with whom we have used the procedures in our studies. Your energy, hard work, and curiosity made us better teachers, and for that we will always be grateful.

ABOUT THE AUTHORS

Jerome Frieman earned his bachelor of arts and master of science degrees from Western Reserve University and his doctoral degree from Kent State University in Ohio. He has been in the Department of Psychological Sciences at Kansas State University since 1968. Over the course of his career, he has engaged in research on operant conditioning in pigeons, rats, and dwarf hamsters; Pavlovian conditioning in rats; social learning in dwarf hamsters; and extraordinary memory in a human participant. He has also taught quantitative methods and experimental design at the graduate level. He is the author of *Learning and Adaptive Behavior* and coauthor of *Memory Search by a Memorist* and *Learning: A Behavioral, Cognitive, and Evolutionary Synthesis* (SAGE, 2016). He is a member of the American Statistical Association and the Psychonomic Society and is a charter member of the Association for Psychological Science.

Donald A. Saucier earned his bachelor's degree in psychology and classical civilization from Colby College in Waterville, Maine, and his master's and doctoral degrees in experimental social psychology from the University of Vermont. He has been in the Department of Psychological Sciences at Kansas State University since 2004. His research interests center on expressions of antisocial and prosocial behavior, with specific emphasis on the individual differences and situational factors that contribute to the justification and suppression of antisocial behavior (e.g., prejudice, aggression) and to decisions to behave prosocially (e.g., to give or withhold help). He is a Fellow of the Society for the Psychological Study of Social Issues (Division 9 of the American Psychological Association) and of the Society for Experimental Social Psychology. His teaching philosophy focuses on maximizing the levels of both teacher and student engagement in the classroom, and he has taught a broad range of classes, from large sections of general psychology to small classes in advanced psychological research methods, at both the undergraduate and graduate levels. Don is a University Distinguished Teaching Scholar. His numerous awards and honors include the Putting Students First Award for Outstanding Service to Students, the University Distinguished Faculty Award for Mentoring of Undergraduate Students in Research, the William L. Stamey Excellence in Undergraduate Teaching Award from the College of Arts & Sciences, the Commerce Bank Outstanding

Undergraduate Teaching Award, the Dr. Ron and Rae Iman Outstanding Faculty Award for Teaching, and the Presidential Award for Excellence in Undergraduate Teaching.

Stuart S. Miller earned a bachelor of science in psychology from the University of Iowa and a master of science from Kansas State University. He plans to complete his doctoral degree in psychology at Kansas State University in 2017. Stuart's research focuses on how individual differences and situational factors are related to perceptions of prejudice and how cognitive mechanisms for moral thought and behavior are involved in the justification and suppression of prejudice. Stuart has taught research methods courses at the graduate level, as well as social and general psychology at the undergraduate level. He has several years of experience in mentoring his graduate and undergraduate colleagues in research, particularly in data analysis techniques and research design.

PROLOGUE

In the aftermath of atrocities, individuals have a desire, even a need, to understand why such atrocities occurred. From events impacting the world (e.g., the Nazi persecution of the Jews, the 9/11 terrorist attacks on the United States, and cyberterrorism) to more localized, and often less severe, antisocial behaviors (e.g., a physical altercation between two teenagers, suicide as a function of cyberbullying, and blatant acts of discrimination), people often want to know the causal agents behind these actions. Questions such as "Who are cyberbullies?" "What variables predict when an employer will discriminate against a minority job candidate?" and "Under what situations are people more aggressive?" are commonplace. The answers to these questions have important implications for all of us, whether we are psychologists, sociologists, parents, students, and/or legislators. The focus of this book will be on how we collect and analyze relevant data that will provide us with information to answer specific research questions akin to those posed above. We try to answer our research questions by constructing hypotheses that reflect possible answers to our questions, collecting data, examining our data, choosing a model that we think represents our data, testing our hypotheses, and drawing conclusions. We are likely to be successful when we are critically reflective, analytical, and prudent in selecting good tools to analyze our data. Our tools include well-conceived research designs and appropriate methods of data analysis.

We also ask increasingly focused and progressive research questions along the way to seek out and gather relevant data. Our subsequent research questions do not occur in a vacuum; rather they are generated against a background of observations, prior research, and theoretical analyses. That is certainly the situation for determining the myriad predictors of antisocial behavior. Therefore, a good place to start is to review the context in which research on antisocial behavior (broadly defined) occurs.

Defining antisocial behavior is complex. However, for the purposes of this book, we echo the thoughts of Simcha-Fagen, Langner, Gersten, and Eisenberg (1975; see Mayer, 1995) who defined *antisocial behavior* as "recurrent violations of socially prescribed patterns of behavior" (p. 7). By adopting this definition, we can begin to understand that antisocial behaviors can manifest themselves in various ways, including aggression, breaking the law, bullying, committing vandalism, engaging in discrimination, and

Figure P.1 ■ Incidents of violent behaviors in American schools.

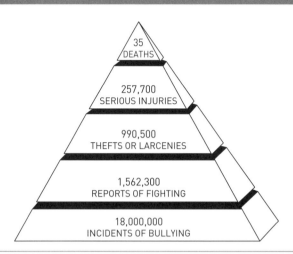

Source: Republished with permission of ABC-CLIO Inc., from D. A. Gentile & A. Sesma, Developmental approaches to understanding media effects on individuals. In *Media Violence and Children* (pp. 19–37). Westport, CT: Praeger Publishers. 2003; permission conveyed through Copyright Clearance Center Inc.

violating social norms. Some antisocial behaviors are more frequent than others. For example, Gentile and Sesma (2003) described an aggression frequency pyramid for incidents of violent behaviors in American schools (see Figure P.1).

As antisocial behaviors become more physically harmful to the victim, these behaviors are often less frequent and are represented in higher positions on the pyramid. For instance, Gentile and Sesma (2003) reported that in 1998, for every 35 deaths that occurred in American schools, there were 257,700 serious injuries, 990,500 thefts or larcenies, 1,562,300 fights, and 18 million reported incidents of bullying. There are several conclusions that can be drawn from these data. First, antisocial behaviors occur at an alarmingly high rate. Second, a plethora of aggressive and antisocial acts occur that are less extreme than one student killing another. Third, this information was specific to youth in the United States. Indeed, antisocial behaviors, independent of how extreme they are, are found all over the world; however, making international comparisons is difficult due to different laws, policies, and definitions (see Anderson & Huesmann, 2003). It is important to remember that crime data from legitimate sources reflect only a small percentage of the actual number of antisocial behaviors that occur. Cyberbullying, rumor spreading, verbal aggression (e.g., yelling, name calling), and other antisocial behaviors are common but are often unreported or do not clearly fit into a country's (or state's) category for criminal law. Therefore, antisocial behaviors are more common than these data initially suggest.

The purpose of this book is not to discuss the nature, predictors, consequences, trends, or interventions of or regarding antisocial behavior. Other publications have addressed these issues (see Anderson & Bushman, 2002; Anderson & Huesmann, 2003; Aquino & Thau, 2009; Archer & Coyne, 2005; Bettencourt, Talley, Benjamin, & Valentine, 2006; Dodge, Coie, & Lynam, 2006; Mayer, 1995). Rather, we will use data from various research labs that have assessed antisocial behaviors to show how statistics can be used to answer important research questions. For instance, how do we know what we know? How do researchers who are interested in studying an antisocial behavior (or any other topic) engage in the research process, use research questions to develop hypotheses, collect and analyze data, and draw appropriate conclusions? Although all of these are important steps in the process, we will focus here on how to use relevant statistical methods to analyze our data based on the questions we ask. In these pages, we have elected to focus on three specific antisocial behaviors: cyberbullying, aggression, and prejudice/discrimination. Briefly, *cyberbullying* is defined as "any behavior performed through electronic or digital media by individuals or groups that repeatedly communicates hostile or aggressive messages intended to inflict harm or discomfort on others" (Tokunga, 2010, p. 278). *Aggressive behavior* is defined as behavior intended to harm someone who is motivated to avoid that harm (Anderson & Bushman, 2002). *Stereotyping*, *prejudice*, and *discrimination* are defined, respectively, as the different ways in which individuals think about, feel about, and treat people from other social groups (Whitley & Kite, 2010). Throughout this textbook, we will apply statistical methods to the examination of data collected to answer research questions related to these theoretically and practically important domains. In so doing, our intent is to demonstrate the great utility of these methods in conducting of research that both improves our understanding of and betters our world.

GETTING STARTED

PART I

THE BIG PICTURE

The research process is a fascinating method for increasing the understanding of our world. The research objectives we may pursue using the research process are virtually limitless. Those who understand and apply this process have the power to determine truths by collecting and evaluating empirical evidence. It is our purpose in this chapter to introduce you to this process at a foundational level.

Let us begin by considering a few questions fundamental to the research process. Why do we collect data in the first place? What research questions do we pursue? How do those research questions inspire us to identify variables to measure as we seek to find out more and more about our questions of interest? How do research questions grow into research programs?

We, as researchers, often identify our research questions by starting with one interesting variable. That variable may be "depression" or "aggression" or "self-esteem," but whatever it is, it is something that we decide we want to know more about. And what we want to know about the variable often relates to a few questions:

What affects this interesting variable?

What is related to this interesting variable?

What does this interesting variable affect?

The first question allows researchers to identify and test other variables as potential antecedents, precursors, or causes of the variable of interest. The second question allows researchers to identify and test potential correlates to the variable of interest. The third question allows researchers to identify and test variables as outcomes of the variable of interest. For each of these questions, researchers collect data and then assess the evidence for the existence of these relationships. As relationships emerge, the research questions often get more complicated, including additional variables as antecedents, correlates, and/or outcomes related to our variable of interest. The models representing, and the analyses consequently used to test, the various relationships become more sophisticated.

But the underlying approach remains the same. In each case, the researchers investigate the extent to which their variables carry information about each other.

Arguably, the objective of all research is to collect and explain information about interesting variables. What this task amounts to, practically, is accounting for variance in our variables. Variables, by definition, take on multiple values, and through our research, we try to determine why these values are not all the same. Researchers attempt to identify other variables that provide some explanation for why these values are not all the same, then test the degree to which the variables share variance. That is, researchers assess how much the variables show some systematic deviation in their values by evaluating the direction and magnitude of relationships among the variables, and researchers build predictive models to summarize these relationships.

This process relies on collecting data to answer these questions; therefore, let's consider the data collection methods of a study investigating the effects of cyberbullying. The question this study attempted to answer was *How do participants feel after being cybervictimized?* (note these are partial data from Barlett, 2015). Participants came into the lab individually and were told that they would be interacting with a "partner" on a group task. Participants were told that they would be completing simple puzzle tasks with their partner. Specifically, participants were instructed to complete a Sudoku puzzle as quickly as they could while their partner waited. Once finished, the partner had to complete the next Sudoku puzzle, and, if it was completed, the participants tried to complete the third, and so forth. All participants were told that they and their partner had a combined 10 minutes to complete as many puzzles as they could. They were also informed that the number of puzzles completed would equal the number of raffle tickets they would receive. Each raffle ticket was an entry to a drawing to win an expensive prize. In actuality, there was no partner. Participants completed these tasks in their own room, having been told that their partner was in the next room. Also, the Sudoku puzzle chosen was unsolvable, and all participants failed. Once the 10-minute time frame had elapsed, participants were allowed to chat online with their partner for a few minutes while the researcher "got the next part of the study ready." Participants were then randomly assigned to receive an insulting ("You Suck") or nice ("It's OK") message from their partner. Finally, participants completed a measure of state hostility. (The instrument measured hostility using 34 items on a 1 = *not at all* to 5 = *extremely* rating scale; scores could range from 34 to 170, with higher scores indicating more hostility.)

The first research question we can ask is whether there was a difference in hostility between those who received the insulting and those who received the nice online messages. We can attempt to answer that question by comparing the hostility scores from the insulted group and the nice group, and we will do that in upcoming chapters. Prior to doing so, though, a good rule of thumb is this: *Look at your data before you do anything else.* We will describe a number of useful techniques for exploring your data in Chapter 2. Statistical techniques aid us in the interpretation and evaluation of our data, and they help us draw conclusions, based on our data, about the variables we study. The purpose of this book is to examine statistical theory and its relationship to research, particularly in the behavioral and social sciences where the use of statistics plays an important role.

An important point to keep in mind throughout this book is that statistical analysis is not an automatic method for interpreting data and drawing conclusions about our research questions and hypotheses. A great deal of subjective evaluation goes into using statistics and interpreting the results of statistical analyses, and the unwary researcher can stumble and be misled in numerous ways.

For example, a statistical formula or test can be applied to any set of numbers regardless of their origin. You can employ a *t*-test statistic to analyze two sets of numbers, derive a value for *t*, and compare that value to the critical values in a *t*-distribution table. How that value should be interpreted depends on the source of the numbers. Your interpretation of the results of a *t*-test on data from two groups of individuals who are either independent samples from different populations or were randomly assigned to conditions should be very different from your interpretation of the results of the same *t*-test comparing the performance of a single participant across a number of repeated observations. In this latter case, the scores in each treatment condition are not independent of each other, and the use of a *t*-statistic here for other than descriptive purposes would be inappropriate. Therefore, it is important to know and understand the assumptions involved in the use of various statistics and how these assumptions affect our interpretations of our data. These assumptions arise from the statistical models we employ to represent the sources of our data. Therefore, we will begin with a discussion of models in general and in statistics.

MODELS

The statistical models we choose to represent our data determine how we analyze and interpret those data. The assumptions we make about our data are based on the models we choose.

A **model** is an *attempt to represent or summarize what we believe to be the true state of affairs.* Accordingly, a model is inspired by the questions we pursue and the interesting variables we measure as part of our application of the research process. Since a model is a *summary* of what we *believe* to be true, it is by definition not a perfect representation of what is being modeled. Nevertheless, models are more than mere guesses. In science and in statistics, they are interrelated sets of concepts that are used to describe data and make predictions, and they are based on systematic observations.

A simple example of a model is a road map that we use to represent the routes and landmarks (rivers, cities, connecting roads, and so forth) between various locations. The road map is useful because it presents the important information in a compact form with many details omitted. If the road map were a perfect representation of the geography of the route, it would be as big as the terrain it represents and too cumbersome to use. Like a road map, a model is an imperfect representation and thus will always be incorrect; however, it can be useful if it helps us to understand the phenomenon we are attempting to model and to communicate that understanding to others.

In science, we construct models to help us to understand and predict. These models can be relatively simple (for example, Newton's laws of motion and Fechner's law in perception) or complex (for example, Freud's psychoanalytic theory of behavior). In either case, because they are models, they are imperfect representations of nature, and while they may be consistent with a large number of observations, we can find situations that they do not represent accurately.

Sometimes there are competing models of the same phenomena (for example, Guthrie's, Hull's, Skinner's, and Tolman's models of learning). Each of these models contributes something to our understanding of learning, and consequently we use them at various times to make predictions or provide explanations while recognizing that each is inadequate as a universal model that accurately represents all data.

The fact that models are not exact representations of reality raises the question of why we bother to use them. There are a number of reasons. First, models help us to organize our data in a meaningful way because they are less complex than the phenomena being modeled. Second, they help us to interpret our data and to derive what appear to be general principles or rules. Finally, a well-specified model can be manipulated mathematically or logically to derive predictions or new ways of viewing our data. We choose among alternative models based on how well they perform with respect to each of the reasons given above. A model is of value when it adds to our understanding and leads to useful predictions, even if it is not completely accurate.

Just as there are models of physical objects and their interactions, and models of the behavior of animals and humans, there are models of numbers and data. In general, there are two classes of statistical models, descriptive models and inferential models.

Descriptive Models

Descriptive models *are used to represent and summarize our data.* Thus, when we say that intelligence test scores have a normal distribution, we are using the normal distribution model to represent those scores. An example of this model is presented in Figure 1.1, which presents the IQ test scores of 3,000 children, ages 2–18, who comprised the standardization group for the 1937 version of the Stanford-Binet.

Clearly, the scores in Figure 1.1 do not create a perfect normal distribution (nor would they even if the sample were larger). When we say that intelligence test scores

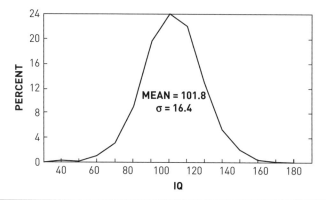

Figure 1.1 ■ The distribution of IQ test scores of the standardization group on the 1937 revision of the Stanford-Binet intelligence test.

Source: From Terman, L. M., & Merrill, M. A. (1973). *Stanford-Binet Intelligence Scale: Manual for the Third Revision, Form L-M.* Boston, MA: Houghton Mifflin.

have a normal distribution, we mean that these data approximate a normal distribution, and we can use the normal distribution model to describe the data. While these scores do not perfectly fit the normal distribution, the fit is good enough for us to use this model as a convenient shorthand way to describe the data and to use the normal distribution tables to calculate percentages of scores within various IQ test score ranges.

Descriptive statistics are as important as inferential statistics for the analysis of data, even if we are not interested in trying to fit a particular descriptive model (such as a normal distribution) to our data. Many researchers overlook the importance of examining their data prior to performing further analyses. Failing to look at how well the data fit the descriptive model that informs the assumptions underlying further analyses can result in misanalysis of our data. New and interesting techniques for describing sets of data, which are useful for the social and behavioral sciences, are not widely used by psychologists and other social scientists because they are not widely known; therefore, we will devote some attention to these techniques in Chapter 2.

Inferential Models

We use **inferential models** *to draw inferences from our data.* By making certain assumptions about the behavior of the researcher with respect to the collection of the data and about certain aspects of the data, these models provide methods for testing statistical hypotheses and drawing conclusions. Analysis of variance, *t*-tests, and other "parametric tests" are based on what we refer to here as the *classical statistical model.* Most of this book will be devoted to the classical statistical model and the implications of that model for data analysis.

A second inferential model, the *randomization model*, will be presented in some detail in Chapters 9, 10, and 14. That model makes different assumptions about the behavior of the experimenter and the data. Interestingly enough, although the assumptions of the randomization model are more realistic with respect to the way experimental research is conducted in psychology, statistical techniques based on this model have not been widely used in psychology for a number of reasons. As mentioned, the most important reason is that most psychologists are also not familiar with this approach—but more about that later.[1]

Given the widespread use of the classical statistical model, we will describe it in some detail now.

THE CLASSICAL STATISTICAL MODEL

The classical statistical model posits that our data are randomly sampled from populations that have certain parameters, some of which are unknown to us. Our task is to use the information in our random samples to estimate the values of the unknown parameters.

The inference model most widely used in social and behavioral science research is the classical statistical model. To use the classical statistical model, one has to make two assumptions, one about the data and one about the behavior of the experimenter.

Assumption about the data:

Populations with certain attributes (called parameters*) exist.*

The elements of these populations can be conceptualized in two ways. We tend to think of the elements of a population as individuals (people, rats, and so forth), and we assume that our study sample is composed of a subset of these individuals. However, in the behavioral sciences, the object of our inquiry is not the individual but the behavior of the individual on the measurement scale we choose to study (e.g., test score, number of correct responses, response rate, and so forth). Therefore, it is more appropriate to think of our study sample as being a subset of the scores or numbers generated by the individuals in our population of interest.

The **parameters** (attributes) of these populations *describe the populations*. These parameters typically include the population mean, population variance, and form or shape of the population (normal distribution, exponential distribution, and so forth).

---

[1] These are not the only two statistical classes of inferential statistical models. Another is the Bayesian model, which is not covered in this book.

Some of these parameters may be assumed to be known to us,[2] and some parameters are assumed to be unknown. The researcher's job is to infer the unknown parameters from the data, using the help of another assumption.

Assumption about the behavior of the experimenter:

Random samples are drawn from the population(s) under study.

In a **random sample**, *each element in the population has an equal chance of being sampled.* The fact that some elements are sampled more frequently than others occurs because more of these elements exist in the population. For example, in a normal distribution, there are more elements in the center of the distribution than at the tails; hence, random samples from normal distributions will tend to contain more elements from the center.

The **purpose of random sampling** is *to obtain a set of scores (a sample) that is representative of the population*, meaning that the sample represents the distribution of the scores in the population. Unless we take the entire population as our sample, we would not expect our sample to match the population exactly. Nevertheless, we hope that by using a random sampling procedure, our sample will adequately reflect the characteristics of the population. We must emphasize that while random sampling does not guarantee that our sample will be representative of our population, a random sample will usually contain enough information for us to make useful inferences about the characteristics of that population.

Despite the importance of the assumption of random sampling for using the classical statistical model, random sampling is a rare event in much of the research in the social and behavioral sciences. Nevertheless, use of the classical statistical model is based on the assumption that random sampling has occurred.

Sometimes, we add the additional assumption that we have *independent* random samples. The assumption that these samples are composed of independent events is of great importance for the correct use of this model in social science research. We have an **independent event** *when the occurrence of one event does not affect the probability of the occurrence of another event.* In terms of sampling, the selection of any element in a sample does not affect the selection of any other element; in other words, the selection of one element does not change the probability that another element might be selected.

Non-independence of events occurs in a number of situations: When sampling is done without replacement, sampling of one element of the population changes the probability that the others will be sampled. Players of card games such as draw poker and blackjack know that the appearance of a given card on the table affects the probability that they will draw another card of the same face value. For example, if no aces are showing (and assuming no aces are

---

[2]For example, Student's *t*-test statistic (see Chapter 7) and analysis of variance (see Chapter 14) are based on assumptions that our data are independent random samples drawn from normal distributions that have equal variances.

already face down on the table), your probability of getting an ace is 4 divided by the number of cards not showing, but if there are already 2 aces face up on the table (and again assuming no other aces are already face down on the table), the probability of drawing another ace is only 2 divided by the number of cards not showing. For the most part, the populations under study in the social and behavioral sciences are (or are assumed to be) so large that sampling without replacement is really not an issue. In the behavioral sciences, non-independent events occur, for example, when we measure the behavior of the same individual more than once. Clearly, there is a relationship between an individual's behavior at one point in time and his or her behavior at a later time. We will examine how to analyze data from non-independent observations later when we discuss the randomization model in Chapter 9.

Having introduced the classical statistical model, let's examine how statistical theory and practice impact how we analyze our data. We will use as an example the experiment we described earlier in this chapter on the effects of online message content on hostility.

DESIGNING EXPERIMENTS AND ANALYZING DATA

In this section, we will examine the steps a researcher would take to design and execute an experiment and analyze the data to try to answer the research question. The researcher must generate a set of experimental hypotheses that specify possible outcomes of the experiment as well as a set of statistical hypotheses to test.

The experiment described at the beginning of this chapter was designed to attempt to answer the following research question: Does being a victim of cyberbullying influence hostility levels? The research design used here is rather simple, and it is not the only possible design or even the most optimal design for this type of study; however, it does allow us to see the issues relevant to designing experiments and analyzing their data clearly.

The first step in any experiment is to decide *specifically* what you want to investigate— in other words, *specifically* what questions you want to ask and hopefully answer. Here the experimenter was interested in whether cybervictimization affects later state hostility. To study this variable, the experimenter had to devise a way to manipulate the participants' behavior through the messages they received and a way to measure the hostility that might result from that experience. Respectively, these components are the independent and dependent variables in this experiment; that is, **independent variables** *are the aspects of the situation the researcher manipulated*, and **dependent variables** *are the participant behaviors the researcher measured.* While these **operational definitions** (the specific ways in which variables are represented or measured in research studies) are properly matters of experimental design, one cannot ask a meaningful question about the effects of cybervictimization on participants' consequent hostility without also considering the context in which the independent variables are presented.

Because an experiment requires at least two levels of the independent variable (e.g., experimental vs. control condition), the experimenter had to select at least two types of electronic communication that were similar in terms of length and number of messages but were very different in terms of content. The idea behind the messages was simple: To possibly elicit hostility from the participant in an ecologically valid and ethical way, the participant had to be cyberbullied. Therefore, the experimenter went to great lengths to convince the participants that they were interacting with another partner they could not see, they were working together to solve the puzzles so that they could win a prize, there would be a raffle and prizes awarded for completing these puzzles, and their partner sent the message they received online.

The experimenter could have used a number of dependent measures to assess the effects of these messages. As described earlier, the experimenter assessed the effects of the "partner's" messages by measuring state levels of hostility after participants received their message from their "partner." Hostility was measured using the State Hostility Scale (SHS; Anderson, Deuser, & DeNeve, 1995), with higher scores being indicative of feeling more hostile. Accordingly, participants were asked to indicate how they felt at that moment by reporting their levels of agreement with several statements, such as *I feel furious*.

Experimental Hypotheses

Experimental hypotheses are possible answers to your research question. They should be mutually exclusive (only one can be true) and exhaustive (these are the only possibilities), and they are stated in terms of the independent and dependent variables in your experiment.

Having defined the task, the next step is to generate a set of **experimental hypotheses**: *Statements about what may or may not be the actual state of affairs in terms of the relationships between the variables you are examining.* Therefore, the experimental hypotheses are phrased in terms of the independent and dependent variables in the experiment and in such a way as to be **mutually exclusive** (they do not overlap such that *only one of them can be true*) and **exhaustive** (*they are the only possibilities*). There are two possibilities for the effects of cybervictimization (message content) on state hostility in this experiment:

1. Cybervictimization (message content) *does not* affect state hostility.

2. Cybervictimization (message content) *does* affect state hostility.

Note that these experimental hypotheses are mutually exclusive and exhaustive because *only one of them can be true* and *they are the only possibilities*. The researcher's task is to discover which of these statements is true. If the researcher knew which experimental hypothesis was true, there would be no reason to conduct the experiment, but because the researcher does not know which statement is true, he or she collects and analyzes data to decide which one is true. However, keep in mind that the number of messages and severity of the derogatory comments in the messages may influence the strength of the effect of cybervictimization on hostility. Thus, the design of the experiment and the operationalization of the variables may affect the outcome and the conclusions about which of the experimental hypotheses is true.

Experimental Design

While many of the details regarding how you conduct an experiment are not statistical issues, they can affect the interpretation of your data, especially if the experiment is not designed properly.

In the experimental design phase of the research process, the researcher decides how to conduct the study. How will the participants be obtained? How many will there be? How many conditions will there be in the experiment? How will the participants be treated in each condition? Exactly what will be measured? With the exception of the questions about how the participants are obtained and the number of participants, the rest of these questions do not involve statistical issues; they are matters of proper experimental procedure.

How we design an experiment that examines the effects of cybervictimization on hostility depends on what we wish to learn about these variables. Because we stated our experimental hypotheses in terms of whether or not cybervictimization has an effect on hostility, a two-group (experimental group and control group) design should be sufficient. In the case of the Barlett (2015) study, one group was designated the experimental group and received insulting messages. The other group was designated the control group and received nice messages. Both groups were treated the same in all other respects; the only difference in their treatment was *in terms of the variable under investigation* (i.e., the type of messages received). That is, participants in both the experimental and control groups received the same instructions, interacted with the same experimenters, used the same equipment, and so forth. If care is not taken to eliminate as many potentially confounding variables as possible from the experimental design, the researcher will not be able to determine whether any of the observed differences between the performance of the participants in these two groups are due to the treatments (such as types of messages) or to other factors (such as the participants' knowledge of the treatment they received or expectations about how they should respond). Again, these points are not statistical issues, but considerations regarding proper experimental design procedures that affect the internal validity of the study and, thus, can impact the interpretation of the study's results.

HOW WILL THE PARTICIPANTS BE OBTAINED? In most experimental research in psychology, participants are recruited as "volunteers" through a system whereby they are enticed to participate by offers of credit toward course requirements, money, or some other compensation for their services. Of course, there are procedures to remove coercion from this process by allowing for alternative methods of earning credit or money, by informing participants of the risks and possible benefits of their participation, and by allowing participants to withdraw at any time without loss of credit or money. Having volunteered, and if they are accepted into the experiment, participants are then assigned to the different conditions of the experiment.

As noted above, one of the assumptions of the classical statistical model is that our data are obtained by random sampling from populations. However, it is obvious that there is nothing remotely random about the manner in which participants are obtained for our experiments. Those who volunteer to be participants do so for various reasons (experimental credit, money, curiosity, and so forth) and are certainly not representative of college students or any other group from which volunteers are solicited. Here is the first instance of a deviation from the assumptions of the classical statistical model. However, this deviation may be somewhat addressed by studying psychological processes that are reasonably assumed to operate similarly in the larger population and by using random assignment to conditions.

RANDOM ASSIGNMENT TO CONDITIONS Random assignment to groups helps us to make up for the fact that we do not use random sampling in experimental research. **Random assignment** is *a procedure for assigning study participants to the various conditions of an experiment, regardless of how the participants are obtained.*

The purpose of the random assignment procedure is to attempt to remove any systematic effects that might produce the observed differences in performance between the groups. For example, we could use the participants' middle initials, flip a coin for each participant (when there are two groups, as in this example), or use a table of random numbers. In this way, the participants in each condition are not systematically different from each other prior to their participation in the study. That is, any differences between the participants in the various conditions prior to the study's manipulations would be random. If, following random assignment, both groups are treated the same—that is, given the same treatment and then tested—the sample statistics (e.g., means, variances, medians) for both groups would tend to be similar (but not necessarily identical), and any differences between the sample statistics for the two groups would presumably not be due to any systematic effects (such as assigning all females to one group, all participants with high IQs to one group, or all older participants to one group). Of course, it is possible for random assignment to produce such a "nonrandom" outcome, but such a possibility is rare; therefore, it should be noted that random assignment (and random sampling) refers to procedures and not to the results of those procedures. Thus, random assignment does not necessarily create groups that are equivalent on the variable of interest. Rather, random assignment attempts to create groups in which the differences on the variable of interest are random, and such randomness (or error) can then be accounted for by the statistical techniques we use to analyze our data.

By using random assignment and then applying different treatments to the two groups, we should feel confident that any large differences in the sample statistics are due to the treatments and not to other factors. Of course, it is possible for there to be another systematic factor operating (that is, a confound), but, as noted above, we can rightly assume such an occurrence is unlikely if we have been careful in how we treat the participants and in how we randomly assigned them to conditions. On the other hand, if we do not use random assignment and we apply different treatments to our two groups, then we will not know whether any large differences in performance are due to the treatments or to any other systematic difference between the groups.

EXPERIMENTAL TREATMENTS Following random assignment to groups, the next steps are the administration of the experimental treatments and the collection of data. The experimental group in our representative experiment received the "insulting" message and then was given the State Hostility Scale to complete.

To assess the effects of cybervictimization on hostility, the researcher needed also to measure the performance of a group that received the "nice" message; this group is the control group. The term *control* is used to indicate that all relevant variables other than the treatment under consideration were controlled; that is, with the exception of the experimental treatment, the two groups were treated identically. If the only difference between the two groups is the presence or absence of the experimental treatment, then the control group provides a baseline against which to compare the data obtained from the experimental group. Any large differences in behavior between these groups would then be attributed to the experimental treatment. For this reason, the control group is sometimes referred to as a *baseline condition or group* (because the results for the control group are what you would expect to observe in a default situation in which the experimental manipulation, in this case the "insulting" message, did not occur) or as a *comparison condition or group*.

Failure to adequately control for other systematic variables compromises the interpretation of the results of the experiment. As in the case of nonrandom assignment, the presence of other systematic differences between groups (such as differential instructions, testing at different times of the day or year, use of different experimenters, and so forth) produces a confounded design. Such a design makes it impossible to determine whether the treatment produced the differences between the groups or the systematic differences that accompanied but did not comprise the experimental manipulation produced the differences between the groups. These are matters of good experimental design procedures and not statistical issues (although nonrandom assignment is a statistical issue);

nevertheless, they should not be overlooked. Statistical methods cannot untangle a confounded design unless the confound is purposely part of the original design.

Data Analysis

Inspection of your data should influence which statistical model you select to analyze your data. If you select the classical statistical model, then your statistical hypotheses will be about the parameters of the populations from which your data were presumably sampled.

After the data are collected, the process shifts to one of analysis. *The first step in any data analysis is to inspect the data.* Inspection of the data is usually facilitated by calculating summary statistics of your data (such as the mean, standard deviation, and median), by organizing the data into tables, and by visually presenting the data using graphs and plots. Inspection of the data in these ways will inform decisions about which inferential statistics to use to analyze the data, and these tables, plots, and graphs may then be used to reinforce the conclusions we will draw from our inferential statistics. We will discuss this step in detail in Chapter 2.

Should it be necessary to employ inferential statistics to decide whether the differences we observe in our data are due to the experimental treatments or to chance, a set of statistical hypotheses have to be developed. These statistical hypotheses parallel our experimental hypotheses. If we decide to use the classical statistical model, *our **statistical hypotheses** will be about the parameters of the populations from which we presumably sampled.*

For our example experiment, there are two experimental hypotheses:

1. Message content (cybervictimization) does not affect hostility.
2. Message content (cybervictimization) does affect hostility.

The researcher's task is to attempt to determine from the data which of these hypotheses is true. As stated, the experimental hypotheses cannot both be true, yet one must be true (because they are both mutually exclusive and exhaustive). For this situation, a corresponding set of statistical hypotheses using the classical statistical model are as follows:

1. $\mu_{\text{insulting message}} = \mu_{\text{nice message}}$. The mean score on the state hostility measure of the population from which the participants who received the insulting message were sampled equals the mean score of the population from which the participants who received the nice message were sampled.

2. $\mu_{\text{insulting message}} \neq \mu_{\text{nice message}}$. The mean score on the state hostility measure of the population from which the participants who received the insulting message were sampled does not equal the mean score of the population from which the participants who received the nice message were sampled.

Note that the statistical hypotheses are phrased in terms of population parameters, *not* in terms of sample statistics.[3] The statement $\overline{X}_{\text{insulting message}} = \overline{X}_{\text{nice message}}$ can be tested directly by inspecting the data: Either the sample means are equal, or they are not. Note that the statement about the difference between the sample means is *not* a correct mathematical formulation of our statistical hypotheses, because hypotheses are about things we cannot directly observe. We can observe whether the sample means are equal or not, but we cannot observe the population means. If we could observe the population means, we would have no reason to collect sample data!

It is on the basis of the results of our statistical hypothesis tests that we use our data to infer which of our various statistical hypotheses is likely to be correct. Using the classical statistical model for our representative experiment, a *t*-test seems most appropriate. We will discuss the rationale for using the *t*-test in this situation in Chapter 7, after we have mastered some basic facts and concepts pertaining to the classical statistical model.

WHERE ARE THE POPULATIONS? With the classical statistical model, we assume that the participants in each condition of our experiment represent a random sample from various populations. While we acknowledge that we rarely use random sampling in experimental research, when we use this model, we identify our participants as being sampled from populations and therefore serving as representatives of those populations. Thus, the hypotheses we test are about the parameters of these populations.

Can we identify the populations from which our participants might be randomly sampled? Where, for example, is the population from which we would draw a sample of participants who are in our experimental group? The answer to these questions is that *these populations do not exist outside of our experiment*. We create both the experimental participants (and the control participants) by giving them the treatments appropriate to their respective conditions. If we want more participants for either condition, we can create them with the appropriate treatment. We could theoretically have 1,000 people receive the insulting message and then randomly sample a small number of them to be in the experimental group. The parameters in our statistical hypotheses would be the attributes of these "created" populations. We call these populations **potential populations** because *although they do not exist outside of our experiments, they could exist if we chose to create them. In other words, they could potentially exist.*

Obviously, we need the concept of potential populations in order to use the classical statistical model. The fact that these populations do not really exist should cause us little concern. The purpose of inferential statistics is not only to test statistical hypotheses but

---

[3]The convention for using Greek letters to represent parameters of a population and Roman letters to represent estimates of those parameters and sample statistics was adopted in the 1920s and 1930s, although there are a few exceptions (some of which will appear in this book).

to make inferences about our experimental hypotheses. In this sense, these populations (and their parameters) are like the hypothetical constructs and intervening variables of many psychological theories; that is, they are useful abstractions that aid us in our work.

From Statistical Hypotheses to Experimental Hypotheses

The goal of research is to answer our research questions. Therefore, an important step is to make correct inferences about our experimental hypotheses from the results of statistical analyses of our statistical hypotheses. We can use good experimental design and perform all of the statistical hypothesis tests correctly yet still not produce a correct answer to our research question.

The results of our statistical hypothesis tests allow us to make inferences from our data to our statistical hypotheses, meaning that we can infer which of our hypotheses we believe to be correct. This, however, is not the end of the story. We conduct our research to learn about the effects of our independent variables on behavior, not to learn about population parameters. *The goal of experimental research is to make inferences about experimental hypotheses*, in this case, the effects of cybervictimization on hostility.

What could the researcher conclude in this experiment if he or she were to accept the statistical hypothesis (on the basis of the statistical hypothesis test on the data) that, for example, $\mu_{\text{insulting message}} \neq \mu_{\text{nice message}}$ (the mean of the population from which the participants who received the insulting message were sampled does not equal the mean of the population from which the participants who received the nice message were sampled)? If, for example, the sample mean for the insulting message group were higher than the sample mean for the nice message group, should we conclude that insulting messages increase hostility? The answer is clearly no! We can only justifiably say that receipt of the insulting message used in this experiment by this group of participants (who may be distinct from other populations in terms of age, gender, social class, educational level, and so forth) affected hostility as measured in this experiment. It would take more data from more experiments to claim more than that. The matter of inference from the results of statistical hypothesis tests to experimental hypotheses is more a matter of logic than statistics; nevertheless, it is an aspect of the research enterprise in which mistakes are frequently made. For an excellent discussion of this topic in the context of statistical hypothesis testing, you should read David Bakan's 1966 paper.

There is also the possibility that the limited conclusion will not stand the test of replication; that is, it may be that results similar to those obtained in one experiment will not occur again when the experiment is repeated. We will discuss the matter of errors in hypothesis testing and the failure to replicate the results of an experiment later in Chapter 6.

Summary

In this chapter, we introduced the purpose of the research process and a general overview of the steps comprising this process. To illustrate the discussion, we used as an example a study examining the effects of cyberbullying.

We noted that all research starts with a research question or questions. For each question, we frame possible answers as experimental hypotheses, statements about the effects of an independent variable (or variables) on dependent variables of interest to us. These hypotheses guide the design of our experiment as we decide how to operationalize our independent and dependent variables. Eliminating possible confounds, while not necessarily a statistical issue, is important because confounds can compromise the effectiveness of our experiments in providing answers to our research questions.

After we collect our data, we need to look at those data to decide what statistical model to use for analysis. The model we choose will determine how we frame our statistical hypotheses. When we use the classical statistical model, which is based on the assumptions that populations of scores exist and we can learn the values of unknown parameters by taking random samples from those populations, our statistical hypotheses are about the parameters of those populations.

Although random sampling from populations is an assumption of the classical statistical model, we do not take random samples when we conduct experiments; rather, we assemble a number of participants and randomly assign them to the conditions in our experiment. We invoke the concept of potential populations, populations that do not exist outside our experiment (but could be created by giving more individuals our experimental treatments) to allow us to use the classical statistical model with experiments.

In Box 1.1, you will find a flowchart that you can use as a guide to the structure of the research process.

BOX 1.1
FLOWCHART FOR EXPERIMENTS

Step 1: Generate your research question

Example: How do participants feel after being cybervictimized?

Step 2: Generate experimental hypotheses as possible answers to your research question

These are statements about what may or may not be the actual state of affairs. They should be mutually exclusive and exhaustive.

Example: Cybervictimization does not produce feelings of hostility.

Cybervictimization produces feelings of hostility.

Step 3: Design your experiment

Choose independent and dependent variables that define the elements of your experimental hypotheses.

Examples: Cybervictimization is defined by the content of the message someone receives. Hostility is measured by responses to the State Hostility Scale (SHS).

Decide what the participants will experience in the different conditions in your experiment.

(Continued)

BOX 1.1 (Continued)

FLOWCHART FOR EXPERIMENTS

Decide who participants will be, how you will recruit or obtain them, how many will be in your experiment, and how they will be assigned to the different conditions.

Step 4: Collect your data

Step 5: Decide what statistical model to use to analyze your data

Step 6: Generate your statistical hypotheses

For the classical statistical model, your statistical hypotheses will be statements about the parameters of the population from which you presumably obtained your samples.

Example: H_0: $\mu_{insulting\ message} = \mu_{nice\ message}$. The mean score on the state hostility measure of the population from which the participants who received the insulting

message were sampled equals the mean score of the population from which the participants who received the nice message were sampled.

H_1: $\mu_{insulting\ message} \neq \mu_{nice\ message}$. The mean score on the state hostility measure of the population from which the participants who received the insulting message were sampled does not equal the mean score of the population from which the participants who received the nice message were sampled.

Step 7: Perform the statistical analyses and draw the appropriate conclusions about your statistical hypotheses

Step 8: Draw the appropriate conclusions about your experimental hypotheses to answer your research question

Questions Raised by the Use of the Classical Statistical Model

The first section of this book will be devoted to answering the following questions about the proper use of the classical statistical model:

1. To test hypotheses about population parameters with the classical statistical model, we must extract information from our samples to estimate these parameters. The question is, *What information from our samples should we use for these estimates?* It is customary to use the sample mean as the "best" estimate of the population mean, but in the case of the estimate of the population variance, the best estimate is not the sample variance. Why that is the case and how we determine the "best" estimates for these parameters is the topic of Chapter 4.

2. The statistical hypotheses in our example experiment are the following:

   a. $\mu_{insulting\ message} = \mu_{nice\ message}$. The mean of the population from which the participants who received the insulting message were sampled equals the mean of the population from which the participants who received the nice message were sampled.

b. $\mu_{\text{insulting message}} \neq \mu_{\text{nice message}}$. The mean of the population from which the participants who received the insulting message were sampled is not equal to the mean of the population from which the participants who received the nice message were sampled.

Hypothesis (a) is usually referred to as the "null hypothesis" and hypothesis (b) as the "alternative hypothesis." Why are they stated as they are and given those names? Questions 2–8 will be addressed in Chapter 6.

3. Even though we might collect data that lead us to reject the null hypothesis ($\mu_{\text{insulting message}} = \mu_{\text{nice message}}$) and accept the alternative hypothesis ($\mu_{\text{insulting message}} \neq \mu_{\text{nice message}}$), can we conclude anything about the *direction* of the effect (whether insulting messages increase or decrease hostility)? And when we expect a result in one direction but not the other, can we state our alternative hypothesis in that direction and accept it only when the difference is in that direction?

4. Our statistical hypotheses, like our experimental hypotheses, are stated so that they are mutually exclusive (only one can be true in a given situation) and exhaustive (there are no other possibilities such that one of these must be true). Because of these properties, if we can reject the null hypothesis on the basis of our data, we can accept the alternative hypothesis. While it is logically possible to accept an alternative hypothesis by testing and rejecting the null hypothesis, why can we not logically test the alternative hypothesis directly?

5. On the basis of what criterion do we reject the null hypothesis?

6. While it is possible to reject the null hypothesis, can we ever accept it? Is non-rejection of the null hypothesis the same as acceptance of it? What conclusion can we draw about our experimental hypotheses when we cannot reject the null hypothesis?

7. When we reject the null hypothesis and accept an alternative, we say that we have found a "significant difference" or that the difference is "statistically significant." What do we mean by this statement?

8. The decision about the number of participants to be included in an experiment is an important one. While it certainly is true that it is easier to demonstrate that the observed difference between two sets of numbers is not due to chance with a large number of participants, the use of large numbers of participants can make small differences "statistically significant." Furthermore, the use of too many participants can be wasteful of time and money when the same inferences could be drawn from a smaller number of participants. How can we decide how many participants to use in an experiment in order to maximize our chances of finding an effect if there is one, while at the same time not finding spurious effects or wasting resources?

9. What are the effects of violating the assumptions of the classical statistical model? We have already briefly looked at the fact that we usually do not draw random samples from populations and how we deal with the violation of that assumption. For the statistical tests based on this

model, assumptions have to be made about the forms of the (potential) populations from which "random samples" are taken. For example, in the case of the t-test suggested for our example experiment, it is assumed that the populations have normal distributions with equal variances. But suppose this is not the case? How would we be able to test these assumptions when our populations really do not exist outside of our experiment? We provide some answers in Chapter 2.

10. What is the appropriate test statistic for testing various statistical hypotheses in different situations? We provide answers in Chapters 6 through 15.

Before we answer these questions, however, we need to step back and learn about some interesting techniques for looking at our data and testing assumptions about our populations. We will accomplish that goal in the next chapter.

Conceptual Exercises

1. Why do we state our statistical hypotheses in terms of population parameters and not in terms of sample statistics?

2. Write the following statement in an English sentence:

$$\mu_1 \neq \mu_2$$

3. What is a potential population? Why do we need this concept for the classical statistical model?

4. What are the two assumptions of the classical statistical model? With respect to these two assumptions, how do we actually do things in psychology?

5. What is the difference between experimental hypotheses and statistical hypotheses? Why do we need both sets of hypotheses when we use the classical statistical model to analyze our data?

6. What is wrong with the following statement?

$$H_0 = \overline{X}_E = \overline{X}_C$$

How should it be written? Write the correct statement in an English sentence.

7. What is the difference between random sampling and random assignment? What is the purpose of each procedure? When do we use each?

8. Self-fulfilling prophecies involve having strong beliefs that something will happen and then unknowingly acting in a way to make it happen. We tried to see if what we told students in an experimental methods class about the intelligence of their rats would affect how long it took students to shape a rat to press a lever. We gave each student a rat and taught them how to shape their rat to press a lever to obtain food. Students in the class were randomly assigned to two groups: One group was told that their rat was bred for superior performance in a maze, and the other group was told that their rat was bred for poor performance in a maze. (In actuality, all rats were the same breed.) Then

all students attempted to shape their rat to press a lever for food. We recorded how many minutes it took them to shape their rat.

One way to analyze the data in this experiment is to use a *t*-test, which is based on the classical statistical model.

a. To use the classical statistical model, we have to make two general assumptions. What are they? How realistic are these two assumptions for this situation? Why?

b. What are the *statistical* hypotheses being tested here? (State them in symbols and in words.)

c. Do we need the concept of a potential population here? Why or why not?

9. In a study of the effects of suggestion on the taste of drinking water, 12 students were recruited from general psychology and randomly assigned to one of two groups. One group drank tap water and rated its taste on a scale from 1 (*very bad*) to 10 (*very good*). The other group also drank tap water but rated it believing it to be a well-advertised, expensive spring water.

a. What are the experimental hypotheses for this experiment?

b. What are the statistical hypotheses being tested here? (State them in symbols and in words.)

c. What is the purpose of random sampling, and how is random sampling related to this situation? Would you consider the participants to be a random sample from a population? Why or why not?

d. Why were the participants in this experiment randomly assigned to conditions? What is the purpose of random assignment, and how is that purpose relevant here?

e. Is there a need to invoke the concept of potential population here? Why or why not?

Student Study Site

Visit the Student Study Site at **https://study.sagepub.com/friemanstats** for a variety of useful tools including data sets, additional exercises, and web resources.

EXAMINING OUR DATA

An Introduction to Some of the Techniques of Exploratory Data Analysis

"There is no single statistical tool that is as powerful as a well-chosen graph."

—Chambers, Cleveland, Kleiner, & Tukey (1983, p. 1)

Sometimes our research questions are about how often something occurs or how some characteristic is distributed in a given population or populations. Sometimes they are about the relationships or correlations between variables. Other times they are about the effects of certain manipulations on the behavior of individuals. No matter what our research question, *the first thing we should do after collecting our data is to look at the numbers and how they are distributed within our data set or sets.* Looking at our data can help us decide what descriptive statistics we should use to summarize our data and what statistical tests we should use to analyze our data. Even if we have already made a preliminary determination of how we will analyze the data, we may want to change our approach after examining them.

To make sense of our data, we need to organize it in some way. Table 2.1 contains some data, along with some standard descriptive statistics, from the experiment by Barlett (2015) described in Chapter 1. The research question in this experiment was *How do participants feel after being cybervictimized?* To investigate that question, the researchers randomly assigned participants to receive either an insulting message or a nice message from their "partner" (really there was no partner) after failure to complete a Sudoku puzzle. This message served as the cybervictimization manipulation. One of the dependent variables in that experiment was the participants' scores on the State Hostility Scale (SHS) after they received the message from their "partner." (See Chapter 1 for additional details of the experiment.)

DESCRIPTIVE STATISTICS

Descriptive statistics provide various ways to describe and summarize a set of numbers. These statistics include measures of central tendency, spread, and shape.

All computer programs for analyzing data provide most, if not all, of the descriptive statistics provided at the bottom of Table 2.1 (see Table 2.2 for definitions of these measures). However, these standard measures of central tendency (mean, median, mode), spread (variance, standard deviation, range), and shape (indices of skewness and kurtosis) do not give us enough information to form a good picture of the data.

For example, a common rule of thumb for deciding whether a set of data is symmetrical is to compare the mean with the median. If the mean and median are identical (or close together), the distribution is supposed to be symmetric; if these sample statistics are far apart (although how far apart depends on the unit of measurement and range of the data), the distribution is suspected to be skewed. However, it is easy to construct counterexamples. The following set of 10 numbers has the same mean and median, but the numbers are not symmetrically distributed around that common value: 1, 1, 1, 1, 2, 2, 2, 2, 3, 5. Do the calculations or construct a histogram, and you will see an asymmetrical distribution.

One way to try to overcome this problem is to use indices of skewness. For the set of 10 numbers above, the index of skewness is 1.718. What does this mean? A perfectly symmetrical set of numbers has an index of skewness of zero. Otherwise, indices of skewness are hard to interpret, except in the ordinal sense that a distribution with a larger index of skewness value has more skew, and the direction of the skew is indicated by the sign.[1] Furthermore, indices of skewness are greatly affected by the presence of outliers in the data. As we will see below, there is an outlier in the After Insulting Message group (142). When this outlier is removed and the index of skewness is recalculated, that value changes from −0.461 to 0.006.

Kurtosis refers to how flat or peaked a set of numbers are relative to a normal distribution, for which kurtosis is zero. Sets of numbers that are more peaked relative to a normal distribution have a positive value for kurtosis, and those that are flatter than a normal distribution have a negative value for kurtosis. Indices of kurtosis are only meaningful for symmetrical distributions, and like indexes of skewness, they too are greatly affected by outliers.[2]

---

[1] A positive value for the index of skew indicates that the sample mean is *higher* than the sample median and the tail of the distribution is on the right side; this is referred to as a **positive skew**, and the distribution is **skewed to the right**. A negative value for the index of skew indicates that the sample mean is *lower* than the sample median and the tail of the distribution is on the left side; this is referred to as a **negative skew**, and the **distribution is skewed to the left**.

[2] When the outlier in the After Nice Message group is removed, the index of kurtosis changes from 1.396 to −0.869.

Likewise, standard deviations and variances are measures of spread, but they too are only useful when we are comparing two sets of data with the same units of measurement. In Chapter 3, we will discuss ways to compare distributions that have different units of measurement.

Looking at the data in Table 2.1, we can see that both the mean and median of the hostility scores for the participants in the After Insulting Message group are higher than

TABLE 2.1 ■ Data From Barlett (2015)

	\multicolumn{10}{c}{State Hostility Scale Scores}
	\multicolumn{5}{c}{After Insulting Message}	\multicolumn{5}{c}{After Nice Message}
	102	66	85	110	65	35	57	46	38	51
	78	93	75	38	103	82	63	59	58	69
	103	39	102	74	75	80	85	97	103	78
	71	44	103	60	73	87	77	100	45	63
	84	71	90	110	65	76	86	57	75	55
	60	78	64	117	114	96	65	142	72	102
	99	86	67	42	80	37	44	83	72	83
	87	49	92	92	101	52	91	55	71	55
	90	90	57	55	94	85	70	53		
	94	79	99	107	43					
	98	102	95	94						
Mean	\multicolumn{5}{c}{81.56}	\multicolumn{5}{c}{70.93}
Median	\multicolumn{5}{c}{85.5}	\multicolumn{5}{c}{71.00}
Mode(s)	\multicolumn{5}{c}{90, 94, 102, 103}	\multicolumn{5}{c}{55}
Sample Standard Deviation	\multicolumn{5}{c}{20.634}	\multicolumn{5}{c}{21.217}
Sample Variance	\multicolumn{5}{c}{425.765}	\multicolumn{5}{c}{450.158}
Range	\multicolumn{5}{c}{79}	\multicolumn{5}{c}{108}
Minimum	\multicolumn{5}{c}{38}	\multicolumn{5}{c}{34}
Maximum	\multicolumn{5}{c}{117}	\multicolumn{5}{c}{142}
Skewness	\multicolumn{5}{c}{−0.461}	\multicolumn{5}{c}{0.734}
Kurtosis	\multicolumn{5}{c}{−0.655}	\multicolumn{5}{c}{1.396}
Count	\multicolumn{5}{c}{54}	\multicolumn{5}{c}{43}

TABLE 2.2 ■ Definitions of Commonly Used Descriptive Statistics			
Name	**Symbol**	**Formula**	**Comments**
Sample mean	X	$$\dfrac{\sum\limits_{i=1}^{n} X_i}{n}$$	Average of a set of scores.
Sample median	Med	Location $= (n+1)/2$	Half of the scores are below this value.
Sample mode	Mo	—	Value that occurs most frequently. This value occurs more than once in a given sample.
Sample variance[a]	s^2	$$\dfrac{\sum\limits_{i=1}^{n}\left(X_i - \overline{X}\right)^2}{n}$$	Average of the squared deviations around the sample mean.
Sample standard deviation	s	$$\sqrt{\dfrac{\sum\limits_{i=1}^{n}\left(X_i - \overline{X}\right)^2}{n}}$$	Square root of sample variance.
Index of skewness	G_1	$$\dfrac{n}{(n-1)(n-2)}\sum\limits_{i=1}^{n}\left(\dfrac{X_i - \overline{X}}{s}\right)$$	There are a number of formulas for calculating skewness. This formula is the one most commonly used in statistical packages.
Index of kurtosis	G_2	(complicated formula)	There are also a number of different formulas for calculating kurtosis.

[a] Many textbooks use the following formula for the sample variance: $\dfrac{\sum\limits_{i=1}^{n}\left(X_i - \overline{X}\right)^2}{n-1}$. For reasons that will be given in Chapter 4, we will use that formula to calculate the unbiased estimator of the population variance (est σ^2) and the formula given in this table to find the sample variance.

the mean and median of the hostility scores of the After Nice Message group; however, there is a great deal of overlap in the hostility scores for the participants in the two groups (which we see from the maximum and minimum scores for both groups). Therefore, it is not obvious from visual inspection that the differences in those measures of central tendency are greater than might occur if you had simply given two groups of participants the same treatment. To draw conclusions about the effects of these two treatments on hostility, we would need to use an inferential statistical test like Student's *t*-test. However, Student's *t*-test is based on the classical statistical model, where certain assumptions are made about the populations from which the data were presumably sampled (i.e., that independent random samples were taken from normal distributions that have the same variance). In this chapter, we will look at various ways to display our data to help us decide whether the use of a procedure like the *t*-test is appropriate for our data.

HISTOGRAMS

Histograms are widely used to provide a graphical representation of a set of data. However, there are better ways to present our information.

Another common practice is to plot a histogram. The data from the two groups in Table 2.1 are plotted as histograms in Figure 2.1. It is clear from these histograms that both sets of data are spread across most of the response scale and the peaks are in different places. While these histograms give us a picture of the distributions of the data in each group, they do so at the expense of submerging the individual scores into broad intervals, and the picture you get depends on the width of the intervals you choose for your histogram. This point is illustrated in Figure 2.2, where the width of the intervals varies from 10 to 30 units. Increasing the width of the intervals affects the overall picture of our data and, in this case, obscures what may be an outlier in the data. There are better ways to plot these data, and we will discuss these alternatives here.

EXPLORATORY DATA ANALYSIS

The techniques collectively called exploratory data analysis *offer a variety of ways to look at our data that provide more information than do histograms.*

Fortunately, there are some excellent techniques for looking at our data. Many of these relatively new techniques were described by John Tukey in his influential 1977 book, *Exploratory Data Analysis*. In that book, Tukey distinguished between exploratory and confirmatory analyses. According to Tukey, **exploratory data analysis** is "numerical detective work," that is, *the search for clues and evidence in our*

FIGURE 2.1 ■ Histograms for the two sets of data in Table 2.1.

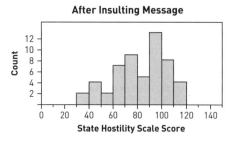
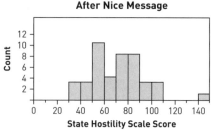

FIGURE 2.2 ■ Three histograms of the After Nice Message group with different interval widths. The interval widths for the top, middle, and lower histograms are 10, 20, and 30, respectively.

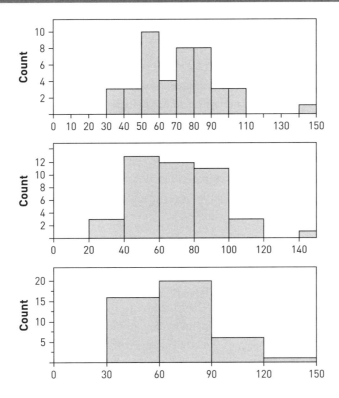

data, while **confirmatory data analysis (inferential statistics)** *assesses the strength of that evidence.* Exploratory data analysis should be the first step in the process of analyzing our data.

It is surprising that many of the techniques to be described here are not included in most quantitative methods textbooks and courses, given these methods' utility and relative ease of construction. In later chapters, we will extend some of these techniques to the comparison of two or more sets of data and will show how they can aid us in confirmatory data analysis (inferential statistics).

There are two ways to display data—in graphs and in tables. Some of the techniques described here for displaying data are pure graphs and some are pure tables. One of the techniques we will describe (the stem-and-leaf display) is both a graph and a table. We will start with a technique that provides us a graphical representation of *all* of the numbers in our data set.

QUANTILE PLOTS

Quantile plots are the simplest graphical representation of data. Every score in the data set is plotted against its ordinal rank. Visually scanning the resulting quantile plot reveals patterns within the data set, discontinuities in the data, outliers, and symmetry or lack of symmetry.

The simplest graphical representation of a set of data is a quantile plot. To create a quantile plot, we rank order our observations from lowest to highest and plot each value against its rank. The result is a graph that includes every observation. This allows us to see the entire data set at a glance. From a quantile plot, we can see whether our data are distributed symmetrically and whether there are any outliers or other characteristics of the data of which we should be aware and that may affect how we should further analyze the data. When we rank order our data from lowest to highest, the location of each number in our data set can be identified by its quantile value.

What Is a Quantile?

If a set of observations X_i is put in rank order from lowest to highest, each observation (X_i) is assigned a rank (r_i), and a certain proportion of the observations (p_i) are below that value and a certain proportion $(1 - p_i)$ above it. Therefore, the location of each X_i can be identified both by its rank (r_i) and by the proportion of scores below it (p_i). This relationship between the relative location of an observation in a ranked set and the value of the observation is usually expressed as follows:

$$Q(p_i) = X_i \qquad (2.1)$$

In words, this is written, "The p_ith quantile of this set of numbers is X_i." This statement tells us that X_i is located p_i of the way from the lowest value in the set. For example, the *median* of a set of numbers (X_{median}) is the data point below which $\frac{1}{2}$ (or 0.50) of the values lie. Therefore, $Q(0.5) = X_{median}$; that is, the 0.5 quantile of this set of numbers is X_{median}. Likewise, the *upper quartile* of a set of numbers is the value below which $\frac{3}{4}$ (or 0.75) of the values lie. Therefore, $Q(0.75) = X_{upper\ quartile}$. It is obvious that quantiles are related to percentiles: Percentiles refer to the percentage of the data below a certain observation, and quantiles refer to fractions (or proportions) of the data below that number.

You may wonder why we even bother referring to quantiles. If we rank order the data from lowest to highest, there will be a one-to-one linear correspondence between the ranks and the proportions. This is because if r_i is the rank, then $p_i = (r_i - 0.5)/n$. If these two values (r_i and p_i) are plotted against each other, the result will be on a straight line. Try it yourself. The reason we use quantiles is that they allow us to compare scores

FIGURE 2.3 ■ Quantile plots for the two groups in Table 2.1.

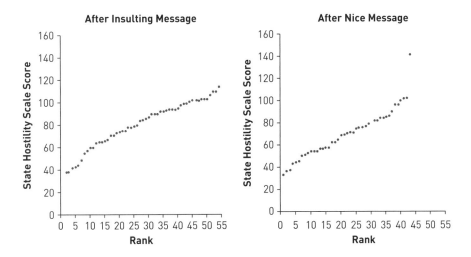

from data sets of different sizes at the same relative locations. The simplest example of this is when we compare the medians [$Q(0.5)$] from different size data sets.

A **quantile plot** is *a graph in which the ordered values are plotted against their corresponding proportions* (p_i) *or their ranks* (r_i). Because of the one-to-one correspondence between r_i and p_i, it is easier to use the ranks when making simple quantile plots.

The data from the two groups in Table 2.1 are graphed as quantile plots in Figure 2.3. To construct these quantile plots, the numbers were first ranked from lowest to highest and then plotted against their ranks. The individual numbers are on the y-axis, and the ranks are on the x-axis. A summary of the procedure for constructing a quantile plot is given in Box 2.1.

BOX 2.1
HOW TO CONSTRUCT A SIMPLE QUANTILE PLOT

Purpose

To provide a graphical representation of our data in which every data point is represented

Procedure

1. Rank order the data from lowest to highest.

2. Put the range of the values on the y-axis (vertical axis) and the ranks from 1 to n on the x-axis (horizontal axis).

3. For each observation, plot a single point at the intersection of its value on the y-axis and corresponding rank on the x-axis.

How to Interpret a Quantile Plot

As we go from left to right on a quantile plot, either the points are next to each other, at the same vertical level, or each successive point is higher than the previous point. In other words, read from left to right, the plot is either level or it rises; it never declines. Can you state why that must be the case?

The vertical distance between successive points is a visual representation of the difference between them. When successive data points are identical, the data points are at the same vertical level; when they are close together, the vertical distance between them is small; and when they are far apart, the vertical distance between them is large. Therefore, where the slope of the plot is flat, the data points all have the same value; where the slope of the plot is shallow, the successive data points are close together in value; and where the slope of the plot is steep, the numbers are far apart from each other. A large vertical gap between two successive data points indicates a discontinuity in the data.

We can also use a quantile plot to give a rough idea of how symmetrical the data are. If we connect the lowest point with the highest point (ignoring outliers), then when the data are symmetrical, the points in the lower half of the plot will be distributed as a mirror image of the points in the upper half of the plot. That is, if the points in the lower half are distributed in a certain way above or below our line from the bottom point to the median, the points in the upper half will be distributed the same way with respect to our line from the top point to the median. When the data are skewed, on the other

FIGURE 2.4 ■ Quantile plots with lines connecting the endpoints (excluding the outliers). The data in the left panel are negatively skewed, and the data in the right panel are not skewed.

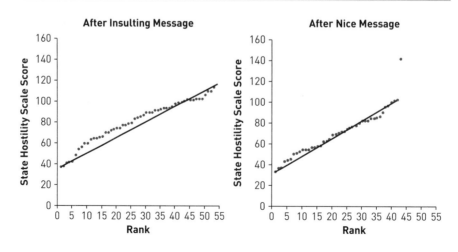

hand, then most of the data points will be either above or below our line connecting the endpoints. When the bulk of the data are above the line, the skew in the data is negative (skewed left), and when the bulk of the data are below the line, the skew in the data is positive (skewed right). Inspection of Figure 2.4 reveals that the After Insulting Message data are skewed left (negatively skewed) and the After Nice Message data are not skewed.

From Figures 2.3 and 2.4, we can see at a glance that the After Nice Message group contains an outlier (142). With the exception of the outlier, both plots cover the same range of values, but the scores in the After Insulting Message group are farther apart at the lower end and closer together at the upper end. This pattern reflects the negative skew. On the other hand, the scores in the After Nice Message group are farther apart at both the lower and upper ends and are closer together in the middle. This pattern reflects the symmetry in the data. A technique that provides a more objective way of identifying outliers will be described below. However, it should be clear that quantile plots are easy to make and easy to read after we become familiar with them.

STEM-AND-LEAF DISPLAYS

Stem-and-leaf displays are tables that list every data point in the data set. A stem-and-leaf display can also function as a histogram, but one in which every data point in an interval is listed. We will describe a number of ways to construct these displays.

Quantile plots are graphs in which every data point in our data set is represented. A stem-and-leaf display is a cross between a table of all of the data points and a graphical representation of the distribution of those data points. On the one hand, it is a table composed of all of the data points in our data set arranged in descending order, with each row in the display (table) representing a different part of the data. On the other hand, it is a graphical representation of our data because it gives us a picture of the relationships among the numbers. If we ignore the values of our data points and just look at the length of each row, we have what amounts to a histogram. But, unlike a histogram, a stem-and-leaf display contains the individual values.

Like quantile plots and histograms, stem-and-leaf displays can tell us at a glance the distribution of our numbers: whether they are spread out or all clumped together, whether and where there are individual clumps, whether and where there are gaps in our data, and whether there appear to be outliers.

To construct a stem-and-leaf display, we take every number in our data set and divide it into two parts: the first part is the stem and the second part the leaf. The choice of where to divide numbers into stems and leaves depends on the data and which resulting display will provide the best picture of the data. For example, we can divide the number 45.3 into 45 as the stem and 3 as a leaf, or we can divide 45.3 into 4 as the stem and 5 as the leaf (throwing away the .3). In the first example, we consider the decimal values to carry important information and keep them for that reason. In the first example, we indicate our choice of where to divide the numbers into stems and leaves in our stem-and-leaf display by saying that the unit = 0.1 and 1 2 = 1.2. In the second example, we consider the first two digits to carry the important information about our data and discard the decimals.[3] Here we indicate that the unit = 1 and 1 2 = 12.

Each line of our stem-and-leaf display will consist of leaves having the same stem. In addition to deciding how to divide data points into stems and leaves, we also have to decide how many lines to use to display the leaves on each stem.

Three examples of stem-and-leaf displays for the data from both groups in Table 2.1 are presented in Figure 2.5. In all three displays of these data from both groups, every data point is split so that the number in the tens column is the stem and the number in the ones column is the leaf. This method for splitting data points is indicated at the top by the statements *Unit = 1* and *1 2 indicates 12*. In the left panel for the After Insulting Message group, the first line of data contains the points that range from 30 to 39. In this case, there are two numbers: 38 and 39. The first two numbers in the left panel for the After Nice Message group are 35 and 37.

The only difference among the three displays for each group is the number of lines per stem. There is only 1 line per stem in the displays on the left, 2 lines per stem (indicated by a · for all leaves with values from 0 to 4 and a * for all leaves with a value from 5 to 9 in the middle displays, and 5 lines per stem in the displays on the right (indicated by a · for leaves with 0 and 1, a *T* for 2 and 3, an *F* for 4 and 5, an *S* for 6 and 7, and a * for 8 and 9).

When there are outliers in our data, as is the case in the After Nice Message group, we avoid having a number of stems with no leaves between the outlying value and the rest of the data by listing those values at the appropriate end of the display preceded by *LO* or *HI*. Here we insert the entire number.

Outliers in our data are indicated as either LO or HI, depending on where they are in the data set. We find any outliers by looking for the LO or HI indicator at the top and/or bottom of the stem, as appropriate. Here we find the entire value. The outlier in the After Nice Message group is indicated by HI = 142. With a stem-and-leaf display, we can tell at a glance whether the data are symmetrical and whether there are any outliers.

To complete a stem-and-leaf display, we add to the left of each line in the display the depths of the values on each line from the closest end of the data set, that is, the total number of leaves on that line and on all the lines between that line and the closer end of the data set. We do this for every line above and below the line that contains the sample median. We put the the number of values on that line in parentheses.

---

[3] Whether a digit contains important information depends on the entirety of the data set and the source of the numbers.

FIGURE 2.5 ■ Stem-and-leaf displays for the data in the After Insulting Message group in the left set of panels and from the After Nice Message group in the right set of panels: (*left*) one line per stem, (*middle*) two lines per stem, and (*right*) five lines per stem.

After Insulting Message Group

```
Unit = 1
1 2 = 12

   1  
   2  
   2   3  89
   6   4  2349
   8   5  57
  15   6  0045567
  24   7  113455889
  (8)  8  04567
  25   9  0002234445899
  12  10  12223337
   4  11  0047
```

```
Unit = 1
1 2 = 12

            3.
      2  *  89
            4.
      5  4. 234
      6  *  9
            5.
      8  *  57
     11  6. 004
     15  *  5567
     19  7. 1134
     24  *  55889
     26  8. 04
    [3]  *  567
     25  5. 0002223444
     16  *  5899
     12 10. 1222333
      5  *  7
      4 11. 0047
```

```
Unit = 1
1 2 = 12

         3.
         T
         F
         S
    2  * 89
         4.
    4  T 23
    5  F 4
    6  * 9
         5.
         T
    7  F 5
    8  S 7
   10  6. 00.
         T
   13  F 455
   15  S 67
   17  7. 11.
   18  T 3
   21  F 455
         S
   24  * 899
   25  8. 0
         T
   12 10. 1.
   11  * 222333
         F
    5  S 7
         *
    4 11. 00.
         T
    2  F 47
         S
         *
```

After Nice Message Group

```
Unit = 1
1 2 = 12

        1
        2
    3   3  578
    6   4  456
   16   5  1235557789
   20   6  3359
  [8]   7  01225678
   15   8  02335567
    7   9  167
    4  10  023
HI = 142
```

```
Unit = 1
1 2 = 12

    1   3. 5
    3   *  78
    4   4. 4
    6   *  56
    9   5. 123
   16   *  5557789
   18   6. 33
   20   *  59
  [4]   7. 0122
   19   *  5678
   15   8. 0233
   11   *  5567
    7   5. 1
    6   *  67
    4  10. 023
HI = 142
```

```
Unit = 1
1 2 = 12

         3.
         T
    1  F 5
    2  S 7
    3  * 8
         4.
         T
    5  F 45
    6  S 6
         *
    7  5. 1
    9  T 23
   12  F 555
   14  S 77
   16  * 89
         6.
   18  T 33
   19  F 5
         S
   20  * 9
  [2]  7. 01
   21  T 22
   19  F 5
   18  S 67
   16  * 8
   15  8. 0
   14  T 233
   11  F 55
    9  S 67
         *
    7  9. 1
         T
         F
    6  S 67
         *
    4 10. 0
    3  T 23
         F
         S
         *
HI = 142
```

The decision about whether to use a one line, two lines, or five lines per stem depends on the range of the data and the number of data points. With large data sets, the number of leaves on some stems becomes exceedingly large. Spreading the leaves across more lines per stem makes the patterns in the data set clearer. Most researchers reserve the five-lines-per-stem figure for very large data sets (those over 500 data points). Which of the three stem-and-leaf displays in Figure 2.5 do you prefer for the data presented here, and what about that stem-and-leaf display appeals to you?

The procedure for creating a stem-and-leaf display is summarized in Box 2.2.

BOX 2.2

HOW TO CONSTRUCT A STEM-AND-LEAF DISPLAY

Purpose

To provide a representation of all of our data that is both a graph and a table

Procedure

1. Rank order the data.

2. Choose a pair of adjacent digit positions to split all numbers in the data set into stems and leafs. For example, the number 623 can be split into 62 3 or 6 2 (throwing away the 3). In the first case, 62 is the stem and 3 is the leaf. In the second case, 6 is the stem and 2 is the leaf. The choice of where to place this split is governed by how the final display will look. Sometimes we may have to compare different stem–leaf splits to find the one that creates the most informative display.

3. Create a column of all of the possible stems from lowest to highest.

4. Draw a vertical line to separate the stems from the leaves. Locate the stem for each number and write the leaf (first trailing digit) on that stem line. The leaves should be arranged in ascending order on each stem.

5. When there is a large number of values, two or more lines can be used per stem. The two most commonly used arrangements are two lines per stem and five lines per stem. The choice of how many lines to use per stem is also dictated by how the final display looks.

   a. *Two lines per stem:* Place leaves 0, 1, 2, 3, and 4 on the first line (indicated by a · after the stem) and leaves 5, 6, 7, 8, and 9 on the second line (indicated by a * alone).

   b. *Five lines per stem:* Place leaves 0 and 1 on a line labeled ·, leaves 2 and 3 on a line labeled *T* (Two and Three), leaves 4 and 5 on a line labeled *F* (Four and Five), leaves 6 and 7 on a line labeled *S* (Six and Seven), and leaves 8 and 9 on a line labeled *.

6. Extreme outliers can be simply listed as *LO* and *HI* on the appropriate end of the distribution. Use the entire number.

7. At the top of the display, indicate the unit of the leaf with a decimal point and by providing an example. If the display splits 623 as 6 2, then write:

   Unit = 10

   1 2 = 120

On the other hand, if 623 were split as 62 3, write:

Unit = 1

1 2 = 12

8. Counting from each end, indicate to the left of each stem the total number of leaves from that line to the nearer end of the data set. These numbers indicate the depth of the values on that line relative to the closer end of the data set. For the stem line that contains the median, count the number of leaves on the stem and put that number in parentheses. If the median falls between two lines, the depths of those two lines will be the same (and each will be half of the total sample size). *Do not put a depth on a line that contains no leaves.*

How to Read a Stem-and-Leaf Display

The unit at the top of the display tells us how to interpret the leaves. When unit = 1 (as in Figure 2.5), the stems are numbers in the tens column (10, 20, 30, and so forth), and each leaf is a number in the ones position. Therefore, when unit = 1, a line that contains 3|578 contains the numbers 35, 37, and 38. However, when unit = 10, the same line contains the numbers 35x, 37x, and 38x (with the units digit disregarded), because the stem is a number in the hundreds position and the leaf a number in the tens position. What would the numbers in the line 3|578 represent when unit = .1?

We find any outliers by looking for the *LO* or *HI* indicator at the top and/or bottom of the stem, as appropriate. Here we will find the entire value. The outlier in the After Nice Message group is indicated by HI = 142. With a stem-and-leaf display, we can tell at a glance whether the data are symmetrical and whether there are any outliers.

The left column in each display contains the depths of the values on each line from the closest end of the data set, that is, the total number of leaves on that line and on all the lines between that line and the closer end of the data set. When we see a number in parentheses, it indicates the line containing the median value, and the value inside parentheses is the number of values on that line.

We can find the value of the median in two steps: First we use the formula $(n + 1)/2$, where n is the total number of values, to find the depth of the median. Then, after noting the depth of the line below the one containing the median, we count over from the left on the line containing the median until we reach the score at the depth of the median. That score is the median. Alternately, we can note the depth of the line above the one containing the median and count over from the right on the line containing the median until we reach the score with the depth of the median. Note that the depth of the line below the median, the number of scores on the line that contains the median, and the depth of the line above the median should add to the total number of scores. If these three numbers do not add to the total number of values, something is either omitted or counted twice. Try to find the median in the left panels of Figure 2.5.

Why Quantile Plots and Stem-and-Leaf Displays Are Better Than Histograms

Although histograms, quantile plots, and stem-and-leaf displays all provide us with an overall picture of our data, the latter two provide a more detailed picture of our data because the numeric value of every score in the data is represented.

LETTER-VALUE DISPLAYS

Letter-value displays provide a way to summarize a set of data by using selected markers in the data. They are especially useful for exploring large data sets. Box plots (the subject of the section following this one) are derived from a subset of those markers.

Quantile plots and stem-and-leaf displays show us every single data point in our data set; however, sometimes we need to summarize our data with a few well-chosen descriptive statistics, which is useful when we are trying to summarize a large number of observations (see the bottom of Table 2.1). Summary statistics tables typically include the mean, median, standard deviation, and range. Sometimes they also include measures of skewness (departure from symmetry) and kurtosis (a measure of how peaked or flat the data are relative to what one would expect if the data came from a normal distribution). While these measures can be and frequently are useful, they really do not give us a good idea of how our data are distributed. The letter-value display does a better job, and it is the basis for the graphical technique called the box plot.

Letter-value displays are based on selected quantiles of our data. The simplest letter-value display, called a **seven-number letter-value display**, *includes the median [Q(.5)], the lower and upper quartiles (called the lower and upper fourths here) [Q(.25) and Q(.75)], the values that mark the lower and upper eighths of the data [Q(.125) and Q(.875)], and the endpoints.* If there is a large number of data points, additional quantiles can be identified by halving the proportions of values between each successive letter (*D, C, B, A, Z, Y, X,* and so forth) and the endpoints. Once these letter values have been identified, it is a simple matter to find the midpoint and the spread between them. A scan of the midpoints tells us whether the data appear symmetrical, and the spreads can be compared to those we would expect if our data came from a normal distribution.

Table 2.3 contains **complete letter-value displays** for the After Insulting Message group and the After Nice Message group data in Table 2.1. Instead of displaying only the 7 values discussed above, these tables show 11 values in the "Lo" and "Hi" columns: the

TABLE 2.3 ■ Seven-Value Letter-Value Displays for the Data in Table 2.1					
After Insulting Message					
(n = 54)					
	Depth	Lo	Hi	Mid	Spread
M	27.5		85.5		
F	14.0	66.0	99.0	82.5	33.0
E	7.5	56.0	103.0	79.5	47.0
D	4.0	43.0	107.0	75.0	64.0
C	2.5	40.5	112.0	76.3	71.5
	1.0	38.0	117.0	77.5	79.0
After Nice Message					
(n = 43)					
	Depth	Lo	Hi	Mid	Spread
M	22.0		71.0		
F	11.5	55.0	84.0	69.5	29.0
E	6.0	46.0	96.0	71.0	50.0
D	3.5	41.0	101.0	71.0	60.0
C	2.0	37.0	103.0	70.0	66.0
	1.0	35.0	142.0	88.5	107.0

median (M), the upper and lower fourths (F), the upper and lower eighths (E), the upper and lower values at D and C, respectively, and the endpoints (depth = 1).

Because the median is the middle score in our data, we locate it by using the formula for its depth, $(n + 1)/2$, as described above. When n is odd, the depth of the median is a whole number, and the median is the middle score. When n is even, the median is half the distance between the two middle scores or, in other words, the average of the two middle scores. The After Insulting Message group contains 54 values; therefore, the depth of the median for that group is 27.5, and the median is 85.5. The After Nice Message group contains 43 values; therefore, the depth of the median for that group is 22, and the median is 71. We enter the median on the M line, and because the median is a single value, we enter it halfway between the "Lo" and "Hi" columns.

Once we have the depth of the median, it is easy to find the fourths. They are the values that divide each half of the distribution in half again so that along with the median they divide the distribution into fourths (quarters). The depth of the fourths is [depth of median + 1]/2, where the [number in brackets] represents the integer value of that number.

For the After Insulting Message group, the depth of the fourths is [27.5 + 1]/2 = 28/2 = 14, and the two fourths (Lo and Hi) are 66 and 99. For the After Nice Message group, the depth of the fourths is a fraction, [22 + 1]/2 = 23/2 = 11.5. Thus, the lower fourth is halfway between the numbers at ranks 11 and 12, and the upper fourth is halfway between the numbers at ranks 32 and 33. Those values are 55 and 84, respectively. These values are entered on the *F* line as "Lo" and "Hi" fourths.

We obtain the values of the eighths and all other letters in the same manner. The endpoints are the highest and lowest values; they have depths of 1.

Once the letter values are obtained, we can find their spread and the midpoint of their spread: The spread for each letter is Hi – Lo, and the midpoint is (Hi + Lo)/2.

The procedure for creating a letter-value display is summarized in Box 2.3.

How to Use a Letter-Value Display

We use letter-value displays to see a tabular representation of our data and how they are distributed. Letter-value displays identify selected quantiles of our data: $M = Q(.5)$,

---

BOX 2.3
HOW TO CONSTRUCT A LETTER-VALUE DISPLAY

Purpose

To provide a summary table for a set of data that contains information about the central tendency, shape, and spread of the data

Procedure

1. Rank order the data from lowest to highest (or start by building a stem-and-leaf display).

2. Find the median (*M*). The depth of the median is (*n* + 1)/2, where *n* is the number of data values. If *n* is odd, the median is the middle score. If *n* is even, the median is half the distance between the two middle scores.

3. Find the fourths (*F*) of the data (the upper or *Hi* fourth and the lower or *Lo* fourth). The fourths are the values that lie halfway between the median and the corresponding endpoints. The depth of the fourths are [depth of median + 1]/2, where the [number in brackets] represents the integer value of that number. If the depth of the fourths is an integer, the fourths are the numbers that occur at that depth counting from each endpoint. If the depth of the fourths is a fraction, average the distance between the corresponding adjacent integers.

4. In a similar manner, find the eighths (*E*) of the data, where the depth of the eighths is [depth of fourth + 1]/2.

5. Continue to define in the same manner as many letter values (*D, C, B, A, Z, X,* etc.) as needed.

6. The endpoints are the highest and lowest values in the data set. The depth of the endpoints is always 1.

7. Find the following for each letter (*F*, *E*, etc.) and the endpoints:

   a. The midpoint between the upper value and the lower value. Use the formula (Hi + Lo)/2.

   b. The spread between the lower value and the upper value. Use the formula Hi – Lo.

8. Create a table in which each letter (*M*, *F*, *E*, . . . , [1]) is on a separate line. The line for the median contains the depth of the median and the median itself in two places: halfway between the Lo and Hi values and in the midpoint column. The lines for the

other letters and the endpoints contain the depth, Lo and Hi values, midpoint between the Lo and Hi values (see 7a above), and the spread between the Lo and Hi values (see 7b above).

To make a seven-number letter-value display, include the median (*M*), fourths (*F*), eighths (*E*), and endpoints along with their corresponding depths, upper and lower values, spreads, and midpoints. To construct a complete letter-value display, continue to find the values that lie halfway between the last letter value (eighths) and the endpoints. The depth of each succeeding letter value is [depth of preceding letter value +1]/2. For letter values smaller than the eighths, use *D, C, B, A, Z, Y, X,* . . . until you reach depth = 1 (which defines the endpoints).

$F = Q(.25)$ and $Q(.75)$, $E = Q(.125)$ and $Q(.875)$, $D = Q(.0625)$ and $Q(.9375)$, $C = Q(.03125)$ and $Q(.96875)$, and so on; each letter value is located at half the depth of the preceding letter value.

An efficient way to begin to look at a letter-value display is to scan down the column labeled "Mid." These values are the midpoints between the Lo and Hi values of each letter. The midpoints will be identical or close together when the distribution is symmetrical. If the midpoints get progressively larger, the data are skewed to the right (positively skewed), and if the midpoints get progressively smaller, the data are skewed to the left (negatively skewed). We also get an idea of where the skew starts from where the midpoints start to diverge. Based on the letter-value displays in Table 2.3, what do you conclude about the data in the two groups? How do these representations of the data compare to the quantile plots in Figure 2.4?

We can also use the spreads in the letter-value display to help assess whether our data might have been sampled from a normal distribution by comparing the letter spreads of our data with those we would expect if the data were obtained from a normal distribution. See Hoaglin (1985) for information on how to make this comparison.

BOX PLOTS

Box plots are graphs based on selected attributes of a set of data (median, upper and lower fourths, and endpoints from a letter-value display). They can also be used to identify possible outliers in your data. Box plots are the most widely used of the exploratory data analysis techniques described in this chapter.

A box plot is a graphical display of data generated from a letter-value display of those data. Box plots tell us at a glance the location, spread, and skewness of our data and can be used to identify outliers. When placed side by side, box plots are far superior to bar graphs or histograms for comparing different groups or sets of data.

There are two types of box plots. The simpler form is called a **skeletal box plot** or a **box-and-whisker plot**. This type of box plot *contains five points from a letter-value display: the median, upper fourth, lower fourth, and two endpoints.* The mean can be added to a box plot to provide additional information. Skeletal (box-and-whisker) plots for the two groups in Table 2.1 are presented in the left panel of Figure 2.6. The box is defined by the fourths,[4] and the line through the box is the median. The mean is indicated by the plus sign.

Interpreting Skeletal (Box-and-Whisker) Box Plots

The median (and the mean) provide measures of central tendency, and the length of the box tells us the location of the middle 50% of our data and provides us with information

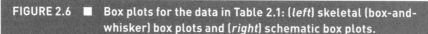

FIGURE 2.6   ■   Box plots for the data in Table 2.1: (*left*) skeletal (box-and-whisker) box plots and (*right*) schematic box plots.

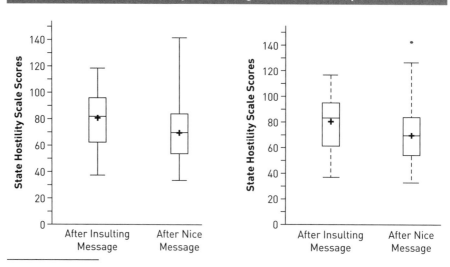

---

[4] The distance between the fourths is called the fourth-spread or simply the F-spread.

about variability in the center of the distribution. Furthermore, the location of the median within the box tells us something about the symmetry of the middle 50% of the data. The median will be in the middle of the box when the data are symmetrical in that part of the data (as for the After Nice Message group). When the median is closer to the lower fourth, scores are closer together between the median and the lower fourth than they are between the median and the upper fourth. On the other hand, when the median is closer to the upper fourth, scores are closer together between the median and the upper fourth than they are between the median and the lower fourth (as for the After Insulting Message group). The whiskers extend to the two endpoints, but they give us no information about the distribution of the numbers outside of the middle 50%. However, one or more outliers are suspected when one whisker is a lot longer than the other. We can remedy this shortcoming of the box-and-whisker plot by drawing a schematic box plot.

Interpreting Schematic (Standard or Fenced) Box Plots

A **schematic box plot** (also called a **standard box plot** or a **fenced box plot**) starts with the box-and-whisker plot but adds fences to identify outliers in the data—any values outside the fences are considered to be outliers. The **inner fences** *are placed 1.5 times the fourth-spread from each fourth* and are connected to the box with a dashed line. When there are no values beyond an inner fence, the dashed line extends to the endpoints. Any points beyond the inner fences are outliers and are identified by a dot (·), and their values may be given. In some box plots, another set of fences may be calculated but not drawn. These are called the **outer fences**, and they *extend an additional 1.5 times the fourth-spread from the inner fence (or 3 times the fourth-spread from the fourths)*. These points are then identified by another symbol (usually an open circle [o]). Schematic box plots for both groups in Table 2.1 are presented in the right panel of Figure 2.6. For the After Nice Message group, the upper fence is at 127.5 [84 + (1.5 × 29)], and there is one data point beyond it (142). There are no values beyond the lower and upper fences in the After Insulting Message group.

The procedure for creating both types of box plots is summarized in Box 2.4.

Box Plots Versus Histograms and Bar Graphs

Box plots can be used in two ways: to look at the distribution of our data and to compare two or more groups of observations. Histograms are the most commonly used graphics to summarize a set of data, and bar graphs are the most commonly used graphics to compare two or more groups of observations. While a histogram can give us more information than a box plot about the distribution of our data, box plots tell us much more than do bar graphs when we are comparing two or more groups of observations.

BOX PLOTS VERSUS HISTOGRAMS: EXAMINING DATA WITHIN A GROUP OF OBSERVATIONS Figure 2.7 compares histograms and schematic box plots of both

BOX 2.4
HOW TO CONSTRUCT A BOX PLOT

Purpose

To provide a graphical display of the data that includes the following features: location, spread, skewness, tail length, and outlying data points

Procedure

From a letter-value display of the data, find the median, fourths, fourth-spread, and endpoints.

To construct a skeletal box plot (box-and-whisker plot), follow these steps:

a. Construct a box between the fourths.

b. Draw a line through this box at the median.

c. Draw a solid line from the fourths to the endpoints.

d. Add the mean (a plus sign [+]) to the figure.

To construct a standard box plot (schematic box plot, fenced box plot), do the following:

a. Construct a box between the fourths.

b. Draw a line through this box at the median.

c. Place the inner fences a distance 1.5 times the fourth-spread from each fourth. Connect these fences to the box with a dashed line. (If there is no value beyond an inner fence, draw the fence at the endpoint.)

d. Values outside the inner fences are denoted by a dot (·), and these values are usually specified.

e. Outer fences can be constructed 1.5 times the fourth-spread from the inner fences (or 3 times the fourth-spread from the fourths). Values outside the outer fences (labeled "far outside values") are denoted by a lowercase o; here again, they are usually specified.

f. If desired, you can add a symbol for the sample mean (usually a plus sign [+]).

FIGURE 2.7 ■ Schematic box plots and histograms for the two groups in Table 2.1.

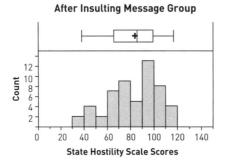

After Insulting Message Group

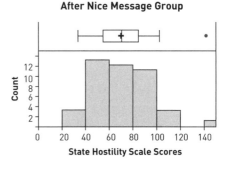

After Nice Message Group

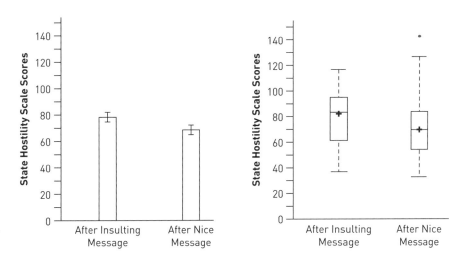

FIGURE 2.8 ■ Comparison of a bar graph (*left*) and box plots (*right*) of the data from the two groups in Table 2.1. The standard error of the mean is depicted for each group on the bar graph.

groups in Table 2.1. Because quantile plots and stem-and-leaf displays give us more information about our data, they are preferred to box plots and histograms when we are trying to examine a group of observations. Histograms provide more information about the shape of the data set than do box plots. However, we use box plots when we want a quick summary of our distribution that includes an indication of central tendency, spread, shape, and the identification of outliers.

BOX PLOTS VERSUS BAR GRAPHS: COMPARING TWO OR MORE GROUPS The most commonly used method for presenting the results of experiments is the bar graph, in which the mean of each group in the experiment is represented by the height of the bar for that group. The standard error of the mean (sample standard deviation divided by the square root of the sample size) is frequently added to each bar to give an estimate of the stability of the sample mean as an estimate of the population mean.

Figure 2.8 contains a comparison of bar graphs and box plots showing the data from the two groups in Table 2.1. Although the means of the After Insulting Message group and the After Nice Message group in the bar graphs on the left are similar, the box plots provide more information about the distributions of the values in each group. Some researchers believe that there is a statistically significant difference between groups when the standard error bars do not overlap, but *that is not true* (see Cumming & Finch, 2005). A graphic that does provide information about which groups are statistically significant from each other (means diamonds) will be presented in Chapter 7. The box plots provide

FIGURE 2.9 ■ Two versions of the box plots in Figure 2.8: (*left*) emphasis on sample means and (*right*) emphasis on variability in the data.

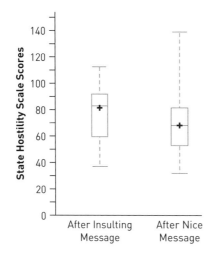
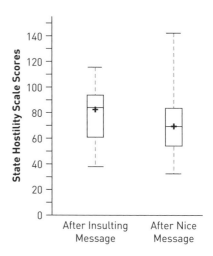

information about the distributions of the data in each group and the presence of outliers. We will see in Chapter 7 that outliers can have dramatic effects on tests of statistical significance.

Lane and Sándor (2009) showed how box plots can be modified to emphasize different aspects of your data. You can emphasize the difference between means in side-by-side box plots by making the means more prominent than the other aspects of the plot. On the other hand, when differences in variability are important, you can make the box and the endpoints more prominent and deemphasize the mean and median (see Figure 2.9).

DID MY DATA COME FROM A NORMAL DISTRIBUTION?

An important assumption of t-tests and analysis of variance is independent random sampling from normal distributions. Three of the techniques developed to answer the question raised in the title of this section are described here.

Many of the statistical tests we use to analyze our data with the classical statistical model are based on the assumption that our data were sampled from a normal distribution. There are a number of approaches to answering the question raised in the title of this section, but only three will be described here. See Conover (1980) and Lehmann (1999) for descriptions and comparisons of all of these various approaches.

Neither of the histograms displayed in Figure 2.1 resemble normal distributions: The data from the After Insulting Message group have a negative skew, which is obvious not only in the histogram but also in the quantile plot, stem-and-leaf display, letter-value display, and box plot for those data. Although the data from the After Nice Message group appear more symmetrical in these various displays, the peak is not in the center of the data, and there is an outlier.

Normal Quantile Plots

We can attempt to answer the question raised here by plotting our data against the corresponding quantiles from a normal distribution. When our data are sampled from a normal distribution, the plotted points will cluster around a straight line and not deviate far from that line.

We can use a variation of the quantile plot to provide a graphic that helps us assess whether our data were sampled from a normal distribution. To construct this graphic, we *plot the ranked values of our data on the y-axis (vertical axis) against the z-scores for the corresponding quantiles from a unit normal distribution* (a normal distribution with a mean [μ] of zero and standard deviation [σ] of 1) on the *x*-axis (horizontal axis). These *z*-scores are obtained from the following formula:

$$z_i = \Phi^{-1}\left[\frac{r_i - 0.5}{n}\right],\qquad(2.2)$$

where

z_i is the approximate *z*-score for the *i*th quantile for scores from a normal distribution,
r_i is the rank for each value in your data set,
n is the total number of values in your data set, and
$\phi^{-1}[\,]$ is the inverse of the cumulative normal distribution probability in the bracket.
(A table for finding the inverse of the cumulative normal distribution probability is in Appendix D at the back of this book.)

Then, we superimpose on this plot a straight line that goes through the point on the plot corresponding to $z = 0$ on the horizontal axis and the sample mean on the vertical axis. The slope of the line is the standard deviation of the data. If the data were sampled from a normal distribution, the plotted values will be distributed on or close to that line. However, because we do not expect that every plotted value will be on that line even when the data were sampled from a normal distribution, we need a way to decide how far our data can deviate from that straight line and still be consistent with the hypothesis that our data were sampled from a normal distribution. A set of confidence bands drawn around the line can provide that information.[5]

The procedure for creating a normal quantile plot is summarized in Box 2.5.

HOW TO INTERPRET A NORMAL QUANTILE PLOT When our data are sampled from a normal distribution, the resulting normal quantile plot should be distributed close to a straight line, and all of our data points should lie within the confidence bands. Therefore, when all of our data are inside the confidence bands, we have *no evidence that our data did not come from a normal distribution*; in other words, our data appear to have been sampled from a normal distribution. On the other hand, we conclude that our data did not come from a normal distribution when some of our data points are outside these confidence bands.

BOX 2.5
HOW TO CONSTRUCT A NORMAL QUANTILE PLOT

Purpose

To assess whether our data may have come from a normal distribution

Procedure

1. Rank order the data from lowest to highest.

2. For each ranked data point, calculate the approximate z-score for each rank for scores from a normal distribution using the following formula: $z_i = \Phi^{-1}\left[\dfrac{r_i - 0.5}{n}\right]$, where r_i is the rank for that value, n is the total number of values in the set, and $\Phi^{-1}[\ ]$ is the inverse normal probability of the value in the bracket.

3. On a sheet of graph paper, put the range of the actual values on the vertical axis and the z-scores on the horizontal axis.

4. For each observation, plot a single point at the intersection of its value on the vertical axis and corresponding z-score from the horizontal axis.

5. Draw a straight line through the point corresponding to $z = 0$ and the sample mean. The slope of this line equals the standard deviation of the sample data.

6. Conclude that there is *no evidence* that your data *did not* come from a normal distribution when one or more of the values in the normal quantile plot are outside the Lilliefors confidence bands.*

---

* These confidence bands are included in the normal quantile plots generated in JMP statistical software.

---

[5] These are called Lilliefors confidence bands (see Lilliefors, 1967). The procedure for calculating a set of confidence bands for this situation is computationally intensive. See Conover (1980) for a good description of that procedure. The program JMP provides the bands for us.

Normal quantile plots for the data in Table 2.1 are presented in Figure 2.10. These plots, which were created in JMP, show the State Hostility Scale scores on the vertical axis, the z-scores for the quantiles from a normal distribution calculated from Equation 2.2 on the top horizontal axis, and the quantiles for a normal distribution on the bottom horizontal axis. The vertical line in the middle of each plot is where $z = 0$. The diagonal line has a slope that equals the standard deviation of the sample data and crosses the line where $z = 0$ at the sample mean.

If these data were sampled from a normal distribution, we would expect the scores to straddle that line and none of the data points to lie outside the confidence bands. We can see in the left panel (After Insulting Message) that large segments of the data do not straddle the straight line very well, although none of the data points is outside the confidence bands (but some are very close or touching). On the other hand, the data in the right panel (After Nice Message) pretty much straddle the diagonal line (with the exception of the points at both ends of the distribution), and none touches or is outside the confidence bands. On the basis of these normal quantile plots, it is hard to decide whether the data in the After Insulting Message group do or do not come from a normal distribution, but we have *no evidence* here to conclude that the data in the After Nice Message group do not come from a normal distribution; that is, we can feel comfortable assuming the data from the latter group come from a normal distribution.

FIGURE 2.10 ■ Normal quantile plots of the State Hostility Scale scores for the After Insulting Message group (*left*) and for the After Nice Message group (*right*).

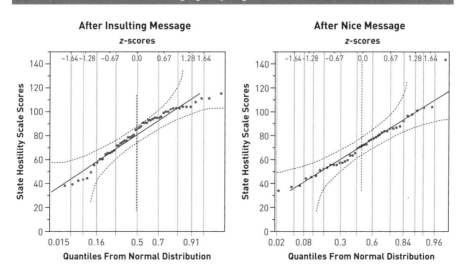

Kolmogorov–Smirnov–Lilliefors Goodness of Fit Test

This test compares the quantiles of your data to those from a normal distribution. When our data are sampled from a normal distribution, the differences between the quantiles will be small.

The normal quantile plot described above is based on the Kolmogorov–Smirnov test for goodness of fit with the Lilliefors correction (now referred to as the K-S-L test). The K-S goodness of fit test was developed to compare how well a theoretical model (like the normal distribution) fits a set of data. This test is performed by comparing the quantiles of your data to the cumulative distribution function[6] for the model you suspect your data fit. The quantiles from your data are plotted against the quantiles from the cumulative distribution function for the model you suspect the data fit. The test statistic for this test is the maximum deviation (D) for the data from the model:

$$D = \max_X [F^*(Y_i) - S_n(Y_i)], \tag{2.3}$$

where,

$S_n(Y_i)$ is the distribution of the ranked sample values (Y_i),

$F^*(Y_i)$ is the value of the corresponding quantile from the cumulative distribution function for the model for each Y, and

D is the maximum difference between these two distributions.

Tables for critical values of this test are available (see Conover, 1980).

The original K-S goodness of fit test uses the parameters of the model (μ and σ) for the test. This leads to a conservative test of the hypothesis that the data came from the theoretical model (normal distribution). Lilliefors (1967) provided a correction that produces a more powerful test by using the sample mean and the estimate of the population standard deviation. Lilliefors's test uses a different set of tables for the critical values (Lilliefors, 1967; see also Conover, 1980). The K-S-L test is provided in SPSS. The procedure for calculating the Kolmogorov–Smirnov–Lilliefors test for a normal distribution is described in Box 2.6.

The null hypothesis for this test is that the data come from a normal distribution. The alternative hypothesis is that the data do not come from a normal distribution. For the data

---

[6]The cumulative distribution function (CDF) for a distribution like the normal distribution gives the probability of obtaining a value less than or equal to any value in that distribution. These probabilities are quantiles. The CDF for a normal distribution is an S-shaped curve. This shape is sometimes called an ogive.

BOX 2.6

HOW TO PERFORM THE KOLMOGOROV–SMIRNOV–LILLIEFORS
GOODNESS OF FIT TEST FOR A NORMAL DISTRIBUTION

Purpose

To test whether our data come from a normal distribution

Procedure

1. Compute the quantile for each z-score from the formula $Q(r_i) = \dfrac{r_i - .5}{n}$.

2. Find the corresponding values for those quantiles from the inverse cumulative normal distribution and create the corresponding cumulative normal distribution, $F^*(Y_i)$.

3. For each score in your sample, find the difference between the $S_n(Y_i)$ and $F^*(Y_i)$ and locate the largest difference $\max_x [F^*(Y_i) - S_n(Y_i)]$.

4. The test statistic is $D = \max_x [F^*(Y_i) - S_n(Y_i)]$.

5. Find the probability of obtaining the computed value of D if our data come from a normal distribution from Table 1 in Lilliefors (1967).

   a. When D is *equal to or greater than* the value for our sample size at the .05 level in Table 1, we conclude that our data were *not* sampled from a normal distribution.

   b. When D is *less than* the value for our sample size at the .05 level in Table 1, we conclude that we have no evidence that our data were not sampled from a normal distribution.

Note: This test is included in SPSS.

in the After Insulting Message group, $D = 0.120$ and $p = .049$. Using $p = .05$ as our cutoff for rejecting the null hypothesis, the value of D leads us to reject the null hypothesis and to conclude that these data *do not* come from a normal distribution. For the data in the After Nice Message group, $D = 0.082$ and $p = .20$. These results do not allow us to reject the null hypothesis that the data in the After Nice Message group come from a normal distribution.

Shapiro–Wilk *W* Test

This test is based on the correlation between our ranked data and corresponding quantiles from a normal distribution. This correlation is close to 1 when our data are sampled from a normal distribution.

The use of Lilliefors confidence bands with normal quantile plots gives us a graphic method for comparing our data to a normal distribution, and the Lilliefors correction to the K-S goodness of fit test provides a test statistic for assessing goodness of fit. The Shapiro–Wilk *W* test provides another approach for detecting deviations from a normal distribution.

The test statistic W is the correlation coefficient between our ranked data and constants that corresponds to what we would expect when the data are from a normal distribution. When the data are perfectly normally distributed, $W = 1$. As the data deviate from a normal distribution, the value of W decreases. Shapiro and Wilk (1965) provided both a table for the corresponding constants from a normal distribution (which they called a) and a table for testing whether the value of W is small enough to reject the hypothesis that our data come from a normal distribution. The general procedure for calculating the Shapiro–Wilk W test is described in Box 2.7.

The null hypothesis for this test is that the data come from a normal distribution, and the alternative hypothesis is that the data do not come from a normal distribution. For the data in the After Insulting Message group, $W = .957$ and $p = .0508$, and for the data in the After Nice Message group, $W = .959$ and $p = .1344$. Using $p = .05$ as our cutoff for rejecting the null hypothesis, the value of W obtained for the data from both the After Insulting Message and After Nice message groups does *not* allow us to reject the null hypothesis that those data come from a normal distribution.

The difference in conclusions between the K-S-L test and the S-W test for the After Insulting group is due to the p-values calculated from each test ($p = .049$ and $p = .0508$, respectively).[7] Most of the time, the conclusions will be the same. For the After Nice Message group, the p-values from both tests, while different from each other, are greater than .05; therefore, they do *not* allow us to reject the null hypothesis that the data in the After Nice Message group come from a normal distribution.

When the results from using normal quantile plots with Lilliefors confidence bands are different from the results of a K-S-L test or a Shapiro–Wilk test, the latter tests are preferred because they are usually more powerful than the Lilliefors confidence bands for detecting departures from normal distributions. However, a note of caution is in order here. As we will see in Chapter 6, the ability of hypothesis tests to detect departures from the hypothesis being tested (the null hypothesis) is a function of sample size: The larger the sample size, the more likely the test will detect departures from the null hypothesis. As we noted in Chapter 1, the normal distribution is a theoretical model for our data, and we rarely expect our data to conform exactly to that model. On the other hand, we will see in Chapter 7, even small departures from the normal distribution assumption that underlies Student's t-test can have an effect on the outcome of that test.

---

[7] How to deal with p-values slightly greater than .05 will be addressed in Chapter 6 in the section "Can a Result Be 'Marginally Significant'?"

BOX 2.7

HOW TO CALCULATE THE SHAPIRO–WILK W TEST STATISTIC

Purpose

To test whether our data come from a normal distribution

Procedure

1. Rank order the scores from lowest to highest.

2. Let $k = n/2$, where n is the number of data values. Compute the difference between the last and first ranked scores $(Y_n - Y_1)$, the second-to-last and second scores $(Y_{n-1} - Y_2)$, and so forth for all k pairs of scores. The formula for the general case is this:

$$Y_{n-i+1} - Y_i, \text{ where } i = 1 \text{ to } k$$

3. Obtain the constants a_{n-i+1} corresponding to each of these k differences from Shapiro and Wilk (1965) Table 5.

4. Compute:

$$b = \sum_{i=1}^{k} a_{n-i+1}\left(Y_{n-i+1} - Y_i\right)$$

5. Compute the sum of the squared deviations of each score from the sample mean:

$$SS = \sum_{i=1}^{n}\left(Y_i - \bar{Y}\right)^2$$

6. Compute the test statistic:

$$W = \frac{b^2}{SS}$$

7. Using Table 6 in Shapiro and Wilk (1965), find the probability of obtaining the computed value of W if our data come from a normal distribution.

   a. When W is *equal to or greater* than the value for our sample size at the .95 level in Table 6, we conclude that we have no evidence that our data were not sampled from a normal distribution.

   b. When W is *less than* the value for our sample size at the .95 level in Table 6, we conclude that our data were *not* sampled from a normal distribution.

Note: This test is included in both SPSS and JMP.

WHY SHOULD WE CARE ABOUT LOOKING AT OUR DATA?

To see why it is important to look at your data before analyzing them, consider the two studies described below. Although these studies deal with a different area of social psychology than we have been discussing, they illustrate the importance of looking at your data before analyzing them.

Buss and Schmitt (1993) asked 75 male and 73 female college students to estimate how many sexual partners they would ideally like to have over a series of time intervals ranging from the next month to the next 30 years. As the length of the time intervals increased, the difference between the men and women who answered that question widened, until over the course of 30 years, the mean ideal number of sexual partners reported by men was 16 and the number reported by women was 4. The differences in reported ideal number of sex partners were statistically significant according to *t*-tests conducted at all time intervals surveyed. On the basis of these results and other findings related to sexual behavior, Buss and Schmitt argued that "because of a fundamental asymmetry between the sexes in minimum levels of parental investment, men devote a larger proportion of their total mating effort to short-term mating than do women" (p. 205).[8]

Pedersen, Miller, Putcha-Bhagavatula, and Yang (2002) questioned that conclusion, even though they replicated the general findings in Buss and Schmitt's paper by asking the same questions of 107 male and 159 female undergraduate students at their university. Looking closely at their data, Pedersen et al. saw that the responses at each of the time periods were highly skewed and there were outliers. In fact, one male participant reported his ideal number of sexual partners over the next 30 years was 6,000! With that number included, the mean ideal number of sexual partners for men was 64.3. When Pedersen et al. used the same procedure as Buss and Schmitt to deal with outliers (that is, replacing values over 99 with 99), they still found a large difference in the mean ideal number of partners between men and women (7.69 vs. 2.78), even though the distributions for men and women were quite similar and, for both genders, the mode and the median of ideal number of partners over 30 years was 1. The difference between the two sample means was due to more men than women claiming an ideal number of sexual partners greater than 10. Clearly, the conclusions one draws depend on what descriptive and inferential statistics are used. Buss and Schmitt might have analyzed their data differently and might have drawn different conclusions had they looked at them first.

Although both Buss and Schmitt and Pedersen et al. found statistically significant results with *t*-tests for these highly skewed data, that outcome does not always happen. Wilcox (2010, 2012) shows how even small departures from normal distributions can dramatically affect the statistical power of *t*-tests when the sample sizes are smaller than those used in these two studies. We will look at this problem in more detail in Chapter 7 and present some alternative statistical tests to overcome that problem. The message here is that those who do not examine their data increase the risk of misinterpreting their findings or performing statistical tests that are not powerful enough to find real differences.

---

[8] Although they did not report it in their paper, they replaced any response over 99 with 99 in their data set. That change to the data reduced, but did not eliminate, the gender differences.

Summary

In Chapter 2, we discussed the importance of examining your data after they are collected and before conducting inferential statistics. We presented a number of procedures for illustrating and evaluating the distributions of your data sets. We learned how to create and use various types of graphical displays, including histograms, letter value plots, stem-and-leaf displays, box plots, and quantile plots to explore your data sets and how to use normal quantile plots and the Kolmogorov–Smirnov–Lilliefors and Shapiro–Wilk tests to decide whether your data are sampled from a normal distribution. We will use these tools to effectively assess the central tendencies, spreads, and shapes of our data sets and to inform our decisions about conducting further analyses in the domain of statistical inference—the topic we will begin to discuss in Chapter 3.

Conceptual Exercises

1. Examine the following stem-and-leaf display and answer the following questions:

   a. What are the *lowest* three values?

   b. What is the median?

   c. Describe the overall shape of this set of data. (Include symmetry/skewness, outliers, and so forth in your answer.) What is it about this stem-and-leaf display that led to your conclusions?

   Unit .01

   1 2 = .12

0*	001112233334
.	55568888999
1*	023444
.	6889
2*	024
.	88
3*	024
.	68
4*	3
.	
5*	
.	
6*	2

2. Examine the following quantile plot. Describe the data set from which it was derived in terms of symmetry, skewness, outliers, etc. What is it about this quantile plot that led to your description?

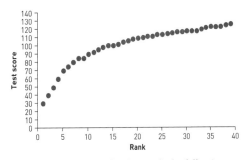

3. Draw a quantile plot for data with the following characteristics: The lowest scores are close together. As you move toward the middle, the scores are progressively farther apart. As you move away from the middle and toward the higher values, the scores become progressively closer together. The entire data set is symmetrical.

4. Examine the following box plot. Describe the data set from which it was derived. (Include symmetry/skewness, outliers, and so forth in your answer.) What is it about this box plot that led to your description?

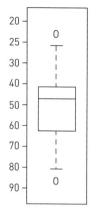

5. Create a schematic box plot for the following data. Include an axis showing the location of the various aspects of your box plot. What does this box plot tell you about the data?

Data			
3	10	14	21
3	10	14	21
4	12	14	24
6	12	17	24
6	12	17	24
7	14	17	37
10	14	19	43

6. What does the following normal quantile plot tell us about the data from which it was drawn? What aspects of this normal quantile plot lead you to your conclusions?

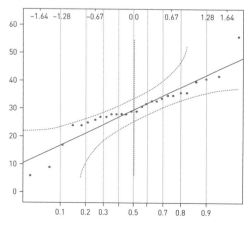

7. What does the following letter value display tell you about the data being summarized here? What aspects of this letter value display lead you to your conclusions?

			$N=200$		
	Depth	*Hi*	*Lo*	*Mid*	*Spread*
M	100.5	115	.68	115.68	
F	50.5	124.55	106.14	115.35	18.41
E	25.5	124.87	93.58	109.23	31.29
D	13	124.16	83.28	103.72	40.88
C	7	122.73	72.77	97.75	49.96
B	4	123.05	67.56	95.31	55.49
	1	125.39	48.00	86.69	77.39

8. Create a schematic box plot from the data in the above letter value display, being sure to include an axis showing the location of the various aspects of your box plot. What does this box plot tell you about the data?

9. Describe in general terms how a normal quantile plot is created from a set of data and what it tells us about the data. Make up an example of a normal quantile plot for data that do *not* come from a normal distribution to illustrate. (Label the axes.)

10. What is a normal quantile plot, and what does it tell you about the data in the plot? Make up an example of a normal quantile plot to illustrate. (Label the axes.)

11. How can you tell whether data are symmetric or skewed from a letter value display? If your data are skewed, how can you tell the direction of the skew?

12. What information do box plots provide about data that bar graphs and line graphs, even those with error bars, do not?

13. Look at the following normal quantile plot. What does it tell you about the data? Why?

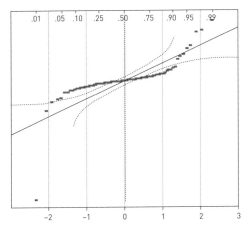

14. Create a normal quantile plot for a set of numbers that were *not* sampled from a normal distribution. Label the axes and indicate what each part of your plot represents.

15. What does the following box plot tell you about the data from which this sample was drawn? What aspects of this box plot lead you to your conclusions?

16. What does the following normal quantile plot tell us about the data from which this sample was drawn? What aspects of this normal quantile plot lead you to your conclusions?

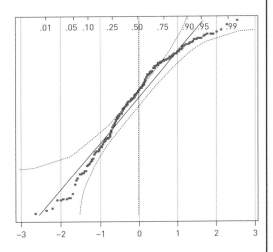

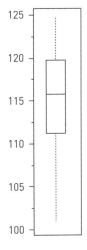

Student Study Site

Visit the Student Study Site at **https://study.sagepub.com/friemanstats** for a variety of useful tools including data sets, additional exercises, and web resources.

THE BEHAVIOR
OF DATA

PART II

PROPERTIES
OF DISTRIBUTIONS

The Building Blocks of Statistical Inference

Before proceeding further on our quest for knowledge of how to answer our research questions using inferential statistics, we need to look at some very important properties of distributions. These properties apply to both populations and samples. *They are the foundations of statistical inference, and it is important that you thoroughly understand them.* Their importance will become obvious shortly.

The properties described here are stated as theorems, and algebraic proofs of these theorems are provided in boxes for those who prefer or require a rigorous proof of the validity of these theorems. Where algebra is used, each step in the proof is annotated.[1] An intuitive explanation is also provided for those who prefer that approach. You can use either (or both) of these modes of explanation to help you understand and accept these theorems. Another way you can convince yourself of the validity of these theorems is to apply them to an arbitrarily chosen set of data. A set of exercises is provided at the end of the chapter. It is important that you understand why these theorems are true and that you be comfortable with them. They provide the basis for the correct understanding and use of inferential statistics.

For the first two theorems, we start with a set of numbers (from a sample or population—it does not matter) and apply the same operation to every number in that set (such as adding a constant to every number) to create a new set of numbers. We are interested in the relationship between the original set of numbers and the new set. In particular, we are interested in the relationship between

---

[1] It will be easier to understand these proofs if you are familiar with the rules of algebra and the rules of summation, which are reviewed in the appendices.

the original mean and the new mean, the relationship between the original variance and the new variance, and whether the operation on the numbers changes the form of the distribution.[2] With respect to an experiment, adding a constant is a way to conceptualize what happens when the experimental treatment affects all of the participants in your experiment the same way (that is, the treatment has an "additive" effect), while multiplying by a constant is one way to conceptualize a "participant-by-treatment interaction" (that is, how the treatment affects the participants depends on who they are). For ease of explanation, these theorems will be described in terms of population parameters (μ, σ^2), but keep in mind that they also are true for sample statistics ($\overline{X}$, s^2).

THE EFFECTS OF ADDING A CONSTANT OR MULTIPLYING BY A CONSTANT

Adding a constant to every value in a set of numbers will shift the mean by that constant, but the variance and form of the set will not change. Multiplying every value in a set of numbers by a constant shifts the mean and changes the variance (we need algebra to tell by how much), but it does not change the form of the distribution of the values.

Theorem 1: Effects of Adding a Constant

Given any set of numbers X_1, X_2, . . ., X_n, that has a mean μ_X and variance σ^2_X, when a constant (C) is added to each score to produce a new set of numbers X_1 + C, X_2 + C, . . . , X_n + C, the mean of this new set of numbers $[\mu_{(X + C)}]$ will be μ_X + C (original mean plus constant), and the variance of the new set of numbers will be σ^2_X (the original variance). Furthermore, the form of the new distribution will be identical to that of the original distribution.

The situation described in Theorem 1 is presented in Figure 3.1.

INTUITIVE EXPLANATION It is apparent that the effect of adding a constant to every number in a distribution is to shift each number the same distance to a new location (X_i + C), thus creating an identical distribution that is displaced to one side of the original distribution. All distances and relationships among the scores are preserved by this transformation; therefore, the variance and form of the distribution are not affected. The mean of the numbers, too, will be shifted the same amount, and the new mean will be μ_X + C.

---

[2] *Form* refers to the distribution of the population of values, that is, whether it is a normal distribution, an exponential distribution, or some other distribution.

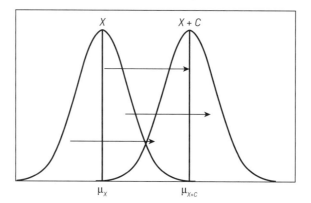

FIGURE 3.1 ■ The effect of adding a constant, *C*, to every number in the distribution on the left is to create a new distribution to the right. The constant is represented by the length of the arrow.

An algebraic proof of the effects on the mean and variance of adding a constant to every number in a distribution of numbers is presented in Box 3.1.

Finally, what is true for addition is also true for subtraction; that is, subtracting a constant from every number in a distribution creates a new distribution with $\mu_{(X - C)} = \mu_X - C$, $\sigma^2_{(X - C)} = \sigma^2_X$, and the form of the new distribution is the same as the form of the original distribution.

Theorem 2: Effects of Multiplying by a Constant

Given any set of numbers X_1, X_2, . . ., X_n, that has a mean μ_X and variance σ^2_X, when each number is multiplied by a constant (C) to produce a new set of numbers CX_1, CX_2, . . . , CX_n, the mean of this new set of numbers $\mu_{(XC)}$ will be $C\mu_X$ (the constant times the original mean), and the variance of this new set of numbers will be $C^2\sigma^2_X$ (the constant squared times the original variance). Furthermore, the form of the new distribution will be the same as the form of the original distribution; that is, if the original distribution X is a normal distribution, for instance, then the distribution of CX will also be a normal distribution.[3]

The situation described in Theorem 2 is presented in Figure 3.2.

---

[3]This last proposition cannot be proved without introducing additional analytic methods that are beyond the scope of this book. While it may seem counterintuitive, it is in fact the case. You can find a formal proof of this assertion in a mathematical statistics text.

BOX 3.1
ALGEBRAIC PROOF OF THEOREM 1

Proof that adding a constant *C* to every number in a distribution creates a new distribution with a mean equal to the original mean plus the constant

The mean of something is "the sum of the somethings divided by the number of somethings." If the mean of the original distribution is $\mu_X = \dfrac{\sum\limits_{i=1}^{n} X_i}{n}$, then the mean of *X* + *C* is as follows:

$$\mu_{X+C} = \frac{\sum\limits_{i=1}^{n}(X_i + C)}{n}$$

If you distribute the summation sign, this becomes the following expression:

$$\frac{\sum\limits_{i=1}^{n} X_i + \sum\limits_{i=1}^{n} C}{n}$$

Using the fact that $\sum\limits_{i=1}^{n} C = nC$, you find

$$\frac{\sum\limits_{i=1}^{n}(X_i) + nC}{n}$$

$$= \frac{\sum\limits_{i=1}^{n} X_i}{n} + \frac{nC}{n}$$

Cancel the *n*'s and use the definition of the mean:

$$\mu_{X+C} = \mu_X + C$$

Proof that adding a constant *C* to every number in a distribution creates a new distribution with a variance equal to the original variance

If the variance of the original distribution is

$$\sigma_X^2 = \frac{\sum\limits_{i=1}^{n}(X_i - \mu_X)^2}{n}, \text{ then variance of } X + C \text{ is as follows:}$$

$$\sigma_{X+C}^2 = \frac{\sum\limits_{i=1}^{n}\left[(X_i + C) - (\mu_X + C)\right]^2}{n}$$

When you remove the parentheses, distributing the negative sign, this becomes

$$= \frac{\sum\limits_{i=1}^{n}(X_i + C - \mu_X - C)^2}{n}$$

Thus,

$$\sigma_{X+C}^2 = \frac{\sum\limits_{i=1}^{n}(X_i - \mu_X)^2}{n} = \sigma_X^2$$

Therefore, if a constant is added to every number in a distribution to create a new distribution, the mean of the new distribution will be $\mu_X + C$ (the original mean plus a constant), and the variance will be σ_X^2 (the original variance). Furthermore, *the form of the new distribution will be identical to the form of the original distribution.*

INTUITIVE EXPLANATION The effect of multiplying every number in a distribution by a constant is to shift the numbers to a new location, but *the distance shifted will depend on the original number*: Low numbers will not be shifted as far as high

FIGURE 3.2 ■ The effect of multiplying every number in the distribution on the left by a constant *C* is to create the new distribution on the right. The arrows represent the distance each score is displaced. Because each number is multiplied by a constant, larger scores are moved greater distances.

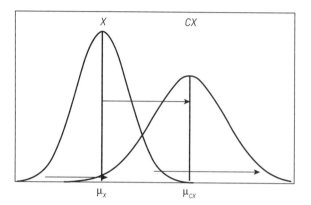

numbers.[4] Therefore, when $C > 1$, the distances between the numbers will increase, and the variance of these numbers will increase; when $C < 1$, the distances between the numbers will decrease. The reason for this behavior of the distribution is tied to the definition of *variance*. We noted earlier that the mean of something is "the sum of the somethings divided by the number of somethings." That makes the variance the "mean of the squared deviations of each score from the mean, that is, the mean of $(X_i - \mu)^2$."[5] Since the variance is the mean of the squared difference between each number and the mean $[(X_i - \mu_X)^2]$, when we increase the difference between X_i and μ_X by a constant (C) that is greater than 1, the variance of those numbers will increase, and when we decrease the difference between X_i and μ_X, the variance of those numbers will decrease. We need the algebraic proof in Box 3.2 to demonstrate that the new variance will be exactly $C^2\sigma_X^2$.

The mean of the numbers in the distribution, too, will be shifted to $C\mu_X$ (the original mean multiplied by the constant).

The algebraic proofs of these assertions are in Box 3.2.

---

[4] Consider two numbers, 4 and 10: When they are both multiplied by 2, 4 becomes 8 and 10 becomes 20. The number 4 is moved a distance of 4 units to become 8, while the number 10 is moved a distance of 10 units to become 20. Now the distance between the new numbers (8 and 20) is *greater* than the distance between the original numbers (4 and 10). On the other hand, if the constant is a fraction, such as 0.5, then 4 becomes 2 and 10 becomes 5. In this case, the distance between the new numbers is *less* than the distance between the original numbers, and the new variance is lower than the original variance.

[5] The term *mean squares* in analysis of variance is short for "mean of the squared deviations."

BOX 3.2
ALGEBRAIC PROOF OF THEOREM 2

Proof that multiplying every number in a distribution by a constant creates a new distribution with a mean equal to the original mean multiplied by the constant

The mean of something is "the sum of the somethings divided by the number of somethings." If the mean of the original distribution is $\mu_X = \dfrac{\sum_{i=1}^{n} X_i}{n}$, then the mean of CX is as follows:

$$\mu_{CX} = \frac{\sum_{i=1}^{n} CX_i}{n}$$

Using the fact that $\sum_{i=1}^{n} CX_i = C\sum_{i=1}^{n} X_i$, you find

$$\mu_{CX} = \frac{C\sum_{i=1}^{n} X_i}{n} = C\mu_X$$

Proof that multiplying every number in a distribution by a constant creates a new distribution with a variance equal to the original variance multiplied by the constant squared

If the variance of the original distribution is

$$\sigma_X^2 = \frac{\sum_{i=1}^{n} (X_i - \mu_X)^2}{n}, \text{ then variance of } CX \text{ is the}$$

following:

$$\sigma_{CX}^2 = \frac{\sum_{i=1}^{n} \left[(CX_i) - (C\mu_X)\right]^2}{n}$$

You can factor out the C from inside the brackets. Because everything in the bracket is squared, you are factoring out C^2.

$$\sigma_{CX}^2 = \frac{\sum_{i=1}^{n} C^2 (X_i - \mu_X)^2}{n} = C^2 \sigma_X^2$$

Therefore, if every number in a distribution is multiplied by a constant to create a new distribution, the mean of the new distribution will be $C\mu_X$ (the original mean multiplied by the constant), and the variance will be $C^2\sigma_X^2$ (the original variance times the constant squared). Furthermore, *the form of the new distribution will be identical to that of the original distribution* (although this latter property is not proved here).

Again, what is true for multiplication is also true for division; that is, dividing every score in a distribution by a constant creates a new distribution with $\mu_{X/C} = \mu_X/C$, $\sigma_{X/C}^2 = \sigma_X^2/C^2$, and the form of the new distribution is the same as the form of the original distribution.

THE STANDARD SCORE TRANSFORMATION

Any set of scores can be converted to standard scores by subtracting the mean of the set from every score and dividing that difference by the standard deviation of the set. Standard scores have a number of uses in statistics and psychological measurement.

We can combine Theorems 1 and 2 to produce a useful metric for comparing scores from different distributions. We subtract the mean of the distribution from each score in the distribution and divide the resulting difference (score – mean) by the standard deviation of the distribution. This produces a new distribution of what are called *standard scores*, where

$$\text{standard score} = \frac{\text{score} - \text{mean}}{\text{standard deviation}} \qquad (3.1)$$

The resulting standard scores are also called z-scores.[6] When the standard score transformation is applied to a population,

$$z = \frac{X - \mu_X}{\sigma_X}, \qquad (3.2a)$$

and when it is applied to a sample,

$$z = \frac{X - \bar{X}_X}{s_X} \qquad (3.2b)$$

Properties of *z*-Scores

The properties of distributions of z-scores come directly from Theorems 1 and 2. When the original numbers come from a normal distribution, we can use the unit normal distribution tables to compute probabilities for ranges of values from normal distributions.

Because of the way z-scores are created (subtracting the mean from every number and dividing by the standard deviation), $\mu_z = 0$ (from Theorem 1) and $\sigma_z^2 = 1$ (from Theorem 2).[7] These equalities are true for all distributions of numbers. Furthermore, the distribution of z-scores will have the same form of distribution as the original distribution. Finally, dividing by the standard deviation puts all z-scores on the same scale; that scale is the number of standard deviations a given value in the original distribution is from the mean of that distribution. For example, $z = 1.5$ indicates that the original score is 1.5 standard deviations above its mean, and $z = -0.5$ indicates that the original value is one half of a standard deviation below its mean. These properties allow us to compare values from different distributions of measurements that may not be on the same scales (such as

---

[6] The term *standard score* is a general term for scores derived to allow researchers to make comparisons on a common scale. z-scores are calculated using Equations 3.2a and 3.2b. As examples, IQ scores and scores on certain academic aptitude tests, such as the SAT and GRE, are derived from z-scores. Other types of derived scores include development standard scores and standard age scores.

[7] These properties of z-scores can be easily verified by substituting Equation 3.2b into the formulas for μ_z and σ_z^2 and applying Theorems 1 and 2.

height and weight or test scores from different tests). That comparability is what makes them "standard" scores.

When the original distribution is a normal distribution, then the distribution of these values converted to z-scores is also a normal distribution with $\mu_z = 0$ *and* $\sigma^2_z = 1$. Called a **unit normal distribution**, it is the basis for the "normal curve" tables in statistics books and in Appendix E here. Transforming normally distributed scores to a unit normal distribution provides information about the proportion of values in the original distribution that are between any given value and the mean, or between any given value and one of the ends of the distribution. The unit normal distribution table (Appendix E) provides values for the areas under the curve as described in Figure 3.3.

To find the area or proportion of the scores between 50 (the mean of the values) and 60 (an example of a given value) in the population shown on the left of Figure 3.3, first convert these values to z-scores with the formula $z = \dfrac{60 - 50}{5} = 2$. Then find the area of the unit normal distribution (distribution of z-scores on the right of Figure 3.3) between $z = 0$ and $z = 2$ using the unit normal distribution table in Appendix E. To do so, first locate the row where $z = 2$ and record the proportion in the tail of the distribution. That proportion is .0228. Then subtract the proportion in the tail (.0228) from .5000 (the area of the normal curve from $z = 0$ to $+\infty$). This result gives .4772 as the proportion of scores between 50 and 60 (between $z = 0$ and $z = 2$). What is the proportion of scores between 40 and 45?

It should be noted that when the original distribution is not a normal distribution, the use of the z-score transformation will *not* produce a normal distribution. It is a common misconception that converting to z-scores always results in a normal distribution, but it can be easily shown that this belief is not correct. Take any set of numbers that is

FIGURE 3.3 ■ On the left is a normal distribution with a mean of 50 and a standard deviation of 5. On the right is the distribution of z-scores.

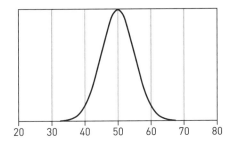
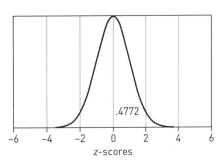

obviously skewed and convert the values to z-scores. The distribution of these z-scores will be in the same form as the original distribution, which is a direct consequence of Theorems 1 and 2. It is possible to transform a non-normal distribution to a normal distribution, but doing so is more complicated than simply converting to z.[8]

Applications of *z*-Scores

There are a number of uses for z-scores, including finding percentile ranks (quantiles) for scores from normal distributions, integrating different measurements into an overall score, and creating test statistics for hypothesis tests for population means.

As noted above, z-scores can be used to find areas under various parts of a normal distribution and to calculate the probability of obtaining scores that fall into different regions of the curve. However, there are several other uses for z-scores.

TO FIND PERCENTILE RANKS (QUANTILES) FOR SCORES FROM A NORMAL DISTRIBUTION Consider the distribution of IQ test scores from the 1937 version of the Stanford–Binet Intelligence Test presented in Figure 3.4. The mean and standard deviation of that sample of 3,000 individuals who comprised the standardization group was very close to the population parameters the designers of the test strove to obtain ($\mu = 100$ and $\sigma = 16$).[9] Suppose someone received a score of 120 on that test. We can compute the z-score for that person and use the unit normal distribution table to determine the proportion of people who score lower than that person (the percentile rank or quantile for that person). For this example, $z = (120 - 100)/16 = 1.25$. From the unit normal distribution table in Appendix E, we see that the area in the tail from $z = 1.25$ to $+\infty$ is .1056. That gives us the proportion of scores above 120. We subtract .1056 from 1.0000 to find the proportion of scores below 120. That proportion is .8944. This tells us that someone with an IQ score on this test scored higher than 89.44% of the population who take this test [$Q(.8944) = 120$]. (See the left of Figure 3.4.) We can also use z-scores to find the proportion of people who have a score below the mean. Suppose someone received a score of 80 on the Stanford–Binet Intelligence Test. In this situation, $z = (80 - 100)/16 = -1.25$. The negative value tells us that this score is below the mean, and the area in the tail from $z = -1.25$ to $-\infty$ is also .1056. That means that this person scored higher than 10.56% of the population who took this test. (See the right of Figure 3.4.) Therefore, we can use the unit normal distribution table to find areas of a normal curve on both sides of the population mean.

---

[8] See Emerson and Stoto (1983) for a good discussion of data transformations.

[9] The standard deviation for the most recent version of the Stanford-Binet Intelligence Scales, Fifth Edition (Roid, 2003) is 15.

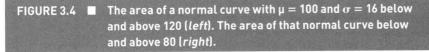

FIGURE 3.4 ■ The area of a normal curve with μ = 100 and σ = 16 below and above 120 (*left*). The area of that normal curve below and above 80 (*right*).

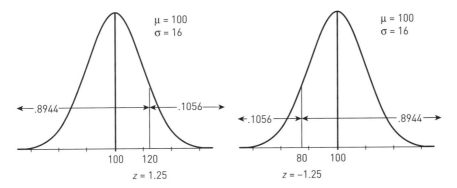

You can also convert quantiles (or proportions) of a normal distribution to raw scores when you know the mean and standard deviation of the original population. For example, if you want to know the IQ score below which 95% of the population scores (the upper 5% of the population), find the corresponding z-score in the unit normal distribution table (1.645 in this case) and substitute it, along with the population mean and standard deviation, into the following equation:

$$X = \mu + z\,\sigma \qquad\qquad (3.3)$$

Equation 3.3 results from applying the rules of algebra to Equation 3.2a. In this example, X = 100 + (1.645 × 16) = 126. Therefore, Q(0.95) = 126.

Note that these procedures to find quantiles (percentile ranks) or to find the scores that correspond to specific quantiles (percentile ranks) only work when the original distribution is, or closely approximates, a normal distribution.

You can do the same with SAT scores. If you know the mean and standard deviation of the test scores (which you do: μ = 500, σ = 100 for the SAT subscales), then you can use Equation 3.2a to find the percentile rank for a given SAT score, and use Equation 3.3 to find the SAT score for a given percentile rank. What is the percentile rank for an SAT score of 650 on the Verbal subscale?

INTEGRATING DIFFERENT MEASUREMENTS INTO AN OVERALL SCORE Many psychological scales are made up of a number of subscales. When the different subscales are measured in different ways using different response scales, the overall score can be constructed by converting each subscale score into z-scores and adding, or averaging, these to obtain the overall score. For example, there are several ways that researchers may measure attitude strength for a given issue, such as gun control or abortion. It may be measured by asking individuals to report how certain they are about their attitudes about the issue, how important their attitudes about the issue are, how much knowledge they have about the issue, etc. (Krosnick, Boninger, Chuang, Berent, & Carnot, 1993). While a case can be made that these dimensions of attitude strength are independent, these various measures are highly correlated (e.g., Saucier, Webster, Hoffman, & Strain, 2014). Accordingly, researchers who are interested in individuals' overall attitude strength for a given issue may be motivated to combine these dimensions into one composite variable. Because the response scales for these dimensions vary, using z-scores makes this combination possible. The reason to use z-scores to compute overall scores is that, if you add or average together two or more response scales that have different ranges (e.g., a 1 to 7 response scale and a 1 to 5 response scale or −3 to +3 response scale), the response scale with the highest possible score will be given greater weight in the average. Converting the scores to z-scores puts the scores on the same scale prior to averaging or adding them.

CREATING TEST STATISTICS FOR HYPOTHESIS TESTS FOR POPULATION MEANS In Chapters 6 and 7, we will use standard scores to create test statistics for testing hypotheses about population means. The hypotheses tested include tests of the hypothesis $\mu_1 - \mu_2 = 0$ (the means of the two populations from which the data were sampled are the same, where the two populations represent the two groups in the experiment) and $\mu = \mu_0$ (the population mean from which the data were sampled equals the value μ_0). When the population variances are known, the test statistic is a z-statistic (Chapter 6). When the population variances are not known and must be estimated from the sample data, the test statistic is a t-statistic (Chapter 7).

THE EFFECTS OF ADDING OR SUBTRACTING SCORES FROM TWO DIFFERENT DISTRIBUTIONS

The next two theorems are concerned with the effects of combining numbers from two different distributions to create a third distribution. They provide the basis for understanding how we perform hypothesis tests for the differences between and among population means.

Theorem 3: Effects of Adding Scores From Two Different Distributions

Given any set of numbers $X_1, X_2, \ldots, X_n$ that has a mean μ_X and variance σ^2_X, and another set of numbers $Y_1, Y_2, \ldots, Y_n$ that has a mean μ_Y and variance σ^2_Y, when a number X_i is randomly selected and added to a randomly[10] selected number Y_i to create a new number $W_i = X_i + Y_i$, and this is done for all possible combinations of X_i and Y_i, the distribution of W will have a mean $\mu_W = \mu_X + \mu_Y$ and a variance $\sigma^2_W = \sigma^2_X + \sigma^2_Y$. Furthermore, when X and Y have normal distributions, then W will also have a normal distribution.

---

[10] The reason for this restriction will be explained in Box 3.3.

The situation described in Theorem 3 is presented in Figure 3.5. That the new mean μ_W should be the sum of the original means, μ_X and μ_Y, should be obvious since μ_X and μ_Y were numbers in the distributions X and Y, respectively. In Figure 3.5, we can see that when numbers are randomly sampled from both X and Y and added together, the

FIGURE 3.5 ■ **The distributions of *X* and *Y* are presented at top and middle, respectively. In each case, the values of X_1, X_2, X_3, X_4, Y_1, Y_2, Y_3, and Y_4 are represented in linear distances from the origin. At the bottom is the distribution of *W*, where the values of *W* are represented as the sum of the linear distances of the *X* and *Y* values.**

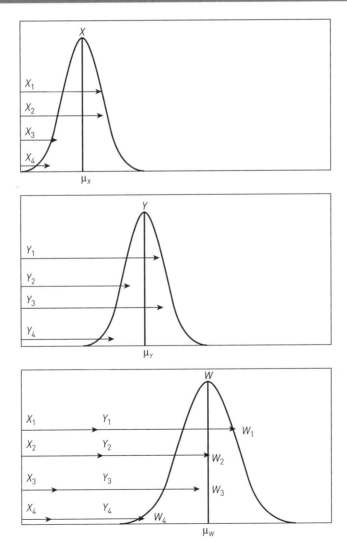

combination of a low score from X and a low score from Y (see W_4) and the combination of a high score from X and a high score from Y (see W_1) will result in a distribution with a larger variance than either of the original distributions. That this new variance is the sum of the original variances requires the algebraic proof given in Box 3.3.

BOX 3.3
ALGEBRAIC PROOF OF THEOREM 3

Proof that the mean of a sum is the sum of the means

Given two distributions X and Y, where

$$\mu_X = \frac{\sum\limits_{i=1}^{n} X_i}{n} \text{ and } \mu_Y = \frac{\sum\limits_{i=1}^{n} Y_i}{n}, \text{ if a number is}$$

randomly selected from each distribution and the two values are added to form a new number $(W_i = X_i + Y_i)$, an infinite number of times, the mean of the distribution of W, μ_W, will be

$$\mu_W = \frac{\sum\limits_{i=1}^{n} W_i}{n}$$

Because $W_i = X_i + Y_i$,

$$\mu_W = \frac{\sum\limits_{i=1}^{n} X_i + Y_i}{n}$$

If we distribute the summation sign,

$$\mu_W = \frac{\sum\limits_{i=1}^{n} X_i + \sum\limits_{i=1}^{n} Y_i}{n}$$

If we distribute the denominator,

$$\mu_W = \frac{\sum\limits_{i=1}^{n} X_i}{n} + \frac{\sum\limits_{i=1}^{n} Y_i}{n}$$

Using the definitions of the mean, we find that

$$\mu_W = \mu_X + \mu_Y$$

Proof that the variance of a sum is the sum of the variances

If the variance of one distribution is σ^2_X and the variance of the other distribution is σ^2_Y, and a number is randomly selected from each distribution and the two values added to form a new number $(W_i = X_i + Y_i)$, an infinite number of times, then the variance of W, σ^2_W, will be

$$\sigma^2_W = \frac{\sum\limits_{i=1}^{n} (W_i - \mu_W)^2}{n}$$

Because $W_i = X_i + Y_i$,

$$\sigma^2_W = \frac{\sum\limits_{i=1}^{n} \left[(X_i - Y_i) - (\mu_X + \mu_Y) \right]^2}{n}$$

When you remove the parentheses and distribute the negative sign, this becomes

$$\sigma^2_W = \frac{\sum\limits_{i=1}^{n} (X_i - Y_i - \mu_X - \mu_Y)^2}{n}$$

We can regroup the terms as follows:

$$\sigma^2_W = \frac{\sum\limits_{i=1}^{n} \left[(X_i - \mu_X) + (Y_i - \mu_Y) \right]^2}{n}$$

When we complete the square on the right $[(a + b)^2 = a^2 + b^2 + 2ab]$, we get

$$\sigma_W^2 = \frac{\sum_{i=1}^{n}\left[\left(X_i - \mu_X\right)^2 + \left(Y_i - \mu_Y\right)^2 + 2\left(X_i - \mu_X\right)\left(Y_i - \mu_Y\right)\right]}{n}$$

When we distribute the summation sign and break this into three parts, we get

$$\sigma_W^2 = \frac{\sum_{i=1}^{n}\left(X_i - \mu_X\right)^2}{n} + \frac{\sum_{i=1}^{n}\left(Y_i - \mu_Y\right)^2}{n}$$

$$+2\frac{\sum_{i=1}^{n}\left(X_i - \mu_X\right)\left(Y_i - \mu_Y\right)}{n}$$

$$= \sigma_W^2 = \sigma_X^2 + \sigma_Y^2 + 2\frac{\sum_{i=1}^{n}\left(X_i - \mu_X\right)\left(Y_i - \mu_Y\right)}{n}$$

Because the numbers to be added together are *randomly* selected from both of the original distributions, there should be no systematic relationship among them. That is, low numbers

for X are just as likely to be added to low numbers from Y as to high numbers from Y, and vice versa. When there is *no relationship* among the numbers being paired, the last term in the last equation equals zero. Those of us familiar with correlation will recognize this last term as the covariance of X and Y, which equals zero when no systematic relationship or correlation exists. Therefore, $\sigma_W^2 = \sigma_X^2 + \sigma_Y^2$. In other words, if numbers are randomly sampled from each distribution and the pairs of values are added to create a new distribution, then the mean of the new distribution equals the sum of the means of the original distributions, and the variance of the new distribution equals the sum of the variances of the original distributions.

It can be proven with more advanced mathematical techniques that when the original populations are normal distributions, the distribution of the sum of numbers from those populations is also a normal distribution. This proof is given in most mathematical statistics book. For now, trust that this statement is true.

Theorem 3 can be generalized to the case in which we add numbers from any number of distributions. In general, it can be said that the *mean of a sum of numbers is the sum of the means* of the distributions from which these numbers are sampled. Likewise, the *variance of a sum of numbers is the sum of the variances* of the distributions from which these numbers are sampled. It is assumed here that all numbers are randomly sampled and there are no systematic relationships among the numbers added together.

Theorem 4: Effects of Subtracting Scores From Two Different Distributions

Given any set of numbers $X_1, X_2, \ldots, X_n$ that has a mean μ_X and variance σ_X^2, and another set of numbers $Y_1, Y_2, \ldots, Y_n$ that has a mean μ_Y and variance σ_Y^2, when a number Y_i is randomly selected and subtracted from a randomly selected number X_i to create a new number $V_i = X_i - Y_i$, and this is done for all possible combinations of

X_i and Y_i, *then the distribution of* V *will have a mean* $\mu_V = \mu_X - \mu_Y$ *and a variance* $\sigma^2_V = \sigma^2_X + \sigma^2_Y$. *Furthermore, when* X *and* Y *are normal distributions, then* V *will also have a normal distribution.*

The situation described in Theorem 4 is presented in Figure 3.6.

FIGURE 3.6 ■ The distributions of *X* and *Y* are presented at top and middle, respectively. In each case, the values of numbers X_1, X_2, X_3, X_4, Y_1, Y_2, Y_3, and Y_4 are represented in linear distances from the origin. At the bottom is the distribution of *V*, where the values of *V* are represented as the difference between the *X* and *Y* linear distances.

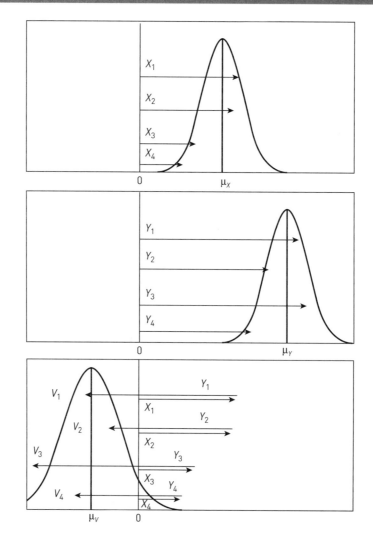

The new mean, μ_V, will be simply the difference $(\mu_X - \mu_Y)$. From Figure 3.6, one can see that if the numbers are randomly sampled from both X and Y, the combination of low X minus high Y (see V_3), and high X minus low Y (see V_2) will result in a distribution with a larger variance than either of the original distributions. While this concept may seem counterintuitive at first, study of Figure 3.6 and some sample calculations of your own should convince you of the reasonableness of this result. The algebraic proof of Theorem 4 is left to you as an exercise. It follows closely the proof of Theorem 3, so use that proof as your guide.

THE DISTRIBUTION OF SAMPLE MEANS

Many of the hypotheses we test with the classical statistical model are about population means, and we test these hypotheses with that model by taking random samples from the populations of interest and computing the means of those samples (see Chapter 1). Our statistical hypothesis tests are based on the properties of the distributions of those sample means.

The **distribution of sample means** is a theoretical distribution. It describes what happens if we could take an infinite number of samples of size n from a population, calculate the means for each of those infinite number of samples, and plot the resulting distribution. Since we obviously cannot take an infinite number of samples, the distribution of sample means is a theoretical distribution.[11] Nevertheless, as we will see shortly, this distribution lies at the heart of the classical statistical model for hypothesis tests about population means. The properties of the distribution of sample means govern how we test those hypotheses with this model.

Theorem 5: The Mean of the Distribution of Sample Means

Given a population of any shape with a mean μ_X and a variance σ^2_X, if an infinite number of samples of size n are drawn with replacement from that population (that is, sampled scores are replaced in the population so that the population is not depleted by the sampling), the mean of the sample means ($\mu_{\bar{X}}$) will be equal to the population mean μ_X; that is, $\mu_{\bar{X}} = \mu_X$.

The key to Theorem 5 is that there is an *infinite number of samples*. If each of those infinite number of samples consists of a single value, the means of each sample would be that value; therefore, the distribution of those sample means would be the same as the distribution of the population, and the mean of those sample means, $\mu_{\bar{X}}$, would be the population mean μ_X. At the other extreme, if each of these infinite number of samples were infinitely

---

[11] The idea of taking an infinite number of samples can be characterized as a "thought experiment," that is, an experiment that could actually be performed given the necessary resources. Although it is not practical to do such an experiment, we can still legitimately do it "in our heads" and ask what the outcome would be. Much of the discussion on hypothesis testing will take this form. You should not be afraid of doing this, as it will help you understand the concepts being presented.

BOX 3.4
ALGEBRAIC PROOF OF THEOREM 5

Proof that the mean of the sample means equals the population mean

By definition, the sample mean $\bar{X} = \dfrac{\sum_{i=1}^{n} X_i}{n}$.

Therefore, the mean of the sample means $(\mu_{\bar{X}})$ can also be written as $\dfrac{\mu \sum X}{n}$. Likewise, we can replace $\sum X$ with $X_1 + X_2 + \cdots + X_n$ and rewrite the mean of the sample means as follows:

$$\mu_{\bar{X}} = \mu_{\frac{\sum X}{n}} = \mu_{\frac{X_1 + X_2 + \dots + X_n}{n}} = \mu_{\frac{X_1}{n} + \frac{X_2}{n} + \dots + \frac{X_n}{n}}$$

Using Theorem 3 (the mean of a sum equals the sum of the means), we get the following:

$$\mu_{\bar{X}} = \mu_{\frac{X_1}{n}} + \mu_{\frac{X_2}{n}} + \dots + \mu_{\frac{X_N}{n}}$$

In each of the terms on the right side, $\dfrac{1}{n}$ is a constant; therefore, using Theorem 2 (the mean of something multiplied by a constant equals the constant times the original mean) yields:

$$\mu_{\bar{X}} = \frac{1}{n}\mu_{X_1} + \frac{1}{n}\mu_{X_{12}} + \dots + \frac{1}{n}\mu_{X_n}$$

Factor the common term $\left(\dfrac{1}{n}\right)$:

$$\mu_{\bar{X}} = \frac{1}{n}\left(\mu_{X_1} + \mu_{X_2} + \dots + \mu_{X_n}\right)$$

To proceed further, we need to determine what the symbol μ_{X_i} represents. X_1 is the first value in each sample drawn from a population that has a mean μ_X. Therefore, if you take an infinite number of samples of size n from that population, that infinite number of X_1's would re-create the original population, and the mean of all those X_1's would be μ_{X_1}; therefore, $\mu_{X_1} = \mu_X$. The same would be true for μ_{X_2}, μ_{X_3}, and so forth. That is, $\mu_{X_2} = \mu_X$, $\mu_{X_3} = \mu_X$, and so forth. Therefore, where there is one μ for each sample value X_i,

$$\mu_{\bar{X}} = \frac{1}{n}\left(\mu + \mu + \dots + \mu\right)$$

$$\mu_{\bar{X}} = \frac{1}{n}\left(n\mu\right) = \mu_X$$

Therefore, the mean of the sample means equals the mean of the population from which the samples were drawn, which is true for all sample sizes.

large,[12] they would include every value in the population, and the mean of each of these samples would be μ_X; therefore, the mean of all these sample means would also be μ_X. What about all other sets of samples with sizes larger than 1 and smaller than ∞? The mean of the sample means, $\mu_{\bar{X}}$, must also equal μ_X, because every value in the population will be included among those infinite number of samples and the mean of all of those values must be μ_X.

An algebraic proof of this theorem is presented in Box 3.4.

---

[12] This outcome can occur because each value is sampled *with replacement*.

Theorem 6: The Variance of the Distribution of Sample Means

Given a population of any shape with a mean μ_X and variance σ_X^2, if an infinite number of samples of size n are drawn with replacement, the variance of all of these sample means $\sigma_{\bar{X}}^2$ equals the variance of the population divided by n, the sample size. That is, $\sigma_{\bar{X}}^2 = \sigma_X^2/n$.

An algebraic proof of Theorem 6 is presented in Box 3.5.

Theorem 6 states that the variance of the sample means $\sigma_{\bar{X}}^2$ is a function of sample size; that is, *the larger the sample size, the smaller the value of $\sigma_{\bar{X}}^2$.* This theorem can be made more intuitively appealing if one considers the effects of drawing samples

BOX 3.5

ALGEBRAIC PROOF OF THEOREM 6

Proof that the variance of the sample means equals the variance of the population divided by the sample size

By definition, the sample mean $\bar{X} = \dfrac{\sum\limits_{i=1}^{n} X_i}{n}$.

Therefore, the variance of the sample means $(\sigma_{\bar{X}}^2)$ can also be written as $\sigma_{\frac{\sum X}{n}}^2$. Likewise, we can replace $\sum X$ with $X_1 + X_2 + \ldots + X_n$ and rewrite the variance of the sample means as follows:

$$\sigma_{\bar{X}}^2 = \sigma_{\frac{\sum X}{n}}^2 = \sigma_{\frac{X_1+X_2+\cdots+X_n}{n}}^2$$

Using Theorem 3 (the variance of a sum equals the sum of the variances), we get this:

$$\sigma_{\bar{X}}^2 = \sigma_{\frac{X_1}{n}}^2 + \sigma_{\frac{X_2}{n}}^2 + \cdots + \sigma_{\frac{X_n}{n}}^2$$

In each of the terms on the right side, $\dfrac{1}{n}$ is a constant; therefore, using Theorem 2 ("variance of something multiplied by a constant equals the constant squared times the original variance") yields the following:

$$\sigma_{\bar{X}}^2 = \frac{1}{n^2}\sigma_{X_1}^2 + \frac{1}{n^2}\sigma_{X_2}^2 + \cdots + \frac{1}{n^2}\sigma_{X_n}^2$$

Factor the common term $\left(\dfrac{1}{n^2}\right)$:

$$\sigma_{\bar{X}}^2 = \frac{1}{n^2}\left(\sigma_{X_1}^2 + \sigma_{X_2}^2 + \cdots + \sigma_{X_n}^2\right)$$

Because the scores $X_1 + X_2 + \ldots + X_n$ are all sample values from a population with a variance σ_X^2, it must be the case that $\sigma_{X_1}^2 = \sigma_X^2, \sigma_{X_2}^2 = \sigma_X^2, \sigma_{X_3}^2 = \sigma_X^2$, and so forth. (See Box 3.4.) Therefore,

$$\sigma_{\bar{X}}^2 = \frac{1}{n^2}\left(\sigma_X^2 + \sigma_X^2 + \cdots + \sigma_X^2\right)$$

$$\sigma_{\bar{X}}^2 = \frac{1}{n^2}\left(n\sigma_X^2\right) = \frac{\sigma_X^2}{n}$$

Therefore, the variance of the sample means equals the variance of the population from which the samples were drawn divided by the sample size.

of various sizes and plotting the means of these samples. For example, if an infinite number of samples with $n = 1$ are drawn from a population, the means of each sample will be just that single sampled value, and the distribution of these sample means will be the same as the original distribution; that is, $\sigma^2_{\overline{X}} = \sigma^2_{\overline{X}}/1 = \sigma^2_{\overline{X}}$. Compare the two distributions at the top of Figure 3.7. On the other hand, if samples of infinite size are drawn from a population (that is, the entire population is sampled each time), all of the same means would be equal to the population mean (μ_X, and $\sigma^2_{\overline{X}} = 0$); that is, there would be no variation among the sample means. See the distribution at bottom left in Figure 3.7.

Given these two extremes, consider the situation in which $n = 2$. Because the mean of a sample size equal to 2 must be halfway between the two sampled values, the only way we can obtain a sample mean far away from the population mean is when both sampled values are from the same far end (tail) of the population distribution, and this event is unlikely. What is more likely is for the two sampled values to be from different locations

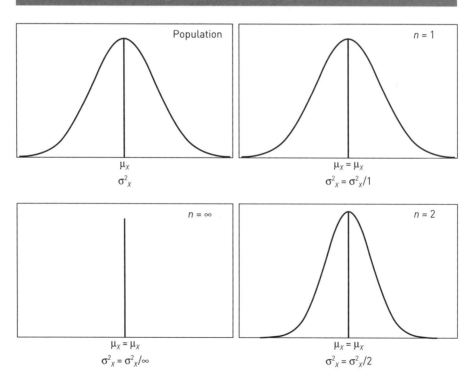

FIGURE 3.7 ■ Given the population in the upper left panel, the distribution of sample means for samples of size 1, ∞, and 2 are presented in the other panels.

in the population distribution, resulting in a sample mean closer to the population mean than to the tails of the population distribution. Therefore, if we take an infinite number of samples of a size equal to 2, $\sigma_{\bar{X}}^2$ will be smaller than σ_X^2. Compare the top left and bottom right panels of Figure 3.7. Theorem 6 tells us how much smaller $\sigma_{\bar{X}}^2$ will be as a function of sample size. This reduction in $\sigma_{\bar{X}}^2$ becomes even more pronounced when you consider larger samples. If $n = 10$, it is very unlikely that all 10 points will even be from the same side of the population distribution. It is more likely that the sampled values will be from both sides of the population, and the mean of those samples will be close to μ_X, thus making the distribution of sample means rather narrow and $\sigma_{\bar{X}}^2$ small.

THE CENTRAL LIMIT THEOREM

The central limit theorem summarizes the properties of the distribution of sample means. Inferences about population means (confidence intervals and hypothesis tests on means) are based on these properties of the distribution of sample means described in Theorem 7.

The previous two theorems define two properties of the distributions of sample means, namely the values of $\mu_{\bar{X}}$ and $\sigma_{\bar{X}}^2$. These theorems will now be combined with a third property, the shape of the distribution of sample means, to complete the **central limit theorem**. This theorem is the most important theorem in the classical statistical model because confidence intervals and hypothesis tests for population means are based on it.

Theorem 7: The Central Limit Theorem

Given a population of any shape with a mean μ_X and variance σ_X^2, if an infinite number of samples of size n are drawn with replacement, the mean of the sample means $\mu_{\bar{X}}$ will be equal to the population mean μ_X, and the variance of the sample means $\sigma_{\bar{X}}^2$ will be equal to σ_X^2/n. The larger the sample size, the more the distribution of sample means will resemble a normal distribution. Furthermore, if the original population is a normal distribution, then the distribution of sample means will have a normal distribution for all sample sizes.

The first parts of the central limit theorem have already been proven in Theorems 5 and 6. While a formal proof of those parts of the central limit theorem that deal with the shape of the distribution of sample means is more involved than is necessary for our purposes here, we will make an attempt to illustrate that it is reasonable that the distribution of sample means becomes more symmetrical (and hence more normal in shape) as sample size increases.

A skewed population with a mean and variance of 2.5 is represented in the upper left of Figure 3.8. The other four distributions are of the sample means of 2,000 random samples of size 1, 5, 10, and 50, respectively, from that population. As sample size increases, the

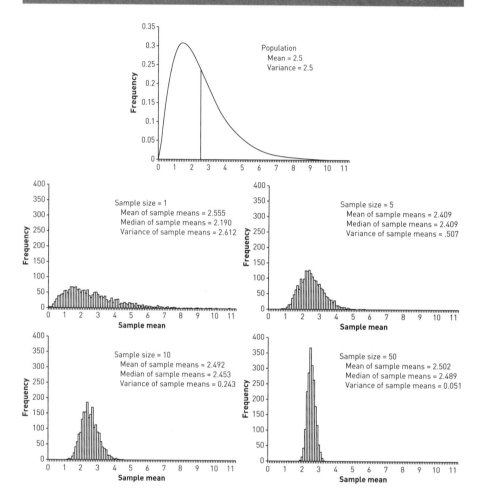

FIGURE 3.8 ■ Distributions of sample means of 2,000 random samples of sample sizes 1, 5, 10, and 50 from the population in the top panel.

distributions of the sample means from these 2,000 samples become more symmetrical around the population mean, and the variance of these distributions decreases.

The argument used to explain why the variance of the sample means decreases as the sample size increases applies here as well. As the sample size increases, the distributions of sample means also become more symmetrical. Consider the case in which the sample size is equal to 5. It is rather unlikely that with a sample size of 5, all five sample points would be obtained from either the extreme right tail or the extreme left tail of the population. It is most likely that the sampled values will be drawn from the region where the bulk of the population occurs, and the means of those samples would be closer to the population

FIGURE 3.9 ■ Normal quantile plots for the sample means of 2,000 random samples of sample sizes 1, 5, 10, and 50 from the population in the distribution at the top of Figure 3.8.

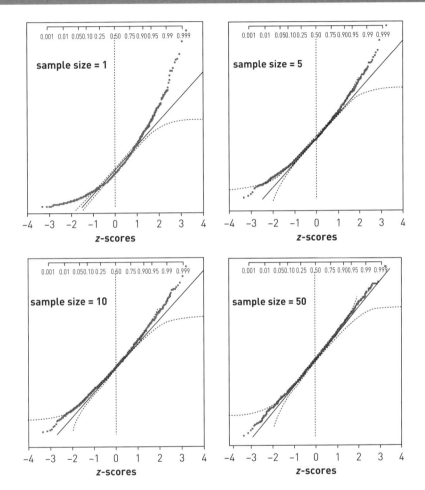

mean, which would tend to reduce the skew in the distribution of sample means. When the sample size is 10, it would be even less likely that all 10 values in your sample would be from the same tail. Instead, one would expect them to be sampled from both sides of the distribution, yielding sample means closer to the population mean. In this way, increasing sample size reduces the variance of the sample means and reduces the tendency for these means to be systematically on one side of the population mean or the other. This outcome becomes even more obvious when the sample size increases to 50.

To determine whether these distributions of sample means become more normal, normal quantile plots for the distributions of sample means in Figure 3.8 are presented in Figure 3.9. What do these normal quantile plots tell us about these distributions of sample means as sample size increases?

The importance of the central limit theorem for inferential statistics that compare population means cannot be overstated. Knowing the mean, variance, and shape of the distribution of sample means allows us to construct confidence intervals and test hypotheses about sample means. How we do these things are the topics of Chapters 4, 6, 7, and 14.

AVERAGING MEANS AND VARIANCES

When the sample sizes are not equal, calculating the average, or mean, of a set of sample means involves weighting each sample mean by its sample size before finding the average. When the sample sizes are equal, the sample means can be added together and divided by the number of sample means to find their average. These same principles apply to averaging sample variances; averaging estimates of the population variance; and finding the variance of the sample means, which we will want to be able to do when we conduct comparisons among means.

The Mean of the Sample Means
When the Sample Sizes Are Not the Same

Theorem 5 (the mean of the sample means equals the population mean) may give you the impression that when you have two or more sample means and want to find the average of them, you need only add them together and divide by the number of means being averaged. This statement is true *only* when all of the means have the same sample size (or all of the means have the same value). When the sample sizes are unequal, there is a potential problem because *the mean of the sample means should equal the mean of all of the scores in all of the samples.* The mean of all the sample scores is called the **grand mean** and is represented by the symbol $\overline{\overline{X}}$. Consider the simple example in Table 3.1 where there are two samples, one containing 2 scores and the other containing 10 scores.

This example illustrates that when we find the mean or average of two or more sample means, we need to take into account the sample sizes, which is accomplished by the following formula:

$$\text{mean of means} = \frac{n_1\overline{X}_1 + n_2\overline{X}_2 + \ldots + n_k\overline{X}_k}{n_1 + n_2 + \ldots + n_k} = \frac{\sum_{j=1}^{k} n_j\overline{X}_j}{\sum_{j=1}^{k} n_j} \qquad (3.4)$$

TABLE 3.1 ■ Averaging Means When the Sample Sizes Are Not the Same			
	Sample 1	**Sample 2**	**All Scores**
	2	3	2, 3
	6	5	6, 5
		7	7
		9	9
		11	11
		13	13
		15	15
		17	17
		19	19
		21	21
Sums	8	120	128
Sample sizes	2	10	12
Means	4	12	10.67

Simple average of the two sample means = (4 + 12)/2 = 16/2 = 8.

Weighted average of the two sample means = [(2 × 4) + (10 × 12)]/(2 + 10) = (8 + 120)/12 = 128/12 = 10.67.

Equation 3.4 tells us that to find the **mean of a group of sample means,** we multiply each sample mean by the number of values that produced it, add these products together, and then divide by the total number of values in all of the samples. If we note that $\overline{X} = \sum(X_i)/n$, then $n \times \overline{X} = \sum(X_i)$. Equation 3.4 can therefore be rewritten as follows:

$$\text{mean of means} = \frac{\sum_{i=1}^{n_1} X_{1i} + \sum_{i=1}^{n_2} X_{2i} + \dots + \sum_{i=1}^{n_k} X_{ki}}{n_1 + n_2 + \dots + n_k}, \qquad (3.5)$$

which instructs us to add all the scores from all of the samples together and divide by the total number of values. This computation has been done in the third column in Table 3.1, and it gives us the grand mean. Therefore, the mean of the sample means is the mean of all the numbers (the grand mean) (Equation 3.5) or is a "weighted average" of the individual sample means (Equation 3.4).

When all of the sample sizes are equal, Equation 3.4 reduces to the following:

$$\text{mean of means} = \frac{\overline{X}_1 + \overline{X}_2 + \cdots + \overline{X}_k}{k} = \frac{\sum\limits_{j=1}^{k} \overline{X}_j}{k}, \tag{3.6}$$

where k is the number of sample means. Equation 3.6 is the simple average of these k means. It is used *only* when the sample means are composed of an equal number of elements.

The mean or average of a number of sample variances when the sample sizes are not the same is obtained in a manner similar to Equation 3.4:

$$\text{mean of sample variances} = \frac{n_1 s_1^2 + n_2 s_2^2 + \cdots + n_k s_k^2}{n_1 + n_2 + \cdots + n_k} = \frac{\sum\limits_{j=1}^{k} n_j s_j^2}{\sum\limits_{j=1}^{k} n_j} \tag{3.7}$$

$$= \frac{\sum\limits_{i=1}^{n_1} \left(X_{1i} - \overline{X}_1\right)^2 + \sum\limits_{i=1}^{n_2} \left(X_{2i} - \overline{X}_2\right)^2 + \cdots + \sum\limits_{i=1}^{n_k} \left(X_{ki} - \overline{X}_k\right)^2}{\sum\limits_{j=1}^{k} n_j} \tag{3.8}$$

Equation 3.7 tells us that to find the mean or average of a number of sample variances, we multiply each variance by its sample size, add these products together, and divide by the total sample size. Equation 3.8 tells us that to find the sum of squares $[\Sigma(X - \overline{X})^2]$ for each sample around each individual sample mean, we add these sums of squares together and divide by the total sample size. This value is *not* the same as the variance of all the numbers.

The *variance of all the numbers* is defined as the sum of squared deviations around the grand mean $(\overline{\overline{X}})$ divided by the total number of scores in all samples. This value can also be expressed as follows:

$$\text{variance of all numbers} = \frac{\sum\limits_{j=1}^{k} \sum\limits_{i=1}^{n_k} \left(X_{ij} - \overline{\overline{X}}\right)^2}{n_1 + n_2 + \cdots + n_k} \tag{3.9}$$

The Mean or Average of the Estimates of Variance

When we perform *t*-tests (see Chapter 7) and analysis of variance (see Chapter 14), we need to find the average of a number of *estimates of the population variance*, that is, the average of $\sum(X - \overline{X})^2/(n - 1)$. We use the same procedure that we use to find the mean (average) of the sample means and the sample variances described above. To find the average of the estimates of the population variance, we can use any of the following equivalent formulas:

$$\text{average of variance estimates} = \frac{(n_1 - 1)\text{est } \sigma_1^2 + (n_2 - 1)\text{est } \sigma_2^2 + \cdots + (n_k - 1)\text{est } \sigma_k^2}{\sum_{j=1}^{k}(n_j - 1)} \tag{3.10a}$$

$$= \frac{n_1 s_1^2 + n_2 s_2^2 + \cdots + n_k s_k^2}{\sum_{j=1}^{k}(n_j - 1)} \tag{3.10b}$$

$$= \frac{\sum_{i=1}^{n_1}\left(X_{1i} - \overline{X}_1\right)^2 + \sum_{i=1}^{n_2}\left(X_{2i} - \overline{X}_2\right)^2 + \cdots + \sum_{i=1}^{n_k}\left(X_{ki} - \overline{X}_k\right)^2}{\sum_{j=1}^{k}(n_j - 1)} \tag{3.10c}$$

When all of the estimates of the population variance are based on samples from the same population, the resulting average is the unbiased estimate of that population variance and is a better estimate than the individual estimates. *The error term for between-groups analysis of variance and the denominator of* t-*tests for group differences is always the average of the within-groups estimates of variance.* We will make use of this fact when we consider the *t*-test in Chapter 7 and analysis of variance in Chapter 14.

The Variance of the Sample Means When the Sample Sizes Are Not the Same

Following the same logic as above, if the sample sizes are not the same, we need to weight each $(X_j - \overline{\overline{X}})$ by n_j when we attempt to find the variance of the sample means. The correct formula for doing so is:

$$\text{variance of sample means} = \frac{\sum_{j=1}^{k} n_j \left(\overline{X}_j - \overline{\overline{X}}\right)}{\sum_{j=1}^{k} n_j} \tag{3.11}$$

Equation 3.6 tells us to find the **variance of the sample means** by computing the squared deviation of each sample mean from the grand mean (symbolized by $\overline{\overline{X}}$), multiplying each squared deviation by the number of scores in that sample, adding all of those weighted squared deviations, and dividing by the total number of scores.

When the sample sizes are the same, Equation 3.11 reduces to

$$\text{variance of sample means} = \frac{\sum_{j=1}^{k}\left(\overline{X}_j - \overline{\overline{X}}\right)^2}{k}, \qquad (3.12)$$

where k is the number of samples.

EXPECTED VALUE

The concept of expected value is used in gambling and in business to determine how much to risk in a game of chance or in a business venture by weighing the possible outcomes. By definition, the expected value is synonymous with the mean. Thus, we can express the theorems about means described in this chapter as expected values.

All of the properties of means described in this chapter can be expressed in terms of expected value notation. We make this connection here because expected value notation is widely used in the literature of statistics, psychology, and economics. Familiarity with the language of expected value will help you become accustomed to thinking in these terms, and you will feel comfortable interpreting the notation when you see it in other papers and books.

Historically, the idea of expected value arose in the context of gambling. Mathematicians were asked to calculate how much a person might "expect" to win (or lose) each time a game is played. When the expected value is negative, we should expect to lose money over the long run and probably should not play (unless we play for enjoyment and not to win money). A fair game (one that favors neither the player nor the "house") is one in which the expected value equals zero; that is, we might expect to neither win nor lose over the long run. Another way to express this idea is that while on every play of the game, we might win or lose, overall these events should balance out so that if we were to play for a very long time (an infinite number of trials), we would win or lose nothing.

The expected value in any situation is defined as follows:

$$E(X) = \Sigma[X \bullet P(X)] \text{ for all values of } X \qquad (3.13)$$

This equation reads, "The expected value of X equals the sum of each possible outcome (X) multiplied by the probability of that outcome occurring [$P(X)$]. The symbol $E(X)$

represents "the expected value of *X*." In a gambling situation, *X* might be the amount of money you would win or lose on any given outcome of the game, and *P(X)* would be the probability that the particular outcome might occur.

To help you understand the concept of expected value, let us consider the "numbers game," a lottery that used to be played in some neighborhoods before legal lotteries were established. Here is how it works: You pick a number from 000 to 999 and bet 25 cents on that number. If that number is the last three digits of the total dollar amount bet at a certain racetrack (or any other mutually agreed upon three-digit number printed in the newspaper), you get back $150. The question is: Is this a fair game, with an expected value of zero? To answer this question, we have to consider what outcomes (*X*) can happen and what their probabilities are. These outcomes are summarized in Box 3.6 along with the calculations.

As we can see in Box 3.6, the expected value for each play of this game is minus 10 cents, which means that every time we play, we can expect to lose 10 cents. Some people may ask, "How can I lose 10 cents when I bet a quarter?" The answer is that 10 cents is the *average loss per play*. Sometimes we lose 25 cents and sometimes we win $149.75. On average, however, we lose 10 cents each time we play. If we play 1,000 times, we can *expect* to lose $100. This $100 represents the average losses of a large number of players for 1,000 plays of the game. On the other hand, if you could play this game an infinite number of times, your total loss would be 10 cents—but you cannot play that many times. No wonder organized crime loves the numbers game! The same logic applies to legal lotteries and casino gambling. In both cases, the expected values are negative numbers. How negative they are depends on the game.

As noted above, the expected value tells us the *average* loss per play. In statistics, the term *expected value* is a synonym for the arithmetic mean or average of a population of values. This identity is illustrated in Box 3.7.

In the definition of expected value, *all possible* values of *X[P(X)]* are summed, which means that either we sum the entire population (as in Box 3.7) or all possible outcomes (as in Box 3.6). We can apply the concept of expected value to flipping a coin and asking, "What is the number of heads we would expect when the coin is flipped 10 times?" The answer is *5*. Although the observed number of heads will vary each time we flip the coin 10 times, in the long run, the average number of heads across those iterations of this task will be 5. Therefore, the expected value is the *theoretical* mean. In other words, when we are asked what number of heads we would expect to occur, we are being asked for the theoretical mean of a binomial distribution, which is the mean for an infinite number of repetitions. We will look closer at the binomial distribution in Chapter 8.

BOX 3.6
CALCULATING THE EXPECTED VALUE FOR "PLAYING THE NUMBERS"

Outcomes [Xi]	Probabilities [P(Xi)]
X_1: You win $150.00 (which means you gain $149.75 because you already had $0.25).	$1/1{,}000 = 0.001$
X_2: You lose $0.25 (that is, −$0.25).	$999/1{,}000 = 0.999$

$$E(X) = \sum X \cdot P(X) \text{ for all values of } X$$
$$= [X_1][P(X_1)] + [X_2][P(X_2)]$$
$$= (\$149.75)(0.001) + (-\$0.25)(0.999)$$
$$= -\$0.10$$

BOX 3.7
THE RELATIONSHIP BETWEEN $E(X)$ AND μ_x

If we have a population of values, we would define the expected value of this population as follows:

$$E(X) = \sum [X \times P(X)] \text{ for all values of } X$$

This formula tells us to take each value in the population (X), multiply it by the probability of that value being sampled from the population, and add up for all values of X. In this situation, $P(X)$ is the *relative frequency* of each X in the population, that is, $\dfrac{\text{frequency of } X}{n}$.

We can rewrite the expected value as

$$E(X) = \sum \left(X \cdot \frac{\text{frequency of } X}{n} \right) \text{ for all } X.$$

The term $\sum (X \times \text{frequency of } X)$ tells us to multiply each value of X in the population by its *relative* frequency and add these products together. This value is equivalent to adding all Xs in the population or, in other words,

$$\sum_{\text{all } X} (X \cdot \text{frequency of } X) = \sum_{i=1}^{N} X_i$$

Therefore,

$$E(X) = \sum_{\text{all } X} [X][P(X)] = \frac{\sum_{i=1}^{N} X_i}{n} = \mu_x$$

THEOREMS ON EXPECTED VALUE

Because of the correspondence between the expected value and the population mean, the theorems at the beginnings of this chapter can be expressed in expected value notation. We will apply these theorems in the next chapter.

Theorem 8: Expected Value of a Sum

If the variable (W) *is the sum of other variables (for example,* W = X + Y + Z*), the expected value of* W, E(W), *is the sum of the individual expected values of* X, Y, *and* Z. *That is,*

$$E(W) = E(X + Y + Z) = E(X) + E(Y) + E(Z)$$

In other words, if we take a score from the distribution of X, a score from the distribution of Y, and a score from the distribution of Z and add these scores together to produce a score W, the average (expected value) of all Ws obtained in this way is the sum of the averages (expected values) of the Xs, Ys, and Zs. (Note the correspondence between this theorem and the part of Theorem 3 that deals with the mean.)

Theorem 9: Expected Value of a Constant Times a Variable

If we have a distribution of numbers (X), *and we multiply each* X *by a constant* (C) *to produce a new distribution of scores* Y = CX, *the expected value of* Y *is* C *times the expected value of* X. *That is,*

$$E(Y) = E(CX) = CE(X)$$

Here again, note the correspondence to the part of Theorem 2 that deals with the mean.

Theorem 10: Expected Value of a Constant

If all of the numbers in a distribution are the same (that is, a constant), the expected value of this distribution is just the constant.

$$E(C) = C$$

If we take Theorem 10 and combine it with Theorem 8, we can arrive at a restatement of Theorem 1; that is, if we have a set of numbers X and we add a constant to every X to form a new distribution $(X + C)$,

$$E(X + C) = E(X) + E(C) \qquad \text{(Theorem 8)}$$

$$= E(X) + C \qquad \text{(Theorem 10)}$$

Theorem 11: The Expected Value of *X* Plus a Constant

(X + C) is the expected value of X *+ the constant.*

$$E(X + C) = E(X) + C$$

Summary

In this chapter, we presented a set of theorems to show basic properties of all distributions of numbers, whether they be populations or samples. These theorems provide the fundamental building blocks for statistical inference, and we will keep referring to them as we develop our discussion of statistical inference. Therefore, it is important that that you know and understand them so that you are comfortable that they are true and you can readily recall them as needed. To help you learn these theorems, we present both intuitive explanations and formal algebraic proofs.

Starting with the effects of adding, subtracting, multiplying, and dividing by a constant, we show that the standard score transformation on any set of numbers will create a new set of numbers that always has a mean = 0 and variance (or standard deviation) = 1. Furthermore, the original set and the transformed set will be the same kind of distribution.

The effects of adding randomly sampled scores from two distributions creates a new distribution in which the mean is the sum of the original means and the variance is the sum of the original variances. Subtracting scores randomly sampled from two distributions creates a new distribution in which the mean is the *difference* between the original means and the variance is the *sum* of the original variances. We used these theorems to understand the properties of the distribution of sample means described by the central limit theorem. *The central limit theorem is the most important theorem for understanding inferential statistics involving means.*

When averaging means and variances, one must take into account whether the samples are the same size. Therefore, a set of formulas is presented for finding the average of a set of means or variances when the sample sizes are unequal. These formulas reduce to simple averages when the sample sizes are the same.

Finally, the theorems on adding, subtracting, multiplying, and dividing by a constant and the theorems on adding and subtracting scores from two different distributions are recast in terms of expected value notation. This notation makes it easier to use these theorems to develop other principles.

In statistical inference, we use data derived from samples to provide information and draw conclusions about the population from which the samples are drawn. Understanding these foundational principles about distributions will provide the basis for much of the statistical inference procedures that follow in later chapters and will make it easier to learn how to test hypotheses in your own research. We will start to use them in the next chapter, where we begin our discussion of statistical inference.

Conceptual Exercises

1. Suppose we have a set of scores $Y_1, Y_2, \ldots, Y_n$ (called Y) that are not normally distributed. Imagine that we subtract the mode of Y from each Y_i and then divide by the standard deviation of Y (S_Y) to create a new variable H, where

$$H_i = \frac{Y - \text{Mode}_Y}{S_Y}$$

   a. Write an equation to express the relationship between the median of H and the median of Y. Explain in words why this is the relationship.

   b. Write an equation to express the relationship between the F-spread of H and the F-spread of Y. Explain in words why this is the relationship.

2. In the proof of the assertion that the mean of the sample means equals the mean of the population, we had to determine the values of $\mu_{X_1}, \mu_{X_2}, \mu_{X_3}, \cdots, \mu_{X_N}$. Explain why it is the case that $\mu_{X_1} = \mu_{X_2} = \mu_{X_3} = \cdots = \mu_{X_N} = \mu_X$.

3. If we repeatedly selected samples of size N from a population that is not normal in form, what is the effect of sample size on the following?

   a. The mean of the sample means

   b. The variance of the distribution of sample means

   Without using algebra, explain why sample size has these effects.

4. In words, explain how we find the variance of the sample means when the sample sizes are unequal.

5. Why does transforming to z-scores not create a normal distribution when the original set of scores is not normally distributed?

6. In the algebraic proof of the theorems about the variance of a sum (σ^2_{X+Y}) and the variance of a difference (σ^2_{X-Y}), we had to deal with the following term:

$$\sum_{i=1}^{N} \frac{(X - \mu_X)(Y - \mu_Y)}{n}$$

   What is this term? Why is it equal to zero in those proofs?

7. In the proof of the assertion that the variance of the sample means equals the population variance divided by the sample size (i.e., $\sigma^2_{\overline{X}} = \frac{\sigma^2_X}{n}$), we had to determine the values of $\sigma^2_{X_1}, \sigma^2_{X_2}, \sigma^2_{X_3}, \cdots, \sigma^2_{Xn}$. Explain why it is the case that $\sigma_{X_1} = \sigma_{X_2} = \sigma_{X_3} = \cdots = \sigma_{Xn} = \sigma_X$.

8. In words, explain how we find the average of a set of sample variances when the sample sizes are unequal. Why would the formula for doing so be different from the formula for calculating the variance of all the scores (from all of the samples)?

9. Suppose we have a set of scores $Y_1, Y_2, \ldots, Y_n$ (called Y) that are *not* normally distributed. We then multiply each Y_i by 10 and then add 50 to create a new variable T, where $T_i = 10Y_i + 50$.

   a. Write an equation to express the relationship between the median of T and the median of Y. Explain in words why this is the relationship.

   b. Write an equation to express the relationship between the range of T and the range of Y. Explain in words why this is the relationship.

10. Using the theorems of expected value, prove that $E[X_i(X_i + a)] = E(X_i^2) + a\mu$, where X_i is a variable, a is a constant, and μ is the mean.

11. Using the theorems of expected value, prove that $E[\mu(X + 1) - \mu^2] = \mu$, where X is a variable and μ (the population mean) is a constant.

Student Study Site

Visit the Student Study Site at **https://study.sagepub.com/friemanstats** for a variety of useful tools including data sets, additional exercises, and web resources.

PART III

THE BASICS OF STATISTICAL INFERENCE

Drawing Conclusions From Our Data

ESTIMATING PARAMETERS
OF POPULATIONS FROM
SAMPLE DATA

There are a number of reasons why someone would engage in cyberbullying. The experiment described in Chapter 1 explores one of these reasons: revenge (or vengeance). Vengeance is "an attempt to redress an interpersonal offense by voluntarily committing an aggressive action against the perceived offender" (McCullough, Bellah, Kilpatrick, & Johnson, 2001, pp. 602). In the case of the cyberbullying experiment described in Chapter 1, the perceived offense was receiving the mean message from the interaction partner. However, beyond the situational motivations, such as offenses and provocations, that may inspire a person to engage in revenge, there are individual differences in how likely a person will engage in revenge. Stuckless and Goranson (1992) created the Vengeance Scale to attempt to assess what they called trait levels of vengeance. The Vengeance Scale is a 20-item questionnaire that asks participants to indicate how much they agree with the items on a 1 (*disagree strongly*) to 7 (*agree strongly*) rating scale. Sample items include "revenge is sweet" and "it's not worth my time or effort to pay back someone who has wronged me." The responses were scored such that higher scores indicated higher levels of vengeance and then were summed. Barlett and Gentile (2012) collected data from 493 college-aged students in the Midwest using a variety of measures that included the Vengeance Scale, as well as scales used to measure aggression and the frequencies of cyberbullying and cybervictimization. They obtained usable data on the Vengeance Scale from 490 participants. Of the participants, 231 (47%) were male and 259 were female. They ranged in age from 16 to 20 (mean = 19.36 years), and 88% classified themselves as Caucasian.

Barlett and Gentile (2012) found that the mean score on the Vengeance Scale for the students who responded to all 20 items on that scale was 63.56 (range 20–115 with a possible range of 20–140).

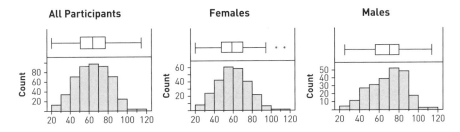

FIGURE 4.1 ■ Histograms and box plots for the scores on the Vengeance Scale by college-aged students from a large Midwestern university. Scale scores are the sum of responses to 20 questions based on a 1 (*disagree strongly*) to 7 (*agree strongly*) rating scale (Barlett, 2015).

The mean for males was 67.96 (range 25–114), and the mean for females was 59.64 (range 20–115). Histograms and schematic box plots of these data are presented in Figure 4.1.

These 490 college students who completed these surveys are a sample (although not a random sample) of all college students in similar schools in the Midwest (the population of interest). Had the researchers given their survey to students at a different set of similar schools, we would expect that they would have obtained similar, but not identical results. Our research question is about the population from which the sample was obtained. In this case, we want to *use the information in our sample (or samples) to estimate the parameters of our population.* That is the problem we will consider here. Such analysis is what we mean by the term **inferential statistics**.

STATISTICAL INFERENCE WITH THE CLASSICAL STATISTICAL MODEL

In the classical statistical model, we use the information in our sample to estimate the unknown parameters of the population from which our sample was obtained. We estimate parameters and test hypotheses with this model.

As was noted in Chapter 1, the classical statistical model is based on two assumptions:

1. Populations with certain characteristics called parameters exist, and some of those parameters are known to us, while others are unknown; and
2. We can estimate the values of the unknown parameters by taking a random sample from the population and using the information in that sample for our estimate.

Stated another way, we know (or can obtain) the information about the sample data; what we do not know are the population parameters.[1] Our task is to use the information we have (the sample data) to estimate the values of those parameters. Because our estimates are based on our sample and not the entire population, we do not expect our estimates to equal the parameter being estimated; however, we want the estimators we use to yield estimates that are close to the population parameter we are trying to estimate.

With respect to the question of how many times American college students cyberbully others, we could in theory ask every American college student about their cyberbullying behavior or experiences and know exactly the characteristics of the cyberbullying population's scores (its mean, standard deviation, form, and so forth), but such a study would not be practical. As noted above, the classical statistical model tells us to take a random sample from that population and use the sample data to *estimate* the population mean and standard deviation. You already know from your basic statistics classes that the *best* estimator of the population mean of a normal distribution is the mean of a random sample from that population ($\bar{X}$). But why is $\bar{X}$ the best estimator? Likewise, when estimating the variance of a normal distribution, you also know that $\sum \dfrac{\left(X - \bar{X}\right)^2}{n-1}$, *not*

$\sum \dfrac{\left(X - \bar{X}\right)^2}{n}$, should be used to estimate that population variance. Why is this so?

In this chapter, these and other questions about estimating parameters will be answered, and the technique most often used to derive estimates of parameters will be described. Before tackling these topics, we will look at the criteria used to select estimators of population parameters.

CRITERIA FOR SELECTING ESTIMATORS OF POPULATION PARAMETERS

Best estimators are unbiased, efficient, and consistent. These properties of estimators are described here.

Statisticians have identified a number of criteria to use to determine which of a number of possible estimators[2] to use. Those estimators that satisfy all of these criteria are considered "best estimators."

---

[1] If we knew the values of the population parameters, we would not have to collect data from samples.

[2] **Estimators** are the formulas we use to calculate our estimates. **Estimates** are the values of an estimator derived from application of that estimator to the sample data at hand. The formula $\dfrac{\sum X_i}{n}$ is the estimator of the population mean. The value of that formula is the estimate of the population mean obtained by applying that formula to the sample data.

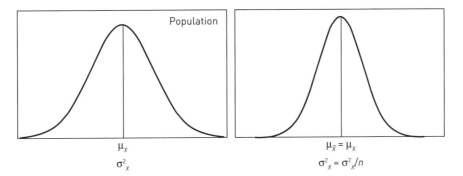

FIGURE 4.2 ■ Given the population on the left, the means of a large number of samples would be distributed as shown on the right. The mean of these means $\mu_{\bar{X}}$ equals μ_X because $\bar{X}$ is an unbiased estimator of μ_X.

Property of Unbiasedness

An estimator is unbiased when the expected value of that estimator equals the parameter being estimated.

An **estimator is unbiased** when the average of an infinite number of estimates (based on an infinite number of samples) is equal to the parameter being estimated. That is, if we take a sample from a population that has a parameter θ and derive an estimate of θ from that sample (called $\hat{\theta}$), take another sample and in a similar manner derive another estimate, and we repeat this process to obtain all possible samples from that population, the estimator $\hat{\theta}$ is said to be unbiased when the average of these estimates is equal to the parameter θ.[3] Using this criterion, the sample mean, $\bar{X}$, is an unbiased estimator of μ, the population mean of a normal distribution. This outcome will occur even though each time we take a random sample from a population and compute $\bar{X}$, those sample means will not equal μ exactly, nor will they all equal each other. However, as we saw in Chapter 3, the mean of the sample means equals the population mean, which is diagramed in Figure 4.2.

We also noted in Chapter 3 that *expected value* is synonymous with *population mean*. Therefore, we can write the definition of an unbiased estimator in mathematical form as follows:

$$E(\hat{\theta}) = \theta, \tag{4.1}$$

where θ is the parameter being estimated and $\hat{\theta}$ is the estimator. As a general rule, an estimator of any parameter is represented symbolically as that parameter with the "hat"

---

[3] When the symbol θ is used to designate a parameter, the symbol $\hat{\theta}$ ("theta hat") is used to designate the estimator of θ.

on it; thus $\hat{\theta}$ represents a *sample statistic* (that is, a value derived from the sample data), and θ represents a population parameter. An algebraic proof demonstrating that the sample mean, $\overline{X}$, is an unbiased estimator of the population mean, μ_X (that is, $E(\overline{X}) = \mu_X$), is presented in Box 4.1.

You are encouraged to study this proof as an example of how to use the expected value operation to prove that an estimator is unbiased. Compare this proof to the one in Box 3.4.

Asymptotically Unbiased Estimators

In some cases, an estimator may be biased, but as sample size increases, the bias is reduced. In this case, we say the estimator is asymptotically unbiased. The sample variance (dividing the sum of squared deviations by n*) is an asymptotically unbiased estimator of the population variance.*

Even when an estimator is biased, it still may have the property of being **asymptotically unbiased**. By asymptotically unbiased, we mean that *although the estimator based on small sample sizes may be biased* ($E(\hat{\theta}) \neq \theta$), *as sample size increases, the amount of bias (the difference between* $E(\hat{\theta})$ *and* θ*) decreases to zero.* In the limit where the sample size is infinite, the bias disappears; that is, the difference between $E(\hat{\theta})$ and θ approaches zero as *n* increases toward infinity. Mathematically, this concept can be represented by the following equations:

$$\lim_{n \to \infty} \left[E(\hat{\theta}) - \theta \right] = 0 \qquad (4.2)$$

or

$$\lim_{n \to \infty} E(\hat{\theta}) = \theta \qquad (4.3)$$

Equations (4.2) and (4.3) both define an asymptotic unbiased estimator in slightly different ways: Equation 4.2 tells us that, as sample size increases, the difference between $E(\hat{\theta})$ and θ decreases to zero, and Equation 4.3 tells us that as sample size increases, $E(\hat{\theta})$ approaches θ.

The sample variance, s^2, is a *biased* estimator of the variance of a normal distribution σ_X^2, but the bias decreases as sample size increases, although the bias only reaches zero when the sample size is infinite or the entire population is sampled. In Box 4.2, we demonstrate that $\dfrac{\sum_{i=1}^{n}(X_i - \overline{X})^2}{n}$ is a biased estimator of σ_X^2, and $\dfrac{\sum_{i=1}^{n}(X_i - \overline{X})^2}{n-1}$ is an unbiased estimator.

BOX 4.1

PROOF THAT THE SAMPLE MEAN ($\bar{x}$) IS AN UNBIASED ESTIMATOR OF THE POPULATION MEAN OF A NORMAL DISTRIBUTION (μ_x), THAT IS, $E(\bar{X})=\mu_X$

Most of us were taught in basic statistics that the mean of a random sample from a normal distribution is an unbiased estimator of the mean of the population from which the sample was drawn. The proof of that assertion is demonstrated by showing that the expected value, or average of the sample means, equals the population mean. This use of expected values could be conceptualized as a thought experiment (see Chapter 3, footnote 12) in which a random sample is drawn from the population and its sample mean calculated, a second sample is drawn and its sample mean calculated, and so forth for an infinite number of samples. If indeed the estimator (in this case $\bar{X}$) is unbiased, then by the definition of unbiasedness, $E(\bar{X})=\mu_X$.

We begin the algebraic proof that $E(\bar{X})=\mu_X$ by replacing $\bar{X}$ with its equivalent, $[\sum(X_i)]/n$, which can also be written as $(X_1 + X_2 + \ldots + X_n)/n$. Thus,

$$E(\bar{X})=E\left(\frac{\sum X_i}{n}\right)=E\left(\frac{X_1+X_2+\ldots+X_n}{n}\right)$$

This formula can be rewritten as follows:

$$E(\bar{X})=E\left(\frac{X_1}{n}+\frac{X_2}{n}+\ldots+\frac{X_n}{n}\right)$$

Because the expected value of a sum equals the sum of the expected values,

$$E(\bar{X})=E\left(\frac{X_1}{n}\right)+E\left(\frac{X_2}{n}\right)+\ldots+E\left(\frac{X_n}{n}\right)$$

Furthermore, because the expected value of a constant times a variable equals the constant times the expected value of the variable,

$$E(\bar{X})=\frac{1}{n}E(X_1)+\frac{1}{n}E(X_2)+\ldots+\frac{1}{n}E(X_n)$$

Factoring out the common terms gives us this:

$$E(\bar{X})=\frac{1}{n}\left[E(X_1)+E(X_2)+\ldots+E(X_n)\right]$$

To proceed further, we must determine what the symbol $E(X_1)$ represents. X_1 is the first value in our sample, and X_1 was drawn from a normal distribution that has a mean μ_X. Therefore, since X_1 is a point from such a normal distribution, $E(X_1) = \mu_X$. Another way to arrive at the same conclusion is to ask, "Suppose we draw an infinite number of samples, and for each sample we identified the first sample points, X_1, what would be the mean or expected value of all of these first sample points?" The answer is $E(X_1) = \mu_X$ because an infinite number of such X_1's would comprise a normal distribution with a mean μ_X. Likewise, $E(X_2) = \mu_X, E(X_3) = \mu_X, \ldots, E(X_n) = \mu_X$.

Therefore,

$$E(\bar{X})=\frac{1}{n}(\mu+\mu+\cdots+\mu)$$

(Note that there are n μ's.)

$$E(\bar{X})=\frac{1}{n}(n\mu)=\mu$$

This formula tells us that $\bar{X}$ is an unbiased estimator of μ_X, the mean of a normal distribution.

BOX 4.2

PROOF THAT THE SAMPLE VARIANCE, $s_X^2 = \dfrac{\sum\limits_{i=1}^{n}(X_i - \bar{X})^2}{n}$ IS AN

ASYMPTOTICALLY UNBIASED ESTIMATOR OF THE POPULATION

VARIANCE OF A NORMAL DISTRIBUTION, AND THAT THE VALUE

$\dfrac{\sum\limits_{i=1}^{n}(X_i - \bar{X})^2}{n}$ IS AN UNBIASED ESTIMATOR OF THE POPULATION VARIANCE

The proof that $s_X^2 = \dfrac{\sum\limits_{i=1}^{n}(X_i - \bar{X})^2}{n}$ is a *biased*

estimator of σ_X^2 involves an algebraic substitution that is not obvious at first glance.[4] After that substitution is made, and by applying the rules of summation and the theorems of expected values, we arrive at the following:

$$E\left(\frac{\sum\limits_{i=1}^{n}(X_i - \bar{X})^2}{n}\right) = \frac{n-1}{n}\sigma^2$$

Thus, the sample variance underestimates the population variance because $(n-1)/n$ is a fraction. While this formula defines a biased estimate, it is obvious that

$$\lim_{n\to\infty} E\left(\frac{\sum\limits_{i=1}^{n}(X_i - \bar{X})^2}{n}\right) = \lim_{n\to\infty}\left(\frac{n-1}{n}\right)\sigma_X^2 = \sigma_X^2$$

Therefore, the sample variance is an asymptotically unbiased estimator of the population variance. As sample size increases, the ratio $(n-1)/n$ becomes closer and closer

to 1, which means that the bias is greatest for small sample sizes, and decreases as sample size increases.

The bias in the sample variance as an estimator of the population variance can be corrected by multiplying both sides of the first equation by $n/(n-1)$:

$$E\left(\frac{n}{n-1}\cdot\frac{\sum\limits_{i=1}^{n}(X_i - \bar{X})^2}{n}\right) = \left(\frac{n}{n-1}\right)\left(\frac{n-1}{n}\right)\sigma_X^2$$

Therefore,

$$E\left(\frac{\sum\limits_{i=1}^{n}(X_i - \bar{X})^2}{n-1}\right) = \sigma_X^2$$

This demonstrates that $\dfrac{\sum\limits_{i=1}^{n}(X_i - \bar{X})^2}{n-1}$ is an

unbiased estimator of σ_X^2, the variance of a normal distribution. Therefore, one should

always use $\dfrac{\sum(X_i - \bar{X})^2}{n-1}$ as the estimator

of that population variance.

---

[4]You can find this proof in most mathematical statistics books.

Property of Consistency

This property is closely related to asymptotical unbiasedness. Consistency *refers to the variance of the estimates generated by an estimator. With a consistent estimator, as sample size increases, the variance of the estimates decreases, and the estimates approach the parameter.*

An estimator is **consistent** *when the estimates tend to get closer to the parameter the estimator is estimating as the sample size increases.* In other words, the variance of a consistent estimator decreases to zero as sample size increases and the estimates approach the parameter being estimated. Consistent estimators are also either unbiased or asymptotically unbiased. The sample mean and the sample median are both consistent estimators of the mean and median of a normal distribution because, in both cases, they are unbiased, and the variance of the estimates decreases as sample size increases. The sample variance and the unbiased estimator of the population variance are also consistent estimators of the variance of a normal distribution. In both cases, the variance of the estimates decreases to zero as sample size increases. The former is an asymptotically unbiased estimate of the population variance of a normal distribution, and the latter is an unbiased estimate.

Property of (Relative) Efficiency

When we have two or more estimators of the same parameter, the estimator with the smallest variance is the most efficient estimator.

Like consistency, *efficiency* also refers to *the variance of estimators*. When there are more than one estimator for the same population parameter, the estimator with the smallest variance is the most efficient estimator.[5] In the lower left of Figure 4.3, distributions of two estimators of the parameter θ are presented, $\hat{\theta}_A$ and $\hat{\theta}_B$. In this case, $\hat{\theta}_A$ is the more efficient estimator. In symbolic form, $\hat{\theta}_A$ is more efficient than $\hat{\theta}_B$ when $\sigma^2_{\hat{\theta}_A} < \sigma^2_{\hat{\theta}_B}$.

When sampling from a normal distribution in which the population mean and population median are the same, the sample mean is a better estimator of the population mean/median, because although both are unbiased estimators of the population mean and median, the sample mean is a more efficient estimator; that is, the variance of the sample mean is less than the variance of the sample median. In fact, when sampling from a normal distribution,

$$\sigma^2_{\bar{X}} < \frac{2}{\pi}\, \sigma^2_{\text{Median}} \tag{4.4}$$

---

[5] For this reason, efficiency is also referred to as **relative efficiency**.

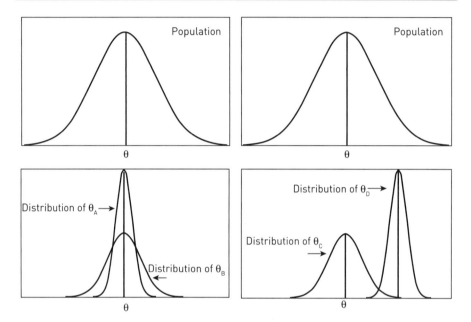

In terms of relative efficiency, the sample mean is 64% more efficient than the sample median (because $2/\pi = 0.636$). This tells us that a sample mean based on a sample size of 64 is as efficient as a sample median based on a sample size of 100 for estimating the mean/median of a normal distribution.

A related question is this: Which estimate of the population mean should we use, a sample mean based on 5 scores or a sample mean based on 50 scores? We should use the sample mean based on 50 scores because it is the more efficient estimator of the population mean. We know this is the case because $\sigma_{\bar{X}}^2 = \dfrac{\sigma^2}{n}$. The larger the sample size, the smaller the value of the variance of the sample means. That is why "larger sample sizes are always better when estimating parameters." This idea is represented in the left panels of Figure 4.3.

The right panels of Figure 4.3 present another issue related to efficiency. In general, an estimator is considered to be a best estimator if it is both unbiased and efficient. However, it is possible that one estimator will be unbiased but have a larger variance than another biased estimator. In this case, the decision as to which is the better estimator will depend on the situation we are in. For the most part, we are more interested in the question of unbiasedness, since that can be directly tested; however, we should not ignore the question of efficiency.

Best estimators *are unbiased, efficient, and consistent estimators.* The sample mean $(\bar{X})$ and the unbiased estimate of the population variance $\left[\sum_{i=1}^{n}(X_i - \bar{X})^2 / (n-1)\right]$ are the best estimators of the mean and variance of a normal distribution, respectively, because they are unbiased, efficient, and consistent estimators of those parameters. These estimators may not be the best estimators of the parameters of other (non-normal) distributions. See Forbes, Evans, Hastings, and Peacock (2011) for information on estimating the parameters of the most commonly used distributions in behavioral science research.

While there are a number of methods for finding estimators of population parameters, only one will be considered here. That method is called *maximum likelihood estimation.* The reason for singling out the maximum likelihood estimation procedure is that when it can be used, it will produce either a best estimator or one that can be easily transformed to a best estimator. The proof of this last assertion is beyond the scope of this book, but we urge you to trust us on this.

MAXIMUM LIKELIHOOD ESTIMATION

Maximum likelihood estimation is a method for finding best estimators of population parameters. When this method can be utilized, it will either produce a best estimator (based on the criteria described above) or an estimator (such as s^2) that can be easily transformed into a best estimator. Maximum likelihood estimation provides the answer to the question "What is the value of the parameter for which the likelihood of having obtained my sample is the highest?" The result is a formula that can apply across all samples from that population.

Maximum likelihood estimation starts with a random sample from a population that has a known form (for example, a normal distribution) but some unknown parameters (for example, the population mean or variance). Samples are composed by drawing individual sample values $(X_1, X_2, \ldots, X_n)$. By knowing what kind of population these values were sampled from, we can find the likelihood[6] of obtaining each of these sample values. These likelihoods are determined by the probability density function for that population and depend on the parameters of that population. A **probability density function** is *an equation that defines the likelihood of any value in that population.* The probability density function for a normal distribution is as follows:

$$f\left(X_i;\mu,\sigma\right) = \frac{1}{\sqrt{2\pi}\sigma}e^{-\frac{1}{2}\left(\frac{X_i-\mu}{\sigma}\right)^2}, \tag{4.5}$$

where X_i is a sampled value and μ and σ are the population mean and standard deviation, respectively. The symbol $f(X_i; \mu, \sigma)$ represents the probability density function that relates to the likelihood of obtaining X_i from a normal distribution with parameters μ and σ. Equation 4.5 generates the familiar bell-shaped normal curve. The height of this curve represents the likelihood for each value of X_i in the population; the higher the curve for a given value X_i, the greater the likelihood for that value.[7] Probability density (likelihood) for any value in $f(X_i; \mu, \sigma)$ is not the same thing as the probability of sampling a value X_i from that population. See Box 4.3 for an explanation of why that is the case.

Therefore, we can use the height of the probability density function to find the likelihood related to a given value of X_i in our sample. To find the likelihood for the entire sample (that is, the likelihood of X_1 and X_2 and X_3 and ... X_n), we multiply the separate likelihoods of each value in the sample. The result is a curve called the likelihood function. A **likelihood function** *describes the likelihood of having obtained the sample you have for different values of the parameter.* Symbolically we represent the likelihood function as

$$L(X_1, X_2, \ldots, X_i, \ldots, X_n; \theta) = f(X_1; \theta) \cdot f(X_2; \theta) \cdots f(X_i; \theta) \cdots f(X_n; \theta), \tag{4.6}$$

where $L(X_1, X_2, \ldots, X_i, \ldots, X_n; \theta)$ stands for the likelihood of $X_1, X_2, \ldots, X_n$ for all possible values of the parameter θ, and $f(X_i; \theta)$ stands for the probability density function for each value of X_i in the sample. The likelihood function for a sample of

---

[6]R. A. Fisher (1925) argued that *likelihood* is the correct term to use when referring to drawing inferences from samples to estimate population parameters. *Probability* refers to future events. It makes no sense to talk about the probability of an event that has already occurred—it either did or did not occur. For example, if I flip a coin, the probability that my flip will result in head is .5. After the coin lands, I do not ask what the probability is that it is a head. I just look at the coin. However, before I look at the coin, I can express how confident I am that it is a head. *Likelihood*, on the other hand, refers to our degree of confidence about an event that has already occurred. Fisher also noted that in everyday discourse, these two terms are frequently used for both situations. We will try to follow Fisher here when using the terms *likelihood* and *probability*.

[7]In Appendix E, the values in the column labeled "Probability Density" are the height of the curve.

BOX 4.3
THE DIFFERENCE BETWEEN LIKELIHOOD AND PROBABILITY

Normal distributions are continuous distributions. *Continuous* means that the values in those distributions are not restricted to discrete whole numbers; therefore, there is an infinite number of values X_i in continuous distributions, and the probability of sampling a specific value for X_i equals $1/\infty = 0$, but that seems counterintuitive. We know there are more values of X_i near the population mean than there are in the tails, so why isn't the probability for sampling a value higher when that value is closer to the population mean?

The answer to that question relates to how we calculate probabilities in a continuous distribution. Probabilities refer to areas under the probability density function between different values. Therefore, while it is not possible to find the probability of sampling a specific value of X_i in a continuous distribution, you can find the probability of sampling a value that exists in a certain range under the curve—for example, between the values 50 and 60, or between the values 9.5 and 10.5—when you know the population mean and standard deviation. We demonstrated in Chapter 3 how to find that area (and probability) using z-scores and the normal distribution table in Appendix E.

For a given range of values, the area and probability are larger when the range is close to the population mean of a normal distribution than when that range of values is in the tail. Furthermore, no matter where the range is

relative to the population mean, if you shrink the difference between the two ends of the range, the area and probability will decrease toward zero. When the range is zero, the probability for that single point is zero.

Probability density refers to the height of the probability density curve. The values in the probability density column in Appendix E are not probabilities. Instead, they are relative measures for expressing the likelihood of that z-score—*the higher the curve, the higher the likelihood of that value.*

Likelihood and probability are related, but they refer to different situations. *Probability* refers to future events, and in continuous distributions such as normal distributions, we can find only the probability of sampling a value that occurs in a certain range in the population when we know the population parameters, not the probability for sampling a specific value. *Likelihood* refers to our level of confidence about the population parameter of the distribution from which we obtained our observed sample value.

To calculate probabilities of sample values from a normal distribution, we need to know the population parameters. With likelihood, we already have the sample value, and we are attempting to assess our degree of confidence about different possible values of the population parameter. In both cases, we use the probability density function to obtain our answer.

five values sampled from a normal distribution is presented in Figure 4.4.[8] The steps for generating this likelihood function are described in Box 4.4.

---

[8]Although this distribution looks like a normal distribution, it is not. The formula for creating this likelihood function is given in Equations 4.7 and 4.8.

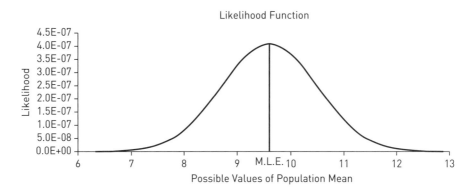

FIGURE 4.4 ■ Likelihood function for the sample 5, 7, 10, 12, 14 drawn from a normal distribution with a variance of 4. On the horizontal axis are various possible values of μ_X, and on the vertical axis are the likelihoods for that sample given different values of μ_X.

BOX 4.4

HOW TO CREATE A LIKELIHOOD FUNCTION FOR A NORMAL DISTRIBUTION

Equation 4.6 provides the formal definition of a likelihood function. To create the likelihood function for a normal distribution, we enter the probability density function in Equation 4.5 into Equation 4.6 for every value of X_i and then multiple these density functions together. Here is the result:

$$L\left(X_1, X_2, \dots X_i, \dots X_n; \mu, \sigma\right) = \prod_{i=1}^{n} \frac{1}{\sqrt{2\pi}\sigma} e^{-\left(\frac{X_i - \mu}{\sigma}\right)^2} \quad (4.7)$$

$$= \left(\frac{1}{\sigma\sqrt{2\pi}}\right)^n e^{-\frac{1}{2}\sum_{i=1}^{n}\left(\frac{X_i - \mu}{\sigma}\right)^2} \quad (4.8)$$

This function can be simulated using an Excel spreadsheet as follows:

1. Start with the sample composed of values $X_1, X_2, \dots, X_i, \dots, X_n$.

2. Enter both a value of X_i and a possible value for the parameter you want to estimate into the probability density function for the population. (For Figure 4.4, that parameter is μ, and the probability density function is Equation 4.5; $\sigma = 2$ was used in all calculations.) The result is the likelihood of that value of X_i and the value of the parameter.

3. Repeat this procedure for all possible values of X_i and multiply the resulting likelihoods together.

4. Repeat steps 2 and 3 for all possible values of the parameter. (For Figure 4.4, the values of μ used ranged from 6 to 13 in increments of 0.1.)

5. Create a graphical representation of these likelihoods across all values of the parameter.

How to Find the Maximum Likelihood Estimator

Once the likelihood function has been obtained, the next step is to find the value of the parameter for which the likelihood function has its maximum value. That is the value on the X-axis, labeled M.L.E. in Figure 4.4. For a random sample from a normal distribution, that value is the sample mean.

Those who know differential calculus know that one can find maximum (or minimum) values on a curve by taking the first derivative of that curve and solving for the value on the X-axis where the slope of the curve = 0.[9] Symbolically, we represent the maximum of the likelihood function as the value of θ for which

$$\frac{dL\left(X_1, X_2, \cdots, X_n\right)}{d\theta} = 0 \tag{4.9}$$

In Equation 4.9, we differentiate with respect to θ, not the X_i's, because here the X_i's are known (and therefore are constants) while θ is the variable we want to estimate. While this approach may at first glance be counterintuitive, some reflection should convince you of the correctness of the procedure because the problem under consideration is to estimate the value of a parameter of the population from which the sample was drawn. The *sample values are known*, and the *population parameter is the unknown quantity*. If the likelihood function has a maximum, we can solve Equation 4.9 to find the value of the parameter at which L is a maximum. This procedure is explained in Box 4.5.

The maximum likelihood estimation procedure will work only when it is possible to create a likelihood function with a maximum value that can be located either with differential calculus or some other procedure. When obtaining such a function is not possible, other methods can be used, such as the method of moments. While the method of moments can produce consistent estimators, they tend to be asymptotically unbiased. See a mathematical statistics book for details on how to use the method of moments. In Chapter 11, we will use another method, the method of least squares, to estimate parameters in linear regression.

The mean of a normal distribution is μ. The maximum likelihood function for μ is the sample mean, which is the best estimator of μ. The variance of a normal distribution is σ^2. The maximum likelihood estimate of σ^2 is the sample variance, $\sum_{i=0}^{n} \frac{\left(X_i - \bar{X}\right)^2}{n}$.

However, the latter can be easily transformed into a best estimator by multiplying it by $n/(n-1)$.

---

[9]This procedure is accomplished through the use of differential calculus. If you do not know how to use this mathematical procedure, skip to the next paragraph and accept that a mathematical technique exists for finding the maximum value of many functions.

BOX 4.5

SUMMARY OF THE PROCEDURE FOR FINDING THE MAXIMUM LIKELIHOOD ESTIMATE OF A PARAMETER Θ THAT HAS A CERTAIN PROBABILITY DENSITY FUNCTION $F(Xi; Θ)$

1. Take a random sample of size n from that population, where the values in that sample are $X_1, X_2, \ldots, X_i, \ldots, X_n$.

2. Multiply the probability densities $f(X_i; \theta)$ for each value in your sample to create the likelihood function (joint probability density function) for your sample:

   $L(X_1, X_2, \ldots, X_i, \ldots, X_n; \theta) = f(X_1; \theta) \cdot f(X_2; \theta) \cdots f(X_i; \theta) \cdots f(X_n; \theta)$

3. Plotting the possible values of the parameter θ on the x-axis and the values of $L(X_1, X_2, \ldots,$ $X_i, \ldots, X_n; \theta)$ on the y-axis, we find the value of θ where the likelihood function has its highest (maximum) value. (See Figure 4.4.)

For many situations, differential calculus can be used to find the maximum value of a function by finding the first derivative of the likelihood function with respect to the parameter being estimated (θ) and solving for the value of θ where that first derivative equals 0:

$$\frac{dL\left(X_1, X_2, \cdots, X_n\right)}{d\theta} = 0$$

CONFIDENCE INTERVALS

Although the mean of an unbiased sample is the best estimator of the mean of a population, we do not expect sample means to equal the population mean. What we can expect is that most of the time, sample means will be close to the means of the populations from which they were sampled. Confidence intervals are statements about the location of parameters. They provide us with a range of values within which we are "confident" that the parameter lies. The width of a confidence interval provides us with information about the stability of our point estimates.

When we select a random sample from a population, our *best* estimate of the mean of that population is the mean of our sample. For example, the mean score on the Vengeance Scale for all of the participants in Barlett and Gentile's (2012) study was 63.56. However, if the researchers had collected a second sample at the same time, it is doubtful that the mean of that second sample would have equaled the mean of the first sample. When we select independent samples from a population, we do not expect the means of those samples to equal each other (although on rare occasions some will). This idea follows from the central limit theorem (Chapter 3). Therefore, when we say that the sample mean is the best estimate of the population mean, it is best given the information in our sample. With a different sample, we will get a different best estimate.

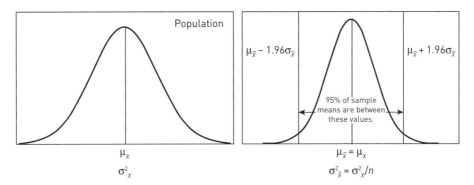

FIGURE 4.5 ■ Given the population on the left, the distribution of means of all possible samples of size *n* drawn from that population is shown on the right.

Sample means provide us with **point estimates** of the population mean, that is, *estimates of the exact location of the parameter*. However, these estimates are rarely, if ever, equal to the parameter being estimated. **Confidence intervals**, on the other hand, are attempts to specify *a range of values within which we are "confident" the parameter lies*; the narrower the range for a given level of confidence, the more precisely we may be able to specify the location of the parameter. Confidence intervals are important supplements to point estimates because of the additional information they provide us about the location of parameters.

However, *confidence* does not mean *certainty*, and how likely the confidence interval we construct will contain the parameter being estimated will depend on the level of confidence we choose. As we will see shortly, the width of a confidence interval is related to the level of confidence we choose—the higher that level of confidence, the wider the confidence interval, but wider intervals provide less precision in specifying the location of the parameter. We can decrease the width of our confidence interval by decreasing our level of confidence, which means that it is less likely that our confidence interval will contain the parameter being estimated.

Confidence Intervals for the Mean of a Normal Distribution When the Population Variance Is Known

Confidence intervals for the mean of a normal distribution are derived from the central limit theorem, which describes the properties of the distribution of sample means.

To understand how the confidence interval for the population mean of a normal distribution is constructed, consider Figure 4.5, in which random samples are repeatedly drawn from a normal distribution with a mean μ_X and variance σ^2_X, and the means of these random samples are calculated. The central limit theorem tells us that the means of all possible

BOX 4.6

THE CONFIDENCE INTERVAL FOR THE MEAN OF A NORMAL DISTRIBUTION WHEN THE POPULATION VARIANCE IS KNOWN

Starting with Equation 4.10, which tells us that the probability is .95 that the mean of a randomly selected sample from a normal distribution with a mean of μ_X will be between the values $\mu_X - 1.96\sigma_{\bar{X}}$ and $\mu_X + 1.96\sigma_{\bar{X}}$, that is,

$$\Pr\left(\mu_X - 1.96\sigma_{\bar{X}} < \bar{X} < \mu_X + 1.96\sigma_{\bar{X}}\right) = .95,$$

we can subtract μ_X from each of the three sections of the inequality to get

$$\Pr\left(-1.96\sigma_{\bar{X}} < \bar{X} - \mu_X < +1.96\sigma_{\bar{X}}\right) = .95$$

This obviously does not change the inequalities or the probability statements. Next subtract $\bar{X}$ from each section of the inequalities. This gives

$$\Pr\left(-\bar{X} - 1.96\sigma_{\bar{X}} < -\mu_X < -\bar{X} + 1.96\sigma_{\bar{X}}\right) = .95$$

If we have two values *a* and *b*, and if $a < b$, then multiplying *a* and *b* by -1 makes $-a > -b$ (for example, if $4 < 7$, then $-4 > -7$). Therefore, multiplying each section of inequalities by -1 will flip the inequality signs, and

$$\Pr\left(\bar{X} + 1.96\sigma_{\bar{X}} > -\mu_X > \bar{X} - 1.96\sigma_{\bar{X}}\right) = .95$$

As it now stands, the larger value ($\bar{X} + 1.96\sigma_{\bar{X}}$)

is on the left, and the smaller value is on the right. To have the inequalities in ascending order from left to right, we rewrite the last equation as follows:

$$\Pr\left(\bar{X} - 1.96\sigma_{\bar{X}} < \mu_X < \bar{X} + 1.96\sigma_{\bar{X}}\right) = .95$$

This notation reflects the confidence interval for the population mean of a normal distribution.

random samples of size n from this population will have the distribution on the right of Figure 4.5. Because the original population is a normal distribution, the distribution of sample means will also be a normal distribution with $\mu_{\bar{X}} = \mu_X$ and $\sigma^2_{\bar{X}} = \sigma^2/n$. Ninety-five percent of the sample means in the right panel will be between the limits $\mu_{\bar{X}} - 1.96\sigma_{\bar{X}}$ and $\mu_{\bar{X}} + 1.96\sigma_{\bar{X}}$. The value 1.96 comes from the unit normal distribution table in Appendix E.[10] In terms of probabilities, this can be expressed symbolically as follows:

$$\Pr\left(\mu_X - 1.96\sigma_{\bar{X}} < \bar{X} < \mu_X + 1.96\sigma_{\bar{X}}\right) = .95 \qquad (4.10)$$

If 95% of the sample means would be expected to be within $\pm 1.96\sigma_{\bar{X}}$ units from μ_X, then we can be reasonably confident that an unknown population mean would be less than that distance from our sample mean. The transformation of Equation 4.10 to a confidence interval is given in Box 4.6.

---

[10]The unit normal distribution table in Appendix E gives you the area for one half of the curve only. The proportion of the data between the $z = 0$ and $z = 1.96$ is .475. When doubled, this value is .95, which is the proportion between −1.96 and +1.96.

The confidence interval for the location of the mean of a normal distribution is

$$\Pr\left(\bar{X} - 1.96\sigma_{\bar{X}} < \mu_X < \bar{X} + 1.96\sigma_{\bar{X}}\right) = .95, \tag{4.11}$$

where $\bar{X} - 1.96\sigma_{\bar{X}}$ is the lower limit of the confidence interval and $\bar{X} + 1.96\sigma_{\bar{X}}$ is the upper limit.

Equation 4.11 is a statement about the location of the population mean. It is *not* a statement about the sample mean, although the value of the sample mean is used to calculate the lower and upper limits of the confidence interval. Instead, Equation 4.11 expresses our degree of confidence about the location of the population mean: In this case, we are 95% confident that the population mean is somewhere within the interval $\bar{X} - 1.96\sigma_{\bar{X}}$ and $\bar{X} + 1.96\sigma_{\bar{X}}$. Our degree of confidence is expressed as a probability statement, but this is *not* because we are saying, "The probability is .95 that our interval contains μ_X." As we have noted earlier in this chapter, *probability* refers to future events. The confidence interval either contains μ_X or it does not; the only probabilities here are 0 and 1. Refer again to Figure 4.5 to consider confidence intervals as probability statements. If we took random samples from the population, calculated $\bar{X}$ for each sample, and constructed a confidence interval around each sample mean using Equation 4.11, 95% of those confidence intervals would contain μ_X and 5% would not. However, when we attempt to estimate the population mean, we take only one sample, and around the mean of that sample we construct only one confidence interval. Our degree of confidence that our interval contains the population mean is based on the probability associated with repeated sampling. See Box 4.7 for more on the relationship between probability and confidence.

Factors That Affect the Width of the Confidence Interval for the Population Mean

The width of the confidence interval for the population mean is a function of the level of confidence selected (the greater the level of confidence, the wider the interval), the population standard deviation (the larger the population standard deviation, the wider the interval), and the sample size (the larger the sample size, the narrower the interval).

Confidence intervals provide us with information about the possible location of population parameters, and they also provide us with information about the stability of our point estimates across repeated samples. The width of a confidence interval reflects the stability of our estimates. Stable estimates are close to each other across different samples, while unstable estimates vary widely. The width of a confidence interval for the mean of a normal distribution is a function of the level

BOX 4.7
THE RELATIONSHIP BETWEEN PROBABILITY AND CONFIDENCE

As noted above, while confidence intervals are written as probability statements, they are not statements of probability. To clarify this relationship between confidence and probability (and the difference between them), consider the following simple situation: Imagine that you thoroughly shuffle a standard deck of 52 playing cards. If asked what the probability is that the first card you draw from the deck will be a heart, you can easily answer 1/4 or .25. If asked for the probability that the first card will be an ace (of any suit), you can answer 1/13 (or .077). Both of these are questions about the probability of future events. Now select a card, but do not turn it over. How confident are you that it is a heart? How confident are you that it is an ace? Clearly, your degree of confidence in selecting a heart (or an ace) is dependent on the probabilities associated with the future occurrence of each event, and you would scale your confidence that you have indeed selected a heart (or an ace) in terms of their respective probabilities.

This approach is similar to what we do with confidence intervals: *Our degree of confidence that the interval contains the parameter in question is measured by the probability that such an interval would contain the parameter in future experiments.* This statement is similar to Fisher's use of the term *likelihood* when drawing inferences from samples to estimate population parameters. The theory of confidence intervals was developed by Neyman, who described the history of confidence intervals in his 1941 paper.

One final note concerns the question of whether you did indeed draw a heart. There is no probability attached to this event; either you did or you did not. By turning the card over, you discover whether you did or not. In scientific investigations, we never get to the point where we know the value of the parameter under investigation. The best we can do is to specify with some degree of confidence a range of values in which we believe the parameter exists.

of confidence we choose, the standard deviation of that normal distribution, and the sample size we select. All three of these pieces of information are to some extent under our control. Ideally, we want to have narrow confidence intervals with high degrees of confidence.

DEGREE OF CONFIDENCE If we want to increase our level of confidence about the location of μ_X from 95% to 99%, we use 2.58 in place of 1.96 in Equation 4.11 because in a unit normal curve, 99% of the area of the curve is contained within the interval -2.58 and $+2.58$. Thus, the 99% confidence interval for μ_X is

$$\Pr\left(\bar{X} - 2.58\sigma_{\bar{X}} < \mu_X < \bar{X} + 2.58\sigma_{\bar{X}}\right) = .99 \qquad (4.12a)$$

While we have increased our confidence that μ_X is contained between the limits $\bar{X} - 2.58\sigma_{\bar{x}}$ and $\bar{X} + 2.58\sigma_{\bar{x}}$, those limits describe a larger interval than in Equation 4.11. Therefore, while we are more confident that μ_X is within the 99% interval, we are less sure about its location because we are dealing with a larger interval. In the extreme, we could have a 100% confidence interval:

$$\Pr\left(\bar{X} - \infty\sigma_{\bar{x}} < \mu_X < \bar{X} + \infty\sigma_{\bar{x}}\right) = 1.00 \qquad (4.12b)$$

but we would not really be able to locate μ_X. Therefore, there is a tradeoff between the level of confidence we select and the width of the resulting confidence interval: the higher the level of confidence, the wider the interval. In other words, we can be more confident that the interval contains the parameter, but less precise in our ability to pin down the location of that parameter.

POPULATION STANDARD DEVIATION As we saw in Chapter 3, the standard deviation of the sample means $\sigma_{\bar{x}} = \dfrac{\sigma}{\sqrt{n}}$. Therefore, Equation 4.11 can be rewritten as follows:

$$\Pr\left(\bar{X} - \frac{1.96\sigma}{\sqrt{n}} < \mu_X < \bar{X} + \frac{1.96\sigma}{\sqrt{n}}\right) = .95, \qquad (4.13)$$

This equation tells us that the width of a confidence interval for the mean of a normal distribution is a direct function of the population standard deviation—the larger the population standard deviation, the wider the confidence interval.

While it may seem counterintuitive, the population standard deviation is partially under our control. This statement is true based on the following:

1. Although we usually think of populations as consisting of individuals, they actually consist of measurements of the behavior of individuals (test scores, responses, and so forth).
2. According to classical measurement theory, such measurements (X) are made up of two parts, a true score (T) and an error component (E). We express this relationship among these elements with the following equation: $X = T + E$. Furthermore, we assume that the errors are normally distributed with $\mu_E = 0$ and $\sigma_E > 0$.
3. From Theorem 3 (Chapter 3), the mean of a sum equals the sum of the means: $\mu_X = \mu_T + \mu_E$, but $\mu_E = 0$; therefore, $\mu_X = \mu_T$. Likewise, the variance of a sum equals the sum of the variances: $\sigma^2_X = \sigma^2_T + \sigma^2_E$.
4. The variance of the true scores reflects the individual differences in your population, but the error variance can be due to a number of factors under our control. These factors include, but are not limited to, the following:

a. How we treat all participants when collecting data, including how we administer the instructions, whether we test participants at the same time of day, and whether the data are collected the same way from all participants.

b. How careful we are when recording our data. Errors in recording can inflate σ^2_E.

Anything we can do to reduce the error variance will reduce the variance of the population of measurements we are collecting and decrease the width of confidence intervals for the population mean.

SAMPLE SIZE Equation 4.13 also shows us that the width of a confidence interval for the population mean is an inverse function of the sample size—the larger the sample, the narrower the confidence interval. Our goal is to create narrow confidence intervals, meaning we have a *high* level of confidence that the parameter we are attempting to estimate is in that interval. Increasing the sample size helps us to achieve that objective as a direct consequence of the central limit theorem, which tells us that the variance of the sample means around the population mean is an inverse function of the sample size $\left(\sigma^2_{\bar{X}} = \dfrac{\sigma^2}{n} \right)$. With large sample sizes, we expect most of our sample means to be close to the population mean.

All other things being equal, increasing the sample size will always decrease the width of the confidence interval; however, there is a law of diminishing returns. Figure 4.6 has a plot of the width of a 95% confidence interval for the mean of a normal distribution as a function of the sample size. The width of the interval decreases rapidly at first but eventually reaches a point where increasingly large sample sizes are required to produce even modest decreases in width. For example, increasing the sample size from 1 to 10 decreases the width of the interval from 58.8 to 18.6 units, a difference of 40 units, but increasing the sample size from 10 to 20 decreases the width of the interval from 18.6 to 13.2, a difference of only 5.4 units. Adding 10 more observations decreases the width to 10.8, a difference of only 2.4 units. Therefore, we should balance our desired level of precision against the resources required to reach that level. For example, increasing our sample size from 30 to 60 observations only gains us a reduction in confidence interval width of 3.2 units (10.8 to 7.6). Is the extra effort worth the gain?

Confidence Interval for the Population Mean of a Normal Distribution When the Population Variance Is Not Known

It is rare that we know the population variance when creating a confidence interval for the population mean of a normal distribution. In this case, we estimate the population variance and use the t-distribution to create our confidence interval.

FIGURE 4.6   ■   **Plot of the width of the confidence interval for the mean of a normal distribution showing width as a function of the sample size (ranging from 1 to 100). The population standard deviation is set at 15.**

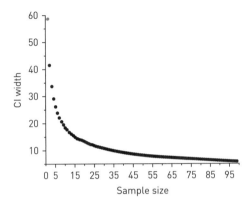

In Box 4.6, the confidence interval for the population mean of a normal distribution when the population variance is *known* was derived. That derivation was done to show you the logic behind the confidence intervals, but in practice, we rarely know the population variance and have to estimate it from the sample data. When we do so, we make the following two substitutions in Equations 4.11, 4.12a, and 4.13: We use the unbiased estimate of the population standard deviation in place of σ and a value from the *t*-table instead of the 1.96 and 2.58 that come from the unit normal distribution table. The value of *t* that we use from the *t*-distribution table (Appendix F) depends on the number of scores in your sample. If *n* is the number of scores in your sample, select the value of *t* with *n* − 1 degrees of freedom for the desired level of confidence.[11] When we do so, the confidence interval for the population mean of a normal distribution when the population variance is not known can be calculated from either of these two equivalent[12] formulas:

$$\Pr\left(\overline{X} - \frac{t_{(.05,n-1\mathrm{df})}\mathrm{est}\,\sigma}{\sqrt{n}} < \mu_X < \overline{X} + \frac{t_{(.05,n-1\mathrm{df})}\mathrm{est}\,\sigma}{\sqrt{n}}\right) = .95 \qquad (4.14a)$$

or

$$\Pr\left(\overline{X} - \frac{t_{(.05,n-1\mathrm{df})}S}{\sqrt{n-1}} < \mu_X < \overline{X} + \frac{t_{(.05,n-1\mathrm{df})}S}{\sqrt{n-1}}\right) = .95 \qquad (4.14b)$$

---

[11] For a 95% confidence interval, we use the column in which .05 is the proportion in two tails.

[12] *Equivalent* means that both formulas produce the same result.

Confidence intervals created by applying Equations 4.14a or 4.14b to the data depicted in Figure 4.1 are presented in Table 4.1.

The Correct Interpretation of Confidence Intervals

Confidence intervals are statements about the locations of fixed population parameters. These confidence intervals, which will vary from sample to sample, are not *statements about sample statistics. We describe three misinterpretations of what confidence intervals tell us, and we highlight the correct interpretations.*

Although Equations 4.11, 4.12a, 4.13, and 4.14 are written in terms of probability, they do *not* tell us the probability is .95 that the specific interval we created (from the calculated lower limit to the calculated upper limit) contains the population mean. The specific interval either contains the population mean or it does not. The 95% probability refers to what would happen if we took repeated samples of size n from that population: *If we take repeated samples of size* n *from a population, calculate the sample means, and construct confidence intervals, 95% of those confidence intervals will contain the population mean, and 5% will not.* But we actually only take one sample, and the most we can say is that we are 95% confident that the interval we created around our sample mean contains the population mean. As noted in footnote 6, the probability that our confidence interval contains the population mean is either 0 or 1; the interval either does or does not contain the population mean. However, if the probability is high that a future confidence interval constructed the same way with another sample will contain the population mean, our level of confidence that the one we created contains the population mean should also be high, even though we have no way of knowing that it does. As noted in footnote 6, *probability* refers to the occurrence of future events, while *confidence* and *likelihood* refer to our subjective appraisal of whether something happened.

TABLE 4.1 ■ Confidence intervals for the population mean in college-aged students in the Midwest on the Vengeance Scale.				
Group	Sample Size	Sample Mean	Lower Bound of CI	Upper Bound of CI
All participants	490	63.56	62.01	65.11
Males	231	67.96	65.66	70.26
Females	259	59.63	57.65	61.62

The *correct* way to read Equation 4.14 with the data for all participants in Table 4.1 is, *I am 95% confident that the population mean on the Vengeance Scale is between 62.01 and 65.11,* (where 62.01 is the lower limit of the interval $\overline{X} - \dfrac{t_{(.05, n-1df)}S}{\sqrt{n-1}}$ and 65.11 is the upper limit of the interval $\overline{X} + \dfrac{t_{(.05, n-1df)}S}{\sqrt{n-1}}$).[13]

This statement does *not* mean that the population mean falls in that interval. The population mean is a fixed but unknown value—it does not change from sample to sample. *Confidence intervals are attempts to define an interval within which we are confident that the fixed parameter lies.*

Another misconception is that if we were to take additional samples and construct confidence intervals around the means of those samples, 95% of those sample means would be contained in the original confidence interval. Cumming, Williams, and Fidler (2004) labeled this statement the "confidence-level misconception (CLM)." Cumming and Maillardet (2006) noted that the probability that the sample means of future samples will be contained in the original confidence interval depends on the location of the original sample mean in relation to the population mean. When the sample mean used to construct the original confidence interval is close to the population mean, the probability that future sample means will be contained in that original confidence interval is close to 95%, but when the original sample mean is far from the population mean, that probability is markedly reduced. Across all possible original 95% confidence intervals, on average only 83.4% of sample means will fall into the original confidence interval (see also Estes, 1977). Confidence intervals are *statements* about population parameters, *not* sample statistics.

BEYOND NORMAL DISTRIBUTIONS AND ESTIMATING POPULATION MEANS

The principles presented in this chapter can be extended to estimating the population variance in a normal distribution and parameters of many other distributions.

Up to this point, the basic principles for finding both point estimates and creating confidence intervals have been presented for estimating the mean of a normal distribution. The maximum likelihood procedure can be used to find estimators of parameters for any population when we can create a likelihood function with a maximum that we can

---

[13] The small size of this confidence interval reflects the large sample size. This confidence interval indicates that the sample mean is likely to be close to the population mean.

find with either differential calculus or some other method; therefore, it can be used with many populations and parameters. With respect to finding confidence intervals for a parameter, we need to know the distribution of the estimator we are using for that parameter. In this chapter, we used the central limit theorem (Chapter 3) to construct the confidence interval for the mean of a normal distribution around the sample mean.

We noted above that the sample variance, s^2, is the maximum likelihood estimate of σ^2, the variance of a normal distribution, and that s^2 can be easily transformed into an unbiased estimate of σ^2. However, s^2 and the unbiased estimate of σ^2 have chi square distributions, not normal distributions. Although chi square distributions are not symmetrical, the principles for creating confidence intervals described in this chapter can be adapted to create confidence intervals for the population variance of a normal distribution using tables for chi square distributions. We can also apply these same principles to constructing confidence intervals for the parameter π (the probability of a success on a single trial) of a binomial distribution (Chapter 8) and the population correlation ρ of a bivariate normal distribution (Chapter 10). The estimators for π and ρ are maximum likelihood estimates.

The situation is not as straightforward when estimating the population median, even when sampling from a normal distribution. The sample median is not a maximum likelihood estimator, and it is not always an unbiased estimator of the population median. Furthermore, there is no formula for the sampling distribution of the sample median, although like the sample mean, its sampling distribution approaches a normal distribution as sample size increases (Wilcox, 2010). As a result, one must use other ways to estimate the population median (Harrell & Davis, 1982) and to create confidence intervals for it. One of these strategies will be described in Chapter 9.

Another problem arises when the data contain outliers that may come from a variety of sources, such as recording errors or sampling from non-normal distributions. We will see in the next chapter that the presence of outliers can have a dramatic effect on sample means and unbiased estimates of the population variance, even when the majority of the numbers are sampled from a normal distribution. Therefore, when deciding which estimator to use, we also need to consider how resistant that estimator is to the presence of outliers in our data. The **resistance of an estimator** is measured by *how much an estimate is influenced by the presence of outliers*. This topic will be covered in the next chapter, in which we consider how to deal with data that do not come from normal distributions or may be contaminated by other sources.

Summary

In the classical statistical model, populations with certain parameters exist, some known (or assumed) and some unknown. We can use the information in a random sample taken from a population to estimate the unknown parameter or parameters of that population. *Point estimators* provide us with ways to use the information in our sample to arrive at a best estimate of the parameter. While it is rare that our point estimate will equal the population parameter being estimated, some point estimators are better than others.

Best estimators are unbiased (the expected value of the estimator equals the parameter being estimated), *efficient* (have the smallest variance among the various estimators), and *consistent* (as sample size increases, the variance of the estimates decreases, and the estimates approach the parameter). Some estimators (like the sample variance) are biased but asymptotically unbiased (bias decreases as sample size increases).

There are a number of techniques for deriving the formulas for estimators. Maximum likelihood estimation is considered the best (when it can be employed) because if a solution can be found, the result will be either a best estimator or one that can be easily transformed to a best estimator. *The maximum likelihood estimator for a parameter is the value of the parameter for which the likelihood of our sample is a maximum.* The sample mean ($\overline{X}$) is the maximum likelihood estimator of the population mean of a normal distribution (μ). The sample variance (s^2) is the maximum likelihood estimator of the population variance of a normal distribution (σ^2). The sample variance is an asymptotically unbiased estimate that can be easily transformed to an unbiased estimate: $\sum_{i=1}^{n}\left(X_i - \overline{X}\right)^2 / \left(n-1\right)$.

Because point estimates such as $\overline{X}$ are rarely equal to the parameter being estimated, we use confidence intervals constructed around our point estimates to provide us with information about the possible location of the parameter and information about the stability of our estimators. Confidence intervals are statements about population parameters. Specifically, *a confidence interval is a statement about the range of values where we are "confident" the parameter under consideration is located.* The parameter may or may not be within that range, but when our chosen level of confidence is high (say .95), we should feel comfortable that the parameter is within that range. Furthermore, the width of the confidence interval tells us something about the stability of our point estimate. The narrower the confidence interval for a given level of confidence, the closer the estimate tends to be to the parameter value. The width of a confidence interval for the population mean from a normal distribution is a direct function of the level of confidence we adopt (the higher the level of confidence, the wider the interval), a direct function of the variance of the population (the greater the variance, the wider the interval), and an inverse function of the sample size (the greater the sample size, the narrower the interval). Because the width of the confidence interval is related to the sample size utilized, we can increase the precision in our estimates by increasing the size of the sample, although there is a diminishing return with respect to the width of the confidence interval with increases in sample size. Therefore, it is important to take into account the sample size when interpreting the width of a confidence interval.

Conceptual Exercises

1. We can apply the concepts in this chapter to many types of distributions. For instance, the Poisson distribution is a discrete distribution that describes the probability of a given number of independent events occurring in a fixed interval of time and/or space. The shape of this distribution depends on a single parameter λ. The probability density function for a Poisson distribution is

$$f\left(X_i;\lambda\right)=\frac{\lambda^X e^{-\lambda}}{X!}$$

Describe how to find the maximum likelihood estimate of λ. (In your answer, describe what a maximum likelihood estimate is, how we find it in this situation, and what it means to say that something is the maximum likelihood estimate of λ.)

2. The maximum likelihood estimate of λ is $\overline{X}$. What does it mean to say that $\overline{X}$ is an unbiased estimator of λ? (In your answer, include the definition of an unbiased estimate and how we determine whether an estimate is unbiased.)

3. Comment on the following statements about the following confidence interval based on a random sample from a normal distribution: $\Pr(2 < \lambda < 5) = .95$. Are they true? Why or why not?

    a. Based on that confidence interval, I am 95% confident that λ lies between 2 and 5.

    b. The probability is .95 that if I take another sample from the same population, the mean of that sample will also be between 2 and 5.

4. What does the statement $\Pr(44.5 < \mu < 61.7) = .95$ tell us about:

    a. The sample mean?

    b. The population mean?

5. Are the following statements true? Why or why not?

    a. Two *SE* bars that do not overlap indicate that there is a statistically significant difference between the two groups represented on the graph.

    b. Two confidence intervals that overlap indicate that there is not a statistically significant difference between the two groups represented on the graph.

6. Why do we say that the sample variance, s^2, is a <u>biased</u> estimate of σ^2 but is an <u>asymptotically unbiased</u> estimate of the same parameter? (Hint: Define what it means to be an unbiased estimate and an asymptotically unbiased estimate as applied to the sample variance.)

7. What is wrong with the following statement: The probability is .95 that the population variance falls between 9.6 and 17.8? How should this statement be written and why?

8. What does it mean to say that the sample variance, s^2, is the maximum likelihood estimate of σ^2, the population variance of a normal distribution? (To answer this question, you should describe what a maximum likelihood estimate is, how we find one <u>in this situation</u>, and what it means to say that s^2 is the maximum likelihood estimate of σ^2.)

9. Reaction times are used to investigate a number of cognitive and perceptual phenomena. Reaction time data can be modeled by a lognormal distribution. The probability density function for the lognormal distribution has two parameters, μ and σ. How would you find the maximum likelihood estimate of μ? (In your answer, describe what a maximum likelihood estimate is, how we find it in this situation, and what it means to say that something is the maximum likelihood estimate of μ.)

10. Comment on the following statements about this confidence interval based on a random sample from a normal distribution: $Pr (20 < \mu < 40) = .95$. Are these statements true? Why or why not?

    a. Based on that confidence interval, I am 95% confident that the population mean lies between 20 and 40.

    b. The probability is .95 that if I take another sample from the same population, the mean of that sample will also be between 20 and 40.

Student Study Site

Visit the Student Study Site at **https://study.sagepub.com/friemanstats** for a variety of useful tools including data sets, additional exercises, and web resources.

RESISTANT ESTIMATORS
OF PARAMETERS

In addition to having his participants complete a number of scales, such as the Vengeance Scale described in the last chapter, Barlett (2015) asked them a number of questions about their use of the Internet for texting, email, and Facebook. The data from the 122 participants (undergraduate students in an introductory psychology course, aged 17–24 years) who responded to the questions about how often they texted others and received texts during various time periods (6 a.m. to 12 p.m., 12 p.m. to 6 p.m., 6 p.m. to 12 a.m., and 12 a.m. to 6 a.m.) during the week and on weekends are summarized in Figure 5.1 as a quantile plot, a stem-and-leaf display, and a schematic box plot. The scores assigned to each participant are based on a formula that provides an overall measure of text messages per week by assigning different weights to the numbers for weekdays and weekends.

These data are highly skewed to the right with a couple of noticeable outliers, and the most common values are on the stem that contains 0–9 texts per week. The sample mean = 41.01, the sample median = 30.25, the sample variance = 1,825.48, and the sample standard deviation = 42.72. The large difference between the sample mean and sample median reflects the extreme skew in these data (index of skewness = 2.69). The 95% confidence interval of the population mean calculated from Equation 4.14 is

$$\Pr (33.32 < \mu < 48.74) = .95 \tag{5.1}$$

Considering the sample size, this is a wide confidence interval.

Although the concepts and procedures described in Chapter 4 apply to estimating the parameters from any population whose form can be specified, most of that discussion was about estimating parameters from normal distributions. That is because many widely used statistical techniques such as *t*-tests, analysis of variance, and regression are based on, and therefore assume, sampling from normal distributions. But real data are rarely sampled from pure normal distributions (Hill & Dixon, 1982; Micceri, 1989;

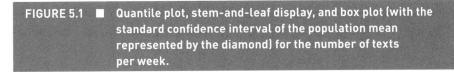

FIGURE 5.1 ■ Quantile plot, stem-and-leaf display, and box plot (with the standard confidence interval of the population mean represented by the diamond) for the number of texts per week.

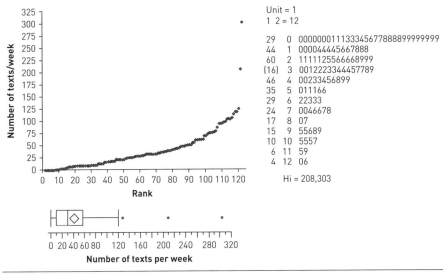

Source: Barlett (2015).

Tukey, 1960). Our data often contain outliers, and the presence of these outliers can distort our estimates of parameters. Outliers can occur for a variety of reasons: recording errors, sampling from distributions that have more values in their tails than normal distributions (that is, "heavy-tailed distributions"), and sampling from nonsymmetrical distributions. The confidence interval in Equation 5.1 is based on the assumption that our data were sampled from normal distributions, but it is clear in Figure 5.1 that they were not.

A CLOSER LOOK AT SAMPLING FROM NON-NORMAL POPULATIONS

Although the distribution of sample means approaches a normal distribution as sample size increases, how quickly this limit is reached depends on the degree of skew in the population.

The central limit theorem (Chapter 3) informs us about the distribution of the means of samples of size n from any population: The mean of the sample means, $\mu_{\bar{X}}$, equals the population mean μ; the variance of the sample means, $\sigma^2_{\bar{X}}$, equals σ^2/n; and the distribution of sample means approaches a normal distribution as sample size increases, even when the population from which the sample was taken is not a normal distribution.

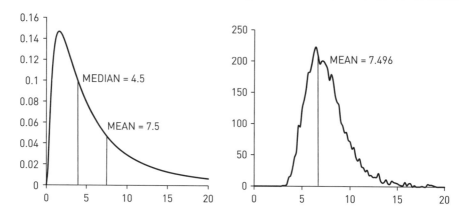

FIGURE 5.2 ■ From the population (*left*), 5,000 samples of size 20 are taken and plotted (*right*).

However, for smaller sample sizes, the distribution of sample means can be quite skewed. We can see this in Figure 5.2, where 5,000 samples of 20 values each are taken from the skewed population of the left and plotted on the right. Note that although the mean of the sample means is close to 7.5, the distribution of sample means is skewed and resembles the original population rather than a normal distribution.

Although the sample mean is close to the population mean, it is clear from the plot in the left panel of Figure 5.2 that the population median better represents the bulk of the scores in that population. It is also clear from the plot in the right panel of that figure that the distribution of the sample means is heavily influenced by the extreme skew and heavy tail on the right side of the population. In this chapter, we will see why the sample mean and the unbiased estimator of the population variance are not "resistant" to the presence of outliers.

Fortunately, there are a number of **resistant estimators** that *reduce the influence of outliers and heavy tails on our estimates of population parameters*. We will explore some of these resistant estimators of location and spread and explain why they are indeed resistant. We will also explore a set of procedures for finding resistant confidence intervals when the population from which the data were obtained is not a normal distribution.

THE SAMPLE MEAN AND SAMPLE MEDIAN ARE L-ESTIMATORS

The reason why sample means are not resistant estimators of the population mean, while sample medians are resistant estimators of population medians, has to do with how they are calculated. Both are L-estimators. That is, they are linear combinations of the sample values. However, sample means give every value in the sample the same weight, while sample medians give all values in the sample except the middle score or middle two scores a weight of zero.

The key to understanding why the sample mean is not a resistant estimator when sampling from populations that are skewed or have heavy tails comes from how the sample mean is calculated:

$$\bar{X} = \frac{\sum_{i=1}^{n} X_i}{n} = \frac{X_1 + X_2 + \cdots + X_n}{n}$$

$$= \frac{X_1}{n} + \frac{X_2}{n} + \cdots + \frac{X_n}{n}$$

$$= \left(\frac{1}{n}\right)X_1 + \left(\frac{1}{n}\right)X_2 + \cdots + \left(\frac{1}{n}\right)X_n \tag{5.2}$$

We see in Equation 5.2 that the sample mean is a linear combination of the values in the sample when each value in the sample has a weight of ($1/n$). For this reason, the sample mean is an example of a linear estimator or **L-estimator**; that is, it is *a linear combination of the observations when each observation is assigned a weight of 1/n.*[1]

The **sample median** is also an L-estimator.[2] In the case of the sample median, after the data are ranked from lowest to highest, when n is an even number, the middle two values ($X_{[(n+1)/2] - 1}$ and $X_{[(n+1)/2] + 1}$) are added together and divided by 2. All of the other $n - 2$ values are given a weight of 0. Therefore, the sample median is also a linear combination of the weighted values in the sample:

$$\text{Sample median} = (0)X_1 + (0)X_2 + \cdots + (0.5)X_{[(n+1)/2] - 1}$$
$$+ (0.5)X_{[(n+1)/2] + 1} + \cdots + (0)X_n \tag{5.3}$$

When n is an odd number, the middle value gets a weight of 1, and all other values get a weight of 0:

$$\text{Sample median} = (0)X_1 + (0)X_2 + \cdots + (1)X_{[(n+1)/2]} + \cdots + (0)X_n \tag{5.4}$$

---

[1]Calculating the sample mean does not require that the values in the sample be rank ordered from lowest to highest. For the sample median and other robust estimators described below, however, the data must be ranked first.

[2]Although the sample mean and the sample median are both L-estimators, they estimate different parameters when the population is skewed. The sample mean is an estimate of the population mean, and the sample median is an estimate of the population median. In symmetrical populations, they estimate the same parameter.

It is clear in Equations 5.3 and 5.4 that the value of the sample median is determined only by the middle one or two values in the sample. In other words, it does not matter what the values from $X_{[(n + 1)/2] + 1}$ through X_n are, the sample median will still be the same. On the other hand, every value in our data affects the value of the sample mean because every value is given the same non-zero weight. Therefore, when the highest score in our sample, X_n, is an outlier above the sample mean, for example, it will cause the value of the sample mean to be larger than it would be if X_n were closer to the rest of the data. This fact gives us a clue to how we might create a robust estimator that is not affected by outliers and still assign non-zero weights to most of the data. We can do so by using what are called "α-trimmed means." An **α-trimmed mean** is an *L-estimator in which the extreme α values on each end of the ranked sample are given weights of 0, while the middle values are given weights of 1/[n(1 − 2α)].* The procedure for calculating α-trimmed means is described below.

Before describing α-trimmed means, we need to consider further how outliers affect the values of estimators.

MEASURING THE INFLUENCE OF OUTLIERS ON ESTIMATES OF LOCATION AND SPREAD

We can use influence functions to provide us with a graphical representation of the effects of outliers in our data on various estimators of location and spread.

How much effect an observation has on an estimator is called its **influence**. We can observe the influence of an observation through the use of an **influence function**, which displays the effect of adding an observation to a data set on the value of various estimators of parameters and sample statistics. Examples of influence functions for the sample mean and sample median are displayed in the top two panels of Figure 5.3. It is clear from these figures that, for the sample mean, the influence of a single data point depends on the value of that data point, and the farther that value is from the rest of the data, the greater is its influence. We can make the sample mean as large as we want by adding a single extreme value to our sample. For the sample mean, the **finite-sample breakdown point**, which is the smallest proportion of the observations that can be changed to make the estimator as large as we want, is $1/n$. On the other hand, the sample median is not readily influenced by outliers. The finite-sample breakdown point for the sample median is $[(n + 1)/2]/n$; that is, roughly half of the values must be changed to make the sample median as large as we want. Thus, the sample median is a resistant estimator, while the sample mean is not.

As noted above, an influence function is a graph in which we plot the effects that adding another score to our data would have on our estimator of location (such as the mean and median) or spread (such as the unbiased estimate of the population variance).

TABLE 5.1 ■ Data for Influence Functions Examples		
Sampled Values – Sample Mean		
−22.79, −19.09, −13.86, −9.63, −8.55, −8.55, −7.31, −2.68, −0.63, −0.05, 2.31, 3.44, 4.65, 5.99, 8.23, 9.76, 13.25, 15.75, 29.77		
Sample Statistics		
$n = 19$	Sample variance = 153.89	
Sample mean = 0.00	Sample standard deviation = 12.40	
Sample median = −0.05	Est. pop. st. dev. = 12.74	
	Est. of population variance = 162.44	

The value of the new score is plotted along the horizontal axis, and the influence of that score is represented on the vertical axis.

To illustrate the effects of "extra" scores on various measures of location and dispersion, a random sample was generated via a computer simulation from a normal distribution with a mean = 50 and a standard deviation = 10. Then the sample mean was subtracted from each sample value to make the sample mean = 0. (Note that the principles described here apply to samples from any population.) The sample mean was shifted (or "centered") to zero by subtracting the original sample mean from each score to make it easier to see the effects of the extra scores on the mean. The resulting values and various sample statistics are in Table 5.1.

To create the influence functions in the following figures, a set of extra scores that ranged from −45 to +45 in increments of 5 units was created. Each extra score was added to the original sample one at a time, and the sample statistics were recalculated.[3] Then the recalculated sample statistics were subtracted from the original sample statistics to find the influence of each extra score. These influence values were then plotted against the extra scores.

Influence Functions for Estimates of Location

The influence functions for the sample mean and sample median, respectively, are plotted in the top two panels of Figure 5.3.

It is clear from the influence function for the sample mean, shown at the top of Figure 5.3, that adding a single score above the sample mean increases the sample mean, and the farther that extra score is from the sample mean, the greater the increase. The same is true for adding a single score below the sample mean. This outcome occurs

---

[3]Only one extra score was included in the calculation each time. Therefore, the recalculated sample statistics were based on 20 scores.

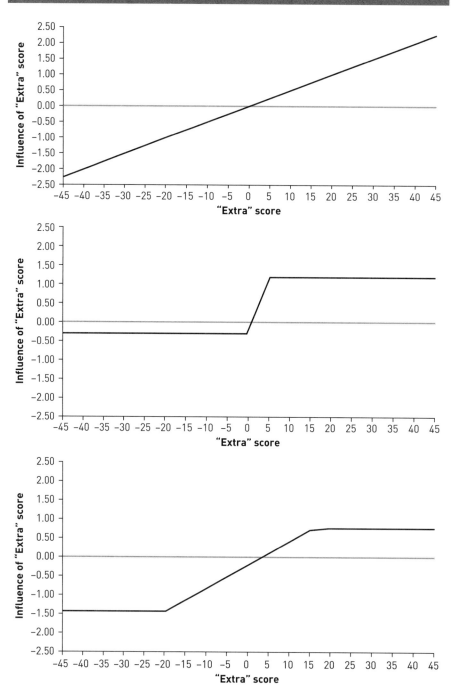

FIGURE 5.3 ■ Influence functions for the sample mean (*top*), sample median (*middle*), and 0.1 α-trimmed mean (*bottom*).

because the sample mean is an L-estimator in which every value is given the same weight ($1/n$). In other words, a single point can dominate the value of the sample mean. If that single point were infinitely large, the sample mean would be infinitely large ($\overline{X} = \infty$). Of course, because each score is weighted by $1/n$, any extra score will have a greater effect on the mean of a small sample than on the mean of a large sample.

We see a very different picture when we look at the influence function for the sample median, shown in the middle of Figure 5.3. Because we give a weight of zero to every score except the middle one when the sample size is an odd number, and except for the middle two numbers if the sample size is an even number, the sample median will shift in the direction of the extra score. However, that shift does not depend on the value of that extra score. It only depends on what becomes the new middle score (or two middle scores). Unlike the sample mean, which we can make as large as we want by adding a sufficiently large score (or moving the largest score a sufficient distance from the rest of the scores), *the only way we can make the median as large as we want it to be is to make at least half of the scores be that large*.[4] Therefore, the finite-sample breakdown point for the median is 0.5.

One might draw the conclusion that the sample median is a better estimator of location than the sample mean, but that conclusion is only true when dealing with skewed distributions or situations in which there are outliers in our data. Consider the distribution of incomes. In many populations, the few very wealthy people inflate the mean so that it does not represent the bulk of the distribution. For this reason, we use median income instead of mean income when representing central tendency for those data. When dealing with normal distributions in which the population mean and population median are the same, the sample mean is a better estimate of both the population mean and population median because, while both the sample mean and sample median are unbiased estimates of the population mean and population median, the sample mean is a more efficient estimate; that is, the variance of the sample mean is less than the variance of the sample median. In fact, when sampling from a normal distribution,

$$\sigma^2_{\overline{X}} = \left(\frac{2}{\pi}\right)\sigma^2_{median} \tag{5.5}$$

However, this pattern only holds for samples from normal distributions. When sampling from heavy-tailed distributions (which produce outliers in our samples) and skewed distributions, the sample median can be the more efficient estimator of central tendency. This fact is obvious in Figure 5.4, in which the population from which the data were sampled was a mixed normal distribution (also called a contaminated normal distribution), that is, a distribution composed of scores from two different normal

---

[4]The actual value of the finite breakdown point is $[(n + 1)/2]/n$.

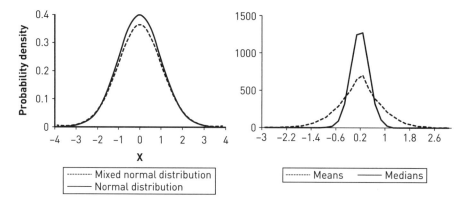

FIGURE 5.4 ■ On the right, a plot of 5,000 sample means and sample medians of samples with size = 20 from the mixed normal distribution such that 90% of the scores are from a normal distribution with $\sigma = 1$ and 10% are from a normal distribution with $\sigma = 10$. These normal distributions are shown on the left. The solid line in the left panel is a unit normal distribution. The dotted line is the mixed normal distribution described in the text.

distributions that have the same mean but different variances. Although both curves look like normal distributions, the mixed distribution is not normal—there are fewer values in the middle of the distribution and more in the tails. The result is that samples tend to have more outliers than we normally observe when sampling from normal distributions.

The sample mean is a more efficient estimator when sampling from a normal distribution, because it gives the same non-zero weight to all of the scores in the sample while the median gives non-zero weights only to the middle or middle two scores. But as we have just seen, the cost of giving the same non-zero weight to all of the scores is to make the sample mean easily influenced by outliers in our data. The use of α-trimmed means provides us with an estimator of location by which we reduce the influence of outliers and still give non-zero weights to most of the scores.

α-TRIMMED MEANS AS RESISTANT AND EFFICIENT ESTIMATORS OF LOCATION

α-trimmed means are created by assigning a zero weight to a certain proportion of the scores on each side of the sample (determined by α), creating an estimator that is resistant to the effects of outliers. α-trimmed means are more efficient than sample medians but less efficient than untrimmed sample means.

An **α-trimmed mean** is *an L-estimator of location in which the extreme* α *values on each end of the ranked sample are given weights of 0, while the middle values are given weights of* $1/n(1 - 2\alpha)$, *where* α *is the proportion of scores trimmed from each end of our data.* Our sample size will determine how many of the values on each end of our sample will get weights of zero. The formula for determining how many values on each end get weights of zero is $g = [\alpha \times n]$, where the number inside the brackets is the integer value of the expression. The procedure for computing α-trimmed means is given in Box 5.1.

The influence function for a 0.1-trimmed mean is presented at the bottom of Figure 5.3. For the 20 scores that include the "extra score," $g = [\alpha \times n] =$ integer value of (0.1 × 20) = 2. Therefore, the two lowest and the two highest scores in the sample (X_1, X_2, X_{19}, and X_{20}) are given weights of zero, and the remaining 16 scores (X_3 through X_{18}) are given weights of 1/16 (decimal value = 0.0625). The details for how these weights are determined are given in Box 5.1. It is clear in Figure 5.3 (bottom) that the values of the most extreme scores have no effect on the value of the 0.1-trimmed mean. However, when the extra score is less than the second highest score in our sample (15.75 in this sample) or more than the second lowest score in our sample (−19.09 in this sample), that score has some influence on the value of the trimmed mean. But in order to make an α-trimmed mean as large as we want it to be, we have to be able to manipulate more than $[\alpha \times n]$ scores on the same side of the sample. Therefore, α-trimmed means are *less* robust than sample medians, but *more* robust than sample means. The finite-sample breakdown point for an α-trimmed mean is $[(\alpha n + 2)/2]/n$.

BOX 5.1

HOW TO COMPUTE AN α-TRIMMED MEAN

Purpose

To find a robust estimate of location by reducing the weights of a certain proportion of the lower and upper values in our sample

Procedure

1. Rank order our data from lowest to highest.

2. Decide what proportion of the data we want to trim from each end of our sample. That proportion is α.

3. Calculate $g = [\alpha \times n]$, where [number in bracket] stands for the integer value of that number. Finding g gives us the number of values on each end of our ranked set of scores that will get a weight of zero.

4. All other scores will get weights of $\frac{1}{n-2g}$.

5. Multiply each score by its appropriate weight as determined in steps 3 and 4. Then add these weighted scores to get the value of the **α-trimmed mean**.

The α-trimmed mean achieves its robustness by giving weights of zero to some proportion of the scores on either end of our sample, but it is still less robust than the sample median (although it is more efficient). It should be noted that when our sample comes from a symmetrical distribution (such as a normal distribution), the sample mean, sample median, and sample trimmed mean are all estimating the same value. However, when the population is skewed, the population median, population mean, and population trimmed mean are not the same values. In this case, the three sample statistics are estimating different parameters.

WINSORIZING: ANOTHER WAY TO CREATE A RESISTANT ESTIMATOR OF LOCATION

Winsorized means are created by replacing a certain proportion of the scores at the end of a ranked sample of numbers with the next score in the sample.

Another resistant estimator of location is the **Winsorized mean**. Winsorizing[5] is similar to trimming except that, instead of giving a certain proportion (α) of the scores at the ends of the data set zero weight, *we replace the [α × n] lowest scores with the next highest score and the [α × n] highest scores with the next lowest score.* For example, when −45 is added to the 20 scores in Table 5.1, the resulting values are −45, −22.79, −19.09, −13.86, −9.63, −8.55, −8.55, −7.31, −2.68, −0.63, −0.05, 2.31, 3.44, 4.65, 5.99, 8.23, 9.76, 13.25, 15.75, 29.77. We can create the 0.1 α-trimmed mean by assigning −45 and −22.79 at the low end and 15.75 and 29.77 at the high end weights of zero and the remaining scores weights of 1/16 [that is, $1/(n − 2g)$]. To Winsorize this same set of scores, we replace −45 and −22.79 with −19.09, and replace 15.75 and 29.77 with 13.25 to create the Winsorized set of scores where the Winsorized values are underlined: −<u>19.09</u>, −<u>19.09</u>, −19.09, −13.86, −9.63, −8.55, −8.55, −7.31, −2.68, −0.63, −0.05, 2.31, 3.44, 4.65, 5.99, 8.23, 9.76, 13.25, <u>13.25</u>, <u>13.25</u>. The Winsorized sample mean is the mean of all 20 scores. It is also an L-estimator where, in this case, the third score from both ends of the original data set now has a weight of $3/20[(g + 1)/n]$, because those three scores from each end of the data set have the same value and the remaining 16 ($n − 2g$) scores have weights of $(1/n)$. The procedure for computing Winsorized means is given in Box 5.2.

The finite-sample breakdown point for an α-Winsorized mean is also $[(αn + 2)/2]/n$, and the efficiency of the Winsorized mean is close to that of the trimmed mean.

---

[5] *Winsorizing* is named after the biostatistician Charles P. Winsor (1895–1951); therefore, it is always written with a capital letter.

BOX 5.2
HOW TO COMPUTE A WINSORIZED MEAN

Purpose

To find a robust estimate of location by replacing proportion scores at both ends of our ranked sample with the next innermost value in our sample

Procedure

1. Rank order our data from lowest to highest.

2. Decide what proportion of the data we want to Winsorize at each end of our sample. That proportion is α.

3. Calculate $g = [\alpha \times n]$, where [number in bracket] stands for the integer value of that number. Finding g gives us the number of values on each end of our ranked set of scores that will be replaced with the next ranked value.

4. The **α-Winsorized mean** is the average of this new set of scores. The formal definition is as follows:

$$\bar{X}_{W} = \frac{1}{n}\left[(g+1)X_{g+1} + X_{g+2} + \cdots + X_{N-g-1} + (g+1)X_{n-g}\right]$$

Although the Winsorized mean is a robust estimate of location, it is typically not used for that purpose. The Winsorized mean is most often used in some other calculations, described below and in later chapters, and we will need the Winsorized mean to find the Winsorized variance described in the next section.

APPLYING THESE RESISTANT ESTIMATORS TO OUR DATA

The various estimators of location described above were calculated for the data in Figure 5.1 and are presented in Table 5.2.

With 122 numbers in the sample, the influence of the outliers on the sample mean does not shift the sample mean much relative to the sample median. Nevertheless, the extreme skew in these data suggests that the sample median is a better measure of central tendency than is the sample mean. With the exception of the 10% Winsorized mean, all of the other resistant estimators are close to the sample median. As noted earlier in this chapter, when data are skewed and contain outliers, the sample median and the 20% trimmed mean can have similar levels of efficiency, and both estimators are more efficient estimators of location than the sample mean. Any of these resistant estimators can be used here, although it should be noted that they are estimating the corresponding population parameter (μ_{t}, μ_{W}), which is not the same as μ_{X}, the population mean.

TABLE 5.2 ■ Estimates of Location for the Number of Texts per Week (Barlett, 2015)	
Estimator	**Estimate**
Sample mean	41.01 (0)
Sample median	30.25 (60)
10% trimmed mean	33.88 (12)
20% trimmed mean	30.97 (24)
25% trimmed mean (sometimes called the midmean or interquartile mean)	29.47 (30)
10% Winsorized mean	37.41 (12)
20% Winsorized mean	33.31 (24)

Note: The numbers in parentheses are the number of values trimmed or Winsorized from each side (*g*).

On the other hand, when data are sampled from normal distributions, the sample mean is more efficient than the sample median. Trimmed means and Winsorized means will change in value depending on the degree of trim, and their efficiency will be reduced under those circumstances. Therefore, the latter two estimators should be used only when outliers have been detected in the data. As noted above, trimmed means and Winsorized means are used in some hypothesis tests when they are applied to data that do not come from normal distributions.

RESISTANT ESTIMATORS OF SPREAD

The influence of outliers on sample variances and unbiased estimates of the population variance are more pronounced than they are on sample means. Winsorized variances and the median of the absolute deviations from the median (MAD) are two resistant estimators of spread.

The influence function for the sample variance[6] is presented in Figure 5.5. Two things are striking about the influence function for the sample variance, and both of them are due to the sample variance being the sum of the squared deviations of each score from the sample mean (and an L-estimator). First, if the extra score is close to the sample mean, the sample variance decreases. Second, as the distance between the extra score and the

---

[6]What is true for the sample variance is also true for the unbiased estimate of the population variance.

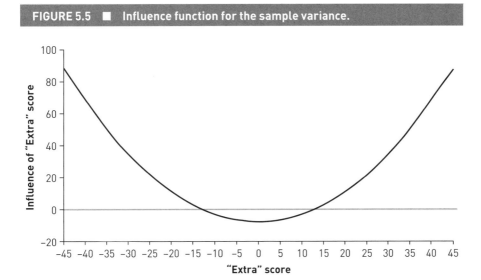

FIGURE 5.5 ■ **Influence function for the sample variance.**

sample mean increases, the influence of the extra score increases at an increasing rate. (Note the difference between the *Y*-axis scale in Figure 5.5 and the *Y*-axis scale of the influence functions for the sample mean, median, and α-trimmed mean in Figure 5.3.) The result of the second observation is that the finite-sample breakdown point for the sample variance is 1/*n*, and the sample variance is easily and dramatically influenced by outliers. The large influence of outliers on the sample variance is a real problem for testing hypotheses using conventional *t*-tests and analyses of variance, because these procedures compare the differences among the sample means with estimates of the population variance from within each sample. We will address ways to deal with this problem in Chapters 7 and 14.

Fortunately, there are robust alternatives for estimating spread. The first one we will consider is the **Winsorized variance**, which is *the sum of the squared deviations of each score in the Winsorized data set subtracted from the Winsorized mean divided by* n.[7] The influence function for the 0.1 Winsorized variance is given in Figure 5.6. It is drawn to the same scale as the influence function for the sample variance in Figure 5.5. Notice the dramatic improvement. The finite-breakdown point of an α-Winsorized variance is α.

Clearly the α-Winsorized variance is a robust estimator of spread, and for that reason, it is used in robust hypothesis tests for population means (see Chapters 7 and 14). It is

---

[7]To calculate the estimate of the population Winsorized variance, divide the sums of squares in the Winsorized set by (*n* − 1).

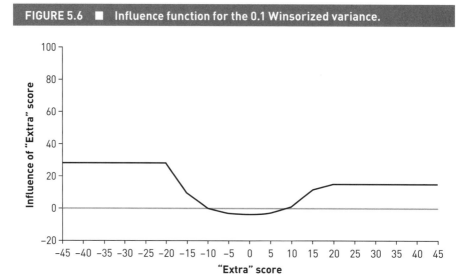

FIGURE 5.6 ■ Influence function for the 0.1 Winsorized variance.

also used to calculate the variance of the α-trimmed mean. The procedure for calculating the Winsorized variance is given in Box 5.3.

Another robust measure of spread is the **median of the absolute deviations from the median (MAD)**.[8] The MAD is computed by finding the absolute value of deviations of each score in our sample from the median of that sample, then finding the median of those absolute deviations. The procedure for calculating the MAD is given in Box 5.4.

Because the MAD is based on the median of the deviations, not on the mean of those deviations (as is the case with the sample variance, which is the mean of the squares of the deviations of each score from the sample mean), outliers that would produce large absolute deviations do not affect the value of the MAD. As with the sample median, over half of the values in our sample would have to be quite large to increase the value of the MAD. The influence function for the MAD is presented in Figure 5.7. Compare the scale on the Y-axis of Figure 5.7 with the scale on the Y-axis in Figures 5.5 and 5.6. As with the sample median, the finite-sample breakdown point for the MAD is 0.5 making the MAD a robust estimator of spread.

---

[8] The abbreviation MAD is also used to represent the statistic $\dfrac{\sum \left| X - \bar{X} \right|}{n}$, the *mean* of the *absolute deviations*.

This index is also a measure of spread, but it is rarely used because unlike the sample variance, which is the mean of the squared deviations, it does not estimate the parameters of the populations we assume underlie our data. Like the variance, it is also not resistant to outliers. Here we are using the abbreviation MAD to represent the median of the absolute deviations from the median: MAD = median $|X_i - \text{median}|$.

BOX 5.3

HOW TO COMPUTE THE WINSORIZED VARIANCE

Purpose

To find a robust estimate of spread by replacing a proportion of scores at both ends of our ranked sample with the next innermost value in our sample

Procedure

1. Rank order our data from lowest to highest.

2. Decide what proportion of the data we want to Winsorize at each end of our sample. That proportion is α.

3. Calculate $g = [\alpha \times n]$, where [number in bracket] stands for the integer value of that number. Solving for g gives us the number

of values on each end of our ranked set of scores that will be replaced with the next ranked value.

4. Calculate the α-Winsorized mean ($\bar{X}_w$; see Box 5.2).

5. Calculate the Winsorized variance by computing the sum of the squared deviations of each score in the Winsorized set from the Winsorized mean and dividing that sum of squared deviations by n.

$$s_W^2 = \frac{\sum_{i=1}^{n}\left(X_{iW} - \bar{X}_W\right)^2}{n}$$

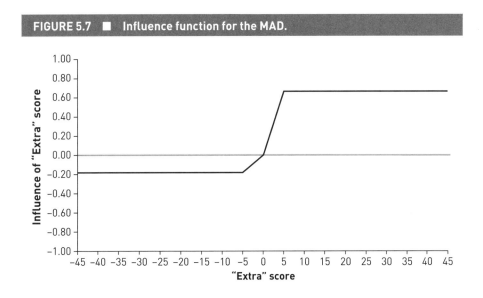

FIGURE 5.7 ■ Influence function for the MAD.

Influence of "Extra" score (y-axis, from −1.00 to 1.00)

"Extra" score (x-axis, from −45 to 45)

BOX 5.4

HOW TO COMPUTE THE MAD (MEDIAN OF THE ABSOLUTE DEVIATIONS FROM THE MEDIAN)

Purpose

To find a robust estimate of spread from our sample

Procedure

1. Find the median of our sample.

2. Find the absolute deviation of each score from the median, that is, $|X_i - \text{median of sample}|$.

3. Find the median of these absolute deviations from the median; that is, MAD = median $|X_i - \text{median of sample}|$.

4. If we believe our data were sampled from a normal distribution, MAD/0.6745 gives us a resistant estimate of the standard deviation of that normal distribution.

Note: F-spread/2 is close to the MAD when sampling from a normal distribution; therefore, F-spread/1.349 can also be used as a resistant estimate of the standard deviation of that normal distribution (1.349 = 0.6745 × 2).[9]

When our data are sampled from a normal distribution, MAD/0.6745 gives us an estimate of the standard deviation of that normal distribution.[10] In the case of a mixed normal distribution or a symmetric distribution with outliers, MAD/0.6745 provides us with a resistant estimate of spread. However, when our data are sampled from a skewed distribution, we need to know what kind of distribution it is to locate $Q(.75)$. This information gives us a value to divide the MAD by to obtain a measure of spread, with which we can estimate the population standard deviation.

APPLYING THESE RESISTANT ESTIMATORS TO OUR DATA (PART 2)

The various estimators of spread described above were calculated for the data in Figure 5.1 and are presented in Table 5.3.

---

[9] The F-spread (or fourth-spread) is the distance between the upper and lower fourth in a letter-value display. It provides the width of the box in a box plot.

[10] The value 0.6745 is $Q(.75)$ in a normal distribution; that is, it is the z-score that separates the bottom 75% of the distribution from the upper 25%. In other words, −0.6745 to +0.6745 brackets the middle 50% of a normal distribution.

TABLE 5.3 ■ Estimates of Location and Spread for the Number of Texts per Week (Barlett, 2015)	
Estimator	**Estimate**
Estimate of the population variance	1,840.57
10% Winsorized estimate of variance	890.38 (12)
20% Winsorized estimate of variance	429.27 (24)
Estimate of the population standard deviation	42.91
10% Winsorized estimate of standard deviation	29.84 (12)
20% Winsorized estimate of standard deviation	20.72 (24)
MAD	20.75
MAD/0.6745	30.76

Note: The numbers in parentheses are the number of values Winsorized from each side (*g*).

As we can see from Table 5.3, the effects of the outliers and the skew in the data have a profound effect on the estimates of the population variance and population standard deviations.[11] This table illustrates the importance of using resistant estimates of spread when dealing with data that are skewed and/or have outliers. In Chapter 7, we will look at a robust hypothesis test for means that uses the 20% trimmed mean and the Winsorized estimate of variance to test hypotheses about population means when sampling from skewed populations and/or populations with heavy tails.

M-ESTIMATORS: ANOTHER APPROACH TO FINDING RESISTANT ESTIMATORS OF LOCATION

M-estimators provide us with another way to create resistant estimators of location. As with maximum likelihood estimation (see Chapter 4), we start with a set of data and try to find the estimate of the parameter that satisfies a certain criterion. The result is a resistant estimator that is sensitive to the data and trims only what is needed to satisfy the chosen criterion.

The problem with trimmed means and Winsorized means is deciding how much to trim. If we do not trim enough, the outliers may still influence the result. But if we trim

---

[11] With the large sample size, the sample variance and standard deviation are close to the unbiased estimates of the population variance and population standard deviations. Therefore, only the unbiased estimates are reported in Table 5.3.

too much, we use less of our sample for our estimate and reduce the efficiency of the estimator. Fortunately, there is another approach to dealing with the problems of outliers and sampling from non-normal distributions. We can use M-estimators of location.

M-estimators provide a method for finding resistant estimators of location that are sensitive to the data at hand and trim only what is needed rather than trimming a certain percentage from both sides. M-estimators are related to maximum likelihood estimation, hence the name (Goodall, 1983). As with maximum likelihood estimation (see Chapter 4), we start with a set of data and try to find a value for the parameter that satisfies a certain criterion. In the case of maximum likelihood estimation, the MLE is the value of the parameter for which the probability of getting our sample is a maximum.[12] An **M-estimator** is *the value for which the sum of a certain function involving the data and the estimator = 0.* We can represent this symbolically in the following way: Let $\psi\left(X_i; \hat{\theta}_M\right)$ be an expression that includes both the individual data points X_i and the M-estimator $\hat{\theta}_M$. The M-estimator is the value of $\hat{\theta}_M$ that makes $\sum_{i=1}^{n} \psi\left(X_i; \hat{\theta}_M\right) = 0$.

The sample mean and the sample median are M-estimators. In the case of the sample mean, the function $\psi\left(X_i; \hat{\theta}_M\right) = \left(X_i - \hat{\theta}_M\right)$, and the sample mean $\overline{X}$ is the value of $\hat{\theta}_M$ for which $\sum_{i=1}^{n}\left(X_i - \hat{\theta}_M\right) = 0$. We can easily verify that for any set of numbers; $\overline{X}$ is the only value we can select for $\hat{\theta}_M$ that makes $\sum_{i=1}^{n}\left(X_i - \hat{\theta}_M\right) = 0$. In the case of the sample median, the function $\psi\left(X_i; \hat{\theta}_M\right)$ is $\text{sgn}\left(X_i - \hat{\theta}_M\right)$.[13] The sample median is the value for which $\sum_{i=1}^{n} \text{sgn}\left(X_i - \hat{\theta}_M\right) = 0$.

When seeking robust M-estimators of location, the general form for the function $\psi\left(X_i; \hat{\theta}_M\right)$ is $\dfrac{X_i - \hat{\theta}_M}{\hat{\tau}}$, where $\hat{\tau}$ is a robust estimate of scale for the data like the MAD. The M-estimator is the value of $\hat{\theta}_M$ for which $\sum \psi\left(\dfrac{X_i - \hat{\theta}_M}{\hat{\tau}}\right) = 0$. Unfortunately, unlike with maximum likelihood estimation in which one can use differential calculus to find the estimator, there is no simple, direct way to find M-estimators. We have to use an iterative method to arrive at an exact solution. However, we can get pretty close to

---

[12] Using differential calculus, this estimate is where the likelihood function has a zero slope.

[13] *Sgn* stands for *signum* (or *sign*). Sgn (of a number) equals +1 when that number is greater than zero, 0 when the number is zero, and −1 when the number is less than zero. For this function to equal 0, the positive and negative values must cancel each other. Because the median is the middle score, the signums cancel each other.

the exact solution by using the procedure described below that involves a single iteration. These are called one-step M-estimators. The one-step M-estimator that appears to give the best result is the **modified one-step M-estimator of location (MOM)**.

The procedure for finding the MOM requires us to use some criterion to *identify the outliers, remove these outliers, and find the average of the remaining values.* A commonly used criterion is based on the sample median and the MAD. An outlier is any value for which

$$\frac{|X - \text{median}|}{\frac{\text{MAD}}{0.6745}} > 1.28 \tag{5.6}$$

This criterion applies to both sides of the data. Let $L =$ the number of scores below the median that satisfy the criterion for being outliers and $U =$ the number of scores above the median that satisfy the same criterion. The one-step M-estimator of location is

$$\frac{1.28 \dfrac{\text{MAD}}{0.6745} (U - L) + \sum\limits_{i=L+1}^{n-U} X_i}{n - L - U} \tag{5.7}$$

BOX 5.5

HOW TO COMPUTE THE MODIFIED ONE-STEP M-ESTIMATOR OF LOCATION (MOM)

Purpose

To find a robust estimate of location from our sample

Procedure

1. Find the median and the MAD for our data and identify the outliers on both the high and low side as those values for which

$$\frac{|X_i - \text{median}|}{\frac{\text{MAD}}{0.6745}} > 1.28$$

2. Let $L =$ the number of scores below the median that satisfy the criterion for being

outliers in step 1 and $U =$ the number of scores above the median that satisfy the same criterion.

3. Calculate the sum of all of the original values *not* identified as outliers based on the criterion in step 1; that is, find $\sum\limits_{i=L+1}^{n-U} X_i$.

4. Substitute the U, L, n, and $\sum\limits_{i=L+1}^{n-U} X_i$ into the following formula to get the modified one-step M-estimator of location:

$$\frac{1.28 \dfrac{\text{MAD}}{0.6745} (U - L) + \sum\limits_{i=L+1}^{n-U} X_i}{n - L - U}$$

The summation in the numerator $\sum_{i=L+1}^{n-U} X_i$ is the sum of the numbers not identified as outliers by Inequality 5.6 above. The procedure for finding the MOM is summarized in Box 5.5.

When there are no outliers in our data identified by Equation 5.6, the MOM in Equation 5.7 reduces to the sample mean.

WHICH ESTIMATOR OF LOCATION SHOULD I USE?

The decision about which estimator to use depends on our data. The sample mean is clearly preferred when samples from normal distributions have no outliers. Sample medians, trimmed means, and M-estimators, such as the MOM, are preferred when our data contain outliers or are highly skewed.

Sample means, sample medians, α-trimmed means, and M-estimators, such as the MOM, have advantages and disadvantages that depend on the situation. When we are sampling from a normal distribution, the sample mean is the most efficient estimator of the population mean (which is also the population median and the population trimmed mean). However, when we are sampling from populations that are skewed or have heavier tails than a normal distribution, the sample mean is not resistant to outliers in the data and is also not efficient relative to the sample median. The sample median, on the other hand, is not efficient relative to the sample mean when we are sampling from normal distributions, but it is more efficient than the sample mean when we are sampling from non-normal populations (Figure 5.4). Trimmed means are also more efficient than the sample mean when sampling from non-normal populations (Figure 5.5).

Wilcox (2010) recommended using a 20% trimmed mean in most situations in which samples are drawn from a non-normal population. The argument for using a 20% trim is based on balancing the reduction of the effects of outliers against the efficiency of the estimates. As we can see in Figures 5.4 and 5.8, the efficiency of the 20% trimmed mean and the sample median are similar when sampling from a mixed normal distribution, and both are more efficient than the sample mean under those circumstances.

Wilcox (2010) also noted that in terms of efficiency, the 20% trimmed mean and the MOM are similar when we are sampling from mixed normal distributions (see Figure 5.9). However, because M-estimators are more sensitive to the data and trim only what and where necessary, they have a breakdown point of 0.5 with no loss

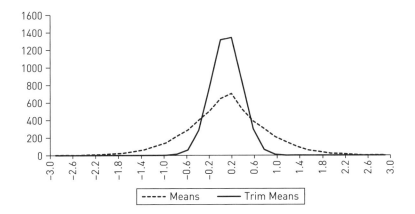

FIGURE 5.8 ■ Plot of 5,000 sample means and 20% trimmed means for sample sizes of 20 from the mixed normal distribution on the left of Figure 5.4.

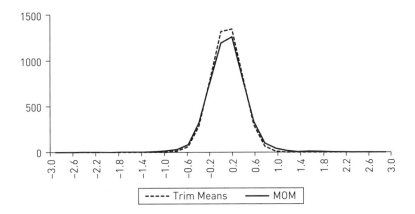

FIGURE 5.9 ■ Comparison of the distribution of a 20% trimmed mean and the MOM when we are sampling from a mixed normal distribution.

in efficiency. Therefore, M-estimators are a better choice when estimating location parameters.

On the other hand, trimmed means might be preferred because they can be used in robust hypothesis tests about population means, a topic we will explore in Chapter 7. Clearly, which estimator we should use depends on what we think is going on with our data.

RESAMPLING METHODS FOR CONSTRUCTING CONFIDENCE INTERVALS

The bootstrap is based on the premise that a random sample reflects the characteristics of the population from which it was randomly sampled. Bootstrap confidence intervals are constructed by resampling with replacement from the original sample to create a distribution of bootstrap estimates. The values at Q(.025) and Q(.975) define the upper and lower intervals of a 95% confidence interval. They can be used to construct confidence intervals for samples for any parameter from any population.

The techniques described above provide us with resistant point estimators of parameters. But as noted in Chapter 4, point estimates are rarely, if ever, equal to the parameters being estimated. We therefore construct confidence intervals around our point estimate in an attempt to measure the magnitude of the possible error in our estimate. The method described in Chapter 4 for creating confidence intervals is based on knowledge of the population from which our sample was obtained and knowledge of the distribution of the estimator used in the confidence interval. When we are sampling from normal distributions, the central limit theorem tells us that the distribution of sample means will be a normal distribution, and from that knowledge, we can use Equations 4.14a or 4.14b to construct confidence intervals for population means. But, we do not always know the kind of population from which our samples were obtained, and we do not always know the distribution of our estimator. Fortunately, there is a way to obtain resistant estimates and confidence intervals that is technically feasible because of the availability of high-speed computers on our desks. That method, called the **bootstrap**, substitutes computer power for theoretical analysis of the behavior of sample statistics from specific populations (Efron, 1979a, 1979b; Efron & Gong, 1983; Efron & Tibhirani, 1986). The bootstrap is one member of a class of resampling procedures that are now possible for all of us to perform.

Bootstrap Methods for Estimating Parameters

As we noted in Chapter 1, the purpose of random sampling is to obtain a sample that is representative of the population from which the scores were obtained. The bootstrap is based on the idea that a random sample from a population reflects the characteristics of the population from which it was obtained. In other words, in the absence of any other information about the population, our sample is our best source of information about that population. This statement is true even when we do not know the shape of the distribution of the population from which our sample was taken. If we carry this logic one step further, then by repeatedly resampling from the original sample, we can generate a distribution of estimates of the population parameter, and from that distribution, we can create confidence intervals.

The bootstrap provides confidence intervals for parameters through random resampling with replacement from our original sample. Because we are using random sampling with replacement, we can generate as many bootstrap samples as we want, compute our bootstrap estimate θ_i^* from each bootstrap sample, and create a distribution of these bootstrap estimates. The distribution of these bootstrap estimates can be used to construct a confidence interval. There are a number of ways to use the information provided by the distribution of bootstrap estimates to construct confidence intervals. Some of these methods are reviewed in Wilcox (2010). The simplest general method is called the **percentile bootstrap method**: Rank order the bootstrap estimates θ_i^* and find the values in that ordered set at $Q(.025)$ and $Q(.975)$ for a 95% confidence interval. The mean of the bootstrap estimates is our point estimate. The procedure for constructing percentile bootstrap confidence intervals is given in Box 5.6.

Improving on the Bootstrap Confidence Interval for the Population Mean

Despite its simplicity and fairly good performance, we can improve on the percentile bootstrap confidence interval for the population mean. One way is called the **percentile-*t***

BOX 5.6
HOW TO FIND PERCENTILE BOOTSTRAP CONFIDENCE INTERVALS

Purpose

To provide estimates of parameters and confidence intervals for any parameter from any distribution, even when the form of the distribution is unknown

Procedure

1. From our original sample, resample *n* values with complete replacement, where *n* is the original sample size. Repeat this procedure a large number of times (for example, 1,000 times).

2. From each of these "bootstrap samples," calculate "bootstrap estimates" of θ, the parameter we want to estimate: $\theta_1^*, \theta_2^*, \theta_3^*, \cdots$ (The distribution of these θ^*'s will approximate the distribution of $\hat{\theta}$.)

3. Rank order the resulting bootstrap estimates (θ^*'s). To find the 95% confidence interval, use $Q(0.025)$ and $Q(0.975)$ of the ranked bootstrap estimates. They will be the lower and upper limits of the 95% bootstrap confidence interval of the parameter being estimated. To find the 90% or 99% confidence interval, use the corresponding quantiles that are the limits for those percentages of the ranked bootstrap sample distribution.

(or **bootstrap-*t***). This is a *combination of the percentile bootstrap described above and the confidence interval for the population mean of a normal distribution when the population variance is unknown* (see Equations 4.14a and 4.14b). To find the confidence interval for the population mean of a normal distribution when we do not know the population variance, we use Student's *t* instead of *z* in the confidence interval. The percentile-*t* uses the bootstrap to approximate the distribution of Student's *t* for the one-sample case in which

$$t = \frac{\overline{X} - \mu}{\dfrac{\text{est } \sigma}{\sqrt{n}}}, \tag{5.8}$$

and then uses quantiles of the bootstrap-*t* distribution for the level of confidence we want in an equation similar to Equations 4.14a and 4.14b. The procedure for constructing a percentile-*t* confidence interval is given in Box 5.7.

Comments on the Use of the Bootstrap

The beauty of the bootstrap is that it can be used to construct confidence intervals for any parameter from any population, even when we do not know the shape of the population. However, when we believe the population is markedly skewed, it is better to take larger samples.

   Although the bootstrap does not require knowledge of the population from which we obtained our sample, to use it to construct a confidence interval, *we have to select an estimator and use that estimator for computing* θ_i^* *for each bootstrap sample.* Therefore, calculate the sample mean from each bootstrap sample as θ_i^* when attempting to estimate the population mean, calculate the sample median from each bootstrap sample as θ_i^* when attempting to estimate the population median, calculate the sample standard deviation from each bootstrap sample as θ_i^* when attempting to estimate the population standard deviation, and so forth. The bootstrap can be used with any estimator. *The bootstrap is only as good as the original sample.* (Remember that random sampling is a procedure; it does not guarantee the outcome.) And as noted in the last chapter, when estimating parameters, the bigger the sample, the better the estimate. Therefore, *the larger the original sample, the smaller the confidence intervals.* However, we can use the bootstrap with samples as small as 10 when the population is close to a normal distribution.

   How many bootstrap samples (resampling with replacement from our original sample) we will want to use depends on the situation. When the original population is a normal distribution or close to a normal distribution, as few as 100 bootstrap samples will suffice. However, because it is so easy to do random sampling with replacement on a computer, it is standard practice to create at least 1,000 bootstrap samples. Note, though, that when the sample size is greater than 20, more bootstrap samples will not improve the estimate.

BOX 5.7
HOW TO FIND PERCENTILE-t (BOOTSTRAP-t) CONFIDENCE INTERVALS

Purpose

To improve on the confidence interval for the population mean, even when the form of the distribution is unknown

Procedure

1. From our original sample, resample n values with complete replacement where n is the original sample size. Repeat this procedure a large number of times (for example, 1,000 times).

2. From each of these "bootstrap samples," calculate the bootstrap sample mean ($\overline{X}^*$) and the bootstrap estimate of the population standard deviation (est σ^*). Then enter them into the following formula:

$$t^* = \frac{\overline{X}^* - \overline{X}}{\dfrac{\text{est}\,\sigma^*}{\sqrt{n}}},$$

where $\overline{X}^*$ is the mean of the bootstrap sample, $\overline{X}$ is the mean of the original sample, est σ^* is the unbiased estimate of

the population variance calculated from the bootstrap sample, and n is the size of the original and bootstrap samples.

3. Rank order the resulting bootstrap-t^*'s. Find the lower and upper quantiles of the ranked bootstrap-t^*'s for the desired level of confidence. For a 95% confidence interval, these boundaries would be the values at $Q(0.025)$ and $Q(0.975)$.

4. The confidence interval is

$$\Pr\left(\overline{X} - \frac{t^*_{upper}\,\text{est}\,\sigma}{\sqrt{n-1}} < \mu < \overline{X} - \frac{t^*_{lower}\,\text{est}\,\sigma}{\sqrt{n-1}}\right)$$

$=$ level of confidence

Note that we use t^*_{upper} to find the lower end of the confidence interval (Wilcox, 1997, 2003). Also note that t^*_{lower} will be negative because it is subtracted to find the upper end of the confidence interval.

The standard confidence interval for the population mean of a normal distribution (Equation 4.14a or 4.14b) for the data described in Figure 5.1 and Table 5.2 is

$$\Pr(33.32 < \mu < 48.74) = .95$$

The percentile bootstrap confidence interval for the same data is

$$\Pr(34.12 < \mu < 48.15) = .95,[14]$$

---

[14] Bootstrap confidence intervals will be slightly different each time we perform a bootstrap.

and the percentile-*t* bootstrap interval is

$$\Pr(32.02 < \mu < 47.39) = .95$$

These three confidence intervals are similar in terms of their spans, despite the fact that the data clearly do not come from a normal distribution. This fact is not surprising given the size of the sample here. As we saw in Chapter 4, the distribution of sample means approaches a normal distribution as sample size increases, even when the population from which the sample is taken is not normally distributed.

According to Wilcox (2010), the standard confidence interval based on Student's *t* (Equations 4.14a and 4.14b) performs as well as the percentile bootstrap-*t* in most, but not all, situations. However, when the sample size is small and the data do not appear to come from a normal distribution, Wilcox recommended using the bootstrap-*t* when making inferences about population means.

A FINAL CAVEAT

Trimming is based on sound statistical theory. It is not the same thing as discarding or replacing data that do not fit our conception of what should occur.

Throughout this chapter, we have discussed various techniques to estimate parameters that are resistant to the influence of outliers, producing what may be more accurate estimates of the population parameters. This is not to say that researchers may delete values in their data sets, or replace values in their data sets, whenever they would like. What we offer are techniques whose purpose is to produce the most resistant estimates of population parameters, which may or may not be the purpose of the researchers' studies. The safest, and most ethical, strategy that we recommend for researchers is to report their data analysis techniques thoroughly, and with justification, to avoid any suspicion of impropriety.

Summary

When our sample data come from populations that have more values in their tails than normal distributions, our data will likely contain outliers. Those outliers will distort our estimates of parameters, such as the sample mean and the unbiased estimate of the sample variance (est σ^2). This adverse effect of outliers occurs because sample means, sample variances, and the est σ^2 are linear estimators; that is, every score in the sample has the same weight in the calculation of the estimate. Therefore, it takes only one extreme value to affect these estimates, and the more extreme the outlier, the greater its influence.

Fortunately, a number of estimators are resistant to the effects of outliers. These include the α-trimmed means, for which a certain proportion of the ranked scores on both ends are given zero weight; Winsorized means and Winsorized variances, for which a certain proportion of the ranked scores on both ends are replaced by the score at the next rank inward; the MAD (*Median* of the *Absolute Deviations* from the median) and the MOM (*Modified One*-step *M*-estimator of location), for which scores that exceed a certain threshold are designated outliers and given zero weight. The sample median is also a robust estimator because it gives zero weight to all values in the sample except the middle one or two. Which of these various estimators is preferred depends on the situation.

Bootstrap confidence intervals can be constructed for any parameter from any population by resampling with replacement the scores in our sample a large number of times, calculating an estimator for that parameter from each resample, and rank ordering the resulting estimates. The endpoints of the middle X% of these bootstrap estimates define the X% confidence interval for that parameter. We can improve our bootstrap confidence intervals of the population mean by putting our bootstrap estimates of the sample mean and population standard deviation into a *t*-statistic (percentile-*t*).

Conceptual Exercises

1. The MOM is an M-estimator of location. Describe in general terms how the MOM is calculated. What is the advantage of the MOM over other trimmed means and Winsorized means?

2. The MAD (median of the absolute deviations from the median) is a robust estimate of spread. What is it about how the MAD is calculated that makes it a robust estimate?

3. Describe how you can construct a confidence interval for the parameter Θ of an exponential distribution with the bootstrap.

4. Describe how you can construct a bootstrap confidence interval for the mean, μ, and for the variance, σ^2, in a population.

5. Do you think that the expression below is a robust estimator of λ? Why or why not? (In your answer, include how we determine whether an estimator is robust.)

$$\frac{N}{\sum\limits_{i=1}^{N} X_i}$$

6. Alpha-trimmed means and the MOM are two different kinds of robust estimators for location. How are they alike? How are they different? Do you see an advantage of using one over the other? If so, which would you prefer and why?

7. Describe how one uses the bootstrap to construct a confidence interval for the population median of a skewed population.

Student Study Site

Visit the Student Study Site at **https://study.sagepub.com/friemanstats** for a variety of useful tools including data sets, additional exercises, and web resources.

GENERAL PRINCIPLES OF HYPOTHESIS TESTING

In Chapter 1, we described an experiment by Barlett (2015) in which he attempted to investigate whether there is a difference in hostility between those who receive insulting or nice online messages by conducting an experiment in which participants received messages that were either insulting or nice and then measuring the participants' levels of hostility. We presented the results of this experiment at the beginning of Chapter 2. In this chapter, we will apply the concepts discussed in preceding chapters to describe the basic principles for testing statistical hypotheses. To make it easier to see those basic principles, we will assume for the moment that we know the population variances. We will postpone the actual analysis of Barlett's data until Chapter 7, where we will use estimates of the population variance in the application of Student's *t*-test.

As we saw in Chapter 1, we start with a research question and generate mutually exclusive and exhaustive experimental hypotheses as possible answers to our research question. Then we design a research study based on our research hypotheses and collect data. By making certain assumptions about the data, we can use a statistical model to assess whether the obtained results reflect real experimental effects or merely random (chance) factors. With the classical statistical model, this assessment is carried out by making assumptions about the shape of the populations from which the data were obtained, setting up statistical hypotheses about the parameters of these populations, and evaluating which hypothesis is best supported by the data. The results of our statistical hypothesis test are then generalized back to our experimental hypotheses to hopefully answer the question originally posed. In this chapter, we will examine the principles involved in testing statistical hypotheses with the classical statistical model, and in Chapter 9, we will do the same with the randomization/permutation model.

EXPERIMENTAL AND STATISTICAL HYPOTHESES

Experimental hypotheses are statements about the relationship between the independent and dependent variables in our experiment. In the classical statistical model, the parallel statistical hypotheses are about unknown parameters in the populations from which our data were sampled.

The independent variable in Barlett's (2015) experiment was the message participants received from their "partner" after failing to solve an unsolvable Sudoku puzzle. This message was either an insulting message ("you suck") or a nice message ("it's OK"). There were a number of dependent variables; the one we discussed was the participants' scores on a scale measuring state hostility (scores could range from 34 to 170, with higher scores indicating more hostility) after they received their "partner's" message. (More details of this experiment are given in Chapter 1.)

Experimental Hypotheses

The experimental hypotheses for Barlett's experiment were:

> Cybervictimization (message content) *does not* affect state hostility.
> Cybervictimization (message content) *does* affect state hostility.

These hypotheses are stated in terms of the independent and dependent variables in the experiment. To analyze his data using the classical statistical model, Barlett had to construct a parallel set of statistical hypotheses about the means of the populations from which the data were presumably sampled.

Statistical Hypotheses

If we assume that the experimental participants were sampled randomly from a normal distribution[1] with a mean of $\mu_{\text{Insulting message}}$ and variance $\sigma^2_{\text{Insulting message}}$, and that the control participants were sampled from a normal distribution with a mean $\mu_{\text{Nice message}}$ and a variance $\sigma^2_{\text{Nice message}}$, then the following statistical hypotheses can be generated to correspond to the experimental hypotheses in the experiment:

$$\mu_{\text{Insulting message}} = \mu_{\text{Nice message}}$$

or

$$\mu_{\text{Insulting message}} - \mu_{\text{Nice message}} = 0$$

---

[1] Here we are using the principle of potential populations we discussed in Chapter 1.

$$\mu_{\text{Insulting message}} \neq \mu_{\text{Nice message}}$$

or

$$\mu_{\text{Insulting message}} - \mu_{\text{Nice message}} \neq 0$$

In words, the first statistical hypothesis reads: "The mean of the population from which the participants in the Insulting message group were sampled is equal to the mean of the population from which the participants in the Nice message group were sampled." This hypothesis can also be stated as "The mean of the population from which the participants in the Insulting message group were sampled *minus* the mean of the population from which the participants in the Nice message group were sampled equals 0." Both versions convey the same information. We will see shortly that the second version fits better with the test statistic we use to test this hypothesis.

The second hypothesis is read in a similar manner, except that the means of the two populations are stated as not being equal; in other words, the difference between them is stated as not being equal to 0. As noted in Chapter 1, with the classical statistical model, statistical hypotheses are statements about the parameters of potential populations created for the purpose of using that model.

The two experimental hypotheses are *mutually exclusive* and *exhaustive*. That is, one of them must be true, but they both cannot be true, and they are the only possibilities: Either being a victim of cyberbullying (through having received an insulting message online) does or does not affect whether someone responds by experiencing hostility. The same logic holds for the statistical hypotheses; either $\mu_{\text{Insulting message}} = \mu_{\text{Nice message}}$ or $\mu_{\text{Insulting message}} \neq \mu_{\text{Nice message}}$.

For ease of exposition and to frame the discussion in this chapter in general terms, the groups in this experiment will be referred to as E and C, denoting experimental and control groups, respectively.

ESTIMATING PARAMETERS

Our statistical hypotheses tell us what parameters we need to estimate to construct a test statistic to help us decide which hypothesis our data support.

Statistical hypotheses are statements about the parameters of the populations from which our samples were obtained. To test these hypotheses, we use the information in our samples to obtain estimates of the unknown parameters. From Chapter 4, we know that the best estimate of the mean of a population is the mean of a random sample from that population. In a two-group experiment, we are concerned with two population means (in this case, μ_E and μ_C); therefore, we must use two estimates, one from the control group ($\bar{X}_C$) and one from the experimental group ($\bar{X}_E$). Since our statistical hypotheses are about the difference between these population means, the value of interest is the difference between the sample means $\overline{X}_E - \overline{X}_C$. Assuming that the sampling is random, we expect that our estimates $\overline{X}_E$ and $\overline{X}_C$ will be close to the parameters μ_E and μ_C.[2] Therefore, if the hypothesis $\mu_E - \mu_C = 0$ is indeed true, we expect that the quantity $\overline{X}_E - \overline{X}_C$ to be close to zero. On the other hand, if the other hypothesis ($\mu_E - \mu_C \neq 0$) is true, then we expect $\overline{X}_E - \overline{X}_C$ to be a non-zero value that is somewhere close to the value of $\mu_E - \mu_C$. Since this other hypothesis says nothing about how far μ_E is from μ_C, the only thing we can say is that a large positive or negative value of $\overline{X}_E - \overline{X}_C$ is more consistent with $\mu_E - \mu_C \neq 0$ than with $\mu_E - \mu_C = 0$.

Therefore, we are faced with trying to answer the following questions: How far can $\overline{X}_E - \overline{X}_C$ be from zero before we conclude that the value is consistent with the hypothesis $\mu_E - \mu_C \neq 0$? How close can $\overline{X}_E - \overline{X}_C$ be to zero before we conclude that it is consistent with the hypothesis $\mu_E - \mu_C = 0$?

THE CRITERION FOR EVALUATING OUR STATISTICAL HYPOTHESES

When we test statistical hypotheses, we select one of the hypotheses and calculate the probability of obtaining (in a future research study) our results, or results even more extreme, assuming that the hypothesis is true. When that probability is below a predetermined level, we reject the hypothesis and accept the other one.

All statistical hypothesis tests are carried out by selecting one of our mutually exclusive and exhaustive hypotheses and calculating the *probability of obtaining (in a future experiment) a similar result, or one even more extreme, assuming that the hypothesis being considered is true.* If the hypothesis we select to test is true, we expect that probability to be high. If our chosen hypothesis is false, we expect that probability to be low (and the probability calculated from the other hypothesis to be higher). To calculate the probability of obtaining our observed difference $\overline{X}_E - \overline{X}_C$ based on the statistical hypothesis we choose to test, we need to create a test statistic to determine the probability of obtaining our data, assuming the statistical hypothesis we chose to test is correct. From the distribution of that test statistic, we can find the probability of obtaining our observed data.

CREATING OUR TEST STATISTIC

Of interest here is the difference between the two sample means, and therefore we need to create a test statistic that allows us to easily determine the probability of

---

[2] As noted in Chapter 1, we rarely expect our estimates to equal our parameters.

obtaining our observed difference between those two sample means based on one of our statistical hypotheses. In the situation under consideration, we apply the standard score transformation to $\overline{X}_E - \overline{X}_C$ *to create our test statistic, z.*

To calculate the probability of obtaining our observed value of $\overline{X}_E - \overline{X}_C$, we need to know the distribution of that difference. From the central limit theorem, we know that when the original populations are normal distributions, the sample means $\overline{X}_E$ and $\overline{X}_C$ will both have normal distributions with means μ_E and μ_C and variances $\sigma^2_{\overline{X}_E} = \dfrac{\sigma^2_E}{n_E}$ and $\sigma^2_{\overline{X}_C} = \dfrac{\sigma^2_C}{n_C} \sigma^2_{\overline{X}_C} = \dfrac{\sigma^2_C}{n_C}$, respectively. Theorem 4 in Chapter 3 can be extended to the present situation in which the numbers under consideration are sample means. Therefore, according to Theorem 4, the distribution of $\overline{X}_E - \overline{X}_C$ has a mean $\mu_E - \mu_C$ and a variance $\sigma^2_{\overline{X}_E} + \sigma^2_{\overline{X}_C}$, and when the original populations are normal distributions, the distribution of $\overline{X}_E - \overline{X}_C$ is also a normal distribution.[3]

Knowing the mean and variance of this normal distribution, we can calculate the probability of obtaining values of $\overline{X}_E - \overline{X}_C$ that occur in any particular region of the distribution by using the normal distribution table in Appendix E. However, to use that table, we must transform the raw scores to a standard score distribution:

$$\text{standard score} = \frac{\text{score} - \text{mean}}{\text{standard deviation}} \tag{6.1}$$

Using Equation 6.1 and substituting $\overline{X}_E - \overline{X}_C$ for the score, $\mu_E - \mu_C$ for the mean, and $\sqrt{\sigma^2_{\overline{X}_E} + \sigma^2_{\overline{X}_C}}$ for the standard deviation, we get the following formula:

$$z = \frac{\left(\overline{X}_E - \overline{X}_C\right) - \left(\mu_E - \mu_C\right)}{\sqrt{\sigma^2_{\overline{X}_E} + \sigma^2_{\overline{X}_C}}} \tag{6.2}$$

The final step is to select a hypothesis to test. In the present situation, only one of our two statistical hypotheses allows us to calculate the probability of obtaining a particular result, and that is the hypothesis $\mu_E - \mu_C = 0$. The other hypothesis, $\mu_E - \mu_C \neq 0$, cannot be used for direct calculation because it does not give a value for the difference between the population means. If that hypothesis were stated with a definite value (such as $\mu_E - \mu_C = 10$), then calculating the probability of that result would be possible.

---

[3]The distribution of $\overline{X}_E - \overline{X}_C$ is a theoretical distribution that could be generated if we perform our research study an infinite number of times. Each time we perform the experiment, we can obtain a value for $\overline{X}_E - \overline{X}_C$. Because the $\overline{X}$'s are estimates of parameters, neither they, nor the values of $\overline{X}_E - \overline{X}_C$, will be the same from study to study. After an infinite number of these replications of the study, we will have a distribution that is normal in shape with a mean $\mu_E - \mu_C$ and a variance $\sigma^2_{\overline{X}_E} + \sigma^2_{\overline{X}_C}$.

The hypothesis that allows us to calculate this probability is called the **null hypothesis** and in this case is written as $H_0: \mu_E = \mu_C$ or $H_0: \mu_E - \mu_C = 0$. *The other hypothesis is called the* **alternative hypothesis** and in this case is written as $H_1: \mu_E \neq \mu_C$ or $H_1: \mu_E - \mu_C \neq 0$.

By substituting $\mu_E - \mu_C = 0$ into Equation 6.2, we arrive at our **test statistic**:

$$z = \frac{\left(\bar{X}_E - \bar{X}_C\right)}{\sqrt{\sigma_{\bar{X}_E}^2 + \sigma_{\bar{X}_C}^2}} \tag{6.3}$$

Equation 6.3 gives us the value we use to find the probability of obtaining our observed results, assuming the null hypothesis (in this case $\mu_E - \mu_C = 0$) is true.

Because the form of a distribution is not changed by the standard score transformation, the distribution of z will be normal when the distribution of $\bar{X}_E - \bar{X}_C$ is normal (which it is when the original populations from which the random samples were taken were normal distributions). Furthermore, when H_0 is true, $\mu_z = 0$ and $\sigma_z^2 = 1$.

DRAWING CONCLUSIONS ABOUT OUR NULL HYPOTHESIS

We can divide the distribution of our test statistic into two regions. Values of our test statistic in one of these regions (called the critical region*) leads us to reject our null hypothesis. The size of the critical region represents the probability of getting a result judged unlikely to have occurred when the null hypothesis is true. The dividing line between these two regions is called the* critical value.

The *p*-Value

The probability of obtaining a particular experimental result or one more extreme, assuming that H_0 is true, is the *p*-**value**. According to Fisher (1925), we can use the *p*-value to assess the correctness of H_0. For Fisher, the *p*-value is a measure of the implausibility of the null hypothesis; that is, the lower the *p*-value, the more implausible the null hypothesis. Therefore, when the *p*-value is lower than a certain value, we should take that as evidence that the null hypothesis is false. Fisher recognized that the null hypothesis might be true even when the *p*-value is a low number. According to Fisher (1956), a low *p*-value means that "either an exceptionally rare event has occurred, or the theory of random distribution [the null hypothesis] is not true" (p. 42). Nevertheless,

Fisher took the position that a low *p*-value should be taken as evidence that the null hypothesis is false.

How small does the p-*value have to be for us to conclude that H_0 is false?* Unfortunately, there is no straightforward answer to that question. Should that probability be .1 (1 chance in 10), or .05 (1 chance in 20), or .01 (1 chance in 100), or .001 (1 chance in 1,000)? While, as we will see later, the choice can depend in part on other considerations, Fisher proposed that we use $p < .05$ as our definition of "a rare event when H_0 is true." In other words, anytime the calculated value of *p* is less than or equal to .05, we reject H_0 and accept the alternative hypothesis H_1. Fisher's proposal has become the standard by which we decide whether to reject H_0. We do not reject H_0 when $p > .05$. As we will see later in this chapter, the latter case does *not* lead us to conclude that H_0 is true.

The value of *z* that divides those results that lead to rejection of H_0 from those that lead to non-rejection is called the **critical value**, and the set of all values of *z* that lead to rejection of H_0 is called the **critical region** (see Figure 6.1).

We use the symbol α to represent the probability of getting a result in the critical region when the null hypothesis is true. We can represent this situation symbolically as follows:

$$\alpha = \text{Pr(test statistic in critical region}|H_0 \text{ true)} \tag{6.4a}$$

or

$$\alpha = \text{Pr(reject } H_0 \text{ when it is true)} \tag{6.4b}$$

Therefore, any value of the test statistic for which $p < \alpha$ leads us to reject H_0.

FIGURE 6.1 ■ Location of the critical value and critical region. Any calculated *z* that is in the critical region leads to rejection of H_0. Calculated values of *z* that are outside the critical region do not lead to rejection of H_0.

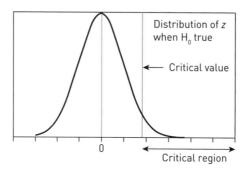

BUT SUPPOSE H$_0$ IS FALSE?

When H$_0$ is false, our test statistic does not come from the distribution based on H$_0$ being true; it comes from another normal distribution that has a mean $\neq$ 0. This other distribution is called the non-central distribution. While the p-value for our test statistic calculated from the distribution based on H$_0$ being true may be low, the probability of getting our data from the non-central distribution will be higher when H$_0$ is false.

The strategy for testing statistical hypotheses described above requires us to assume that the hypothesis we test (the null hypothesis) is true and to use the distribution of our test statistic (in this case z) to calculate the probability of obtaining our data. But suppose H$_0$ is false?

When H$_0$ is false, the distribution of z will also be a normal distribution with variance equal to 1, but the mean will *not* be equal to zero. The formulas for μ_z and σ_z^2 when H$_0$ is both true and false are derived in Box 6.1.

BOX 6.1

ALGEBRAIC DERIVATION OF THE MEAN AND VARIANCE OF THE z-TEST STATISTIC

The mean of the test statistic $z = \dfrac{\bar{X}_E - \bar{X}_C}{\sqrt{\dfrac{\sigma_E^2}{n_E} + \dfrac{\sigma_C^2}{n_C}}}$ is

found by repeatedly drawing samples from the two populations, finding $\bar{X}_E - \bar{X}_C$ for each set of samples, converting to z using Equation 6.3, and then averaging all of the resulting z-statistics. Using the definition of the mean, we find that

$$\mu_z = \frac{\sum\limits_{i=1}^{K} z_i}{K}$$

where K is the number of z-scores generated by this procedure. Substituting Equation 6.3 for z produces

$$\mu_z = \frac{\sum\limits_{i=1}^{K} \dfrac{\bar{X}_E - \bar{X}_C}{\sqrt{\dfrac{\sigma_E^2}{n_E} + \dfrac{\sigma_C^2}{n_C}}}}{K}$$

Because the term under the square root sign is a constant with respect to the summation,

$$\mu_z = \frac{1}{\sqrt{\dfrac{\sigma_E^2}{n_E} + \dfrac{\sigma_C^2}{n_C}}} \cdot \left[\frac{\sum\limits_{i=1}^{K}\left(\bar{X}_E - \bar{X}_C\right)}{K} \right]$$

We can distribute the summation sign to get the following:

$$\mu_z = \frac{1}{\sqrt{\dfrac{\sigma_E^2}{n_E} + \dfrac{\sigma_C^2}{n_C}}} \cdot \left[\frac{\sum_{i=1}^{K} \bar{X}_E}{K} - \frac{\sum_{i=1}^{K} \bar{X}_C}{K} \right]$$

The values in the brackets represent $\mu_E - \mu_C$. Therefore,

$$\mu_z = \frac{\mu_E - \mu_C}{\sqrt{\dfrac{\sigma_E^2}{n_E} + \dfrac{\sigma_C^2}{n_C}}}$$

When H_0 is true, $\mu_E - \mu_C = 0$, and $\mu_z = 0$. When H_0 is false, the value of μ_z depends on the actual difference between μ_E and μ_C, the population variances, and the sample sizes.

The variance of the z-test statistic can be found in a similar manner. Start with the definition of the variance as the mean of the squared deviations of scores from their means:

$$\sigma_z^2 = \frac{\sum_{i=1}^{K} (z_i - \mu_z)^2}{K}$$

We can substitute $z = \dfrac{\bar{X}_E - \bar{X}_C}{\sigma_{\bar{X}_E - \bar{X}_C}}$ and $\mu_z = \dfrac{\mu_E - \mu_C}{\sigma_{\bar{X}_E - \bar{X}_C}}$ to get this:

$$\sigma_z^2 = \frac{\sum_{i=1}^{K} \left[\left(\dfrac{\bar{X}_E - \bar{X}_C}{\sigma_{\bar{X}_E - \bar{X}_C}} \right) - \left(\dfrac{\mu_E - \mu_C}{\sigma_{\bar{X}_E - \bar{X}_C}} \right) \right]^2}{K}$$

Because the term $\sigma_{\bar{X}_E - \bar{X}_C}^2$ occurs in both parts and is a constant with respect to the summation,

$$\sigma_z^2 = \frac{1}{\sigma_{\bar{X}_E - \bar{X}_C}^2} \cdot \frac{\sum_{i=1}^{K} \left[(\bar{X}_E - \bar{X}_C) - (\mu_E - \mu_C) \right]^2}{K}$$

(Note: $\sigma_{\bar{X}_E - \bar{X}_C}^2$ is squared because it comes from a squared expression.)

The summation term is, by definition of variance, $\sigma_{\bar{X}_E - \bar{X}_C}^2$. Therefore, $\sigma_z^2 = 1$ both when H_0 is true and when H_0 is false.

The distributions of our test statistic when H_0 is true and when H_1 is true are represented in Figure 6.2. The two curves are presented separately because they are two *mutually exclusive possibilities*; that is, they cannot both happen at the same time: Either H_0 is true, in which case our calculated z (Equation 6.3) comes from the top distribution, or H_1 is true, in which case our calculated z (Equation 6.3) comes from the bottom distribution.[4]

---

[4] Although our alternative hypothesis is two tailed (that is, $\mu_E - \mu_C \neq 0$), this difference can only be on one side when the null hypothesis is false: Either $\mu_E - \mu_C > 0$ or $\mu_E - \mu_C < 0$. In the first situation, z is greater than 0, and in the second situation, z is less than zero. For the discussion here, we will assume the true state of affairs is that $\mu_E - \mu_C > 0$ and $z > 0$.

FIGURE 6.2 ■ Location of the critical value and critical region. Any calculated z that is in the critical region leads to the rejection of H_0. Calculated values of z that are outside the critical region do not lead to the rejection of H_0.

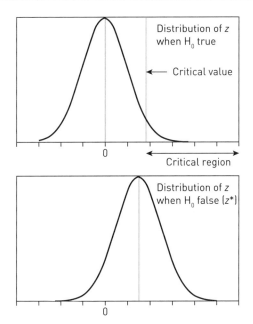

We decide whether to reject or not reject H_0 by calculating the probability of obtaining our observed value of z from the H_0 (top) distribution. When H_0 is true, the probability of getting a result in the critical region is low. On the other hand, when H_0 is false and H_1 is true, our test statistic comes from the bottom distribution, and our getting a result in the critical region is more likely to occur. The bottom distribution in Figure 6.2 is called the **non-central z distribution** and is symbolized as z^* (z-star).

ERRORS IN HYPOTHESIS TESTING

There are two types of errors we might make when testing statistical hypotheses. One error is to reject H_0 when it is true, which is called a type I or alpha error. The other error is to not reject H_0 when it is false, which is called a type II or beta error. We can only make a type I error when H_0 is true and our test statistic is in the critical region. We can only make a type II error when H_0 is false and our test statistic is not in the critical region.

Although we reject H_0 when the *p*-value is lower than our predetermined definition of an improbable event, there is the possibility that H_0 is indeed true. In this case, our rejection of H_0 leads to an error.[5] Following Neyman and Pearson (1928a, 1928b), this error is called a **type I** or **alpha error** and is represented by the part of the distribution based on H_0 being true that is in the critical region. *We can only make a type I error (or an alpha error) when H_0 is true and we obtain a result that falls in the critical region. The error is that we will decide to reject H_0 when it is indeed true.* The probability that we might make a type I or alpha error is α (see Equations 6.4a and 6.4b).

There is another kind of error we can make, namely, when H_0 is false and our data do not lead us to reject it; that error will occur when our test statistic does *not* fall in the critical region. We use the symbol β to represent *the probability of getting a result that is not in the critical region when the null hypothesis is false.* We can represent this situation symbolically as follows:

$$\beta = \text{Pr(test statistic is not in the critical region}|H_0 \text{ false)} \tag{6.5a}$$

or

$$\beta = \text{Pr(do not reject } H_0 \text{ when it is false)} \tag{6.5b}$$

This probability is represented by the portion of the z^* distribution that is *outside* the critical region. This error is called a **type II** or **beta error**. Since the probability of making a type II error (or beta error) is dependent on how much of the z^* curve is outside the critical region, which in turn is dependent on the unknown mean of z^*. It is not possible to calculate the probability of making a type II error. Nevertheless, there are ways to minimize this error, and these will be discussed in the next section.

When H_0 is false and the calculated value of z is in the critical region, then H_0 will be correctly rejected. This is not an error; it is a correct decision. The probability that one will correctly reject H_0 when it is false is represented by the area of the z^* curve that is in the critical region. *The probability of correctly rejecting H_0 when it is false* is called **power**; that is,

$$\text{Power} = \text{Pr(test statistic in critical region}|H_0 \text{ false)} \tag{6.6a}$$

or

$$\text{Power} = \text{Pr(reject } H_0 \text{ when it is false)} \tag{6.6b}$$

Since power and beta (probability of a beta or type II error) represent those parts of the z^* distribution that are inside and outside the critical region, respectively, they are related by the

---

[5] It is easy to make the mistake of stating that "there is such and such a probability that H_0 is true or not true." H_0 is either true or not, there is no probability attached to the truth or falseness of H_0; the only probability here is associated with obtaining a given result (in a future experiment) assuming H_0 is true.

FIGURE 6.3 ■ Relationship between the critical region, the probability of making a type I error (alpha), the probability of making a type II error (beta), and power (the probability of rejecting H_0 when it is false).

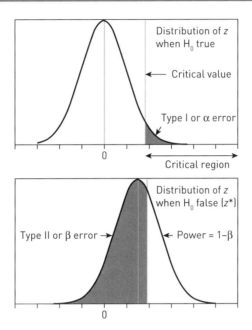

formula, power $= 1 -$ beta. Therefore, those things that increase power also decrease beta, and vice versa. The relationships described here are represented in Figure 6.3.

Finally, when H_0 is true and the calculated z does not fall in the critical region, one has no reason to reject H_0. Does this outcome mean that H_0 can be accepted? The answer is no, since logically one cannot prove a hypothesis true by finding evidence consistent with it. It may be that the hypothesis is actually false, but the data are still technically consistent with that hypothesis (or just not inconsistent enough with the hypothesis to warrant its rejection). We will discuss the reasons why one cannot prove H_0 to be true and what one can do with results that do not lead to the rejection of H_0 (see the section in this chapter titled "What Should We Do (or Not Do) When Our Data Do Not Allow Us to Reject the Null Hypothesis?").

POWER AND POWER FUNCTIONS

If our experimental question involves trying to determine whether two treatments have different effects on behavior, then we want to design an experiment in which the probability of rejecting a false null hypothesis (the power of our test) is high. Although we cannot calculate the power of our statistical hypothesis test, we know what factors affect the power, and we can use that information to design our experiment to maximize its power. Power functions provide us with a way to decide how large a sample size to use when we design our experiment.

Power is defined as the probability of rejecting H_0 when it is false. It is represented in Figure 6.3 as that area of the z^* distribution that lies in the critical region. To determine the power of a hypothesis test, we would have to know the form and location of the z^* distribution. Because z^* is a normal distribution with variance $= 1$ (see Box 6.1), the location of z^* is determined by the mean of the distribution, which is shown in Box 6.1 to be

$$\mu_{z^*} = \frac{\mu_E - \mu_C}{\sqrt{\dfrac{\sigma_E^2}{n_E} + \dfrac{\sigma_C^2}{n_C}}} \tag{6.7}$$

From Equation 6.7, it can be seen that the location of the z^* distribution (and hence the power of the test) is dependent on

1. the difference between the population means ($\mu_E - \mu_C$),
2. the population variances (σ_E^2 and σ_C^2), and
3. the sample sizes (n_E and n_C).

In addition, power will depend on

4. the critical value for the test that is based on the value of α we select as defining an improbable result when H_0 is true.

Of these four things, all but the value $\mu_E - \mu_C$ are known for any given experiment for which the z-test statistic can be used. Therefore, while we do not know what μ_{z^*} is, we certainly know how to change its value and to influence the power of the test.

The Population Variances

We tend to think of the population variances as fixed values not under our control, but that belief is not entirely true. The scores under consideration are measurements of behavior. From classical measurement theory, we know that an observed score is made up of two components, a true score and an error component. Although we cannot directly measure the true score, we can estimate it as the expected value of an infinite number of the measurements. The error component is assumed to be randomly distributed around the true score so that the mean of the errors $= 0$. The observed score can thus be represented by the following formula:

$$Y = T + Error, \tag{6.8}$$

where $\mu_{Error} = 0$.

From Theorem 3 in Chapter 3, the mean of a sum is the sum of the means, and the variance of a sum is the sum of the variances. Therefore,

$$\mu_Y = \mu_T + \mu_{Error} = \mu_T \tag{6.9}$$

$$\sigma_Y^2 = \sigma_T^2 + \sigma_{Error}^2 \tag{6.10}$$

The variance of the true scores is a function of the variation of the individuals being measured. Homogeneous groups (such as when all members of the group share the same gender, same age, same background, and so forth) will have lower values for σ_T^2. Heterogeneous groups will have larger values. For this reason, we try to use homogeneous groups in our experiments. We will see in Chapter 14 how we can apply analysis of variance to the possible sources of variance mentioned above to reduce the variances of the observed scores.

The variance of the errors is affected by the reliability of our measuring instrument and how consistently the participants in a given group are treated. *Reliability* refers to getting the same value each time we take the measurement. A perfectly reliable measuring instrument yields the same value every time we use it (assuming the true score does not change over time). An unreliable measuring instrument yields different values each time the measurement is taken. An extreme example of using an unreliable measuring instrument is using a rubber band to measure the length of an object. Therefore, it is important to choose measuring instruments that have high reliability.

The other factor that affects σ_{Error}^2 involves whether the conditions under which participants are treated and tested are held constant. Sloppy experimental procedures (not administering the treatments or instructions to our participants in the same way, or otherwise handling the participants in different ways that are not directly connected to the manipulation of the independent variables in our experiment) increase σ_{Error}^2, and thus in turn decrease the power of our statistical test. To improve the power of our statistical test, all experiments should be conducted in a way that ensures all participants in a given condition are treated the same.

It is clear from Equation 6.7 that anything we can do to *decrease* σ_E^2 and σ_C^2 will *increase* the μ_z. and therefore move the non-central distribution to the right. Doing so will increase the power of our statistical test, which uses the z in Equation 6.3 as the test statistic.

The Sample Sizes

It is clear in Equation 6.7 that μ_z. is also a function of the sample size. The larger the sample size (for any given difference $\mu_E - \mu_C$ and any given values of σ_E^2 and σ_C^2), the larger the value of μ_z. and the greater the power of our z-test. This relationship is illustrated in Figure 6.4. Power is represented by the shaded area of the distributions on which H_0 is assumed to be false.

Clearly, as sample size increases, more and more of the distribution of the test statistic when H_0 is false falls in the critical region of the distribution based on H_0 being true, thus increasing the power. In this case, because the form and variance of the H_1 distribution do not change, the location of that distribution must shift further into the critical region. This concept is illustrated in both sides of Figure 6.4. The difference between the two sides of Figure 6.4 reflects the size of the difference between μ_E and μ_C. In these examples, the difference between μ_E and μ_C on the right is twice as large as that on the left; hence, the power of the test at any given sample size is greater for detecting the larger difference. It should be noted, however, that if the sample sizes were large enough, the

FIGURE 6.4 ■ In the top panels, there are distributions of the test statistic (Equation 6.3) when H_0 is true, and in the middle and bottom panels, when the null hypothesis is false. In the middle panels, $n_E = n_C = 8$, and in the bottom panels, $n_E = n_C = 18$. On the left, $\mu_E - \mu_C = 5$, and on the right, $\mu_E - \mu_C = 10$. In all cases, $\alpha = .05$ and $\sigma_E^2 = \sigma_C^2 = 10$.

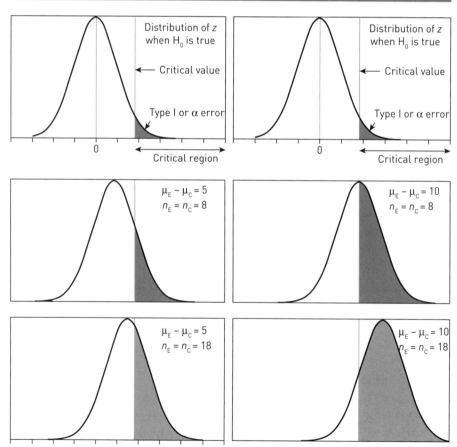

H_1 distribution would shift far enough into the critical region to allow detection of the difference between μ_E and μ_C, even if that difference were small. Therefore, any test can be made powerful enough to detect the smallest differences by increasing the sample size. We will have much more to say about this in the section "The Use of Power Functions" later in this chapter.

The Value of α Selected for Our Test

Finally, if the critical value were shifted to the right by decreasing the probability of making a type I error from $\alpha = .05$, where the critical value is 1.64, to $\alpha = .01$, where the critical value increases to 2.33, the power of the statistical test would decrease because less of the H_1 distribution would be in the critical region.

Power Functions

A **power function** is a *functional relationship between the power of a test and various possible values of the alternative hypothesis for a given sample size.* It is conventional to express the alternative hypothesis $\mu_E - \mu_C \neq 0$ in terms of the number of standard deviations μ_E is from μ_C. This index is the **standardized effect size**, where

$$ES = \frac{\mu_E - \mu_C}{\sigma} \tag{6.11}$$

The horizontal axis of the power function graph is in units of the standardized effect size $\left(\dfrac{\mu_E - \mu_C}{\sigma}\right)$, and the power is on the vertical axis.

To construct a power function, we must find the area of the alternative distribution curve (in this case, z^*) that lies in the critical region for various possible values of $\mu_E - \mu_C$. Thus, if we adopt a certain critical value (based on our choice of alpha) and particular sample sizes (n_E and n_C), we can examine the probability that our test would reject H_0 for different values of $\mu_E - \mu_C$. If we chose a different sample size and again looked at different values of $\mu_E - \mu_C$, we would construct another curve that would reflect the power at that sample size. In fact, if we chose many different values of n, we could construct a *family* of power functions. Similarly, we could hold sample size constant and vary alpha to construct another family of power functions that reflect the effects of that factor. Examples of these power functions are given below.

In the case of the z-test statistic under consideration, the power of the test can easily be found because we know that the distribution of z^* is normal with a known mean (see Equation 6.8) and variance ($\sigma_z^2 = 1$). Therefore, we can find the area of this normal curve that lies in the critical region by using the standard score transformation so that we can use the unit normal curve tables. The method for finding the power for the two-sample z-test is given in Box 6.2. The derivation in Box 6.2 is provided to illustrate how various factors affect the power of a test. All of these factors have similar effects in

BOX 6.2

FORMULA FOR THE POWER FUNCTION FOR THE TEST OF THE NULL HYPOTHESIS

H_0: $\mu_E - \mu_C = 0$ with the z-test statistic.

The power of a test is defined as the probability of rejecting H_0 when it is false. In this case, it is represented by the area of the z^* distribution that lies in the critical region (see Figure 6.4). Because z^* is a normal distribution, we can find the power by converting to standard scores again and finding the area of the curve from the critical value to $+\infty$. To do this, we substitute into the following formula:

$$\text{standard score} = \frac{\text{score} - \text{mean}}{\text{standard deviation}}$$

$$z' = \frac{z - \mu_{z^*}}{\sigma_{z^*}}$$

We will designate this standard score as z' (z-prime) to differentiate it from the other z-values used in this section. (The symbol z represents the test statistic in Equation 6.3 and the distribution of Equation 6.3 when H_0 is true; z^* represents the distribution of the z-test statistic when H_0 is false.) From Box 6.1 we know that

$$\mu_z = \frac{\mu_E - \mu_C}{\sqrt{\dfrac{\sigma_E^2}{n_E} + \dfrac{\sigma_C^2}{n_C}}}$$

and $\sigma_z^2 = 1$.

This deviation can be simplified if the following assumptions are made:

1. $\sigma_E^2 = \sigma_C^2$. (The two population variances are equal; this is called homogeneity of variance.)

2. $n_E = n_C$. (The sample sizes are equal.)

If we drop the subscripts on σ^2 and n to denote that they are equal,

$$\mu_{z^*} = \frac{\mu_E - \mu_C}{\sqrt{\dfrac{2\sigma^2}{n}}} = \frac{\mu_E - \mu_C}{\sigma} \cdot \sqrt{\frac{n}{2}}$$

Because we want to find the area to the right of the critical value (c.v.),

$$z' = \frac{c.v. - \mu_{z^*}}{\sigma_{z^*}}$$

$$z' = \frac{c.v. - \dfrac{\mu_E - \mu_C}{\sigma} \cdot \sqrt{\dfrac{n}{2}}}{1}$$

$$z' = c.v. - \frac{\mu_E - \mu_C}{\sigma} \cdot \sqrt{\frac{n}{2}}$$

The value of z' determines the area of the z^* curve that lies in the critical region. The smaller the value of z', the greater the area of z^* in the critical region and the greater the power. Note that when z' is a negative number, the power is greater than .5.

all hypothesis tests. This derivation applies only to situations in which the distribution where H_0 is false is normal. When that distribution is not normal, other methods must be used. Some of these strategies will be described in subsequent chapters.

From the formula derived in Box 6.2, we can readily construct a set of power functions for any z-test of the hypothesis $H_0: \mu_E - \mu_C = 0$. Two examples of such functions are given below. In the first example, the probability of a type I (α) error is set at .05 and sample size is varied (see Table 6.1 and Figure 6.5). In the second example, sample size is held constant at 8 participants in a group and the value of α is varied (see Table 6.2 and Figure 6.6).

TABLE 6.1 ■ Power for the Test of $H_0: \mu_E - \mu_C = 0$ Against $H_1: \mu_E - \mu_C > 0$ With a z-Statistic for Various Standardized Effect Sizes. $\alpha = .05$, and Sample Size (n) Is Varied							
n	\multicolumn{7}{c}{Standardized Effect Size $\dfrac{\mu_E - \mu_C}{\sigma}$}
	0	0.5	1.0	1.5	2.0	2.5	3.0
2	.05	.13	.26	.44	.63	.80	.91
8	.05	.26	.63	.91	.99	.99	.99
18	.05	.44	.91	.99	.99	.99	.99

FIGURE 6.5 ■ Power functions for the z-test of $H_0: \mu_E - \mu_C = 0$ against $H_1: \mu_E - \mu_C > 0$ with $\alpha = .05$.

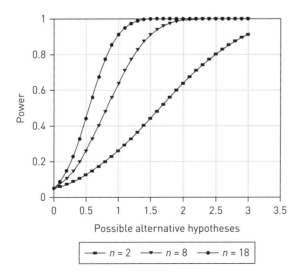

TABLE 6.2 ■ Power for the Test of $H_0: \mu_E - \mu_C = 0$ Against $H_1: \mu_E - \mu_C > 0$ With a z-Statistic for Various Standardized Effect Sizes (Sample Size = 8; α Is Varied)							
α	Standardized Effect Size $\dfrac{\mu_E - \mu_C}{\sigma}$						
	0	0.5	1.0	1.5	2.0	2.5	3.0
.05	.05	.26	.63	.91	.99	.99	.99
.01	.01	.09	.37	.75	.95	.99	.99
.001	.001	.02	.14	.46	.82	.97	.99

FIGURE 6.6 ■ Power functions for the z-test of $H_0: \mu_E - \mu_C = 0$ against $H_1: \mu_E - \mu_C > 0$ with sample size = 8.

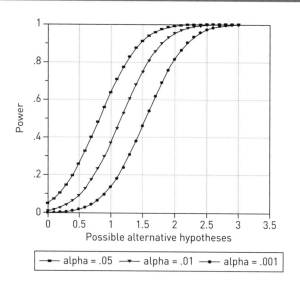

THE USE OF POWER FUNCTIONS

When used properly, power functions can help us decide how large a sample size to use to find a treatment effect of a certain size at a given level of α. *Too large a sample size can be wasteful of resources, while too small a sample size will not result in a test with enough power to consistently detect a real difference between the population means.*

If we are going to commit time and resources to an experiment, we want to do so in a way that maximizes our chances of finding an effect that we predicted. In view of the proceeding discussion about power, it is apparent that the sample size one chooses has a great deal to do with this.

Too small a sample size will lead to an experiment in which the power of the test (probability of rejecting H_0 when it is false) is also too small. For example, if the effect size $\frac{\mu_E - \mu_C}{\sigma} = 1$, then an experiment with a sample size of 8 in a group will have a power of .63 when alpha = .05 (see Table 6.1 and Figure 6.5). Thus, if the experiment were repeated a large number of times, over *one third* of these replications would not lead us to reject H_0 even though μ_E and μ_C are one standard deviation apart (a rather large difference). If, however, the sample size is increased to 18 in a group, the power increases to .91, which means that less than 1 in 10 replications would *not* lead us to reject H_0. In this case, the risk of making a type II error (not rejecting H_0 when it is false) is at an acceptably small level.

On the other hand, too large a sample size can be wasteful of resources. For example, if the sample size above were increased from 18 per group to 25 (that is, 50 participants in all), the power would increase from .91 to .97, a gain in power that, while useful, might not be worth the added expense of the additional participants. In general, when the power of a test is around .9, adding more participants does little to increase it because there is so little room for further increase.

Clearly, the choice of sample size is an important matter. Too small a sample can lead to a test that possesses little power and consequently will most likely not lead to rejection of H_0 even when it is false (type II error). This situation is most apt to occur when the difference between μ_E and μ_C is small (see Figures 5.5 and 5.6 where $\frac{\mu_E - \mu_C}{\sigma}$ is a small number). Too large a sample size, on the other hand, creates a different problem. Note that in Figure 6.5, where $\frac{\mu_E - \mu_C}{\sigma}$ is a large number, the power is very high and almost the same for a wide range of sample sizes. Thus, the smaller sample sizes lead to tests as powerful as the larger ones.

The major problem with using power functions to aid in the determination of sample size for an experiment is that one needs to have some estimate of the size of the difference between the population means. Because this unknown value is what the experimenter is attempting to find, power functions can only be useful if some thought is given to how small a difference one wants to look for. For example, would a difference of 0.1 standard deviation $\left(\frac{\mu_E - \mu_C}{\sigma} = 0.1 \right)$ be worth looking for? If so, it would be possible to choose a sample size large enough to have a test with power = .9 when that is the difference between μ_E and μ_C. In this situation, one would need 1,717 participants in a group. (As an exercise, you should try to verify this value.) Whether such a difference is worth looking for can only be decided in the context of a particular research area. Such a choice is not a statistical decision. The statistical model merely tells us what sample size to use to obtain a test with a certain power when the actual difference between μ_E and μ_C is of a particular magnitude. After we decide how large a difference between μ_E and μ_C to look for, the power function can be consulted to determine the smallest sample size necessary to achieve a test of a certain power. Fortunately, there are power functions available for all of the test statistics used in the social sciences that researchers can consult.

p-VALUES, α, AND ALPHA (TYPE I) ERRORS: WHAT THEY DO AND DO NOT MEAN

The p-value, α, and a type I (α error) are not the same thing. Unfortunately, many people inappropriately use these terms interchangeably. The problem is that the p-value was introduced by R. A. Fisher in his hypothesis-testing paradigm. Alpha and alpha error were introduced by Jerzy Neyman and Egon Pearson to test statistical hypotheses. Although we use concepts from both models, it is important for us to understand where they come from and what they mean and do not mean.

The model for testing statistical hypotheses presented here is a combination of two competing and perhaps contradictory paradigms, one by R. A. Fisher (1925, 1935) and the other by Jerzy Neyman and Egon Pearson (1928a, 1928b). Fisher's paradigm is called *significance testing*, and Neyman and Pearson's paradigm is called *hypothesis testing*. The concepts of significance, null hypothesis, and *p*-values come from Fisher, and the concepts of alternative hypotheses, α and β errors, and power come from Neyman and Pearson.

With Fisher's significance-testing paradigm, we propose a null hypothesis that the sample comes from a specific infinite population, and the *p*-value is a measure of how unlikely it is that our data came from that population. Fisher adopted $p < .05$ as his criterion for an unlikely event when the null hypothesis is true. He called his paradigm a significance test and argued that, although obtaining a result where $p < .05$ could mean we have observed an unlikely event, such rare events can be taken as evidence that the null hypothesis is false. For Fisher, the smaller the observed *p*-value, the stronger the evidence against the null hypothesis. Fisher said nothing about alternative hypotheses, α, β, or power.

On the other hand, with Neyman and Pearson's hypothesis-testing paradigm, we set up two competing hypotheses, the null hypothesis (H_0) and the alternative hypothesis (H_1), and test H_0 against H_1. These researchers introduced the probabilities of committing two types of errors: type I or alpha errors (rejecting true null hypotheses) and type II or beta errors (retaining false null hypotheses). Rather than conceptualizing an experiment as sampling from an infinite population, they built their paradigm on repeated random sampling from a population. Therefore, α is the probability of getting results that fall in the critical region when H_0 is true if we repeat the same experiment a large number of times. The same is the case for β with respect to getting results that do not fall in the critical region when the H_0 is false. Neyman and Pearson also introduced the concept of the power of the test, or the probability of rejecting a false null hypothesis. Because the power of a test depends of a number of factors, such as sample size and effect size, they argued that we can improve our experiments by considering what the power of our test might be to detect a particular effect size in the population.

Because the concepts we use to describe statistical hypothesis testing come from these two competing paradigms, there is a lot of confusion about the proper understanding of p-values, α, β, and power (Hubbard, 2004; Hubbard & Bayarri, 2003; Huberty, 1993).

Differentiating *p*-Values From α Levels

With the Neyman–Pearson paradigm, we select an α-level (the probability of getting results in the critical region and rejecting H_0) prior to conducting the experiment. Therefore, α is a fixed value. On the other hand, the p-value is not fixed; instead, it is a value that varies depending on our data. It is the probability of getting the value of our test statistic (or one more extreme), assuming the null hypothesis is true. As noted in this chapter, when the null hypothesis is false, we can make the p-value as small as we want by increasing the sample size. The p-value is *not* the probability of making, or having made, a type I error. We connect these two concepts by saying that we will reject the null hypothesis when the p-value is less than α (the value we selected to define the critical region), a statement that neither Fisher nor Neyman and Pearson would have made.

Can we calculate the probability that we might make a type I or α error? *The answer to this question is no!* What we *can* determine is the probability that we might make a type I or α error when the null hypothesis is true. That probability is α, the probability of getting a result in the critical region when the null hypothesis is true (see Equation 6.5). Alpha is *not* the probability that a result in the critical region is a type I or α error. It is *not* the probability that we *might* make a type I or α error, because we can only make a type I or α error when the null hypothesis is true *and* our test statistic is in the critical region. As Pollard and Richardson (1987) noted, the probability that the null hypothesis is true and our test statistic is in the critical region equals the probability that the null hypothesis is true times the probability of getting a test statistic in the critical region when the null hypothesis is true.[6] Using the symbol H_0 for the null hypothesis is true and D^* for data in the critical region, Pollard and Richardson (1987) expressed this idea as follows:

$$Pr(H_0 \text{ and } D^*) = Pr(H_0) \times Pr(D^*|H_0) \tag{6.12}$$

$Pr(D^*|H_0)$ is α, and $Pr(H_0)$ is an unknown value between 0 and 1 because we have no idea of how often the null hypothesis is true across all possible experiments that can be performed; therefore, the probability that we might make a type I or α error is less than α, but we have no way of calculating that value.

Can we calculate the probability that we did make a type I or α error when we rejected the null hypothesis? *The answer to this question is also no!* As Pollard and Richardson (1987) noted, "When the null hypothesis is rejected, the probability of *having made* a Type I error is a probability about the null hypothesis because a Type I error has been made if and only if the null hypothesis is in fact true" (p. 160; emphasis added). This question is really about estimating the proportion of experiments in which the null hypothesis is true *and* the test statistic is in the critical region, that is, $Pr(H_0|D^*)$. The formula for calculating a posterior (after-the-fact) probability is Bayes' theorem:

$$Pr\left(\mu_0|D^*\right) = \frac{Pr\left(D^*|\mu_0\right) \times Pr\left(\mu_0\right)}{Pr\left(D^*\right)} \tag{6.13}$$

It is clear from Equation 6.13 that to calculate the probability that the null hypothesis is true when our test statistic falls in the critical region, we need to know the probability that the null hypothesis is true (H_0) and the probability of getting data that fall in the critical region in any experiment. Both of these values are unknown; therefore, there is no way to know after the fact whether our result that fell in the critical region occurred because the null hypothesis is false or because we made a type I or α error.

A WORD OF CAUTION ABOUT ATTEMPTING TO ESTIMATE THE POWER OF A HYPOTHESIS TEST AFTER THE DATA HAVE BEEN COLLECTED

Power is the probability of correctly rejecting the null hypothesis when that hypothesis is false. Because probability refers to future events, we use power functions to help us

---

[6]This logic is based on the addition law of probability: $Pr(A \text{ and } B) = Pr(A) \times Pr(B|A)$.

design our experiments so that when the null hypothesis is false, the probability that we will reject it will be high. Therefore, trying to calculate the power of a statistical test from the sample data gives us no more information than we already have.

The words of caution are simple: Do not do this! As noted above, the power of a hypothesis test is the probability of rejecting the null hypothesis when it is false. Although we cannot know the power of our test because we do not know the location of the distribution of our test statistic (the non-central distribution) when the null hypothesis is false, we do know the factors that affect the power of our test (the true difference between the population means; the sample size; the value for α we select; whether we are performing a one- or two-tailed test; and, in the case of hypothesis tests on population means, the population variance). We demonstrated that we can use power functions to select the sample sizes for an experiment when we are attempting to look for a given effect size (or one larger). *We estimate the power of a hypothesis test before we perform the experiment, not afterward.* See Lenth (2001) for some practical advice for selecting the appropriate sample sizes.

The issue of attempting to estimate the power of our statistical hypothesis test arises when the results of an experiment have been analyzed and the test statistic did not fall in the critical region. The failure to reject the null hypothesis could have been because of low power (due to a variety of factors noted above) even though there actually is an effect. On the other hand, if we could show that the power is indeed high, this information might be taken as evidence that the null hypothesis is true. A number of statistical software packages provide retrospective or post hoc (after-the-fact) power analyses based on the observed data. These analyses are based on the premise that the observed differences between sample means and the observed estimate of variance are *perfect* estimates of the parameters of the populations. However, as Hoenig and Heisey (1991) and Lenth (2007) observed, this type of analysis is doomed to failure. The reason is simple: The observed power (that is, the power calculated from the observed data) is a monotonic function of the *p*-value for that experiment; that is, the larger the *p*-value, the lower the observed power, and vice versa. Therefore, when $p > .05$, power will always be less than .5. In fact, .5 is the maximum value of the observed power when the null hypothesis is not rejected.

One possible use of a retrospective or post hoc power analysis is to try to determine what sample size we would need to reject the null hypothesis for the observed differences between sample means and the observed estimate of variance, assuming they are perfect estimates of the population effect size and variance, an assumption that is almost always false. While we could calculate how large a sample size we would need to find that effect size *in a future experiment,* it is *not appropriate* to use that information to add more participants to our sample. In fact, using the classical statistical model, it is *never appropriate* to keep collecting data until we have enough data to reject the null hypothesis!

IS IT EVER APPROPRIATE TO USE A ONE-TAILED HYPOTHESIS TEST?

One-tailed tests are always more powerful than two-tailed tests when the difference between the sample means is in the predicted direction, but what will you do when there is a large difference in the opposite direction? Changing your theory and statistical hypothesis to accommodate that situation increases the probability of making a type I error. To discourage that practice, journal editors often advise authors to not use one-tailed tests. However, there are situations in which one-tailed tests are appropriate.

The answer to this question is "it depends." One-tailed hypothesis tests are designed to test a directional hypothesis, for instance, that the mean of Group 1 is greater than the mean of Group 2. In such a situation, the null hypothesis would only be rejected if the mean for Group 1 were larger than the mean of Group 2 and large enough to result in the test statistic falling in the critical region. In this situation, the critical region would reside on only one side of the distribution such that, conventionally, 5% of the distribution on one side, but 0% of the distribution on the other side, would comprise the critical region. This circumstance would provide the most powerful test of the directional hypothesis, which was likely based on good theoretical foundations.

Such an outcome seems to be the optimal situation, with researchers being rewarded for their good theoretical foresight in predicting the direction of the mean difference with increased power to reject the null hypothesis in detecting it. However, researchers are often unsuccessful in their predictions (as researchers will begrudgingly admit). Sometimes the effect manifests differently than extant theory would suggest, such as when the mean of Group 1 is substantially less than the mean of Group 2 in our example above. Were the researchers using a one-tailed test, they would have no opportunity (that is, no power) to reject the null hypothesis in this case because there would be no critical region on that side of the distribution for their test statistic.

In thinking about their counterintuitive results, the researchers may, being bright and creative individuals, create a reasonable (nay, compelling!) explanation for why they would get results opposite to that which they predicted. Further, they may even convince themselves that they should have known that the results would turn out that way. Consequently, they may change their analytical approach to a two-tailed test in an effort to reject the null hypothesis, or they may even adopt a one-tailed test with a directional hypothesis opposite to their original directional hypothesis.

The problem with this hypothesizing after the results are known, or "HARKing" (Kerr, 1998), is that the probability of making a type I or alpha error has increased. The original one-tailed test in the wrong direction carried with it a 5% chance of making a type I error if the null hypothesis were true. Following this one-tailed test with a two-tailed test raises that to a 7.5% chance of making a type I error if the null hypothesis were true (with the initial 5% critical region on one side of the distribution added to the subsequent 2.5% critical region on the other side of the distribution). Following the initial one-tailed test with a one-tailed test in the other direction similarly raises the probability of making a type I error if the null hypothesis were true to 10%. Given the severity of the consequences of making type I errors, it should be obvious that practices that may be exploited to increase these error rates are not things to be considered casually. And given the bias for the publication of significant effects and the "publish or perish" mentality that researchers too often face, the researchers may decide that the downsides of making type I errors are temporarily overshadowed by the short-term rewards of finding significant results.

For these reasons, it has become standard practice for many psychology journals to require authors to use two-tailed tests almost exclusively, thereby more explicitly controlling the probability of making type I errors when the null hypothesis is true. It is our opinion that one-tailed tests are valuable, particularly when an effect in the opposite direction is as meaningful as no effect (such as when a new therapy has either no effect or makes the clients' situations worse—in either case, the therapy would be discontinued). However, researchers who intend to use them should be well prepared to justify why they were appropriate to use, and we recommend that researchers do so proactively.

WHAT SHOULD WE MEAN WHEN WE SAY OUR RESULTS ARE STATISTICALLY SIGNIFICANT?

When R. A. Fisher described the results of an experiment as significant, he meant that the result was unlikely to occur by chance if the tested hypothesis were true. That does not mean that the observed difference is important or of consequence. Furthermore, statistical significance is not the same as practical significance. What is the correct way to deal with situations in which our p-value is slightly larger than the criterion we adopted for judging the result of our experiment as unlikely?

We say our results are "statistically significant" when our test statistic falls in the critical region and we reject our null hypothesis in favor of our alternative hypothesis. What should we mean when we say our results are statistically significant?

It is unfortunate that Fisher used the term *significance testing* to describe his paradigm for statistical inference because in everyday discourse, *significance* and *significant* mean something very different than they do in statistics. The dictionary definitions of these terms include the language "important" and "of consequence." Such a definition is not what Fisher meant when he applied those terms to experiments. As noted above, Fisher used those terms to describe the situation in which the obtained p-value is below a certain level judged to be improbable when the null hypothesis is true, which is all *significance* means in the context of statistical inference and hypothesis testing. Unfortunately, we tend to drop the adjective *statistically* and just say a result is "significant," adding to the confusion.

Fisher went on to argue that the smaller the observed p-value, the stronger the evidence against the null hypothesis, and some people take that to mean that the smaller the p-value, the more significant the results are in terms of their importance. But as we have seen in this chapter, as long as the null hypothesis is false, the p-value can be made as small as we want by increasing the sample size. David Bakan (1966) made a persuasive argument that the null hypothesis is never true; that is, anything we do that treats the participants in our experiments differently will have some effect, even if that effect is small. Furthermore, in the Neyman and Pearson hypothesis-testing paradigm, we reject the null hypothesis whenever our test statistic falls in the critical region, but it does not matter where in that region the test statistic falls. Therefore, it is not correct to say that a result is "more significant" when the p-value is small or that a small p-value is a reflection of a large treatment effect.

Can a Result Be "Marginally Significant"?

As noted above, Fisher used the p-value as a measure of the strength of the evidence against the null hypothesis, and he proposed the use of $p < .05$ as the threshold beyond which the result of an experiment is considered to be unlikely when the null hypothesis is true. He would have treated $p < .049$ and $p < .051$ as similar results. On the other hand, Neyman and Pearson set the value of $\alpha = .05$ to differentiate those results in the critical region that lead us to reject the null hypothesis from those that do not. Clearly, the decision to adopt Fisher's $p < .05$ as the threshold is arbitrary. As Rosnow and Rosenthal (1989) commented, "Surely, God loves the .06 nearly as much as the .05." So what does it mean, and what should we do, when the p-value in our experiment is slightly greater than .05? Such results are sometimes referred to as *marginally significant*, *approaching significance*, *nearly significant*, or *trending*. It has become more common over the past 40 years for psychologists to use these terms to describe those situations (Pritschet, Powell, & Horne, 2016).

One argument for using such terms is to convey to the reader that the researcher is not confident that the null hypothesis is false but still thinks there is something worth reporting, and by using terms like *marginally significant*, the researcher can highlight findings that do not fall in the region of rejection so that the reader can decide how to interpret those findings. Researchers who use these terms need to be careful about how they characterize these findings, because, despite the arbitrary nature of the .05 threshold, these findings do not result in rejection of the null hypothesis, and researchers should not make strong conclusions as if they did.

Statistical Significance Versus Practical Significance

Statistical significance is not the same as practical significance, or importance. The importance of the results of an experiment depends on the context and other nonstatistical aspects of an experiment, even when the treatment effects are small (Prentice & Miller, 1992). In Chapter 7, we will look at how to estimate the effect size, and in Chapter 13 we will look at another way to estimate the effect size. In both cases, the measure of effect size is not affected by the sample size. It has long been the recommendation of the American Psychological Association, and it is being required by more and more journals, that researchers accompany their significance tests with effect sizes when reporting the results of their studies. But even then, researchers should be careful not to overstate the implications of their "significant" findings and the effect sizes they compute.

What Should We Do (or Not Do) When Our Data Do Not Allow Us to Reject the Null Hypothesis?

This situation happens to all of us. We carefully consider how many participants to use when we design our experiment to find an effect size of at least a certain magnitude, and we conduct our study carefully. But our obtained results are not in the critical region, and therefore we cannot reject our statistical null hypothesis. Where do we go from here?

When we have not rejected our null hypothesis, we have *not* provided evidence that the null hypothesis is true. As we have discussed earlier, when our null hypothesis is false, our statistical test result is not always in the critical region. That is, we may have made a type II (or beta) error.

There are a number of perspectives to consider in determining what this finding allows us to conclude. Bakan (1966) argued that the null hypothesis is never true because it is hard to conceive of a situation in which different treatments will have *exactly* the same effects on behavior. And logically it makes sense that a firm stance on any prediction that a predetermined exact value is true is unlikely to be verified by our findings. Therefore, it should be obvious that non-rejection of a null hypothesis, which does not allow us to say that predetermined exact value is true, is not evidence that the null hypothesis is true. We can only conclude that we do not have sufficient evidence to demonstrate that it is false.

In Fisher's (1925, 1928) significance-testing model, obtaining a result with a $p < .05$ can be taken as evidence that the null hypothesis is false, but obtaining a result with $p > .05$ cannot be taken as evidence that the null hypothesis is true. In this model, a non-significant result could be due to a number of possibilities, from the null hypothesis being true to the treatment effect being small. Under these circumstances, we cannot draw a firm conclusion about the null hypothesis. At best, we can say the results of our experiment are inconclusive.

On the other hand, Neyman and Pearson (1928a, 1928b) viewed the situation as a test between two competing hypotheses, H_0 and H_1. According to their perspective, we can reject the null hypothesis and accept the alternative when our test statistic is in the critical region. On the other hand, we "accept" the null hypothesis when the data are not in the critical region. However, according to them, "accepting" the null hypothesis does not mean that we are concluding that the null hypothesis is true. Their position is that we should "act" as if the null hypothesis is true until we get more data to indicate otherwise.

Bakan (1966) provided a justification for Neyman and Pearson's approach to non-rejection of the null hypothesis by distinguishing between "sharp" and "loose" null hypotheses. A sharp null hypothesis is that there is absolutely no difference between the population parameters; as he noted, this situation rarely, if ever, occurs. A loose null hypothesis is a range of values around a sharp null hypothesis such that any difference in the interval is too small for us to conclude that the null hypothesis is false. By adopting this approach, we do not accept the sharp null hypothesis; rather we say that the difference is too small to be meaningful for us.

In summary, when our research yields findings that do not fall in the critical region, we fail to reject the null hypothesis. Therefore, we "retain" it, but we do not officially "accept" it. Failing to find an effect is not the same as verifying that the effect does not exist. Indeed, absence of evidence is not evidence of absence. We recommend that researchers who have strong theoretical reasons to predict an effect, but do not find it in their studies, consider conducting their studies again with stronger manipulations, more reliable measures, and generally greater power. If the effect is out there and is strong enough to warrant interest (that is, it has a nontrivial effect size), you will likely find it. On the other hand, if your data from multiple well-designed studies fail to allow you to reject the null hypothesis, then the effect may be too small to be of value, or, possibly, the null hypothesis may be true—whether or not you can technically conclude that is the case.

A FINAL WORD

Although the principles described in this chapter were developed for the two-sample z-test for population means when the population variance is known, they apply to all statistical hypothesis tests using the classical statistical model. The two-sample z-test was chosen to illustrate those basic principles in a direct way. In subsequent chapters, we will apply these principles to other test statistics. Therefore, it is important that we master these basic principles before moving forward.

In the next chapter, we will use Student's t to analyze the results from Barlett's (2015) two-group experiment described in Chapter 1. As we will see, the shape of the t-distribution is affected by the sample size, and the shape and location of the non-central t-distribution is affected by the sample size and the effect size. Nevertheless, the basic principles described here apply.

Summary

Starting with our research question, we generate a set of mutually exclusive and exhaustive experimental hypotheses stated in terms of the independent and dependent variables in our research study. With the classical statistical model, we create a parallel set of statistical hypotheses stated in terms of the unknown parameters of the populations from which our random samples are obtained. We obtain estimates of these unknown parameters from our samples. (See the summary flowchart in Figure 6.7.)

In a two-group experiment in which the statistical hypotheses are about the difference between the means of the populations ($\mu_E - \mu_C$), the data of interest are $\bar{X}_E - \bar{X}_C$. Assuming that the populations are normal distributions with known variances, the distribution of $\bar{X}_E - \bar{X}_C$ is a normal distribution. To find the probability of obtaining our observed value of $\bar{X}_E - \bar{X}_C$, we apply the z-score transformation. Then, we create our test statistic by assuming the hypothesis we can test (the null hypothesis) is true. When our null hypothesis is true, our test statistic has a normal distribution with $\mu_z = 0$ and $\sigma_z^2 = 1$, and we can create a critical region (based on our definition of an improbable event) such that, if the value of our test statistic fell in this region, we would reject our null hypothesis. The procedure for creating our test statistic and performing our statistical test is summarized in the flowchart in Figure 6.7.

When our null hypothesis is false, our test statistic is a non-central normal distribution (symbolized as z^*) with $\mu_{z^*} \neq 0$ and $\sigma_{z^*}^2 = 1$. The value of μ_{z^*} is a function of the actual value of $\mu_E - \mu_C$, the variances of the populations, and the sample sizes. The greater the value of μ_{z^*}, the greater the power of our test (probability of rejecting a false null hypothesis). We can use power functions to help us decide how large a sample size to use to obtain a high level of power.

When our null hypothesis is true, a result falling in the critical region will lead us to make a type I error or α error (we reject the null hypothesis when it is true). On the other hand, when our null hypothesis is false, a result falling outside the critical region will lead us to make a type II error or β error (we do not reject the null hypothesis when it is false). The convention is to use $\alpha = .05$ as our definition of an improbable event when the null hypothesis is true. We do not know the probability of making a β error, but because power $= 1 - \beta$, those factors that increase the power also decrease the probability of making a β error.

The method for hypothesis testing described in this chapter is a hybrid of models described by R. A. Fisher and by J. Neyman and E. S. Pearson. Because these two models are in some ways incompatible, we need to be careful about how we use concepts like p-value, α, and α error.

FIGURE 6.7 ■ Summary flowchart

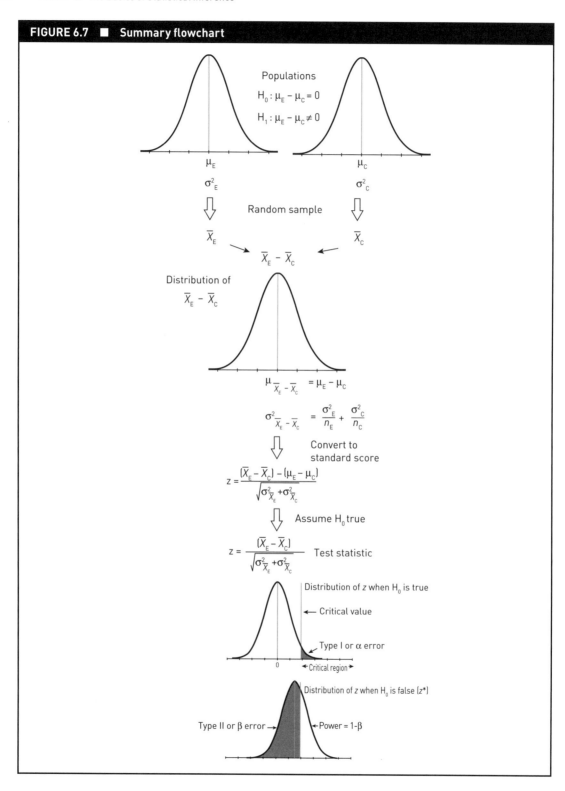

Conceptual Exercises

1. Your test statistic is in the critical region, and you reject the null hypothesis. What is the probability that you made a type I or α error? Why?

2. Comment on the appropriateness of the following statement:

   My test statistic is not in the critical region, but the observed power of my test is high; therefore, the data indicate that I should accept the null hypothesis.

3. Fisher argued that the smaller the p-value, the stronger the evidence against the null hypothesis. That is, $p < .001$ indicates stronger evidence against the null hypothesis than $p < .01$. Does it follow that $p < .001$ indicates a larger treatment effect than $p < .01$? Why or why not?

4. Are you more likely to make an alpha (or type I) error with a large sample size or with a small sample size? Why or why not?

5. What are the effects of increasing sample size on:

   a. the probability of making a type I (or alpha) error?

   b. the probability of making a type II (or beta) error?

   Why in each case?

6. What does $p < .05$ tell us about the null hypothesis? About the alternative hypotheses?

7. Comment on the following statements and explain what, if anything, is wrong:

   a. We will make a type I error a small proportion of the time—the exact proportion being specified by our alpha level.

   b. Although I did not reject the null hypothesis, the power of my test indicates that I would have rejected the null hypothesis if I had enrolled 5 more participants in each group.

   c. If the sample sizes are equal, then a p-value of .001 represents a larger treatment effect than does a p-value of .05.

8. In general terms, how does one construct a power function for a statistical test? (Hint: Define the *power* of a test. What part of what distribution contains the power? How is this fact then translated into a power function?)

9. Why does a test statistic for which $p < .001$ not necessarily represent a large treatment effect?

10. Although we usually expect to collect data to support a research hypothesis that more closely matches the alternative hypothesis, the hypothesis we actually test is the null hypothesis. What are the two reasons for why we do so?

11. Respond to the following statement:

    I am not convinced that there really is a difference here because the sample size is so small. We all know that with small sample sizes, there is a lot of variability in the sample means; the central limit theorem tells us that! Therefore, I am not convinced that the significant result is real. If the experimenter had used a larger sample size and gotten a significant result, then I would believe that there is something there.

    In your response, be sure to respond to the assertions about the sample size and the variability of the sample means, as well as the other parts of the statement. What false assumptions is the author making, and why are they false? What is the correct state of affairs? How should we interpret the significance of an experimental result?

Student Study Site

Visit the Student Study Site at **https://study.sagepub.com/friemanstats** for a variety of useful tools including data sets, additional exercises, and web resources.

SPECIFIC TECHNIQUES TO ANSWER SPECIFIC QUESTIONS

THE INDEPENDENT GROUPS *t*-TESTS FOR TESTING FOR DIFFERENCES BETWEEN POPULATION MEANS

I n Chapter 6, we reviewed the general principles for testing statistical hypotheses in a two-group experiment. Now we will apply those principles to Barlett's (2015) experiment described in Chapter 1. Briefly, participants were randomly assigned to receive either an insulting message over instant messenger or a nice message from their "partner" (who did not actually exist) regarding their failure on a puzzle task. Cyberbullying was measured by the hostility of the participant's response to the partner. To test what psychological variable(s) are related to message content, Barlett measured state levels of hostility after participants received their message from their partner. Hostility was measured using the State Hostility Scale (SHS; Anderson, Deuser, & DeNeve, 1995). The SHS is a 35-item measure that uses a Likert scale [1 (*not at all*) to 5 (*extremely*)], with higher scores being indicative of feeling more hostile. Participants were asked to indicate how they "feel right now" using this scale. A sample item is "I feel furious."

The experimental hypotheses for this experiment are as follows:

Cybervictimization (message content) *does not* affect state hostility.

Cybervictimization (message content) *does* affect state hostility.

The corresponding statistical hypotheses are:

H_0: $\mu_{\text{insulting}} - \mu_{\text{nice}} = 0$. The mean hostility score of the population from which the participants in the After Insulting Message group were sampled minus the mean hostility score of the population from which the participants in the After Nice Message group were sampled equals 0.

H_1: $\mu_{\text{insulting}} - \mu_{\text{nice}} \neq 0$. The mean hostility score of the population from which the participants in the After Insulting Message group were sampled minus the mean hostility score of the population from which the participants in the After Nice Message were sampled does not equal 0.

The data from this experiment are reprinted in Table 7.1.

The general principles for testing statistical hypotheses in Chapter 6 were developed for testing the statistical hypothesis $\mu_E - \mu_C = 0$ against the alternative $\mu_E - \mu_C \neq 0$ when we know the population variances σ_E^2 and σ_C^2. However, we do not know the population variances in the experiment under consideration; in fact, it is rarely the case that we know those population variances. Therefore, we cannot use the *z*-test developed in Chapter 6 to analyze most of the data we collect from experiments such as this one with two independent groups of participants. Student's *t*-test[1] provides us a way to deal with this situation. Student's

TABLE 7.1 ■ Data From Barlett (2015)									
State Hostility Scale Scores									
After Insulting Message					**After Nice Message**				
102	66	85	110	65	35	57	46	38	51
78	93	75	38	103	82	63	59	58	69
103	39	102	74	75	80	85	97	103	78
71	44	103	60	73	87	77	100	45	63
84	71	90	110	65	76	86	57	75	55
60	78	64	117	114	96	65	142	72	102
99	86	67	42	80	37	44	83	72	83
87	49	92	92	101	52	91	55	71	55
90	90	57	55	94	85	70	53		
94	79	99	107	43					
98	102	95	94						
Mean		81.6					70.9		
Median		84.5					71.00		
Sample Variance		425.765					450.158		
Count		54					43		

[1] *Student* is a pseudonym for William S. Gossett (1876–1937), who was employed by the Guinness brewery in Dublin. Gossett developed the statistical test that can be applied to small samples when we do not know the population variance and the estimates of variance are not efficient. Guinness had a policy that obligated Gossett to use a pseudonym when he published his work (Cowles, 2001).

t-test, like the *z*-test, utilizes a standard score transformation of the data, but instead of using the population variances, we use *estimates* of those variances. To use Student's *t*-test correctly, we need to understand the logic and the assumptions that underlie it.

STUDENT'S *t*-TEST

We use Student's t-*test for two-group experiments when we do not know the population variances and have to estimate them from our sample data. Estimating the population variances affects the variance and form of the distribution of* t.

Student's *t*-test is based on three assumptions:

1. The populations from which the samples were obtained are normal distributions.
2. The variances of these populations are identical.[2]
3. The estimates of the parameters come from independent random samples from each population.[3]

As we saw in Chapter 6, to test the hypothesis $\mu_E - \mu_C = 0$ against the alternative $\mu_E - \mu_C \neq 0$, we need to estimate the two population means and compare the values of those estimates. When the hypothesis $\mu_E - \mu_C = 0$ is true, we expect that $\bar{X}_E - \bar{X}_C$ will be close to 0, and when the hypothesis $\mu_E - \mu_C \neq 0$ is true, we expect $\bar{X}_E - \bar{X}_C$ to be far from 0. How far from 0 does $\bar{X}_E - \bar{X}_C$ have to be before we conclude that $\mu_E - \mu_C \neq 0$? To answer that question, we have to perform a standard score transformation on the distribution of $\bar{X}_E - \bar{X}_C$.

By definition,

$$\text{standard score} = \frac{\text{score} - \text{mean}}{\text{standard deviation}} \tag{7.1a}$$

In this situation, the scores are $(\bar{X}_E - \bar{X}_C)$, the mean is $(\mu_E - \mu_C)$, and the standard deviation is $\sigma_{\bar{X}_E - \bar{X}_C}$. However, because we do not know $\sigma_{\bar{X}_E - \bar{X}_C}$ we have to estimate it. When we put est $\sigma_{\bar{X}_E - \bar{X}_C}$ into the standard score transformation, we get this formula:

$$t = \frac{\left(\bar{X}_E - \bar{X}_C\right) - \left(\mu_E - \mu_C\right)}{\text{est } \sigma_{\bar{X}_E - \bar{X}_C}} \tag{7.1b}$$

---

[2]This assumption is called *homogeneity of variance.*

[3]In an independent random sample, each score sampled does not affect the selection of any other score.

The logic of the *t*-test parallels the logic of the *z*-test (and that of all hypothesis testing). We have two hypotheses that are mutually exclusive (if one is true, then the other must be false) and exhaustive (these hypotheses are the only possibilities); therefore, we select one of these hypotheses to test. If our data lead us to reject that hypothesis, we can accept (or at least retain) the other. The two hypotheses we are considering are $\mu_E - \mu_C = 0$ and $\mu_E - \mu_C \neq 0$. Only the first one gives us a value to test, and that hypothesis becomes our null hypothesis. Therefore, by testing $\mu_E - \mu_C = 0$, our test statistic becomes

$$t = \frac{\bar{X}_E - \bar{X}_C}{\text{est } \sigma_{\bar{X}_E - \bar{X}_C}} \tag{7.2}$$

We know that $\sigma_{\bar{X}_E - \bar{X}_C} = \sqrt{\sigma_{\bar{X}_E}^2 + \sigma_{\bar{X}_C}^2}$ and $\sigma_{\bar{X}}^2 = \frac{\sigma_X^2}{n}$. Because we do not know the values of σ_E^2 and σ_C^2, we can estimate them with $\text{est } \sigma_E^2$ and $\text{est } \sigma_C^2$, respectively.[4] Therefore,

$$t = \frac{\bar{X}_E - \bar{X}_C}{\sqrt{\dfrac{\text{est } \sigma_E^2}{n_E} + \dfrac{\text{est } \sigma_C^2}{n_C}}} \tag{7.3}$$

As noted earlier, one of the assumptions of Student's *t*-test is that the two population variances, σ_E^2 and σ_C^2, are equal (homogeneity of variance[5]). If σ_E^2 and σ_C^2 are equal, then $\text{est } \sigma_E^2$ and $\text{est } \sigma_C^2$ must be estimating the same value (which we will call σ^2). Therefore, we can replace $\text{est } \sigma_E^2$ and $\text{est } \sigma_C^2$ with $\text{est } \sigma^2$. Under these circumstances, *t* becomes

$$t = \frac{\bar{X}_E - \bar{X}_C}{\sqrt{\text{est}\sigma^2 \left(\dfrac{1}{n_E} + \dfrac{1}{n_C} \right)}}, \tag{7.4}$$

where $\text{est } \sigma^2$ is an unbiased estimate of the variances of both populations that are assumed to be equal. Because we have two samples that come from populations with the same variance, we can consider the estimates of variance from each sample to be estimates of the same value, and we can combine these two estimates by averaging them. As we saw in

---

[4] $\text{est } \sigma^2 = \displaystyle\sum_{i=1}^{n} (X_i - \bar{X})^2 / (n-1)$

[5] Why this assumption is a reasonable one to make in experimental situations will be discussed later.

Chapter 3, we do so by weighting the sample variances (or the estimates of variance) by their sample sizes, thereby giving us the following formulas, all of which are equivalent (that is, they produce the same answer):

$$\text{est } \sigma^2 = \frac{n_E s_E^2 + n_C s_C^2}{n_E + n_C - 2} \tag{7.5a}$$

$$\text{est } \sigma^2 = \frac{(n_E - 1)\text{est } \sigma_E^2 + (n_C - 1)\text{est } \sigma_C^2}{n_E + n_C - 2} \tag{7.5b}$$

Because $s^2 = \dfrac{\sum\limits_{i=1}^{n}(X_i - \overline{X})^2}{n}$ and $\text{est } \sigma^2 = \dfrac{\sum\limits_{i=1}^{n}(X_i - \overline{X})^2}{n - 1}$, both of these equations reduce

to the following:

$$\text{est } \sigma^2 = \frac{\sum\limits_{i=1}^{n_E}(X_i - \overline{X}_E)^2 + \sum\limits_{i=1}^{n_C}(X_i - \overline{X}_C)^2}{n_E + n_C - 2} \tag{7.5c}$$

All three of these equations produce the same value for est σ^2 (the unbiased estimate of the common population variance obtained from the information in both samples). This result is sometimes called a "pooled estimate of variance" because the information from both samples is pooled to provide the estimate. Clearly the pooled estimate is better than the individual estimates because it is based on more values. The pooled estimate is not only more efficient than the estimates of variance from each sample considered separately, but it is also unbiased; that is, the expected value of all of these three estimates (est σ^2) equals the common population variance σ^2. You should be able to prove that all of these three pooled estimates of variance (7.5a, 7.5b, and 7.5c) are unbiased estimates of σ^2 by using the theorems on expected value at the end of Chapter 3.

Substituting Equation 7.5a (the first of these estimates of variance) into Equation 7.4 gives us a formula for calculating t based on the sample means, sample variances, and sample sizes:

$$t = \frac{\overline{X}_E - \overline{X}_C}{\sqrt{\dfrac{n_E s_E^2 + n_C s_C^2}{n_E + n_C - 2}\dfrac{1}{n_E} + \dfrac{1}{n_C}}} \tag{7.6}$$

BOX 7.1
DEGREES OF FREEDOM

Degrees of freedom is a parameter in a number of distributions, and it can be defined in a number of ways. We will use two definitions here.

Definition 1: How many scores are "free to vary" (that is, be any value) before the rest are fixed (and hence not free to vary)

We can understand this definition by considering the definition of the sample mean:

$$\bar{X} = \frac{\sum_{i=1}^{n} X_i}{n} = \frac{X_1 + X_2 + \cdots + X_{n-1} + X_n}{n}$$

Clearly, there are a great many samples of size *n* that have the same sample mean. We could generate any of them by arbitrarily selecting values for $X_1, X_2, …, X_{n-1}$, but once we have gotten that far, it is clear that X_n is *not* free to vary because $\sum_{i=1}^{n} X_i$ must add up to a certain value. Therefore, when we have *n* values in our sample, the degrees of freedom for that sample are *n* – 1.

Definition 2: How many scores we need to get some "freedom" (or variance) in our sample

Here we consider the definition of the sample variance:

$$s^2 = \frac{\sum_{i=1}^{n}\left(X_i - \bar{X}\right)^2}{n}$$

If we have only one score in our sample, then the mean of our sample is that score, and $\sum_{i=1}^{n}\left(X_i - \bar{X}\right)^2 = 0$. In other words, when *n* = 1, s^2 = 0. However, when *n* = 2, s^2 = 0 only when both scores are the same value. When they are not the same value (which is the more likely situation), s^2 > 0. Therefore because we need to have at least 2 values in our sample to have some variance (freedom), the degrees of freedom for a sample of *n* values is *n* – 1.

In the *t*-test and in any situation in which we have a sample or samples of values from a normal distribution, both definitions apply and lead to the same result. In Chapter 11, we will come across situations in which one definition applies but the other one does not.

When the null hypothesis is true, this test statistic (Equation 7.6) has a *t*-distribution with $\mu_t = 0$ and the value of σ_t^2 depending on a parameter called *degrees of freedom*, where

$$\sigma_t^2 = \frac{df}{df - 2} \tag{7.7}$$

See Box 7.1 for the meaning of *degrees of freedom* in this context.

Degrees of freedom are related to the sample sizes (n_C and n_E), and because sample sizes can vary across different experiments, there is a family of *t*-distributions, all with

FIGURE 7.1 ■ The distribution of *t* for degrees of freedom 2, 5, 10, and 20

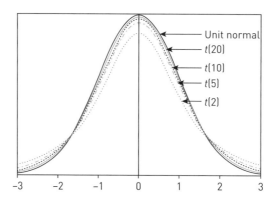

the same mean but different variances. In Figure 7.1, *t*-distributions with 2, 5, 10, and 20 degrees of freedom are compared to a unit normal distribution (*z*, where $\mu_z = 0$, $\sigma_z^2 = 1$). From Figure 7.1, we can see that the distribution of *t* is symmetrical but wider than a normal distribution. As degrees of freedom (sample sizes) increase, the distribution of *t* approaches the unit normal *z*-distribution.

Because the variance of the *t*-distribution is a function of the degrees of freedom, and degrees of freedom is a function of sample size, in order to keep α constant, the critical value for *t* depends on the sample size. As degrees of freedom (sample sizes) increase, the critical value gets smaller and approaches the critical value for a *z*-distribution. We can see this from the *t*-table in Appendix F. Each entry in that table is the critical value for rejecting the null hypothesis for a given level of α (represented in the table's columns: proportion in the tails of the distribution) and a given number of degrees of freedom (represented in the table's rows). To use this table for hypothesis tests, we locate the row with the degrees of freedom for our experiment and the column for our alpha level. *When the value of our test statistic (Equation 7.6) is larger than the critical value in the table for our degrees of freedom and alpha, we reject H_0.*

As we scan down each column in the *t*-table, we see that once we get past the degrees of freedom being equal to 1 or 2, the differences in the critical values of *t* do not change very much as degrees of freedom (samples sizes) increase. Note that the last row is for degrees of freedom = ∞. The critical values on that row are the critical values for a *z*-test. Therefore, as degrees of freedom increase, σ_t^2 approaches 1, and the distribution of *t* approaches the distribution of *z*.

DISTRIBUTION OF THE INDEPENDENT GROUPS *t*-STATISTIC WHEN H_0 IS TRUE

When H_0 is true, Student's t has a symmetrical, but not normal, distribution, with $\mu_t = 0$ and σ_t^2 being a function of the sample sizes. Therefore, the critical value of a t-test is affected by the sample size. As the samples increase in size, the σ_t^2 approaches 1 (σ_z^2), the critical value for t approaches the critical value for z, and the distribution of t approaches the distribution of z.

When the null hypothesis ($\mu_E - \mu_C = 0$) is true, our test statistic is Equation 7.2 (which is equivalent to Equations 7.4 and 7.6). This test statistic has a *t*-distribution that is symmetrical with $\mu_t = 0$ and $\sigma_t^2 = \dfrac{df}{df - 2}$ (see Figure 7.1).

The reason the distribution *t* is symmetrical around $\mu_t = 0$ when H_0 is true is that if we repeated our experiment an infinite number of times, sometimes ($\bar{X}_E - \bar{X}_C$) would be a positive number because $\bar{X}_E$ would be greater than $\bar{X}_C$, and sometimes ($\bar{X}_E - \bar{X}_C$) would be a negative number because $\bar{X}_C$ would be greater than $\bar{X}_E$. The average of these infinite number of differences would be 0.

The reason the variance of *t* is greater than 1 *and* is a function of the sample sizes (degrees of freedom) is that we have to estimate the variances of the populations. The efficiency of those estimates is a function of sample size: The bigger the sample sizes, the more efficient the estimates. When the samples sizes are small, the sample variances can be far from the population variances. If the sample variances *over*estimate the population variances (are *much larger* than the population variances), the effect will be to *reduce* the value of *t* because the denominator of Equations 7.2, 7.4, and 7.6 will be large. This situation is not a problem when H_0 is true because small values of *t* do not lead us to reject H_0. On the other hand, if the sample variances *under*estimate the population variances (are much *smaller* than the population variances), the effect will be to *increase* the value of *t* because the denominator will be small. This situation is a problem because large values of *t* lead us to reject H_0. If we simply used the critical values from the distribution of *z*, we would reject H_0 more often than our stated alpha level.

With larger sample sizes, the estimates of variance become more efficient and are likely to be closer to the population variance. As a result, with larger sample sizes, the values of *t* (calculated with estimates of the population variance) will be closer to the values of *z* (assuming we know the population variance).

FIGURE 7.2 ■ **Flowchart for generating the test statistic for Student's *t*-test.**

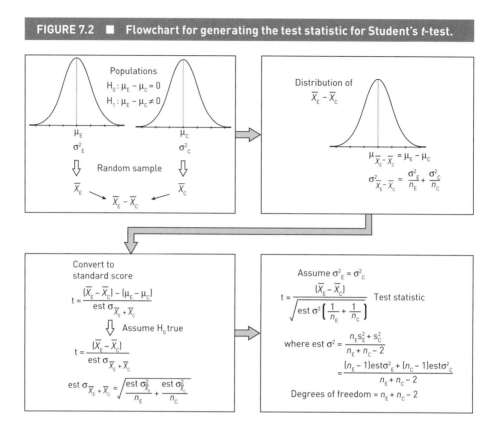

Gossett ("Student") derived the *t*-distribution to take this expected pattern into account. As we can see in Figure 7.1, the distribution of *t* is wider than the distribution of *z*, and as degrees of freedom (sample sizes) increase, the distribution of *t* approaches the distribution of *z*. Therefore, we may adjust the critical value of *t* to keep α equal to .05 (or whatever level we choose). Figure 7.2 shows the process of generating Student's *t*-statistic.

DISTRIBUTION OF THE INDEPENDENT GROUPS *t*-STATISTIC WHEN H$_0$ IS FALSE

The non-central t-distribution (t*) is not symmetrical. The mean and variance of this distribution are determined by the true difference between the population means, the population variances, and the sample sizes.

When H$_0$ is false, the distribution of our test statistic (Equation 7.2) is a **non-central *t*-distribution (*t**)**. The mean of *t** (μ_{t^*}) does not equal zero because of how we derived our test statistic: We started with the standard score transformation in Equation 7.1 and assumed H_0 is true. Therefore, we set $\mu_E - \mu_C = 0$. When H_0 is true, subtracting this constant moves the distribution of our test statistic and centers it around 0 (so that $\mu_t = 0$). But when $\mu_E - \mu_C \neq 0$, subtracting 0 will not center the distribution of our test statistic around 0. In other words, when H_0 is false, $\mu_E - \mu_C \neq 0$, and the numerator of our test statistic will be either a positive or negative number (depending on whether $\mu_E > \mu_C$ or $\mu_E < \mu_C$). If we were to perform our experiment an infinite number of times when H_0 is false, $\mu_{t^*} \neq 0$. The mean of t^* is a function of the degrees of freedom and what is called the noncentrality parameter δ. The noncentrality parameter δ can be obtained by substituting the parameters being estimated (μ_E for $\overline{X}_E$, μ_C for $\overline{X}_C$, and σ^2 for est σ^2) for the sample statistics in Equation 7.4.

$$\delta = \frac{\mu_E - \mu_C}{\sqrt{\sigma^2 \left(\dfrac{1}{n_E} + \dfrac{1}{n_C} \right)}} \tag{7.8a}$$

The exact value of the mean of t^* is calculated as follows:

$$\mu_{t^*} = \delta \sqrt{\frac{df}{2}} \frac{\Gamma\big[(df - 1)/2\big]}{\Gamma(df/2)}, \tag{7.8b}$$

where $\Gamma()$ is the gamma function for the value in the parentheses.[6] μ_{t^*} will always be slightly larger than δ; however, as the degrees of freedom increase, the difference between μ_{t^*} and δ decreases. Therefore, we can use δ as a close approximation of the actual value of μ_{t^*}.

Because we have to estimate the variance of the populations from which our samples are taken, the non-central *t*-distribution is skewed, and the $\sigma_{t^*}^2$ is a complex formula consisting of the degrees of freedom and the noncentrality parameter δ.[7] Thus, it is more difficult to calculate the power of a *t*-test and create power functions as we can do with the *z*-test. A non-central *t*-table is needed to calculate the power of a *t*-test.

---

[6] There are calculators online for calculating gamma functions. These functions can also be calculated in Excel and JMP.

[7] $\sigma_{t^*}^2 = \left[\dfrac{df}{df - 2}(1 + \delta) \right] - \left(\dfrac{df}{2}\delta^2 \right)\left(\dfrac{\Gamma[(df - 1)/2]}{\Gamma(df)/2} \right)$

FACTORS THAT AFFECT THE POWER OF THE INDEPENDENT GROUPS *t*-TEST

Like the two-group z-test, the power of Student's t-test is a function of the critical value and location of the non-central distribution. In both situations, the critical value depends on the level of α chosen and whether a one- or two-tailed test is performed; however, in the case of the t-test, the critical value also depends on the degrees of freedom. In both situations, the location of the non-central distribution depends on the true difference between the population means, the population variances, and the sample sizes. Because the non-central t-distribution is not a normal distribution, we need to use a non-central t-table to create a set of power functions.

Like the independent groups *z*-test, the power of the *t*-test depends on the critical value and the location of the non-central *t*-distribution (which is dependent on the value of μ_{t^*}). However, *unlike* the *z*-distributions (where $\sigma_z^2 = 1$), the variance of the *t*-distribution when H_0 is true depends on the sample sizes ($\sigma_t^2 = \dfrac{df}{df-2}$), which therefore affects the critical value.

Critical Value

The critical value of *t* is determined by three things: what we choose for alpha; whether we have a one-tailed or a two-tailed alternative hypothesis; and the degrees of freedom, which are a function of the sample sizes. As sample sizes increase, $\dfrac{df}{df-2}$ approaches 1, and the critical value of *t* approaches the critical value of *z*. This pattern is evident when we scan down the rows of the table of critical values for the *t*-test (Appendix F). With $df = \infty$, the critical value of a one-tailed *t*-test with α = .05 is 1.645, which equals the value of *z* when 5% of the *z*-distribution is in one tail, and the critical value of a two-tail *t*-test with α = .05 is 1.96, which equals the value of *z* when 2.5% of the *z*-distribution is in each tail of the distribution.

Location of the Non-Central *t*-Distribution

From Equations 7.8a and 7.8b, it is obvious that the power of the independent groups *t*-test is also a function of the true difference ($\mu_E - \mu_C$), the population variances, and the sample sizes:

a. The larger the difference between the population means ($\mu_E - \mu_C$), the greater the power of the test. This is because, all other things being equal, the larger this difference, the larger the value of μ_{t^*}, and more of the non-central *t*-distribution is in the critical region.

b. The smaller the population variances, the greater the power of the test. The denominator of Equation 7.8a is larger when the value of σ^2 (which represents the two equal population variances) is smaller. Therefore, the entire fraction becomes larger (which makes μ_{t^*} larger) and puts more of the non-central *t*-distribution in the critical region.

c. As sample sizes increase, two things happen: First, the critical value will move slightly in the direction of the critical value of *z*, because the variance of the *t*-distribution will decrease slightly. Second, the non-central *t*-distribution shifts more into the critical region. This second factor has the greater effect on power: As sample sizes increase, the denominator of Equation 7.8a decreases. As a result, the entire fraction becomes larger (which makes μ_{t^*} larger) and puts more of the non-central *t*-distribution in the critical region. (For this same reason, the mean of z^* increases as sample size increases.)

Creating a Power Function for the *t*-Test

Because the non-central distribution (t^*) is not a normal distribution, we *cannot* simply use the kind of formula we used for the *z*-tests to find the area of the non-central distribution in the critical region and from that area create a power function. Fortunately, there are tables for the non-central *t*-distribution that allow us to find those areas and create a power function for the *t*-test.

THE ASSUMPTION BEHIND THE HOMOGENEITY OF VARIANCE ASSUMPTION

Homogeneity of variance occurs when the treatment adds a constant to every score in the original population to create a new population. When the treatment is conceptualized as something else (like multiplying every score in the original population), homogeneity of variance will not be the result.

The standard *t*-test as derived by Student is based on the assumption that the data being analyzed are independent random samples from two normal distributions that have the same variances. In the context of an experiment, this assumption means that originally there were two identical populations of scores. These two populations had the parameters (means, variances, and forms) of the control condition in the experiment. One of these populations was then modified by giving every individual in that population the experimental treatment, making it the experimental population. If we assume that *the treatment affected every individual in the same way, then a constant was added to (or subtracted from) each individual's score to create the experimental population*. This effect is called **additivity**, and it is the assumption behind the assumption of homogeneity of variance.

From what we know about the properties of distributions (Chapter 3), adding a constant to every score in a distribution moves that distribution to a new location. The new mean is the original mean plus the constant, the new variance is the same as the original variance, and the form of the distribution does not change. In other words, *additivity of treatment effects produces homogeneity of variance.*

But suppose the effects of the treatment result in multiplying each individual's score by a constant? Again, from what we know about the properties of distributions, multiplying each score in a distribution by a constant also moves that distribution to a new location. Although the form of the distribution does not change, the new mean is the original mean multiplied by the constant, and the new variance is the original variance multiplied by the constant squared. Therefore, *homogeneity of variance will not occur when the treatment effect is multiplicative.*

When the treatment effect is additive, each individual responds in the same way to the treatment. When the treatment effect is multiplicative, *how an individual responds to the treatment depends on his or her original score*, which is referred to as a **participant-by-treatment interaction**. Such interactions complicate hypothesis testing with a *t*-test. On the one hand, if the effects of the experimental treatment increase the population variance (the standard effect of multiplying by a constant), then the power of the *t*-test will be reduced because the pooled estimate of variance will be too large, which in turn will make the denominator too large and the calculated value of the *t*-statistic too small. On the other hand, there could be floor or ceiling effects. There is a floor effect when scores cannot be reduced below a certain level. As a result, individuals with higher initial scores reduce their performance further than those with lower scores. Similarly, there is a ceiling effect when scores cannot be increased above a certain level. Here, those with higher original scores cannot perform much higher, but those with lower scores can raise their performance quite a bit. In both of these situations, the experimental condition will have a much smaller variance. In this case, the pooled estimate of variance will decrease, which in turn will make the denominator too small and the calculated value of the *t*-statistic larger. Although it appears that the power of our test would increase, it also increases the probability that we will make an α error. We can spot such possible problems by looking at our data.

GRAPHICAL METHODS FOR COMPARING TWO GROUPS

In addition to using side-by-side box plots and back-to-back stem-and-leaf displays, we can use empirical quantile–quantile plots to tell us whether the experimental treatment is additive or multiplicative, and we can use means diamonds to provide a graphical way to determine whether the observed difference should lead us to reject the null hypothesis.

There are a number of graphical methods for exploring our data in the two independent groups situation. In all cases, the purpose is to compare the two sets of data to see whether they are similar. One method is to construct **side-by-side box plots** for both groups (see Figure 2.5). As noted in Chapter 2, these plots give us a picture that reveals differences in location and dispersion as well as the presence of outliers. Another approach is to compare the stem-and-leaf displays for both groups by presenting them as **back-to-back stem-and-leaf displays**. Because stem-and-leaf displays include every value in the data set, we get a more detailed picture of how the two groups compare when the data are presented in this way. A back-to-back stem-and-leaf display for the data in Table 7.1 is presented in Figure 7.3. As is the case in Figure 2.5, the back-to-back stem-and-leaf display shows us how the data from the After Insulting Message group compare with the data from the After Nice Message group, but we get more information here.

A third technique that provides a different look at the data is an **empirical quantile–quantile plot**. An empirical quantile–quantile plot can be created by *plotting the quantiles from two sets of data against each other*. In other words, rank order the scores, and when there is an equal number of scores in both sets, plot each successive value in one set against the corresponding ranked value in the other set.[8] When both sets of data are similar, the resulting quantile–quantile plot will straddle a line drawn from the origin

FIGURE 7.3 ■ Back-to-back stem-and-leaf display for the data in Table 7.1 from Barlett (2015).

Insulting		Nice
	Unit = 1	
	1 2 = 12	
	1	
	2	
98	3	578
9432	4	456
75	5	1235557789
7655400	6	3359
988554311	7	01225678
76540	8	02335567
99855444322000	9	167
73332221	10	023
7400	11	
		HI = 142

---

[8] When the sample sizes are not equal, we have to approximate the quantiles for one of the sets.

with a slope of 1 (Figure 7.4, *top left*). Deviations from that standard line represent the effect of the treatment and/or the presence of outliers in our data. An additive treatment effect is indicated when our data are parallel to this line but displaced either above or below it. When our data are above the line, the vertical displacement from the line is the size of the treatment effect (Figure 7.4, *top right*). When our data are below the line, the horizontal displacement from the line is the size of the treatment effect. A multiplicative treatment effect is indicated when our data are on a straight line that is not parallel to this line (Figure 7.4, *bottom*), meaning that one set of data has a smaller variance than the other. The procedure for constructing empirical quantile–quantile plots is described in Box 7.2.

An empirical quantile–quantile plot for the data in Table 7.1 is presented in Figure 7.5. Except for the outlier, most of the data points are at or above the diagonal line. From this plot, it appears that the insulting message raised the State Hostility score for the participants in that group relative to those who received the nice message. This effect appears to be an additive effect. We need to calculate Student's *t* to decide whether there is a statistically significant difference.

Although empirical quantile–quantile plots are superior to histograms, side-by-side box plots, and back-to-back stem-and-leaf displays, none of these displays provides a graphical way to determine whether the groups are statistically significantly different from each other. That deficit can be overcome with **means diamonds**.

Means diamonds indicate the location of the sample mean and the endpoints of the 95% confidence interval for each group. In addition, means diamonds include overlap marks that indicate whether two groups with equal sample sizes are statistically significantly different at $p < .05$ based on Student's *t*-test. These overlap marks are $\frac{\sqrt{2}}{2} \times \frac{CI}{2}$ above and below the group mean for each group. When these overlap marks overlap, the difference between groups is not statistically significant at $p < .05$. When they do not overlap, the difference between groups is statistically significant.

The confidence interval and overlap points for the data in Table 7.1 are presented in Table 7.2.

Although the two 95% confidence intervals overlap, the overlap marks do not because the lower overlap mark for the After Insulting Message group is higher than the upper overlap mark for the After Nice Message group. This example is presented graphically in Figure 7.6.

Therefore, the difference between the groups in Figure 7.6 is statistically significant. This result is confirmed by calculating Student's *t*-test for these data. The value of Student's *t* for the data in Figures 7.4 and 7.5 is –2.46, $df = 95$, $p = .0156$ (two-tail test). As noted in Chapter 4, confidence intervals can overlap, yet the difference be statistically significant. It is the overlap marks that determine statistical significance, not the endpoints of the confidence intervals.

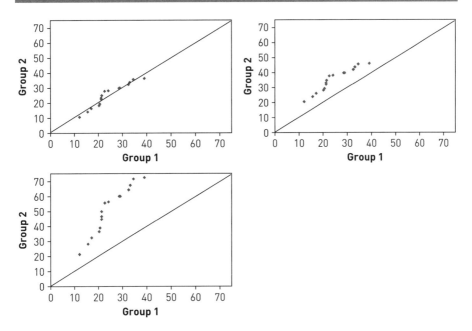

FIGURE 7.4 ■ Empirical quantile–quantile plots for three situations: (*top left*) Group 1 and Group 2 are two samples from the same population; (*top right*) an *additive effect* is created by adding 10 to each value in Group 1; (*bottom*) a *multiplicative effect* is created by multiplying each value by 2 in Group 1.

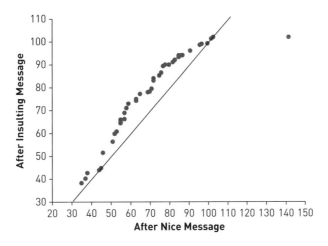

FIGURE 7.5 ■ Empirical quantile–quantile plot for the data in Table 7.1 from Barlett (2015).

BOX 7.2
HOW TO CONSTRUCT AN EMPIRICAL QUANTILE–QUANTILE PLOT

Purpose

To provide a graphical comparison of two sets of data

Procedure

1. Rank order the data in both sets.

2. If the sample sizes are the same, plot the ordered values from each set of observations against each other.

3. If the sample sizes are not equal, convert to quantiles and plot the corresponding quantiles against each other. Starting with the smaller group, try to match the scores with the same or similar quantiles. We will have to use interpolation to match the quantiles. The maximum number of points will be the smaller sample size. (See Chambers, Cleveland, Kleiner, and Tukey (1983) for more on this procedure.)

4. Draw a line with a standardized slope of 1. This line represents completely overlapping distributions.

5. Compare our data to the line from step 4.

   a. If our data overlap this line, then the two sets are similar.

   b. If our data are parallel to this line but displaced either above or below it, then the treatment effect is additive. When our data are above the line, the vertical displacement from the line is the size of the treatment effect. When our data are below the line, the horizontal displacement from the line is the size of the treatment effect.

   c. If our data are on a straight line that is not parallel to this line, then the treatment effect is multiplicative. In this circumstance, one set has a smaller variance than the other.

   d. We can easily detect outliers as values that deviate from the straight line for our data.

TABLE 7.2 ■ Confidence Interval and Overlap Points for the Data in Table 7.1		
	After Insulting Message	**After Nice Message**
Mean	81.56	70.93
Upper 95% CI	87.24	77.54
Lower 95% CI	75.87	64.32
Upper overlap mark	85.58	75.60
Lower overlap mark	77.54	66.26

FIGURE 7.6 ■ Means diamonds for comparing the data in Table 7.1 from Barlett (2015).

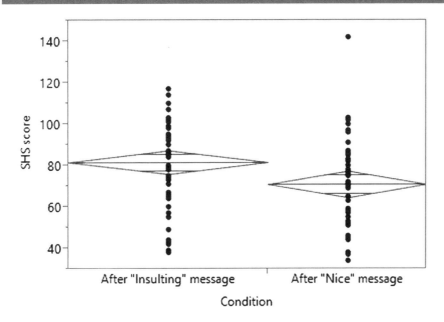

BOX 7.3

HOW TO CREATE MEANS DIAMONDS

Purpose

To provide a graphical comparison of groups that includes a way to determine whether the groups are statistically significantly different from each other

Procedure

1. Calculate the mean and the limits of the 95% confidence interval for each group using Equation 4.14a or 4.14b in Chapter 4.

2. Calculate the overlap marks at $\dfrac{\sqrt{2}}{2} \times \dfrac{CI}{2}$ above and below the group mean for each group (where CI is the length of the confidence interval).

3. Either superimpose the confidence intervals (drawn as a diamond) and overlap marks onto the graph of the data points of each group or simply draw them for each group.

SUPPOSE THE POPULATION VARIANCES ARE NOT EQUAL?

When we have reason to believe that the population variances are not equal, the Welch–Satterthwaite approximation is preferred to Student's t-test.

As noted above, the derivation of the formula for the independent groups *t*-test (Equations 7.4 and 7.6) is based on the assumption that the population variances are equal (that is, there is homogeneity of variance). When homogeneity of variance is assumed, the common population variance is estimated by averaging the estimates of variance from both samples (see Equations 7.5a–7.5c). Averaging estimates of variance from different samples to create a pooled estimate of variance makes sense for estimates of the same value because pooling produces a more efficient estimate based on more numbers. But suppose $\sigma_E^2 \neq \sigma_C^2$. That outcome can happen, and when it does, Equations 7.4 and 7.6 are not appropriate for testing the hypothesis that the population means are equal.

A simple solution would appear to be to use the value produced by Equation 7.3 as our test statistic, but the value produced by Equation 7.3 does not have a *t*-distribution. A number of solutions to this problem have been proposed, none of which is universally accepted. The most popular of these was proposed independently by Satterthwaite (1946) and Welch (1947), and the resulting procedure is commonly referred to as the Welch–Satterthwaite approximation. The test statistic is

$$t_{\text{W-S}} = \frac{\bar{X}_E - \bar{X}_C}{\sqrt{\dfrac{\text{est } \sigma_E^2}{n_E} + \dfrac{\text{est } \sigma_C^2}{n_C}}} \tag{7.9}$$

Satterthwaite showed that the distribution of this test statistic approximates a *t*-distribution with

$$df = \frac{\left(\text{est } \sigma_{\bar{X}_E}^2 + \text{est } \sigma_{\bar{X}_C}^2\right)^2}{\sqrt{\dfrac{\left(\text{est } \sigma_{\bar{X}_E}^2\right)^2}{n_E - 1} + \dfrac{\left(\text{est } \sigma_{\bar{X}_C}^2\right)^2}{n_C - 1}}}, \tag{7.10}$$

where

$$\text{est } \sigma_{\bar{X}_E}^2 = \frac{\text{est } \sigma_E^2}{n_E} \quad \text{and} \quad \text{est } \sigma_{\bar{X}_C}^2 = \frac{\text{est } \sigma_C^2}{n_C}$$

To find the critical value of $t_{w\text{-}s}$, round the approximate *df* in Equation 7.10 to the nearest whole number before consulting the *t*-table.

It is clear from Equation 7.10 that the approximate degrees of freedom for the Welch–Satterthwaite approximation is a function of both the difference between the estimates of the population variances and the difference between the sample sizes. When both are similar, the approximate degrees of freedom will be slightly lower (never higher) than the degrees of freedom for Student's *t*. The greater the differences between the estimates of the population variances and the sample sizes, the greater the difference between the degrees of freedom for the two tests.

When applied to the data in Table 7.1, the Welch–Shatterthwaite approximation $t = -2.45$, $df = 88.95$, $p < .0161$. For these data, the value of the Welch–Satterthwaite approximation *t* is very close to the value of Student's *t* (–2.462 vs. –2.454). These two values are not that far apart because the sample sizes and the estimates of the population variances for the two groups are very similar (433.79 vs. 460.876). Although the degrees of freedom for the Welch–Satterthwaite approximation *t* are lower than the degrees of freedom for Student's *t* (95 vs. 88.95), they are similar because the estimates of variance and the sample sizes are similar.

Consider the following situation in which the sample sizes and estimates of the population variances are quite different: Barlett and Gentile (2012) surveyed 493 students enrolled in psychology classes at a large Midwestern university. Of the students, 224 were men. The majority of those men were Caucasian (83.7%), and their average age was 19.5 years. Among the questions asked was a yes-or-no question about whether they had cyberbullied others in the past year. They also completed an Anonymity subscale consisting of five items scored on a 1–5 scale; examples of items include "Sending mean e-mails or text messages is easy to do because I am not face-to-face with the other person," and "I feel comfortable sending mean text messages or e-mails to anybody no matter if I know them or not." The summary data for these two variables are presented in Table 7.3.

For these data, Student's $t = 1.961$, $df = 222$, $p = .0511$. Using $p < .05$ as the criterion for rejecting the null hypothesis (that the mean Anonymity subscale scores are equal for men who did and did not cyberbully others), we would not reject it.[9] However, when the same data are analyzed with the Welch–Satterthwaite approximation, $t = 2.264$, $df = 24.608$, $p = .0326$. Although the degrees of freedom value for the Welch–Satterthwaite approximation is much less than for Student's *t*-test, the increase in the value of $t_{w\text{-}s}$ allows

[9] As we noted in Chapter 6, Fisher's proposal that we use $p < .05$ to define our critical region for rejecting a null hypothesis has become the standard practice. Strict adherence to that standard requires us to not reject the null hypothesis here. However, we should acknowledge that the choice of $p < .05$ is arbitrary, and a less stringent standard could easily be justified.

TABLE 7.3 ■ Data on the Effects of Anonymity on Whether Men Cyberbullied Others (from Barlett and Gentile, 2012)		
Cyberbullied Others	Number Answering	Score on Anonymity Subscale
Yes	20	Mean = 12.70; est σ^2 = 9.17
No	204	Mean = 11.06; est σ^2 = 13.01

us to reject the null hypothesis and conclude that men's attitudes about the anonymity are related to their tendencies to engage in cyberbullying.

Which *t*-Test Statistic Should We Use?

When the sample variances (or the individual estimates of variance) are close to each other, Student's *t*-test and the Welch–Satterthwaite approximation produce similar results when the sample sizes are similar. But when the sample variances (or the individual estimates of variance) are very different, the degrees of freedom computed with Equation 7.10 for the Welch–Satterthwaite approximation can be much smaller. Although this equation results in a more extreme critical value, the test statistic is frequently larger, resulting in a more powerful test with better control for the probability of making an alpha error.

Unfortunately, there is no simple way to decide based on our sample variances (or estimates of variance) whether they are so far apart that the Welch–Satterthwaite should be used in place of Student's *t*-test. Furthermore, neither test statistic works well when both the sample variances and the sample sizes are very different from each other; this is especially true when the smaller sample has the larger variance. Therefore, the Welch–Satterthwaite approximation is highly recommended when the sample variances seem very far apart and the sample sizes are similar. A bit of good news is that both test statistics perform better under all conditions with larger sample sizes.

STANDARDIZED GROUP DIFFERENCES AS ESTIMATORS OF EFFECT SIZE

As we saw in Chapter 6, the p*-value cannot provide us with a measure of the effect size in an experiment because the* p*-value is a function of sample size. We can overcome that problem by estimating the standardized group difference from our data. This index allows us to compare the results of different experiments with different sample sizes. Three different standardized estimates of effect size are described.*

In our discussion of power in Chapter 6, we defined the effect size for a two-condition experiment in terms of the standardized difference between the population means:

$$\delta = \frac{\mu_E - \mu_C}{\sigma}, \tag{7.11}$$

Defining effect size in this manner allows us to create power functions that can be used across different two-group experiments. After the data are collected, we can substitute sample statistics to estimate the effect size in our experiment. Three slightly different sample statistics have been proposed to estimate effect size as defined in Equation 7.12: Cohen's *d*, Hedges' *g*, and Glass's Δ. The basic form of all of these estimates of effect size is as follows:

$$\frac{\overline{X}_E - \overline{X}_C}{\text{est } \sigma} \tag{7.12}$$

where est σ is an estimate of the population variance.

Cohen (1962, 1969) proposed the following formula for the standardized group difference estimator of effect size:

$$d = \frac{\overline{X}_E - \overline{X}_C}{\sqrt{\dfrac{s_E^2 + s_C^2}{2}}} \tag{7.13}$$

Hedges (1982) proposed the following formula for that same estimate:

$$g = \frac{\overline{X}_E - \overline{X}_C}{\sqrt{\dfrac{n_E s_E^2 + n_C s_C^2}{n_E + n_C - 2}}} \tag{7.14}$$

Hedges (1982) demonstrated that both Cohen's *d* and Hedges' *g* are biased estimators of the population effect size δ (in the direction of overestimating the population effect size).

The bias can be reduced, but not eliminated, by multiplying *d* by $\left(\dfrac{N-3}{N-2.25} \right)\left(\sqrt{\dfrac{N-2}{N}} \right)$

and *g* by $\dfrac{N-3}{N-2.25}$. In both cases, $N = n_E + n_C$, and in both cases, the bias decreases as

sample sizes increase.

Both Cohen's *d* and Hedges' *g* can be easily transformed to the other measure:

$$d = g\sqrt{\frac{n_E + n_C}{n_E + n_C - 2}} \text{ , and } g = d\sqrt{\frac{n_E + n_C - 2}{n_E + n_C}}$$

Furthermore, it is easy to calculate d and g directly from t and vice versa:

$$d = t \frac{n_E + n_C}{\sqrt{(n_E + n_C - 2)(n_E n_C)}} \text{, and } t = d \frac{\sqrt{(n_E + n_C - 2)(n_E n_C)}}{n_E + n_C}$$

Likewise,

$$g = t \sqrt{\frac{n_E + n_C}{n_E n_C}} \text{, and } t = g \sqrt{\frac{n_E n_C}{n_E + n_C}}$$

A potential problem with using Cohen's d and Hedges' g is that both are based on the assumption of homogeneity of variance. However, when the treatment has a multiplicative effect, that assumption is violated, and the bias goes in the opposite direction (by underestimating the treatment effect). To overcome that problem, Glass (1977) proposed the following measure for estimating effect size:

$$\Delta = \frac{\bar{X}_E - \bar{X}_C}{s_C}, \tag{7.15}$$

where s_C is the standard deviation of the control group. Unfortunately, there is no way to directly calculate t from Δ and vice versa.

Which One Should We Use?

With respect to Cohen's d and Hedges' g, it does not matter which one we use as long as *we clearly specify which one we are using* and we believe that the homogeneity of variance assumption of Student's t-test is not violated. Both indexes are biased estimates of the population effect size. With small sample sizes, Hedges' g has less bias because it uses the unbiased estimate of the common population variance. However, both the bias and the difference between these two estimates decrease as sample sizes increase. Furthermore, one can easily transform Cohen's d to Hedges' g and vice versa. On the other hand, Glass's Δ is preferred when we have reason to believe that the experimental treatment affects not only the population mean of the experimental condition but also the population variance for that condition.

Although these indexes are commonly used measures of effect sizes for Student's t, they are not the only ones that have been created. Another class of effect size estimators based on correlations will be presented in Chapter 13, along with a discussion of the proper use of all of these measures.

Confidence Intervals for Effect Size Estimates

Measures such as *d*, *g*, and Δ are point estimates of the effect size for the population. Therefore, in addition to calculating the estimate of effect size, we should also provide a confidence interval to give us an idea of the accuracy of our point estimate. There are two approaches to finding confidence intervals for *d*. One approach makes use of the non-central *t*-distribution. Unfortunately, it is not easy to calculate the limits of the confidence interval this way. The alternative is to use the percentile bootstrap to find the confidence interval (see Chapter 5).

ROBUST HYPOTHESIS TESTING

> *The power of both Student's* t-test *and the Welch–Satterthwaite approximation can be greatly compromised when the original populations are not normally distributed and/or there are outliers in our data. Yuen's* t-test *provides a robust alternative with more power when the assumptions of those other tests are not met.*

We saw in Chapter 5 that the occurrence of outliers in our data affects both the estimates of the population means and the estimates of the population variances. Outliers also affect the power of both Student's *t*-test and the Welch–Satterthwaite approximation. This effect occurs because the numerator of both Student's *t*-test and the Welch–Satterthwaite approximation is the difference between the two group means (which are estimates of the means of the populations from which the samples were obtained), and the denominator of both tests is an estimate of the standard deviation of the difference between the population means based on estimates of the population variance from *within* each group.

The problem occurs primarily because the within-groups estimates of the population variance are extremely sensitive to the presence of outliers. One way to think about outliers is to imagine that *the population from which we are sampling is a mixture of two sources of data, both of which could be normal distributions with different variances*. This situation is called a **contaminated normal distribution**. Although most of the scores in that population come from a normal distribution with a small variance, it does not take too many scores from the normal distribution with the larger variance to produce outliers relative to the other normal distribution. Tukey (1960) reported that the estimate of the population variance of a contaminated normal distribution like that just described is severely inflated when only 0.18 percent of the scores are sampled from the wider normal distribution [$\mu = 0$, $\sigma^2 = 10$] and 99.82 percent are from a unit normal [$\mu = 0$, $\sigma^2 = 1$] (see also Hampel, 1973). Because this inflated estimate is in the denominator of Student's t and the Welch–Satterthwaite approximations, calculated values of t are smaller than when the estimates of variance are based on sampling from regular normal distributions, thereby compromising the power of both t-tests.

This situation can be illustrated by considering the two distributions in Figure 7.7. They both look like normal distributions, but only one actually is. The other distribution was created by mixing scores from two normal distributions that have the same mean but different variances. The contaminated normal distribution was created by combining a unit normal distribution ($\mu = 0$; $\sigma = 1$) with a normal distribution in which $\mu = 0$ but $\sigma = 10$ in the following proportions: 0.9 from the unit normal ($\mu = 0$, $\sigma = 1$) and 0.1 from the wider normal distribution ($\mu = 0$, $\sigma = 10$). Both curve types (the unit normal and the contaminated normal) are symmetrical bell curves that appear to be almost identical. But visual comparisons are deceiving. The additional variance contained in the contaminated normal distribution creates the heavy tails; that is, the scores are more widely distributed than those in a normal distribution. In other words, the contaminated normal distribution may look like a normal distribution, but it is not a normal distribution. Furthermore, samples from the contaminated normal distribution are more likely to contain outliers. As noted above, the presence of outliers in data reduces the power of the test.

The consequences of the effects of outliers in our data on the power of Student's t-test is illustrated in Table 7.4, which reports the results of computer simulations of sampling from normal and contaminated normal distributions. Pairs of normal distributions and pairs of

FIGURE 7.7 ■ Probability density functions for a unit normal distribution [$N(0, 1)$] (solid curve) and a contaminated normal distribution (dashed curve). The contaminated normal distribution is $0.9\ N(0, 1) + 0.1\ N(0,10)$.

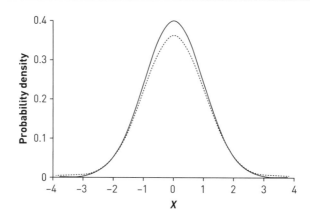

TABLE 7.4 ■ Power of Student's *t*-Test When Sampling From Normal and Contaminated Normal Distributions				
Sample Size	Population	Effect Size		
		0.5	1.0	1.5
10	normal	.190	.546	.891
10	contaminated normal	.040	.184	.329
20	normal	.347	.863	.995
20	contaminated normal	.097	.247	.390
30	normal	.477	.967	.999
30	contaminated normal	.081	.268	.468

approximately normal distributions were created, and 1,000 random samples of various sizes and of various effect sizes were taken from each pair. Student's *t*-test was calculated for each of these 1,000 pairs of samples, and the power of the test was estimated by counting how many of these 1,000 tests led to the correct rejection of the null hypothesis. Effect sizes were scaled in terms of the distance between the population means in standard deviation units. There were three effect sizes (differences between the population means of 0.5, 1.0, and 1.5 standard deviations based on the unit normal distribution) and three sample sizes (*n* = 10, *n* = 20, and *n* = 30). These combinations produced 18 separate distributions of *t*-test results based on the two types of distributions (normal or contaminated normal distributions) from which the samples were taken, the three effect sizes, and the three sample sizes.

The power of Student's *t*-test is lower when sampling from the contaminated normal distribution in Figure 7.7 under all combinations of effect and sample sizes used here (see Table 7.4). The effect is most dramatic with larger effect sizes and larger sample sizes. For example, when we are sampling from normal distributions with 30 participants per sample, the power of the *t*-test to detect a mean difference of 1.0 standard deviation is .967. However, when we sample from contaminated normal distributions and use the same parameters as were used when sampling from the normal distribution, the power drops to .268.

A Robust Alternative to the *t*-Test

Yuen (1974) described a procedure for analyzing data that contain outliers and suffer from other consequences of sampling from non-normal distributions. With Yuen's procedure, the *t*-test statistic is modified by using trimmed means in the numerator and Winsorized estimates of variance in the denominator. The resulting test statistic has a *t*-distribution with degrees of freedom adjusted to reflect the amount of trimming and the Winsorized

Sample Size	Population	Test Statistic	Effect Size		
			0.5	1.0	1.5
10	normal	Student's *t*	.190	.546	.891
		Yuen's *t*	.137	.415	.784
10	contaminated normal	Student's *t*	.040	.184	.329
		Yuen's *t*	.127	.353	.666
20	normal	Student's *t*	.347	.863	.995
		Yuen's *t*	.273	.793	.986
20	contaminated normal	Student's *t*	.097	.247	.390
		Yuen's *t*	.244	.706	.956
30	normal	Student's *t*	.477	.967	.999
		Yuen's *t*	.429	.933	.999
30	contaminated normal	Student's *t*	.081	.268	.468
		Yuen's *t*	.333	.854	.997

TABLE 7.5 ■ Comparing the Power of Student's *t*-Test and Yuen's *t*-Test When Sampling From Normal and Contaminated Normal Distributions

estimates of variance. The procedure for calculating Yuen's *t*-statistic and the appropriate degrees of freedom are presented in Box 7.4.

The value of using Yuen's *t*-test statistic with contaminated distributions is illustrated in Table 7.5, where her procedure was applied to the 18 combinations of populations (normal and contaminated normal), sample sizes (10, 20, and 30 cases per sample), and effect sizes (0.5, 1.0, and 1.5 standard deviations) using a 20% trim from each tail. As noted above, a Student's *t*-test to detect an effect size of 1.0 standard deviation with 30 cases per sample collected from contaminated normal distributions has a power of only .268. However, when Yuen's *t*-test is applied to the same data, the power jumps from .268 to .854. A similar increase in power occurs for all other combinations of effect sizes and sample sizes. Furthermore, Yuen (1974) found that the probability of making a type I error with her test statistic is closer to the stated α-level when sampling from a wide variety of non-normal distributions than it is with a standard *t*-test. However, as Table 7.5 also shows, Student's *t*-test is always more powerful than Yuen's *t*-test when the underlying populations are normal distributions.

TABLE 7.6 ■ Student's *t* and Yuen's *t* for the Data in Table 7.1					
	Nice Message	**Insulting Message**		**Nice Message**	**Insulting Message**
Means	70.93	81.56	Trim means	69.78	83.71
Variances	450.16	425.77	Winsorized var.	139.21	218.58
Degrees of freedom	95		Degrees of freedom	60.07	
Student's *t*	2.46		Yuen's *t*	3.02	
	p < .0157			*p* < .0037	

For the data in Table 7.1, the relevant statistics for Student's *t* and Yuen's *t* are presented in Table 7.6. The trimmed means are farther apart than the sample means, and the Winsorized variances are smaller than the sample variances. While the degrees of freedom are reduced, the value of Yuen's *t* is larger than Student's *t*, and the *p*-value for Yuen's *t* is $p < .0037$ for a two-tailed test. This outcome occurs because the heavy tails on both sides of the data have been eliminated.

Which *t*-Test Statistic Should We Use? (Reprise)

When all three assumptions of Student's *t*-test are met (that is, by independent random sampling from normal distributions with equal population variances), Student's *t*-test will always be more powerful than Yuen's *t*-test. When the sample variances (or the individual estimates of variance) are close to each other, Student's *t*-test and the Welch–Satterthwaite approximation produce similar results when the sample sizes are similar. But when the sample variances (or the individual estimates of variance) are very different, the Welch–Satterthwaite approximation can be more powerful than Student's *t*-test, with better control for the probability of making a type I error. As noted above, neither Student's *t*-test nor the Welch–Satterthwaite approximation works well when both the sample variances and the sample sizes are very different from each other, especially when the smaller sample has the larger variance; however, both test statistics perform better under all conditions with larger sample sizes.

On the other hand, when the data contain outliers or come from heavy tail distributions, both of which produce inflated sample variances, Yuen's *t*-test will always be more powerful than both Student's *t*-test and the Welch–Satterthwaite approximation. These examples illustrate why it is so important to look at our data before analyzing it. In Chapter 9 we will look at another robust technique for analyzing these same data.

BOX 7.4
HOW TO COMPUTE YUEN'S *t*-TEST

Purpose

To provide a hypothesis test for the difference between population means when there are outliers and other problems with the data (due to sampling from non-normal distributions).

Procedure

1. Calculate the trimmed mean for each group by rank ordering the scores and trimming a certain proportion of the scores from each side of each sample. We denote the number of scores we trim as g where $g = [\alpha \times n]$. The [number in brackets] stands for the integer value of that number. This calculation gives us the number of values on each end of our ranked set of scores that will get a weight of zero. The trimmed mean is the sum of the middle $(n - 2g)$ scores divided by $(n - 2g)$. It is customary to substitute the symbol h for $(n - 2g)$. The symbol for a trimmed mean is $\bar{X}_{jt}$, where j designates the group and t stands for *trimmed*.

2. Calculate the Winsorized mean for each group: Winsorizing is another method for reducing the effects of outliers and heavy tails in our data. To Winsorize a set of scores, rank order them and replace the lowest g scores with the score in the $(g + 1)$ position. Do the same on the other side of the sample, replacing the highest g scores with the score in the $(n - g)$ position. The result is a set of n scores where the highest and the lowest $(g + 1)$ scores are the same. The Winsorized mean is the sum of these n scores divided by n.

3. For each group, calculate the sum of the squared deviations of each score in the Winsorized set from the Winsorized mean and divide these sums of squared deviations, SSD_w, by $h(h - 1)$, producing a quantity called c_j.

4. Calculate Yuen's *t*-test statistic: The formula for Yuen's *t*-test involves substituting trimmed means $(\bar{X}_{jt})$ and c for each group into the following formula:

$$t_y = \frac{\bar{X}_{1t} - \bar{X}_{2t}}{\sqrt{c_1 + c_2}}$$

5. Calculate the degrees of freedom for Yuen's *t*-test:

$$\text{degrees of freedom} = \frac{\left(c_1 + c_2\right)^2}{\left(c_1^2 / h_1\right) + \left(c_2^2 / h_2\right)}$$

RESISTANT ESTIMATES OF EFFECT SIZE

The commonly used standardized estimates of effect size are based on sample means and sample variances that are not resistant to the effect of outliers. However, we can use trimmed means and Winsorized variances in our estimates of effect size when outliers are detected in our data.

Because all measures of standardized effect sizes are the ratio of the difference between the sample means divided by an estimate of the population variance (see Equation 7.12), these estimates of the population effect size are not resistant to the presence of outliers in our data (Algina, Keselman, & Penfield, 2005). As noted in Chapter 5, the sample variance and the unbiased estimate of the population variance are both seriously affected by outliers in our data. The result is that these sample statistics are inflated by outliers. When they are in the denominator of t, d, or g, the resulting fraction is reduced, lowering the power of both Student's t and the Welch–Satterthwaite t and underestimating the estimate of the population effect size. To get around this problem in t-tests, Yuen (1974) proposed a t-test using trimmed means and Winsorized variances (see above).

Algina et al. (2005) proposed the following alternative to Cohen's d using 20% trimmed means and 20% Winsorized variances:

$$d_R = .642 \left(\frac{\overline{X}_{t2} - \overline{X}_{t1}}{S_W} \right) \qquad (7.16)$$

where $S_W^2 = \dfrac{\sqrt{(n_1 - 1)S_{W1}^2 + (n_2 - 1)S_{W2}^2}}{n_1 + n_2 - 2}$. The constant 0.642 is in the formula for d_R

so that d_R also estimates the population effect size when the data are sampled from normal distributions (as opposed to contaminated normal distributions that introduce outliers into our sample data).[10] When the normal distribution assumptions for the t-test are met, d and d_R are estimating the same effect size parameter for the populations. For that reason, Algina et al. (2005) advocated using their measure and the percentile bootstrap for the confidence interval.

Summary

We use a t-test for a two-group experiment when we do not know the population variances, as is usually the case. Student's t is based on the assumptions that our data were sampled from normal distributions with equal variances (homogeneity of variance). We use the Welch–Satterthwaite approximation when we have reason to believe that the population variances are not equal. Both of these t-tests lose power when there are outliers in our data. Yuen's t provides a robust alternative when our samples come from non-normal distributions or contain outliers. The degrees of freedom for the Welch–Satterthwaite approximation and Yuen's t are adjusted downward so that those test statistics have approximate t-distributions. These latter two test statistics provide us with additional ways to compare the means from two groups in our research studies when the assumptions of Student's t-test are not met. Most journals require that we, in addition to reporting the values of the t-tests and the resulting p-values for our data, include an estimate of the effect sizes. Some standardized effect size estimators are described here. Another class of effect size estimators will be described in Chapter 13 along with a discussion of their proper use.

---

[10] This approach is similar to dividing the MAD (median of the absolute deviations from the median; see Chapter 5) to get an unbiased estimate of the population variance when sampling from a normal distribution.

Conceptual Exercises

1. Why does *not* treating every subject in a given condition in an experiment the same reduce the power of statistical hypothesis tests about population means?

2. What is it about the way Student's *t*-test is calculated that makes it not robust when there are outliers in your data? How does Yuen's *t*-test get around this problem?

3. Why does the variance of the *t*-distribution depend on the degrees of freedom (that is, the sample size[s])?

4. Do women discriminate against other women? To answer this question, female English majors were randomly assigned to one of two groups. The 13 women in one group read an essay presented as being written by "John McKay" and then rated the essay for quality of writing style on a scale from 1 to 10, with higher scores indicating greater perceived quality. The other group ($n = 15$) read and rated the same essay but were lead to believe it was written by "Joan McKay."

   a. What are the experimental and statistical hypotheses here? (Write the statistical hypotheses in symbols and in words. Use the information in the problem for both your experimental and statistical hypotheses. Do not state the general case.) Indicate whether there is a direction to the alternative hypotheses and why (or why not).

   b. What is the appropriate test statistic for this situation and why?

   c. Describe the distribution of this test statistic when H_0 is true and when H_0 is false. (Include the mean, variance, and form of these distributions.)

   d. Describe the effects of increasing sample size on both these distributions. How does increasing sample size affect the power of this test?

5. Describe in *general* terms how you might construct a power function for the situation described above. (In your answer, define the *power of a test* and describe how one finds the power of the test.) Draw a power function for this situation and label the axes.

6. Why is the variance of a *t*-test larger than the variance of a *z*-test, even though the sample sizes are the same and the data come from the same population?

7. Are children more persistent at trying to solve a problem when one of their parents is present? To investigate this question, you could randomly assign children at a preschool to one of two conditions and give them the task of trying to solve an unsolvable problem. The children assigned to one group would work in the presence of one of their parents, and the children assigned to the other group would work in the presence of a stranger. The dependent measure would be how long each child works on the problem before quitting.

   a. What are the experimental and statistical hypotheses being tested in this experiment? State the statistical hypotheses in both symbols and words.

   b. Indicate which test statistic you would use to analyze these data and explain why you would use it here.

   c. Describe the distributions of this test statistic when the null hypothesis is true and when it is false. (Include the means, variances, and kinds of distributions.)

d. What are the effects of increasing sample size on:

i. the probability of making an alpha error?

ii. the probability of making a beta error? Why in each case?

e. Describe in *general* terms how you might construct a power function for the situation described above. (In your answer, define the *power of a test* and how one finds the power of the test.) Draw a power function for this situation and label the axes.

8. Suppose for the situation described in the previous question you set $\alpha = .05$.

a. If your test statistic is in the critical region and you reject the null hypothesis, what is the probability that you made a type I or α error? Why?

b. How can you determine the power of your test based on the value of your test statistic? What information does that value provide you about your test?

9. You can use Student's *t* to test whether treatments given to two groups of participants in an experiment have the same effects on behavior.

a. What measure can you use to estimate the strength of the treatment effects in your experiment? Why did you choose that measure?

b. Is this measure of strength of the treatment effects influenced by sample size? Why or why not?

Student Study Site

Visit the Student Study Site at **https://study.sagepub.com/friemanstats** for a variety of useful tools including data sets, additional exercises, and web resources.

TESTING HYPOTHESES WHEN THE DEPENDENT VARIABLE CONSISTS OF FREQUENCIES OF SCORES IN VARIOUS CATEGORIES

D ata can come in various formats. The data we have been exploring and analyzing in previous chapters consist of scores on some measure of behavior, such as the State Hostility Scale (SHS). This scale consists of 35 items like "I feel furious." Participants indicate the extent to which they agree or disagree with these mood statements on a 1–5 scale, where 1 indicates the individual strongly disagrees and 5 indicates the individual strongly agrees. The scoring of some items, such as "I feel friendly," is reversed, and the scores are summed so that higher total scores are indicative of feeling more hostile.

However, not all data come in this format. Another frequently used format is counts of the number of individuals in different categories. Here, individuals' scores are not numbers but the names of the categories they are in. In this chapter, we will look at how to analyze these kinds of data. But before doing so, we need to look at the characteristics of the various data formats we use in our research.

CLASSIFYING DATA

The statistical procedures we use to describe and analyze data depend on the format of those data. The most widely used system for classifying data was proposed by Stevens (1946). He described four formats: nominal, ordinal, interval, and ratio.

Stevens (1946) classified data into four formats[1] depending on the operations we can perform on the data. He labeled these data formats nominal, ordinal, interval, and ratio and argued that certain statistical procedures are appropriate for each data format. Hence, it is important to understand the differences among these formats. These formats are generally held to be in a hierarchy, with the highest-order category including the data on which the most operations can be conducted.

The term **nominal** is invoked *when the only thing you can do is to sort the data into categories*. This operation is referred to as classification. All items or individuals placed in the same category are considered equal for the purpose of analysis. This format is the lowest level in the hierarchy. The data we will consider in this chapter are nominal data.

The next level is **ordinal**. *Here we can rank order the data in some way.* The 1–5 scale for each item on the State Hostility Scale is ordinal in the sense that the person is telling us something about his or her mood, but it is not clear how different a choice of 1 is from 2, 2 is from 3, 3 is from 4, and 4 is from 5. At best, the result of analyzing such data indicate ordering, not meaningful differences.

We use the term **interval** for data *when the distances between the numbers are equal.* Here the difference between a 1 and a 2 equals the distance between a 3 and a 4 and so forth across the entire set of scores. One could argue that the overall State Hostility Score obtained for each person represents an interval format by adding up the individual ratings on all items.[2] Although the intervals between the numbers are equal, we cannot say, for example, that a person with an SHS score of 100 is feeling twice as hostile as a person with an SHS score of 50, which leads us to the final format in this schema, the ratio format.

A **ratio** format describes data with *equal distances between the numbers as well as an absolute zero.* It is the absolute zero that allows us to make ratio statements, such as "Someone who responds at a rate of 10 responses per minute is responding twice as fast as someone who is responding at a rate of 5 responses a minute."

Why the Format of Data Matters

Stevens's 1946 paper started a long-standing debate among data analysts over whether the format of the data matters when choosing what statistical procedures to use. On the one hand, there are those like Lord (1953) and Gaito (1980) who argued that "numbers do not know where they came from." From that perspective, data format does not matter. On the other hand, there are those like Townsend and Ashby (1984) who, in their reply to Gaito, argued that it does. Over the years, this debate has focused on whether one can use *t*-tests and analysis of variance to analyze ordinal data. Nevertheless, all are agreed that

---

[1] Stevens used the term *scales of measurement* to describe these different formats, and this designation is the most commonly used term to describe them. Carifio and Perla (2007) argued that the term *scale* has lots of meanings and it is easy to confuse these meanings. For example, we use the term *scale* when referring to the way we measure psychological processes such as hostility, but Stevens used the term in a different way. To avoid this problem, we will use the less ambiguous term *format*.

[2] This assertion is based on the central limit theorem (see Chapter 3), which tells us that the means of the ratings are normally distributed or become normally distributed as the sample size increases. The same should apply to the sum of the rating, because the mean is the sum divided by the number of ratings being summed (Norman, 2010).

the statistical techniques one uses to describe and analyze nominal data are different from those used for data in the other three formats. The remainder of this chapter is devoted to analyzing nominal data.

TESTING HYPOTHESES WHEN THE DEPENDENT VARIABLE CONSISTS OF ONLY TWO POSSIBILITIES

When there are only two categories, we can use the binomial distribution to test hypotheses about the proportion of individuals in a population who are in one of those categories.

Sometimes the dependent variable in your study consists of only two possibilities or categories, such as a participant being correct or incorrect on a given trial, a voter choosing candidate A or candidate B for office, a citizen opting to vote or not vote in the election, a survey participant answering yes or no to a question, a consumer purchasing or not purchasing a certain item, an individual possessing or not possessing a certain characteristic (for example, being male or female, being depressed or not depressed, being or not being a member of a minority group), and so forth. In these situations, we gather a number of observations (called *trials*) and count how many of our participants or observations are in each category. Because there are only two possibilities or categories, when we gather n total observations and X are in one category, then $(n - X)$ must be in the other category. Therefore, knowing the total number of observations (n) and the number in one category (X) gives us the number in the other category $(n - X)$. It is thus convenient to focus on one category and call X the number of "successes." Stating this category of outcomes in this way does not mean that the other category consists of "failures." The term is used to mean only that we are focusing on how many cases among our total number of observations are in the first category. Data collected in this manner are called *binomial data*, and we use the binomial distribution to analyze these data.

An interesting question that would produce binomial data is whether or not people "get" a joke they are told. Inevitably, some people understand the meaning of a joke they hear, while others do not. This distinction may be especially important when a person's understanding, versus not understanding, the intended meaning of a joke changes the joke's message from potentially positive to accidentally negative. This situation could occur when the joke makes some reference to race. To address this question, Saucier, Strain, Miller, Till, and O'Dea (2016) investigated individuals' responses to racial humor across a series of studies. Their overall objective was to examine the interpretation, perceptions, and effects of various types of racial humor. Most importantly, the researchers were interested in examining how likely it would be for individuals to perceive racial humor intended to be subversive as subversive (that is, how often the individuals "got" the joke versus did not "get" the joke). Subversive humor attempts to confront or challenge racism, rather than to reinforce it (Saucier, O'Dea, & Strain, 2016; Strain, Martens, & Saucier, 2016). Accordingly, researchers approached participants on campus and asked whether they would be interested in hearing a joke. In the subversive joke conditions, the researchers told a version of a riddle, beginning with the question, "What do you call a Black guy who flies a plane?" After pausing for a moment, the researchers provided the answer, "A pilot, you racist!" This riddle was used because the question, asked in the context of a racial joke, is likely to arouse stereotypes in the mind of the participants, and the answer then confronts this stereotypic thinking.

After hearing the joke, the participants reported who they thought was the target, or the "butt," of the joke, and the researchers coded the responses into two categories. The "Subversive Response" category consisted of responses in which the participants interpreted the joke as subversive by identifying the target of the joke to be racists or themselves (these participants "got" the joke). The "Nonsubversive Response" category consisted of responses in which the participants failed to interpret the joke as subversive (such as by identifying the target of the joke as Black people); these participants did not "get" the joke. The data consisted of the number of participants whose responses were coded as "Subversive Responses" or "Nonsubversive Responses."

THE BINOMIAL DISTRIBUTION

The formula for generating a binomial distribution gives us the probability of obtaining X successes in n trials for all values of X from 0 to n. The binomial distribution has one parameter, π, the probability of a success on a single trial. The maximum likelihood estimate of π is $\dfrac{X}{n}$, the observed number of successes in n trials. $\mu = n\pi$ and $\sigma^2 = n\pi(1 - \pi)$.

Suppose for the moment that we have only five participants ($n = 5$) and X is the number of participants who are coded as giving Subversive responses, where X can vary from 0 to 5. If we keep track of the data as they are collected, there are 32 different possible outcomes in terms of how the 5 participants responded to the question. These are listed in Table 8.1.

Table 8.1 contains all possible patterns of Subversive and Nonsubversive responses that can be produced by the 5 participants. We observe one of those possible patterns when we collect the data. Clearly, the probability of getting any one of these patterns is 1/32, but our interest is in how many Subversive responses (X) we get, not the order in which they occur. For example, there are 10 different ways we can get 3 Subversive responses and 2 Nonsubversive responses. Therefore, the probability of getting 3 Subversive responses from 5 participants is 10/32 = .3125. Rather than enumerating all of the possible patterns

TABLE 8.1 ■ The Possible Ways (Subversive [S] or Nonsubversive [N]) in Which 5 Participants Responded to the Question			
	Possible Outcomes	**Number**	**Probability**
5 S and 0 N	SSSSS	1	1/32
4 S and 1 N	SSSSN, SSSNS, SSNSS, SNSSS, NSSSS	5	5/32
3 S and 2 N	SSSNN, SSNSN, SNSSN, NSSSN, SSNNS, SNSNS, NSSNS, SNNSS, NSNSS, NNSSS	10	10/32
2 S and 3 N	SSNNN, SNSNN, SNNSN, SNNNS, NSSNN, NSNSN, NSNNS, NNSSN, NNSNS, NNNSS	10	10/32
1 S and 4 N	SNNNN, NSNNN, NNSNN, NNNSN, NNNNS	5	5/32
0 S and 5 N	NNNNN	1	1/32
Total Number of Possible Outcomes		32	

and counting those that meet your criterion, you can use the following formula to get the same information:

$$\Pr(X\,|\,n) = \frac{n!}{X!(n-X)!}\pi^{X}(1-\pi)^{n-X} \tag{8.1}$$

where n is the number of trials (number of participants questioned in our example), X is the number of successes (number of Subversive responses in our example), π is the probability of a success on a single trial $(0 < \pi < 1)$, and $n! = n \times (n - 1) \times (n - 2) \times \ldots \times 1$.

This formula also gives us the probability density function for a binomial distribution based on n trials with parameter π; that is, it generates the probability for a given parameter value π of all the possible numbers of successes (X) in n trials. In other words, it gives us the probability of obtaining 0 successes, 1 success, 2 successes, and so forth to X successes in n trials for a given parameter value π. From this formula, we can also determine the probability of getting X or more successes in n trials or X or fewer successes in n trials. The probability density function for a binomial distribution with n trials and $\pi = .5$ is represented in Figure 8.1.

The mean of a binomial distribution $\mu = n\pi$, and the variance $\sigma^2 = n\pi(1 - \pi)$. In the situation represented by Figure 8.1, $\mu = (5)(0.5) = 2.5$ and $\sigma^2 = (5)(0.5)(1 - .5) = 1.25$. The formulas for the mean and variance of a binomial distribution, $\mu = n\pi$ and $\sigma^2 = n\pi(1 - \pi)$, tell us that both values are a function of the sample size n and the parameter π: Both the mean and variance increase as n increases. The mean also increases as π increases from 0 to 1, but for any given value of n, the variance is at its largest value when $\pi = .5$.

We can also use Equation 8.1 to test hypotheses about the parameter π, the probability of a success on a single trial. To do so, we consider the observations a random sample from

FIGURE 8.1 ■ Probability density function for a binomial distribution with $n = 5$ trials and $\pi = .5$.

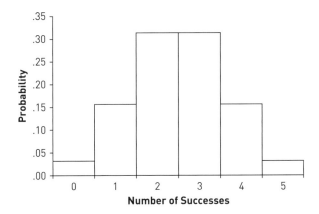

a population and use the observed number of successes (X) in n trials to test hypotheses about the proportion of the population that is successes. We use the symbol π to represent that parameter of the population. The maximum likelihood estimate of π is $\hat{\pi}$ is $\dfrac{X}{n}$, the observed number of successes in n observations or trials. It is a simple matter to demonstrate using the rules of expected value and the fact that the $E(X)$ for a binomial distribution is $n\pi$ that $E(X/n) = \pi$, that is, to demonstrate that (X/n) is an unbiased estimate of π.

TESTING HYPOTHESES ABOUT THE PARAMETER π IN A BINOMIAL EXPERIMENT

To test the null hypothesis that $\pi = $ a certain value π_0 for a certain number of trials, we substitute π_0 and n into Equation 8.1, generate the binomial distribution, and define the critical region. The test statistic is X, the observed number of successes. We reject the null hypothesis when X is in the critical region. The non-central distribution is also a binominal distribution where $\pi \neq \pi_0$. The power of the test is that area of the non-central distribution in the critical region. Power is a function of the chosen value of α, whether the test is one or two tailed, the number of trials, and the true difference between π and π_0.

The Experimental or Research Question

The research question in the situation described above is whether people will interpret racial humor intended to be subversive as subversive. Suppose for the sake of this discussion that 20 individuals were asked to respond.

Experimental Hypotheses

The experimental hypotheses for this experiment are as follows:

> *Individuals are as likely to interpret a subversive racial joke as subversive as they are to interpret it as nonsubversive.*

> *Individuals are more likely to interpret a subversive racial joke as subversive than as nonsubversive.*

Statistical Hypotheses

The statistical hypotheses for the binomial situation are statements about the value of the parameter π, the probability of being correct on each trial. These hypotheses take the following form:

> $H_0: \pi = \pi_0$. In words, this mathematical statement says, "The probability of being correct on each trial *equals* a certain value (represented by the symbol π_0)," and it represents the general form of the null hypothesis. For the situation described above, π_0 is .5 if an individual is just as likely to interpret a subversive racial joke as subversive as nonsubversive.

The alternative hypothesis will depend on the situation and the question being asked. For the situation described above, when individuals are more likely to interpret a subversive racial joke as subversive than as nonsubversive, the alternative hypothesis, in general terms, is as follows:

> $H_1: \pi > \pi_0$. In words, this mathematical statement reads, "The probability of an individual perceiving the subversive joke as subversive *is greater than* a certain value (represented by the symbol π_0)," where, in this case, $\pi_0 = .5$.

The reason for using a one-tailed hypothesis here is that we expect an individual to perform better than chance in determining whether a joke is subversive when he or she is told a subversive joke; in other words, for that person, $\pi > .5$. When an individual performs worse than chance, we do not attribute his or her interpretation to an inability to perceive the subversive nature of the joke—we attribute such poor performance to chance (and bad luck). There are other situations in which a two-tailed alternative is appropriate. In those cases,

> $H_1: \pi \neq \pi_0$. In words, read this as "The probability of an individual perceiving the subversive joke as subversive *is not equal* to a certain value (represented by the symbol π_0)."

Clearly, the choice of which version of H_1 is appropriate depends on the research question being asked and the experimental hypotheses generated as possible answers. How do we decide which statistical (and corresponding) experimental hypothesis is correct? What evidence (data) would lead you to conclude that the first experimental hypothesis is true? What evidence (data) would lead you to conclude that the second experimental hypothesis is true?

Defining the Test Statistic and Finding the Critical Region and Critical Value

We can answer our research question by seeking responses from, for example, 20 individuals and coding their responses. As noted above, the maximum likelihood estimate of π, the probability of being correct on a single trial, equals $\hat{\pi} = X / n$. Therefore, our **test statistic** *is simply* X, *the number of successes in* n *trials*. Because the null hypothesis is that π equals a certain value π_0 (.5 in this case), we can test the null hypothesis by calculating the probability of getting our observed data (*X* successes in *n* trials). If that probability < .05, we will reject the null hypothesis that $\pi = .5$ and accept the alternative that $\pi > .5$. Because $\hat{\pi}$ is an unbiased estimate of π, we expect $\hat{\pi}$ to be close to π_0 (.5 in this case) when the null hypothesis is true and far from π_0 when the null hypothesis is false.

The probability density function (the distribution of the number of successes, *X*, in *n* trials) for $n = 20$ and $\pi = .5$, is presented in Figure 8.2. This function represents the distribution of our test statistic *X* (the number of successes in 20 trials) when the null hypothesis is true ($\pi = .5$ in this case). Because the mean of a binomial distribution $\mu = n\pi$ and the variance $\sigma^2 = n\pi(1 - \pi)$, when $n = 20$ and $\pi = .5$, $\mu = 10$ and $\sigma^2 = 5$.

When the null hypothesis ($\pi = .5$) is true, 8, 9, 10, 11, and 12 successes (in 20 trials) are the most likely outcomes, and 0, 1, 2, 18, 19, and 20 successes are very unlikely. Therefore, we identify the **critical region** and **critical value** by *starting at the ends of the distribution and adding the probabilities for each possible outcome, moving toward the center until the probabilities sum to a value close to .05*. We do so on one side of the distribution when testing against a one-tailed alternative hypothesis. With a two-tailed alternative, we add the probabilities of each possible outcome on both sides to get probabilities of .025 on each side. Because the values of *X* (number of successes in *n* trials) are whole numbers, it is usually not the case that the critical region will be exactly .05 (or .025 on each side for tests of a two-tailed alternative). In Figure 8.2, the probability of getting 14 or more successes in 20 trials is .058. In other words, the critical value for testing the hypothesis that $\pi = .5$ against the alternative that $\pi > .5$ with $n = 20$ is 14, and the critical region contains all values of *X* from 14 to 20. The probability of getting a result in this critical region (rounded to three digits) is .058 (see Table 8.2).

Therefore, we *reject* the statistical null hypothesis that $\pi = .5$ and accept the alternative hypothesis that $\pi > .5$ when individuals are correct 14 or more times in 20 trials. This outcome also leads us to accept the experimental hypothesis that individuals are more likely to perceive a subversive joke as subversive. We do not reject the statistical null hypothesis (and the experimental hypothesis) that individuals are equally likely to perceive a subversive joke as subversive or nonsubversive when the group of 20 participants is correct fewer than 14 times. The probability of making an alpha error here when $n = 20$ and $\pi = .5$ is .058.

FIGURE 8.2 ■ Probability density function for a binomial distribution with n = 20 and π = .5 (critical region indicated).

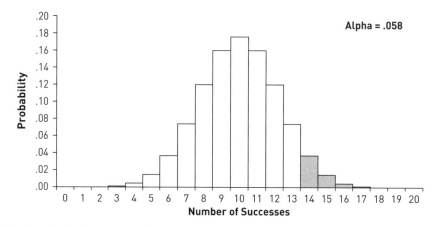

Note: The critical region is on one side because the alternative hypothesis is π > .5.

TABLE 8.2 ■ Finding the Critical Region for Testing the Hypothesis That π = .5 with n = 20 Against the One-Tailed Alternative π > .5

Number of Successes in 20 Trials (X)	Probability of Getting X Successes (Pr[X])	Cumulative Probability From the Right Side of the Distribution
20	.0000010	.0000010
19	.0000191	.0000201
18	.0001812	.0002013
17	.0010872	.0012885
16	.0046206	.0059091
15	.0147858	.0206947
14	.0369644	.0576591
13	.0739288	.1315880
12	.1201344	.2517223
11	.1601791	.4119015
10	.1761971	.5880985

Note: Only one half of the distribution is given here.

It is also clear from Table 8.2 that the critical value for a two-tailed test with $n = 20$ and $\pi = .5$ is 15 or more correct on the right side and 5 or fewer on the left side. The probability of getting data in either of those two regions of the binomial distribution under these conditions is .041. This area defines the probability of making an alpha error (rejecting the null hypothesis when it is true) when testing against a two-tailed alternative when $n = 20$ and $\pi = .5$. The procedure for performing a test of the hypothesis $H_0: \pi = \pi_0$ using the binomial distribution is presented in Box 8.1.

Power of the Test

Power is the probability of correctly rejecting the null hypothesis when it is false. We represent the power of a statistical hypothesis test as that part of the non-central distribution in the critical region. In the case of the binomial distribution, the non-central distribution is also a binomial distribution, but one for which $\pi \neq \pi_0$.

BOX 8.1

HOW TO PERFORM A HYPOTHESIS TEST WITH THE BINOMIAL DISTRIBUTION PURPOSE

Purpose

To test the hypothesis $H_0: \pi = \pi_0$ (the probability of being correct on each trial equals a certain value π_0), where there are only two possible outcomes of each trial

Procedure

1. Decide whether your alternative hypothesis is one-tailed or two-tailed.

2. If you are doing a two-tailed test, use your observed number of successes, X, in n trials to decide whether to do your calculations on the left or right tail. If $X/n < n\pi_0$, use the left (lower side) of the binomial distribution. If $X/n > n\pi_0$, use the right (higher side) of the binomial distribution. For a one-tailed test, use the side in the direction of your alternative hypothesis.

3. Define the critical region by starting at the end of the binomial distribution and using the binomial distribution formula

$$\Pr\left(X \mid n\right) = \frac{n!}{X!\left(n-X\right)!}\pi^X\left(1-\pi\right)^{n-X} \text{ to find the}$$

probability of getting X successes in n trials for each succeeding value of X. Add those probabilities until you get a total probability close to your chosen value for alpha for a one-tailed test or close to alpha/2 for a two-tailed test. (That probability can be slightly higher than alpha [or alpha/2].)

4. Your critical value is the last value of X you used to define the critical region in step 3.

5. Is your observed value of X in the critical region? If so, reject H_0.

If, for example, the true value of $\pi = .8$, with $n = 20$ trials, the non-central distribution is a binomial distribution with $\mu = (20)(0.8) = 16$ and $\sigma^2 = (20)(0.8)$ $(1 - 0.8) = 3.2$. The central and non-central distributions for the test of H_0: $\pi = .5$ against H_1: $\pi > .5$, where $n = 20$ trials and where the true value of $\pi = .8$ are presented in Figure 8.3. For this situation, the critical region is 14 or more correct out of 20 trials, and the probability of that outcome occurring when the null hypothesis is true $=$ .058. The power of the test $= .914$.

The power of a binomial test depends on the following:

- *The number of trials* (n). All other things being equal, the greater the number of trials, the greater the power.
- *The level of alpha*. All other things being equal, the higher the alpha level set, the greater the power.
- *A one-tailed or a two-tailed test*. All other things being equal, the one-tailed test will always be more powerful.
- *The actual value of* $(\pi - \pi_0)$. The greater this difference, the greater the power.

Unlike the situation with the z- and t-tests described in Chapters 6 and 7, respectively, the population variance does not play an independent role in the power, because $\sigma^2 = n\pi(1 - \pi)$. In other words, the population variance is itself a function of the sample size, which we have seen directly affects the power.

Why the Number of Trials Affects the Power of a Binomial Test

As with t- and z-tests, the power of the binomial test increases as sample size (number of trials in the binomial case) increases, but for a different reason.

In the case of the z-tests, the central z-distribution does not change ($\mu_z = 0$ and $\sigma_z^2 = 1$ for all sample sizes), keeping the critical value and the size of the critical region constant. Likewise, the variance of the non-central z-distribution stays the same, but the mean of the non-central distribution moves away from zero, thereby putting more of that non-central distribution in the critical region.

In the case of the t-tests, as sample size increases, $\mu_t = 0$, but σ_t^2 decreases toward 1 as sample size increases. In this case, the critical value of t moves toward the critical value of z, which increases the size of the critical region. The variance of the non-central t-distribution also decreases toward 1 as sample size increases, and the mean of the non-central distribution moves away from zero. Therefore, more of that non-central distribution appears in the critical region.

However, binomial distributions are different. As the number of trials (the sample size) increases, both the mean and variance of the central null-hypothesis-true binomial distribution increase because $\mu = n\pi$ and $\sigma^2 = n\pi(1 - \pi)$. In other words, the null-hypothesis-true binomial distribution spreads out and becomes flatter to accommodate the increased number of possible outcomes with the larger sample size. Because the lower end of a binomial distribution is anchored at $X = 0$, as n increases, the mean increases as the entire distribution spreads to the right. The total area still equals 1, but it contains more possible outcomes in the critical region. You can see this pattern in Figure 8.3 (where $n = 20$) and Figure 8.4 (where $n = 10$).[3] The calculations that generated those figures are in Table 8.3.

FIGURE 8.3 ■ Power of the binomial test when $\pi = .8$ and $n = 20$ if the null hypothesis is true (*top*) and if it is false (*bottom*).

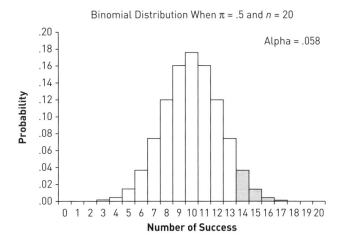

Binomial Distribution When $\pi = .5$ and $n = 20$

Alpha = .058

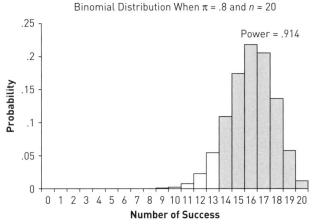

Binomial Distribution When $\pi = .8$ and $n = 20$

Power = .914

---

[3]It may not be immediately apparent from comparing Figures 8.3 and 8.4 that the null-hypothesis-true distribution flattened, because the scales of the figures' vertical axes are different.

Consider first the *null-hypothesis-true distributions*. When $n = 10$ (Figure 8.4 and Table 8.3, *top*), the critical region consists of only three possible outcomes (8, 9, and 10 successes), and the total probability of getting any one of those outcomes when the null hypothesis is true is .058. In other words, it takes a minimum of 8 out of 10 successes (80% correct) to reject the null hypothesis. Those three outcomes comprise 27% (3/11) of the total possible outcomes for the experiment.

But when $n = 20$ (Figure 8.3 and Table 8.3, *bottom*), there are seven possible outcomes in the critical region (14, 15, 16, 17, 18, 19, and 20 successes), and the total probability of getting any one of these outcomes when the null hypothesis is true is .055. In other

---

FIGURE 8.4 ■ Power of the binomial test when $\pi = .8$ and $n = 10$ if the null hypothesis is true (*top*) and if it is false (*bottom*).

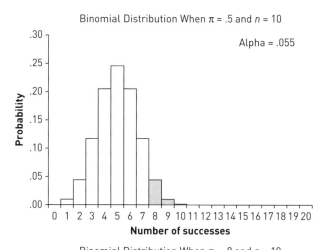

Binomial Distribution When $\pi = .5$ and $n = 10$

Alpha = .055

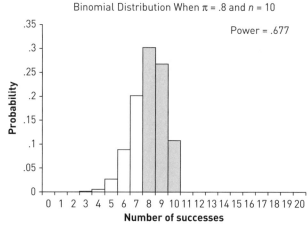

Binomial Distribution When $\pi = .8$ and $n = 10$

Power = .677

TABLE 8.3 ■ **The Power of the Binomial Test of H_0: $\pi = .5$ When the True Value of $\pi = .8$**

			$n = 10$			
			Number of Successes (X)			
	5	6	7	8	9	10
$\pi = .5$	.246	.205	.117	.044	.010	.001
					$\alpha = .055$	
$\pi = .8$	.026	.088	.201	.302	.268	.107
				power = .677		
				critical region = 27.27% (3 out of 11) of the total possible outcomes		

					$n = 20$					
					Number of Successes (X)					
	11	12	13	14	15	16	17	18	19	20
$\pi = .5$	.160	.120	.074	.037	.015	.005	.001	.0002	.00002	.0000009
							$\alpha = .058$			
$\pi = .8$	.007	.022	.055	.109	.175	.218	.205	.137	.058	.012
			power = .914							
			critical region = 33.33% (7 out of 21) of the total possible outcomes							

words, it takes a minimum of 14 out of 20 successes (70% correct) to reject the null hypothesis. Those seven outcomes comprise 33% (7/21) of the total possible outcomes for the experiment.

Power is that part of the *null-hypothesis-false distribution* in the critical region. We calculate the power using Equation 8.1 for the values of X in the critical region (see Table 8.3). When $n = 10$ and the true value of $\pi = .8$, the power of the binomial test of the hypothesis H_0: $\pi = .5$ against H_1: $\pi > .5$ is .677 (see Figure 8.4 and Table 8.3, *top*). Increasing n to 20 stretches and flattens both the null-hypothesis-true distribution and the null-hypothesis-false distribution. As noted above, when the null-hypothesis-true distribution spreads out, the number of possible outcomes in the critical region increases both in absolute terms (from 3 to 7 in our example) and in relative terms (from 27% of the total possible to 33%), although the probability of making an alpha error remains around .05. As the null-hypothesis-false distribution spreads out, more of it is pulled into the critical region. In our example, the power increases from .677 to .914. Therefore, *the power of a binomial test increases as the number of trials increases*, because the critical region is composed of more possible outcomes and, as the null-hypothesis-false distribution stretches and flattens, more of it is in the critical region.

THE NORMAL DISTRIBUTION APPROXIMATION TO THE BINOMIAL DISTRIBUTION

As the number of trials increases, the generation of the binomial distribution becomes increasingly tedious; however, as n *increases, the binomial distribution can be approximated by a normal distribution in the form of a z-statistic. With a correction for the fact that we are fitting a normal distribution that is a continuous distribution onto a binomial distribution made up of discrete whole numbers, the approximation provides probabilities that are very close to the actual binomial probabilities. All of the principles for testing hypotheses with a z-statistic described in Chapter 6 apply here.*

The procedure for testing hypotheses about the parameter π described above and summarized in Box 8.1 gets extremely tedious as the number of trial increases. The research examining how individuals respond to subversive humor described at the beginning of this chapter involved many more than 20 participants. Fortunately, as the number of trials increases, the binomial distribution approaches a normal distribution, even when $\pi \neq .5$. This pattern can be illustrated by comparing Figure 8.4 (where $n = 10$) with Figure 8.3 (where $n = 20$). When $n = 20$, both the binomial distributions for $\pi = .5$ and $\pi = .8$ look more like normal distributions than when $n = 10$. We can capitalize on this fact by fitting a normal distribution to a binomial distribution and using that fitted normal distribution to approximate the area under the binomial distribution. This strategy will give us a simple way to test hypotheses about the parameter π. We will see that the approximation is pretty close to the actual probability when we make a simple correction for the fact that we are fitting a continuous normal distribution to the discrete binomial distribution.[4]

Therefore, we can overlay a normal curve on top of a binomial distribution and convert to standard scores (*z*-scores), where

$$\text{standard score} = \frac{\text{score} - \text{mean}}{\text{standard deviation}}$$

and

$$z = \frac{X - \mu_X}{\sigma_X} \tag{8.2}$$

---

[4]The binomial distribution is a **discrete distribution** because the *values of X are discrete whole numbers*: One can have 14 successes or 15 successes, but not 14.28 successes. The normal distribution is a **continuous distribution** because, at least theoretically, *the values of X consist of all possible values between* $-\infty$ *and* $+\infty$.

In this situation, the scores are X, the mean $\mu_x = n\pi$, and the standard deviation $\sigma_X = \sqrt{n\pi(1-\pi)}$. Substituting into the z-score formula, we get

$$z = \frac{X - n\pi}{\sqrt{n\pi(1-\pi)}} \qquad (8.3)$$

To test the null hypothesis that $\pi = \pi_0$, we substitute the hypothesized value for π into Equation 8.3 to get the following test statistic:

$$z = \frac{X - n\pi_0}{\sqrt{n\pi_0(1-\pi_0)}} \qquad (8.4a)$$

What kind of distribution does the formula in Equation 8.4a have when the null hypothesis is *true*? What are its mean and variance? What kind of distribution does the formula in Equation 8.4a have when the null hypothesis is *false*? What are its mean and variance?

We saw earlier that when calculating directly from the binomial distribution, the probability of getting 8 or more successes in 10 trials is .058 (See Table 8.3). When we substitute $X = 8$, $n = 10$, and $\pi = .5$ into Equation 8.4a, we get $z = 1.898$. From the unit normal distribution table, we find that $p = .0287$, which is not close to the exact value of .055. Why the difference? The answer has to do with the difference between a discrete distribution and a continuous distribution (see footnote 4). In a discrete distribution, there are only whole numbers (7, 8, 9, and so forth). Each of these numbers occupies a distance along the x-axis (see Figures 8.1, 8.2, 8.3, and 8.4a). In a continuous distribution, as in the normal distribution, each of the infinite number of values is a single point on the x-axis. The distance covered by the number 8 in a discrete distribution is the same as the distance between 7.5 and 8.5 in a continuous distribution. Therefore, to get a closer approximation to the binomial distribution, we need to *adjust* Equation 8.4a *for the fact that we are approximating a discrete distribution with a continuous distribution*. This adjustment is called a **correction for continuity**.[5] We perform this correction by subtracting 0.5 from the distance between the score X and the mean in the numerator of the equation. The new test statistic becomes

$$z = \frac{|X - n\pi_0| - 0.5}{\sqrt{n\pi_0(1-\pi_0)}} \qquad (8.4b)$$

Substituting the same values into this test statistic yields $z = 1.582$, for which $p = .0571$. Much better!

Equations 8.4a and 8.4b use X as the score to test the hypothesis. Because the null hypothesis is stated in terms of π and the maximum likelihood estimate $\hat{\pi} = X/n$, if we divide the numerator and denominator of Equations 8.4a and 8.4b by n, we get the following set of test statistics:

---

[5] The correction for continuity was first proposed by Yates (1934) for the χ^2 test described later in this chapter.

$$z = \frac{\hat{\pi} - \pi_0}{\sqrt{\dfrac{\pi_0\left(1-\pi_0\right)}{n}}} \qquad (8.5a)$$

$$z = \frac{\left|\hat{\pi} - \pi_0\right| - \dfrac{0.5}{n}}{\sqrt{\dfrac{\pi_0\left(1-\pi_0\right)}{n}}} \qquad (8.5b)$$

It is clear from Equation 8.5b that the correction for continuity has its greatest effect with small numbers of trials. As n increases, the effect of the correction is lessened because the binomial distribution becomes more like a normal distribution as n increases.

Equations 8.5a and 8.5b are equivalent to Equations 8.4a and 8.4b respectively; that is, they give the same answers for the same values entered. Use the test statistic that is more convenient for you.

Finally, can you explain why all of the things that affect the power of a binomial test affect the power with the test statistic in Equation 8.5a?

Confidence Intervals for the Parameter π

We can use the normal distribution approximation to the binomial distribution and the procedures described in Chapter 4 to construct confidence intervals for π, the unknown parameter in a binomial distribution. From Equations 8.5a and 8.5b, we see that the standard deviation of $\hat{\pi}$, the estimate of π, is

$$\hat{\sigma}_{\hat{\pi}} = \sqrt{\frac{\hat{\pi}\left(1-\hat{\pi}\right)}{n}} \qquad (8.6)\,[6]$$

Equation 4.10 is the confidence interval for μ, the mean of a normal distribution. The corresponding confidence interval for π is

$$\Pr\left(\hat{\pi} - 1.96\sqrt{\frac{\hat{\pi}\left(1-\hat{\pi}\right)}{n}} < \pi < \hat{\pi} + 1.96\sqrt{\frac{\hat{\pi}\left(1-\hat{\pi}\right)}{n}}\right) = .95 \qquad (8.7a)$$

---

[6] π here refers to the actual value of the parameter, not the hypothesized value (π_0) in Equations 8.5a and 8.5b.

We can improve the precision of this interval by adding the correction for continuity described above:

$$\Pr\left(\hat{\pi} - 1.96\sqrt{\frac{\hat{\pi}(1-\hat{\pi})}{n}} - \frac{0.5}{n} < \pi < \hat{\pi} + 1.96\sqrt{\frac{\hat{\pi}(1-\hat{\pi})}{n}} + \frac{0.5}{n}\right) = .95 \quad (8.7b)$$

Analysis of the Responses to Diversity Initiatives Study

A recent study examined how White individuals would respond when given the opportunity to provide feedback on a proposed diversity initiative. O'Dea, Miller, and Saucier (2016) had 152 White participants, all of whom were college students, read a list of goals they were told comprised a diversity initiative that was proposed for implementation at their campus. The specific initiative the participants read was varied: Half the participants read about a diversity initiative that proposed to provide minority students additional information about the application process and scholarships, and half the participants read about a diversity initiative that proposed to lower the standards for admission for minority students. For our purposes here, we will collapse the data across these two conditions. The participants were then informed that they would have the opportunity to provide constructive feedback about the diversity initiative they had just read, but they could choose to either discuss their feedback verbally in a 5-minute conversation with the experimenter or write their feedback in a one-page response. This choice was the dependent variable in the study; in actuality, the participants neither engaged in the conversations nor wrote the response papers. The data from this study are presented in Table 8.4. The experimental question in this example is: Do students prefer expressing criticisms of a proposed diversity initiative by talking with an experimenter or by writing a one-page paper?

The experimental hypotheses are as follows:

Individuals are as likely to choose to submit verbal responses as they are to choose to submit written responses.

Individuals are not as likely to choose to submit verbal responses as they are to choose to submit written responses.

The corresponding statistical hypotheses are:

H_0: $\pi_{\text{Verbal responses}} = 0.5$ The proportion of individuals in the population who choose to submit verbal responses equals 0.5.

H_1: $\pi_{\text{Verbal responses}} \neq 0.5$ The proportion of individuals in the population who choose to submit verbal responses does not equal 0.5.

Inserting the values in Table 8.4 into Equation 8.4b or 8.5b yields $z = 3.24$. The critical value for a two-tailed z-test is 1.96. Therefore, based on these results, we reject the null hypothesis that $\pi_{\text{Verbal responses}} = 0.5$. We conclude that the participants were more likely to

TABLE 8.4 ■ Data From Experiment 2 (O'Dea, Miller, & Saucier, 2016)			
Verbal	**Written**	**Total**	**Proportion Verbal**
96	56	152	.63

prefer expressing criticisms of a proposed diversity initiative verbally with an experimenter than by writing a one-page paper. Another way to test our null hypothesis in this situation is to construct a 95% confidence interval for $\pi_{\text{Verbal responses}}$ and test whether this confidence contains 0.5 (the value specified by the null hypothesis). The confidence interval for $\pi_{\text{Verbal responses}}$ is $\text{Pr}(.55 < \pi < .71) = .95$. Because this 95% confidence interval does not contain 0.5, we can reject the null hypothesis and accept the alternative hypothesis.

TESTING HYPOTHESES ABOUT THE DIFFERENCE BETWEEN TWO BINOMIAL PARAMETERS ($\pi_1 - \pi_2$)

We can also use a z-statistic to test whether two samples come from binomial distributions with the same parameter π.

We can also use the normal distribution approximation to the binomial to construct a hypothesis test for the hypothesis $H_0: \pi_1 = \pi_2$ or its equivalent form, $H_0: \pi_1 - \pi_2 = 0$. The test statistic is

$$z = \frac{\hat{\pi}_1 - \hat{\pi}_2}{\sqrt{\dfrac{\hat{\pi}_1\left(1 - \hat{\pi}_1\right)}{n_1} + \dfrac{\hat{\pi}_2(1 - \hat{\pi}_{2)}}{n_2}}} \tag{8.8}$$

This equation was derived by starting with the definition of a standard score and then substituting $(\hat{\pi}_1 - \hat{\pi}_2)$ for the scores and $\pi_1 - \pi_2$ for the mean of $(\hat{\pi}_1 - \hat{\pi}_2)$. The standard deviation of $(\hat{\pi}_1 - \hat{\pi}_2)$ is the square root of the sum of the individual standard deviations for $\hat{\pi}_1$ and $\hat{\pi}_2$.

Can you show how those substitutions lead to the test statistic in Equation 8.8? What kind of distribution does the formula in Equation 8.9 have when the null hypothesis is *true*? What are its mean and variance? What kind of distribution does the formula in Equation 8.8 have when the null hypothesis is *false*? What are its mean and variance? Can you explain why all the things that affect the power of a binomial test affect the power of the test statistic in Equation 8.8?

In the O'Dea et al. (2016) study discussed above, there was an additional manipulation: the experimenter was either White or Black. The researchers wondered whether the

TABLE 8.5 ■ Data From O'Dea, Miller, and Saucier (2016)				
Condition	**Verbal**	**Written**	**Total**	**Proportion Verbal**
Black	44	36	80	0.55
White	52	20	72	0.72

participants would choose different methods for conveying their feedback about the diversity initiatives as a result of the experimenter's race. In particular, the researchers wondered if White participants would prefer to provide their feedback in writing more when the experimenter was Black to avoid criticizing the diversity initiative in person, and potentially appearing racist as a result, to the Black experimenter. The results of this experiment with both the categories of the experimenter's race and the categories of the method chosen to provide feedback are presented in Table 8.5.

The experimental hypotheses are as follows:

The race of the experimenter does not affect individuals' preference for choosing to submit verbal responses.

The race of the experimenter does affect individuals' preference for choosing to submit verbal responses.

The corresponding statistical hypotheses are as follows:

$H_0: \pi_{\text{Black experimenter}} = \pi_{\text{White experimenter}}$ — The proportion of the population of individuals who choose to respond verbally to a Black experimenter equals the proportion of the population of individuals who choose to respond verbally to a White experimenter.

$H_1: \pi_{\text{Black experimenter}} \neq \pi_{\text{White experimenter}}$ — The proportion of the population of individuals who choose to respond verbally to a Black experimenter does *not* equal the proportion of the population of individuals who choose to respond verbally to a White experimenter.

Inserting the proportions and sample sizes in Table 8.5 into Equation 8.8 yields $z = -2.25$. There is evidence here to reject the null hypothesis that the race of the experimenter does not have an effect on the choice to submit verbal (rather than written) criticisms of a proposed diversity initiative. The results clearly show that the White participants chose to provide their feedback to the experimenter verbally at lower rates, electing to instead provide their feedback in writing at higher rates, when the experimenter was Black than when the experimenter was White. The researchers concluded that the participants were more hesitant to criticize the diversity initiatives in a conversation with the Black experimenter, in particular, due to their anxiety about the potential interracial interaction in which they may have thought the experimenter was more likely to perceive their criticism as racist.

TESTING HYPOTHESES IN WHICH THE DEPENDENT VARIABLE CONSISTS OF TWO OR MORE CATEGORIES

The most commonly used test statistic for testing hypotheses about the proportions of individuals in different categories in a population when there are three or more categories is the χ^2 statistic. This test statistic compares the observed data to the proportions in the population model represented by the null hypothesis.

The binomial tests described above can only be used where there are only two categories. When there are more than two categories, we need to use a different approach. The most commonly used test statistic for that purpose is the chi square (χ^2) statistic:

$$\chi^2 = \sum \frac{\left(\text{observed} - \text{expected}\right)^2}{\text{expected}} \tag{8.9}$$

The χ^2 test statistic compares the observed frequencies of individuals in different categories of our sample with what would be expected from a theoretical model. Although this test statistic can also be used when there are only two categories, it is more versatile than the binomial distribution test because the χ^2 test statistic can be used when there are more than two categories and when the categories are composed of combinations from two dimensions (like race and gender). We will explore how to analyze those kinds of data in Chapter 10.

There is also a distribution called chi square. The χ^2 test statistic has an approximate chi square distribution when the null hypothesis is true and the assumptions underlying the chi square distribution are satisfied. To understand how to properly use the χ^2 test statistic, we need to understand how the chi square distribution is generated.

The Chi Square Distribution

The distribution of the χ^2 test statistic when the null hypothesis is true can be approximated by a chi square distribution. The chi square distribution is generated by taking random samples from a normal distribution.

The chi square distribution, like the *t*-distribution, is a family of distributions that differ in shape depending on their degrees of freedom. As we will see later in this chapter, how

FIGURE 8.5 ■ A chi square distribution with *n* degrees of freedom is generated by taking an infinite number of random samples of size *N* from a unit normal distribution and summing the squared *z*-scores for each sample.

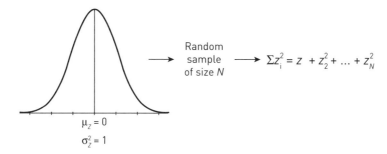

the chi square distribution is generated informs the proper use of the χ^2 test statistic. The chi square distribution is generated by taking a random sample of size *n* from a unit normal distribution (mean = 0 and variance = 1; that is, a distribution of *z*-scores), squaring each *z*-score in the sample, and adding these squared values together. The resulting sum has a chi square distribution with *n* degrees of freedom. The sample size *n* can be any number from 1 to infinity. This procedure is diagramed in Figure 8.5.

Figure 8.6 contains chi square distributions for 1, 2, 3, 4, and 8 degrees of freedom. Note that as the number of scores in the random sample from a unit normal distribution increases, the chi square distribution shifts to the right and becomes more symmetrical. Can you explain why this outcome occurs based on how chi square distributions are generated? Can you also explain why the range of all of these chi square distributions is from 0 to $+\infty$, even though half the values in a unit normal distribution are negative?

It is also apparent in Figure 8.6 that as degrees of freedom increase, both the mean and variance of the chi square distribution increase. As a result, the critical value for hypothesis tests also increases (see "Chi Square Distribution" in the appendix). This pattern is similar to that of the binomial distribution (see Figures 8.3 and 8.4). *The mean of a chi square distribution is the degrees of freedom, and the variance of a chi square distribution is 2 times the degrees of freedom.*

Testing Hypotheses About Proportions of Individuals in a Population With the χ^2 Test Statistic

We use the χ^2 test statistic to evaluate how well our data conform to the population model described in our null hypothesis.

We can use the χ^2 test statistic to test hypotheses about the proportions of individuals in a population who possess certain characteristics. We perform such a test by taking a random

FIGURE 8.6 ■ **Probability density functions for chi square distributions with 1, 2, 3, 4, and 8 degrees of freedom.**

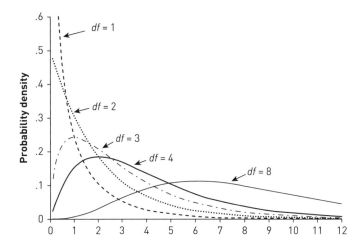

sample from a population and using the χ^2 test statistic to compare what we observe in the sample with what we expect based on our theoretical model of the population. This approach is an example of a **goodness-of-fit test**. We *reject* the null hypothesis when the calculated value of χ^2 is *larger* than the critical value. When we reject the null hypothesis, we conclude that our theoretical model is not correct. On the other hand, we *do not reject* the null hypothesis when the calculated value of χ^2 is *smaller* than the critical value. When we do not reject the null hypothesis, we conclude that we have no evidence that the model is incorrect. Of course, the null hypothesis could be false, but our sample size may be too small to detect a statistically significant difference. As sample size increases, the power of the test increases, and it is easier for smaller deviations from the null hypothesis to result in its rejection.

Although the chi square test is referred to as a nonparametric test in many textbooks, it is a parametric test because it involves taking random samples from populations and testing hypotheses about the characteristics of those populations. Furthermore, how well the distribution of the χ^2 test statistic approximates a chi square distribution depends on how well the assumptions involved in generating the chi square distribution described above are satisfied. We will address that point at the end of this chapter.

An example of how to use the χ^2 test statistic to test for goodness of fit is presented in Box 8.2.

The goodness-of-fit test is designed to determine how well the data fit the theoretical model. The expected values do not have to be equal (as they are in the example in Box 8.1). In general, the degrees of freedom for goodness-of-fit tests are the number of categories minus 1 (as in the example in Box 8.1). However, there are a few situations in which this general rule does not hold. For example, suppose we wanted to ask whether the heights of

BOX 8.2

EXAMPLE OF A GOODNESS-OF-FIT TEST USING THE χ^2 TEST STATISTIC

The experimental question in this example is as follows: Do students prefer expressing criticisms of a proposed diversity initiative by speaking with an experimenter or by writing a one-page paper? The experimental hypotheses are as follows:

The distribution of preferences for verbal responses or written responses is random; that is, both options are equally preferred.

The distribution of preferences for verbal responses or written responses is not random; that is, one option is more preferred than the other.

Using $\pi_{\text{Preference}}$ to indicate the proportion of individuals in the population who indicate a preference for a certain type of response, the corresponding statistical hypotheses are the following:

H_0: $\pi_{\text{Prefer verbal responses}} = \pi_{\text{Prefer written responses}}$.

H_1: At least one $\pi_{\text{Preference}}$ is different from the others.[7]

The data (O'Dea et al., 2016) in Table 8.6 again represent the decisions of the 152 undergraduate students who chose how to provide their feedback about diversity initiatives: 96 participants chose to express their criticisms verbally, and 56 participants chose to express their criticisms by writing a one-page paper. These numbers are the *observed* values. If the null hypothesis is true, we would *expect* to see equal numbers of individuals choosing each option. Do these observed values deviate enough from the expected values for us to conclude that the null

hypothesis is false? We use the following test statistic to answer the question:

$$\chi^2 = \sum \frac{\left(\text{observed} - \text{expected}\right)^2}{\text{expected}}$$

The calculation of the value of the χ^2 test statistic is facilitated by arranging the data in Table 8.6.

TABLE 8.6 ■ Data From O'Dea, Miller, and Saucier (2016)			
	Verbal	**Written**	**Total**
Observed (O)	96	56	152
Expected (E)	76	76	152
O − E	20	−20	
(O − E)²	400	400	
(O − E)²/E	5.26	5.26	

The sum of the last row in the table is $\chi^2 = 10.52$. To determine whether these data will lead us to reject the null hypothesis, we need to know the degrees of freedom. As with most goodness-of-fit tests, *the degrees of freedom are the number of categories minus 1*. For this situation, the degrees of freedom are $2 - 1 = 1$. The critical value for chi square with 1 degree of freedom at $\alpha = .05$ is 3.841. Therefore, these data lead us to reject the null hypothesis in favor of the alternative hypothesis and conclude that the distribution of preferences for verbal responses and written responses is not random in this population.

---

[7]This statement represents the general form of the alternative hypothesis for the χ^2 test statistic because there can be more than two categories of responses. When there are only two categories, as is the case here, the alternative hypothesis can be written as $\pi_{\text{prefer verbal responses}} \neq \pi_{\text{prefer written responses}}$.

all the students at a given university fit a normal distribution. To test the hypothesis that they do, we would take a random sample of students, measure their heights, and count how many fit into different categories (for example, 55–59 inches, 60–64 inches, and so forth). In that situation, degrees of freedom equal the number of categories minus 3, because a normal curve has two additional parameters, the population mean and variance, that limit the degrees of freedom of the data.

The Use and Misuse of the χ^2 Test Statistic

Guidelines for the correct use of the χ^2 test statistic to test hypotheses about population proportions are based on how the chi square distribution is generated from random sampling from a normal distribution.

The distribution of the χ^2 test statistic *approximates* a chi square distribution when the null hypothesis is true and the chi square distribution is based on independent random sampling from a normal distribution. Therefore, it is important to keep that assumption in mind when using the χ^2 test statistic. Failure to do so can lead to misuse. The two ways that the assumption of independent random sampling is violated are when the scores used in the calculation of the χ^2 test statistic are not independent and when the calculation uses proportions or percentages.

INDEPENDENCE OF SCORES Proper use of the χ^2 test statistic requires that the observations be independent, that is, they each come from a different participant. Therefore, there should never be more scores than participants, with each participant providing one, and only one, score. Having more scores than participants artificially inflates the sample size and violates the assumption of independent random sampling.

USE FREQUENCIES, NOT PROPORTIONS OR PERCENTAGES, TO CALCULATE χ^2 Although your statistical hypotheses are in terms of proportions (for example, H_0: $\pi_1 = \pi_2 = .5$), you have to convert the expected values to *frequencies* on the basis of the sample size to calculate the χ^2 test statistic. The examples in Table 8.7 illustrate what happens if you incorrectly calculate χ^2 based on observed and expected proportions or percentages rather than correctly using frequencies. Using proportions will never lead to the rejection of the null hypothesis, while using percentages will inflate the value of χ^2 if you have fewer than 100 observations, because the test statistic is being calculated as if there were 100 observations.

SAMPLE SIZE AND POWER As the sample size (n) (not the degrees of freedom) increases, the calculated value of χ^2 increases. Therefore, it is easier to reject H_0 when the sample size (n) is large (assuming H_0 is false). This point is illustrated in Table 8.8.

TABLE 8.7	■	Why You Should Always Use Frequencies to Calculate χ^2

$H_0: \pi_1 = \pi_2 = .5$

$n = 10$

Critical value for $\alpha = .05$ with 1 degree of freedom = 3.84

		Category 1	Category 2	
Frequencies	O	7	3	$\chi^2 = 1.6$
	E	5	5	
Proportions	O	.7	.3	$\chi^2 = 0.16$
	E	.5	.5	
Percentages	O	70	30	$\chi^2 = 16$
	E	50	50	

TABLE 8.8	■	The Proportion of Scores in Both Categories Required to Reject the Null Hypothesis That $\pi_1 = \pi_2$ as a Function of Sample Size

Sample Size	Proportion in Category 1	Proportion in Category 2
10	.90	.10
20	.75	.25
40	.68	.33
80	.61	.39
100	.60	.40
200	.57	.43
500	.54	.46
1,000	.53	.47
10,000	.51	.49

CORRECTION FOR CONTINUITY The χ^2 test statistic is based on frequencies that are discrete values, but the chi square distribution is based on sampling from a normal distribution, which is continuous. When the degrees of freedom = l, the approximation of the distribution of the χ^2 test statistic to a normal distribution can be improved by subtracting 0.5 from the absolute value of each $O - E$ difference before squaring. This correction can be achieved with the following formula:

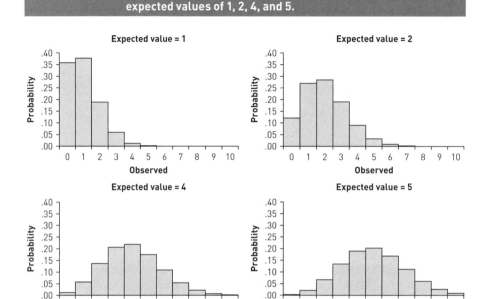

FIGURE 8.7 ■ Distributions of observed values for expected values of 1, 2, 4, and 5.

$$\chi^2 = \sum \frac{\left(|O - E| - 0.5\right)^2}{E} \tag{8.10}$$

ASSUMPTION OF NORMAL DISTRIBUTIONS OF O − E *One is cautioned not to use the χ^2 test statistic when more than 20% of the expected values (E) are less than 5* (Cochran, 1954). The reason for this caution is that when the expected values are small, the observed values will not be symmetrically distributed around the expected values.[8] This potential problem is illustrated in Figure 8.7. It is important that researchers use these and any other data analytic procedures with appropriate regard for the advantages, as well as the limitations, of their use.

Summary

We use the binomial distribution to test hypotheses about the proportion of trials or individuals in a population that have a certain characteristic (π).

When the number of trials or individuals is small, we can use the discrete binomial distribution to calculate probabilities and perform hypothesis tests,

---

[8]This problem does not occur with the binomial distribution test because the binomial test is an exact probability test while the χ_2 test statistic has an approximate chi square distribution. The only problem there is that tests with small sample sizes may have low power.

but when the number of trials or individuals is large, we can use the normal distribution approximation (with a correction for continuity) to calculate those same probabilities with precision and to construct confidence intervals for π. We can also use the normal distribution approximation to test hypotheses about the values of π from two different binomial populations.

The chi square distribution and the χ^2 test statistic provide us with another way to analyze nominal data that consist of frequencies of

individuals in different categories, especially when there are more than two categories. The χ^2 test allows us to test the distribution of observed frequencies against a hypothesized distribution of expected frequencies.

Accordingly, these procedures provide researchers with the opportunity to test meaningful hypotheses even when they collect data in nominal categories, precluding the use of other commonly used data analysis procedures.

Conceptual Exercises

1. For the *exact* binomial test of the hypothesis $H_0: \pi = \pi_0$

   a. What is the test statistic?
   b. Describe the distributions of this test statistic when H_0 is true and when H_0 is false, including the kinds of distributions, the means, and the variances of both distributions.
   c. Explain why the power increases as sample size increases in this situation.

2. For the *normal distribution approximation* test of the hypothesis $H_0: \pi = \pi_0$

   a. What is the test statistic?
   b. Describe the distributions of this test statistic when H_0 is true and when H_0 is false, including the kinds of distributions, the means, and the variances of both distributions.
   c. Explain why the power increases as sample size increases in this situation.

3. Describe the chi square distribution and the non-central chi square distribution. Make a diagram of the shapes, including the means of these distributions and range of possible values that can occur. What happens to both distributions as degrees of freedom increase?

4. Why should one not use percentages as the expected values in a goodness of fit test using the χ^2 test statistic?

5. There is a rule of thumb that no more than 20% of the expected values should be less than 5 when you use the χ^2 test statistic. What assumption is violated when too many expected values are less than 5? Why does having more than 80% of the expected values greater than 5 solve this problem?

6. Why is it a misuse of the χ^2 test statistic to have more data points than subjects?

Student Study Site

Visit the Student Study Site at **https://study.sagepub.com/friemanstats** for a variety of useful tools including data sets, additional exercises, and web resources.

THE RANDOMIZATION/ PERMUTATION MODEL

An Alternative to the Classical Statistical Model for Testing Hypotheses About Treatment Effects

ll of the statistical hypothesis tests we have reviewed to this point are based on the classical statistical model. However, as noted in Chapter 1, although the classical statistical model assumes random sampling from populations, this assumption is often not satisfied when we perform experiments. The participants in the experiments described in Chapters 1, 2, 6, and 7 were obtained through convenience sampling; that is, they signed up to participate in the experiment, probably to satisfy the experimental participation requirement of an introductory psychology course or possibly because they were paid money for their participation. After they decided to participate in the experiment, they were randomly assigned to conditions. Our purpose here is to consider an alternative model called the **randomization model** (also known as the **permutation model**). *This model is based on the assumption that the participants in our experiments are randomly assigned to conditions, not randomly sampled from populations.* In fact, we do not even talk about populations when we use this model.

The **randomization model** employs resampling techniques similar to those we encountered when we studied the bootstrap in Chapter 5. Like the bootstrap, the techniques based on the randomization model are computationally intensive and require a computer. For this reason, they were not widely used or known by many researchers until recently, although they were first described long ago by R. A. Fisher (1935, Chapter 3). That has changed with the development of the personal computer. As with the bootstrap, we do not have to make any assumptions about populations when we use the randomization model. To appreciate the randomization model, we need to contrast it with the classical statistical model.

THE ASSUMPTIONS UNDERLYING THE CLASSICAL STATISTICAL MODEL

The classical statistical model is based on random sampling from populations; therefore, with this model, statistical hypotheses are stated in terms of population parameters.

In Chapter 1, we learned that the classical statistical model is based on two assumptions, one about the data (or the source of the data) and the other about the behavior of the researcher:

1. *Assumption about the data:* Populations that have certain attributes (called parameters) exist. Some of these characteristics (such as the form or kind of population) are known, and some are unknown.
2. *Assumption about the behavior of the researcher:* We can estimate the values of the unknown parameters by taking random samples from the population.

These two assumptions are the basic assumptions underlying the z-test in Chapter 6 and the t-tests in Chapter 7. When we use Student's t-test, we also assume that the populations are normally distributed with equal variances.

We have already discussed the fact that normal distributions do not exist and that we rarely take random samples. Although the above assumptions do not fit what we do when we perform experiments, the classical statistical model seems to give us the correct answer about the effects of different treatments when we randomly assign participants to conditions, when we use similar sample sizes, and when the treatment effects are large.

THE ASSUMPTIONS UNDERLYING THE RANDOMIZATION MODEL

The randomization model requires only that a participant's performance reflects the treatment given to that individual and that participants be randomly assigned to the treatment conditions.

Like the classical statistical model, the randomization model for testing whether different treatments have the same or different effects on behavior is based on two assumptions, one about the data and the other about the behavior of the researcher:

1. *Assumption about the data:* Each participant's behavior will reflect the treatment given to him or her. In other words, if we give someone a treatment, it is going to somehow show up in his or her behavior.

2. *Assumption about the behavior of the researcher:* Participants are randomly assigned to conditions.

Both of these assumptions are quite reasonable. In fact, we implicitly make the first assumption when we use the classical statistical model to analyze data from experiments, although we do not state it as such. The second assumption matches an important aspect of how we conduct experiments.

These two assumptions can be combined into the primary assumption of a randomization test, sometimes referred to as exchangeability. In the context of a randomization test for testing hypotheses about treatment effects, **exchangeability** means that *if the treatments in the experiment have the same effect (that is, the null hypothesis is true—see below), then a participant would perform the same no matter what treatment group they were assigned to.*

HYPOTHESES FOR BOTH MODELS

The experimental hypotheses regarding the independent and dependent variables in our experiments are the same for both models. They differ in that the statistical hypotheses for the classical statistical model are about the parameters of populations, while the statistical hypotheses for the randomization model are about the effects of the treatments on the behavior of the participants.

Experimental Hypotheses

Our experimental hypotheses are the same in both models:

Null hypothesis: The effects of the treatments are the same; in other words, the experimental treatment does not have an effect on behavior that is different from the control treatment.

Alternative hypothesis: The effects of the treatments are different; in other words, the experimental treatment has an effect on behavior that is different from that of the control treatment.

We collect data to decide which of these two statements is true.

Statistical Hypotheses in the Classical Statistical Model

Because the classical statistical model deals with populations, our statistical hypotheses are about population parameters. For a two-group experiment, the statistical hypotheses that correspond to the experimental hypotheses are the following:

$$H_0: \mu_E = \mu_C \text{ or } \mu_E - \mu_C = 0$$

$$H_1: \mu_E \neq \mu_C \text{ or } \mu_E - \mu_C \neq 0$$

Statistical Hypotheses in the Randomization Model

Because the randomization model does not deal with populations or population parameters, the statistical hypotheses are not about population parameters; they are about the effects of the treatments on behavior. For a two-group experiment, the statistical hypotheses that correspond to the experimental hypotheses are as follows:

H_0: Each participant would have responded the same if given the other treatment. We would expect this outcome if the treatments or conditions had the same effect on behavior. In other words, "No matter which group an individual was assigned to, his or her behavior would be the same." This statement reflects the exchangeability assumption, described above.

H_1: Some of the participants would have responded differently had they received the other treatment.

These two hypotheses are reasonable because they are stated in terms of exactly what we want to learn from our experiment. Here, we are generalizing about the effects of the treatments, not about populations.

There are two general kinds of randomization tests: exact tests and approximate tests. With an **exact test**, we *generate all possible arrangements of our data*. The exact test is not too difficult to do when the sample sizes are relatively small, but the number of possible arrangements of the data can become overwhelming. In such a case, we have to use the approximate test. With an **approximate test**, we *take a random sample from the total possible arrangements*. The principles are the same whichever test we do.

THE EXACT RANDOMIZATION TEST FOR TESTING HYPOTHESES ABOUT THE EFFECTS OF DIFFERENT TREATMENTS ON BEHAVIOR

For the exact randomization test, start with all possible ways the obtained scores can be arranged in the two conditions and rank order them in terms of how much the two sets of scores overlap. The 5% of possible orders with the least amount of overlap constitute the critical region. We reject the null hypothesis when the original arrangement of scores is in that critical region.

After we obtain our participants and randomly assign them to groups, we administer the treatment and collect the data. Then we have to determine the probability of getting our data, assuming that the null hypothesis is true.

The following example illustrates how we calculate that probability and perform the hypothesis test with this model: Suppose we have 9 individuals who have been randomly assigned to two groups with 5 individuals in one group and 4 in the other. The scores for the individuals in both groups after the treatments are administered are as follows:

Group A	Group B
0	16
11	19
12	22
0	24
	29

What is the probability of getting this particular outcome, assuming that the null hypothesis is true? When the null hypothesis is true, the effects of the treatments are the same, and we expect that the two groups of scores would have a high degree of overlap. In other words, when the null hypothesis is true, the probability of getting overlapping sets of scores is high. On the other hand, when the null hypothesis is false, we expect the two groups of scores to be different and not overlap much or at all. Therefore, groups with a high degree of overlap have a high probability of occurring when the null hypothesis is true, and groups with little or no overlap have a low probability of occurring when the null hypothesis is true. Inspection of the data here reveals that the scores overlap. Does the amount of overlap lead us to reject the null hypothesis? The *t*-test works in a similar fashion: When the null hypothesis is true and we perform a *t*-test on the data, we expect to see sample means close together and sets of scores that overlap a lot. As we do with the classical statistical model, we need to have a way to calculate the probability of getting our data, assuming the null hypothesis is true.

With the randomization model, we calculate that probability in the following way: When the null hypothesis is true, each individual behaves the same no matter what treatment he or she is given (or what group he or she is assigned to). Therefore, first we calculate how many different ways we can arrange the scores for all of the individuals in our experiment so that we have n_1 individuals in one group and n_2 individuals in the other group (where $N = n_1 + n_2$, the total number of individuals). Then we generate all possible arrangements of our data and rank order them using some criterion for scaling the degree of overlap, define the critical region, and check whether our observed data are in the critical region.

Calculating the Total Number of Arrangements and Defining Our Critical Region

To come up with all of the different ways that the above scores can be arranged so that we have 4 (n_1) scores in one group and 5 (n_2) in another, we have to calculate the number of combinations of N things taken X at a time $\left(C_{n_1 n_2}^N \right)$. The formula for calculating this value is as follows:

$$C_{n_1 n_2}^N = \frac{N!}{n_1!(n_2)!} \tag{9.1}$$

Returning to our example, to determine how many ways we can arrange our 9 scores so that there are 5 in one group and 4 in the other, we substitute those numbers into this formula to obtain the following:

$$C_{5,4}^9 = \frac{9!}{5!4!} = \frac{9 \cdot 8 \cdot 7 \cdot 6 \cdot 5!}{5! \cdot 4 \cdot 3 \cdot 2 \cdot 1} = 126$$

Thus, there are 126 different ways that we could arrange our 9 scores so that 4 of them are in one group and 5 in the other. Out of the 126 different ways we can assign the 9 participants, *which ones would lead us to reject the null hypothesis*?

If we set our α = .05, then 5% of the total possible outcomes from our experiment will constitute the critical region. When the null hypothesis is true, the high-probability events are two sets of scores that overlap a lot. The low-probability events when the null hypothesis is true are two sets of scores that either do not overlap at all or overlap only a little. We choose as our critical region the 5% of the total possible outcomes that are unlikely to occur when the null hypothesis is true.

In our example, there are 126 possible arrangements of the 9 scores. Then 5% of 126 is 6.3. Because 6.3 is not an integer, we round down to the nearest integer (in this case 6).[1] The critical region will consist of those $\left(\alpha \text{ times } C_{n_1 n_2}^N \right)$ outcomes that have the least amount of overlap. The problem then is to determine which of the total number of outcomes are in the critical region (in our example, those 6 with least amount of overlap).

Identifying Those Arrangements in the Critical Region

Before we can identify those arrangements in the critical region, we need to generate the entire set of possible arrangements (126 in our example). We can do this by putting the lowest scores in one group and the highest in the other and then systematically exchanging first one score between each group, then two scores, and so forth until we have all of the lowest scores in the other group. See Table 9.1 for an example. In the first row, all of the low

---

[1] Clearly, having to round down the next integer will reduce alpha. In this example, alpha = 6/126 = .048.

TABLE 9.1 ■ Rank-Ordered Arrangements of the 126 Possible Outcomes of Our Experiment

Group A				Group B					$\sum A$	$\sum B$	$\bar{X}_A$	$\bar{X}_B$	$\bar{X}_A - \bar{X}_B$	t
0	11	12	16	19	20	22	24	29	39	114	9.75	22.80	−13.05	−3.61
0	11	12	19	16	20	22	24	29	42	111	10.50	22.20	−11.70	−2.77
0	11	12	20	16	19	22	24	29	43	110	10.75	22.00	−11.25	−2.56
0	11	12	22	16	19	20	24	29	45	108	11.25	21.60	−10.35	−2.20
0	11	12	24	16	19	20	22	29	47	106	11.75	21.20	−9.45	−1.90
.	.	.	.	.	.	.	.	.						
.	.	.	.	.	.	.	.	.						
.	.	.	.	.	.	.	.	.						
.	.	.	.	.	.	.	.	.						
16	22	24	29	0	11	12	19	20	91	62	22.75	12.40	10.35	2.20
19	20	24	29	0	11	12	16	22	92	61	23.00	12.20	10.80	2.37
19	22	24	29	0	11	12	16	20	94	59	23.50	11.80	11.70	2.77
20	22	24	29	0	11	12	16	19	95	58	23.75	11.60	12.15	3.01

248

scores are in Group A and all of the high scores are in Group B. The second row was created by exchanging the 16 in Group A with the 19 in Group B. The third row was generated by restoring the first row and then exchanging the 16 in Group A with the 20 in Group B. Although not shown in Table 9.1, this process was continued until every number in Group A was exchanged with a number in Group B. Each time, the data were restored to the row 1 state before the exchange was made. Then two numbers from Group A were exchanged with two numbers in Group B (again restoring the data to the row 1 state before the next exchange). The last three lines of the table show how four numbers were exchanged until all of the highest numbers were in Group A and the lowest in Group B.

Then we have to order these arrangements in terms of how much they overlap. There are a number of ways to do so, all of which will result in the same ordering. Six of these orderings are presented on the right side of Table 9.1. The simplest way is to calculate the sum of all of the scores in Group A ($\sum A$) or the sum of all of the scores in group B ($\sum B$). Clearly, the $\sum A$ is lowest when all of the low scores are in Group A (first row) and highest when all of the high scores are in Group A (last row). The same is true for $\sum B$: This value is highest when all of the high scores are in Group B (first row) and lowest when all of the low scores are in Group A (last row). The same pattern is true if we use the group means ($\bar{X}_A$ or $\bar{X}_B$). The last two columns use the difference between the means ($\bar{X}_A - \bar{X}_B$) and Student's t. Both sets of values are large negative numbers when all of the low scores are in Group A and all of the high scores are in Group B (first row). When the two groups overlap, both measures are close to zero. At the other end, both sets of values are large positive numbers. Which of these five measures ($\sum A$, $\sum B$, $\bar{X}_A$, $\bar{X}_B$, t) should we use? All will work, but using t allows us to easily compare our results to those of the standard t-test; therefore, this statistic is preferred.

We have already determined that for $\alpha = .05$, the critical region will contain six arrangements. When we want to perform a one-tailed test, then our critical region is the six arrangements on the side of the set of ordered arrangements consistent with our alternative hypothesis. When we want to perform a two-tailed test, we have to divide our critical value between the two ends of the set of ordered arrangements. In this case, the critical region is the three arrangements on each end.

Suppose, however, that the integer value of (α times C_X^N) is an odd number. We cannot split an odd number into two equal integers. In this case, we round (α times C_X^N) down to the next lower even integer and split the critical region as described above.[2]

Inspection of Table 9.1 reveals that the original data are on the third line. They are in the critical region for both a one-tailed test and a two-tailed test. Therefore, given these data, we reject the null hypothesis and conclude that the treatment had an effect.

---

[2] This procedure will reduce alpha for this test, but you can easily recompute alpha.

The Problem of Ties

Although it did not happen here, ties can occur, such that the value of t is the same for two or more arrangements of the data, and some of the tied scores may be in the critical region and the others may be outside the critical region. Consider the following set of rank-ordered t-scores where the integer value of (α times C_X^N) makes the critical region the lowest five t-scores:

-3.90
-2.69
-2.69
-2.30
<u>-2.30</u>
-2.30
-2.30
-1.70

If the t-score for our original data is -2.30, it is not clear which -2.30 is generated by our data. To deal with this situation, we adjust the critical value down to -2.69 and compute the actual value of α. In this situation, we cannot reject the null hypothesis at $\alpha = .05$.

The Effects of Sample Size on the Power of This Test

Although sample size affects the size of the critical region in terms of the number of possible arrangements contained in it, sample size has *no effect* on the probability of making an alpha error, because α is set by the experimenter and sample size does not affect this choice. However, sample size does affect the power of the test. The reason is that with larger sample sizes, groups with more overlap (and presumably smaller treatment effects) will lead to rejection of the null hypothesis. This concept is illustrated in Table 9.2.

TABLE 9.2 ■ The Relationship Between Sample Size and the Number of Arrangements in the Critical Region			
Sample Sizes		Total Number of Combinations	.05 × # Combinations
A	B		
3	3	20	1
4	4	70	2.5
4	5	126	6.3
5	5	252	12.6
10	10	184,756	9,237.8

When we have 3 participants in each group (total of 6 participants), the total number of possible arrangements is 20, and 5% of 20 is 1. Therefore, when we have only 3 participants in each group, the critical region only has one possible outcome in it. That outcome is the one in which there is no overlap between the scores (for example, all the higher scores are in one group and all the lower scores are in the other). In this case, we cannot perform a two-tailed test because if we have only one possible arrangement, it would be in the critical region. We cannot split that one possible arrangement in half to do a two-tailed test. Furthermore, we cannot perform a randomization test with only 2 participants in each group because 5% of the total possible arrangements would not equal even one arrangement in the critical region (although we could perform a standard t-test).

With 4 participants in each group (total of 8 participants), we have 2.5 possible arrangements in the critical region. To keep α at .05 or below, we round the number of possible arrangements in the critical region down to 2. For a two-tailed test, we have one possible arrangement in the critical region on either side. With 5 participants in each group (10 total), we have 12.6 possible arrangements in the critical region (one-tailed test). We round that number down to 12 arrangements to keep α at .05 or below. For a two-tailed test, we have 6 possible arrangements in the critical region on either side. Therefore, when we add 2 participants (1 to each group to increase the number of participants from 4 to 5 in each group), the number of possible arrangements in the critical region increases from 2 to 12. With 10 participants in each group (total of 20 participants, probably the most common sample size in psychology), we have 184,756 possible combinations, with 9,237.8 of them in the critical region.

Therefore, with a small sample size, the only results that will allow us to reject the null hypothesis are those in which there is complete nonoverlap or very small overlap. However, with larger sample sizes, much more overlap will allow us to reject the null hypothesis; that is, the larger the sample size, the smaller the differences between the two groups that will allow us to reject the null hypothesis. This outcome occurs because the number of possible arrangements in the critical region is getting larger and larger as sample size increases, even though the probability of making an alpha error remains the same.

Although the exact randomization test is a nonparametric test (because it is not a test about the parameters of a population), the power of this test is the same as the power of Student's t-test when all of the assumptions of that t-test are met. However, the power of an exact randomization test may be greater when the assumptions of Student's t-test are not met. For example, suppose that the last data point in Group B above was 290 instead of 29. In this case, the value of Student's t would be -1.035. With 7 degrees of freedom, the critical value for a two-tailed test with $\alpha = .05$ is 2.365, and $p > .05$. However, when we perform a randomization/permutation test with that substitution, the six most extreme values of t on the low side of the distribution of permutations are:

−1.069

−1.044

−1.035 (t for observed data)

−1.018

−1.009

−1.001

Even when 29 has been replaced by 290, t for our observed data has the same ordinal location in the critical region as before. Although this value of t would not be statistically significant with Student's t-test, it is significant with the randomization/permutation test.[3]

BOX 9.1

HOW TO USE THE EXACT RANDOMIZATION TEST TO TEST HYPOTHESES ABOUT THE EFFECTS OF DIFFERENT TREATMENTS ON BEHAVIOR

1. Obtain participants, randomly assign them to groups, administer the appropriate treatments, and collect the data.

2. Use the following formula to calculate the total number of ways our N data points from both groups can be arranged so that there are n_1 scores in one group and n_2 in the other:

$$C^N_{n_1 n_2} = \frac{N!}{n_1! n_2!}$$

3. Generate all possible arrangements of our data and rank order them using some criterion for scaling the degree of overlap. (Calculating the standard t-statistic for each possible arrangement is recommended.)

4. Determine the number of arrangements in the critical region by calculating the integer value of $\left(\alpha \text{ times } C^N_{n_1 n_2} \right)$.

a. When a one-tailed test is performed, the critical region is all of the $\left(\alpha \text{ times } C^N_{n_1 n_2} \right)$ arrangements on the side of our rank-ordered set of arrangements consistent with our alternative hypothesis.

b. When performing a two-tailed test, find the largest even number below $\left(\alpha \text{ times } C^N_{n_1 n_2} \right)$. The critical region is distributed so that half of those arrangements are on each end of our rank-ordered set of arrangements.

5. Reject H_0 when our obtained data are in the critical region.

---

[3] Even though the means and sample variances are farther apart when the last data point in Group B is 290, the Welch–Satterthwaite approximation $t = -1.17$ is not statistically significant when compared to the t-distribution with 4 degrees of freedom.

Therefore, the randomization/permutation test can be a robust alternative to Student's t when the amount of overlap between the two groups is the same even when one group has an outlier. Because of the large sample sizes in the experiment by Barlett (2015) on the effects of message type on state hostility scores described at the beginning of Chapter 7, we cannot use the exact randomization test to analyze the data unless we have a very powerful computer. Instead, we will have to use the approximate randomization test described below.

THE APPROXIMATE RANDOMIZATION TEST FOR TESTING HYPOTHESES ABOUT THE EFFECTS OF DIFFERENT TREATMENTS ON BEHAVIOR

For the approximate randomization test, take a random sample from the total possible arrangements of the obtained scores and rank order them in terms of how much the two sets of scores overlap. The 5% with the least amount of overlap constitute the critical region. We reject the null hypothesis when the original arrangement of scores is in that critical region.

The exact randomization test described above is based on all possible arrangements of the data, and for that reason it is preferred. However, as noted in Table 9.3, even with sample sizes of 10 in a group (a modest sample size), the number of possible arrangements is 184,756, and the number of arrangements in the critical region for $\alpha = .05$ is 9,237.8. Furthermore, the number of arrangements increases rapidly with each additional participant added to both groups: With 11 participants in both groups, the number of combinations is 705,432, and the number of arrangements in the critical region for $\alpha = .05$ is 35,271.6. Although it is possible to write a computer program to handle such quantities of arrangements, there reaches a point where the numbers get out of hand. Fortunately, there is a way to handle these situations with an approximate randomization test.

With an **approximate randomization test**, we *take a random sample from the total possible arrangements*. Fortunately, we can obtain such a sample without generating all of the possible arrangements (which would defeat the purpose of using an approximate test) with the following procedure: Calculate t for our data. Combine the scores from both groups into one long string of numbers and shuffle them. Then, use a random assignment procedure (such as flipping a coin) to assign each number to one of two groups (for example, heads to Group A and tails to Group B), making sure we end up with the same numbers of scores in each of these new groups as in the original groups. Calculate t for each new arrangement of scores. Put the scores back into the one string of numbers, reshuffle them, and repeat the random assignment procedure at least 200 times, rank ordering the values of t. With $\alpha = .05$, the 5% most extreme values of t on one side constitute the critical region for a one-tailed test. For a two-tailed test, the 2.5% most extreme t's on each side constitute the critical region. With 200 resamples and $\alpha = .05$, the critical region is comprised of the 10 values on the end for a one-tailed test and the 5 values on each side for a two-tailed test. We reject the null hypothesis if the value of t for the original set of data would be in the critical region.

When we perform this procedure, our original data may not be one of the possible outcomes listed in the critical region, but as long as it is somewhere within those values, we can reject the null hypothesis. If we took our same data and did this again, we would get slightly different critical regions because the computer might not generate the same arrangements the second time around as it did the first time. But we would expect that if the null hypothesis were false, our original value of t would be somewhere within that region each time.

The procedure just described mimics starting with a population of, for example, 184,756 possible combinations of 20 numbers taken 10 at a time and randomly sampling 200 of those 184,756 possible combinations. The 200 random samples would provide an adequate representation of the 184,756 possible combinations.

Power of the Approximate Randomization Test

As is the case with all statistical hypothesis tests, power increases here as the sample sizes increase. This power increase occurs with the approximation test just described for the following reasons: As we saw in Chapter 7, when the null hypothesis is false, the value of t-statistics increase as sample sizes increase (even when the difference between the sample means does not increase). The 10 values that comprise the critical region(s) will be large values of t. Therefore, as sample sizes increase, the original t-value will tend to increase and be more likely to be among those in the critical region(s). The point is that although increases in sample sizes do not increase the number of values in the critical region (as with the exact test), the power increases because the original value of t is more likely to be among those in the critical region.

There is however, a price we pay when we perform an approximate rather than an exact randomization test: The power of the exact test will always be higher than the power of an approximate test, but the difference in power is small.

BOX 9.2

HOW TO USE THE APPROXIMATE RANDOMIZATION TEST TO TEST HYPOTHESES ABOUT THE EFFECTS OF DIFFERENT TREATMENTS ON BEHAVIOR

1. Obtain participants, randomly assign them to groups, administer the appropriate treatments, and collect the data.

2. Calculate *t* for our data.

3. Combine the scores from both groups into one long string of numbers and shuffle them. Then use a random assignment procedure (such as flipping a coin) to assign each number to one of two groups (for example, heads to Group A and tails to Group B), making sure to end up with the same numbers of scores in each of these new groups as in the original groups.

4. Calculate *t* for each new arrangement of scores.

5. Put the scores back into the one string of numbers, reshuffle them, and repeat the random assignment procedure at least 200 times.

6. Rank order the values of *t*. With $\alpha = .05$, the 5% most extreme values of *t* on one side constitute the critical region for a one-tailed test. For a two-tailed test, the 2.5% most extreme *t*'s on each side constitute the critical region.

7. Reject H_0 when the value of *t* for the original set of data would be among those in the critical region.

We can analyze the data from Table 7.1 easily by shuffling the data and distributing the scores between the two conditions 1,000 times. Each time we complete our shuffle, we calculate Student's *t*, put each of those 1,000 values of *t* in a column, and rank order them (sorting from lowest to highest). When we use $p < .05$ as our criterion for whether to reject the null hypothesis, the highest 25 and the lowest 25 values define the two-tailed critical region, and the highest 50 values of *t* define the one-tailed critical region. The highest 50 values from one application of the procedure just described are presented in Table 9.3. The obtained value for Student's *t* for the original data is 2.46. That value, although not in Table 9.3, is in the critical region. Repeating the procedure would yield a different set of 50 values for the critical region, but the obtained value of 2.46 would still be in the critical region. Note that these results would also lead us to reject the null hypothesis with a two-tailed test, because 2.46 is still among the top 25 values of *t* in this case. The presence of the same values of *t* in Table 9.3 is due to the number of tied scores in the original data.

TABLE 9.3 ■ **One-Tailed Critical Region Based on 1,000 Shuffles of the Data in Table 7.1**

Rank (high to low)	t	Rank (high to low)	t	Rank (high to low)	t	Rank (high to low)	t	Rank (high to low)	t
1	3.24	11	2.50	21	2.10	31	1.93	41	1.73
2	3.08	12	2.43	22	2.09	32	1.92	42	1.71
3	2.99	13	2.39	23	2.09	33	1.92	43	1.70
4	2.94	14	2.35	24	2.08	34	1.89	44	1.69
5	2.91	15	2.33	25	2.07	35	1.78	45	1.68
6	2.85	16	2.33	26	2.01	36	1.77	46	1.66
7	2.75	17	2.33	27	2.01	37	1.76	47	1.65
8	2.62	18	2.25	28	2.00	38	1.76	48	1.64
9	2.61	19	2.17	29	1.95	39	1.74	49	1.64
10	2.52	20	2.14	30	1.95	40	1.73	50	1.64

USING THE RANDOMIZATION MODEL TO INVESTIGATE POSSIBLE EFFECTS OF TREATMENTS

We can investigate whether our experimental treatment results in an additive or a multiplicative effect by performing a randomization test on the difference between the two variances.

As noted in Chapter 7, treatments can affect behavior in a number of ways. The simplest is that the experimental treatment adds a constant to the scores of individuals (*additive effect*). In this case, the measures of central tendency (mean and median) are also shifted by that constant, and the difference between the group means or medians of the experimental and control groups is an estimate of the experimental treatment's effect on behavior (relative to the control condition). The variances of the experimental and control groups should be similar because adding a constant does not affect the variance of the new set of scores.

On the other hand, when the experimental treatment multiplies pretreatment scores by a constant (*multiplicative effect*), the mean and median are both multiplied by that constant, and the variance of the scores in the experimental group is increased by the constant squared. Because multiplicative effects result in different individuals' scores changing by different amounts, we say a *participant-by-treatment interaction* occurs. Participant-by-treatment interactions are not restricted to multiplicative effects; they occur anytime different participants are affected differently by the experimental treatments.

Student's *t*-test described in Chapter 7 assumes independent random sampling from normal distributions that have the same variance. This homogeneity of variance occurs when there is an additive treatment effect. The presence of a participant-by-treatment interaction can reduce the power of Student's *t*-test. The Welch–Satterthwaite test is an attempt to maintain the power of the *t*-test when the two group variances are different.

In contrast to its role in the classical statistical model, Student's *t* is a descriptive statistic in the randomization test described here. When the statistic is used in this way, homogeneity of variance is *not* required, and the lack of homogeneity of variance does not reduce the power of the test. However, the occurrence of a participant-by-treatment interaction should be of interest because it tells us that the two treatments (experimental and control) have different effects on different individuals' behaviors. If we suspect such an interaction, we can use empirical quantile–quantile plots (Chapter 7) to reveal it. We can also use a randomization test with differences between group variances as our test statistic to test whether the treatments employed had differential effects on the spread of our data. The null hypothesis in this case is that the effect of the experimental treatment is additive, and the alternative hypothesis is that the effect of the experimental treatment is multiplicative. This test can supplement the permutation (randomization) test with Student's *t* for the null hypothesis that the effects of the treatments are the same. In the first case, we are focusing on the group means, and in the second case, on the group variances. Taken together, both tests reveal how the experimental treatment affects the behavior of the participants relative to the control treatment. That is information worth knowing!

SINGLE-PARTICIPANT EXPERIMENTAL DESIGNS

An important assumption underlying Student's t *and other parametric tests is that the resulting scores are independent from each other. We violate that assumption when we test a single individual repeatedly under two (or more) experimental conditions. Therefore, Student's* t-*test is not appropriate for analyzing data generated in that manner. For this common research design in applied behavioral analysis research, the randomization test is appropriate.*

An important assumption that underlies hypothesis tests using the classical statistical model is that independent random sampling from populations has occurred. Although we do not use random samples when we conduct experiments, we still assume that our data consist of independent observations. We do not satisfy this condition when we test a single participant a number of times across different experimental conditions. The simplest single-participant design consists of repeatedly testing an individual under a baseline or control condition, then applying an experimental treatment and testing that same individual repeatedly under the experimental treatment. The result is two sets of scores, one for the control condition and one for the experimental condition. The problem is that the scores obtained under each condition are not independent of each other; that is, the score on one trial can have an effect on the score on a subsequent trial within the same condition. This lack of independence can inflate the probability of making a type I error when we analyze these data using Student's *t*. Randomization tests do not require that the scores be independent; therefore, they are appropriate for analyzing data and drawing conclusions from single-participant experiments in which the behavior of a single individual is studied over time under different experimental conditions. See Dugard, File, & Todman (2012) for examples that illustrate how to use randomization (permutation tests) for various single-participant experimental designs.

Summary

Randomization tests do not require assumptions about independent random sampling from populations; therefore, they are nonparametric tests. The only assumptions required for randomization tests are that participants' performance reflects the treatment given to them and they are randomly assigned to the treatment conditions. When the assumptions underlying Student's *t*-test are met, randomization tests have the same power as Student's *t*-test. However, when the assumptions underlying Student's *t*-test are not met, randomization tests can be more powerful than Student's *t*-test for detecting treatment effects. Randomization tests can also be used to analyze data from single-participant experiments. Additional examples of randomization tests will be given in subsequent chapters. Overall, these tests are flexible and useful techniques for researchers across a variety of situations.

Conceptual Exercises

1. What is the assumption of exchangeability for a randomization test? How is this assumption related to the assumptions of the classical statistical model?

2. Compare the experimental hypotheses and the statistical hypotheses for the classical statistical and randomization models. Are they the same or different? Why or why not?

3. What are the differences between exact and approximate randomization tests?

4. How are arrangements used in the exact randomization model? If we have 5 scores in one group and 6 scores in another group, how many ways can we arrange our 11 scores across those two groups? How would you create and use a critical region to engage in hypothesis testing in this example?

5. Which is more powerful, an exact randomization test or an approximate randomization test? Explain your answer.

6. Describe how to perform an *approximate randomization (permutation) test* on whether a treatment has an effect (whether it is different from the control treatment). Include the following in your answer:

   a. The experimental and statistical hypotheses for this test

   b. The test statistic you would use

   c. How you would create the distribution of the test statistic when the null hypothesis is true and how you would define the critical region

   d. How and why sample size affects power of this test

Additional Resources

Edgington, E. S., & Onghena, P. (2007). Randomization tests (4th ed.). Boca Raton, FL: Chapman Hall/CRC.

Good, P. H. (2001). Resampling methods: A practical guide to data analysis (2nd ed.). Boston, MA: Birkäuser.

Student Study Site

Visit the Student Study Site at **https://study.sagepub.com/friemanstats** for a variety of useful tools including data sets, additional exercises, and web resources.

EXPLORING THE RELATIONSHIP BETWEEN TWO VARIABLES

Correlation

U p to this point, we have focused on research questions that involve whether different treatments have the same or different effects on behavior and questions about whether a population parameter is a certain value. In this chapter, we turn our attention to research questions about whether there is a relationship between two variables. Although the questions are different, the ways we attempt to answer them make use of the principles developed in the first part of this book. We will focus on the most commonly used descriptive statistics for measuring the relationship between two variables and then illustrate how we can test hypotheses about the relationship.

To illustrate the assessment of relationships between variables, we will examine a study in the domain of social prejudice. Individuals of many social groups face prejudice and discrimination. McManus, Feyes, and Saucier (2011) were interested in the factors that would predict prejudicial attitudes toward individuals with intellectual disabilities. Using a sample of 125 undergraduate students, they assessed the quantity of contact the participants had with individuals with intellectual disabilities (e.g., *In high school, I had frequent interactions with people with intellectual disabilities*), the quality of contact they had with individuals with intellectual disabilities (e.g., *Overall, I have had positive experiences with people with intellectual disabilities*), and the amount of knowledge they thought they possessed about intellectual disabilities (e.g., *I think I know more about intellectual disabilities than other people*). The participants reported their agreement with various statements to assess the quantity of contact, quality of contact, and perceived knowledge on scales from 1 (*strongly disagree*) to 9 (*strongly agree*). Their responses were averaged to produce scores for each of these three factors such that higher scores reflected higher levels of quantity of contact, quality of contact, and perceived knowledge, respectively. The participants' levels of prejudicial attitudes toward individuals with intellectual disabilities were measured using the Mental Retardation Attitude Inventory–Revised (MRAI-R; Antonak & Harth, 1994). On this measure, the participants used the same response scale from 1 (*strongly disagree*) to 9 (*strongly agree*) to report their levels of agreement with statements such as *The child who has an intellectual disability should be integrated into regular classes at school*. Again, the participants' responses were averaged, with higher scores reflecting more positive (i.e., less prejudicial) attitudes toward individuals with intellectual disabilities.

McManus et al. (2011) hypothesized, and indeed found, that participants' levels of quantity of contact with individuals with intellectual disabilities, quality of contact with individuals with intellectual disabilities, and perceived knowledge about intellectual disabilities were positively correlated with their scores on the MRAI-R. That is, as their levels of quantity of contact, quality of contact, and perceived knowledge increased, so did their positive attitudes toward individuals with intellectual disabilities. However, the researchers expected that the participants' quality of contact with individuals with intellectual disabilities would be particularly important as a factor relating to their attitudes toward such individuals. Accordingly, we will focus on this relationship in the following example, in which we measure the degree of relationship between participants' quality of contact with individuals with intellectual disabilities and their scores on the MRAI-R. In Chapter 11, we will focus on using the participants' quality of contact with individuals with intellectual disabilities to predict their scores on the MRAI-R.

MEASURING THE DEGREE OF RELATIONSHIP BETWEEN TWO INTERVAL-SCALE VARIABLES

We can use the Pearson product-moment correlation coefficient as a descriptive statistic for measuring the degree of relationship between two variables when there is a monotonic relationship between the variables. We describe how this correlation coefficient captures the degree of relationship and the factors that affect the value of this coefficient.

When two variables are related, changes in one variable are accompanied by changes in the other. For example, there is a relationship between the IQs of parents and the IQs of their children (Kagan & Moss, 1959): Parents with higher IQs tend to have children with higher IQs, and parents with lower IQs tend to have children with lower IQs. The relationship is not perfect, but it does exist. We can use a **coefficient of correlation** to *measure the degree of relationship (or association) between the variables*. The most commonly used measure of a monotonic relationship[1] between interval scale variables such as IQ is the **Pearson product-moment correlation coefficient**:

$$r = \frac{\sum \left(X - \overline{X} \right)\left(Y - \overline{Y} \right)}{n S_X S_Y} \tag{10.1}$$

The Pearson product-moment correlation coefficient[2] can be used as a descriptive statistic to describe the degree of relationship between two variables, very much as we use the sample mean to describe the central tendency of a set of numbers and the sample variance to describe the dispersion among a set of numbers.

We calculate the Pearson product-moment correlation coefficient from Equation 10.1 as follows: The data are pairs of observations measured on both the X scale (the first variable) and the Y scale (the second variable). First, calculate the mean and standard deviation of the X-values of all of the pairs of observations (ignoring the Y-values). Do the same for the Y-values. Then, for each pair of observations, multiply the difference between the X-value and the mean of $X (X - \overline{X})$ by the difference between the Y-value and mean of $Y \left(Y - \overline{Y} \right)$. Sum these products and divide the sum by n times the standard deviations of X and Y (that is, S_X times S_Y). The reason for dividing by S_X and S_Y is to create a measure that is independent of the scales on which X and Y are measured (that is, a standardized measure like the z-score). This index allows us to compare the degree of relationship for two different sets of measurements (for example, to determine whether the correlation between mother's IQ and child's IQ is larger or smaller than the correlation between mother's IQ and father's IQ). Furthermore, r is constrained to be between −1 and +1. How the Pearson product-moment correlation coefficient reflects the relationship between X and Y is based on Figure 10.1.

Whether each $(X - \overline{X})(Y - \overline{Y})$ is a positive or a negative number depends on which quadrant of Figure 10.1 it is in. When a score is in either the lower left or upper right quadrants, $(X - \overline{X})(Y - \overline{Y})$ will be a *positive number*, and when a score is in either the upper left and lower right quadrants, $(X - \overline{X})(Y - \overline{Y})$ will be a negative number. Therefore, according to Equation 10.1, when *more* of the scores are in the lower left and upper right quadrants (as opposed to the upper left and lower right quadrants), the Pearson product-moment correlation coefficient will be positive. On the other hand, Equation 10.1 also tells us that

---

[1] In a monotonic relationship, as one variable changes in a given direction (increases or decreases), the other variable changes in the same or the opposite direction. In the example of the IQs of parents and children, both variables change in the same direction, which demonstrates a positive monotonic relationship.

[2] Although Karl Pearson's name is attached to this measure of the degree of relationship or association, he was not the first person to employ the product-moment formulation (that honor goes to Bravais [1846]) or to develop a practical way to create a single measure of correlation (that honor goes to Francis Galton [1888]). Pearson's contribution was to derive the formula we use today. This is a "product-moment correlation coefficient" because the term in the numerator is the sum of the products of what are called the "first moments" around the mean: $X - \overline{X}$ and $Y - \overline{Y}$.

FIGURE 10.1 ■ The signs (+ or −) of $X - \bar{X}$, $Y - \bar{Y}$, and their products for each of the four quadrants in this figure. The cross products for each quadrant are in brackets.

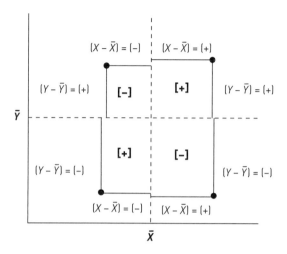

when *more* of the scores are in the upper left and lower right quadrants (as opposed to the lower left and upper right quadrants), the Pearson product-moment correlation coefficient will be negative. When the scores are evenly distributed among all four quadrants, there will be a zero (or close to zero) correlation, because the positive and negative cross products will sum to zero (or close to zero). The value of the Pearson product moment correlation coefficient will be +1 when all of the scores are on a straight line that extends from the lower left quadrant to the upper right quadrant, and it will be −1 when all of the scores are on a straight line that extends from the upper left quadrant to the lower right quadrant.

Returning to our example of IQs of parents and IQs of their children, there is a positive correlation. If we took a group of parents and ranked them in order from most intelligent to least intelligent, and we then took their children and ranked them from most intelligent to least intelligent, the parents and children with the highest scores would be generally associated with each other, and the parents and children with the lowest scores would generally be associated with each other. Thus, most of the parent–child pairs would be in the upper right and lower left quadrants of Figure 10.1. If the correlation were a perfect positive correlation, then the parent with the highest IQ would have the child with the highest IQ, the parent with the next highest IQ would have the child with the next highest IQ, and so forth until we got to the parent with the lowest IQ having the child with the lowest IQ. On the other hand, if there were no correlation between IQs of parents and IQs of their children, then if we ranked the parents in order from most intelligent to least intelligent, their children's IQs would be distributed randomly with respect to their parents' IQs. A high-IQ parent would be just as likely to have a child with

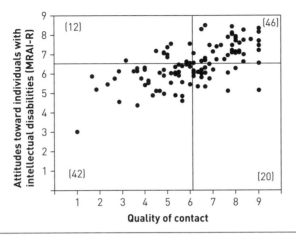

> FIGURE 10.2 ■ Scatterplot of the data from McManus et al. (2011) on the relationship between quality of contact and scores on the MRAI-R scales; $r = .615$.

Note: The total number of data points in each quadrant is in parentheses.

a high IQ (and be in the upper right quadrant) or a low IQ (and be in the lower right quadrant), and so forth.

Therefore, the Pearson product-moment correlation coefficient measures the degree of relationship by taking into account which quadrants most of the scores lie in. The value of the Pearson product-moment correlation coefficient ranges between −1 and +1 (−1 ≤ r ≤ +1). The value of r is zero when there is no relationship between the variables. The value of r is +1 when there is a perfect positive correlation, and it is −1 when there is a perfect negative correlation.

The data collected by McManus et al. (2011) on the relationship between participants' quality of contact with individuals with intellectual disabilities and their scores on the MRAI-R are presented in Figure 10.2. Because the pairs of scores are the same in many places, the scatterplot contains fewer plotted points than the total number of pairs of scores. The actual numbers of points in each quadrant are indicated in parentheses in the corners of each quadrant.[3] It is clear that more data points are in the lower left and upper right quadrants than in the upper left and lower right quadrants. For these data, $r = +.615$.

Attributes of Data That Affect the Pearson Product-Moment Correlation

As noted above, the value of the Pearson product-moment correlation coefficient depends on how the scores are distributed among the four quadrants in Figure 10.1. In particular, the value of the Pearson r depends on the following:

---

[3] Only 120 students completed both the quality of contact and the MRAI-R scales.

FIGURE 10.3 ■ Perfect linear relationship (*top*; *r* = 1.00); perfect monotonic but nonlinear relationship (*bottom*; *r* = .95).

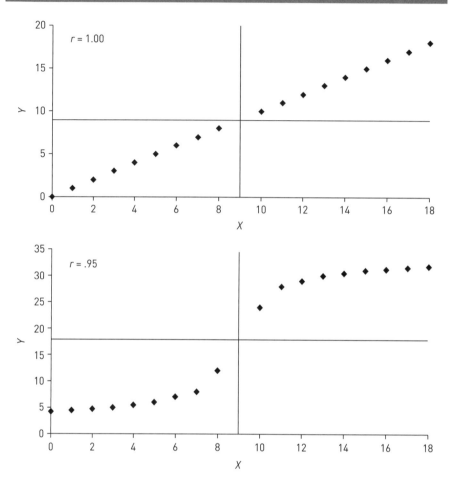

- the form of the relationship (for the same spread of scores, the value of the Pearson *r* is highest when there is a linear relationship);
- how close the scores are to the line depicting the relationship (the closer the scores are to the line, the higher the value of the Pearson *r*);
- the slope of the line depicting the relationship (the steeper the slope, the higher the value of the Pearson *r*);
- the presence of outliers, which decrease the value of the Pearson *r*; and
- the range of scores on both measures.

We can see the effects of these characteristics of the distribution in Figures 10.3, 10.4, and 10.5.

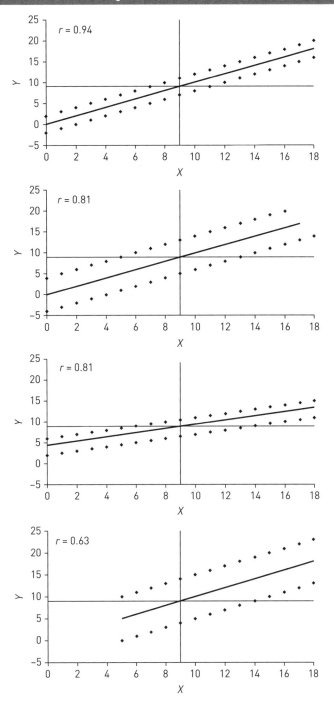

EFFECT OF THE FORM OF THE RELATIONSHIP On the top of Figure 10.3, you see a situation in which there is a perfect positive correlation ($r = 1.00$). Note that all of the scores are in the upper right and lower left quadrants and no scores are in the other two quadrants. However, as we see on the bottom of Figure 10.3, there is a positive monotonic relationship between X and Y and all of the scores are in the upper right and lower left quadrants, yet the value of r is not quite 1.00 ($r = .95$). Therefore the Pearson $r = 1.00$ *only* when all of the scores are on a straight line.

EFFECTS OF THE SPREAD OF THE SCORES, THE SLOPE OF THE RELATIONSHIP, AND THE DATA RANGE Figure 10.4 depicts four situations. In the top panel, there is a linear relationship with the scores distributed equally on either side of a straight line ($r = .94$).

In the second panel, the slope is the same, but the scores are further from the line ($r = .81$). It is clear from these examples that the value of the Pearson r depends on the spread of the scores around a straight line. The Pearson r decreases when the scores are further from a straight line because more of them are in the upper left and lower right quadrants.

In the third panel, the scores have the same spread around the line as in the top panel, but the slope of the line is shallower ($r = .81$). Thus, the value of the Pearson r depends on

FIGURE 10.5 ■ The effect of an outlier on the value of the Pearson r depends on the location of the outlier.

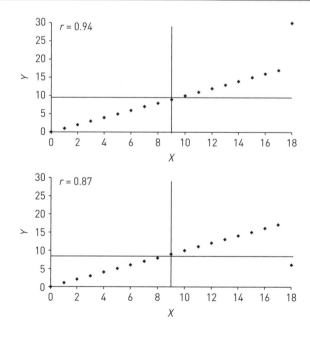

the slope of the relationship, because more scores are in the upper left and bottom quadrants when the slope is more shallow than when it is steeper.

Finally, in the bottom panel, the spread of the scores is the same as in the second panel, but the range of the data has been restricted to the highest 14 X values and $r = .63$.

EFFECTS OF OUTLIERS Two examples of outliers are presented in Figure 10.5. In both cases, the relationship is perfectly linear except for the last point. In the top panel, the outlier is 12 units above the straight line (producing a value of $r = .94$), and in the bottom, it is 12 units below the straight line (producing a value of $r = .87$). In both cases, the Pearson r is reduced, but it is reduced more in the second case, no doubt because the outlier is in the lower right quadrant.

All of the effects described above complicate the interpretation of the value of the Pearson r as a measure of the degree of relationship between two variables (Wilcox, 2003).

RANDOMIZATION (PERMUTATION) MODEL FOR TESTING HYPOTHESES ABOUT THE RELATIONSHIP BETWEEN TWO VARIABLES

We can use the randomization (permutation) model to test whether there is a monotonic relationship between two variables without making any assumptions about the source of the data. The only assumption we have to make is that when there is no relationship, any X can be paired with any Y.

In the preceding section, we saw how the Pearson product-moment correlation coefficient can be used as a descriptive statistic for measuring the degree of relationship between two interval-scale variables. We can use the randomization (permutation) model to construct a hypothesis test to determine whether there is a relationship between two interval-scale variables without making any assumptions about the source of the data (that is, distributions of the variables, random sampling, or the form of the relationship). The research hypotheses for this test are as follows:

There is no relationship between the two variables.

There is a relationship between the two variables.

We need only one assumption to use the randomization (permutation) model to test these hypotheses: *When there is no relationship, any X could occur with any Y.* This assumption is called **exchangeability**.

Here are the statistical hypotheses:

H_0: There is no relationship between the two variables; in other words, any X could be paired with any Y.

H_1: There is a relationship between the two variables; in other words, only certain Xs will be paired with certain Ys.

To decide which of these hypotheses is true, we have to determine the probability of getting our data, assuming that the null hypothesis is true.

When the null hypothesis is true and there is no relationship between the two variables under consideration, then no matter what the X-score, the Y-score can be any possible value in the range of Y. In other words, the individual with a certain X-score is just as likely to have any Y score as any other. Therefore, under the null hypothesis, we can calculate the total possible number of ways that we could pair up all the Xs with all of the Ys, rank order those XY pairs according to some criterion of degree of relationship, calculate α times the total number of ways we can pair X and Y, and then ask, "Of those possible ways we could pair them together, which of them would lead us to reject the hypothesis that there is no relationship?" The ones that would lead us to reject the null hypothesis would be the ones in which high Xs are paired with high Ys and those in which low Xs are paired with low Ys (or high Xs are paired with low Ys, and vice versa, for a negative correlation). As is the case with the randomization (permutation) test for whether a treatment has an effect, there are an *exact* test and an *approximate* test.

Exact Randomization (Permutation) Test for Whether There Is a Relationship Between Two Variables

Suppose we have the following five pairs of scores:

X	Y
1	6
2	7
3	8
4	9
5	10

What is the total number of possible ways we could take these five X values and pair them with every Y value? The answer is $n!$[4] In this case, $5! = 120$. We need a way to rank order these 120 possible arrangements of X and Y in terms of the degree of relationship. Here again there are a number of possible candidates, all of which yield the same ordering:

---

[4] Recall that $n!$ represents the factorial operation by which a value is computed by multiplying all of the positive integers up to and including the value of N (e.g., $5! = 1 \times 2 \times 3 \times 4 \times 5 = 120$).

$$\Sigma XY \tag{10.2a}$$

$$\sum \left(X - \bar{X}\right)\left(Y - \bar{Y}\right) \tag{10.2b}$$

$$\sum \frac{\left(X - \bar{X}\right)\left(Y - \bar{Y}\right)}{n} \tag{10.2c}$$

$$r = \frac{\sum \left(X - \bar{X}\right)\left(Y - \bar{Y}\right)}{nS_X S_Y} \tag{10.2d}$$

We could use any of these formulas to rank order our $n!$ possible arrangements of X and Y, but the Pearson r is preferred because it gives us a measure that is easiest to interpret.

The critical region consists of α times $n!$ scores. We rank order the 120 possible arrangements and compute how many of them constitute 5% of that number. In this case, 5% of 120 is 6 pairs of scores. Now we determine whether our original sample is one of those six most extreme pairs. If it is, we reject the null hypothesis. This process is described in Box 10.1.

BOX 10.1

HOW TO USE THE EXACT RANDOMIZATION (PERMUTATION) TEST TO TEST HYPOTHESES ABOUT WHETHER THERE IS A RELATIONSHIP BETWEEN TWO VARIABLES

1. Obtain data from n participants measured on two different variables (X and Y).

2. Calculate the total number of ways we could pair the measurements so that every X value is paired with every Y value. That number is **$n!$**

3. Generate all $n!$ possible arrangements of your data and rank order them using some criterion for scaling the degree of relationship for each set of arrangements. (Calculating the Pearson product moment correlation coefficient (r) is recommended.)

4. Determine the number of arrangements in the critical region by calculating the integer value of α level $\times$ $n!$.

a. When performing a one-tailed test, the critical region is all of the α level $\times$ $n!$ arrangements on the side of our rank-ordered set of arrangements consistent with our alternative hypothesis.

b. When performing a two-tailed test, find the largest even number below α level $\times$ $n!$. The critical region is distributed so that half of the α level $\times$ $n!$ arrangements is on each end of our rank-ordered set of arrangements.

5. Reject H_0 when our obtained data are in the critical region.

Approximate Randomization (Permutation) Test for Whether There Is a Relationship Between Two Variables

Most research on the relationship between two variables involves many more than five pairs of scores. It is quite clear from Table 10.1 that the number of arrangements of the data ($n!$) gets very large very fast.

Most of the time, therefore, we have to resort to an *approximate* randomization (permutation) test to use this model. As was the case with the randomization (permutation) model used to test hypotheses about the effects of different treatments, the procedure is to take a random sample of, say, 200 of the total possible arrangements of our data, rank order these arrangements according to some criterion for scaling the degree of relationship, construct a critical region based on whether we have a one-tailed or a two-tailed test, and determine whether our original arrangement is in the critical region. This process is described in Box 10.2.

When we apply the approximate randomization test to the data in Figure 10.2, using 1,000 shuffles, the top 25 values of r constitute the critical region for a two-tailed test with $\alpha = .05$ on the positive side, and the 25 values on the negative side make up the remainder of the two-tailed critical region. The critical value on that side is .175. With $r = .620$, we can reject the hypothesis that there is no relationship between participants' quality of contact with individuals with intellectual disabilities and their scores on the MRAI-R.

TABLE 10.1 ■ The Relationship Between Sample Size and the Number of Arrangements in the Critical Region		
Number of Pairs of Scores (n)	**Number of Arrangements (n!)**	**.05 Times No. of Arrangements**
5	120	6
6	720	36
7	5,040	252
8	40,320	2,016
9	362,880	18,144
10	3,628,800	181,440
15	1.3×10^{12}	6.5×10^{10}
20	2.4×10^{18}	1.2×10^{17}
30	2.6×10^{32}	1.3×10^{31}
40	8.1×10^{47}	4.0×10^{46}
50	3.0×10^{64}	1.5×10^{63}
493	1.6×10^{1115}	8.1×10^{1113}

BOX 10.2

HOW TO USE THE APPROXIMATE RANDOMIZATION (PERMUTATION) TEST TO TEST HYPOTHESES ABOUT WHETHER THERE IS A RELATIONSHIP BETWEEN TWO VARIABLES.

1. Obtain data from n participants measured on two different variables (X and Y).

2. Calculate r for your data.

3. Shuffle the measurements on one of the variables and calculate r on the new arrangement.

4. Repeat step 3 at least 200 times.

5. Rank order the values of r. With $\alpha = .05$, the 5% most extreme values of r on one side constitute the critical region for a one-tailed test. For a two-tailed test, the 2.5% most extreme rs on each side constitute the critical region.

6. Reject H_0 when the value of r for the original set of data would be among those in the critical region.

Power of the Randomization (Permutation) Tests for the Relationship Between Two Variables

When the null hypothesis is false, the power of a statistical test is a direct function of the sample size—the larger the sample size, the higher the power. The same relationship is true here. With the exact randomization test described above, the number of arrangements increases as sample size increases, and the size of the critical region (5% of the total number of arrangements) increases. The result is that smaller values of the Pearson r will be in the larger critical region.

However, with the approximate randomization test, the number of shuffles is fixed, and 5% of that number is independent of the sample size. Nevertheless, as sample size increases, the chances that we will reject a false null hypothesis also increase. In Chapter 7, we saw that the reason the power of the randomization test for the difference between two experimental treatments increases with increasing sample sizes can be explained by the effects of sample size on the calculated value of Student's t: For a given difference between sample means, the value of Student's t increases as sample size increases. But the value of the Pearson r does *not* increase as sample size increases, even though n is in the denominator. The reason r does not increase is that with increasing sample size, there are also more cross products in the numerator. The numerator and denominator balance out to prevent r from changing in one direction.

The reason why the power of this randomization test increases as sample size increases is related to what happens in the exact randomization test. Because taking these shuffles is like taking random samples of the total number of arrangements, the critical region will contain smaller values of r when the sample size is larger. Consequently, the observed value of r is more likely to be among those values in the critical region with a larger sample size.

The randomization (permutation) model can be used to test hypotheses about whether there is a relationship between two variables, but that is all we can do with it. To test other hypotheses and construct confidence intervals, we have to use the classical statistical model. There are two classical statistical models that allow us to do these things, the bivariate normal distribution model and the linear regression model. We will look at each in turn.

THE BIVARIATE NORMAL DISTRIBUTION MODEL FOR TESTING HYPOTHESES ABOUT POPULATION CORRELATIONS

The bivariate normal distribution is a theoretical population consisting of pairs of measurements on two dimensions. The Pearson r is the maximum likelihood estimate of the population parameter ρ, the correlation between these measurements in the population. Because the shape of the distribution of Pearson r's taken from this population depends on the value of ρ and is not a normal distribution, we use Fisher's r to z_r transformation to create a normal distribution with a known mean and variance. This transformation allows us to use z-scores to construct test statistics to test a number of different hypotheses about ρ.

The first classical statistical model we will consider is the **bivariate normal distribution model**. Here we *assume* that a population called the **bivariate normal distribution** exists. That population consists of pairs of Xs and Ys and has the following characteristics:

1. *The two variables (X and Y) have normal distributions.* That is to say, if you projected all of the Y values on the Y-axis, the distribution of those Y values would be a normal distribution. The same is true for the X values.
2. *The relationship between X and Y is linear.* In other words, a straight line defines the relationship.
3. The variance of each variable around that straight line is the same at every point on that line. For every value of X, the variance of the Y-scores is the same, which is called homoscedasticity.

A drawing of a bivariate normal distribution is presented in Figure 10.6.

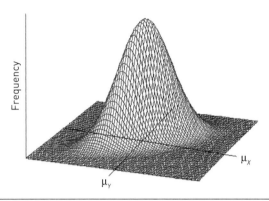

Source: Adapted from Penn State University, https://onlinecourses.science.psu.edu/stat505/node/33

The bivariate normal distribution is a three-dimensional object. The *X*- and *Y*-axes are along the base of this figure, and the vertical axis is the frequency of each *XY* pair in the population. A consequence of the three characteristics of the bivariate normal distribution is that if we make a slice in this three-dimensional object perpendicular to the *X*-axis or the *Y*-axis, we get slices that look like normal curves, and no matter where we make the slices, out toward the tails or near the center, these normal distribution slices all have the same variance (homoscedasticity). The slices near the tails would be narrower and shorter than the ones near the center, but they would have the same variance.

The bivariate normal distribution is generated by the following formula:

$$f(X,Y) = \frac{1}{2\pi\sigma_X\sigma_Y\sqrt{1-\rho^2}} e^{-\frac{1}{2(1-\rho^2)}\left[\left(\frac{X-\mu_X}{\sigma_X}\right)^2 - 2\rho\frac{(X-\mu_X)(Y-\mu_Y)}{\sigma_X\sigma_Y} + \left(\frac{Y-\mu_Y}{\sigma_Y}\right)^2\right]} \qquad (10.3)$$

This equation that describes this population has five parameters: μ_X, μ_Y, σ_X, σ_Y, and ρ. If we draw a random sample from this population, we can estimate those parameters from that random sample. The maximum likelihood estimators of these population parameters are the following:

$$\hat{\mu}_X = \overline{X} \qquad (10.4a)$$

$$\hat{\mu}_Y = \overline{Y} \qquad (10.4b)$$

$$\hat{\sigma}_X^2 = s_X^2 \qquad (10.4c)$$

$$\hat{\sigma}_Y^2 = s_Y^2 \qquad (10.4d)$$

$$\hat{\rho} = r \qquad (10.4e)$$

Like s_X^2 and s_Y^2, which are asymptotically unbiased estimates of σ_X^2 and σ_Y^2, respectively, r is also an asymptotically unbiased estimate of ρ. When $\rho = 0$, there is no bias, but when $\rho = .8$, the estimate is biased to one side. (The formulas to correct the bias in this estimate will be described later in this chapter.)

The bivariate normal distribution in Figure 10.6 has $\rho = .8$. When $\rho = 0$, the base is a circle. When $\rho \neq 0$, the base is an ellipse. The closer the value of ρ is to $+1$ or -1, the narrower that ellipse.

Testing Hypotheses About the Parameter ρ, the Population Correlation Between the Two Variables

When we test hypotheses about μ (the population mean), we start with the sample mean (which is the maximum likelihood estimate of μ). The central limit theorem tells us what the distribution of the sample means is, and we convert to z- or t-scores to get a test statistic for which we can find the probability of getting our data when the null hypothesis is true. The distribution of the test statistic (z or t) depends on the distribution of the sample means, which in turn depends on the form of the population (per the central limit theorem).

When we test hypotheses about ρ, we start with the Pearson r because that is the maximum likelihood estimate of ρ. To continue, we need to know the attributes of the distribution of the Pearson r. Unfortunately, the distribution of the Pearson r depends on the value of the population correlation, ρ, as well as the sample size. When $\rho = 0$, the distribution of the sample correlations from a bivariate normal distribution is a symmetrical distribution with values ranging from -1 to $+1$ and a mean at 0, but it is *not* a normal distribution. Furthermore, when $\rho \neq 0$, the distribution of the Pearson r is skewed. For example, when $\rho = .8$, most of the sample correlation coefficients will be around .8. The distribution of these Pearson rs is skewed because you cannot get a value for r greater than 1 but you can get values of r as low as -1 (although a value of r that low would be very unlikely to occur when $\rho = .8$). Therefore, it is difficult to find the probability of getting certain values of r because the distribution of r has a different shape for every possible value of ρ. Fortunately, there is a solution to our problem.

Fisher's r to Z$_r$ Transformation

We have a problem here: The distribution of r depends on the value of ρ. But the problem is not insurmountable because R. A. Fisher found a way to *transform the distribution of* r *to a normal distribution with a known mean and a known variance*. This is called **Fisher's r to Z$_r$ transformation**, where

$$Z_r = \frac{1}{2}\ln\left(\frac{1+r}{1-r}\right)$$

(10.5)

$$\mu_{Z_r} = \frac{1}{2}\ln\left(\frac{1+\rho}{1-\rho}\right) \tag{10.6}$$

$$\sigma_{Z_r} = \frac{1}{\sqrt{n-3}} \tag{10.7}$$

Because Z_r has a normal distribution with a known mean and known variance, we can convert Z_r to standard scores, where

$$z = \frac{\text{score} - \text{mean}}{\text{standard deviation}} \tag{10.8}$$

In this situation, the score is Z_r, the mean is μ_{Z_r}, and the standard deviation is σ_{Z_r}. Substituting these terms into Equation 10.8, we get the following:

$$z = \frac{Z_r - \mu_{Z_r}}{\sigma_{Z_r}} \tag{10.9}$$

Case I: Research Question "Is There a Relationship Between the Two Variables?"

The statistical hypotheses for this research question are the following:

$H_0: \rho = 0$

$H_1: \rho \neq 0$

The Pearson r is the maximum likelihood estimate of the maximum estimate of ρ. What would you expect to observe about the value of r if H_0 were true? What would you expect to observe about the value of r if H_0 were false? What is the criterion we use to decide whether to reject or not reject H_0?

If we assume that the null hypothesis is true, then $\rho = 0$ and $\mu_{Z_r} = \frac{1}{2}\ln 1 = 0$, and $\sigma_{Z_r} = \sqrt{\frac{1}{n-3}}$. If we substitute the values for μ_{Z_r} and σ_{Z_r} into Equation 10.9, the test statistic becomes this:

$$Z = \frac{Z_r}{\sqrt{\dfrac{1}{n-3}}} \tag{10.10}$$

This formula can easily be rewritten as follows:

$$z = Z_r\sqrt{n-3} \tag{10.11}$$

What do you know about the distribution of this test statistic when the null hypothesis is true? When it is false? What factors affect the power of this test? How can we construct a power function for this hypothesis test?

For the data in Figure 10.2, $r = +.62$, $z_r = +0.725$, $n = 120$, and the value for the z-statistic in Equation 10.11 $= 7.845$. The critical value for z with $\alpha = .05$ for a two-tailed test is 1.96. Therefore we *reject* the null hypothesis of no correlation in the population between participants' quality of contact with individuals with intellectual disabilities and their scores on the MRAI-R. We conclude that these two variables are indeed correlated.

Case II: Research Question "Does the Population Correlation Equal a Certain Value?"

The statistical hypotheses for this research question are as follows:

H_0: $\rho = \rho_0$

H_1: $\rho \neq \rho_0$

Case II is the general case for testing hypotheses with the bivariate normal distribution model. (Case I is the special case when the null hypothesis is $\rho = 0$.) As we do with Case I, we take a random sample from the bivariate normal distribution, calculate r, and convert r to z_r. This procedure yields a statistic that has a normal distribution with a known mean and standard deviation. We convert to standard scores, and the test statistic for this test is

$$z = \frac{z_r - \frac{1}{2}\ln\frac{1+\rho_0}{1-\rho_0}}{\sqrt{\frac{1}{n-3}}} \tag{10.12}$$

We know the distribution of this test statistic when the null hypothesis is true and when it is false, and we know what affects the power of this test. We can construct a power function for the H_0 false distribution, and we can create confidence intervals for the population parameter.

Case III: Research Question "Does the Correlation Between Two Variables in Population 1 Equal the Correlation Between Two Variables in Population 2?"

This situation arises when we take two samples from two different bivariate normal distributions and ask whether the two population correlations are the same. In that case, our statistical hypotheses are the following:

H_0: $\rho_1 = \rho_2$

H_1: $\rho_1 \neq \rho_2$

To test the null hypothesis, we obtain two samples, one from each population. Then we calculate r_1 and r_2, convert both to z_r, and substitute these values into the following test statistic:

$$z = \frac{Z_{r_1} - Z_{r_2}}{\sqrt{\dfrac{1}{n_1 - 3} + \dfrac{1}{n_2 - 3}}} \tag{10.13}$$

In this case, the variances of the variables in your bivariate normal distributions will not affect the power, because the correlation is independent of the variance of the bivariate normal distribution.

McManus et al. (2011) collected data from 75 female participants and 45 male participants for both the quality of contact measure and the MRAI-R. The Pearson r for the relationship between these two measures for female participants was .6094, and the Pearson r for the relationship for male participants was .6982. We can use Equation 10.13 to ask whether the correlation between quality of contact and attitudes toward individuals with intellectual disabilities, as measured by the MRAI-R, is the same or different for the populations from which the participants in this study were sampled. The value of the z-statistic in Equation 10.13 for these data equals .802. In this case, we would *not reject* the null hypothesis that the correlation between quality of contact and attitudes toward individuals with intellectual disabilities, as measured by the MRAI-R, for female participants equals the correlation for male participants.

Power of the Hypothesis Tests for ρ With the Bivariate Normal Distribution Model

The three z-test statistics described above all have a unit normal distribution ($\mu = 0$ and $\sigma = 1$) when the null hypothesis being tested is true. When that null hypothesis is false, the z-test statistics have non-central normal distributions with $\sigma_{z^*} = 1$. Following are the means of those non-central distributions:

$$\text{Case I: } \mu_{z^*} = \tfrac{1}{2}\ln\left(\frac{1+\rho}{1-\rho}\right)\sqrt{n-3} \tag{10.14a}$$

$$\text{Case II: } \mu_{z^*} = \frac{1}{2}\ln\left(\frac{1+\rho}{1-\rho}\right)\left(\frac{1-\rho_0}{1+\rho_0}\right)\sqrt{n-3} \tag{10.14b}$$

$$\text{Case III: } \mu_{z^*} = \frac{\dfrac{1}{2}\ln\left(\dfrac{1+\rho_1}{1-\rho_1}\right)\left(\dfrac{1-\rho_2}{1+\rho_2}\right)}{\sqrt{\dfrac{1}{n_1-3} + \dfrac{1}{n_2-3}}} \tag{10.14c}$$

where ρ is the true value of the parameter, ρ_0 is the hypothesized value of ρ in Case II, and ρ_1 and ρ_2 are the true values of the population parameters in Case III.

In all three cases, $\mu_{z^*} = 0$ when the null hypothesis is true. In Case I, the value of μ_{z^*} is a function of ρ and n. In Case II, μ_{z^*} is a function of the difference between ρ and ρ_0 and the sample size (n). In Case III, μ_{z^*} is a function of the difference between ρ_1 and ρ_2 and the two sample sizes (n_1 and n_2). These factors affect the power of these hypothesis tests for ρ when using the bivariate normal distribution model.

CREATING A CONFIDENCE INTERVAL FOR THE POPULATION CORRELATION USING THE BIVARIATE NORMAL DISTRIBUTION MODEL

Because the distribution of z_r is a normal distribution, we can construct a confidence interval for μ_{Z_r} and then convert from z_r to r to obtain a confidence interval for ρ.

In Chapter 4, we derived the confidence interval for the mean of a normal distribution. The resulting equation for that confidence interval was based on the fact that the distribution of sample means is a normal distribution with $\mu_{\bar{X}} = \mu$ and $\sigma_{\bar{X}}^2 = \sigma^2 / n$. When we know the population variances, that equation is

$$\Pr\left(\bar{X} - 1.96\sigma_{\bar{X}} < \mu < \bar{X} + 1.96\sigma_{\bar{X}}\right) = .95 \tag{10.15a}$$

We read this expression as "We are 95% confident that the population mean is contained somewhere within the interval between $\bar{X} - 1.96\sigma_{\bar{X}}$ and $\bar{X} + 1.96\sigma_{\bar{X}}$."

We can use the fact that Z_r also has a normal distribution with a known mean $\left[\mu_{Z_r} = \frac{1}{2}\ln\left(\frac{1+\rho}{1-\rho}\right)\right]$ and a known variance $\sigma_{Z_r}^2 = \frac{1}{n-3}$ to create a similar confidence interval for μ_{Z_r}. That confidence interval would be

$$\Pr\left(Z_r - 1.96\sigma_{Z_r} < \mu_{Z_r} < Z_r + 1.96\sigma_{Z_r}\right) = .95 \tag{10.15b}$$

We read this expression as "We are 95% confident that μ_{Z_r} is contained somewhere within the interval between $Z_r - 1.96\sigma_{Z_r}$ and $Z_r + 1.96\sigma_{Z_r}$."

But we are interested in the confidence interval for ρ, not for μ_{Z_r}. Because Z_r and r are related through Fisher's r to Z_r transformation, we can transform the two values that we calculate with Equation 10.15a [$Z_r - 1.96\sigma_{Z_r}$ and $Z_r + 1.96\sigma_{Z_r}$] from the Z_r scale to the r scale. The result is a confidence interval for ρ:

$$\Pr(\text{lower limit of CI} < \rho < \text{upper limit of CI}) = .95 \tag{10.16}$$

See Box 10.3 for an example of how to compute this confidence interval.

BOX 10.3

HOW TO FIND THE 95% CONFIDENCE INTERVAL FOR ρ BASED ON R = .62 AND n = 120

When $r = .62$, $Z_r = .725$, and $\sigma_{Z_r} = 0.0925$, we can construct a 95% confidence interval for ρ by substituting the obtained values for r, Z_r, and σ_{Z_r} into the following:

$$\Pr\left(Z_r - 1.96\sigma_{Z_r} < \mu_{Z_r} < Z_r + 1.96\sigma_{Z_r}\right) = .95$$

For this example, the equation becomes

$$\Pr\left(\left[0.725 - 1.96(0.0925)\right] < \mu_{Z_r} < \left[0.725 + 1.96(0.0925)\right]\right) = .95$$

$$\Pr\left(0.554 < \mu_{Z_r} < 0.907\right) = .95$$

This expression gives us a confidence interval for μ_{Z_r}. To get the confidence interval for ρ, we convert .554 and .907 from the Z_r scale to the r scale. This gives us the following:

$$\Pr(.496 < \rho < .719) = .95$$

BOOTSTRAP CONFIDENCE INTERVALS FOR THE POPULATION CORRELATION

We can use the percentile bootstrap procedure to find confidence intervals for ρ when we are concerned that our data may not have come from a bivariate normal distribution.

The bootstrap (see Chapter 5) provides an alternative approach to finding confidence intervals for ρ, especially when we have reason to be concerned that the assumptions of the bivariate normal distribution model described above are violated by our data. The Pearson r is not a robust estimator of ρ because it is greatly influenced by outliers and by the distributions of X and Y. Contamination in either or both distributions can have dramatic effects on the value of r. This fact, in turn, can affect confidence intervals for ρ. One way we can deal with this issue is to use the percentile bootstrap procedure to estimate ρ and to compute confidence intervals. The procedure here is a straightforward application of the bootstrap procedures described in Chapter 5 (Box 5.6). How this approach is adapted for finding confidence intervals for ρ is described in Box 10.4. See Lunneborg (1985) for a detailed description of the use of bootstrap confidence intervals for ρ.

BOX 10.4
HOW TO FIND PERCENTILE BOOTSTRAP ESTIMATES FOR ρ

Purpose

To create a confidence interval for the population correlation ρ when the assumptions of the bivariate model have not been met

Procedure

1. Starting with the bivariate original sample, resample rows with replacement. Do this a large number of times (for example, 1,000 times).

2. From each of these bootstrap samples, calculate r^*, the bootstrap estimates of ρ.

3. Rank order the resulting bootstrap estimates and find $Q(.025)$ and $Q(.975)$ for these estimates; those two values will be the lower and upper limits of the 95% bootstrap confidence interval for ρ. The mean of the bootstrap estimates (r^*) is your point estimate of ρ.

A 95% percentile bootstrap confidence interval for the data in Figure 10.2 is

$$Pr(.4904 < \rho < .728) = .95$$

This interval is similar to the confidence interval obtained with the bivariate normal distribution model in Box 10.3. This fact is not surprising given that the original data appear to satisfy the assumptions of the bivariate normal distribution model.

UNBIASED ESTIMATORS OF THE POPULATION CORRELATION

The Pearson r is a biased estimate of ρ. We give two equations for correcting for that bias.

As noted earlier, the Pearson r is the maximum likelihood estimate of ρ, but it is an asymptotically unbiased estimate. R. A. Fisher (1915) showed that

$$E(r) = \rho - \frac{\rho\left(1-\rho^2\right)}{2n} \tag{10.17}$$

Equation 10.17 can be rearranged to give the following unbiased estimate of the population correlation from a bivariate normal distribution,

$$\text{est } \rho = r\left(1 + \frac{1 - r^2}{2n}\right) \tag{10.18}$$

Olkin and Pratt (1958) found that the following equation provides a better estimate:

$$\text{est } \rho = r\left[\frac{1 + \left(1 - r^2\right)}{2(n-3)}\right] \tag{10.19}$$

Equation 10.17 tells us that the Pearson r is an unbiased estimator when $\rho = 0$, and for all other values of ρ, the bias $(E[r] - \rho)$ decreases as sample size increases. For sample sizes in the range of 10 to 20, the bias is around $-.01$ to $-.02$ when r is between .2 and .3. The bias increases to around $-.03$ when $n = 10$ and the correlation is between .4 and .6. The bias is highest at $\rho = \pm.577$. This means that the Pearson r systematically *underestimates* ρ.

Most researchers ignore the bias because it is small $(.01-.038)$ even when the sample size is small. You should use the unbiased estimate when your purpose is to obtain an accurate estimate of ρ.

ROBUST ESTIMATORS OF CORRELATION

We describe three robust estimators of the population correlation: The Winsorized correlation coefficient uses the Pearson r formula to compute the correlation after Winsorizing both sets of scores. The Spearman rank-order correlation coefficient is calculated by applying the formula for the Pearson r to the ranked data. Kendall's rank-order correlation coefficient is calculated using the difference between the number of ranks for X and Y that are in the same order (concordant) and the number that are in different order (discordant) in our sample.

Because outliers in our data can reduce the value of the Pearson r, especially when the sample sizes are small, the Pearson r is not a robust estimator of the population correlation.

To explore this idea further, consider the hypothetical data in Table 10.2 and Figure 10.7. The set of numbers on the left of Table 10.2 does not contain an outlier, while the set on the right does. All data points in both sets are the same *except* for those in the last row.

Using Equation 10.11 as our test statistic for the data on the left of Table 10.2, $z = 3.241$, $p < .001$. For the data on the right of that table, $z = 0.885$, $p = .364$. Clearly, the outlier has a dramatic effect on the value of the Pearson r and the conclusion you

TABLE 10.2 ■ Hypothetical Data for Considering the Effects of Outliers on Correlation Coefficients			
Without Outlier		**With Outlier**	
X	**Y**	**X**	**Y**
10	8.04	10	8.04
8	6.95	8	6.95
13	7.58	13	7.58
9	8.81	9	8.81
11	8.33	11	8.33
6	7.24	6	7.24
4	4.26	4	4.26
12	10.84	12	10.84
7	4.82	7	4.82
5	5.68	5	5.68
14	**9.96**	**28**	**7.00**

would draw from the test of the null hypothesis that $\rho = 0$. Fortunately, there are a number of robust measures of correlation we can use to minimize the influence of such outliers in bivariate situations.

Winsorized Correlation Coefficient

As we saw in Chapter 5, one of the ways to reduce the influence of outliers in a set of numbers is to Winsorize that set by ranking the numbers and replacing a certain proportion of the scores at both ends of the ranked numbers with the next score in the set (see Box 5.2). We can *Winsorize both variables in a bivariate situation* to produce the **Winsorized correlation coefficient.** This approach is illustrated in Table 10.3, where the data set with outliers is presented on the left and the Winsorized values are presented on the right.

Using $\alpha = .2$, the Winsorized correlation for the data in Table 10.3 is .685. The procedure for computing the Winsorized correlation coefficient is summarized in Box 10.5.

The Winsorized correlation coefficient, r_W, is an estimate of the population Winsorized correlation, ρ_W, and we can use the following test statistic to test the hypothesis that $\rho_W = 0$:

$$t = r_W \sqrt{\frac{n-2}{1-r_W^2}} \qquad (10.20)[5]$$

---

[5] We will see in Chapter 11 that a similar test statistic can be used with the Pearson *r*.

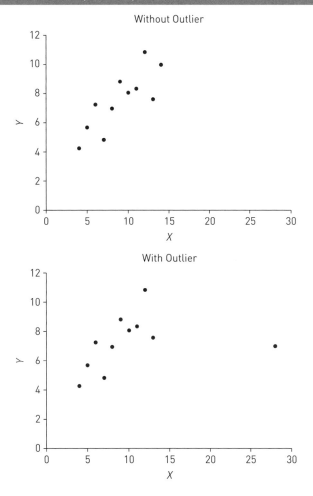

FIGURE 10.7 ■ **Scatterplots for the data in Table 10.2: (*top*, no outlier)**
$r = .816$; (*bottom*, outlier) $r = .303$.

For the data on the right of Table 10.2, where $r_W = .685$, $t = 3.228$, we use the *t*-table (Appendix E) with degrees of freedom = (number of values *not* Winsorized) − 2 to find the critical value. In Table 10.2, $n = 11$, and with $\alpha = .2$, the number of values *not* Winsorized is 7; therefore, the degrees of freedom for testing the Winsorized correlation here are $7 - 2 = 5$, and the critical value of *t* for a two-tailed test with 5 degrees of freedom and $\alpha = .05$ is 2.571. Therefore, we can reject the null hypothesis that $\rho_W = 0$ and conclude there is a relationship between the variables *X* and *Y* for the data on the right of the table, which include the outlier.

TABLE 10.3 ■ Example of How the Winsorized Correlation Coefficient Is Calculated			
Original Data With Outliers (ranked on the x-axis)		Winsorized Scores on Both Axes	
X	Y	X	Y
4	**4.26**	**6**	**5.68**
5	5.68	**6**	5.68
6	7.24	6	7.24
7	**4.82**	7	**5.68**
8	6.95	8	6.95
9	8.81	9	**8.83**
10	8.04	10	8.04
11	8.33	11	8.33
12	10.84	12	**8.83**
13	7.58	**12**	7.58
28	7.00	**12**	7.00
$r = .303$		$r_w = .685$	

Note: Winsorized values are in **bold**.

BOX 10.5

HOW TO COMPUTE THE WINSORIZED CORRELATION COEFFICIENT

Purpose

To create a robust correlation coefficient that is not affected by outliers

Procedure

1. Starting with pairs of X and Y values, Winsorize the X values, keeping the original

pairs of items together. Wilcox (2003) recommended using $\alpha = .2$.

2. Winsorize the Y values, again keeping the paired items together.

3. Apply the formula for calculating the Pearson r to the Winsorized values.

Spearman Rank-Order Correlation Coefficient

As we noted at the beginning of this chapter, the degree of relationship between two variables can be conceptualized in terms of how well the ranks on the two variables match. When there is a perfect positive correlation, the ranks for each pair of scores are identical, and when there is no relationship between these variables, the ranks on one variable are randomly distributed with respect to the ranks on the other variable. The **Spearman rank-order correlation coefficient** (also referred to as **Spearman ρ**, or simply r_s) is calculated by *applying the formula for the Pearson r to the ranks of the scores on each variable* (rather than their original values). This procedure is illustrated in Table 10.4. The procedure for calculating Spearman's rank-order correlation coefficient is described in Box 10.6.

Applying the Spearman rank-order correlation coefficient to the data in Table 10.2, we find that $r_s = .818$ for the data on the left and .627 for the data on the right. We can test the hypothesis that $\rho_s = 0$ in one of the following ways:

TABLE 10.4 ■ Example of How the Spearman Rank-Order Correlation Coefficient Is Calculated			
Original Data With Outliers (ranked on the x-axis)		**Ranks**	
X	Y	X	Y
4	4.26	1	1
5	5.68	2	3
6	7.24	3	6
7	4.82	4	2
8	6.95	5	4
9	8.81	6	10
10	8.04	7	8
11	8.33	8	9
12	10.84	9	11
13	7.58	10	7
28	7.00	11	5
$r = .303$		$r_s = .627$	

1. Use either the exact or approximate randomization test described earlier in this chapter with the ranks.
2. Use the tables for the critical values of r_s in Siegel and Castellan (1988).
3. Use the following test statistic:

$$t = r_s \sqrt{\frac{n-2}{1-r_s^2}} \qquad (10.21)$$

where degrees of freedom = $n - 2$ degrees of freedom and sample size > 10.

The critical value for r_s from the table in Siegel and Castellan (1988) is .618. Applying Equation 10.21 to the data on the right yields $t = 3.080$, $p < .01$. Therefore, with either test, we can reject the null hypothesis that $\rho_s = 0$ and conclude there is a relationship between the variables X and Y.

BOX 10.6

HOW TO COMPUTE THE SPEARMAN RANK-ORDER CORRELATION COEFFICIENT (SPEARMAN ρ OR r_s)

Purpose

To create a robust correlation coefficient that is not affected by outliers

Procedure

1. Starting with pairs of X and Y values, convert the X values to their corresponding ranks, keeping the original pairs of items together. In the case of ties, assign the average of the ranks for the tied scores.

2. Convert the Y values to their corresponding ranks, again keeping the paired items together.

In the case of ties, assign the average of the ranks for the tied scores.

3a. Apply the computational formula for Pearson's r to the ranked scores to obtain the Spearman rank-order correlation coefficient.

or

3b. Use the following formula: $r_s = 1 - \dfrac{6 \sum_{i=1}^{n} d_i^2}{n^3 - n}$,

where d_i = the difference between the ranks for a given pair of numbers.[6]

---

[6] If there is a perfect correlation, then the ranks line up perfectly and $d_i = 0$ for every pair of ranks. Thus, $\sum_{i=1}^{n} d_i^2 = 0$ and $r_s = 1$. The larger the difference between the paired ranks, the larger the $\sum_{i=1}^{n} d_i^2$ and the smaller the value of r_s. When there is a perfect negative correlation, $\dfrac{\sum_{i=1}^{n} d_i^2}{n^3 - n} = 2$.

When there are ties in the data, the average of the tied ranks is used with the Pearson r applied to the ranks, but Equation 10.21 has to be modified to accommodate the ties. Siegel and Castellan (1988) described the procedure for this modification. However, in general, the Spearman rank-order correlation coefficient is not appropriate when there is a large number of ties in the data.

Kendall Rank-Order Correlation Coefficient (Kendall's Tau)

The logic behind Kendall's tau[7] is related to how we conceptualize measuring the degree of relationship between two variables in terms of how well the ranks for the pairs of scores match. Going back to the example at the beginning of this chapter of the correlation between the IQs of parents and the IQs of their children, if we ranked the parents' IQs from lowest to highest and if there were a perfect correlation with the IQs of their children, the ranks of the children's IQs would match perfectly those of their parents. But if the correlation were less than perfect, there would be some instances in which the ranks of the children would be inverted; that is, the parent with the lowest IQ might have the child with the second or third lowest IQ. The higher the correlation, the fewer the number of inversions we would find in the ranks of the children relative to the ranks of their parents. On the other hand, if there were no correlation between the IQs of parents and children, when the IQs of the parents are ranked from lowest to highest, the ranks of the children would be assorted randomly; that is, the ranks for the children of any two of the ranked parents could be in the same direction or the opposite direction. Kendall's tau measures the degree of correlation between two variables.

To compute Kendall's tau, we rank order the scores on one variable[8] (keeping the pairs of scores together). We then count the number of times the order of the ranks on the second variable are in the same direction (that is, rank of Y_i < rank of Y_j) as the first variable. We also count the number of times the order of ranks on the second variable is in the opposite direction (that is Y_i > Y_j). *Those ranks in the same order on the second variable* are said to be **concordant**, and *those ranks in the opposite order on the second variable* are said to be **discordant**. We subtract the number of discordant ranks for the second variable from the number of concordant ranks for the second variable (number of concordant ranks for the second variable − number of discordant ranks for the second variable).

When there is a perfect positive correlation, the order of the ranks is identical on both variables (all are concordant), and inserting the number of concordant ranks and the number of pairs of scores into Equation 10.22 yields $\tilde{\tau} = 1$. When there is no relationship between the two variables, the number of times the order of the ranks on the second variable is in

---

[7] To differentiate between the population parameter and the sample statistic, we will use τ for the population parameter and $\tilde{\tau}$ for the sample statistic.

[8] Rank of X_1 < rank of X_2 < ... < rank X_i < rank of X_j < ... < rank of X_n.

the same direction (concordant) will be offset by the number of times the rank order is in the opposite direction (discordant), and the value of $\tilde{\tau} = 0$ (or is close to 0). When there is a negative relationship, $\tilde{\tau}$ is a negative number, because the number of discordant ranks is greater than the number of concordant ranks. This pattern is illustrated in Table 10.5.

The data from the right panel of Table 10.2 are presented on the left of Table 10.5, with the X scores ranked from lowest to highest. The determination of the number of concordant and discordant ranks is carried out on the right of the table. A 1 is entered where a comparison of ranks is concordant, and a −1 is entered where a comparison of ranks is discordant. For example, in the first column on the right (and the first row on the left), the rank of X is 1 and the rank of Y is 1. Every row in that column gets a 1 because all of the ranks of Y are greater than 1. In the second column on the right (the second row on the left), the rank of X is 2, and the rank of Y is 3. With one exception (row 4), all of the ranks in that column are above 3. The row where the rank of $Y = 2$ gets a −1 because $2 < 3$, and all other rows get a 1 because their ranks on Y are > 3. This process is repeated for each succeeding row. The entries in each column are summed.

When there are no ties in the data (and the ranks), the formula for calculating $\tilde{\tau}$ is

$$\tilde{\tau} = \frac{2\sum(\text{column sums})}{n(n-1)} \tag{10.22}$$

When there are ties in the data, we use the mean of the tied ranks and put a 0 in the table when comparing them. Under that circumstance, the formula for calculating $\tilde{\tau}$ is

$$\tilde{\tau} = \frac{2\sum \text{column sums}}{\sqrt{n(n-1)(\#\ \text{ties in } X)}\sqrt{n(n-1)(\#\ \text{ties in } Y)}} \tag{10.23}$$

Kendall's tau is preferred to Spearman's r_s when there are more than a few ties in the data.

For the data in Table 10.5, $\tilde{\tau} = .455$. As is the case when testing the hypothesis $\rho_s = 0$ with the Spearman rank-order correlation coefficient, we can test the hypothesis that $\tau = 0$ in one of the following three ways:

1. Use either the exact or approximate randomization test described earlier in this chapter with $\sum(\text{column sums})$.
2. Use the tables for the critical values of r_s in Siegel and Castellan (1988).
3. Use the following test statistic:

$$z = \frac{3\tilde{\tau}\sqrt{n(n-1)}}{\sqrt{2(2n+5)}} \tag{10.24}$$

When $n > 10$ and $\tau = 0$, the distribution of this test statistic approximates a normal distribution.

TABLE 10.5 ■ Calculation of Kendall's Tau for the Data in Table 10.2 (*right*)

Rank (X)	X	Y	Rank (Y)	Rank (X)										
				1	**2**	**3**	**4**	**5**	**6**	**7**	**8**	**9**	**10**	**11**
			Rank (Y)	1	3	6	2	4	10	8	9	11	7	5
1	4	5.68	1	1										
2	5	5.68	3	1	1									
3	6	7.24	6	1	1	1								
4	7	5.68	2	1	−1	−1	1							
5	8	6.95	4	1	1	−1	1	1						
6	9	8.83	10	1	1	1	1	1	1					
7	10	8.04	8	1	1	1	1	1	−1	1				
8	11	8.33	9	1	1	1	1	1	−1	1	1			
9	12	8.83	11	1	1	1	1	1	1	1	−1	−1		
10	13	7.53	7	1	1	1	1	1	−1	−1	−1	−1	−1	
11	28	7	5	1	1	1	1	1	−1	−1	−1	−2	−1	5
			Σ [Column]	10	7	2	7	6	−3	0	−1	−2	−1	0

291

For the data in Table 10.5, the critical value for a two-tailed test with $\alpha = .05$, using the table in Siegel and Castellan (1988), is .491. Using Equation 10.24 to calculate the test statistic produces $z = 1.946$, $p = .0516$. Using the strict criterion $p < .05$ for rejecting the null hypothesis, we would not reject the null hypothesis when we used Kendall's tau.

Why Is $\tilde{\tau}$ Lower Than r_s?

Although $\tilde{\tau}$ and r_s are calculated from the same set of ranks, they are measuring the relationship between two variables in different ways and therefore are not directly comparable. Spearman's rank-order correlation coefficient is a Pearson product-moment correlation applied to the ranks. Kendall's tau is the difference between the number of X and Y ranks that are in the same order (concordant) and the number that are in a different order (discordant) in our sample, divided by the total number of possible comparisons of the ranks. Most of the time, $\tilde{\tau}$ and r_s lead to the same conclusion. However, this outcome does not always occur, as we see here.

ASSESSING THE RELATIONSHIP BETWEEN TWO NOMINAL VARIABLES

We can use the χ^2 test statistic described in Chapter 8 to test the null hypothesis that there is no relationship between two nominal variables.

There are times when we are interested in whether there is a relationship between two nominal variables. For example, in Chapter 8 we described a study by O'Dea, Miller, and Saucier (2016) in which White undergraduate students, after reading about a proposed diversity initiative, chose to provide their critical feedback either verbally (via a five-minute conversation with the experimenter) or in writing (via a one-page essay). In this study, the race of the experimenter was varied so that the experimenter was White half the time and Black half the time.

The experimental question in this example is: Are students' preferences for expressing criticisms of a proposed diversity initiative by speaking with an experimenter or by writing a one-page paper related to whether the experimenter is Black or White? The experimental hypotheses are as follows:

There is no relationship between the race of the experimenter and the students' preferences to provide verbal responses versus written responses.

There is a relationship between the race of the experimenter and the students' preferences to provide verbal responses versus written responses.

TABLE 10.6 ■ Observed Frequencies in the O'Dea, Miller, and Saucier (2016) Experiment			
	Verbal	Written	Total
Black	44	36	80
White	52	20	72
Total	96	56	152

The corresponding statistical hypotheses are:

H_0: The population correlation between race of the experimenter and preferences for verbal responses versus written responses = 0.

H_1: The population correlation between race of the experimenter and preferences for verbal responses versus written responses ≠ 0.

The observed frequencies of people choosing to express their criticisms of the proposed diversity initiative by speaking to the experimenter or by writing a one-page paper are given in Table 10.6.

Table 10.6 is called a **contingency table**. Contingency tables are *used to record the number of individuals who possess combinations of characteristics measured on two or more nominal scales*. Each cell in the table represents a unique combination of the attributes measured. By examining the numbers of individuals in each cell, we can determine whether there is a relationship between these attributes in a population. That is, we decide whether the combinations of characteristics are dependent (systematically related) or independent (random).

Using the χ^2 Test Statistic With Contingency Tables

Up to this point in our discussion of correlation coefficients, we have identified the coefficient and then illustrated how to test the null hypothesis (that the population correlation = 0). That procedure is reversed with contingency tables. Here we calculate the test statistic and, from that statistic, derive the correlation coefficient. The test statistic for tests of association in contingency tables is this:

$$\chi^2 = \sum \frac{\left(\text{Observed} - \text{Expected}\right)^2}{\text{Expected}}$$

(10.25)

The expected values are calculated from the marginal totals in the contingency table, that is, the sums of each row and each column (labeled "Total" in Table 10.6). For each cell in a contingency table, the **expected value** is *the row total for that cell times the*

TABLE 10.7 ■ Expected Values ([row total × column total]/grand total) for the Data in Table 10.6			
	Verbal	Written	Total
Black	50.5	29.5	80
White	45.5	26.5	72
Total	96	56	152

column total for that cell divided by the total number of scores in the table (called the grand total). Using this procedure, the expected value for the cell in which 44 participants opted to provide verbal feedback about the diversity initiative to a Black experimenter is $(80 \times 96)/152 = 50.5$. The expected values for all four cells in Table 10.6 are given in Table 10.7.

The row and column totals for the expected values must be equal to those for the observed values. Applying Equation 10.25 to these data, the value of $\chi^2 = 4.33$. To determine whether these data will lead us to reject the null hypothesis, we need to know the degrees of freedom. The *degrees of freedom for most contingency table tests are (the number of rows − 1) × (the number of columns − 1)*. For this situation, the degrees of freedom are $(2 − 1) \times (2 − 1) = 1$. The critical value for chi square with 1 degree of freedom at $\alpha = .05$ is 3.841. Therefore, these data lead us to reject the null hypothesis in favor of the alternative hypothesis and conclude that there is a relationship between race of the experimenter and preferences for verbal responses or written responses, such that participants are less likely to prefer to provide their feedback about the diversity initiative verbally (vs. in writing) to the Black than to the White experimenter.

THE FISHER EXACT PROBABILITY TEST FOR 2 × 2 CONTINGENCY TABLES WITH SMALL SAMPLE SIZES

The Fisher exact probability test provides us with a way to test for association in 2 × 2 contingency tables when the sample sizes are small.

In Chapter 8, we were cautioned not to use the χ^2 test statistic when more than 20% of the expected values (*E*) are less than 5. Fisher (1934), Yates (1934),[9] and Irwin (1935) all described a way to calculate the exact probability of obtaining a set of observed

---

[9]Yates (1934) acknowledged that the idea that the probability that any observed set of values in a 2 × 2 contingency table can be exactly determined was suggested to him by Fisher.

TABLE 10.8 ■ Depiction of a 2 × 2 Contingency Table for Calculating the Fisher Exact Probability Test			
	Category of Response		
Group	**1**	**2**	**Totals in Each Group**
I	A	B	A + B
II	C	D	C + D
Totals in Each Condition	A + C	B + D	N

frequencies in a 2 × 2 contingency table by not violating the normal distribution assumption underlying the distribution of the χ^2 test statistic. That exact probability can be calculated by applying the hypergeometric distribution[10] to a 2 × 2 contingency table depicted in Table 10.8, where the letters A, B, C, and D refer to the number of observations in each cell.

The exact probability for any arrangement of frequencies in Table 10.8 is given by the following hypergeometric distribution formula:

$$p = \frac{\dfrac{(A+B)!}{A!B!}\dfrac{(B+D)!}{B!D!}}{\dfrac{N!}{(A+C)!((B+D)!}}$$

This expression can be simplified for purposes of computation to the following formula:

$$p = \frac{(A+B)!(C+D)!(A+C)!(B+D)}{N!A!B!C!D!}$$

In the original formulations for this test, the marginal totals ($A + B$, $C + D$, and so forth) were predetermined by the researcher. In practice, that is rarely the case, especially for the two conditions. However, this test is useful when at least one set of marginal totals is predetermined (e.g., the number of participants in each group is set by the researcher, but the numbers in each category are determined by the participants' responses) and the expected values are low due to small sample sizes.

---

[10] The hypergeometric distribution is similar to the binomial distribution, but it is different in one important respect: With the binomial distribution, the sampling is with replacement from an infinitely large population, and the probability of a success on each trial is the same. With the hypergeometric distribution, the sampling is from a small population without replacement, meaning that the probability of success is not the same on each trial.

CORRELATION COEFFICIENTS FOR NOMINAL DATA IN CONTINGENCY TABLES

After performing the χ^2 test described in the previous section, we can assess the degree of relationship between the two nominal variables using either the contingency coefficient (C) or Cramér's coefficient (V).

There are a number of possible correlation coefficients we can use to provide an index of the strength of the relationship between the two variables in a contingency table. The two most commonly used measures are the contingency correlation coefficient (C) and Cramér's coefficient (V). Both indexes can be computed directly from the value of χ^2.

Contingency Coefficient (C)

The formula for calculating the contingency correlation is

$$C = \sqrt{\frac{\chi^2}{\chi^2 + N}} \tag{10.26}$$

The value of C for the data in Table 10.7 is .175. Although C can be used as a measure of relationship for contingency tables, it can never equal 1 (because of the N in the denominator). Furthermore, the maximum value for C increases toward 1 as the dimensionality of the contingency table (that is, the number of rows and columns) increases. The formula for computing the maximum value for C is

$$C_{max} = \sqrt{\frac{k-1}{k}}, \tag{10.27}$$

where k is the smaller of the number of rows and columns. Therefore, we can use C to compare the strength of relationship across only two contingency tables of the same dimensionality, but the value of C will underestimate the strength of the relationship.

Some researchers attempt to overcome this problem by computing C/C_{max} to obtain a value that can vary between 0 and 1 for all contingency tables. For the data in Table 10.7, where $k = 2$, $C_{max} = 0.707$, and the ratio $C/C_{max} = 0.247$. Although this procedure appears to overcome the problem, many statisticians question whether it can be justified on theoretical grounds. Therefore, we rarely see it used in practice.

Cramér's Coefficient (*V*)

An alternative to *C* that partially overcomes that problem is Cramér's coefficient (*V*):[11]

$$V = \sqrt{\frac{\chi^2}{N(k-1)}} \tag{10.28}$$

where *k* is the smaller of the number of rows and columns. Unlike *C*, *V* can vary between 0 and 1, but it can equal 1 only when the number of rows equals the number of columns (for any size contingency table). The maximum value of *V* will be less than 1 when the number of rows does not equal the number of columns. *V* gives us the proportion of the maximum possible variation between the two variables. For the data in Table 10.7, *V* = .178.

The value of χ^2 allows us to directly calculate the values for the contingency coefficient (*C*) and Cramér's coefficient (*V*). These values allow us to represent the strength of the relationship between two nominal variables in much the same way as correlation coefficients do for variables that are not nominal (i.e., ordinal, interval, or ratio). Further, squaring these values provides the proportion of variance shared by the two variables. Together, these values provide us with simple, yet meaningful, ways to both better understand and communicate the results of our research.

Summary

We can use the Pearson product-moment correlation coefficient (*r*) as a descriptive statistic of the measure of the relationship between two variables when the relationship between them is either monotonically increasing or decreasing. The value of the Pearson *r* is affected by how far the relationship between the two variables deviates from a straight line, the spread of the scores in the *Y* direction, the slope of the scores, the range of the scores, and the presence of outliers.

We can use a randomization (permutation) test with the Pearson *r* to test the null hypothesis that there is no relationship between the two variables. The only assumption required to use this statistic is that when there is no relationship between them, any *X* can be paired with any *Y*. This assumption is called exchangeability.

The Pearson *r* is the maximum likelihood estimate of the parameter ρ in a bivariate normal distribution of the population of pairs of scores.

---

[11] The symbol φ_C is also used for Cramér's coefficient because it has the same value as the phi coefficient (φ), which can be used to measure the correlation between two dichotomous variables (that is, when there are only two rows and two columns). When *k* = 2, $\varphi = \sqrt{\frac{\chi^2}{N}}$.

Using the classical statistical model, we can take a random sample from that population and calculate r. Because the distribution of r depends on the value of ρ and is not a normal distribution, we use Fisher's r to z_r transformation to create a normal distribution with a known mean and known variance. We can use this normal distribution to create z-test statistics to test hypotheses about the value of ρ and determine whether two bivariate normal distributions have the same value for ρ. We can also use the distribution of z_r to create confidence intervals for ρ.

When we are concerned that our data may not have come from a bivariate normal distribution, we can use the percentile bootstrap procedure to find confidence intervals for ρ.

When there are outliers in the data, we can use any of the following correlation coefficients to measure the degree of relationship and test hypotheses about the population correlations: Winsorized correlation coefficient, Spearman rank-order correlation coefficient, and Kendall's rank-order correlation coefficient (Kendall's tau).

We can also compute correlation coefficients to assess the association between two nominal variables arranged in a contingency table. Here we start by calculating the χ^2 statistic for those data and then use the χ^2 in a formula to calculate a correlation coefficient. The most commonly used correlation coefficients for these data are the contingency coefficient and Cramér's V.

So far we have dealt with two of the three models for testing hypotheses about correlations. First we dealt with the randomization (permutation) model, in which we did not make any assumptions about populations. Then we explored the bivariate normal distribution, in which we drew random samples from populations and used the samples to test hypotheses about the population correlation (per the classical statistical model). In the next chapter, we will discuss a model, the linear regression model, that is a little less restrictive than the bivariate normal distribution in terms of its assumptions about the population. Linear regression is also more useful in that it allows us to do more things, and it provides the basis for analysis of variance, multiple regression, and other multivariate analysis techniques.

Conceptual Exercises

1. We can use the Pearson product-moment correlation coefficient to measure the degree of relationship between two variables (e.g., to measure the degree of relationship between the amount of television teenagers watch and the amount of aggressive behaviors they exhibit 7 years later).

   a. Using the formula for r, describe how r measures the degree of relationship between these two variables.

   b. Explain how r can reflect the degree of positive relationship between these two variables.

   c. Explain how r might reflect the possibility that there is no relationship here.

2. We can use the following test statistic from the bivariate normal distribution model to test the hypothesis that the population correlation $\rho = 0$:

   $$z = z_r \sqrt{n-3}$$

   a. Explain why this statistic is appropriate for testing that hypothesis. Starting with a bivariate normal distribution (you do not have to state the assumptions of the model), explain why this statistic is appropriate for this test. Include the answers to the following questions in your answer:

  i. What is z_r and why do we need to use it in this formula?
  ii. Why is the test statistic a z-statistic?
  iii. Why is $n - 3$ in the formula?

  b. What is the distribution of this test statistic when the null hypothesis is true *and* when it is false?

3. Describe a test of the hypothesis that the observed correlation between two variables is not due to chance when you make no assumptions about random sampling. In your answer, include the following:

  a. The assumptions you need to make
  b. The null and alternative hypotheses you can test
  c. The test statistic you would use and the steps in performing the test
  d. The effect of increasing sample size on the power of this test and why sample size has this effect

4. Answer the following questions about testing the null hypothesis $H_0: \rho_1 = \rho_2$.

  a. What is the test statistic?
  b. Describe the distributions of this test statistic (including the kinds of distributions, means, and variances) when H_0 is true *and* when H_0 is false.
  c. Explain why power increases as sample size increases in this situation.

5. List the steps used to create a bootstrap confidence interval for ρ.

6. Using the *bivariate normal distribution model* to test the hypothesis $H_0: \rho = \rho_0$:

  a. What is the test statistic?
  b. Describe the distributions of this test statistic (including the kinds of distributions, means,

and variances) when H_0 is true *and* when H_0 is false.

  c. Explain why power increases as sample size increases in this situation.

7. Describe how you would construct a confidence interval for the population correlation with the bivariate normal distribution model. Starting with a brief description of the population, describe the steps you would go through to derive this confidence interval.

8. Why do we have to convert to z_r in order to test hypotheses or construct confidence intervals with the bivariate normal distribution model?

9. We can also use the following test statistic from the bivariate normal distribution model to test the hypothesis that the population correlation $\rho = \rho_0$:

$$z = \frac{z_r - \frac{1}{2}\ln\frac{1+\rho_0}{1-\rho_0}}{\sqrt{\frac{1}{n-3}}}$$

  a. Explain why this statistic is appropriate for testing that hypothesis. Starting with a bivariate normal distribution (you do not have to state the assumptions of the model), explain why this statistic is appropriate. What is z_r and why do we need to use it in this test statistic? Why is the test statistic a z-statistic? Why do we subtract $\frac{1}{2}\ln\frac{1+\rho}{1-\rho}$? Why do we divide by $\sqrt{\frac{1}{n-3}}$?

  b. What is the distribution of that test statistic when the null hypothesis is true *and* when it is false?

  c. Why does increasing sample size increase the power of this test?

Student Study Site

Visit the Student Study Site at **https://study.sagepub.com/friemanstats** for a variety of useful tools including data sets, additional exercises, and web resources.

EXPLORING THE RELATIONSHIP BETWEEN TWO VARIABLES
The Linear Regression Model

In the last chapter, we reviewed two models for testing hypotheses about the relationship between two variables. By making one simple assumption (i.e., when there is no relationship between the two variables, any X-value in our data could occur with any Y-value in our data), we can perform a randomization (permutation) test. We can also use the classical statistical model to conduct hypothesis tests about the parameter of a bivariate normal distribution called ρ, which describes the degree of relationship between the two variables for that population. The latter tests are not restricted to whether or not there is a relationship between the two variables (does $\rho = 0$?); we can also test hypotheses about the specific value of ρ (for example, does $\rho = .5$?) and about whether the population correlations are the same or different in different bivariate normal distributions (does $\rho_1 = \rho_2$?).

In this chapter, we will explore another classical statistical model for the relationship between two variables called the **linear regression model**. This model makes different assumptions about the population from which we sample. Although we can only test the hypothesis that $\rho = 0$ with this model, it is more useful because it provides the foundation for analysis of variance, multivariate analysis, and hypothesis tests when the relationship is not linear.

To illustrate the use of the linear regression model, we will return our focus to the research study conducted by McManus, Feyes, and Saucier (2011) that we introduced in Chapter 10. Recall that the researchers were interested in examining the factors associated with prejudicial attitudes toward individuals with intellectual disabilities. As we previously described, they used a sample of 125 undergraduate students and assessed their quantity of contact with individuals with intellectual disabilities, their quality of contact with individuals with intellectual disabilities, and the amount of knowledge they reported that they possessed about intellectual disabilities. The participants reported their levels of these variables on several items on scales from 1 (*strongly disagree*) to 9 (*strongly agree*), and their responses were averaged to produce scores for each of these three factors, with higher scores reflecting higher levels of quantity of contact, quality of contact, and perceived knowledge, respectively. The researchers assessed the participants' levels of prejudicial attitudes toward individuals with intellectual disabilities using the Mental Retardation Attitude Inventory–Revised (MRAI-R; Antonak & Harth, 1994). This measure also employed several items using scales from 1 (*strongly disagree*) to 9 (*strongly agree*), and the participants' responses were averaged, with higher scores reflecting more positive (i.e., less prejudicial) attitudes toward individuals with intellectual disabilities.

As we previously noted, consistent with their predictions, McManus et al. (2011) found that participants' levels of quantity and quality of contact with individuals with intellectual disabilities and their perceived knowledge about intellectual disabilities were positively correlated with their scores on the MRAI-R. Thus, as levels of quantity and quality of contact increased and as perceived knowledge increased, so did positive attitudes toward individuals with intellectual disabilities.

In Chapter 10, we focused on the relationship between the participants' quality of contact with individuals with intellectual disabilities and their attitudes toward individuals with intellectual disabilities. In this chapter, we will again focus on this relationship by using the participants' quality of contact with individuals with intellectual disabilities as a predictor variable and the participants' scores on the MRAI-R as a criterion variable.

ASSUMPTIONS FOR THE LINEAR REGRESSION MODEL

Unlike with the bivariate normal distribution model, we make no assumptions about the distribution of the values on the X-axis. However, we assume that for every value of X, the Y scores are normally distributed around a straight line $Y' = \alpha + \beta X$ and the variances of those normal distributions are equal.

In the linear regression model, we make *no assumptions about the distribution of the variable we call* X *or how we obtain the values of* X: X can have a normal distribution as in the bivariate normal distribution model, and we can randomly sample the values of X (as in that model). On the other hand, X could be a nominal variable for which the values are preselected. However, no matter what the distribution of X is or how we obtain the values of X, in this model, we do assume the following for each X: the values of Y are normally distributed, all of these normal distributions of Y values have the same variance, and the means of these normal distributions lie on a straight line. We can estimate the parameters and test hypotheses by taking a random sample from this population. These assumptions can be summarized as follows:

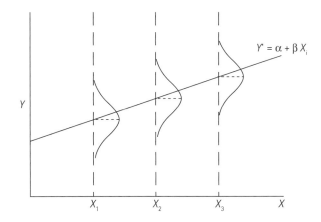

Figure 11.1 ■ This population consists of three values of X (X_1, X_2, X_3). For each X_i, the Y-values have a normal distribution. The variances of these normal distributions are the same, and the means of these normal distributions are on the line $Y' = \alpha + \beta X$.

1. The variable we call X can have any distribution, and it does not matter whether the values of X were obtained by random sampling or were preselected.
2. For every value of X, the associated values of Y have a normal distribution.
3. The means of these normal distributions of Y values lie on a straight line. The equation for that line is $Y' = \alpha + \beta X$, where α is the Y-intercept of the line and β is the slope. This line is called **population regression line**.
4. These normal distributions of Y scores all have the same variance around that straight line. (This assumption is called **homoscedasticity**.)
5. We can estimate the values of the two parameters α and β by taking a random sample from this population.

These assumptions are represented graphically in Figure 11.1.

In Figure 11.1, we can locate every Y-value in any of the normal distributions from the following equation:

$$Y_i = \alpha + \beta X_i + \varepsilon_i \tag{11.1}$$

where Y_i is the Y-value we are seeking, α is the Y-intercept of the line on which the means of the normal distributions of the Y-values lie, β is the slope of that line, X_i is the X-value for the normal distribution in which we are seeking the Y-value, and ε_i is the distance the particular Y-value is above or below the line. These components are shown on the graph in Figure 11.2.

According to Equation 11.1, we locate the point in the normal distribution for any X_i by going up a distance α, then go up another distance βX_i. That takes you to the mean

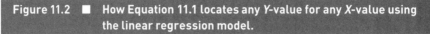

Figure 11.2 ■ How Equation 11.1 locates any Y-value for any X-value using the linear regression model.

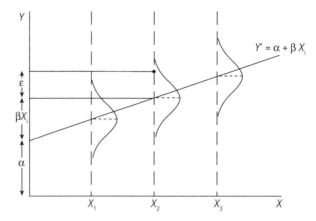

of the Y-values for X_i. Then go up or down the distance ε_i to get to Y_i. Every point (X_i, Y_i) can be defined that way.

The symbol ε_i in Equation 11.1 represents the distance each Y-value is from the mean of the normal distribution in which it resides. Because those means are on the line $Y' = \alpha + \beta X$, ε represents the distance each Y value is from the line, that is $\varepsilon = Y - Y'$. Clearly, if Y has a normal distribution for each X, then ε also has a normal distribution with $\mu_\varepsilon = 0$ and $\sigma_\varepsilon^2 = \sigma_Y^2$ for each X (homoscedasticity).

ESTIMATING PARAMETERS WITH THE LINEAR REGRESSION MODEL

We use the method of least squares to estimate the intercept and slope of the population regression line $Y = \alpha + \beta X$. *We start by taking a random sample from the population and finding the values of the estimators of* α *and* β *(A and B respectively) that minimize the function* $\Sigma[Y - (A + BX)]^2$.

The relationship between the two variables X and Y is described by the population line $Y' = \alpha + \beta X$. There are two parameters in this equation (α and β). To estimate these parameters, we take a random sample from the population and attempt to find the line that best fits the sample data. The equation for that line is $Y' = A + BX$, where A is the estimate of α and B is the estimate of β. Clearly, there are an infinite number of lines that can be drawn on top of the sample data. Some of these lines fit the sample data better than others. What criterion should we use to choose among these lines? The criterion that has been adopted is the **least squares criterion**, which instructs us to *find the values for* A *and* B *that minimize the sum of the squared deviations of the data points from the line*. Put simply, we are attempting to identify the line that comes the closest to all of the data points collectively. Applying this criterion is the basis for the **method of least squares**.

The method of least squares works as follows:

1. Draw a random sample from the population.
2. Try to fit the equation $Y' = A + BX$ to the sample data by finding values for A and B that minimize the value of $\Sigma[Y - (A + BX)]^2$. Because $Y' = A + BX$, this expression can be rewritten as finding the values for A and B that minimize $\Sigma(Y - Y')^2$ (that is, finding the values that minimize the sum of the squared deviations between the sample values, Y, and the corresponding value on the sample regression line, Y').

The reader who is familiar with differential calculus can use that technique to find A and B: Find the first derivative of $\Sigma[Y - (A + BX)]^2$ with respect to A and again with respect to B. Set these terms equal to zero, thereby yielding two simultaneous equations with two unknowns. You can use algebra to find the values of A and B that satisfy those two simultaneous equations. The reader who is not familiar with differential calculus will have to take on faith that the following formulas give us the values of A and B that make $\Sigma[Y - (A + BX)]^2$ a minimum:

$$A = \bar{Y} - r\left(\frac{S_Y}{S_X}\right)\bar{X} \tag{11.2}$$

$$B = r\left(\frac{S_Y}{S_X}\right) \tag{11.3}$$

Substituting these expressions into the equation for the sample regression line ($Y' = A + BX$), we get the following formula:

$$Y' = \left[\bar{Y} - r\left(\frac{S_Y}{S_X}\right)\bar{X}\right] + \left[r\left(\frac{S_Y}{S_X}\right)X\right] \tag{11.4a}$$

Equation 11.4 is the **sample regression line**. It is based on five easily obtainable sample statistics: $\bar{Y}$, $\bar{X}$, S_Y, S_X, and r. When there is a non-zero correlation between X and Y, we can use Equation 11.4 to help us predict Y-scores from knowledge of X-scores.

REGRESSION AND PREDICTION

We can use the sample regression line to predict values on the Y-axis for any value on the X-axis. We scale the accuracy of our prediction in terms of the variance in the observed scores around the predicted scores. The higher the value of the Pearson r, the lower the variance, and the closer our predicted scores are to the observed scores. We can also use the method of least squares to find a regression line for predicting the X-scores from the Y-scores. The phenomenon of regression toward the mean is a consequence of using the method of least squares to estimate the population regression line with the resulting sample regression line.

Equation 11.4a is the sample regression line. When two variables are related, knowledge of an individual's score on one variable should help us to predict his or her score on the other variable; that is, after we find the sample regression line for one sample from a population, we can use that regression line to predict the Ys from the Xs for other individuals sampled from that population. The predicted value will be the value of Y' from Equation 11.4a for a given value of X.

For the data from McManus et al. (2011), $\bar{X}_{Quality} = 6.13$, $\bar{Y}_{MRAI-R} = 6.52$, $\sigma_{Quality} = 1.78$, $\sigma_{MRAI-R} = 1.04$, and $r = .615$. Inserting these values into Equation 11.4a yields the following sample regression line:

$$Y' = 4.35 + 0.35X \qquad\qquad (11.4b)$$

where Y' is the predicted score on the MRAI-R scale and X is the individual's score on the quality of contact scale. This sample regression line has 4.35 as the Y-intercept and 0.35 as the slope. These values are the least squares estimates for the parameters α and β of the population regression line. Therefore, if someone scores 7 on the quality of contact scale, we predict the score on the MRAI-R scale would be 6.79. The value of Y' is our best prediction for someone's score on the MRAI-R scale (indicating the positivity of their attitudes toward individuals with intellectual disabilities) given their score on the quality of contact (indicating the quality of their past experiences with individuals with intellectual disabilities). This prediction demonstrates that, consistent with the positive relationship between these variables, individuals' relatively high scores on quality of contact are associated with their having relatively high levels of positive attitudes. More importantly, this result is consistent with the researchers' hypothesis that higher levels of quality of contact with individuals with intellectual disabilities would be associated with more positive attitudes toward individuals with intellectual disabilities. This relationship suggests that positive interactions with members of a stigmatized group may contribute to lower levels of prejudice toward them.

When we are talking about prediction in the case of regression, we are talking about it in the sense that when there is a correlation between X and Y, knowing something about a participant's score on X, while not necessarily allowing you to predict Y exactly, tells you something about the Y-score for a given individual: In the case of high positive correlation, higher Xs tend to go with higher Ys, and lower Xs tend to go with lower Ys. In the case of attitudes toward individuals with intellectual disabilities, a positive relationship such that higher levels of quality of contact are associated with more positive attitudes does not mean every participant with higher levels of quality of contact necessarily has more positive attitudes.

This situation raises a question. We know that our predicted scores for individuals are not going to be identical to their observed scores. We need some way to scale the accuracy of our predictions. We scale the accuracy of our predictions by looking at the *variation* of the observed scores from the predicted scores. Consider any given value of X. Equation 11.4a gives us a single predicted value for that X, but there are a large number of possible values associated with that X. The following formula gives us a measure of the accuracy of our predictions:

$$S^2_{Y|X} = \frac{\sum (Y - Y')^2}{n} \tag{11.5}^1$$

When using Equation 11.5 as the measure of the accuracy of our predictions, we are *not* defining accuracy as the number or percentage of exact predictions we make. It is rare that we are going to predict the observed score exactly. Instead, Equation 11.5 measures accuracy of prediction in terms of the average of the sum of the squared deviations of the observed scores from the predicted scores. The closer the observed scores are to the predicted scores (and the regression line), the more accurate your predictions; the more spread out the observed scores are around the regression line, the poorer your predictions.

When $r = 1$, we would have perfect predictions because all of the observed scores would be on the regression line ($Y = Y'$); that is, all of the observed scores would equal the predicted scores. When this situation occurs, $S^2_{Y|X} = 0$. But when $r \neq 0$, then there

---

[1] The square root of Equation 11.5 is the *standard error of the estimate*.

will be some variation between the observed scores and predicted scores and $S^2_{Y|X} > 0$. Therefore, the smaller the value of $S^2_{Y|X}$, the better our predictions.

When $r = 0$, Equation 11.3 tells us that $B = 0$, Equation 11.2 tells us that $A = \bar{Y}$, and Equation 11.4 tells us that $Y' = \bar{Y}$. This means that when $r = 0$, our best prediction for the value of Y is $\bar{Y}$ because that value minimizes the $\Sigma(Y - Y')^2$. Because our observed scores are scattered all over the place when $r = 0$, the sum of the squared deviations of the observed scores from the predicted scores is going to be the largest it can be for those data. Substituting $\bar{Y}$ for Y' in Equation 11.5 makes $S^2_{Y|X} = S^2_Y$.

The higher r is, the better our prediction. The better our prediction, the smaller the deviation of the observed scores from the predicted scores when you average them over all of the data. Therefore, there is an obvious relationship between $S^2_{Y|X}$ and r: As r increases, $S^2_{Y|X}$ decreases. Furthermore, when $r = 0, S^2_{Y|X} = S^2_Y$, and when $r = 1, S^2_{Y|X} = 0$. The exact form of the relationship between r and $S^2_{Y|X}$ is

$$S^2_{Y|X} = S^2_Y\left(1 - r^2\right) \tag{11.6}$$

Predicting in the Other Direction

When two variables are correlated, we should be able to make predictions in either direction (from X to Y and from Y to X). To make predictions from X to Y, we use the method of least squares to find the values of A and B in the equation $Y' = A + BX$ such that $\Sigma(Y - Y')$ is a minimum. If we want to make predictions from Y to X, the corresponding equation would be $X' = A^* + B^*Y$ (where A^* is the X-intercept and B^* is the slope), and we use the method of least squares to find the values of A^* and B^* such that $\Sigma(X - X')^2$ is a minimum. Here is the analytic solution:

$$A^* = \bar{X} - r\left(\frac{S_X}{S_Y}\right)\bar{Y} \tag{11.7}$$

and

$$B^* = r\left(\frac{S_X}{S_Y}\right) \tag{11.8}$$

Substituting these two terms into the equation for the sample regression line ($X' = A^* + B^*Y$), we get the following formula:

$$X' = \left[\bar{X} - r\left(\frac{S_X}{S_Y}\right)\bar{Y}\right] + \left[r\left(\frac{S_X}{S_Y}\right)Y\right] \tag{11.9}$$

BOX 11.1
REGRESSION TOWARD THE MEAN

An interesting thing happens when r is between 0 and ± 1: Suppose we take a value X_1 and use it to predict the value of Y_1'. Notice that the difference between X_1 and $\bar{X}$ and Y_1' and $\bar{Y}$ are not the same: $(Y_1'-\bar{Y})$ is smaller than $(X_1-\bar{X})$. Now take Y_1' and go back in the other direction to predict X. When we do that, the predicted value for $X(X_1')$ is closer to $\bar{X}$ than X_1 is; that is, $X_1'-\bar{X}<X_1-\bar{X}$. Furthermore, $X_1'-\bar{X}<Y_1'-\bar{Y}$. In other words, *the predicted score is always closer to its mean than the score from which we started*, no matter which direction we go. This phenomenon is **regression toward the mean**.

Frances Galton discovered the phenomenon of regression toward the mean. He noticed that the average height of the children of tall parents was less than the average of the height of their parents and, for short parents, the average height of their children was greater than the average height of the parents. Furthermore, the average heights of the children of both tall and short parents were closer to the mean of all children than the average heights of the parents were to the average heights of all parents. There is a biological explanation for this phenomenon: Two things determine height. One is genetics (tall people tend to have tall children), and the other is nutrition. The nutritional factor accounts for the fact that in recent history, successive generations have tended to be taller than their parents.

Galton was showing the effects of heredity and the environment in the following way. A person who is quite tall is so for two possible reasons. One is the genetic component, and the other is a favorable nutrition program. What were the chances in the next generation that such a combination would occur again? It is likely that the genetics will be passed on. But when the favorable nutritional environment is not repeated in the next generation, the height of the children of tall parents will be lower. Likewise, the children of short parents tend to be taller because, although the genes for shortness are passed on, better nutrition in the second generation would cause the children to be a little taller than their parents. Thus, in both cases, the fact that the nutritional environment was likely to vary from generation to generation leads to differences in height between parents and children. Of course, not all short parents had taller children and not all tall parents had shorter children, but the average height of the children was shorter or taller than the average height of their parents. The fact that the environmental factors can change from generation to generation allows researchers to separate the effects of heredity and the environment.

The same phenomenon is observed with IQ. Parents with high IQs will not necessarily have children whose IQs are higher than average. The children's IQ scores could be higher than average, of course, but not necessarily. The environment is an important factor also. In a constant environment, you would observe purely genetic factors at work.

Implicit in the formula for Y' is this idea of regression to the mean. This pattern becomes obvious when we convert both X and Y to standard scores. The resulting equations are $z_Y'=rz_X$ and $z_X'=rz_Y$. Clearly, the slopes of those lines are always going to be some value less than 1. Thus, since the slope of the regression line is less than 1, when you predict Y from X, the predicted value will be closer to the mean (zero in the case of z-scores). See Senn (2011) for more details about Galton's discovery of regression to the mean and its implications.

These two lines, X' and Y', are always different *except* when $r = +1$ or -1. On the other hand, when $r = 0$, $Y' = \bar{Y}$ and $X' = \bar{X}$. Therefore, when $r = 0$, the lines are perpendicular to each other and cross at the point $(\bar{X}, \bar{Y})$. When r is between 0 and ± 1, the two lines cross at the point $(\bar{X}, \bar{Y})$ with the angle between them less than $90°$. The greater the absolute value of r, the smaller the angle between these two regression lines. When $r = \pm 1$, they are the same line. An interesting thing happens when r is between 0 and ± 1 (see Box 11.1).

VARIANCE AND CORRELATION

We can partition the variance of the Y-scores into two parts: the variance of the predicted scores around the mean of Y (variance due to regression or explained variance) and the variance of the observed scores around the regression line (residual variance or unexplained variance). The proportions of the variance in Y that are due to regression and the residual variance are both functions of the Pearson r for a given set of data.

In our sample data, the deviation of every Y-value from $\bar{Y}$ $(Y - \bar{Y})$ is the sum of the deviation of that Y-value from the predicted value of $Y (Y - Y')$ and the deviation of each predicted value Y' from $\bar{Y}$ $(Y' - \bar{Y})$. That is,

$$\left(Y - \bar{Y}\right) = \left(Y - Y'\right) + \left(Y' - \bar{Y}\right) \tag{11.10}$$

This concept is illustrated in Figure 11.3.

If we square both sides of Equation 11.10, add up all of the squared deviations on both sides, and divide by the sample size (n), we get the following:

$$\sum \frac{(Y - \bar{Y})^2}{n} = \sum \frac{[(Y - Y') + (Y' - \bar{Y})]^2}{n} \tag{11.11}$$

If we complete the square on the right side of Equation 11.11 and distribute the summation sign and the division by n, we get the following equation:

$$\sum \frac{(Y - \bar{Y})^2}{n} = \sum \frac{(Y - Y')^2}{n} + \sum \frac{(Y' - \bar{Y})^2}{n} + 2\sum \frac{(Y - Y')(Y' - \bar{Y})}{n} \tag{11.12}$$

The term to the left of the equal sign is the variance of the Y-scores. We call this the **total variance** of $Y (S_Y^2)$. The first term after the equal sign is the variance of the Y-scores

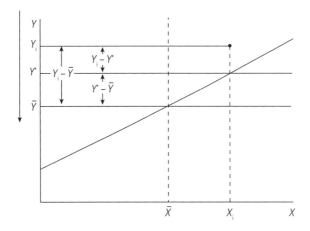

FIGURE 11.3 ■ The deviation of every *Y*-score from $\bar{Y}$ $(Y - \bar{Y})$ is the sum of the deviation of that *Y*-value from the predicted value of *Y* $(Y - Y')$ and the deviation of each predicted value *Y'* from $\bar{y}$ $(y' - \bar{y})$.

around the regression line. This term is referred to as either the **unexplained variance** or the **residual variance**. The symbol for this variance is $S_{Y|X}^2$. The second term after the equal sign is the variance of the scores on the line (predicted scores) around the mean of *Y*. This term is called the **explained variance**. The symbol for this variance is $S_{Y'}^2$. Substituting these symbols into Equation 11.12, we get the following:

$$S_Y^2 = S_{Y|X}^2 + S_{Y'}^2 + 2\sum \frac{(Y - Y')(Y' - \bar{Y})}{n} \tag{11.13}$$

The last term in Equations 11.12 and 11.13 is the covariance between the deviations of the *Y* scores around the regression line $(Y - Y')$ and the deviations of the predicted scores around the mean of *Y* $(Y' - \bar{Y})$. As noted in the previous chapter, the covariance is related to the correlation between two variables, and the only time the correlation is zero is when there is no relationship between the two variables (correlation = 0). In this case, the covariance term in Equations 11.12 and 11.13 equals zero. In this case, there is no relationship between the deviations of the observed score from the line $(Y - Y')$ and the deviations of the points on the line from the mean of *Y* $(Y' - \bar{Y})$. If they were positively correlated, then where the deviation between *Y'* and $\bar{Y}$ is small, the deviation *Y* around the line (Y') would also be small, and where $(Y' - \bar{Y})$ is large, $(Y - Y')$ would also be large. In this case, we could not have equal variance around the line (homoscedasticity), because homoscedasticity means that the variance around the regression line is the same everywhere along that line. This situation can only occur when the correlation (covariance) between $(Y - Y')$ and $(Y' - \overline{Y}) = 0$. Therefore,

$$S_Y^2 = S_{Y|X}^2 + S_{Y'}^2 \qquad (11.14)$$

Equation 11.14 tells us that the *total variance* in Y (S_Y^2) is made up of two parts: One part is the *explained variance* $(S_{Y'}^2)$, which is variation due to the correlation between X and Y; that is, this is the variance in Y that is due to or explained by variation in X (this component is also referred to as *variation due to regression*). The other part is the *unexplained or residual variance* $(S_{Y|X}^2)$ which is the variation in Y that is not explained by variation in X.

We saw in Equation 11.6 that the value of $S_{Y|X}^2$ depends on the correlation between X and Y. When $r = 1$, all of the Y-scores are on the regression line, and there is no variation around that line; that is, there is no residual variance. In other words, when $r = 1$, all of the variation in Y is explained by the correlation with X, nothing is unexplained, and $S_{Y|X}^2 = 0$. On the other hand, when $r = 0$, $Y' = \overline{Y}$. In this case, no matter what the value of X, the predicted score is the same; in other words, there is no variation in the Y' values. Therefore, *all* of the variation in Y is unexplained variation or residual variance and $S_{Y|X}^2 = S_Y^2$.

Substituting Equation 11.6 into Equation 11.14 and rearranging the terms gives us the following equation:

$$S_{Y'}^2 = r^2 S_Y^2 \qquad (11.15)$$

Equation 11.15 tells us that the explained variance is also a function of the correlation between X and Y (due to regression): When $r = 1$, $S_{Y'}^2 = S_Y^2$, and when $r = 0$, $S_{Y'}^2 = 0$.

We can rearrange Equation 11.15 to get the following important relationship:

$$r^2 = \frac{S_{Y'}^2}{S_Y^2} \qquad (11.16)$$

Equation 11.16 tells us that the *square of the Pearson* r *equals the proportion of variance in* Y *explained by the correlation with* X. In other words, the higher the correlation, the greater the proportion of the total variance in Y that is explained by variation in X.

We can perform a similar arrangement of Equation 11.16 to get the following relationship:

$$r^2 = 1 - \frac{S_{Y|X}^2}{S_Y^2} \qquad (11.17)$$

Equation 11.17 tells us that the square of the Pearson r equals 1 minus the proportion of variance that is not explained by the correlation with X (the residual variance).

TESTING HYPOTHESES WITH THE LINEAR REGRESSION MODEL

We use the ratio of two estimates of variance, one based on the variation among the predicted Y-scores and the other based on the variation of the Y-scores around the regression line. When ρ = 0, both are estimating the variance of Y. When ρ ≠ 0, they are estimating different things. The test statistic is an F-ratio. This concept is the basis of analysis of variance.

We can test the hypothesis that $\rho = 0$ by comparing two estimates of the variance. One estimate is based on the deviations of the predicted scores of Y from $\overline{Y}$ in your sample, and the other is based on the deviations of the observed scores from the predicted scores in your sample. The test statistic is the ratio of those two estimates of variance. When the null hypothesis is true, both of these estimates are estimating the variance of Y for the population (σ_Y^2). When $\rho \neq 0$, one of those estimates of variance is estimating something greater than σ_Y^2, and the other is estimating something less than σ_Y^2.

In the linear regression model, all of the normal distributions of the Y values for each X value lie on a straight line $Y' = \alpha + \beta X$. Equations 11.2 and 11.3 give us the values of A and B (the least square estimates of α and β). It is also the case that

$$\alpha = \mu_Y - \rho\left(\frac{\sigma_Y}{\sigma_X}\right)\mu_X \text{ and } \beta = \rho\left(\frac{\sigma_Y}{\sigma_X}\right) \tag{11.18}$$

Therefore, $\beta = 0$ when $\rho = 0$. In this case, testing the hypothesis $H_0: \rho = 0$ is equivalent to testing the hypothesis $H_0: \beta = 0$.

We can construct a test for the hypothesis $H_0: \rho = 0$ from the following facts:

1. The total sum of the squared deviations of all of the Y-scores around the mean of Y can be divided into two additive parts: the sum of the squared deviations for each Y-score around the predicted value for that Y-value (Y') and the sum of the squared deviations of these predicted values (Y') from the mean of all of the Y-scores:

$$\sum\left(Y - \overline{Y}\right)^2 = \sum\left(Y - Y'\right)^2 + \sum\left(Y' - \overline{Y}\right)^2 \tag{11.19a}$$

The sums of squared deviations to the left of the equal sign is called SS_{Total}, the first sum of squared deviations to the right of the equal sign is called the $SS_{Unexplained}$ or $SS_{Residual}$, and the second sum of squared deviations to the right of the equal sign is called the $SS_{Explained}$. Therefore,

$$SS_{Total} = SS_{Unexplained} + SS_{Explained} \tag{11.19b}$$

2. The total degrees of freedom equal sample size minus 1: $df_{\text{Total}} = n - 1$. We can use both of the definitions for degrees of freedom developed in an earlier chapter to arrive at this value.[2] The total degrees of freedom can be divided into two additive parts:

   a. *Degrees of freedom explained* ($df_{\text{Explained}}$) *or degrees of freedom regression* ($df_{\text{Regression}}$). The sums of squares explained involves the deviations' predicted values around the mean of Y. Those predicted values are all on a straight line. We know from Euclid's axioms in geometry that one and only one straight line can be drawn between two points. The regression line Y' goes through the point $(\bar{X}, \bar{Y})$. Therefore, using the first definition of degrees of freedom (how many of those predicted scores we have to know before we can know all the rest), if we know one other point on the line, we know the location of all of the points on the line. Therefore, $df_{\text{Explained}} = 1$.

   b. *Degrees of freedom unexplained* ($df_{\text{Unexplained}}$) *or degrees of freedom residual* (df_{Residual}). We use the second definition of degrees of freedom to find the unexplained degrees of freedom, which are related to the deviations of observed scores around the regression line: When we have only one point, we can draw an infinite number of regression lines through that point, and the sum of the squared deviations around the regression line is zero because the regression line has to go through that point based on the method of least squares. When we have two points, we minimize the sum of the squared deviations around the line by drawing the regression line through those two points. Here $r = 1$, and the sum of the squared deviations is zero. Therefore, we must have *at least three values* before the sum of squared deviations of the scores around the regression line can be a non-zero value. Therefore, $df_{\text{Unexplained}} = (n - 2)$.

   We can summarize this relationship with the following equation:

   $$(n - 1) = (n - 2) + 1 \tag{11.20a}$$

   $$df_{\text{Total}} = df_{\text{Unexplained}} + df_{\text{Explained}} \tag{11.20b}$$

3. Dividing sums of squares by degrees of freedom produces estimates of variance, and we can use the definition of unbiased estimates to determine what variances are being estimated:

   a. $\dfrac{\sum\left(Y - \bar{Y}\right)^2}{n - 1}$ is an unbiased estimate of σ_Y^2. Therefore,

   $$E\left[\frac{\sum\left(Y - \bar{Y}\right)^2}{n - 1}\right] = \sigma_Y^2 \tag{11.21}$$

---

[2] The two definitions of *degrees of freedom* are (1) how many scores you need to know before all the rest are fixed and (2) how many scores you need to have before the sum of squares could be a non-zero value.

BOX 11.2

THE EXPECTED VALUE OF $\dfrac{\sum(Y-Y')^2}{n-2}$

$\dfrac{\sum(Y-Y')^2}{n-2}$ is an unbiased estimate of the unexplained (residual) variance in the population $\sigma^2_{Y|X}$. We saw earlier that the unexplained (residual) variance of the sample, $S^2_{Y|X}$, is a function of the value of the Pearson r:

$S^2_{Y|X} = S^2_Y(1-r^2)$. The value of $\sigma^2_{Y|X}$ is a function of the population correlation ρ in a similar way; that is, $\sigma^2_{Y|X} = \sigma^2_Y(1-\rho^2)$. Combining these two pieces of information we arrive at the following equation:

$$E\,\frac{\sum(Y-Y')^2}{n-2} = \sigma^2_{Y|X} = \sigma^2_Y\left(1-\rho^2\right)$$

When $\rho = 0$, $E\,\dfrac{\sum(Y-Y')^2}{n-2} = \sigma^2_Y$; that is,

$E\,\dfrac{\sum(Y-Y')^2}{n-2}$ is estimating σ^2_Y.

When $\rho \neq 0$, $E\,\dfrac{\sum(Y-Y')^2}{n-2}$ is estimating something *smaller* than σ^2_Y.

b. When $\rho = 0$,

$$E\left[\frac{\sum(Y-Y')^2}{n-2}\right] = \sigma^2_Y \qquad\qquad (11.22)$$

Therefore, when $\rho = 0$, this formula is estimating σ^2_Y. When $\rho \neq 0$, this formula is estimating something *smaller* than σ^2_Y. (See Box 11.2.)

c. When $\rho = 0$,

$$E\left[\frac{\sum(Y'-\overline{Y})^2}{1}\right] = \sigma^2_Y \qquad\qquad (11.23)$$

Therefore, when $\rho = 0$, this formula is estimating σ^2_Y. When $\rho \neq 0$, this formula is estimating something *larger* than σ^2_Y. (See Box 11.3.)

BOX 11.3

THE EXPECTED VALUE OF $\sum \frac{\left(Y'-\bar{Y}\right)}{1}$

We can derive the expected value of $\dfrac{\sum\left(Y-\bar{Y}\right)^2}{1}$ by starting with Equation 11.19a:

$$\sum\left(Y-\bar{Y}\right)^2 = \sum\left(Y-Y'\right)^2 + \sum\left(Y'-\bar{Y}\right)^2$$

We can rearrange the terms to get

$$\sum\left(Y'-\bar{Y}\right)^2 = \sum\left(Y-\bar{Y}\right)^2 - \sum\left(Y-Y'\right)^2$$

If we take the expected value of both sides and use the fact that the expected value of a difference is the difference in the expected values, we arrive at the following relationship

$$E\left[\sum\left(Y'-\bar{Y}\right)^2\right] = E\left[\sum\left(Y-\bar{Y}\right)^2\right] - E\left[\sum\left(Y-Y'\right)^2\right] \tag{A}$$

We saw earlier that $E\left[\dfrac{\sum\left(Y-\bar{Y}\right)^2}{n-1}\right] = \sigma_Y^2$. Applying the rules of algebra and expected values, we

get $E\left[\sum\left(Y-\bar{Y}\right)^2\right] = (n-1)\sigma_Y^2$.

It is also the case that because

$$E\left[\frac{\sum\left(Y-Y'\right)^2}{n-2}\right] = \sigma_Y^2\left(1-\rho^2\right),$$

$$E\left[\sum\left(Y-Y'\right)^2\right] = (n-2)\sigma_Y^2\left(1-\rho^2\right)$$

Substituting these into Equation A above, we get this:

$$E\left[\sum\left(Y-Y'\right)^2\right] = (n-1)\sigma_Y^2 - (n-2)\sigma_Y^2\left(1-\rho^2\right) \tag{B}$$

By applying the rules of algebra, we obtain the following:

$$E\left[\sum\left(Y'-\bar{Y}\right)^2\right] = \sigma_Y^2\left[1+(n-2)\rho^2\right] \tag{C}$$

Thus, when $\rho = 0$, $E\left[\dfrac{\sum\left(Y'-\bar{Y}\right)^2}{1}\right] = \sigma_Y^2$; that is, $E\left[\dfrac{\sum\left(Y'-\bar{Y}\right)^2}{1}\right]$ is estimating σ_Y^2, and when $\rho \neq 0$,

$E\left[\dfrac{\sum\left(Y'-\bar{Y}\right)^2}{1}\right]$ is estimating something *larger* than σ_Y^2.

We can use the results in Boxes 11.2 and 11.3 to construct a hypothesis test for $\rho = 0$ by comparing the two estimates of variance $\dfrac{\sum(Y - Y')^2}{n-2}$ and $\dfrac{\sum(Y' - \bar{Y})^2}{1}$. When $\rho = 0$, we expect

$$\frac{\sum(Y - Y')^2}{n-2} \approx \frac{\sum(Y' - \bar{Y})^2}{1} \tag{11.24}$$

And when $\rho \neq 0$, we expect

$$\frac{\sum(Y - Y')^2}{n-2} << \frac{\sum(Y' - \bar{Y})^2}{1} \tag{11.25}$$

We can compare these two estimates of variance by forming their ratio. The symbol for this ratio is F (after R. A. Fisher, who derived its distribution). When the null hypothesis is true, the value of the F-ratio should be close to 1. If we put the value we expect to be larger in the numerator when the null hypothesis is false, the value of F will be a lot larger than 1 when the null hypothesis is false. When the null hypothesis is true, the F-ratio has an F-distribution. The exact shape of the central F-distribution depends on both the degrees of freedom for the estimate in the numerator and degrees of freedom for the estimate in the denominator. Because F is the ratio of two estimates of variance, which must be positive given that they are squared values, $F \geq 0$. When the null hypothesis is true, $\mu_F = \dfrac{df_{\text{denominator}}}{df_{\text{denominator}} - 2}$. The variance of F is a complicated formula that depends on both $df_{\text{numerator}}$ and $df_{\text{denominator}}.$[3] As either degrees of freedom increase, σ_F^2 decreases, and the distribution of F becomes narrower (see Figure 11.4).

We reject the null hypothesis when F is a large number. Therefore, the critical region for an F-test is always in the right tail of the null hypothesis true distribution (central F-distribution). When the null hypothesis is false, the F-ratio has a non-central F-distribution with

$$\mu_{F^*} = \left(\frac{df_{\text{den}}}{df_{\text{den}} - 2}\right)\left(\frac{df_{\text{num}} + \delta}{df_{\text{num}}}\right), \tag{11.26}$$

---

[3] $\sigma_F^2 = \dfrac{2\,df_{\text{den}}^2\left(df_{\text{num}} + df_{\text{den}} - 2\right)}{df_{\text{num}}\left(df_{\text{den}} - 2\right)^2\left(df_{\text{den}} - 4\right)}$ when $df_{\text{denominator}} > 4$.

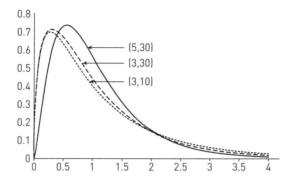

FIGURE 11.4 ■ Probability density functions for *F* for various degrees of freedom. In the parentheses, the first numbers are $df_{numerator}$, and the second numbers are $df_{denominator}$.

where δ is the noncentrality parameter. For this situation,

$$\delta = n\left[\frac{\rho^2}{(1-\rho)^2}\right] \tag{11.27}$$

where ρ is the true population correlation.

When H_0 is true, $\rho = 0$ and $\delta = 0$, and μ_{F^*} reduces to μ_F.

Therefore, to test H_0: $\rho = 0$ when the relationship between the variables is linear, the *F*-ratio is as follows:

$$F = \frac{\sum(Y' - \bar{Y})^2 / 1}{\sum(Y - Y')^2 / (n - 2)} \tag{11.28}$$

As noted in Equation 11.24, when the null hypothesis is true, the numerator and denominator are both estimating σ_Y^2, but when the null hypothesis is false (Equation 11.25), the numerator is estimating a value *larger* than σ_Y^2, and the denominator is estimating a value *smaller* than σ_Y^2. Therefore, large values of F lead to rejection of the null hypothesis.

Presenting the Results of an *F*-Test

When people perform *F*-tests, they may display the results in a standard format called an ***F*-table** (see Table 11.1). The *F*-table starts with the sums of squares and degrees of freedom for each component of the *F*-ratio, combines them into estimates of variance (called *mean squares*), and finally forms the *F*-ratio from the ratio of the mean squares.

The column labeled "Source of Variance" contains the names of the sources of variance that have been identified as adding up to the total variance in the situation under study.

TABLE 11.1 ■ *F*-Table				
Source of Variance	Sums of Squares	Degrees of Freedom	Mean Square	*F*
Source 1	SS_1	df_1	$MS_1 = SS_1/df_1$	$F = MS_1/MS_2$
Source 2	SS_2	df_2	$MS_2 = SS_2/df_2$	
Total	SS_{Total}	df_{Total}		

How many sources of variance there are depends on the situation. The sums of squares and degrees of freedom in the second and third columns must add to the total sums of squares and degrees of freedom, respectively. Mean squares are estimates of variance for each source of variance in the table. They are the obtained by dividing the sums of squares by the corresponding degrees of freedom. Finally, the value of *F* is the ratio of two mean squares (estimates of variance).

In the test of the hypothesis that $\rho = 0$ for the linear regression situation, the *F*-table would look like Table 11.2.

The sums of squares for regression and residual in Table 11.2 are not easy to calculate. Equivalent formulas that are easier to use are presented in Box 11.4.

The results from Box 11.4 lead to Table 11.3.

By dividing the numerator and denominator of the *F*-ratio in the Table 11.3 by SS_{Total}, the test statistic can be simplified to the following:

$$F = \frac{r^2/1}{(1-r^2)/(n-2)} \tag{11.29}$$

TABLE 11.2 ■ *F*-Table for the Hypothesis That $\rho = 0$				
Source of Variance	Sums of Squares	Degrees of Freedom	Mean Square	*F*
Regression	$\sum(Y'-\bar{Y})^2$	1	$\sum(Y'-\bar{Y})^2/1$	$\dfrac{\sum(Y'-\bar{Y})^2/1}{\sum(Y-Y')^2/(n-2)}$
Residual	$\sum(Y-Y')^2$	$n-2$	$\sum(Y-Y')^2/(n-2)$	
Total	$\sum(Y-\bar{Y})^2$	$n-1$		

BOX 11.4

COMPUTATIONAL FORMULAS FOR THE SUMS OF SQUARES FOR THE F-TEST OF $H_0: \rho = 0$

The sums of squares regression and residual in the table can be calculated from the Pearson r and the sums of squares total (SS_{Total}). The derivation of these formulas for the hypothesis test under consideration can be generalized to a wide variety of situations.

Equation 11.15 tells us that the explained variance (variance due to regression [$S^2_{Y'}$]) is equal to r^2 times the total variance in Y; that is,

$$S^2_{Y'} = r^2 S^2_Y$$

where S^2_Y is the total variance in Y (S^2_{Total}).

Because variance equals sums of squares divided by sample size (n), the above equation can be written as follows:

$$\frac{SS_{Regression}}{n} = r^2 \left(\frac{SS_{Total}}{n} \right)$$

Multiplying both sides of this equation by n leaves

$$SS_{Regression} = r^2 \cdot SS_{Total}$$

where $SS_{Total} = \Sigma \left(Y - \bar{Y} \right)^2$.

We can derive a similar formula for $SS_{Residual}$. Equation 11.17 can be rewritten as

$$S^2_{Y|X} = (1 - r^2) S^2_Y$$

Applying the same logic as above,

$$\frac{SS_{Residual}}{n} = (1 - r^2) \left(\frac{SS_{Total}}{n} \right)$$

and

$$SS_{Residual} = (1 - r^2) \cdot SS_{Total}$$

TABLE 11.3 ■ *F*-Table for the Hypothesis That $\rho = 0$				
Source of Variance	Sums of Squares	Degrees of Freedom	Mean Square	F
Regression	$r^2 SS_{Total}$	1	$r^2 SS_{Total} / 1$	$\dfrac{r^2 SS_{Total} / 1}{(1 - r^2) SS_{Total} / (n - 2)}$
Residual	$(1 - r^2) SS_{Total}$	$(n - 2)$	$(1 - r^2) SS_{Total} / (n - 2)$	
Total	SS_{Total}	$(n - 1)$		

Therefore, we may now perform our hypothesis test using only r and n.

When the degrees of freedom numerator $= 1$ in an F-ratio, the square root of $F = t$, with degrees of freedom $= df_{\text{denominator}}$. Therefore, one can also use the following t-statistic to test H_0: $\rho = 0$:

$$t = \frac{r\sqrt{n-2}}{\sqrt{1-r^2}} \tag{11.30}$$

When the null hypothesis is true, Equation 11.30 has a t-distribution with $(n-2)$ degrees of freedom. When the null hypothesis is false, Equation 11.30 has a non-central t-distribution. We can use the t-test in Equation 11.30 to conduct one-tailed tests where the alternative hypothesis is $\rho > 0$ or $\rho < 0$. The F-test only allows for two-tailed tests because it uses r^2. That is, while the F-distribution only has one tail, it does not allow for the testing of directional tests that are typically referred to as "one-tailed."

Summary

The linear regression model starts with the population regression line $Y = \alpha + \beta X + \varepsilon$, which describes the relationship between the two variables X and Y (where X is the predictor and Y is the criterion) in the population. After drawing a random sample from that population, we can use the method of least squares to estimate the parameters α and β. The result is a line $Y' = \alpha + \beta X$, which minimizes the sum of the squared deviations between the individual data points in the sample (Y) and the corresponding points on the line (Y'). After the sample regression line (Y') is located, the total variance in the Y-values (S_Y^2) can be partitioned into two parts, the explained variance and the unexplained or residual variance. The explained variance is the variance of the points on the sample regression line (Y') around the mean of the Y-values in the sample $(\bar{Y})$. It is called *explained* because it is the variance in Y that is due to variance in X. The higher the value of the sample correlation (Pearson r), the greater the explained variance. The symbol for the explained variance is $S_{Y'}^2$. The unexplained, or residual, variance is the variance of the individual data points Y around Y'. It is that part of the variance in Y that is *not* due to the correlation, and the higher the value of the Pearson r, the less the residual variance. The symbol for the residual variance is $S_{Y|X}^2$.

The value of the square of the Pearson r can be calculated from the following two formulas:

$$r^2 = \frac{S_{Y'}^2}{S_Y^2}$$

and

$$r^2 = 1 - \frac{S_{Y|X}^2}{S_Y^2}$$

We can use r^2 to test the null hypothesis that the population correlation $= 0$ with the following test statistic:

$$F = \frac{\dfrac{r^2}{1}}{\dfrac{1-r^2}{n-2}}$$

The ideas summarized here can be generalized to situations in which there are more than one predictor (multiple regression) and in which the relationship between two variables is not linear. These ideas also provide a link between correlation and hypothesis tests on means, a connection that is the basis for measures of effect sizes in t-tests and analysis of variance. Finally, these ideas lay the foundation for the analysis of variance. We will show how these ideas apply to nonlinear situations and to situations in which there is more than one predictor (multiple regression) in the next chapters.

Conceptual Exercises

1. Describe how the method of least squares can be used to estimate parameters in the linear regression model. Indicate what parameters are being estimated. (You do *not* have to describe all the assumptions of this model to answer the question.)

2. Why does $df_{\text{residual}} = n - 2$ when testing the hypothesis that the slope of the regression line = 0?

3. In the *F*-test of the hypothesis $H_0 : \rho = 0$ with the linear regression model, the numerator is:

$$\frac{\sum \left(Y' - \bar{Y}\right)^2}{1}$$

What does this term represent (or estimate) when H_0 is true *and* when H_0 is false?

4. Why is the test statistic for the hypothesis $H_0 : \rho = 0$ of the following form?

$$\frac{\dfrac{\sum \left(Y' - \bar{Y}\right)^2}{1} / 1}{\sum \left(Y - Y'\right)^2 / (n - 2)}$$

(Hint: Think in terms of expected values.)

5. Why does $\dfrac{\sum \left(Y' - \bar{Y}\right)^2}{1}$ not necessarily equal 0 when $\rho = 0$?

6. We encounter two similar terms when discussing the linear regression model:

$$\frac{\sum \left(Y' - \bar{Y}\right)^2}{n} \quad \text{and} \quad \frac{\sum \left(Y' - \bar{Y}\right)^2}{1}$$

What do these terms represent?

7. To test the hypothesis $H_0 : \rho = 0$ against the alternative hypothesis $H_1 : \rho \neq 0$ using the linear regression model, we could use either of the following test statistics:

$$F = \frac{\sum \left(Y' - \bar{Y}\right) / 1}{\sum \left(Y' - \bar{Y}\right)^2 / (n - 2)}$$

$$F = \frac{r^2 / 1}{\left(1 - r^2\right) / (n - 2)}$$

   a. Describe the distributions of these test statistics when H_0 is true *and* when H_0 is false (their means, degrees of freedom, and forms). Also draw a diagram.

   b. Why does the power of this test increase as sample size increases?

   c. Describe how you could create a power function for this test statistic. Also, make a diagram and label the axes. (Your answer should indicate your understanding of the task here.)

   d. In the case of the *F*-statistic on the top, what can you say about the terms in the numerator and denominator when H_0 is true *and* when H_0 is false. That is, what are the terms estimating?

8. What do the sample statistics $s^2_{Y|X}$ and $s^2_{Y'}$ represent? (They are variances of what around what?) What are their values when $r = 0$ and $r = 1$? Why?

Student Study Site

A CLOSER LOOK AT LINEAR REGRESSION

The bivariate normal distribution model described in Chapter 10 provides us with test statistics we can use to test hypotheses about the correlation between two variables and a method for constructing confidence intervals for population correlations in bivariate normal populations. The linear regression model described in Chapter 11 provides us with test statistics for testing hypotheses about the linear relationship between two variables. Both models include assumptions about the source of the data. When these assumptions are violated, the results of our analyses and the conclusions we draw may be incorrect. Therefore, it is important to look at our data before calculating correlation coefficients or fitting regression lines.

For the linear regression model, the critical assumptions are that the *Y*-scores at each value of *X* are random samples from normal distributions that all have the same variance and whose means are all on a straight line (see Chapter 11, Figure 11.1). In this chapter, we will explore why these assumptions are important and the effects ignoring them can have on the interpretation of our data. The assumption of linearity is especially important. We can improve our accuracy of prediction and get a good estimate of the population correlation by fitting the appropriate function to our data.

THE IMPORTANCE OF LOOKING AT OUR DATA

By graphing our data and examining these graphs, we can identify patterns in our data that might lead us to identify outliers or nonlinear trends. By doing so, we may make better decisions about how to analyze the relationship between two variables.

In an influential paper, Anscombe (1973) illustrated the importance of graphing data first. He created four very different sets of data that all have the same correlation (see Figure 12.1).

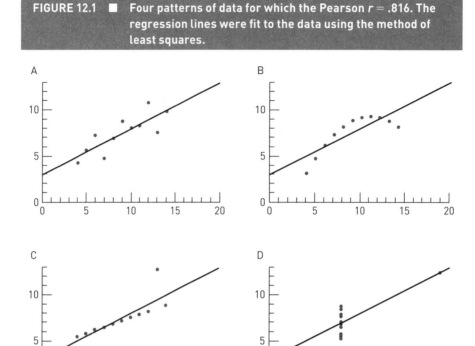

FIGURE 12.1 ■ **Four patterns of data for which the Pearson $r = .816$. The regression lines were fit to the data using the method of least squares.**

Source: Figures 1, 2, 3, 4 on pp. 19 & 20 from Anscombe, F. J. (1973). Graphs in Statistical Analysis. *American Statistician, 27*, 17–21, reprinted with permission of the American Statistical Association, www.amstat.org

The data represented in panel A of Figure 12.1 appear appropriate for the linear regression model, because the relationship appears to be linear and there appears to be homoscedasticity around the regression line. On the other hand, fitting a straight line to the data in panel B underestimates the strength of the relationship. If instead we use the method of least squares to fit a quadratic function ($Y' = A + BX + CX^2$) to the data, the fit will be close to perfect, and the value of the resulting correlation will be close to 1.0. We will look at how to fit such a function later in this chapter.

In panel C, there is an almost perfect linear relationship for all except one point. This example demonstrates the influence certain outliers can have on the Pearson r (and measures of correlation in general). On the other hand, panel D shows us how the presence of a single outlier can lead us to believe there is a correlation between two variables when, in fact, there is none.

The examples in panels B, C, and D are rather dramatic, and simply plotting the data readily reveals the inappropriateness of fitting a straight line using the method of least squares without plotting and looking at our data first.

With that idea in mind, consider the data from the following study that further examines how individuals perceive racial humor intended to confront or subvert, rather than to reinforce or support, racism (Miller & Saucier, 2016b). In the study, 89 White participants were recruited online. They first completed a measure of their tendencies to perceive racial prejudice, the Propensity to Make Attributions to Prejudice Scale (PMAPS; Miller & Saucier, 2016a). This measure consists of 15 items to which participants report their agreement on a scale from 1 (*strongly disagree*) to 9 (*strongly agree*). A sample item is *Racist behavior is more widespread than people think it is*. In the study, after the relevant items were reverse scored, the researchers averaged participants' scores to provide composite scores representing the overall tendency to attribute others' behaviors to prejudice. The participants then read either a joke that was intended to reinforce prejudice by disparaging Blacks or a joke that was intended to subvert prejudice by confronting stereotypic thinking (see Chapter 8). After reading the joke, participants rated how funny they thought the joke was, how offensive it was, the extent to which it contained an antiracism message, and so on. The researchers were most interested in examining whether participants' tendencies to make attributions to prejudice, as measured by the PMAPS, were related to the extent to which the participants who read the subversive joke perceived it to be subversive. These data are given below in Table 12.1 and Figure 12.2.

FIGURE 12.2 ■ Scatterplot of the data in Table 12.1 with a straight line fitted to the data.

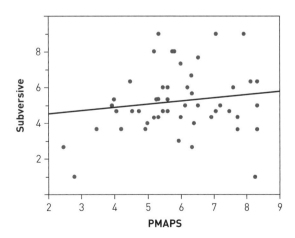

TABLE 12.1 ■ Data From Miller and Saucier (2016b)

PMAPS	Subversive	PMAPS	Subversive	PMAPS	Subversive	PMAPS	Subversive
5.73	8.00	2.47	2.67	7.07	4.67	6.33	5.67
7.73	4.33	5.93	3.00	4.00	5.33	6.00	7.33
6.00	4.33	4.53	4.67	4.47	6.33	6.53	5.00
6.93	4.33	4.20	3.67	2.80	1.00	3.53	8.00
8.33	5.00	3.47	3.67	8.27	1.00	8.33	6.33
6.20	6.00	5.47	4.67	4.93	3.67	7.60	6.00
5.80	8.00	6.13	5.00	7.47	4.67	5.33	4.33
5.60	5.33	5.33	9.00	6.53	7.67	5.47	6.00
6.40	4.00	7.73	3.67	5.60	6.00	5.33	5.33
7.93	9.00	4.73	4.67	4.07	4.67	5.60	4.67
5.20	4.33	8.33	3.67	6.33	2.67	7.20	5.00
5.27	5.33	7.07	9.00	3.93	5.00	8.13	6.33
6.33	6.67	5.20	8.00	5.00	4.00		

For these data, the Pearson $r = .14$, $p = .32$. If we stopped here, we would conclude that there is no relationship between PMAPS and perceiving the subversive joke as subversive, but perhaps that conclusion is premature.

USING RESIDUALS TO CHECK ASSUMPTIONS

By plotting and examining the residuals (deviations) from the regression line, we can examine whether our data violate assumptions of normality, homoscedasticity, and linearity.

Proper use of the linear regression model requires that the Y-scores be normally distributed with equal variance (homoscedasticity) around the population regression line for each value of X. One way to check whether our data appear to reflect sampling from populations that possess these attributes is to plot the **residuals**, that is, *the differences between the observed* Y-scores and the predicted Y-scores $(Y - Y')$ for every value in the data. Sometimes violations of the normal distribution, homoscedasticity, and linearity assumptions are immediately obvious from examination of the residuals, which is clearly the case with Anscombe's examples (1973; Figure 12.1): Only the data in panel A are distributed around the regression line across the range of values of X. It is also possible to perform additional analyses of the residuals using techniques from Chapter 2 to look more closely for violations of these assumptions. Some of these approaches will be described below.

The value of plotting the residuals is best illustrated by Figure 12.2, where the data are not distributed uniformly across the range of PMAPS values; rather, they appear to be evenly distributed around the regression line except at the lowest and highest values of X. The residuals $(Y - Y')$ are plotted in Figure 12.3. The horizontal line is where the observed and predicted scores are the same; that is, the value of the residual would be zero. This plot of the residuals makes it easier to see that the data are *not* uniformly distributed around the regression line across the entire range of X values displayed. Clearly, there are more values above the line between the PMAPS values of 4 and 7, and below 4 and above 7 there are more values below the line. This pattern of residuals suggests that the relationship is not linear. There are a number of ways to test for linearity, and two of those methods will be described later in this chapter.

Homoscedasticity refers to *the assumption that the variances of the* Y-scores around the regression line are the same at all values of X. Plots of the residuals can reveal gross departures from homoscedasticity. Such plots are illustrated in Figure 12.4. The plot of the data on the left of Figure 12.4 exhibits a pattern consistent with homoscedasticity, because the spread of the Y-scores appears to be the same across the range of X values exhibited.

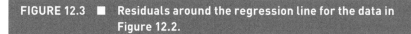

FIGURE 12.3 ■ **Residuals around the regression line for the data in Figure 12.2.**

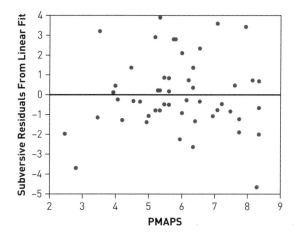

However, the pattern in the residuals on the right does not reflect homoscedasticity, because the variance in the Y-scores increases across the range of X values.

Looking back at the data in Figure 12.3, we can see that it does not appear to reflect homoscedasticity. Although this technique is a crude way to look for homoscedasticity, it is the best we can do most of the time. There are some statistical tests one could use, but they are not very useful in most situations.

On the other hand, we can check for departures from the normal distribution assumption by using some of the techniques described in Chapter 2. These approaches include creating quantile plots, stem-and-leaf displays, box plots, and normal quantile plots of the residuals. We can apply the box plot and normal quantile plot to the residuals to check the normal distribution assumption (see Figure 12.5).

FIGURE 12.4 ■ **Example of homoscedasticity (*left*) and example of nonhomoscedasticity (*right*).**

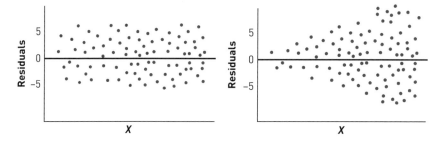

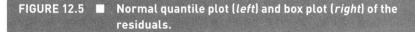

FIGURE 12.5 ■ Normal quantile plot (*left*) and box plot (*right*) of the residuals.

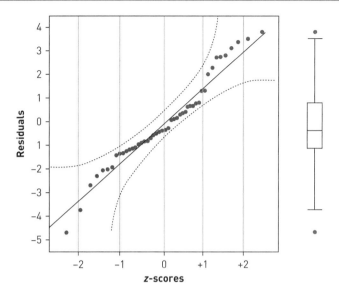

The box plot of the residuals on the right of Figure 12.5 is fairly symmetrical with one outlier at each end. That by itself is not evidence that the data came from populations that are normally distributed around the population regression line, but a clearly nonsymmetrical box plot would suggest that the underlying distributions are not normal. A more sensitive technique is the normal quantile plot, in which the residuals are plotted against the quantiles from a normal distribution. When the points in that plot are close to the line and within the Lilliefors confidence bands, we feel more comfortable that these data do not violate the assumption that the underlying distributions of Y-scores are normally distributed. We can test the hypothesis that the residuals are normally distributed with the Shapiro–Wilk test (See Chapter 2). For the data in Figure 12.5, $W = .966$, $p < .15$; therefore, the Shapiro–Wilk test confirms what we see in Figure 12.5 with the normal quantile plot.

TESTING WHETHER THE RELATIONSHIP BETWEEN TWO VARIABLES IS LINEAR

We can use inferential tests to assess the extent to which a linear equation fits our data by partitioning the residual sums of squares and degrees of freedom and testing whether the data deviate from the regression line more than would be expected by chance.

As was noted earlier, we assume that the *Y*-scores at each value of *X* are random samples from normal distributions that all have the same variance and whose means are all on a straight line (see Chapter 11, Figure 11.1). The regression line in Figure 12.2 is the least squares estimate of the regression line that goes through the means of those normal distributions from which the data were sampled. Because these data are sample data, we would not expect the means of the *Y*-scores at each value of *X* to be on a straight line, but we would expect those means to be close to a straight line. Any deviations from that line would represent sampling error. In Figure 12.6, the means of the *Y*-scores are plotted for each value of *X* where there is more than one value of *Y*.

Those means are based on between two or three values; therefore, it is not surprising that many of them deviate from the best-fitting line because they are not efficient estimates of the population means. Nevertheless, there is a pattern here that warrants a closer look: The means of the Subversive scores are mainly above the regression line between PMAPS 5 and 7, while those above 7 are mostly below the regression line. Unfortunately, there are no means for PMAPS below 5 because there are no PMAP values below 5 where there are at least two Subversive scores. This is one of the limitations of this approach.

However, when there are sufficient numbers of *Y*-scores across the range of the *X*-axis, we can extend the procedures for partitioning sums of squares and degrees of freedom and for hypothesis testing developed in Chapter 11 to test whether the data deviate from the regression line more than would be expected by chance. We test this possibility by comparing the variation of the sample means from the regression line to the average variation of the *Y*-scores around those means (where there is more than one *Y*-score at a given value for *X*).

FIGURE 12.6 ■ Means of the Subversive scores for those values of PMAPS where there is more than one Subversive score (*black dots*) have been superimposed on Figure 12.2.

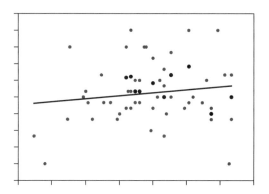

This procedure, described in Box 12.1, is possible because the residual sums of squares and degrees of freedom can be partitioned into two independent parts similarly to how we partition the total sums of squares.

BOX 12.1

PARTITIONING THE RESIDUAL SUMS OF SQUARES AND DEGREES OF FREEDOM TO TEST WHETHER A STRAIGHT LINE IS THE APPROPRIATE MODEL FOR THE DATA

As noted in the last chapter (Equation 11.19a), the sum of the squared deviations of each Y-score from the mean of all of the Y-scores in the sample data (SS_{Total}) can be partitioned into two parts:

$$\sum(Y-\bar{Y})^2 = \sum(Y-Y')^2 + \sum(Y'-\bar{Y})^2 \quad (12.1a)$$

$$SS_{Total} = SS_{Residual} + SS_{Regression} \quad (12.1b)$$

$SS_{Regression}$ is the sum of squared deviations of the predicted scores for each value of X from the mean of all of the Y-scores. $SS_{Residual}$ is the sum of squared deviations of the Y-scores around the regression line at each value of X.

$SS_{Residual}$ can also be partitioned into two parts. One part is the sum of squared deviations of the Y-scores around their mean at each value of X, and the other part is the sum of squared deviations of those means from the regression line. This partitioning can be represented by the following equation:

$$\sum_{All\ Y}(Y-Y')^2 = \sum_{j=1}^{m}\sum_{i=1}^{n_j}(Y-\bar{Y}_j)^2 + \sum_{j=1}^{m}(\bar{Y}_j-Y')^2 \quad (12.2a)$$

where the symbol $\bar{Y}_j$ represents the mean of the Y-scores for the jth value of X, n_j is the

number of Y-scores at the jth value of X, and m is the total number of X values that have more than one Y-score. The term to the left of the equal sign is $SS_{Residual}$. The first term to the right of the equal sign is *the sum of the squared deviations of the Y-scores around their mean ($\bar{Y}_j$) for all values of X where there is more than one Y-score*. This term is called **pure error** because it is determined without reference to the regression line. It is an estimate of the inherent variation in the data at each value of X. The second term on the right is the *sum of the squared deviations of each $\bar{Y}_j$ from the regression line*. This term is called **lack of fit** because it represents the deviation from perfect fit (which would occur when $Y_j = Y'$ at all values of X). Therefore,

$$SS_{Residual} = SS_{Pure\ error} + SS_{Lack\ of\ fit} \quad (12.2b)$$

As we saw in the last chapter, degrees of freedom can also be partitioned. The degrees of freedom corresponding to Equation 12.1 are as follows:

$$(N-1) = (N-2) + 1 \quad (12.3a)$$

$$df_{Total} = df_{Residual} + df_{Regression} \quad (12.3b)$$

Degrees of freedom for the residual $(N-2)$ are also composed of two parts: degrees

(Continued)

BOX 12.1 (Continued)

PARTITIONING THE RESIDUAL SUMS OF SQUARES AND DEGREES OF FREEDOM TO TEST WHETHER A STRAIGHT LINE IS THE APPROPRIATE MODEL FOR THE DATA

of freedom for pure error and degrees of freedom for lack of fit. The computation for degrees of freedom for pure error is straightforward: If there are n_j different Y-scores for a given value of X_j, then the degrees of freedom for the Y-scores of that value of X_j equal $(n_j - 1)$. We add the degrees of freedom for the Y-scores for each X_j to obtain the degrees of freedom for pure error. Here is the formula for degrees of freedom for pure error:

$$\sum_{j=1}^{m}(n_j - 1),\qquad (12.4)$$

where m is the number of values of X that have more than one Y-score and n_j is the number of Y-scores for those values of X where there is more than one Y-score. Degrees of freedom for lack of fit are the difference between the degrees of freedom for the residual and degrees of freedom for pure error. Therefore,

$$N-2=\sum_{j=1}^{m}(n_j-1)+(N-2-df_{\text{Pure error}})\qquad (12.5a)$$

$$df_{\text{Residual}} = df_{\text{Pure error}} + df_{\text{Lack of fit}}\qquad (12.5b)$$

Dividing the sums of squares by the corresponding degrees of freedom gives us

$MS_{\text{Pure error}}$ and $MS_{\text{Lack of fit}}$. When the relationship between X and Y is linear, $MS_{\text{Pure error}} \approx MS_{\text{Lack of fit}}$, and when the relationship is not linear, $MS_{\text{Pure error}} \ll MS_{\text{Lack of fit}}$ because each Y_j will not be close to the straight line generated by the method of least squares. The test for whether the form of the relationship we chose (a linear relationship in this example) is appropriate is also an F-test, where $F = MS_{\text{Lack of fit}} / MS_{\text{Pure error}}$.

The null and alternative hypotheses for this test are as follows:

H_0: The model chosen ($Y_i = \alpha + \beta X_i + \varepsilon_i$) is appropriate.

H_1: The model chosen ($Y_i = \alpha + \beta X_i + \varepsilon_i$) is *not* appropriate.

If we suspect the relationship might not be linear, we should test for lack of fit *before* testing the slope of the regression line (β) to determine whether the variation in the Y-scores is due to the correlation with X. Whether we continue and test whether the slope of the straight line we fit to the data (β) equals 0 depends on how much we judge the data deviate from that line.

The F-table for both tests (lack of fit and $\beta = 0$) is presented in Table 12.2.

TABLE 12.2 ■ F-Table for Testing for Lack of Fit to a Linear Relationship

Source of Variance	Sums of Squares	Degrees of Freedom	Mean Square	F
Regression	$\sum(Y'-\bar{Y})^2$	1	$\sum(Y'-\bar{Y})^2/1$	$\dfrac{\sum(Y'-\bar{Y})^2/1}{\sum(Y-Y')^2/(N-2)}$
Residual	$\sum(Y-Y')^2$	$(N-2)$	$\sum(Y-Y')^2/(N-2)$	
Lack of fit	$\sum_{j=1}^{m}\left(\bar{Y}_j-Y'\right)^2$	$(N-2)-df_{\text{Pure error}}$	$\sum_{j=1}^{m}\left(\bar{Y}_j-Y'\right)^2/(N-2-df_{\text{pe}})$	$\dfrac{\sum_{j=1}^{m}\left(\bar{Y}-Y'\right)^2/(N-2-df_{\text{pe}})}{\sum_{j=1}^{m}\left[\sum_{i=1}^{n_j}\left(Y-\bar{Y}_j\right)^2\right]\Big/\sum_{j=1}^{m}(n_j-1)}$
Pure error	$\sum_{j=1}^{m}\left[\sum_{i=1}^{n_j}\left(Y-\bar{Y}_j\right)^2\right]$	$\sum_{j=1}^{m}(n_j-1)$	$\sum_{j=1}^{m}\left[\sum_{i=1}^{n_j}\left(Y-\bar{Y}_j\right)^2\right]\Big/\sum_{j=1}^{m}(n_j-1)$	
Total	$\sum(Y-\bar{Y})^2$	$(N-1)$		

THE CORRELATION RATIO: AN ALTERNATE WAY TO MEASURE THE DEGREE OF RELATIONSHIP AND TEST FOR A LINEAR RELATIONSHIP

Because the correlation ratio does not assume linearity, we can use it to test the degree of relationship between two variables when that relationship is nonlinear. The value of the correlation ratio can be compared to the value of the Pearson r to test whether the relationship is linear.

The test for whether the relationship between two variables is linear described in the last section can only be used when there is more than one Y-score at a number of levels of X. Unfortunately, this situation is somewhat rare, as we saw with the data in Table 12.1. Fortunately, there are other ways to test for linear relationships. One way is to use the statistic called the correlation ratio, for which the symbol is the Greek letter eta (η). The correlation ratio can be used as a coefficient of correlation and to test for whether the relationship is linear.

Assumptions Underlying the Correlation Ratio as a Measure of Correlation

The correlation ratio (η) has less restrictive assumptions than the Pearson r and for that reason can be used in some situations where the Pearson r would not be appropriate. Although both the correlation ratio (η) and the Pearson r assume that the data were obtained from populations where the underlying distributions of the Y-scores for each value of X are normal distributions with equal variances, the correlation ratio (η) *does not* require that the values of X be ordered (that is, the X values can be nominal categories) or that the relationship between X and Y be linear (even when the values of X are on an ordinal, interval, or ratio scale). Therefore, the correlation ratio is a more general measure of the degree of relationship. It can be used as a measure of the relationship between two variables when the relationship is linear, when it is nonlinear, or when the X-axis consists of nominal categories. Therefore, the correlation ratio does not involve fitting a line (or any other function) to the data.

How the Correlation Ratio Is Related to the Pearson *r*

In Chapter 11, we saw that when the relationship is linear, we can use the method of least squares to fit the regression line to the data and then calculate the Pearson r from either of the following equations:

$$r^2 = 1 - \frac{S_{Y|X}^2}{S_Y^2}, \tag{12.6}$$

where $S_{Y|X}^2$ is the variance of any observed Y-scores around the regression line for each value of X, or

$$r^2 = \frac{S_{Y'}^2}{S_Y^2}, \tag{12.7}$$

where $S_{Y'}^2$ is the variance of the predicted scores (which are on the regression line) around $\overline{Y}$. In both equations, S_Y^2 is the variance of all of the Y-scores around $\overline{Y}$.

Equation 12.6 tells us that when there is a linear relationship between Y and X, the square of the Pearson r is an *inverse* function of the variance of the Y-scores around the regression line relative to the total variance of Y; that is, r is high when the variance of the Y-scores around the regression line is small relative to the total variance of Y, and r is low when the variance of the Y-scores around the regression line is close to the total variance of Y.

Likewise, Equation 12.7 tells us that the Pearson r is a *direct* function of the variation of the scores on the regression line (the predicted scores) when there is a linear relationship between Y and X; that is, r is high when the variance of the predicted scores is close to the total variance of Y, and r is low when the variance of the predicted scores is low relative to the total variance of Y.

Like the Pearson r, the correlation ratio (η) is also calculated by comparing a measure of variation similar to the residual and comparing it to the total variance of Y, but the measure of residual variation used here is *not* calculated from deviations from a regression line (because we do not fit a line to the data). The first step in the calculation of the correlation ratio is to divide the X-axis into categories or arrays (if they are not already nominal categories) and calculate the means for each array. The reason for dividing the values on the X-axis into arrays is to provide a number of values from which one can calculate the means and variances of the arrays. This procedure is represented in Figure 12.7 for the data in Table 12.1. It is clear in Figure 12.7 that the means of the Subversive scores in each array are close to the regression line, but the pattern of the means suggests that the relationship between PMAPS and Subversive scores is curvilinear.

How many arrays to create and how many scores should be in them will depend on the total number of Y-scores. If there are very few scores in the arrays, the means and variances are not going to be efficient estimates of the corresponding population

FIGURE 12.7 ■ Scatterplot of the data in Table 12.1 where the values on the PMAPS axis are divided into arrays 2 units wide. The means of the Subversive scores in each array are designated by the large black dot. The line was fit to the original data with the method of least squares.

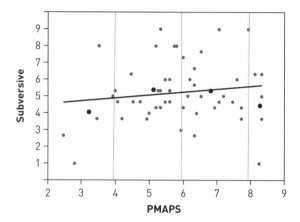

parameters. On the other hand, we get a better idea of the relationship when there are many arrays.

Eta-squared can be calculated in a manner similar to that of the Pearson r that was presented in Equations 12.6 and 12.7. Instead of computing $S_{Y|X}^2$, as is done in Equation 12.6, we calculate the average variance within arrays (average $S_{\text{within arrays}}^2$) using the procedures described in Chapter 3 for finding the average variance when the sample sizes are unequal (see Equations 3.11a–c).[1] The formula for calculating η^2 is the following:

$$\eta^2 = 1 - \frac{\text{average } S_{\text{within arrays}}^2}{S_Y^2} \tag{12.8}$$

The correlation ratio can also be calculated in a manner similar to Equation 12.7 by comparing the variance of the sample means to the total variance in the Y-scores:

$$\eta^2 = \frac{\text{average } S_{\text{array means}}^2}{S_Y^2} \tag{12.9}$$

---

[1] This procedure is the same one used to calculate pure error.

Here again, to calculate the variance of the array means, each mean must be weighted by the number of scores in that array.

The calculation of η^2 for the data in Table 12.1 and Figure 12.7 is illustrated in Box 12.2. The variance of the array means was computed from the following equation:

$$S^2_{\text{array means}} = \frac{\sum_{j=1}^{k} n_j \left(\bar{Y}_j - \bar{Y}\right)^2}{\sum_{j=1}^{k} n_j} \tag{12.10}$$

where k is the number of arrays, n_j is the number of scores in the jth array, $\bar{Y}_j$ is the mean of the Y-scores in the jth array, and $\bar{Y}$ is the mean of all of the Y-scores. Equation 12.10 tells us to compute the squared deviation of each array mean from $\bar{Y}$, multiply each squared deviation by the number of scores in that array (n_j), add up these products for all arrays, and divide by the total number of scores $\left(\sum_{j=1}^{k} n_j\right)$. This value is divided by the total variance in the Y-scores to obtain η^2 (see Equation 12.9).

The correlation ratio η^2 can also be obtained by finding the average variance within arrays and substituting that value into Equation 12.8. The average variance within arrays is computed from the following equation:

$$\text{average } S^2_{\text{within arrays}} = \frac{\sum_{j=1}^{k} n_j S_j^2}{\sum_{j=1}^{k} n_j} \tag{12.11}$$

where k is the number of arrays, n_j is the number of Y-scores in the jth array, and S_j^2 is the variance in the jth array. Equations 12.8 and 12.9 yield the same value for η^2.

Using the Correlation Ratio to Test Whether There Is a Relationship Between Two Variables

The correlation ratio (η) can vary between 0 and 1; it cannot have a negative value because of the way it is calculated (see Equations 12.8 and 12.9). In the case of the Pearson r, a negative value indicates that the regression line has a negative slope, but with η, there is no line and hence no slope. The value of η is 0 when all of the array means are the same; that is, all of the array means are on a horizontal line. The value of η is between 0 and 1 when at least one of the array means is different from the others.

BOX 12.2
CALCULATION OF η^2 FOR THE DATA IN TABLE 12.1 AND FIGURE 12.6

		Arrays			
		2.00–3.99	4.00–5.99	6.00–7.99	8.00–9.99
		2.67	5.33	4.33	6.33
		1.00	4.67	7.33	1.00
		3.67	3.67	5.00	5.00
		8.00	6.33	6.00	3.67
		5.00	4.67	6.67	6.33
			4.67	2.67	
			3.67	5.67	
			4.00	4.00	
			4.33	7.67	
			8.00	5.00	
			5.33	4.33	
			9.00	9.00	
			4.33	4.67	
			5.33	5.00	
			4.67	4.67	
			6.00	6.00	
			5.33	4.33	
			6.00	3.67	
			4.67	9.00	
			8.00		
			8.00		
			3.00		
Array sizes		5	22	19	5
Array means		4.07	5.41	5.53	4.47
Variance within arrays =		5.57	2.43	2.86	3.98

Mean of all $Y =$	5.23
Variance of all $Y =$	3.29
Variance of array means $=$	0.24
Avg variance within arrays $=$	3.05

$\eta^2 = 0.24/3.29 = 0.071893$ (from Equation 12.9)

$\eta^2 = 1 - 3.05/3.29 = 0.071893$ (from Equation 12.8)

Finally, $\eta = 1$ when there is no variance around the array means and at least one of them is different from the others.

Because the correlation ratio does not require that the relationship between two variables be linear, it can be used as a general test for whether there is a relationship between two variables. The null and alternative hypotheses for this test are as follows:

H_0: population $\eta = 0$

H_1: population $\eta > 0$

As noted above, the alternative hypothesis can only be $\eta > 0$. The value of η does not tell us anything about the direction or form of the relationship between X and Y, only that they are related and that knowledge of an individual's score on X helps us predict how he or she will perform on Y. As is the case with the Pearson r, the same value for η can occur with very different patterns of data.

The test statistic here is similar to the F-ratio for testing the null hypothesis that $\rho = 0$ (see Equation 11.29):

$$F = \frac{\eta^2 / (k-1)}{\left(1 - \eta^2\right) / (N - k)} \qquad (12.12)$$

where k is the number of arrays or categories and N is the total number of scores. When the null hypothesis is true, this test statistic has an F-distribution with $(k - 1)$ degrees of freedom for the numerator and $(N - k)$ degrees of freedom for the denominator. For the data in Table 12.1 (see Box 12.2), $\eta^2 = .0719$, $k = 4$, $N = 51$, and $F = 1.214$.

The critical value of F with 3 and 47 degrees of freedom is 2.304. Therefore, we cannot reject the null hypothesis, and we cannot conclude there is a relationship between X and Y.

Comparing the Values η^2 and r^2

The value of r^2 for the data in Box 12.3 is .02, and the value of η^2 is .0719. *The value of η^2 will always be equal to or greater than* r^2 (even when the relationship is linear). The reason has to do with how η^2 and r^2 are calculated. This relationship is best illustrated by comparing Equation 12.6 with Equation 12.8. The formula for r^2 uses $S^2_{Y|X}$, which is the sum of the squared deviations of the Y-scores around the regression line, and η^2 uses the average $S^2_{\text{within arrays}}$, which is the average of the sums of squared deviations of the Y-scores in each array around the mean of that array. For any set of numbers, the sum of the squared deviations ($\sum(X-a)^2$) will *always* be a minimum when $a = \bar{X}$. Therefore, average $S^2_{\text{within arrays}}$ will *always* be equal to or smaller than $S^2_{Y|X}$, making η^2 larger than r^2. The only time they will be the same value is when *all* of the array means are on the regression line. We can use this fact to construct a hypothesis test for whether the relationship is linear.

Using the Correlation Ratio to Test for Linearity

Although η^2 is usually larger than r^2, the two coefficients of correlation will be similar in value when the relationship is linear. However, when the relationship is not linear, η^2 will be a lot larger than r^2. Therefore, we can test for linearity by comparing η^2 and r^2. The null and alternative hypotheses for that test are the following:

H_0: The relationship is linear.

H_1: The relationship is not linear.

Here is the test statistic:

$$F = \frac{\left(\eta^2 - r^2\right)/(k-2)}{\left(1-\eta^2\right)/(N-k)} \tag{12.13}$$

For the data in Table 12.1 and Figure 12.6, $\eta^2 = .078$ with 4 arrays, $r^2 = .0196$, and $F = 1.324$. The critical value of F with 2 and 47 degrees of freedom is 2.802. We cannot reject the hypothesis that the relationship between X and Y for these data is linear.

WHERE DO WE GO FROM HERE?

The results of the statistical analyses we just completed are contradictory. On the one hand, for these data, we could not reject the null hypothesis $\rho = 0$ and the null hypothesis that $\eta = 0$, yet the plots of the data in Figures 12.2, 12.6, and 12.7 suggest that there may be a relationship between the individuals' PMAPS scores and their ratings of the subversive jokes as subversive, but it is not linear. Were the test for $\eta = 0$ (Equation 12.12) and the test for linearity (Equation 12.13) statistically significant, we would be searching for a nonlinear equation to fit these data. Nevertheless, let's explore that possibility.

WHEN THE RELATIONSHIP IS NOT LINEAR

When the relationship between two variables is not linear, we can use nonlinear functions to describe and fit our data to assess the degree of relationship.

Fitting a straight line to the data with the method of least squares is the most commonly used procedure with bivariate data, even when the relationship is not strictly linear but there is a strong linear trend in the data. That approach may be satisfactory if our purpose is to determine that a relationship exists; however, we can improve both our estimation of the size of the correlation (and the proportion of variance explained) and our predictions of performance by fitting a nonlinear function to the data with the method of least squares. This procedure can be accomplished by generalizing the principles and procedures described above and in Chapter 11.

Applying the Method of Least Squares to Nonlinear Relationships

In the linear regression situation, we use the method of least squares to fit a line ($Y' = A + BX$) to our sample data, where A and B are estimates of the parameters of the Y-intercept (α) and slope (β) of the population regression line. After we fit a line to the data, we can calculate the Pearson r with either Equation 12.6 or 12.7.

We can generalize those procedures to fit any function to our data. The problem is figuring out what is the appropriate function. There are two general approaches to selecting a function. The first approach is to select a function on theoretical grounds. For example, we might decide, as is commonly done, to fit a logarithmic function ($Y' = A + B \ln X$) to perceptual data. Such an approach is the most desirable, with many precedents for doing so, but unfortunately there are many situations in which we do not have solid theoretical rationale for selecting the model to fit our data ahead of time. Therefore, most of the time we are forced to select a function after looking at our data. That situation is the case for the data in the example at the beginning of this chapter. Figures 12.6 and 12.7 suggest that we should explore trying to fit a quadratic function to our data. (See Figure 12.8 for examples of various types of relationships.)

The left of Figure 12.9 shows the least squares fit of a cubic equation ($Y' = A + BX + CX^2 + DX^3$) to the data in Table 12.1, and the right shows the residuals around the fitted

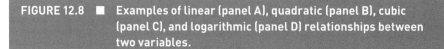

FIGURE 12.8 ■ Examples of linear (panel A), quadratic (panel B), cubic (panel C), and logarithmic (panel D) relationships between two variables.

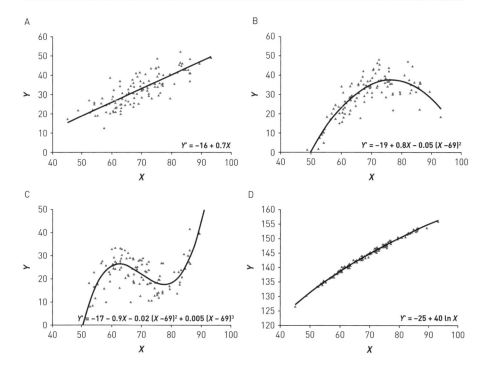

cubic equation. The residuals appear to be more uniformly distributed around the cubic function than was the case with the straight line in Figure 12.2.

The correlation between X and Y for any fitted function using the method of least squares can be calculated from the following equation:

$$\text{correl}^2 = 1 - \frac{S_{Y|X}^2}{S_Y^2}, \tag{12.14}$$

where $S_{Y|X}^2$ is the variance of the residuals around the fitted function. Fitting a quadratic function to the data in Table 12.1 and Figure 12.2 yields $\text{correl}^2 = .123$. The Pearson r^2 (based on fitting a straight line to the same data) is .02. There is a definite improvement in the proportion of variance explained.

We can test the null hypothesis that the population correlation = 0 with the following test statistic:

FIGURE 12.9 ■ **The data in Table 12.1: (*left*) a quadratic function fit to the data with the method of least squares; (*right*) residuals fitted around the curve.**

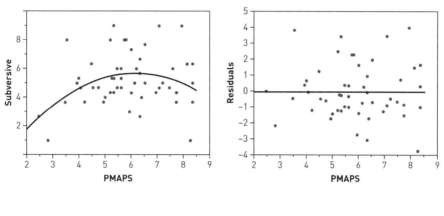

$$F = \frac{\left(\text{correl}^2\right) / \left(\# \text{ parameters estimated} - 1\right)}{\left(1 - \text{correl}^2\right) / \left(n - \# \text{ parameters estimated}\right)} \tag{12.15}$$

For these data, $F = 3.378$, $p < .0424$. This result leads us to reject the null hypothesis that the population correlation $= 0$, and we conclude that there is a quadratic relationship between the participants' scores on the PMAPS and their ratings of the subversive jokes as subversive.

Is Fitting a Curve to the Data Worth the Effort?

This question is quite reasonable to ask. Although the quadratic function fits the data here better than a straight line, the difference between the two correlation coefficients is not large ($r^2 = .02$ and $\text{correl}^2_{\text{quadratic}} = .123$). Does it matter? There are two ways to answer that question. The first is to determine whether the increase in proportion of variance accounted for is due to chance or reflects a real increase. The second is to ask whether a statistically significant increase is meaningful.

We can determine whether the increase is statistically significant by comparing the two correlation coefficients with the following test statistic:

$$F = \frac{\left(r_p^2 - r_q^2\right) / \left(df_p - df_q\right)}{\left(1 - r_p^2\right) / \left(n - df_p - 1\right)}, \tag{12.16}$$

where r_p^2 is the correlation coefficient with the greater number of parameters estimated and r_q^2 is the correlation coefficient with the smaller number of parameters estimated. The degrees of freedom for p and q are the corresponding degrees of freedom numerator used to test whether there is a relationship. For this example, r_p^2 is correl^2 = .123 and r_q^2 is the Pearson r^2 = .02, df_p = 2 and df_q = 1, and F = 5.637. The critical value of F with 1 and 48 degrees of freedom = 4.043. Therefore, we conclude that the increase in the correlation is statistically significant.

Now we move on to the next consideration: Is the increase meaningful? In this situation, the answer is yes, because had we stopped after looking only at a linear fit, we would not have uncovered an interesting relationship between our two variables. What we find here is that individuals scoring at both the low and high ends of the PMAPS response scale were more likely to report the subversive jokes as less subversive than were those individuals scoring more in the middle of the PMAPS response scale. It may be the case that the participants on the extremes of the scale were more biased by their predispositions to make or not make attributions to prejudice in evaluating the jokes than were those in the middle. Those participants at the low end of the scale may be less likely to believe that prejudice exists in society and may thus not perceive the subversive intent of the joke because there is little need to subvert something that does not exist. Those participants at the high end of the scale may be more sensitive to cues that indicate prejudice and may thus perceive a racial joke, even one with subversive intentions, as racist rather than subversive in its intention. The potential for these very different cognitive biases to lead to similar responses could inspire interesting and important research questions that we would have missed had we not examined the fit of a curvilinear function to our data. But the point should not be lost that it is important to look at our data before fitting a line to them; if the data appear not to be linear, we can use the method of least squares to fit a function, to calculate a correlation coefficient, and to test whether there is a statistically significant relationship based on the function we chose.

THE EFFECTS OF OUTLIERS ON REGRESSION

The degree to which outliers affect our estimates of the relationship between two variables depends on the amount of leverage and influence outliers have on the fit of the regression line.

The effect of a given observation on regression depends on its leverage and influence. **Leverage** is *the potential effect of a given data point on how well a regression line will fit the data*. Data far from the center of the values on the *x*-axis have *high leverage* because

FIGURE 12.10 ■ The effects of outliers on regression: an outlier with high leverage but low influence (*upper right*); the effects of outliers with low leverage and low influence (*middle left*) and high influence (*middle right*); the effects of an outlier with high leverage and high influence (*bottom*).

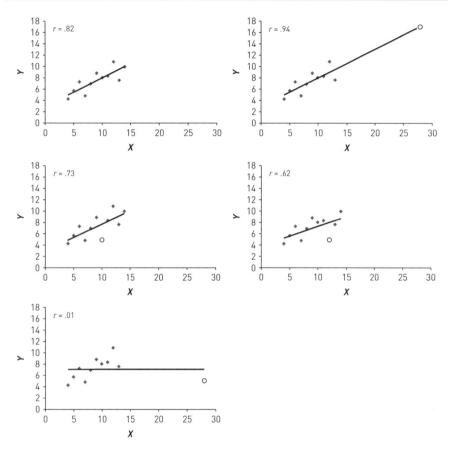

they pull the regression line toward themselves. There are two kinds of leverage points, sometimes called "good" leverage points and "bad" leverage points. A *good leverage point* is an outlier on the *x*-axis, but it is *not* an outlier with respect to the regression line for the rest of the data. Good leverage points *increase* the value of the Pearson product-moment correlation coefficient and make it appear that there is a stronger relationship between the two variables (see the upper right of Figure 12.10). On the other hand, a *bad leverage point* is one that is not only an outlier on the *x*-axis but also *is* an outlier with respect to the regression line for the rest of the data. Bad leverage points *decrease* the value of the Pearson product moment correlation coefficient and deflect the regression line away from the other data points (see the bottom of Figure 12.10). The result is a poor fit of the regression line to the data and a misrepresentation of the relationship.

The **influence** of a data point is *the actual impact of that data point on how well the regression line will fit the data.* A data point with high leverage can have low influence. Similarly, a data point with low leverage can nevertheless have high influence on the regression line. These situations are depicted in Figure 12.10. The starting point for the various situations in that figure is the pattern from Anscombe (1973) depicted in panel A of Figure 12.1. Note the effects of the outliers on the Pearson r and the slope of the regression line in each case. It is clear that a single point can distort our interpretation of our data if we only look at the Pearson r and not the plot of the data.

ROBUST ALTERNATIVES TO THE METHOD OF LEAST SQUARES

There are a number of robust alternatives available to minimize the influence of outliers and nonhomoscedasticity, which can occur when there are outliers in our data.

All of the regression lines in Figure 12.10 were fitted to the values using the method of least squares (sometimes referred to as ordinary least squares or OLS). There are a number of robust alternatives available to minimize the influence of outliers and nonhomoscedasticity, which can occur when there are outliers in our data. While no single alternative has been found to be best in all situations, they all work better than OLS when the assumptions of the linear regression model are violated. Unfortunately, all of them are labor intensive and require special routines to obtain solutions. Wilcox (2003) described them in more detail.

Least Median Squares

With the method of least squares (OLS), we find the regression line slope and intercept that minimizes the sum of the squared deviations of the Y-scores from the line (that is, the residuals). With least median squares, we *find the regression line slope and intercept where the median of the sum of the squared deviations of the Y-scores from the line is a minimum.* This method does not perform as well as some of the others described below.

Least Trimmed Squares

This method involves trimming the largest and smallest residuals $(Y - Y')$ and then applying OLS to the remaining values to find the slope and intercepts of the best-fitting line. Identifying the residuals to be trimmed requires an iterative trial-and-error process. The recommended amount of trimming is 0.2.

Least Trimmed Absolute Value

This method is similar to the method of least trimmed squares except that we *minimize the sum of the remaining absolute residuals* instead of the sum of squares. Again, the optimal amount of trimming is 0.2.

Theil–Sen Estimator

The Thiel–Sen estimator uses the fact that the slope of the regression line in OLS is the mean of the slopes of all possible pairs of points in the data set. In other words, we can connect any pair of data points in a scatterplot with a straight line. If we apply this procedure for all possible pairs of points and find the average of the slopes of those points, we will have the slope of the overall regression line. Because the sample mean is not a robust estimator, OLS does not provide a robust estimate of the overall slope. The **Thiel–Sen estimator** *uses the median of the slopes of the lines connecting all possible data points to estimate the overall slope of the regression line (*B_{ts}*).* The *y*-intercept is estimated by the following formula:

$$A_{ts} = \text{Median}_Y - B_{ts} \times \text{Median}_X$$

Wilcox (1998) indicated that although the Thiel–Sen estimator is not always the best choice in all situations, it appears to have advantages over other robust methods for regression, including those described above.

A QUICK PEEK AT MULTIPLE REGRESSION

The regression equations we use to test the relationship between two variables can be extended to assess the extent to which multiple variables predict values of another variable.

Up to this point, we have considered only the situation in which there are two variables and we want to determine the degree of relationship between them and perhaps predict the impact of one of these variables on the other. We call *the variable we want to predict* the **criterion** and *the variable we use to predict performance on the criterion* the **predictor**. For example, as McManus, Feyes, and Saucier (2011) did and as we began to discuss in Chapter 11, we can try to predict attitudes toward individuals with intellectual disabilities as reported on the Mental Retardation Attitude Inventory–Revised (MRAI-R; Antonak & Harth, 1994) from the participants' quantity of previous contact with individuals with intellectual disabilities by using the method of least squares to fit a line (or other function) to the data. But we might do better if we added another predictor, such as the participants' quality of previous contact with individuals with intellectual disabilities. **Multiple regression** involves *a regression equation with more than one predictor.* The basic principles involved in the use of multiple regression can be generalized from Chapter 11 and the current chapter. In fact, simple linear regression is the special case of multiple regression where there is only one predictor.[2]

In multiple regression, the structural model that defines the relationship between the criterion and the predictors for the population is

$$Y_i = \beta_0 + \beta_1 X_{i1} + \beta_2 X_{i2} + \cdots + + \beta_k X_{ik} + \varepsilon_{ij} \tag{12.17}$$

where the i stands for each individual who is measured on the k predictors. Therefore, X_{ij} refers to the score on predictor j for individual i. The parameters β_1, β_2, ..., β_k are the slopes of the planes for each predictor, and β_0 is the point where the planes cross the y-axis when the values of all of the predictors are 0. ε_{ij} is the sum of the residuals in the population for each predictor. We can use the method of least squares to find the estimates of these parameters and the sample regression equation:

$$Y' = b_0 + b_1 X_1 + b_2 X_2 + \cdots + + b_k X_k \tag{12.18}$$

We can use either of the following ways to find the value of the sample multiple correlation:

$$R^2_{Y \bullet X_1 X_2 \cdots X_k} = 1 - \frac{S^2_{Y \bullet X_1 X_2 \cdots X_k}}{S^2_Y} \tag{12.19}$$

where $S^2_{Y \bullet X_1 X_2 \cdots X_k}$ is the variance of the residuals $(Y - Y')$ or

$$R^2_{Y \bullet X_1 X_2 \cdots X_k} = \frac{S^2_{Y'}}{S^2_Y} \tag{12.20}$$

where $S^2_{Y'}$ is the variance of the predicted scores.

---

[2]The assumptions for multiple regression are extensions of those for linear regression (see Chapter 11); that is, there is a linear relationship between each predictor and the criterion and, for each predictor, the values of the criterion are normally distributed with equal variances. However, each predictor adds another physical dimension, which means we are no longer talking about lines but rather planes in a multidimensional space. This situation reduces to a line in two-dimensional space when there is one predictor.

Here is the test statistic for the hypothesis test that the population multiple correlation = 0.

$$F = \frac{\left(R^2_{Y \cdot X_1 X_2 \cdots X_k}\right) / \left(\# \text{ predictors}\right)}{\left(1 - R^2_{Y \cdot X_1 X_2 \cdots X_k}\right) / \left(n - \# \text{ predictors} - 1\right)} \qquad (12.21)$$

Furthermore, we can use Equation 12.16 to decide whether the addition of another predictor (e.g., participants' quality of contact with individuals with intellectual disabilities) improves (in a statistically significant sense) how well we can predict the participants' scores on the criterion above and beyond the level of prediction offered by the original predictor (e.g., quantity of contact).

There is a lot more to say about the use of multiple regression, but for now it is important to see that we use the same principles to find the best-fitting functions, to measure the degree of correlation, and to construct hypothesis tests for linear regression, nonlinear regression, and multiple regression.

Summary

We use correlation and linear regression to assess the strength of the relationship between variables, but how well that works for us depends upon whether the assumptions of the linear regression model are met. Therefore, the first thing we must do is plot and review our data. We can plot the residuals to check that the homoscedasticity and normal distribution assumptions are met. There are various ways to determine if the relationship between our variables is linear. One is to calculate the correlation ratio (η^2) and compare it to r^2 through an F-test. Another is to try to fit a curve to our data using the method of least squares, calculate a measure of correlation (called "correl^2"), and test if the proportion of variance accounted for with correl^2 is greater than with r^2. If it is, we should use the fitted curve to represent our data.

Outliers can distort the value of r and the slope of the linear regression line. We briefly discussed a number of robust alternatives.

We can use multiple regression when there is more than one predictor. The basic principles for calculating the multiple correlation coefficient and fitting multiple regression to our data are extensions of those described in Chapter 11 and in this chapter.

The basic principles for using regression models can be summarized as follows:

1. Plot our data to get an idea of the form of the relationship between the two variables. Plot and examine the residuals to get a better idea of the relationship.

2. Select a model (function) and fit it to the data using the method of least squares.

3. Compute the correlation using one of the following formulas:

$$\text{correlation coefficient}^2 = 1 - \frac{S^2_{\text{residuals}}}{S^2_Y}$$

or

$$\text{correlation coefficient}^2 = \frac{S^2_{Y'}}{S^2_Y}$$

4. The test statistic to test the null hypothesis that the population correlation = 0 is as follows:

$$F = \frac{\left(\text{correlation coefficient}^2\right)/\left(\# \text{ parameters estimated}\right)}{\left(1 - \text{correlation coefficient}^2\right)/\left(n - \# \text{ parameters estimated} - 1\right)}$$

We can use this test statistic for multiple regression instead of Equation 12.21 because the # parameters estimated = # predictors + 1.

5. The *F*-test to determine whether adding predictors significantly improves prediction in multiple regression or whether the curve significantly improves prediction in a bivariate situation is this:

$$F = \frac{\left(r_p^2 - r_q^2\right)/\left(df_p - df_q\right)}{\left(1 - r_p^2\right)/\left(n - df_p - 1\right)}$$

6. Use one of the robust regression methods when outliers distort the relationship. The Theil–Sen appears to have advantages over other robust methods for regression.

Conceptual Exercises

1. Is there a relationship between anxiety level and test performance? To answer this question, 40 students recruited from introductory psychology classes completed the Taylor Manifest Anxiety Scale (MAS) and the quantitative portion of the ACT (ACT-Q). This yielded two numbers for each participant: the participant's score on the MAS and the participant's score on the ACT-Q. There are a number of ways that you can analyze the resulting data, depending on how well the data reflect the assumptions of the various possible models.

   a. What test would be appropriate to perform to determine whether the relationship between these two variables is linear? What is the appropriate test statistic, and why is this test statistic appropriate?

   b. How can you determine whether the homoscedasticity assumption of the linear regression model has been violated?

2. Suppose you determine that the ACT-Q scores are normally distributed but the relationship between the ACT-Q and MAS scores is *not* linear.

   a. You could try to fit a curve to the data (for example, $Y' = A + BX^2$, $Y' = A + B \log X$). Describe the procedure for finding the values of *A* and *B* for the best fitting curve. Use *X* to represent the MAS scores and *Y* to measure the ACT-Q scores.

   b. Using the curve you fit above, what measure of correlation should you use to measure the degree of relationship between the two variables in this situation? Write the formula for that correlation coefficient. Why did you choose it?

c. What test statistic would you use to test whether the population correlation above equals zero? Write the formula for that test statistic. Why did you choose it?

d. What is the distribution of this test statistic when the null hypothesis is true *and* when it is false? Make a diagram of the shapes, including the means of these distributions and the ranges of possible values that can occur.

e. Describe the effects of increasing sample size on both these distributions. Why does increasing sample size affect the power of this test?

3. One of the assumptions of the linear regression model is that the relationship between the two variables we are studying is linear.

a. What do *pure error* and *lack of fit* refer to in the linear regression model? How do we use these two sources of variance to test for linearity? What should we observe when the relationship is linear? When it is not linear?

b. What is the formula for the correlation ratio (η)? How does this statistic measure the degree of correlation between two variables? How can we use η to test for linearity?

c. Describe in words how you would find the estimates of the parameters for a *nonlinear* relationship between two variables.

4. What test statistic can you use to test for linearity of regression? Why does this test statistic provide a test for linearity of regression?

5. After looking at the scatterplot of your data, you decide the relationship is quadratic. Therefore, you could use the following equation to represent the relationship in

the population from which the data were obtained: $Y' = \alpha + \beta X + \gamma X^2$.

a. Describe the procedure for finding the estimates for α, β, and γ in the above population regression equation.

b. Write the formula for the statistic you would use to estimate the population correlation in this situation.

c. Write the formula for the test statistic you could use to test whether the population correlation equals zero.

d. What is the distribution of this test statistic when the null hypothesis is true *and* when it is false? Make a diagram of the shapes, including the means of these distributions and ranges of possible values that can occur.

e. Describe the effects of increasing sample size on both these distributions. Why does increasing sample size affect the power of this test?

6. All of the regression models we studied are based on the assumption that the residuals are normally distributed. What are the residuals? How can you test whether they are normally distributed?

7. You can test for whether you have selected the correct model by partitioning the residual or unexplained sums of squares into two parts, partitioning the degrees of freedom, creating estimates of variance (mean squares) for each part, and comparing the estimates of variance with the following test statistic:

$$F = \frac{\sum_{j=1}^{m}(\bar{Y} - Y')^2 \Big/ (N - 2 - df_{pe})}{\sum_{j=1}^{m}\left[\sum_{i=1}^{n_j}(Y - \bar{Y}_j)^2\right] \Big/ \sum_{j=1}^{m}(n_j - 1)}$$

a. What do the numerator and denominator of this F-ratio represent?

b. If the model chosen is *not* correct (that is, the null hypothesis is false), which estimate of variance should be bigger? Why?

8. Is the size of your brain an indicator of your mental capacity? In an attempt to answer this question, Willerman, Schultz, Rutledge, and Bigler (1991) used magnetic resonance imaging (MRI) to determine the brain size of their participants. They took into account gender and body size to draw conclusions about the relationship between brain size and intelligence. Forty participants drawn from an introductory psychology course were given the Wechsler Adult Intelligence Scale–Revised (1981).

a. Because the participants are college students and not a sample from the entire population, describe how you can decide whether the obtained IQ scores came from a normal distribution.

b. How can you test whether the relationship between these two variables is linear? What

is the appropriate test, and why is this test appropriate?

c. What test statistic should you use to test whether the population correlation equals zero?

d. What are the experimental *and* statistical hypotheses associated with this hypothesis test?

e. How can you measure the proportion of variance in IQ scores explained by variation in MRI scores?

9. Adding extra parameters to the regression equation will increase the proportion of variance explained. How can we determine whether the increase represents a real improvement in prediction?

10. A study was carried out in Alachua County, Florida, to investigate the relationship between a mental health index and several possible explanatory variables. The criterion measure was an index of psychiatric impairment (IPI) that incorporates several dimensions of psychiatric symptoms, including aspects of anxiety and depression. Scores on this measure can range from 0 to 50; higher scores indicate greater psychiatric impairment. The three explanatory variables in this study were a life events score (LE), socioeconomic status (SES), and educational level. If Y is the score on the IPI, X_1 is LE, X_2 is SES, and X_3 is educational attainment, the structural model for each score in the population would be $Y = \beta_0 + \beta_1 X_1 + \beta_2 X_2 + \beta_3 X_3 + \varepsilon$.

a. Describe how you would find the best estimates of the parameters β_0, β_1, β_2, and β_3. Start with how you obtain your data according to the statistical model.

b. Once you have the sample regression equation, what measure of correlation would you use? Write the formula for that correlation coefficient.

c. What test statistic would you use to evaluate whether the population correlation in part (b) equals 0? Write the formula for that test statistic. Why did you choose it?

d. What are the distributions of that test statistic when the null hypothesis is true *and* when it is false? Give the names, means, and variances (if known) of these distributions.

e. Adding another predictor will increase the proportion of variance explained. How can we determine whether that increase represents a real improvement in prediction?

Student Study Site

Visit the Student Study Site at **https://study.sagepub.com/friemanstats** for a variety of useful tools including data sets, additional exercises, and web resources.

ANOTHER WAY TO SCALE THE SIZE OF TREATMENT EFFECTS

In a simple two-group experiment with an experimental group and a control group, the statistical null hypothesis is $H_0: \mu_E = \mu_C$, and under appropriate conditions, we can use a t-test to decide whether to reject or not reject this null hypothesis (see Chapter 7). When the value of the test statistic leads us to reject the null hypothesis, we say the results of an experiment are "statistically significant," but as we saw in Chapter 6, a statistically significant difference does not mean that the effect size is large. As we have seen repeatedly, the p-value (the probability of getting our data assuming that the null hypothesis is true) is a function not only of the effect size but also of the sample size when the null hypothesis is false: *For any given effect size, the p-value decreases as sample size increases.* To overcome this problem, we can use standardized effect sizes (Cohen's d, Hedges' g, and Glass's Δ) as estimates of the population effect size. In this chapter, we will look at another way to scale the size of treatment effects.

This other way is to reformulate our hypothesis test on means as a regression problem in which the independent variable in the experiment is the predictor and the dependent variable is the criterion. If the effects of the treatment are different, then knowing what treatment an individual received (the independent variable) should help us predict his or her performance on the dependent variable (see Table 13.1 and Figure 13.1).

THE POINT-BISERIAL CORRELATION COEFFICIENT AND THE *t*-TEST

As an alternative to the t-test, we can use the point-biserial correlation coefficient to test whether there is a relationship between a dichotomous variable and a continuous variable. The point-biserial correlation coefficient also gives us an estimate of the size of the effect of a two-level independent variable on a continuous dependent variable.

Table 13.1 presents data from Barlett (2015) that have been discussed earlier in Chapters 1 and 7. Figure 13.1 presents those data as a scatterplot with the two experimental conditions on the *x*-axis and the dependent variable (State Hostility Scale scores) on the *y*-axis. For these data, $t = -2.46$. The critical value for *t* for a two-tailed test with 95 degrees of freedom at $\alpha = .05$ is 1.985. The exact *p*-value for $t = -2.46$ is .0157. Therefore, we reject the null hypothesis and accept the alternative hypothesis that the treatment given to the experimental group had an effect relative to the performance of the control group on this dependent variable.

When we have two variables, one a continuous variable and the other a dichotomy, the appropriate correlation coefficient is called the **point-biserial correlation** (r_{pb}). There are

TABLE 13.1 ■ Data From Barlett (2015)									
	State Hostility Scale Scores								
	After Insulting Message					After Nice Message			
	102	66	85	110	65	35	57	46	38	51
	78	93	75	38	103	82	63	59	58	69
	103	39	102	74	75	80	85	97	103	78
	71	44	103	60	73	87	77	100	45	63
	84	71	90	110	65	76	86	57	75	55
	60	78	64	117	114	96	65	142	72	102
	99	86	67	42	80	37	44	83	72	83
	87	49	92	92	101	52	91	55	71	55
	90	90	57	55	94	85	70	53		
	94	79	99	107	43					
	98	102	95	94						
Mean	81.56					70.93				
Median	84.5					71.00				
Sample Variance	425.765					450.158				
Count	54					43				

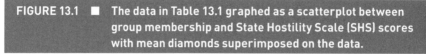

FIGURE 13.1 ■ The data in Table 13.1 graphed as a scatterplot between group membership and State Hostility Scale (SHS) scores with mean diamonds superimposed on the data.

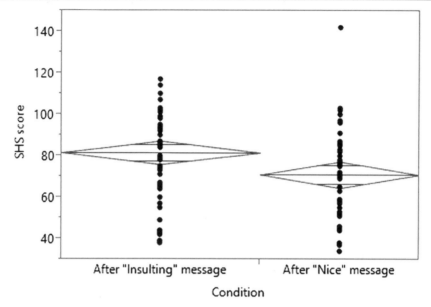

a number of equations for calculating the point-biserial correlation coefficient. One such equation is

$$r_{pb} = \frac{\left(\bar{X}_1 - \bar{X}_2\right)\sqrt{p_1 p_2}}{S_Y},$$ (13.1)

where p_1 is the proportion of the total number of scores in group 1, p_2 is the proportion of the total number of scores in group 2, and S_Y is the standard deviation of all of the dependent variable scores in both groups.

We can also obtain the value of r_{pb} by calculating the Pearson r. We do so by assigning 1 as the value of X for every individual in one group, assigning 2 for every individual in the other group, and then calculating the Pearson r. This alternative approach will give us the same value as does Equation 13.1.

The value of r_{pb} can be either positive or negative. The sign of r_{pb} indicates the direction of the slope of a line that connects the two sample means. The statistic is positive when the mean of the group on the right is higher than the mean of the group on the left, and it is negative when the opposite is true. For the data in Table 13.1, $r_{pb} = -.159$.[1]

---

[1] In this example, the value of r_{pb} is negative because the participants in the After Insulting Message group were assigned a value of 1 as their condition and those in the After Nice Message group were assigned a value of 2.

We can test the null hypothesis that the population point-biserial correlation (ρ_{pb}) equals 0 with the following test statistic:

$$t = \frac{r_{pb}\sqrt{df}}{\sqrt{1 - r_{pb}^2}} \tag{13.2}$$

Note the similarity of this test statistic to Equation 11.30. When the null hypothesis is true, Equation 13.2 has a t-distribution with $(n_1 + n_2 - 2)$ degrees of freedom. Substituting $r_{pb} = -.159$ and $df = 95$ into Equation 13.2 yields $t = -2.46$, the same value obtained with Student's t-test of the null hypothesis $H_0: \mu_E = \mu_C$. Therefore, we also reject the null hypothesis that $\rho_{pb} = 0$ and accept the alternative hypothesis that $\rho_{pb} \neq 0$. This result also tells us that there is a correlation between the independent variable and the dependent variable. We can estimate the size of that correlation with the point-biserial correlation coefficient and use the square of r_{pb} to obtain an estimate of the proportion of variance in the dependent variable that is due to the differences in how the groups were treated (that is, estimate the size of the treatment effect). For these data, $r_{pb}^2 = .0727$.

Equation 13.2 can be rearranged to yield the following equation, which allows us to calculate the point-biserial correlation coefficient directly from the value of t:

$$r_{pb} = \sqrt{\frac{t^2}{t^2 + df}} \tag{13.3}$$

Therefore, after performing a t-test, we can calculate the point-biserial correlation coefficient with Equation 13.3. Again, squaring r_{pb} gives us an estimate of the proportion of variance in the dependent variable that is due to the difference between the treatments. Although the p-value is very low, the estimated proportion of variance in the SHS scores due to the two treatments administered is .07.

The relationship between the point-biserial correlation coefficient and the t-test means that when we perform a t-test on the data from a two-group experiment, we are in fact testing two parallel sets of null hypotheses:

$H_0: \mu_E - \mu_C = 0$

$H_0: \rho_{pb} = 0$

The point-biserial correlation coefficient can also be used with a z-test to test the null hypothesis that the population means are equal when the population variances are known. In this case, the point-biserial correlation coefficient can be obtained from the following formula:

$$z = \frac{r_{pb}\sqrt{N}}{\sqrt{1 - r_{pb}^2}} \tag{13.4}$$

Friedmann (1968) described similar indices of effect size for χ^2 tests for association (see Chapter 8) and analysis of variance (see Chapter 14).

Equations 13.2 and 13.3 tell us that hypothesis tests on population means and the correlation between the independent and dependent variables in our experiments are two sides of the same coin: When we are testing the experimental hypothesis that the effects of our treatments are the same, we are testing not only the statistical hypothesis that the population means are equal but also the statistical hypothesis that there is no correlation between our independent variable (what treatment our participants received) and the dependent variable (how they performed on a task we measured).

When the null hypothesis about the population means is false, the calculated value of our test statistic gets larger as sample size increases. As a result, very small treatment effects will be judged to be statistically significant with very large sample sizes. Furthermore, for any given situation in which the null hypothesis is false, the p-value can be made as small as we want by increasing the sample size. Therefore, the p-value cannot be used as a measure of the size of the treatment effect.

On the other hand, the sample correlation coefficient is an estimate of the population correlation. When sample sizes increase, the sample correlation coefficient becomes a better estimate of the population correlation, because sample correlation coefficients are both more efficient and the bias in the estimates of the population correlation is reduced.[2] Therefore, as sample size increases, sample correlations approach the value of the population correlation, regardless of whether the null hypothesis is true or false. Because correlation coefficients do not get systematically larger or smaller as sample size increases (rather they become better estimates of the population correlations), we can use them to scale the size of the treatment effect, and the square of the correlation coefficient gives us an estimate of the proportion of variance in the dependent variable that is explained by variation in the independent variable. For that reason, these correlation-based estimates of effect size are sometimes called **variance-accounted-for measures** or **relational indices**.

In Chapter 7, we saw how we can use standardized group difference measures to estimate the size of the treatment effect in a two-group experiment using Cohen's d, Hedges' g, and Glass's Δ. In the next chapter, we will look at some variance-accounted-for measures for experiments in which there are more than two groups.

---

[2] As noted in Chapter 10, the Pearson r is a biased estimate of ρ. The same is true for r_{pb} and η with respect to their corresponding population correlations.

ADVANTAGES AND DISADVANTAGES OF ESTIMATING EFFECT SIZES WITH CORRELATION COEFFICIENTS OR STANDARDIZED GROUP DIFFERENCE MEASURES

Estimating effect sizes with correlation coefficients gives us a more flexible measure of effect size that is the basis of the linear model and has a more direct relationship with the power of our tests. However, other measures of effect size may be more intuitive in some situations.

McGrath and Meyer (2006) considered this issue. They noted that it is relatively easy to transform Cohen's d into r_{pb} and vice versa; however, each measure emphasizes different aspects of our data.

McGrath and Meyer identified three advantages of correlation coefficients like r_{pb} over standardized group differences, such as d and g, for estimating effect sizes:

1. *The relationship between r_{pb} and power is more direct.* It is clear from Equation 13.1 that the value of r_{pb} is determined by both the difference between the two sample means and the proportions of values in the two groups (p_1 and p_2). The product $p_1 p_2$ is highest when $p_1 = p_2 = .5$. The value declines as the values of p_1 and p_2 diverge. While it is rarely mentioned, the values of Student's t and the Welch–Satterthwaite t are also affected by the differences between the two sample sizes. For a given difference between group means, the values of r_{pb} and t are both highest when the proportion of the total number of scores $= .5$, and both decrease as the proportions and group sizes diverge. This relationship affects the power of a t-test because large values of t lead to rejection of the null hypothesis. Standardized group differences (d and g) are not affected by the differences in group sizes and proportions of scores in each group. Therefore, when we use standardized estimates of effect sizes, there can be a disconnect between the estimate of effect size and the power of our test.

2. *Correlation coefficients are more flexible measures of effect size because they can be used with a variety of test statistics.* The standardized measures described above are restricted to two-group experiments. In Chapter 14, we will look at estimates of effect sizes for when there are more than two groups (analysis of variance).

3. *The general linear model involves correlation coefficients.* As we saw in Chapter 11, The general linear model is the basis of linear regression, nonlinear regression, multiple regression, and analysis of variance.

However, it is a mistake to believe that there are no advantages of standardized measures such as d and g over r_{pb}. McGrath and Meyer noted that *standardized mean differences may be relevant and perhaps intuitive when thinking about treatment effects.* As noted in Chapter 7, the noncentrality parameter is a standardized difference between the population means; therefore, the standardized estimates of effect size are a direct way to estimate the actual effect size.

CONFIDENCE INTERVALS FOR EFFECT SIZE ESTIMATES

Effect sizes are point estimates. Confidence intervals for effect size estimates provide us with information about the accuracy of the point estimate.

Measures like d, g, and r_{pb}, are point estimates of the effect size for the population. Therefore, in addition to calculating the estimate of effect size, we should also provide a confidence interval to give us an idea of the accuracy of our point estimate. In Chapter 7, we looked at how to create confidence intervals for population standardized effect sizes. The situation is easier with r_{pb}. Because the distribution of r_{pb} is approximately normal when the distributions for the two groups are normal and the total sample size is greater than 25, we can use the following formula to find the 95% confidence interval for the population point-biserial correlation ρ_{pb}:

$$\Pr(r_{pb} - 1.96\sigma_{r_{pb}} < \rho_{pb} < r_{pb} + 1.95\sigma_{r_{pb}}) = .95 \tag{13.5}$$

where $\sigma^2_{r_{pb}} = \dfrac{r^2_{pb} + 2p_1p_2\left(2 - 3r^2_{pb}\right)}{4np_1p_2}\left(1 - r^2_{pb}\right)^2$ (Tate, 1955). However, if these assumptions cannot be met, then the percentile bootstrap is a better method of finding the confidence interval for ρ_{pb}.

FINAL COMMENTS ON THE USE OF EFFECT SIZE ESTIMATORS

In the same manner that researchers have adopted conventions for significance testing (e.g., p < .05), many researchers refer to conventional interpretations of effect sizes when trying to understand and communicate the significance of their findings. However, we should also consider what a meaningful effect size is in the context of the variables we study before making conclusions about the significance of our research.

Cohen (1969, 1988) proposed a set of benchmarks for interpreting d as a measure of effect size and introduced these benchmarks with the following caution:

The terms "small," "medium," and "large" are relative not only to each other but to the area of behavioral science or even more particularly to the specific content and research method being employed. . . . [T]here is a certain risk inherent in offering conventional operational definitions for these terms for use . . . in as diverse a field of inquiry as behavioral science. (1988, p. 25)

Later in the same book, Cohen wrote:

These proposed conventions were set forth throughout with much diffidence, qualifications, and invitations not to employ them if possible. . . . They were offered as conventions because they were needed in a research climate characterized by a neglect of attention to issues of [effect size] magnitude. (1988, p. 532)

Despite his cautions about using his benchmarks for interpreting d as a measure of effect size, these benchmarks are widely used to judge the importance of research findings. However, there are strong arguments for not doing so.

Prentice and Miller (1992) described two research strategies in which the effect size can be small but the research findings important. Their first research strategy involved experiments that involved minor manipulations of the independent variable (e.g., Tajfel, Billig, Bundy, & Flament's (1971) experiment on the effects of group membership on preferences). The second research strategy involves using a difficult-to-influence dependent variable. Asch's (1951) experiment on conformity to group pressure provides a well-known example of this strategy. These and other experiments cited in Prentice and Miller's paper illustrate that estimated effect sizes are not the only way to evaluate the importance of a research finding.

Abelson (1985) made a compelling case for why effect size in terms of percent of variance explained may understate the importance of a variable. His example involved asking how much of the variance in a baseball batter's getting a hit during an at bat is due to skill. Assuming the batter has a .270 batting average, Abelson calculated that the percent of variance in a single official at bat that is due to skill is one third of 1%. Does that mean that skill does not matter in whether a batter gets a base hit? The answer is clearly "no" because, as Abelson points out, over the course of a season, the effects of skill accumulate both within an individual and a team as a whole. The result is that teams with more skilled players win more games. Abelson's point is that there are situations in which a variable contributes little to the proportion of variance explained but that variable may still be important.

Finally, Thompson (2001) commented:

If people interpreted effect sizes with the same rigidity with which α = .05 has been used in statistical testing, we would merely be being stupid in another metric. Moreover, effect size reporting is not a panacea that will intrinsically guarantee that all research will both be thoughtful and address only important questions. (pp. 82–83)

This statement does not mean that we should not include effect size measures in our descriptions of our results. It means that we should use caution when interpreting measures of effect size.

Summary

When we conduct an experiment and perform a hypothesis test on population means, we are also performing a hypothesis test on the correlation between the independent variable and the dependent variable in our experiment. When we reject the null hypothesis test that the population means are equal, we can also reject the null hypothesis test that the correlation between our independent and dependent variables in our experiment equals zero. For t-tests on population means, the corresponding correlation coefficient is the point-biserial correlation (r_{pb}). Formulas exist for translating t to r_{pb} and vice versa. Although the value of Student's t when the null hypothesis is true increases as sample size increases, r_{pb} becomes a better estimate of the population point-biserial correlation ρ_{pb} as sample size increases. Because we can use the square of r_{pb} to estimate the proportion of the variance in our participants' scores on our dependent variable that is attributed to the different conditions in our experiment (our independent variable), this statistic provides us with another way to estimate the size of our treatment effects. In the next chapter, we will use similar procedures to estimate the size of the treatment effects where there are more than two groups in our experiment.

Conceptual Exercises

1. It is possible that we might get a statistically significant result when performing a t-test or an analysis of variance even though the differences among the sample means is small. What statistic can we use to measure the strength of the treatment effects in this situation? What is the effect of sample size on this measure of the strength of the treatment effects?

2. What is the relationship between the null hypothesis for the population point-biserial correlation and the null hypothesis for a t-test?

3. How does an increase in sample size influence a p-value differently than a sample correlation coefficient, both in terms of the size of these values and their meaning?

4. Suppose the proportion of variance explained in an experiment is small. Should that fact lead you to be concerned about the importance of your result? Why or why not?

5. What are the advantages of using correlation-based measures, such as r_{pb}, instead of standardized group difference measures, such as Cohen's d?

6. What are the advantages of using standardized group difference measures, such as Cohen's d, instead of correlation-based measures, such as r_{pb}?

Student Study Site

Visit the Student Study Site at **https://study.sagepub.com/friemanstats** for a variety of useful tools including data sets, additional exercises, and web resources.

ANALYSIS OF VARIANCE FOR TESTING FOR DIFFERENCES BETWEEN POPULATION MEANS

At the beginning of Chapter 7, we looked at an experiment by Barlett (2015) in which he investigated the effects of message content on how people responded to the State Hostility Scale. The details of that experiment are described in Chapter 1 and in Chapter 7, and the results are presented again here in Table 14.1.

In Chapter 7, Student's t was used to test the null hypothesis that $\mu_{insulting} = \mu_{nice}$ against the alternative that $\mu_{insulting} \neq \mu_{nice}$. In this chapter, we will look at another way to test that null hypothesis. The concepts described here can be expanded to test null hypotheses that involve more than two treatment conditions. However, we will start by applying them to the two-group experiment in Table 14.1 and then expand them to situations in which there are more than two groups. The procedure described in this chapter is called **analysis of variance (ANOVA)**.

WHAT ARE THE SOURCES OF VARIATION IN OUR EXPERIMENTS?

The key to understanding analysis of variance is to identify what produces variation (differences) between the scores of individuals in our experiment.

What Produces Variation *Within* Groups?

Select any two numbers in the After Insulting Message data on the left of Table 14.1. Why are these two numbers different given that they are scores from two individuals who were given the same

TABLE 14.1 ■ Data From Barlett (2015)									
State Hostility Scale Scores									
After Insulting Message					**After Nice Message**				
102	66	85	110	65	35	57	46	38	51
78	93	75	38	103	82	63	59	58	69
103	39	102	74	75	80	85	97	103	78
71	44	103	60	73	87	77	100	45	63
84	71	90	110	65	76	86	57	75	55
60	78	64	117	114	96	65	142	72	102
99	86	67	42	80	37	44	83	72	83
87	49	92	92	101	52	91	55	71	55
90	90	57	55	94	85	70	53		
94	79	99	107	43					
98	102	95	94						

	After Insulting Message	After Nice Message
Mean	81.56	70.93
Median	84.5	71.00
Sample Variance	425.765	450.158
Count	54	43

treatment? There are a number of reasons why individuals given the same treatment may behave differently on the dependent variable:

Unreliability of measuring instruments. Taking the same measurement on the same individual under the same circumstances may still lead to differences due to the unreliability of the measuring instrument.

Behavioral variability. Even in an unchanging environment and with perfectly reliable measuring instruments, individuals do not perform actions exactly the same way every time they have the opportunity to perform them.

Individual differences. Different individuals rarely perform the same on the same task under the same circumstances.

We lump all of these causes for variation among scores of individuals under the same conditions under the term **error variance**. The sample variance is a measure of the error variance in a set of numbers. The estimate of the population variance estimates the error variance in the population from which the scores were presumably randomly sampled.

What Produces Variation *Between* Groups?

Now select a single score from each group. Why are these two numbers different?

Here again, individual differences, unreliability of measurement instruments, and behavioral variability play a role, but these are *not* the only reasons why these two numbers may be different.

The other reason is that the two individuals from whom these scores were obtained were given different treatments and the treatments may have had different effects on behavior. If the effects of the treatments are the same, then any differences between scores in different groups are only due to error variance. On the other hand, if the effects of the treatments are different, then the difference between scores in different groups is due to *both* error variance and the different treatments received.

Why Are the Means of the Groups Different?

The answer is the same: error variance and possibly variation due to the treatments. The analysis of variance procedure is designed to help us decide whether the variation among the mean scores of individuals given different treatments is due only to error variance or is due to error variance plus variance due to the different treatments given.

EXPERIMENTAL AND STATISTICAL HYPOTHESES

As is the case in all experiments, the experimental hypotheses are about the effects of the treatments on behavior. Because analysis of variance is based on the classical statistical model, the statistical hypotheses are about the means of the populations from which our data were sampled.

For the two-group experiment being considered here, the experimental hypotheses are as follows:

The effects of the treatments are the same; that is, receiving insulting messages has the same effect as receiving nice messages on how hostile a person feels afterward.

The effects of the treatments are not the same; that is, receiving insulting messages does not have the same effect as receiving nice messages on how hostile a person feels afterward.

The corresponding statistical hypotheses are the following:

$H_0: \mu_{insulting} = \mu_{nice}$ The mean hostility score of the population from which those who received the insulting message were sampled *equals* the mean hostility score of the population from which those who received nice messages were sampled.

$H_1: \mu_{insulting} \neq \mu_{nice}$ The mean hostility score of the population from which those who received insulting messages were sampled is *not equal to* the mean hostility score of the population from which those who received the nice messages were sampled.

ESTIMATING VARIANCES

The test statistic for analysis of variance (F) is the ratio of two estimates of the variances of the populations from which our data were sampled. The denominator of this ratio is calculated by averaging the estimates of the variances from the different samples (conditions in our experiment), and the numerator uses the variation among the sample means to construct the estimate of the population variances.

When the null hypothesis is *true*, we have samples that come from identical (or the same) populations. We can estimate the variances of these populations in two ways.

We can estimate the common population variance for both conditions by averaging the individual estimates of the population variances using Equations 3.11a−c in Chapter 3. We can do so whether the null hypothesis is true or false because individuals in each group all received the same treatment; therefore, differences between individuals within each group only reflect error variance and not different treatment effects. For the data in Table 14.1, the estimates of the population variance for the two groups are 433.80 and 460.88. The average of these estimates of the population variances is 445.80. This value is the **mean square within groups** or **mean square error**.

When the null hypothesis is true, we can also estimate the common population variance from the variance of the sample means using Equation 3.11c in Chapter 3. When the null hypothesis is true, the treatments have the same effect, and any differences between the sample means reflect only individual differences.

On the other hand, when the null hypothesis is false, the mean square between groups is estimating something larger than the common population variance because it contains error variance and variance due to the treatments. For the data in Table 14.1, the estimated variance of the sample means is 2702.56. This value is the **mean square between groups**. The computations that produce this statistic are presented in Box 14.1.

We compare these two estimates of variance with an *F*-test statistic:

$$F = \frac{\text{mean square between groups}}{\text{mean square error}} = \frac{\text{error variance} \left[+ \text{ possible treatment effects} \right]}{\text{error variance}}$$

BOX 14.1
COMPUTATIONS FOR ANALYSIS OF VARIANCE OF DATA IN TABLE 14.1

	After Insulting Message	After Nice Message
Sample means	81.56	70.93
Estimates of population variance	433.80	460.88
Sample sizes	54	43
Grand mean	76.85	
Variance of sample means	(54)(81.56 − 76.85) + (43)(70.93 − 76.85) = 2,702.56	
Average estimate of population variance	[(54 × 433.80) + (43 × 460.88)]/(54 + 43) = 445.80	

TABLE 14.2 ■ Analysis of Variance for the Data in Table 14.1

Source of Variance	df	MS	F
Between Groups	1	2,702.56	6.062
Within Groups	95	445.80	
Total	96		

The results of the analysis of variance for the data in Table 14.1 are presented in Table 14.2. When there is only 1 degree of freedom numerator, $\sqrt{F} = t$. For the data in Table 14.1, $\sqrt{6.062} = 2.46$, which is the value of t for those data (see Chapter 7).

WHEN THERE ARE MORE THAN TWO CONDITIONS IN YOUR EXPERIMENT

We can extend the procedures described above to situations in which we have more than two conditions to compare. We describe the general format for performing an analysis of variance here.

When we conduct an experiment in which there are only two conditions (typically just a treatment and a control condition), we can use Student's t-test (Chapter 7) or the randomization (permutation) model (Chapter 9) to test whether the effects of the treatments are the same. However, it is more often the case that there are more than two treatment conditions in an experiment, and for these situations, the t-test (or t-tests for all possible pairs of groups) will not suffice. To handle this situation, we can use either ANOVA or an extension of the randomization model to more than two groups. We will demonstrate the latter procedure later in this chapter.

We turn now to an experiment by Sharp, Sheeley, and Saucier (2004) concerning how people react to highly salient opinions, either highly prejudiced or nonprejudiced statements, by either well-known White or Black people. The participants in this experiment were divided into four conditions and, depending on the condition, were given packets to read containing a photograph and quotation from either former Louisiana state representative David Duke, Minister Louis Farrakhan, Doctor Martin Luther King Jr., or Pope John Paul II. David Duke and Pope John Paul II were White; Minister Louis Farrakhan and Doctor Martin Luther King, Jr., were Black. David Duke and Minister Louis Farrakhan made highly prejudiced statements; Pope John Paul II and Doctor Martin Luther King Jr. made nonprejudiced statements. The quotations used are presented in Box 14.2.

After reading the statements, the participants completed a number of rating scales that measured their reactions to the individual, their evaluations of the individual, their performance on numerous racism measures, and their affective reactions. Of interest here are the affective reactions of the participants to what they read. A composite score based on three affective items (Embarrassed, Guilty, and Ashamed) that loaded highly on a factor analysis was used as the dependent variable. The ratings for each affective item were on a 9-point scale from 1 (*not at all*) to 9 (*very much*). These ratings were then summed to produce the dependent measure. A summary of the results of this experiment are presented in Table 14.3 and Figure 14.1.

It is clear from the means and medians in Table 14.3 and the box plots in Figure 14.1 that the affective reactions to the statements by David Duke were stronger in some participants than were reactions to the statements from the other three individuals. However, it is also clear from the minimum and maximum scores that there is a lot of overlap among the scores in the four groups. We can use analysis of variance to decide whether the differences in means are statistically significant. Before analyzing these data, we need to understand in more detail the logic that underlies this procedure.

Consider the situation in Table 14.4 where there are k groups of participants with n participants per group, and each group of participants received a different treatment (although the effects of the different treatments on the participants' behavior may or may

BOX 14.2

QUOTATIONS USED IN THE SHARP ET AL. (2004) EXPERIMENT

Minister Louis Farrakhan

White people are potential humans. . . . They haven't evolved yet.

— *Philadelphia Inquirer*, March 18, 2000

According to a journalist's account, "Farrakhan called 'the white man' the 'anti-Christ' to rousing applause."

— Jackson, Mississippi, September 19, 1997, reported in the *Clarion-Ledger*, September 21, 1997

Former Louisiana State Representative David Duke

What we really want to do is to be left alone. We don't want Negroes around. We don't need Negroes around. We're not asking—you know, we don't want to have them, you know, for our culture. We simply want our own country and our own society. That's in no way exploitive at all. We want our own society, our own nation...

— Duke interviewed in March 1985 by doctoral student Evelyn Rich, who traveled around the country with Duke while conducting research for her dissertation on the KKK

Dr. Martin Luther King Jr.

I have a dream that one day this nation will rise up and live out the true meaning of its creed, "We hold these truths to be self-evident, that all men are created equal.". . . I have a dream that my four little children will one day live in a nation where they will not be judged by the color of their skin but by the content of their character.

— Address given on August 28, 1963, at the March on Washington for Jobs and Freedom

Pope John Paul II

The Holy See and the Catholic Church as a whole are deeply committed to co-operating with the State of Israel "in combating all forms of anti-Semitism and all kinds of racism and of religious intolerance, and in promoting mutual understanding among nations, tolerance among communities and respect for human life and dignity"

— Fundamental Agreement, Article 2, 1

TABLE 14.3 ■ Summary Statistics for the Sharp et al. (2004) Experiment				
	Condition			
	David Duke	**Louis Farrakhan**	**John Paul II**	**M. L. King**
Mean	13.16	5.86	4.18	4.86
Median	15.5	4.5	3	3
Variance	56.02	14.98	4.22	7.75
Minimum	3	3	3	3
Maximum	27	18	10	12

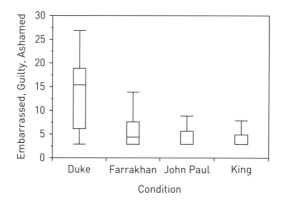

FIGURE 14.1 ■ Box plots for the four conditions in the Sharp et al. (2004) experiment.

TABLE 14.4 ■ Depiction of a Set of Data in Which There Are k Groups With n Participants in Each Group

Group							
1	**2**	**3**	...	**j**	...	**k**	
Y_{11}	Y_{12}	Y_{13}	...	Y_{1j}	...	Y_{1k}	
Y_{21}	Y_{22}	Y_{23}	...	Y_{2j}	...	Y_{2k}	
⋮	⋮	⋮		⋮		⋮	
Y_{i1}	Y_{i2}	Y_{i3}	...	Y_{ij}	...	Y_{ik}	
⋮	⋮	⋮		⋮		⋮	
Y_{n1}	Y_{n2}	Y_{n3}	...	Y_{nj}	...	Y_{nk}	
$\overline{Y}_1$	$\overline{Y}_2$	$\overline{Y}_3$		$\overline{Y}_j$		$\overline{Y}_k$	$\overline{\overline{Y}}$

Note: Number of groups $(k \geq 2)$. n = number of participants in each group $(n \geq 2)$. Y_{ij} is the ith participant in the jth group, where $i = 1$ to n, and $j = 1$ to k. $\overline{Y}_j$ is the mean of the jth group, and $\overline{\overline{Y}}$ is the grand mean (the mean of all the values and the mean of the group means).

not be different). The only restriction on the number of groups (k) is that it be 2 or more, and the only restriction on n is that it be 2 or more.[1]

As we saw in Chapter 11, the deviation of each Y_{ij} from the grand mean $(\overline{\overline{Y}})$ can be partitioned into additive parts. In analysis of variance, the two parts are the deviation of

---

[1] We will assume in the discussion that follows that the sample sizes are the same. That restriction is not required for performing an analysis of variance, as we saw above, but it will simplify the presentation.

each Y_{ij} from the mean of the group that score is in ($\overline{Y}_j$) and the deviation of each group mean ($\overline{Y}_j$) from the grand mean ($\overline{\overline{Y}}$):

$$(Y_{ij} - \overline{\overline{Y}}) = (Y_{ij} - \overline{Y}_j) + (\overline{Y}_j - \overline{\overline{Y}}) \tag{14.1}$$

If we square both sides of Equation 14.1, add up the squared deviations on both sides within each group (from $i = 1$ to n) and across all groups ($j = 1$ to k) and apply the rules of summation, we obtain the following equation:

$$\sum_{j=1}^{k}\sum_{i=1}^{n}(Y_{ij} - \overline{\overline{Y}})^2 = \sum_{j=1}^{k}\sum_{i=1}^{n}(Y_{ij} - \overline{Y}_j)^2 + n\sum_{j=1}^{k}(\overline{Y}_j - \overline{\overline{Y}})^2$$
$$+2\sum_{j=1}^{k}\sum_{i=1}^{n}(Y_{ij} - \overline{Y}_j)(\overline{Y}_j - \overline{\overline{Y}}) \tag{14.2}$$

The last term in Equation 14.2 is the numerator of the covariance of the deviation of each score from its group mean and the deviation of each group mean from the grand mean. Based on what we have seen in earlier chapters, this covariance = 0. Therefore, Equation 14.2 reduces to

$$\sum_{j=1}^{k}\sum_{i=1}^{n}(Y_{ij} - \overline{\overline{Y}})^2 = \sum_{j=1}^{k}\sum_{i=1}^{n}(Y_{ij} - \overline{Y}_j)^2 + n\sum_{j=1}^{k}(\overline{Y}_j - \overline{\overline{Y}})^2 \tag{14.3}$$

where the term to the left of the equal sign is the *total sum of squares* (SS_{Total}), the term immediately to the right of the equal sign is the *sum of squares within groups* ($SS_{Within\ groups}$ or SS_{Error}), and the second term on the right is the *sum of squares between groups* ($SS_{Between\ groups}$):

$$SS_{Total} = SS_{Within\ groups} + SS_{Between\ groups} \tag{14.3a}$$

As we saw in Chapter 11, degrees of freedom can also be partitioned. In Table 14.3, there are n scores in k different groups. Therefore, the *total degrees of freedom* is $kn - 1$. Within each group, there are $n - 1$ degrees of freedom. Therefore, the *degrees of freedom within groups (or degrees of freedom error)* equals $k(n - 1)$. Finally, with k groups, the *degrees of freedom between groups* is $k - 1$:

$$kn - 1 = k(n - 1) + (k - 1) \tag{14.4a}$$

$$df_{Total} = df_{Within\ groups} + df_{Between\ groups} \tag{14.4b}$$

Dividing sums of squares by degrees of freedom yields estimates of variance. *In ANOVA, these estimates of variance are called* **mean squares**. The two mean squares we need to consider are the $MS_{\text{Between groups}}$ and the $MS_{\text{Within groups}}$ (or MS_{Error}), and we need to determine what they estimate when the null hypothesis is true and when it is false.

ASSUMPTIONS FOR ANALYSIS OF VARIANCE

Starting with the assumption that our data are based on independent random samples from normal distributions that have the same variances, we create a structural model that uniquely specifies every value in those normal distributions. The mean squares within groups and between groups are developed from these assumptions and the structural model.

The correct use of analysis of variance is based on the assumption that the data to be analyzed are independent random samples from normal distributions that have the same variance (homogeneity of variance). Based on this assumption, every score (Y_{ij}) in each of these k populations is uniquely specified by the following **structural model**:

$$Y_{ij} = \mu + \tau_j + \varepsilon_{ij} \tag{14.5}$$

where the following hold:

μ is the grand mean of all of the scores in all of the populations in the experiment.

τ_j is the treatment applied to the jth group.

ε_{ij} is the deviation of each Y_{ij} from the mean of the population from which it was sampled (μ_j). The assumption of independent random sampling from normal distributions with equal variances (homogeneity of variance) means that the ε_{ij}'s in each population are normally distributed around the mean of each population (μ_j), and the variance of the ε_{ij}'s is the variance of those populations (which is assumed to be the same for all of the k populations).

In what is called the **fixed-effects model**, *the treatment effects are the differences between the means of the populations and the grand mean* ($\tau_j = \mu - \mu_j$), *and* $\sum_{j=1}^{k} \tau_j = 0$.

TESTING HYPOTHESES ABOUT DIFFERENCES AMONG POPULATION MEANS WITH ANALYSIS OF VARIANCE

We use the mean squares within groups and between groups to test hypotheses about the differences among population means. When the null hypothesis (the population means are the same) is false, then the mean squares between groups will be greater than the mean squares within groups.

The experimental hypotheses for this situation are as follows:

The effects of the treatments are the same.

The effects of the treatments are not the same.

And here are the corresponding statistical hypotheses:

H_0: $\mu_1 = \mu_1 = \ldots \mu_j \ldots = \mu_k$
H_1: At least one μ_j is different from the others.

To test the null hypothesis, we compare the mean square between groups with the mean square within groups by forming the ratio between them. When the null hypothesis is true, they are both estimating the same thing. When the null hypothesis is false, the mean square between groups is estimating something larger. This background information leads us to the following questions.

What Does the Mean Square Within Groups (Mean Square Error) Estimate?

The mean square within groups is $\dfrac{\displaystyle\sum_{j=1}^{k}\sum_{i=1}^{n}(Y_{ij}-\overline{Y}_j)^2}{k(n-1)}$. By rewriting this expression

as $\displaystyle\sum_{j=1}^{k}\dfrac{\displaystyle\sum_{k=1}^{n}\left(Y_{ij}-\overline{Y}_j\right)^2/(n-1)}{k}$, we see that it represents the *average of the estimates of*

population variances. As noted above, the sample variance within groups reflects only error variance, regardless of whether the null hypothesis is true or false. Therefore, under all conditions,

$$E\dfrac{\displaystyle\sum_{j=1}^{k}\sum_{i=1}^{n}(Y_{ij}-\overline{Y}_j)^2}{k(n-1)} = \sigma_\varepsilon^2 \tag{14.6}$$

What Does the Mean Square Between Groups Estimate?

The mean square between groups is $n \dfrac{\sum_{j=1}^{k}(\overline{Y}_j - \overline{\overline{Y}})^2}{k-1}$ By rewriting this formula as

$n\left[\dfrac{\sum_{j=1}^{k}(\overline{Y}_j - \overline{\overline{Y}})^2}{k-1}\right]$, we can see that this is n *times the estimate of the variance of the* k

population means. As noted above, the variance of the sample means reflects error variance *and* the differential effects of the different treatments *when the null hypothesis is false.*

When the null hypothesis is true, the variance of the sample means reflects only error variance. Therefore, when the null hypothesis is *true,*

$$E\left[\frac{n\sum_{j=1}^{k}(\overline{Y}_j - \overline{\overline{Y}})^2}{k-1}\right] = \sigma_\varepsilon^2, \tag{14.7a}$$

and when the null hypothesis is *false,*

$$E\left[\frac{n\sum_{j=1}^{k}(\overline{Y}_j - \overline{\overline{Y}})^2}{k-1}\right] = \sigma_\varepsilon^2 + \sigma_\tau^2 \tag{14.7b}$$

Therefore, when the null hypothesis is true, $MS_{\text{Between groups}} \approx MS_{\text{Within groups}}$, and when the null hypothesis is false, $MS_{\text{Between groups}} > MS_{\text{Within groups}}$. As noted in Chapter 11, we use an F-ratio to compare these two estimates of variance. In this case,

$$F = \frac{n \cdot \sum_{j=1}^{k}(\overline{Y}_j - \overline{\overline{Y}})^2 / (k-1)}{\sum_{j=1}^{k}\sum_{i=1}^{n}(Y_{ij} - \overline{Y}_j)^2 / k(n-1)} \tag{14.8}$$

When the null hypothesis is true, Equation 14.8 has an F distribution with $k - 1$ and $k(n - 1)$ degrees of freedom, such that

$$\mu_F = \frac{df_{\text{denominator}}}{df_{\text{denominator}} - 2}, \tag{14.9}$$

and, when $df_{\text{den}} > 4$,

$$\sigma_F^2 = \frac{2\left(df_{\text{den}}^2\right)\left(df_{\text{num}} + df_{\text{den}} - 2\right)}{df_{\text{num}}\left(df_{\text{den}} - 2\right)^2\left(df_{\text{den}} - 4\right)} \tag{14.10}$$

TABLE 14.5 ■ Analysis of Variance Summary Table for One-Way Analysis of Variance

Source of Variance	Sums of Squares	Degrees of Freedom	Mean Square	F
Between Groups	$n\sum_{j=1}^{k}\left(\bar{Y}_j - \bar{\bar{Y}}\right)^2$	$k-1$	$\dfrac{n\sum_{j=1}^{k}\left(\bar{Y}_j - \bar{\bar{Y}}\right)^2}{k-1}$	$F = \dfrac{n \cdot \sum_{j=1}^{k}\left(\bar{Y}_j - \bar{\bar{Y}}\right)^2 / (k-1)}{\sum_{j=1}^{k}\sum_{i=1}^{n}\left(Y_{ij} - \bar{Y}_j\right)^2 / k(n-1)}$
Within Groups	$\sum_{j=1}^{k}\sum_{i=1}^{n}\left(Y_{ij} - \bar{Y}_j\right)^2$	$k(n-1)$	$\dfrac{\sum_{j=1}^{k}\sum_{i=1}^{n}\left(Y_{ij} - \bar{Y}_j\right)^2}{k(n-1)}$	
Total	$\sum\left(Y_{ij} - \bar{\bar{Y}}\right)$	$kn-1$		

TABLE 14.6 ■ Analysis of Variance Summary Table for the Sharp et al. (2004) Experiment

Source of Variance	Sums of Squares	Degrees of Freedom	Mean Square	F	p	η^2
Condition	1,608.61	3	536.20	24.88	<.0001	.187
Within Conditions	2,327.64	108	21.55			
Total	3,936.25	111				

The results of a one-factor analysis of variance are commonly summarized in a format such as Table 14.5. The value of F is close to 1 when H_0 is true and much greater than 1 when H_0 is false. The p-value for any calculated value of F depends on the degrees of freedom for the numerator and the degrees of freedom for the denominator.

Applying the formulas in Table 14.5 to the experiment by Sharp et al. (2004) yields the analysis of variance results presented in Table 14.6.

The sums of squares are obtained by applying the formulas in Table 14.5 to the data from the Sharp et al. (2004) experiment. With 4 conditions and 28 participants in each condition, the total degrees of freedom is $(4 \times 28) - 1 = 111$, the degrees of freedom for conditions is $4 - 1$, and the degrees of freedom for within conditions (error) is $4 \times (28 - 1) = 108$. The critical value ($\alpha = .05$) for F with 3 and 108 degrees of freedom is 2.689. Clearly, the observed value of F obtained here is in the critical region.

Figure 14.1 displays these data using mean diamonds. Note that the mean diamonds use the $MS_{\text{Within groups}}$ for the estimate of variance for all four conditions. The mean diamonds in Figure 14.2 clearly show that the participants' affective response to David

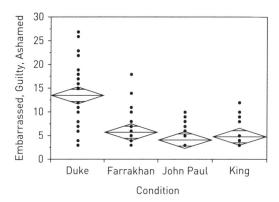

FIGURE 14.2 ■ Graph of the data from the Sharp et al. (2004) experiment.

Duke is statistically significantly different from responses to the other three individuals, which are not statistically different from each other.[2]

FACTORS THAT AFFECT THE POWER OF THE *F*-TEST IN ANALYSIS OF VARIANCE

The power of the F-*test in analysis of variance increases when the sample sizes increase, the treatments result in more variation among the population means, and the variances of the population decrease.*

As is the case with all hypothesis tests under the classical statistical model, the power of the *F*-test for differences among population means is a function of the critical value and the location of the non-central distribution. *For any selected value for* α, *the critical value of* F *is determined by the* F-*distribution when* H_0 *is true, which is a function of the degrees of freedom for the numerator and the degrees of freedom for the denominator* (see Figure 11.4). Although it may not be immediately obvious from Equation 14.10, σ_F^2 *decreases* as both $df_{\text{numerator}}$ and $df_{\text{denominator}}$ *increase*, and the critical value of *F* moves toward 1.

When the null hypothesis is *false*, the test statistic in Equation 14.8 has a non-central *F* distribution with

---

[2]See Chapter 7 for a discussion of how to interpret mean diamonds in the context of statistical hypothesis tests on means.

$$\mu_{F^*} = \left(\frac{df_{den}}{df_{den} - 2} \right) \left(\frac{df_{num} + \delta}{df_{num}} \right), \tag{14.11}$$

where the noncentrality parameter

$$\delta = n \frac{\sum_{j=1}^{k} \tau_j^2}{\sigma_\varepsilon^2} = n \frac{\sum_{j=1}^{k} \left(\mu_j - \mu \right)^2}{\sigma_\varepsilon^2} \tag{14.12}$$

The noncentrality parameter δ is a function of the sample size (n); the variation of the population means (μ_j) around the grand mean (μ), which represents the effects of the different treatments (τ_j); and the variance of those populations (σ_ε^2), which are assumed to be the same (homogeneity of variance). It is clear from Equation 14.12 that the power of this test increases when

1. the sample sizes increase,
2. the treatments result in more variation among the population means, and
3. the variances of the population decrease.

As we saw with the t-test (Chapter 7), the power of this F-test also increases as sample sizes increase for two reasons. The major reason is that as sample sizes increase, μ_{F^*} increases, and the non-central F-distribution shifts to the right away from the central F-distribution. The second reason is that as sample sizes increase, $df_{denominator}$ increases [$df_{denominator} = k(n - 1)$], which causes the variance of the central F-distribution to decrease (see Equation 14.10) and the critical value of F to move toward 1. Therefore, even when the effects of the different treatments are small relative to each other, we can make the power of the test as large as we want by increasing the sample sizes.

Creating a Power Function for the *F*-Test

As we saw with the t-test, the non-central distribution (F^*) is not a normal distribution. Therefore, in order to create a power function for F, we need to consult a non-central F-distribution to find the area of F^* in the critical region.

Because the power of the F-test is a function of the population variances (see #3 above), the presence of outliers in the data for any one of the groups will *increase* the estimate of the population variances (the denominator of Equation 14.8) and will result in a smaller value of F. Thus, outliers will reduce the probability of rejecting the null hypothesis when it is false and hence the power of the test.

RELATIONAL EFFECT SIZE MEASURES FOR ANALYSIS OF VARIANCE

There are a number of relational effect size numbers we can use for analysis of variance. The three most commonly used indexes are the correlation ratio (η^2), epsilon squared (ε^2), and omega squared (w^2), all of which are estimates of the population correlation ratio.

In Chapter 7, we reviewed a number of standardized group difference measures (i.e., Cohen's *d*, Hedges' *g*, and Glass's Δ) to measure the treatment effect size in two-group experiments analyzed with Student's *t*. Then in Chapter 13, we looked at the point-biserial correlation coefficient to provide variance-accounted-for measures (relational indices) of effect size for those same two-group experiments. Unfortunately, those standardized effect size measures only work with two-group experiments. Fortunately, there are a number of variance-accounted-for measures (relational indices) we can use when we perform experiments that have more than two groups.

Eta Squared (η^2)

In Chapter 12, we saw how the correlation ratio (η) can be used as a measure of the correlation between a continuous variable (on the *y*-axis) and a set of three or more categories or groups (called arrays there) on the *x*-axis. This situation is the same as that encountered with one-way analysis of variance. Calculating the correlation ratio (η) with our data after performing an analysis of variance gives us a measure of the degree of relationship between the independent and dependent variables, and the square of the correlation ratio gives us an estimate of the proportion of variance in the dependent variable that is explained by the different levels of the independent variable. Therefore, we can use the correlation ratio as a variance-accounted-for (relational index) analysis of variance. This approach works even when there are only two groups, and the result is identical to what we obtain by calculating the point biserial correlation coefficient.

As noted above, the experimental hypotheses and statistical hypotheses for analysis of variance are the following:

Experimental Hypotheses	Statistical Hypotheses
The effects of the treatments are the same.	$H_0: \mu_1 = \mu_2 = \ldots \mu_j \ldots = \mu_k$
The effects of the treatments are not the same.	H_1: At least one μ_j is different from the others.

The statistical hypotheses for the correlation ratio are the following:

H_0: population $\eta = 0$

and

H_1: population $\eta > 0$,

where the population in these statistical hypotheses consists of the set of potential populations from which the participants in our experiment were sampled.

When we reject the statistical null hypothesis for analysis of variance ($\mu_1 = \mu_2 = \ldots = \mu_k$), we conclude that at least one of the treatments had a different effect on our dependent variable than the others. When we reject the statistical null hypothesis that $\eta = 0$, we conclude that there is a correlation between what we did to the participants in our experiment and how they performed on the dependent variable and that the sample correlation ratio is an estimate of the population correlation ratio. These conclusions are two sides of the same coin.

As we saw in Chapter 12, we can use the following F-ratio to test the null hypothesis that the population $\eta = 0$:

$$F = \frac{\eta^2/(k-1)}{(1-\eta^2)/(N-k)}, \tag{14.13}$$

where k is the number of treatment conditions (groups) and N is the total number of participants.

We can rearrange Equation 14.13 to yield the following equation, which allows us to calculate η^2 directly from the F-ratio from an analysis of variance:

$$\eta^2 = \frac{df_{\text{numerator}}F}{df_{\text{numerator}}F + df_{\text{denominator}}} \tag{14.14}$$

where $df_{\text{numerator}} = (k - 1)$, and $df_{\text{denominator}} = (N - k)$.

We saw in Chapter 12 that we can also calculate η^2 with the following formula:

$$\eta^2 = 1 - \frac{\text{average } S^2_{\text{Within groups}}}{S^2_Y} \tag{14.15}$$

We use the procedures described in Chapter 3 to find the average $S^2_{\text{Within groups}}$ when the sample sizes are unequal (see Equation 3.4).

Maxwell, Camp, and Arvey (1981) noted that the sample η^2 can be calculated directly from the $SS_{\text{Between groups}}$ and the SS_{Total} from Table 14.5:

$$\eta^2 = \frac{SS_{\text{Between groups}}}{SS_{\text{Total}}} \qquad (14.16)$$

Just as r is a biased estimate of ρ, the sample η is a biased estimate of the population η, which means that η^2 is a biased estimate of the proportion of variance in the dependent variable accounted for by variation in the independent variable. This fact is readily apparent when one considers that even when the population $\eta^2 = 0$, the sample means will rarely be identical, and the sample η^2 will be greater than 0 (Maxwell, Camp, & Arvey, 1981). We describe a method of attempting to address this bias below.

Epsilon Squared (ε^2)

Kelley (1935) attempted to overcome the bias in η^2 as an estimator of the population η^2 by substituting unbiased estimators for the population within group variances $S^2_{\text{Within groups}}$ and the total population variance of Y (σ^2_Y). The formula for the resulting estimator of the population η^2 is

$$\varepsilon^2 = 1 - \frac{\text{average est } \sigma^2_{\text{Within groups}}}{\text{est } \sigma_Y}, \qquad (14.17)$$

where

$$\text{average est } \sigma^2_{\text{Within groups}} = \frac{SS_{\text{Within groups}}}{n - J}$$

and

$$\text{est } \sigma^2_Y = \frac{SS_{\text{Total}}}{n - 1}$$

Glass and Hakstian (1969) derived the following computational formula for ε^2:

$$\varepsilon^2 = \frac{SS_{\text{Between groups}} - (J - 1)MS_{\text{Within groups}}}{SS_{\text{Total}}}, \qquad (14.18)$$

where J is the number of groups. Although Kelley used unbiased estimators in both the numerator and denominator to derive ε^2, that does not make ε^2 an unbiased estimator of the population η^2.

Omega Squared (ω^2)

Hays (1963) employed a slightly different approach to derive an unbiased estimator of the population η^2, and although his estimator is less biased than ε^2, it too is a biased estimator. The computational formula Hays derived is:

$$\omega^2 = \frac{SS_{\text{Between groups}} - (J - 1) MS_{\text{Within groups}}}{SS_{\text{Total}} + MS_{\text{Within groups}}} \qquad (14.19)$$

Comparing These Three Estimators of the Population η^2

As is the case with the sample η^2, there are formulas for converting the F from a one-way analysis of variance into ε^2 and ω^2. These conversions are presented in Table 14.7 along with the computational formulas from above.

It is clear from the formulas in the above table that for the same set of data, $\eta^2 \geq \varepsilon^2 \geq \omega^2$. For that reason, ω^2 is the most conservative, and is therefore the most commonly used, of these three relational estimators of effect size. However, it should be noted that as sample sizes increase, all three indexes converge on the same value. When η^2 is reported, it is because it provides a descriptive statistic for the proportion of variance accounted for in the data. Epsilon squared (ε^2) is the adjusted R^2 reported in many data analysis programs. What should be clear at this point is that calculating and reporting the proportion of variance that we account for in our research studies is an effective and convenient way to report the strength of our effects.

TABLE 14.7 ■ Formulas for Computing η^2, ε^2, and ω^2	
Computational Formulas From Analysis of Variance Tables	**Formulas for Converting Analysis of Variance F-Ratios to Relational Indices**
$\eta^2 = \dfrac{SS_{\text{Between groups}}}{SS_{\text{Total}}}$	$\eta^2 = \dfrac{df_{\text{numerator}} F}{df_{\text{numerator}} F + df_{\text{denominator}}}$
$\varepsilon^2 = \dfrac{SS_{\text{Between groups}} - (J - 1) MS_{\text{Within groups}}}{SS_{\text{Total}}}$	$\varepsilon^2 = \dfrac{df_{\text{numerator}} (F - 1)}{df_{\text{numerator}} (F - 1) + df_{\text{Total}}}$
$\omega^2 = \dfrac{SS_{\text{Between groups}} - (J - 1) MS_{\text{Within groups}}}{SS_{\text{Total}} + MS_{\text{Within groups}}}$	$\omega^2 = \dfrac{df_{\text{numerator}} (F - 1)}{df_{\text{numerator}} (F - 1) + \text{Total number of scores}}$

RANDOMIZATION TESTS FOR TESTING FOR DIFFERENTIAL EFFECTS OF THREE OR MORE TREATMENTS

The randomization tests for experiments in which there are more than two groups are a direct extension of the randomization test described in Chapter 9.

As was noted above, the correct use of analysis of variance is based on the assumption that the data to be analyzed are independent random samples from normal distributions that have the same variance (homogeneity of variance). We saw in Chapter 7 that the power of Student's t-test is greatly compromised when the populations from which the data are sampled are not normal distributions and/or outliers are present in the data. The same situation is the case here. One way to deal with these situations is to use the randomization model (also known as the permutation model) introduced in Chapter 9.

Assumptions

The assumptions for the randomization model for testing whether three or more treatments have the same or different effects are the same as those described in Chapter 9 for the two-group situation:

> Each participant's behavior will reflect the treatment given to him or her.
>
> Participants are randomly assigned to conditions.

These two assumptions can be reduced to the simple assumption called **exchangeability**: *If the treatments in the experiment have the same effect, all participants would perform the same no matter what treatment group they were assigned to.*

Experimental Hypotheses

The experimental hypotheses are as follows:

> *The effects of the treatments are the same.*
>
> *The effects of at least one of the treatments are different from the effects of one or more of the other treatments.*

Statistical Hypotheses

Because the randomization model does not deal with populations or population parameters, the statistical hypotheses are not about population parameters; they are about the effects of the treatments on behavior. The statistical hypotheses for the randomization test for whether treatments have the same or different effects are as follows:

> H_0: No matter which group an individual was assigned to, his or her behavior would be the same. This is the exchangeability assumption described above.
>
> H_1: Some of the participants would have responded differently had they received a different treatment.

The *Exact* Randomization Test

Following the general principle that we base our decision whether to reject H_0 based on the probability of getting our data assuming that H_0 is true, we can calculate that probability by performing a randomization test:

1. Calculate how many different ways the participants in our experiment could have been randomly assigned to the different treatment conditions (that is, the number of combinations of N things divided into different groups).
2. Calculate a test statistic that we can use to rank order the number of combinations from most extreme to least extreme.
3. Define the critical region as the 5% most extreme of the total possible outcomes assuming H_0 is true (using the metric in step 2).
4. Check whether the outcome we observed in our experiment is one of those 5% in the critical region. If it is, we reject H_0.

There are a number of possible metrics we can use here to rank order the possible arrangements from most extreme to least extreme. When the numbers of participants in each group are the *same*, we can use the F-statistic in Equation 14.8 as that metric. This statistic has the advantage of being able to directly compare the result of the randomization test with that of the classical statistical model test. However, when the numbers of participants in each group are *different*, it is recommended that we use the **sum of the absolute deviations of each group mean from the grand mean** as our test statistic:

$$\sum_{j=1}^{k}\left|\overline{X}_j - \overline{\overline{X}}\right| \tag{14.20}$$

The grand mean is calculated using Equation 3.5 or 3.6 in Chapter 3.

In Chapter 9, where there were only two treatment conditions, we used the **binomial coefficient** $C_{n_1,n_2}^{N} = \dfrac{N!}{n_1!n_2!}$ to calculate the total number of ways (combinations) the N participants in our experiment could have been randomly assigned to the two conditions with n_1 participants in one group and n_2 participants in the other.[3]

When there are more than two groups, we use the **multinomial coefficient**,

$$C_{n_1 n_2 \cdots n_j \cdots n_k}^{N} = \frac{N!}{n_1!n_2!\cdots n_j!\cdots n_k!} \tag{14.21}$$

to calculate the number of ways N participants can be randomly assigned to the different groups.[4] The number of ways to randomly assign participants (combinations) increases rapidly as the number of groups increases, as illustrated by the following examples:

- The number of combinations of 10 participants randomly assigned to two groups with 5 in each group = 256.

---

[3] This formula for calculating the number of combinations is sometimes called the *binomial coefficient* due to its use for calculating probabilities in a binomial distribution.

[4] Equation 14.21 is the general case for determining the number of ways to randomly assign N subjects to k groups. It reduces to the binomial coefficient when $k = 2$.

BOX 14.3

HOW TO USE THE APPROXIMATE RANDOMIZATION TEST TO TEST HYPOTHESES ABOUT THE EFFECTS OF DIFFERENT TREATMENTS ON BEHAVIOR

1. Randomly assign participants to groups, administer the appropriate treatments, and collect the data.

2. Select a test statistic, $\sum_{j=1}^{k} \left| \overline{X}_j - \overline{\overline{X}} \right|$, the sum of the absolute deviations of the group means from the grand mean. (We can also use Equation 14.8 when the sample sizes are the same.)

3. Combine the scores from both groups into one long string of numbers and shuffle them. Then use a random assignment procedure to assign each number to one of the groups, making sure you end up with the same numbers of scores in each of these new groups as in the original groups.

4. Calculate your test statistic for each new arrangement of scores.

5. Put the scores back into one string of numbers, reshuffle them, and repeat the random assignment procedure at least 200 times.

6. Rank order the values of the test statistic. With $\alpha = .05$, the 5% most extreme values of the test statistic (largest values) constitute the critical region.

7. Reject H_0 when the value of the test statistic for the original set of data would be among those in the critical region.

- Randomly assigning those 10 participants to three groups with 3, 3, and 4 subjects increases the number of combinations to 4,200.
- Adding a third group with 5 participants to the original two 5-participants groups increases the total number of participants to 15 and the number of combinations to 756,756.
- The number of combinations of 30 participants randomly assigned to three groups with 10 participants per group = 5,550,996,791,340 (5.55×10^{12}).

Therefore, we need to use an approximate randomization test for most applications of the randomization model with more than two groups.

The *Approximate* Randomization Test

We perform an approximate randomization test by taking a random sample of at least 200 of the total possible combinations, rank ordering these according to some measure of extremity under the null hypothesis, constructing a critical region based on whether we

TABLE 14.8 ■ Critical Region for the Randomization Test on Data From Sharp et al. (2004) Experiment Based on 1,000 Shuffles for $\alpha = .05$									
Rank	Σ|dev|	Rank	Σ|dev|	Rank	Σ|dev|	Rank	Σ|dev|	Rank	Σ|dev|
1	8.036	11	6.500	21	6.071	31	5.714	41	5.643
2	7.571	12	6.357	22	6.036	32	5.714	42	5.571
3	7.357	13	6.357	23	6.000	33	5.714	43	5.571
4	7.143	14	6.357	24	6.000	34	5.714	44	5.571
5	7.071	15	6.286	25	5.893	35	5.679	45	5.571
6	6.929	16	6.250	26	5.857	36	5.679	46	5.571
7	6.786	17	6.214	27	5.857	37	5.679	47	5.571
8	6.643	18	6.214	28	5.786	38	5.679	48	5.536
9	6.643	19	6.214	29	5.714	39	5.643	49	5.536
10	6.500	20	6.071	30	5.714	40	5.643	50	5.536

Note: Σ\|dev\| is $\sum \left| \overline{Y}_j - \overline{\overline{Y}} \right|$.

have a one-tailed or a two-tailed test, and determining whether our original arrangement is in the critical region. See Box 14.3.

The value of $\sum_{j=1}^{k} \left| \overline{X}_j - \overline{\overline{X}} \right|$ for the data in the Sharp et al. (2004) experiment is 12.964. With 1,000 resamplings of the data, the 5% critical region contains the highest 50 values from the resamplings. We reject the null hypothesis when the observed value of the test statistic is higher than the 50th value, which clearly is the case here, as shown in Table 14.8.

Power of the Randomization Test

Because the randomization model does not assume that the data are random samples from normal distributions with equal variances, violations of those assumptions, such as non-normal distributions, the presence of outliers, and nonhomogeneity of variance, do not necessarily adversely affect the power of this test. Because the randomization test uses the actual data, the exact test is as powerful as an ANOVA when all of the assumptions of the ANOVA are met, and the randomization test can be more powerful when those assumptions are violated. The approximate randomization test is slightly less powerful than an ANOVA when all of the assumptions of ANOVA are met, but as sample sizes increase, the difference between the two techniques decreases (Edgington & Onghena, 2007).

USING ANOVA TO STUDY THE EFFECTS OF MORE THAN ONE FACTOR ON BEHAVIOR

Analysis of variance can be used to study the effects of two or more sets of conditions or factors applied at the same time to participants. Such a factorial design allows us to investigate possible interactions between those factors.

One of the many advantages of using analysis of variance is that it allows us to investigate separately the effects of more than one factor in an experiment. The Sharp et al. (2004) experiment described above actually contains two independent variables, race and prejudice level of the famous individuals, as represented in Table 14.9. With this arrangement of the data, we can investigate the effects of the race of the famous individual on the participants' affective scores by summing the participants' scores down each column and comparing the means of those columns with an *F*-ratio. We can also investigate how high- and low-prejudice statements affect the dependent variable by summing the participants' scores across the rows and comparing those means with an *F*-ratio.

Another important advantage of this design is that it allows us to determine whether the effects of the different factors (race and prejudice level of the famous individuals) **interact** with each other, that is, whether the effect of one factor depends on the level of the second factor.

This type of experimental design is called a **factorial design** when *all combinations of the two or more factors are included in the experiment*, as they are here.

What Is an Interaction, and Why Is It Important?

An interaction occurs when what we observe for the mean of a cell is not what we would expect from the combination of the levels of the factors that define that cell based on the individual (i.e., main) effects of those factors. Put another way, the effect

TABLE 14.9 ■ Sharp et al. (2004) Experiment as a Two-Factor Experiment		
	Race of Source of Statements	
	White	**Black**
High-prejudice statements	*n* = 28	*n* = 28
Low-prejudice statements	*n* = 28	*n* = 28

of one factor depends on the level of the other factor.[5] For example, using Table 14.9, we can assess whether the effect of the content of the statements (high or low in prejudice) is the same or different when the source is Black or White. If there is *no* interaction between the level of prejudice in the statements and the source's race, then the pattern of cell means for both levels of prejudice will look the same (or similar) for both races. This possibility is portrayed on the top left of Figure 14.3, where, although the mean affective score is higher when the statements are highly prejudicial, the difference in means for high- and low-prejudice statements is the same for both races. The parallel lines portray that situation. Observing this pattern of cell means would tell us that the participants react to the prejudice in the statements similarly for both Black and White sources.

On the other hand, we observe an **interaction** *when the pattern of cell means for both races is different. In this case, the lines will not be parallel (or close to parallel).* There are two possibilities: The first possibility is that the lines are not parallel, but they do *not* cross. This is called an **ordinal interaction** *because the rank order of the cell means for one factor is the same within each level of the second factor.* This situation is portrayed in the upper right of Figure 14.3. Here again, although the mean affective scores are higher for high-prejudice statements, it is much higher when the source is White than when the source is Black. This outcome would indicate that the level of prejudice in the statements has a stronger effect on the participants' affective reactions when the source is White.

The other type of interaction is called a **disordinal interaction** because *the rank order of cell means is not the same within each level of the second factor.* This situation is portrayed on the bottom panel of Figure 14.3 where the lines cross.[6] In this scenario, the mean affective score for high-prejudice statements is *higher* when the source is White but *lower* when the source is Black. Here, the effect of the prejudice level of the statements is fundamentally different for White and Black sources. Clearly, the pattern of cell means provides us important information about how the participants react to the combination of the two factors in this experiment.

How to Interpret the Pattern of Cell Means

When there is *no interaction*, the interpretation is straightforward: Each factor has an independent effect on the dependent variable, and we can easily interpret the main effects of the factors with an *F*-test as we would if there were only one factor. However, the presence of a statistically significant interaction complicates the interpretation of our data.

---

[5] Each cell represents the unique combination of one level of each factor.

[6] Disordinal interactions are also called *crossover interactions*.

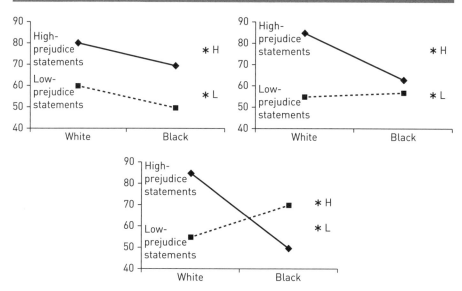

FIGURE 14.3 ■ **Stylized representations of a two-factor experiment with no interaction (upper *left*), an ordinal interaction (*upper right*), and a disordinal interaction (*bottom*). The stars on the right side of each panel are the means for high and low levels of prejudice in the statements across the two races of the sources.**

In the case of the *ordinal interaction* portrayed in the upper right of Figure 14.2, the difference between the cell means of the White sources may be statistically significant, but there does not appear to be such a difference for the Black sources. We will require separate tests on the difference between the means of the high- and low-prejudice statements for White and for Black sources to interpret these results. These tests are called simple effects tests and will be described later.

The situation with a disordinal interaction is even more complicated. The pattern displayed on the bottom of Figure 14.1 suggests that there may be a statistically significant difference between the levels of prejudice for both races, but the differences are in the opposite direction. Furthermore, the pattern suggests that the difference between the means for high- and low-prejudice statements when averaged over the two races may not be statistically significant. The means for the two levels of prejudice are indicated by the stars on the right side of each panel. The difference between these means is larger in the left and middle panels. We will have more to say about interpreting interactions and main effects when we look closely at the data.

PARTITIONING VARIANCE FOR A TWO-FACTOR ANALYSIS OF VARIANCE

The principles and procedures described above can be easily adapted to situations in which there are two or more factors.

Table 14.10 depicts a two-factor experiment where A and B are the factors and there are n participants in each cell (AB combination). It does not matter whether A and B are experimental treatments or classification variables, but to simplify the presentation, it is assumed that there are equal numbers of participants in each cell.[7]

The location of each value (Y_{ijk}) in Table 14.10 is indicated by the three subscripts i, j, and k, where i tells us the level of the A factor, j tells us the level of the B factor, and k tells us which participant we are looking at in each cell in the table (combination of A and B factors). The total number of levels of the A factor is a, the total number of levels of the B factor is b, and the number of participants in each cell is n. Therefore, $i = 1$ to a for the A factor, $j = 1$ to b for the B factor, and $k = 1$ to n for each participant in a cell (AB combination).

The deviation of each Y_{ijk} from the grand mean can be partitioned into four parts:

$$\left(Y_{ijk} - \overline{\overline{Y}}\right) = \left(Y_{ijk} - \overline{Y}_{ij}\right) + \left(\overline{Y}_i - \overline{\overline{Y}}\right) + \left(\overline{Y}_j - \overline{\overline{Y}}\right) + \left(\overline{Y}_{ij} - \overline{Y}_i - \overline{Y}_j + \overline{\overline{Y}}\right) \quad (14.22)$$

The first term on the right side of this equation is the deviation of each score from the mean of the cell (AB combination) it is in, the second term is the deviation of each row mean from the grand mean, the third term is the deviation of each column mean from the grand mean, and the fourth term includes the deviation of the mean of each AB combination from what we would expect it to be based on the row and column it is in; that is, $\overline{Y}_{ij} - E\left(\overline{Y}_{ij}\right)$, where the expected value of a cell is the row mean + the column mean − the grand mean,[8] This relationship is expressed mathematically as follows:

$$E\left(\overline{Y}_{ij}\right) = \overline{Y}_i + \overline{Y}_j - \overline{\overline{Y}} \quad (14.23a)$$

Therefore, the interaction term is

$$\overline{Y}_{ij} - E\left(\overline{Y}_{ij}\right) = \left(\overline{Y}_{ij} - \overline{Y}_i - \overline{Y}_j + \overline{\overline{Y}}\right) \quad (14.23b)$$

---

[7] As will be discussed later, unlike in the situation in which there is only one factor, having unequal numbers of participants changes the way the ANOVA must be performed.

[8] This calculation is similar to how the expected value is computed in the chi-square analysis of a contingency table described in Chapter 10 ([row sum × column sum]/total n). For ANOVA, the expected value is determined by adding and subtracting rather than by multiplying and dividing.

| TABLE 14.10 ■ Depiction of a Two-Factor Experiment With a Levels of Factor A, b Levels of Factor B, and n Participants in Each Cell (AB combination). |

			Factor B			
	B_1	B_2	...	B_j	...	B_b	
	Y_{111}	Y_{121}	...	Y_{1j1}	...	Y_{1b1}	
	Y_{112}	Y_{122}	...	Y_{1j2}	...	Y_{1b2}	
A_1	⋮	⋮		Y_{1jk}	⋮	$\bar{Y}_{1..}$	
	Y_{11n}	Y_{11n}	...	Y_{1jn}	...	Y_{1bn}	
	$\bar{Y}_{11.}$	$\bar{Y}_{12.}$	...	$\bar{Y}_{1j.}$	...	$\bar{Y}_{1b.}$	
	Y_{211}	Y_{221}	...	Y_{2j1}	...	Y_{2b1}	
	Y_{212}	Y_{222}	...	Y_{2j2}	...	Y_{2b2}	
A_2	⋮	⋮		Y_{2jk}	⋮	$\bar{Y}_{2..}$	
	Y_{21n}	Y_{22n}	...	Y_{2jn}	...	Y_{2bn}	
	$\bar{Y}_{21.}$	$\bar{Y}_{21.}$	...	$\bar{Y}_{2j.}$	...	$\bar{Y}_{2b.}$	
A_i				Y_{ijk}		$\bar{Y}_{i..}$	
	Y_{a11}	Y_{a21}	...	Y_{aj1}	...	Y_{ab1}	
	Y_{a12}	Y_{a22}	...	Y_{aj2}	...	Y_{ab2}	
A_a	⋮	⋮		Y_{ajk}	⋮	$\bar{Y}_{a..}$	
	Y_{a1n}	Y_{a2n}	...	Y_{ajn}	...	Y_{abn}	
	$\bar{Y}_{a1.}$	$\bar{Y}_{a2.}$	...	$\bar{Y}_{aj.}$	...	$\bar{Y}_{ab1.}$	
	$\bar{Y}_{.1.}$	$\bar{Y}_{.2.}$	...	$\bar{Y}_{.j.}$	...	$\bar{Y}_{.b.}$	$\bar{\bar{Y}}$

Note: b = number of levels of B factor (columns), a = number of levels of A factor (rows), n = number of participants in each cell. Y_{ijk} is the kth subject in the cell composed of the combination of A_i and B_j. A_i is the mean of the ith level of Factor A, $\bar{Y}_j$ is the mean of the jth level of Factor B, and $\bar{\bar{Y}}$ is the grand mean (the mean of all the values).

You can see that the left side of Equation 14.22 equals the right side by removing the parentheses and performing the appropriate cancellations.

By summing and squaring both sides of Equation 14.22, we obtain Equation 14.24a,[9] where the term to the left of the equal sign is called the *total sum of squares* (SS_{Total}), the term immediately to the right of the equal sign is the *sum of squares within cells* ($SS_{\text{Within cells}}$ or SS_{Error}), the second term on the right is the *sum of squares for the A factor* (SS_A), the third term on the right is the *sum of squares for the B factor* (SS_B), and the final term on the right is the *sum of squares for the interaction between the A and B factors* (SS_{AB}):

$$\sum_{i=1}^{a}\sum_{j=1}^{b}\sum_{k=1}^{n}\left(Y_{ijk}-\overline{\overline{Y}}\right)^{2} = \sum_{i=1}^{a}\sum_{j=1}^{b}\sum_{k=1}^{n}\left(Y_{ijk}-\overline{Y}_{ij}\right)^{2} + nb\sum_{i=1}^{a}\left(\overline{Y}_{i}-\overline{\overline{Y}}\right)^{2}$$

$$+ an\sum_{j=1}^{b}\left(\overline{Y}_{j}-\overline{\overline{Y}}\right)^{2} + n\sum_{i=1}^{a}\sum_{j=1}^{b}\left(\overline{Y}_{ij}-\overline{Y}_{i}-\overline{Y}_{j}+\overline{\overline{Y}}\right)^{2} \qquad (14.24a)$$

$$SS_{\text{Total}} = SS_{\text{Within cells}} + SS_A + SS_B + SS_{AB} \qquad (14.24b)$$

As we saw earlier, degrees of freedom can also be partitioned. With equal sample sizes in each cell, there are *n* scores in each cell, and there are $a \times b$ cells. Therefore, the total number of observations is $a \times b \times n$, and the *total degrees of freedom* is $abn - 1$. Within each cell, there are $n - 1$ degrees of freedom. Therefore, the *degrees of freedom within cells (or degrees of freedom error)* equals $ab(n - 1)$. With *a* levels of the A factor, the *degrees of freedom for A* is $a - 1$, and with *b* levels of the B factor, the *degrees of freedom for B* is $(b - 1)$. Finally, because in each row, there are *b* columns, and the mean of each row is the mean of the cells in that row, the degrees of freedom across the rows is $(b - 1)$. Similarly, because in each column, there are *a* rows, and the mean of each column is the mean of the cells in that column, the degrees of freedom across the columns is $(a - 1)$. Therefore, the degrees of freedom for the AB interaction is $(a - 1)(b - 1)$, and the total degrees of freedom can be represented by the following equation:

$$(abn - 1) = ab(n - 1) + (a - 1) + (b - 1) + (a - 1)(b - 1) \qquad (14.25a)$$

$$df_{\text{Total}} = df_{\text{Within cells}} + df_A + df_B + df_{AB} \qquad (14.25b)$$

Dividing sums of squares by their corresponding degrees of freedom yields estimates of variance called mean squares. For a two-factor ANOVA, the following are the corresponding mean squares for the terms on the right:

$$MS_{\text{Within cells}} = \frac{\sum_{i=i}^{a}\sum_{j=1}^{b}\sum_{k=1}^{n}\left(Y_{ijk}-\overline{Y}_{ij}\right)^{2}}{ab(n-1)} \qquad (14.26a)$$

---

[9] As was the case with Equations 14.2 and 14.3, the cross products all equal 0 because the respective terms are uncorrelated. This situation may not be the case when the sample sizes in each AB combination are not equal. As we will see later, having unequal cell sizes introduces complications for performing the ANOVA.

$$MS_A = \frac{nb\sum_{i=1}^{a}\left(\overline{Y}_i - \overline{\overline{Y}}\right)^2}{a-1} \qquad (14.26b)$$

$$MS_B = \frac{na\sum_{j=1}^{b}\left(\overline{Y}_j - \overline{\overline{Y}}\right)^2}{b-1} \qquad (14.26c)$$

$$MS_{AB} = \frac{n\sum_{i=1}^{a}\sum_{j=1}^{b}\left(\overline{Y}_{ij} - \overline{Y}_i - \overline{Y}_j + \overline{\overline{Y}}\right)^2}{(a-1)(b-1)} \qquad (14.26d)$$

To perform an analysis of variance, we need to determine what each of these terms estimates when the null hypothesis is true and when it is false.

TESTING HYPOTHESES WITH TWO-FACTOR ANALYSIS OF VARIANCE

What we use as the denominator of an F-*ratio (error term) when we have two or more factors depends on which of our factors are fixed (we are only interested in the levels of the factors in our experiment) or random (the levels are a sample from a larger set). We describe a useful algorithm for deciding what to use as the error term below.*

Hypothesis tests with two-factor analysis of variance are based on several assumptions. Every value in Table 14.10 can be specified by the structural model

$$Y_{ijk} = \mu + \alpha_i + \beta_j + \alpha\beta_{ij} + \varepsilon_{ijk}$$

where the following hold:

μ is the grand mean of all of the scores (Y_{ijk}) in all of the populations in the experiment.

α_i is the level of the A factor for that score, and $\alpha_i = \mu_i - \mu$.

β_j is the level of the B factor for that score, and $\beta_j = \mu_j - \mu$.

$\alpha\beta_{ij}$ is the unique effect that might occur for that combination of A and B. This is the interaction, where $\alpha\beta_{ij} = \mu_{ij} - \mu_i - \mu_j + \mu$.

ε_{ijk} is the deviation of each Y_{ijk} from the mean of the population from which it was sampled (μ_{ij}). It is assumed that that these populations are *normally distributed with equal variances and the scores in our experiment were randomly sampled from those populations.*

An additional consideration is whether the conclusions we want to draw based on our results apply only to the levels of the factors in our experiment or to those as well as to other levels not being tested. With a **fixed effect**, we are *only interested in the levels of that factor in our experiment.* In the experiment under consideration, both level of prejudice and race of

BOX 14.4

HOW TO DETERMINE THE EXPECTED MEAN SQUARES [$E(MS)$] WITH FIXED AND RANDOM FACTORS

1. List all of the sources of variance down the page.

2. Write the main effects and whether they are fixed or random across the top of the page. Place an *a* in every row where A does not occur.

3. Place a 1 in all other rows if A is random, 0 in all other rows if A is fixed. (Exception: Place a 1 in every row where the letter is in parentheses.)

4. Repeat for variables B, C, D, and so forth.

5. Starting with the first row, cover the columns that correspond to the letters in that row.

6. For each row that contains the letter(s) of the target row, multiply the entries in the uncovered columns together.

7. Copy onto the target row the non-zero product of letters from every row that contains the letter(s) of the target row. Use these as the coefficients for the $E(MS)$s for that row.

Example

	A (fix)	B (ran)	C (fix)	S (ran)	$E(MS)$
A	0	b	c	n	$\sigma^2_{S(ABC)} + cn\sigma^2_{AB} + bcn\sigma^2_A$
B	a	1	c	n	$\sigma^2_{S(ABC)} + acn\sigma^2_B$
AB	0	1	c	n	$\sigma^2_{S(ABC)} + cn\sigma^2_{AB}$
C	a	b	0	n	$\sigma^2_{S(ABC)} + an\sigma^2_{BC} + abn\sigma^2_C$
AC	0	b	0	n	$\sigma^2_{S(ABC)} + n\sigma^2_{ABC} + bn\sigma^2_{AC}$
BC	a	1	0	n	$\sigma^2_{S(ABC)} + an\,\sigma^2_{BC}$
ABC	0	1	0	n	$\sigma^2_{S(ABC)} + n\sigma^2_{ABC}$
S(ABC) [within cell]	1	1	1	1	$\sigma^2_{S(ABC)}$

Note: A is fixed, B is random, C is fixed, S is subjects (always random).

source were considered fixed effects. On the other hand, in an experiment in which various concentrations of a drug are tested, the research might want to generalize the results to other concentrations. This is possible, for instance, when the factor is a continuous variable such as concentration. Concentration would be a **random effect** because the *levels in the experiment are sampled from a larger set of possibilities, such as those that exist along a continuum.*

When we treat A and B as **fixed effects** where $\alpha_i = \mu_i - \mu$ and $\beta_j = \mu_j - \mu$, the following constraints also apply: $\sum_{i=1}^{a}\alpha_i = 0$, and $\sum_{j=1}^{b}\beta_j = 0$. Under these circumstances, $\sum_{i=1}^{a}\alpha\beta_{ij} = 0$ and $\sum_{j=1}^{b}\alpha\beta_{ij} = 0$. On the other hand, when a factor is a random effect, the sum of all of the levels will not equal zero (for example, $\sum_{i=1}^{a}\alpha_i \neq 0$ and $\sum_{i=1}^{a}\alpha\beta_{ij} \neq 0$).

This fact can have an effect on the how the *F*-ratio is constructed for testing the other factor. A simple algorithm for how to determine the expected mean squares when there are fixed and random factors is presented in Box 14.4. For the discussion that follows, we will assume that both A and B are fixed effects.

TESTING HYPOTHESES ABOUT DIFFERENCES AMONG POPULATION MEANS WITH ANALYSIS OF VARIANCE

Below we describe the procedures for deriving the expected mean squares when all of the factors are fixed.

In a two-factor analysis of variance, there are three sets of experimental and statistical hypotheses:

Experimental Hypotheses	Statistical Hypotheses
Main effect of A factor	
The effects of the levels of A factor are the same.[10]	$H_0: \mu_1 = \mu_2 = \ldots = \mu_a$.
The effects of the levels of A factor are not the same.	H_1: At least one μ_i is different from the others.
Main effect of B factor	
The effects of the levels of B factor are the same.[11]	$H_0: \mu_1 = \mu_2 = \ldots = \mu_b$.

[10] When the null hypothesis is true, it is also the case that the null hypothesis is $\alpha_1 = \alpha_2 = \ldots = \alpha_a$.

[11] When the null hypothesis is true, it is also the case that the null hypothesis is $\beta_1 = \beta_2 = \ldots = \beta_b$.

Experimental Hypotheses	Statistical Hypotheses
The effects of the levels of A factor are not the same.	H_1: At least one μ_j is different from the others.
Interaction between factors A and B	
There is no interaction between A and B	H_0: $\alpha\beta_{11} = \alpha\beta_{12} = \ldots = \alpha\beta_{ab}$
There is an interaction between A and B	H_1: At least one $\alpha\beta_{ij}$ is different from the others.

What Does the Mean Square Within Cells (Mean Square Error) Estimate?

$$MS_{\text{Within cells}} \text{ equals } \frac{\sum\limits_{i=i}^{a} \sum\limits_{j=1}^{b} \sum\limits_{k=1}^{n} \left(Y_{ijk} - \overline{Y}_{ij}\right)^2}{ab(n-1)} \text{ (Equation 14.26a)}.$$

This expression can be rewritten as

$$\sum\limits_{i=1}^{a} \sum\limits_{j=1}^{b} \frac{\left[\dfrac{\sum\limits_{k=1}^{n}\left(Y_{ijk} - \overline{Y}_{ij}\right)^2}{n=1}\right]}{ab}$$

The numerator of this expression is the estimate of the population variance within each cell, and these estimates are averaged across all cells. Therefore, the $MS_{\text{Within cells}}$ is the average of the estimates of the common population variance in the cells. In ANOVA, this term is called the error variance. This term is used regardless of whether the null hypotheses for the factors and the interaction are true or false or whether the sample sizes within each cell are the same or different. Therefore, under all conditions,

$$E\left[\frac{\sum\limits_{i=1}^{a}\sum\limits_{j=1}^{b}\sum\limits_{k=1}^{n}\left(Y_{ijk} - \overline{Y}_{ij}\right)^2}{ab(n-1)}\right] = \sigma_\in^2 \qquad (14.27)$$

What Do the Mean Squares for Factors A and B Estimate?

We can rewrite the right-hand expression in $MS_A = \dfrac{nb\sum\limits_{i=1}^{a}\left(\overline{Y}_i - \overline{\overline{Y}}\right)^2}{a-1}$ (Equation 14.26b) as $nb\left(\dfrac{\sum\limits_{i=1}^{a}\left(\overline{Y}_i - \overline{\overline{Y}}\right)^2}{a-1}\right)$, where the expression in the parentheses is the estimate of the variance of the population means for the A factor. From the central limit theorem, we know that multiplying the estimate of the variance of the population means by the sample size provides an estimate of the population variance (in this case, the error variance). Here the sample size for each A mean is *nb* (the number of scores in each cell times the number of cells in a given row). Therefore, the MS_A is nb *times the estimate of the variance of the A means.* As noted earlier in this chapter, the mean square for a factor reflects the error variance and, when the null hypothesis is false, the differential treatment effects of that factor on the dependent variable. Therefore, when the null hypothesis for the A factor is *true*, the variance of the A factor means reflects only the error variance. That is,

$$E\left(\frac{nb\sum_{i=1}^{a}\left(\overline{Y}_i-\overline{Y}\right)^2}{a-1}\right)=\sigma_\epsilon^2 \tag{14.28a}$$

However, when the null hypothesis is *false*,

$$E\left(\frac{nb\sum_{i=1}^{a}\left(\overline{Y}_i-\overline{\overline{Y}}\right)^2}{a-1}\right)=\sigma_\epsilon^2+\sigma_\alpha^2 \tag{14.28b}$$

The same is true for the B factor:

$$E\left(\frac{na\sum_{j=1}^{b}\left(\overline{Y}_j-\overline{\overline{Y}}\right)^2}{b-1}\right)=\sigma_\epsilon^2+\left[\sigma_\beta^2\right] \tag{14.28c}$$

What Does the Mean Square Interaction Estimate?

We saw in Equation 14.26d that $MS_{AB}=\dfrac{n\sum_{i=1}^{a}\sum_{j=1}^{b}\left(\overline{Y}_{ij}-\overline{Y}_i-\overline{Y}_j+\overline{\overline{Y}}\right)^2}{(a-1)(b-1)}$. Mean squares are sums of squares divided by degrees of freedom, where the sums of squares are the sum of the squared deviations of the score from its expected value.[12] The same is true for MS_{AB}: The scores are $\overline{Y}_{ij}$, and $E\left(\overline{Y}_{ij}\right)=\overline{Y}_i+\overline{Y}_j-\overline{\overline{Y}}$ (see Equation 14.26a).

We can rewrite MS_{AB} as $n\dfrac{\sum_{i=1}^{a}\sum_{j=1}^{b}\left(\overline{Y}_{ij}-\overline{Y}_i-\overline{Y}_j+\overline{\overline{Y}}\right)^2}{(a-1)(b-1)}$. Applying the same logic used above for $E(MS_A)$ and $E(MS_B)$, MS_{AB} is n (the number of scores in each cell) times the estimate of the variance of the AB cell means. When the null hypothesis is *true*, the variation among the cell means only reflects error variance:

---

[12] In Equation 14.26a, the scores are Y_{ijk}, and $E(Y_{ijk})=\overline{Y}_{ij}$. In Equations 14.26b and 14.26c, the scores are factor means ($\overline{Y}_i$ and $\overline{Y}_j$), and the expected value for both is $\overline{\overline{Y}}$.

$$\mathrm{E}\left(\frac{n\sum_{i=1}^{a}\sum_{j=1}^{b}\left(\overline{Y}_{ij}-\overline{Y}_{i}-\overline{Y}_{j}+\overline{\overline{Y}}\right)^{2}}{(a-1)(b-1)}\right)=\sigma_{\varepsilon}^{2} \tag{14.29a}$$

and, when the null hypothesis is false:

$$\mathrm{E}\left(\frac{n\sum_{i=1}^{a}\sum_{j=1}^{b}\left(\overline{Y}_{ij}-\overline{Y}_{i}-\overline{Y}_{j}+\overline{\overline{Y}}\right)^{2}}{(a-1)(b-1)}\right)=\sigma_{\varepsilon}^{2}+\sigma_{\alpha\beta}^{2} \tag{14.29.b}$$

The means for the Sharp et al. (2004) data are presented in Table 14.12. Applying the formulas in Table 14.11 to the experiment by Sharp et al. (2004) yields the analysis of variance summary table presented in Table 14.13.[13] These results are presented two ways in Figure 14.4.

Compare the results in Table 14.13 with those in Table 14.6, where these data were analyzed as a one-way analysis of variance. The sum of squares total is the same in both tables. Likewise, the sum of squares for the error terms (within conditions and within cells) is the same. If we add the three sources of variance (race of source, level of prejudice, and interaction between race of source and level of prejudice), we will get the sum of squares for conditions. Therefore, the $\sum\left(Y_{ijk}-\overline{\overline{Y}}\right)^{2}$ can be divided in various ways depending on how we characterize the experimental design. Additionally, we see that the error term is the average of the within-cell (or condition) estimates of variance.

It is clear from Table 14.13 and Figure 14.4 that there is an interaction between the race of the source and the level of prejudice expressed in the statements made by these individuals. This interaction is due to one condition in this experiment, the high-prejudice statements from David Duke. That one condition produced the statistically significant interaction and the two statistically significant main effects in this experiment. Given that the other three cell means are all close to each other, we have to interpret the statistically significant main effects with caution because they are due to the interaction. Therefore, when interpreting the results of this experiment, we need to focus on the interaction and not the main effects.

In experiments such as this one, where there is an interaction, we may want to look closely at **simple effects**, or *the differences among the cell means at each level of one of the*

---

[13] It is important to note that the data used here are derived from Likert-type scales and are thus technically ordinal. ANOVA and other data analytic procedures can deal with any numerical values you choose to analyze, regardless of what they represent, because the equations themselves are not judgmental. It is up to you as the researcher to determine whether the results produced by ANOVA will be useful and meaningful given the nature of your measured variables.

TABLE 14.11 ■ Analysis of Variance Summary Table for a Two-Factor Analysis of Variance With Fixed Effects

Source of Variance	Sums of Squares	Degrees of Freedom	Mean Square	F
A factor	$nb\sum_{i=1}^{a}\left(\bar{Y}_i - \bar{\bar{Y}}\right)^2$	$a-1$	$\dfrac{nb\sum_{i=1}^{a}\left(\bar{Y}_i - \bar{\bar{Y}}\right)^2}{a-1}$	$\dfrac{MS_A}{MS_{\text{Within cell}}}$
B factor	$na\sum_{j=1}^{b}\left(\bar{Y}_j - \bar{\bar{Y}}\right)^2$	$b-1$	$\dfrac{na\sum_{j=1}^{b}\left(\bar{Y}_j - \bar{\bar{Y}}\right)^2}{b-1}$	$\dfrac{MS_B}{MS_{\text{Within cell}}}$
AB interaction	$n\sum_{i=1}^{a}\sum_{j=1}^{b}\left(\bar{Y}_{ij} - \bar{Y}_i - \bar{Y}_j + \bar{\bar{Y}}\right)^2$	$(a-1)(b-1)$	$\dfrac{n\sum_{i=1}^{a}\sum_{j=1}^{b}\left(\bar{Y}_{ij} - \bar{Y}_i - \bar{Y}_j + \bar{\bar{Y}}\right)^2}{(a-1)(b-1)}$	$\dfrac{MS_{AB}}{MS_{\text{Within cell}}}$
Within cell	$\sum_{i=1}^{a}\sum_{j=1}^{b}\sum_{k=1}^{n}\left(Y_{ijk} - \bar{Y}_{ij}\right)^2$	$ab(n-1)$	$\dfrac{\sum_{i=1}^{a}\sum_{j=1}^{b}\sum_{k=1}^{n}\left(Y_{ijk} - \bar{Y}_{ij}\right)^2}{ab(n-1)}$	
Total	$\sum_{i=1}^{a}\sum_{j=1}^{b}\sum_{k=1}^{n}\left(Y_{ijk} - \bar{\bar{Y}}\right)^2$	$abn-1$		

TABLE 14.12 ■ Table of Means for the Sharp et al. (2004) Experiment Arranged as a Two-Factor Experiment			
	Race of Source of Statements		
	White	**Black**	**Row Means**
High-prejudice statements	13.60	5.85	9.73
Low-prejudice statements	4.17	4.85	4.51
Column means	8.89	5.36	7.12 ($\bar{\bar{Y}}$)

main effects. We do this by looking across all levels of one of the factors while holding the other factor constant at one of its levels. There are a number of ways to test simple effects. The easiest is to look at the mean diamonds. The difference is statistically significant when the overlap bars do not overlap, as is the case with the difference between the mean reactions to the low- versus high-prejudice statements when the source is held constant at White, as shown on the left of Figure 14.4. On the other hand, the overlap bars do overlap for the reactions to the low- versus high-prejudice statements when the source is held constant at Black. Therefore the level of prejudice effect is significant when the source is White, but not when the source is Black, and it is this differential pattern among the simple effects that explains the significant interaction.

Another way to test for simple effects is to perform a one-factor analysis of variance for all levels of one of the factors at each level of the other factor, but using the $MS_{\text{Within cell}}$ as the error term.[14] In the experiment under consideration here, $F(1, 108) = 57.757$ for the difference in the means between the levels of prejudice holding the source constant at White, and $F(1, 108) = 0.650$ for the difference between the levels of prejudice holding the source constant at Black. In both cases, the critical value of $F = 3.929$ for $\alpha = .05$. This outcome confirms the picture given by the mean diamonds, with the level of prejudice only reaching significance when the source of the statement is White.

In summary, how participants responded to the statements in terms of their experiences of negative self-directed affect (e.g., guilt) depended on both the race of the source and the prejudice level of the statement. When the source was Black, the participants, who were White, did not show different levels of negative affect. However, when the source was White, the participants who were exposed to a high-prejudice

---

[14] We use $MS_{\text{Within cell}}$ as the error term because it is the average of the within cell variances for all groups in the experiment. It is therefore based on more observations and provides a better estimate of the population variance. When the assumption of homogeneity of variance is met, this produces a more powerful test than if we used only the data from the cells at the level being tested.

TABLE 14.3 ■ Analysis of Variance Summary Table for the Sharp et al. (2004) Experiment Analyzed as a 2-Factor Experiment							
Source of Variance	Sums of Squares	Degrees of Freedom	Mean Square	F	p	η^2	Expected MS
Race of source	350.03	1	350.03	16.24	<.0001	.131	$\sigma_\varepsilon^2 + \sigma_\alpha^2$
Level of prejudice	761.29	1	761.29	35.32	<.0001	.246	$\sigma_\varepsilon^2 + \sigma_\beta^2$
Race × Level	497.29	1	497.29	23.07	<.0001	.176	$\sigma_\varepsilon^2 + \sigma_{\alpha\beta}^2$
Within cell	2,327.64	108	21.55				σ_ε^2
Total	3,936.25						

statement felt higher levels of negative affect than did those participants who were exposed to a low-prejudice statement. These results suggest that when a member of one's own racial group expresses prejudice, which is often (rightfully) considered socially inappropriate, the individual will internalize some degree of negative self-directed affect; that is, the individual feels guilty for the bad behavior of the in-group member. These results have implications for theories of social identity and responses to norm violations.

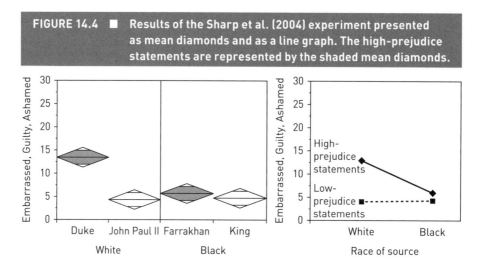

FIGURE 14.4 ■ Results of the Sharp et al. (2004) experiment presented as mean diamonds and as a line graph. The high-prejudice statements are represented by the shaded mean diamonds.

DEALING WITH UNEQUAL SAMPLE SIZES IN FACTORIAL DESIGNS

The procedures we described above for factorial experiments are only appropriate when all of the groups in our experiment have the same sample size. This situation is called a balanced design. We present one way to analyze data from an unbalanced design in the next chapter.

In the Barlett (2015) experiment described in Chapters 1 and 7 and at the beginning of this chapter, his treatment was message content, and he looked at whether message content (nice or insulting) had different effects on levels of hostility as measured by the State Hostility Scale (SHS). His sample included both men and women. We can use analysis of variance to investigate the effects of both message content and gender and whether the effects of message content are the same or different for men and women (see Table 14.14).

In Table 14.14, there are two types of factors: experimental treatments and classification variables.[15] **Experimental treatments** are *the independent variables in our experiment.* **Classification variables** consist of *groups of individuals who have the same characteristics* (e.g., men and women). Sometimes we are interested in the differences between the levels of the classification factors, but a common use of classification factors is to remove any variance within the dependent variable for each experimental treatment that is due to the classification variable. This procedure usually reduces the within-cell variance (mean

TABLE 14.14 ■ A Factorial Design for Studying the Effects of Message Content and Gender on the Dependent Variable (SHS score) in the Experiment			
	Message Content		
	Insulting Messages	**Nice Messages**	**Totals**
Women	40 women received Insulting messages	26 women received Nice messages	Total # women = 66
Men	14 men received Insulting messages	17 men received Nice messages	Total # men = 31
Totals	Total # receiving Insulting message = 54	Total # receiving Nice message = 43	

---

[15] It is common to refer to *the individual factors in a factorial experiment* as the **main effects**.

square error), which can increase the power of the *F*-test to detect different effects of the experimental treatments.

In Barlett (2015), the numbers of men and women in each condition are not equal, thereby producing complications for analyzing and interpreting the data. The problem arises because, unlike the situation where there are equal sample sizes in the AB combinations, as described in the previous section, the variation among the means for the A factor and the means of the B factor are *not* independent of each other. In other words, *when the sample sizes are equal, increasing the differences between the A means does not have an effect on the variation of the B means.* This situation is called a **balanced design**. When there are unequal sample sizes in each cell, increasing the differences between the A means affects the variation of B means. Therefore, the procedures described in this chapter will work only for factorial designs with equal sample sizes in all cells. We need to use other procedures to analyze the data in an **unbalanced design**. Those procedures are the focus of the next chapter.

Summary

We can use analysis of variance to analyze the effects of two or more treatments as well as to analyze the effects of combinations of treatments (factorial experiments). Factorial experiments also allow us to explore whether there are interactions among the various factors.

Analysis of variance is based on comparing two estimates of variance by way of an *F*-ratio. When the null hypothesis is true, both the numerator and denominator of an *F*-ratio are estimating the same thing (the variance of the populations [error variance]). When the null hypothesis is false, the numerator is estimating both the error variance and the treatment effects.

We use a relational measure to estimate the size of the treatment effects when we have more than two conditions in our experiments. The most common measures are eta squared (η^2), epsilon squared (ε^2), and omega squared (ω^2). While all three overestimate the population effect size, ω^2 is the most conservative and is therefore the most commonly used.

We can also use the randomization model when we are concerned that the assumptions underlying analysis of variance are not met or when there are outliers in our data that compromise the power of analysis of variance. This is a straightforward extension of the procedures for exact and approximate randomization tests for treatment effects described in Chapter 9.

Analysis of variance allows us to analyze the effects of two or more sets of factors applied at the same time to participants. An important advantage of this type of experimental design is that it allows us to investigate whether there are interactions among the factors in our experiment.

In all single factor and factorial between-groups experiments, the error term is always the average of the estimates of the within-groups variances. This is true even when the sample sizes are not equal. However, we need to use a different approach for finding the mean squares between groups when the sample sizes are not equal. We will describe this procedure in the next chapter.

Conceptual Exercises

1. Explain why individuals, both within and between groups, may differ on their scores on a dependent variable.

2. How are variances estimated within and between groups? How are these two variances compared to test the null hypothesis that there are no mean differences between groups?

3. Explain the differences between a fixed-effects model and a random effects model.

4. When is power increased for the *F*-test in analysis of variance? Explain your answer.

5. Describe and compare the three most commonly used measures of relational effect size for the analysis of variance.

6. Suppose that you perform an experiment in which you test how well students in research methods courses learn data analytic procedures after engaging with the material in different ways. You randomly assign each of 200 participants to one of four groups. Group 1 only reads about the data analytic procedures. Group 2 only completes an online tutorial on the procedures. Group 3 both reads about the procedures and completes the online tutorial. Group 4 is a control group that neither reads about the data analytic procedures nor completes the online tutorial.

   It is possible to get a statistically significant result here (especially given the rather large sample sizes), even though the different methods of processing the words might not have very different effects.

   a. What are the experimental hypotheses in this experiment? What are the statistical hypotheses?

   b. What criterion would we use to decide which hypothesis is true? (Note: The answer is *not p* < .05.)

   c. We know that if the null hypothesis is false, the *p*-value decreases as sample size increases. Therefore, the *p*-value does not measure the size of the treatment effect. What is the appropriate measure for the size of the treatment effect here? Why does this measure not suffer from the same problem as the *p*-value when sample size increases?

   d. Suppose the proportion of variance explained here is small. Should we be concerned about the importance of the result? Why or why not?

   e. What do we mean when we say that the results of this experiment are "statistically significant"?

7. In an analysis of variance, why should the *F*-ratio be much greater than 1 when the null hypothesis is false?

8. What does it mean to say that we have an interaction between two of the factors in our study? How do interactions differ from main effects? How do ordinal interactions differ from disordinal interactions?

9. Describe the structural models for the one-factor and two-factor versions of the analysis of variance.

10. Imagine that you conducted a study to examine the effects of the gender of a performer (identifying as female or male), the type of task completed (stereotypically feminine or stereotypically masculine), and these variables' interaction on the mean attribution score for how skilled an observer perceived the performer to be. Use the graphs in Figure 14.5 to estimate the possible effects for each of three sets of hypothetical results you may have found in your study. For each set of results, answer these questions and explain why or why not:

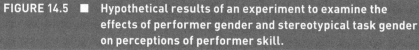

FIGURE 14.5 ■ Hypothetical results of an experiment to examine the effects of performer gender and stereotypical task gender on perceptions of performer skill.

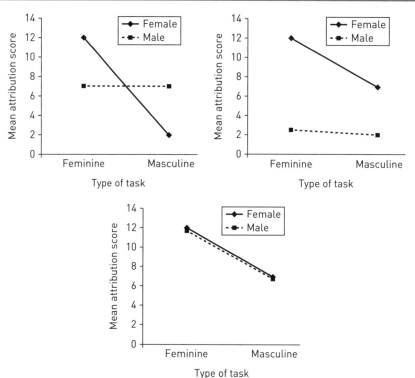

a. Is there evidence for a main effect of the gender of performer?

b. Is there evidence for a main effect of the type of task?

c. Is there evidence for an interaction between the gender of performer and the type of task?

11. How does a factorial design allow us to separate the effects of two (or more) independent variables that are present in the same research study?

12. We make three assumptions in ANOVA: one about the form of the populations from which the data are presumably sampled, one about the variances of these populations, and one about the relationships among the scores in these samples.

a. What are the consequences of violating these assumptions?

b. Briefly, what should one do when each of these are violated and why?

13. Complete Table 14.15 by calculating the degrees of freedom, means squares, and F-values for each effect and generating the $E(MS)$ for each effect. Then perform the appropriate F-tests to determine which effects

are statistically significant. There are three levels of variable A, four levels of variable B, five levels of variable C, and four participants in each cell. Variables A and B are random, and variable C is fixed.

14. In a two-factor experiment, what problem can arise if you have an unequal number of scores in each AB combination (i.e., in each cell of the combinations of your two factors)?

TABLE 14.15 ■ Source Table for the Main Effects and Interaction Effects of Three Variables

Source	SS	df	MS	F	E(MS)
A	864				
$B(A)$	504				
C	468				
CA	120				
$CB(A)$	608				
$S(ABC)$	3,420				

Student Study Site

Visit the Student Study Site at **https://study.sagepub.com/friemanstats** for a variety of useful tools including data sets, additional exercises, and web resources.

15

MULTIPLE REGRESSION AND BEYOND

To this point, we have discussed how various analytic techniques can be applied to data to test hypotheses and draw conclusions. In Chapters 10 to 12, we explored how we use correlation and regression to describe the relationship between two continuous variables (that is, variables that can take on any value within their range of coverage) and to test hypotheses about these relationships in populations. In Chapters 7 and 14, we discussed how to test hypotheses about population means. In these situations, the independent variables are categorical (that is, they consist of discrete categories, such as experimental conditions). In Chapter 13, we saw that hypothesis tests about differences among population means and hypothesis tests on population correlations are two sides of the same coin; that is, when we test the null hypothesis that the population means are the same, we are also testing the null hypothesis that the population correlation between the independent variable and the dependent variable is equal to 0. In this chapter, we will expand the discussion to include ways to examine how multiple variables, both categorical and continuous, can be used, individually and together, to predict the values of dependent variables.

In Chapter 11, we discussed the results of a study by McManus, Feyes, and Saucier (2011) in which they assessed factors that they predicted would be associated with prejudicial attitudes toward individuals with intellectual disabilities. These factors included the quantity of contact their participants had with individuals with intellectual disabilities, the quality of that contact, and the amount of knowledge the participants thought they possessed about intellectual disabilities. Each of these factors was represented by scores averaged across the relevant items that could range from 1 to 9, with higher scores indicating higher levels of quantity of contact, quality of contact, and knowledge, respectively. The researchers used the Mental Retardation Attitude Inventory–Revised (MRAI-R; Antonak & Harth, 1994) as their measure of prejudice. Participants used response scales from 1 (*strongly disagree*) to 9 (*strongly agree*) to report their agreement with statements such as *The child who has an intellectual disability should be integrated into regular classes at school*. Participants' responses were averaged, with higher scores reflecting more positive (i.e., less prejudicial) attitudes toward individuals with intellectual disabilities. In Chapter 11, we confined our examination of the McManus et al. (2011) data to their results regarding quality of contact as a predictor of prejudicial attitudes. In Chapter 12, we discussed the possibility of including the additional factors as predictors of prejudicial attitudes. In this chapter, we will do just that, by using multiple regression to examine how quality of contact, quantity of contact, and knowledge predict, individually and in combination, participants' levels of prejudicial attitudes toward individuals with intellectual disabilities.

We will now expand our discussion of ways to analyze data by focusing on an approach that is common to many techniques, and we will describe how that approach is used generally in discovering the stories in data. We will focus less on specific techniques and how they are conducted, and instead provide an overview of an overarching method of examining data that provides the foundation for multiple regression in both its simpler and more complex forms. Our discussion here will be focused at the overview level, because it is beyond the scope of this textbook to do these techniques justice at the level of detail with which we have treated earlier techniques. In fact, there are entire textbooks devoted to the information we will dip into in this chapter. Therefore, it will be our intention to illustrate multiple regression more conceptually than mathematically and to focus more on what it may offer as a technique in terms of the questions it can address than on its operations.

The objective of all research is to collect information about the relationships between and among interesting variables and to use that information to help us understand how some of these variables affect other variables. The analytic approach to this goal is to assess the direction and magnitude of relationships among variables and to build predictive models that summarize these relationships. These models take the form of equations constructed to predict some outcome (or criterion) variable using the information provided by one or more predictor variables. Such models include the structural equations in regression (see Chapter 11) and analysis of variance (see Chapter 14). We can tie these two approaches together through the general linear model (GLM).

OVERVIEW OF THE GENERAL LINEAR MODEL APPROACH

The general linear model (GLM) is an approach to data analysis in which we construct predictive equations using predictor and criterion variables of any type. We can apply this universal approach to almost any type of data.

The GLM is a universal approach to data analysis that allows for multiple predictors of virtually any type (categorical or continuous) as well as multiple dependent measures of any type (categorical or continuous). The various combinations of predictor and criterion variables give birth to the various specific techniques and procedures that we use to analyze our data from different research designs. The simplest use of the GLM to analyze data is simple regression (both linear and nonlinear), where there is one continuous variable for the predictor and one continuous variable for the criterion. Multiple regression involves more than one predictor, and the predictors can be both continuous and categorical variables. As we saw in Chapter 13, the *t*-test can be conceptualized as a correlation between a single categorical predictor that has only two levels and a dependent variable (criterion) that is a continuous variable. We use the one-factor analysis of variance when the single categorical predictor has more than two levels and the higher-order analysis of variance where there is more than one categorical predictor. Furthermore, the analysis of variance can be extended to situations in which some of the predictors are continuous variables and where more than one dependent variable is simultaneously analyzed. The GLM provides us with a common conceptual basis to assess these relationships among variables and to evaluate how much information our predictors provide for our criterion variables.

With the GLM approach, the relationships among predictor and criterion variables are evaluated using equations in which criterion variables are estimated by the values of the predictor variables weighted by the strength of their relationships with the criterion variables. Stronger predictive models are composed of predictors that account for greater levels of explained variance in the criterion variable(s). The strength of the predictive model is assessed by looking at the relationship between the values the predictive model estimates for the criterion variable(s) and the actual value of the criterion variable(s).

Each predictor is added into the equation that estimates the value of the criterion variable(s) and is evaluated for its own contribution to that estimation. Predictors entered into the equation may take the form of individual predictor variables, but they may also take the form of polynomials (e.g., a squared or cubed variable to test for relationships between predictors and criteria that may take quadratic or cubic functions, respectively) or product terms (e.g., to carry the interaction between two or more predictor variables). But the logic is the same; each predictor is entered into the equation and is tested for its ability to improve the estimation of the criterion(s). When the predictor does not contribute to this estimation, the weight of its effect (i.e., its slope) will be close to zero, and researchers consequently may decide to eliminate this predictor from the equation.

There are many ways to construct these equations, depending on the decisions we make as a researcher. For instance, how we decide to prioritize our predictor variables as we use them to account for variance in our criterion variable(s) will change the procedure that we choose. We will now consider how these general principles manifest in regression.

REGRESSION

We can use regression to test how well our predictor variables predict our criterion variables, both individually and as sets.

Regression is a technique that allows researchers to test how well predictor variables, individually and collectively, account for variance in criterion variables. It allows for much more flexibility in how researchers build their models and conduct their tests than typically would be allowed by techniques such as the analysis of variance (ANOVA). As such, regression provides more opportunities for researchers to examine their research questions and test their hypotheses using variables of different types and predictors of many forms.

ANOVA allows for main effects of categorical predictors, and interactions between them, to be tested in terms of their ability to account for variance in a dependent measure. Main effects (i.e., the ability of a predictor to account for variance in a dependent measure independently of the other predictors) and interactions (i.e., situations in which a predictor's relationship with the dependent variable changes at different levels of the other predictor(s)) are undeniably important and frequently interesting. However, other types of effects also may be important and interesting. Accordingly, techniques beyond ANOVA must be considered to explore and assess the predictive value of variables that consist not of categorical levels or groups but along continua.

ANOVA assesses how categorical predictors account for variance in a dependent measure. Only categorical predictors may be used, which is fine when the predictors of interest are naturally categorical. But when predictors are not categorical, researchers may not simply plug them into ANOVA. There are techniques that researchers have used to convert their predictors that fall on some sort of continuum into categorical predictors (whether or not the predictors are truly continuous). This approach is a bad idea (see Box 15.1).

SIMPLE VERSUS MULTIPLE REGRESSION

We can use simple regression to test how well a single predictor variable predicts a criterion variable. We can use multiple regression to test how well more than one predictor variable predicts a criterion variable.

As we saw in Chapter 11, simple regression is a technique in which researchers use only one predictor variable to estimate the value of the criterion variable. The resulting regression equation contains a slope that represents the relationship between the predictor variable and the criterion variable, as well as an intercept that provides the predicted value of the criterion when the predictor's value is zero. While it is important to assess the relationship

BOX 15.1
WHY MEDIAN SPLITS ARE A BAD IDEA

Median splits result when *researchers take predictor values along a continuum and recode them into "low" and "high" groups depending on whether the values are below or above the middle score of the predictor's distribution, respectively.* While this technique allows researchers to use ANOVA with a predictor that has been measured on a continuous scale by producing convenient group means to compare, this technique is fundamentally flawed.

One big problem with median splits is that they produce groups that are not really groups. Median splits, which are often performed on data that are at least approximately normally distributed, treat every member of the "low" group as equally low and every member of the "high" group as equally high on the construct of interest. Thus, the precision of measurement that shows that some scores are very low, while others are moderately low, and still others are barely low (i.e., just below the median value) is completely lost. This loss of precision is mirrored in the scores comprising the "high" group. Further, all scores in the "low" group are treated as if they are categorically different from all scores in the "high" group, which is especially problematic for scores just below and just above the median. These scores will be closer in value to each other than they will be to the more extreme values in their own groups. And given an approximately normal distribution, there will be many scores in these situations, meaning that the assumption that different groups comprise the data on the distribution is patently false. Not only is this loss of precision

of measurement, and consequent creation of artificial groups, suboptimal, but it is also unnecessary, as we will discuss later.

Another problem with median splits is that they are associated with the commission of errors in hypothesis testing. First, because of the artificiality of the group assignments created by the large proportions of scores just below and just above the median value, the tests of group differences (at the main effect level) are often underpowered. This situation results in higher rates of type II errors, by which researchers fail to show that the predictor variables account for variance in the criterion. Second, median splits may produce spurious interaction effects (i.e., type I errors), which could result in researchers reporting conclusions that are unlikely to be replicated in future research. Such results could inspire not only the researchers themselves to chase these false effects in their future studies but also others to undertake these unachievable quests.

It then should come as no surprise that researchers find different effects and come to different conclusions when they conduct ANOVAs with median split predictor groups than when researchers conduct regression analyses with the predictors left on their original continuous scales in the same data sets. Given the legacy that comes from the findings that researchers produce, researchers should be motivated to employ the most precise and reliable techniques at their disposal. And with continuous predictors, regression is the more precise and reliable option.

between the predictor and the criterion, that same information can be provided by a correlation coefficient. In fact, the value of the standardized regression coefficient (i.e., the slope of the simple regression line when the predictor and criterion variables are computed as z-scores) equals the value of the correlation coefficient for the relationship between the predictor and criterion.

Regression Line Equations

The **unstandardized regression equation** is $Y' = BX + A$. In this equation, Y' is the value of the criterion estimated by the regression line, and B is the **unstandardized regression coefficient**, or the **slope of the regression line** that indicates the degree of relationship between Y and X. Specifically, this value is the amount that Y will change for each one-unit increase in the value of X, which is the predictor variable. A is the **Y-intercept**, or value of Y when the value of X is zero. In Chapter 11 (Equations 11.2 and 11.3), we saw that $B = r\dfrac{s_Y}{s_X}$ and $A = \overline{Y} - r\dfrac{s_Y}{s_X}\overline{X}$.

The applications of GLM in this chapter will use the **standardized regression equation**, *where the predictor's and criterion's values are converted to z-scores*. This conversion is given in Box 15.2.

In the standardized regression equation z'_Y is the value of the standardized criterion estimated by the regression line. Although the slope of the standardized regression equation is the Pearson r, it is common to use the symbol β for that slope. Therefore, β is the **standardized regression coefficient**, or **slope of the standardized regression line**. This value is the amount that z'_Y will change, in standard deviation units, for each one standard deviation increase in the value of z_X. Again, the value of β represents the degree and direction of relationship between the predictor and criterion. Further, in simple regression, the value of β will equal the value of the zero-order correlation coefficient (r). The intercept for the standardized regression line will always equal zero, because the

BOX 15.2
THE STANDARDIZED REGRESSION EQUATION

Starting with the unstandardized regression equation $Y' = \left(\overline{Y} - r\dfrac{s_Y}{s_X}\overline{X}\right) + r\dfrac{s_Y}{s_X}X$, subtract $\overline{Y}$ from both sides to yield $Y' - \overline{Y} = -r\dfrac{s_Y}{s_X}\overline{X} + r\dfrac{s_Y}{s_X}X$.

Divide both sides by s_Y and rearrange the remaining terms on the right to yield the following:

$$\frac{Y' - \overline{Y}}{s_Y} = r\frac{\left(X - \overline{X}\right)}{s_X}$$

Standard scores are $\dfrac{\text{score} - \text{mean}}{\text{standard deviation}}$.

Therefore, $z'_Y = rz'_X$ is the standardized regression equation.

regression line will always pass through (and rotate on) the *point represented by the mean of the predictor and the mean of the criterion* (also known as the **centroid**). When the predictor and criterion are standardized as *z*-scores, these means must equal zero.

Given that the standardized regression coefficient is equal to the *r* value of the relationship between *X* and *Y*, calculating the unstandardized regression coefficient and the unstandardized regression line is simply a matter of converting the *z*-scores back to their original scales.[1]

For the McManus et al. (2011) data, the unstandardized regression line using quality of contact (represented by *Qual*) to estimate the levels of prejudice (represented by *Prej*) is as follows:

$$Prej' = 0.35Qual + 4.41$$

The standardized regression line is this:

$$z'_{prej} = 0.62z_{Qual}$$

Here the standardized regression coefficient (which equals the zero-order correlation) indicates that there is a positive relationship between participants' reported quality of contact with individuals with intellectual disabilities and their more positive (less prejudicial) attitudes toward individuals with intellectual disabilities.

Advantages of Simple Regression

There are a few advantages to simple regression beyond the information that would be provided by a correlation coefficient. First, simple regression allows researchers to explicitly identify one of their variables as a predictor and the other as a criterion (or outcome). This distinction is important in terms of theory building and hypothesis testing. And while the extent to which researchers may draw causal conclusions about the relationships among their variables depends on the design of the research study, simple regression provides results in a form that facilitates the discussion of the variables in the context of theory.

Second, simple regression allows for the estimation of values for the criterion based on specified values for the predictor. Third, not trivially, simple regression allows for a more direct illustration of how regression techniques fit within the general linear model. Simple regression directly produces the information needed to create the line equations that are the foundation of the GLM. This point illustrates nicely the linearity and additivity

---

[1] It should be noted that unstandardized and standardized regression lines and coefficients carry the same information. The only difference is that the unstandardized regression lines and coefficients will be reported on the variables' original measurement scales, while the standardized regression lines and coefficients will be reported with the variables converted to *z*-scores. Standardized regression coefficients often are the preferred values for reporting these relationships due to removal of scaling differences among variables.

components of the GLM and provides a good basis for understanding more complicated techniques within the GLM.

MULTIPLE REGRESSION

There is a natural extension from simple regression to multiple regression. Rarely is it the case that we, as researchers, are satisfied to investigate only one predictor as a source of information in estimating the value of a criterion. More often, we envision multiple factors as explanations for their outcome variables, and we are eager to use them to collectively predict as much variance as they can in the outcomes. Further, we are eager to pit the predictors against each other in a "statistical cage match" to see which of them can account for the most unique variance in the prediction, which is where multiple regression shines as an approach.

Simple regression produces a line equation to estimate the criterion with only one predictor added into the equation. Multiple regression produces a very similar line equation to estimate the criterion with more than one predictor added into the line equation. The values that are produced provide both an assessment of the collective predictor value of the model and an assessment of the individual predictors in accounting for unique variance in the criterion.

The unstandardized regression line equation that uses two predictors (X_1 and X_2) to estimate Y would be given as follows:

$$Y' = B_1 X_1 + B_2 X_2 + A \tag{15.1}$$

And the standardized regression line equation that uses two predictors (X_1 and X_2) to estimate Y would be this:

$$Z'_Y = \beta_1 Z_{X_1} + \beta_2 Z_{X_2} \tag{15.2}$$

Prediction by the Overall Model

The predictive value of the model overall is indicated by R and R^2 values. R is the multiple correlation coefficient, and it represents the value of the relationship between the values of Y as they are estimated by the predictors using the regression line equation (i.e., $\hat{Y}$) and the actual values of Y. Because it is not possible for a regression line equation to predict values of Y that would be negatively correlated with the actual values of Y, the value of R varies from 0 (indicating that the estimated values of Y are completely unrelated to the actual values of Y) to 1 (indicating that the estimated values of Y are perfectly related to the actual values of Y). The value of R (when estimating the value of Y using two predictors, X_1 and X_2) would be calculated using this equation:

$$R = \sqrt{\frac{r_{YX_1}^2 + r_{YX_2}^2 - 2r_{YX_1}r_{YX_2}r_{X_1X_2}}{1 - r_{X_1X_2}^2}} \qquad (15.3)$$

Squaring the value of R to produce R^2 should provide a value representing the total amount of variance in Y that is predicted by the model containing the predictors; however, there are a number of problems with simply using R^2 to estimate the explained variance. First, as was noted in Chapter 10, the $E(r)$ is a biased estimate of ρ, because the fit to the data is optimized for the sample that produced the regression line equation and, logically, would be expected to generalize less well to any other sample. The same idea is true with R. Second, adding more predictors will almost always increase the value of R, and this effect is most pronounced when the sample size is small. To deal with these problems, we use the **adjusted R^2** (or **shrunken R^2**):

$$\text{adjusted } R^2 = 1 - \left(1 - R^2\right)\frac{n-1}{n-k-1}, \qquad (15.4)$$

where n refers to the sample size and k refers to the number of predictors in the model.

This equation clearly shows that the correction is greater with smaller sample sizes, which makes sense given that fewer members of the population would be contributing to the regression line equation, and in particular that the correction is greater as the ratio of predictors to sample size increases.

Prediction by the Individual Predictors

The regression coefficients provide an assessment of the unique predictive value of each of the predictors in accounting for variance in the criterion that is not accounted for by the other predictors in the model. This assessment is done by removing the overlapping variance the predictors share with each other in estimating the criterion in the calculation of these regression coefficients. This approach is illustrated in the equations given below for the standardized and unstandardized regression coefficients for X_1. The process could be repeated to calculate the regression coefficients for X_2 by simply reversing the positions of X_1 and X_2 in these equations.

To calculate the standardized regression coefficient for X_1, use this equation:

$$\beta_1 = \frac{r_{YX_1} - r_{YX_2}r_{X_1X_2}}{1 - r_{X_1X_2}^2} \qquad (15.5)$$

The unstandardized coefficient for X_1 simply converts the predictor back to its original scale:

$$B_1 = \beta_1 \, \frac{s_Y}{s_{X_1}} \tag{15.6}$$

It is clear in the equations above how the relationship between X_1, for instance, and the other predictor X_2, as well as the relationship between X_2 and the criterion Y, are **partialled out** in assessing the unique relationship between X_1 and Y. What is left is the value of the relationship between X_1 and Y, in this case, that can only be attributed to X_1 (i.e., not to X_1's overlap with X_2). Stated differently, this value reflects the relationship of X_1 and Y *above and beyond* X_2.

In the McManus et al. (2011) study, the researchers tested a model that used the three predictors of quality of contact, quantity of contact, and knowledge to estimate the participants' levels of prejudice. Each of these predictors was correlated significantly with participants' MRAI-R scores, and the predictors each correlated with each other:

Quality–Quantity	$r = .54$	Quality–MRAI-R	$r = .62$
Quality–Knowledge	$r = .55$	Quantity–MRAI-R	$r = .34$
Quantity–Knowledge	$r = .58$	Knowledge–MRAI-R	$r = .34$

This model produced an R value equal to .62. This value indicates the degree of correlation between the participants' actual scores on the MRAI-R and the MRAI-R scores predicted for the participants based on their levels of quality of contact, quantity of contact, and knowledge. The R^2 value of .39 indicated the amount of variance that these three predictors accounted for in MRAI-R scores, and the adjusted R^2 value of .37 indicated how much variance in MRAI-R scores these three predictors would be expected to account for in the population.

The unstandardized regression line for this model is as follows:

$$Prej' = 0.36Qual + 0.02Quan - 0.02Know + 4.34$$

And here is the standardized regression line for this model:

$$Z'_{Prej} = 0.62Z_{Qual} + 0.03Z_{Quan} - 0.03Z_{Know}$$

As McManus et al. (2011) reported, only the regression coefficient for the participants' quality of contact reached significance as a unique predictor of participants' MRAI-R scores when the other predictors were also included in the model. This result indicates that while quantity of contact and knowledge had significant zero-order correlations with the participants' MRAI-R scores, neither of those variables provided explanation for the variance of the participants' MRAI-R scores that was not already accounted for by the other variable or by the participants' quality of contact.

TYPES OF MULTIPLE REGRESSION

There are several ways in which we can use regression models to test the value of multiple predictors. These approaches differ in terms of how the predictors are given the opportunity to account for variance in the criterion.

Typically, researchers will examine the zero-order correlations between their predictors and criterion prior to building a multiple regression model, generally including only those predictors that were correlated with the criterion in building that multiple regression model. This approach is usually a logical course of action (unless the researchers are hypothesizing suppression effects, which are not common), and because the researchers do not need to use degrees of freedom from the error terms to test predictors of little value, it results in more powerful analyses. Further, leaving out the unrelated predictors reduces the possibility that relationships among the predictors could produce stronger (but often theoretically meaningless) relationships in the regression model than were shown in the zero-order correlations as the partitioning of shared variance is performed. Leaving these unrelated predictors out of the multiple regression, then, provides some control for the possibility of type I errors.

Simultaneous Regression

Researchers use **simultaneous regression** *to use more than one predictor to estimate the criterion while entering each of the predictors into the model (and regression equation) at the same time.* In this technique, each predictor is given an equal opportunity to account for variance in the criterion. None of the predictors is given an advantage, or put at a disadvantage, in terms of its ability to account for variance in the criterion. Simultaneous regression allows researchers to determine how well the set of predictors accounts for variance in the criterion overall. But simultaneous regression also allows researchers to determine how well each individual predictor accounts for a *unique* portion of the variance in the criterion *above and beyond* that offered by the other predictors. That is, researchers can assess how much they need each individual predictor to maximize their prediction of the criterion. It may be that predictors are associated with the criterion in such a way that they account for the same variance in the criterion due to the relationships that exist among the predictors themselves. This degree of relationship among the predictors can mean that there is **redundancy** *in their subsequent overlap with the criterion*, and the researchers may not then need all of the predictors in the model.

Stepwise Regression

Researchers use **stepwise regression** *to build predictive models based on the empirical relationships that emerge between the predictors and the criterion, rather than on theoretical* *relationships that may be hypothesized by the researchers.* The purpose here is to refine the predictive model so that it contains only the predictors that it needs to maximize the prediction of the criterion and leaves out those predictors that fail to offer unique prediction of variance in the criterion. **Backward stepwise regression** *may be conducted by first entering all of the possible predictors into the model and then trimming the model down.* In the trimming process, the weakest unique predictor is removed from the model, and the model's consequent ability to account for variance in the criterion is assessed. If the model is not significantly reduced in terms of its ability to account for variance in the criterion, then the next weakest unique predictor is removed, and the process continues. The trimming stops when removing the predictor would significantly decrease the model's overall ability to account for variance in the criterion. Conversely, **forward stepwise regression** *adds variables into the predictive model one at a time, starting with the strongest unique predictor.* The model's consequent ability to account for the variance in the criterion is assessed. If the addition of the predictor to the model significantly increases the model's ability to account for variance in the criterion, then the next strongest unique predictor is added. The process continues until the addition of the next strongest predictor fails to significantly strengthen the model's ability to account for variance in the criterion.

One of the disadvantages of stepwise regression is that its process is not optimal for testing specific hypotheses. It builds models based on empirical, not theoretical, relationships.

Stepwise regression is a good technique for optimizing the model to account for variance in the criterion for the sample that produced the data. Its use inferentially, though, is less reliable. Especially when there are high degrees of **multicollinearity** (*relationships among the predictors*), the model and line equation that emerge do not replicate well due to the potential for variability among both the relationships among the predictors and the relationships between the predictors and the criterion. For these reasons, stepwise regression is best used when researchers have more descriptive than inferential objectives (i.e., intending to use the predictive model that emerges only for the sample that produced it), when the analyses are exploratory in nature, and with large samples. If researchers do want to use the model that emerges inferentially, it is important that they replicate the model with another sample. One way to accomplish this objective would be by dividing their initial sample into two groups, then using the first sample in the initial stepwise regression and using the second sample (called a **hold-out sample**) to **cross-validate** the model.

Hierarchical Regression

Possibly the most flexible and exciting of the multiple regression techniques is **hierarchical regression**. Using this technique, researchers may order their predictors, individually or as sets, and allow them to account for variance in the criterion in a prearranged pattern.

This technique allows researchers to build their models in steps, assessing the amount of additional variance that may be explained by the addition of the predictor(s) at each step above and beyond the predictor(s) that have already been entered into the model (given by the change in R^2, or ΔR^2, value). This technique provides the basis for testing for several types of sophisticated patterns of relationships among predictor and criterion variables, including testing for indirect effects, mediation, and curvilinear effects.

There are many ways in which researchers may choose to order their variables in hierarchical regression. For instance, researchers may choose to enter their strongest predictors (i.e., those that have the largest correlation with the criterion, or those that are most theoretically important) first, to give them the best opportunity to account for variance in the criterion. Conversely, researchers may choose to enter *variables they want to control* as **covariates** in the first step(s) and evaluate their more theoretically important variables later, after having eliminated the shared variance with less important or potentially confounding variables. This latter strategy may be used to establish the **incremental validity** of a new measure (i.e., *to show that scores on the new measure account for unique portions of variance in an important criterion even after controlling for existing measures of the same or similar constructs*). By putting the new measure at this obvious disadvantage, the researchers make a compelling case for its use if it still accounts for unique variance in the criterion.

However, what remains constant is that predictors entered into the model at later steps have a disadvantage in accounting for variance in the criterion. This disadvantage is because the predictors at earlier steps have already accounted for some of the criterion's variance and have been assessed for their predictive value with greater power (because, with fewer predictors in the model at that point, more degrees of freedom remain in the error term). Further, the earlier predictors in the model have accounted for, and been credited for, any overlapping prediction they share with predictors entered later in the model. Thus, the guiding rule for hierarchical regression is *"Order is everything."* It is typical for researchers to examine the ability of a predictor to account for unique variance in the criterion only at its point of entry. However, researchers will sometimes, such as when testing for mediation, assess how a predictor's unique predictive value is changed when another predictor is entered later into the model.

Predictors may be entered individually in each step, or they may be entered into the model together as sets. There are two types of sets. **Functional sets** consist of *predictor variables that share a common theme and may be argued to represent aspects of a higher order construct.* For example, researchers could use participants' sex, ethnicity, and age in a functional set of demographic predictors. Or researchers could use participants' scores on the various aspects of the five-factor model of personality (i.e., openness, neuroticism, agreeableness, conscientiousness, and extraversion) in a functional set of personality predictors. This strategy would allow the researchers to examine the predictive ability of the set (e.g., of demographics overall or of personality overall) as well as the unique predictive ability of the individual predictors comprising the sets.

Structural sets consist of *predictor variables that are actually not distinct, but exist only to measure the full range of values for an individual predictor.* An example may be when a researcher measures participants' political affiliation on a categorical measure of Republican (R), Democrat (D), or independent (I). Assigning these three levels values of 1, 2, and 3 would make little sense because there is no obvious order to these groups. Instead the researcher may use $(g - 1)$ dummy variables to represent the categorical predictor in a structural set, where g is equal to the levels of the categorical predictor.[2] This representation scheme might be operationalized like this:

	Dum$_1$ ("R-ness")	*Dum$_2$* ("D-ness")	*Dum$_3$* ("I-ness")
Republicans	1	0	0
Democrats	0	1	0
Independents	0	0	1

In this operationalization, three dummy variables are used to represent the three aspects of political affiliation as the researcher categorized them. The first dummy variable (Dum_1) distinguishes Republicans from the other participants by assigning scores of 1 to the Republicans in the sample and scores of 0 to the Democrats and independents. The second dummy variable (Dum_2) distinguishes Democrats from the other participants by assigning scores of 1 to the Democrats in the sample and scores of 0 to the Republicans and independents. Finally, the third dummy variable (Dum_3) distinguishes independents from the other participants by assigning scores of 1 to the independents in the sample and scores of 0 to the Republicans and Democrats. With this recoding, the researcher then needs only two of these dummy variables to know the political affiliations of the participants. For Dum_1 and Dum_2, for instance, Republicans would receive scores of 1 and 0, Democrats would receive scores of 0 and 1, and independents would receive scores of 0 and 0, respectively. These unique combinations then fully carry the aspects of the three categories that comprise the entirety of the categorical predictor political affiliation.

To evaluate the predictive ability of political affiliation, a structural set containing two of these dummy variables would be entered into the predictive model, and the additional variance accounted for in the criterion by this structural set would indicate the predictive value of political affiliation. Further, the regression coefficients for the individual dummy

---

[2]Given that our categorical variable has three levels, we would then need only two dummy variables to represent the entire range of the variable in the study. We are providing all three possibilities for the dummy variables here because having all three is necessary for making all of the comparisons among the various levels of the dummy-coded categorical variable possible.

variables would test the categorical levels against each other. For instance, if the researcher entered Dum_1 and Dum_2 as the structural set, then the test of the regression coefficient for Dum_1 would test for mean differences between Republicans and independents (referred to as the **zero group**, or **comparison group**, *having received zeros on the scoring of both dummy variables*). Similarly, in this case, the test of the regression coefficient for Dum_2 would test for mean differences between Democrats and independents.

To complete the testing, the researcher would rerun the analysis with either Democrats as the zero group (entering Dum_1 and Dum_3 as the structural set representing political affiliation) or Republicans as the zero group (entering Dum_2 and Dum_3 as the structural set representing political affiliation). Either of these structural sets would allow for the test of mean differences between Republicans and Democrats on the criterion.

It should be noted that this dummy coding may only be used if the categories comprising the categorical predictor are both mutually exclusive and exhaustive. That is, no participant may be in more than one level, and all levels of the categorical predictor must be represented in the dummy coding.[3]

INTERACTIONS IN MULTIPLE REGRESSION

One of the most exciting things that we can do in multiple regression is to test for interactions among our predictors in estimating the values of the criterion. This approach has most often been associated historically with analysis of variance techniques, but analysis of variance restricts us to the use of categorical predictors. Regression sets no such constraints and allows us to test the predictive value of product terms that can carry interactions between continuous variables, between categorical variables, or between categorical and continuous variables.

Testing Interactions in Multiple Regression

The general strategy for testing interactions in multiple regression consists of using hierarchical regression to assess the ability of product terms that carry the interactions between predictors to explain variance in the criterion that is not explained by the individual (main) effects of the predictors. If these product terms significantly improve the predictive model above and beyond the individual effects of the predictors in a design with two predictors, for instance, then researchers can conclude that the relationship between one of the predictors and the criterion is moderated by the other predictor. This design is illustrated as follows:

---

[3]The dummy-coding procedure described here is a general, and common, approach. However, other procedures for coding (such as effects coding, contrast coding, and nonsense coding) do exist for creating sets of variables to carry the levels of categorical predictors and to make comparisons among these levels.

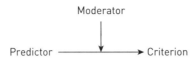

This depiction emphasizes that interactions occur when a moderator is associated with a change in the relationship between a predictor and criterion, rather than impacting the predictor or criterion values directly. In regression, the relationship between the predictor and the criterion is represented as a slope.

The full regression line equation for a model that tests the main effects of and interactions between two predictors (X_1 and X_2) is given below:

$$Y' = B_1 X_1 + B_2 X_2 + B_3 X_1 X_2 + A \tag{15.7}$$

Here the product term $X_1 X_2$ carries the interaction between X_1 and X_2 and tests the interaction $X_1 \times X_2$ when the individual effects of X_1 and X_2 are partialled out. The test of the interaction's significance is provided by the assessment of the R^2 change (or ΔR^2) when the product term is added to the model following the main effects.[4] If the interaction were found to be significant, probing the pattern of effects would be facilitated by reorganizing the equation above so that the criterion is estimated as a function of the predictor variable (rather than of the moderator). For this example, we will identify X_1 as the predictor and X_2 as the moderator to produce the reorganization below:

$$Y' = (B_1 + B_3 X_2) X_1 + (B_2 X_2 + A) \tag{15.8}$$

In this equation, the slope representing the relationship between X_1 and Y' is indicated by $(B_1 + B_3 X_2)$, and the intercept is indicated by $(B_2 X_2 + A)$.

Using Simple Slopes to Probe Interactions

When an interaction occurs, it means that the slope of the regression line that we use to estimate the value of the criterion from the predictor's value will change at different values of the moderator. To assess how this pattern occurs (i.e., how the relationship changes), researchers identify levels of the moderator at which they will hold the moderator's value constant and then calculate the resultant slopes (called **simple slopes**). This procedure is conceptually the same as holding one level of an independent variable constant and assessing the full effect of another independent variable when performing **simple effects** to probe interactions that emerge from ANOVA. Accordingly, different values of X_2 may be inserted into Equation 15.8 to calculate the simple slopes and intercepts of these simple regression equations to see how the relationship between X_1 and Y' varies.

---

[4] To test whether there is a significant increase in R^2, see Equation 12.16 in Chapter 12.

BOX 15.3

GENERAL OVERVIEW OF THE PROCEDURE FOR TESTING INTERACTIONS USING HIERARCHICAL REGRESSION

1. Dummy code any categorical predictors using $g - 1$ dummy variables for each.

2. Center (or standardize) any continuous predictors.

3. Compute the necessary product terms to carry the interactions between any of the predictors for which you wish to test for interaction effects.

4. Enter the main effects of each predictor into the first step(s) of the hierarchical regression either individually or as sets, as dictated by theory and logic. Evaluate the main effect of each predictor using the regression coefficient produced at the step in which the predictor is entered.

5. Enter the product term(s) carrying the interaction(s) among predictors in the step(s) following the entry of those predictors' main effects. Evaluate the interaction effect(s) using the ΔR^2 value for the step(s) at which the product term(s) are entered.

6. Probe the interactions by calculating the simple slopes. The procedure you will choose from those described later in this chapter depends on whether your interaction occurs between categorical variables, between continuous variables, or between categorical and continuous variables.

In Equation 15.8, it is important to notice that the equation simplifies considerably when the value of X_2 is zero:

$$Y' = B_1 X_1 + A$$

This modification facilitates probing immensely. We will discuss this concept more below in the context of testing interactions of varying types of predictors. But before commencing that discussion, we offer two important recommendations to establish the foundation of your process. First, know where your zeros are, both in terms of what the zeros represent in your dummy-coded categorical predictors and what the zeros represent in terms of the values of your continuous predictors. Knowing what the value of zero represents for your moderating variable is the key to probing interactions in regression. Second, know how to (and that you can) move your zeros. Transforming and recoding your X_2 values to have the zero point reflect other levels of X_2 will allow for simple production and interpretation of your simple slopes to probe interactions.

The general strategy above will hold for all forms of interactions in multiple regression. However, testing the various specific combinations of predictors involves a few nuances that deserve a bit more discussion. One caveat prior to proceeding to that discussion: Just because it is possible for us to test interactions between our predictor variables does not mean that we should. Researchers should be judicious in both their research designs and analyses to make sure they are testing effects that make sense to test, such as those that directly test their hypotheses, and are not just fishing in their data.

The procedure for testing interactions using hierarchical regression, described in Box 15.3, applies to the sections that follow.

CONTINUOUS × CONTINUOUS INTERACTIONS

We can use multiple regression techniques to examine how well our continuous predictor variables predict our criterion variable, both individually and interactively.

In estimating the criterion, researchers may easily test interactions between two or more predictors using the procedures described above. Main effects of the predictors are entered in the early steps of a hierarchical regression, either together or in a predetermined order. Following the entry of the main effects, a product term carrying the interaction between the predictors is entered into the model, and the interaction is tested in terms of the unique variance it accounts for in the criterion, above and beyond that predicted by the singular effects of the predictors. Simple slopes are then calculated by solving the equation for one of the predictor variables, identifying the other as the moderator, substituting specific values for the moderator, and examining how the slopes representing the relationship between the predictor and criterion change at different levels of the moderator.

Centering the Predictor Variables

But prior to performing this process, the values of the continuous predictors should be **centered** so that *the mean of each of the continuous predictors equals zero.* Centering is accomplished by subtracting the mean value from each of the continuous predictor's scores. This procedure will not change the values of the continuous variable's relationships with the other predictors or with the criterion. But doing so will provide the dual advantages of reducing the degree of multicollinearity that the predictor's main effect will have with the product term(s) carrying the interaction(s) and of making the simple slopes easier to calculate and interpret, as discussed earlier. Further, standardizing the values of the continuous predictors (i.e., converting them to *z*-scores) has the added advantage of making the standard deviations of the continuous predictors equal 1, aiding in the calculation and interpretation of the simple effects.

Testing the Simple Slopes

Once the continuous predictors are centered (or standardized), the product term(s) to carry the interaction(s) should be calculated using the centered (or standardized) values. If the interaction is significant, simple slopes may be calculated using the procedures described above to probe the interaction. The regression coefficient that accompanies the predictor variable will provide the simple slope, which indicates the relationship between the predictor and criterion when the moderator's value is zero. It would then be necessary to test the simple slope at other specified values of the moderator.

Conventionally, the other values of the moderator to be tested would be a specified value that is objectively low and a specified value that is objectively high. These values are often operationalized to be values of the moderator that are one standard deviation below the mean and one standard deviation above the mean, respectively.[5] When the value of the moderator is standardized, these values are easy to calculate given that the standard deviation equals 1. To move the zero value for the standardized moderator to 1 standard deviation above the mean, a value of 1 is subtracted from all values of the moderator. To move the zero value for the standardized moderator to 1 standard deviation below the mean, a value of 1 is added to all values of the moderator. Thus, the general rule is that moving the zero value to a specified value of the moderator is performed by subtracting the specified value from all values of the standardized moderator. In the case above, in which we would add a value of 1 to all values of the moderator to move the zero to 1 standard deviation below the mean (to the value previously equal to –1), we are actually subtracting the value of –1 from all values of the standardized moderator (i.e., – (–1) = + 1). Please note that new product terms would need to be calculated using these transformed moderator values to include when rerunning our analyses to produce the new simple slopes.

In the McManus et al. (2011) study, it is possible that the relationship between participants' quantity of contact with individuals with intellectual disabilities and their attitudes toward individuals with intellectual disabilities would be moderated by the quality of that contact. For instance, these predictors may interact such that higher levels of quantity of contact are associated with more positive attitudes toward individuals with intellectual disabilities when quality of the contact is high, but with less positive attitudes toward individuals with intellectual disabilities when quality of the contact is low.

To test this, we standardized the quantity and quality of contact variables and calculated a product term to carry the interaction between these variables. We entered the individual effects together into the first step of a hierarchical regression to estimate the participants' scores on the MRAI-R, and we entered the product term carrying the interaction into the second step of the regression. The individual effects entered in step 1 accounted for a significant portion of the variance, with $R^2 = .39$. The regression coefficients indicated that only the participants' quality of contact was a unique predictor of scores on the MRAI-R, with $\beta = .61$; higher scores on quality of contact were associated with more positive attitudes toward individuals

---

[5] Other techniques, such as using various quantiles of the distribution of the moderator, exist for identifying values of the moderator when performing simple slopes, but examining simple slopes at one standard deviation above and below the mean of the moderator is the most common method.

with intellectual disabilities. With $\beta = .01$, participants' quantity of contact failed to predict unique variance in MRAI-R scores above and beyond participants' quality of contact.

However, the addition of the product term in the second step significantly improved the model, producing $\Delta R^2 = .03$. This result indicated that the interaction between quality and quantity of contact predicted participants' scores on the MRAI-R above and beyond the individual effects of those predictors. That is, the relationship between participants' reported levels of quantity of contact and their attitudes toward individuals with intellectual disabilities was different at different levels of quality of contact. Therefore, we needed to calculate simple slopes to identify the pattern of effects producing this interaction.

The unstandardized regression line equation is as follows:

$$Prej' = -0.02Quan + 0.65Qual + 0.19QuanQual + 6.41$$

Solving this equation to estimate MRAI-R scores as a function of quantity of contact produces this equation:

$$Prej' = (-0.02 + 0.19Qual)Quan + (0.65Qual + 6.41)$$

For mean levels of quality of contact, which equals zero given that we standardized this variable, the equation simplifies to

$$Prej' = (-0.02)Quan + 6.41$$

This simple slope indicates that the relationship between participants' quantity of contact and their attitudes toward individuals with intellectual disabilities is close to zero at mean levels of quality of contact. The interaction indicates that this slope will change at other levels of quality of contact. As noted above, we conventionally calculate simple slopes by setting the levels of the moderator (quality of contact in this case) at values 1 standard deviation below the mean (as a low value) and 1 standard deviation above the mean (as a high value) to observe the pattern of change across these simple slopes.

When we specify the zero level as 1 standard deviation below the mean by subtracting –1 from (which is the same as adding 1 to) each of the standardized scores of quality of contact, the simple slope equation becomes

$$Prej' = (-0.21)Quan + 5.76$$

This simple slope indicates that the relationship between participants' quantity of contact and their attitudes toward individuals with intellectual disabilities is negative at low levels of quality of contact.

When we specify the zero level as 1 standard deviation above the mean by subtracting 1 from each of the standardized scores of quality of contact, the simple slope equation becomes

$$Prej' = (0.18)Quan + 7.06$$

This simple slope indicates that the relationship between participants' quantity of contact and their attitudes toward individuals with intellectual disabilities is positive at high levels of quality of contact. Together, these results show that when participants have low levels of quality of contact, increases in quantity of contact are associated with less positive attitudes toward individuals with intellectual disabilities, but when participants have high levels of quality of contact, increases in quantity of contact are associated with more positive attitudes toward individuals with intellectual disabilities. In essence, more contact is only better when the contact is good. This pattern of effects is shown in Figure 15.1.

Results such as these may be summarized in tables that report the effects for each step of the hierarchical regression (see Table 15.1).

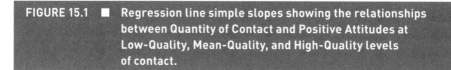

FIGURE 15.1 ■ Regression line simple slopes showing the relationships between Quantity of Contact and Positive Attitudes at Low-Quality, Mean-Quality, and High-Quality levels of contact.

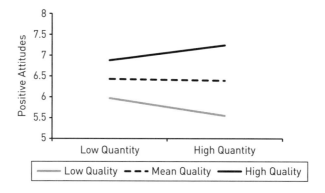

TABLE 15.1 ■ Summary of the Analysis of the Data in the McManus et al. (2011) Study

Step	R^2	ΔR^2	B	β
Step 1	.39	.39		
Quantity of Contact			0.01	.01
Quality of Contact			0.63	.61
Step 2	.42	.03		
Quantity × Quality			0.19	.19

CATEGORICAL × CONTINUOUS INTERACTIONS

We can also use multiple regression techniques to examine how well our continuous and categorical predictor variables predict our criterion variable, both individually and interactively.

Testing the Interaction

For testing interactions between categorical and continuous predictors, the same procedure described above will be conducted. However, our earlier discussion of using structural sets to represent categorical predictors having more than two levels will again be relevant. Let's begin by considering a situation in which two predictors will be used to estimate a criterion variable, and both the main effects of, and the interaction between, the predictors will be tested. We will identify *Cat* as a categorical predictor with two levels, and we will code those levels as 0 for Group A and 1 for Group B in keeping with our recommendations about knowing and manipulating our zero values.[6] We will identify *Con* as a continuous variable and will have either centered or standardized this value prior to testing these effects. Thus, we produce the familiar regression line equation from above, but with Cat and Con inserted as labels in place of X_1 and X_2, respectively:

$$Y' = B_1Cat + B_2Con + B_3CatCon + A$$

If the addition of the interaction term[7] improved the predictive model above and beyond the main effects, then it would indicate that the relationship between the continuous predictor and the criterion varies at different levels of the categorical predictor.

Testing the Simple Slopes

Accordingly, we would calculate simple slopes to test the relationships between the continuous predictor and the criterion variables at each of the levels of the categorical variable (i.e., for Group A versus Group B in this case).[8] This procedure may

---

[6] It should be noted that categorical predictors may be either experimental or classification variables (e.g., person variables, such as sex or race). Further, the need to have perfect balance (equality) between the sample sizes of the levels of the categorical variable is much less essential for regression analyses than for ANOVA. Unbalanced designs in ANOVA create relationships among the factors, violating ANOVA's independence of observation assumption. Using regression is a solution to this issue.

[7] In this case, the regression coefficient for the interaction term is the difference in the slopes of the continuous variable between Group A and Group B.

[8] In cases when it makes more theoretical sense to treat the continuous variable as the moderator, we can also probe the interaction at high and low levels of the continuous moderator to examine the differences in means on the categorical variable at high and low levels of the moderator. This approach is useful when,

be accomplished by solving the regression line equation for the continuous variable's relationship with the criterion; we insert values for the categorical variable into this equation to test the various simple slopes:

$$Y' = (B_2 + B_3 Cat)Con + (B_1 Cat + A)$$

For Group A, which has been assigned a value of 0 for the categorical variable, the regression equation simplifies to the following:

$$Y' = B_2 Con + A$$

In this equation, the B_2 coefficient is the value of the simple slope representing the relationship between the continuous predictor and the criterion variable for Group A. To test the simple slope representing the relationship between the continuous predictor and the criterion variable for Group B, all we would have to do is repeat this procedure, now assigning a value of 0 to Group B and a value of 1 to Group A, and recalculate the product term accordingly.

When the categorical variable has more than two levels, this process is a bit more complicated because the categorical variable must now be represented by more than one dummy variable. Let's consider the case in which the categorical variable has three levels for Groups A, B, and C. We can adapt the example in which we used Republicans, Democrats, and independents in our discussion of structural sets for this more general case. As we discussed then, we would need two dummy variables to represent our categorical group variable, because it is composed of three levels, and we could operationalize these levels as in this table.

	Dum_1 ("A-ness")	Dum_2 ("B-ness")	Dum_3 ("C-ness")
Group A	1	0	0
Group B	0	1	0
Group C	0	0	1

We have created all three possible dummy variables but only need to use two at a time. Our selection of these dummy variables would identify one of the groups as the zero group. This designation will assist in testing the simple slopes if we were to find the interaction significant. To test the interaction of our categorical variable (again noted as

---

for example, we want to know boundary conditions of an experimental treatment based on values of a continuous subject variable (e.g., age).

Cat) and our continuous variable (previously centered or standardized and noted as *Con*), the regression equation becomes this:

$$Y' = B_1 Dum_1 + B_2 Dum_2 + B_3 Con + B_4 Dum_1 Con + B_5 Dum_2 Con + A$$

The test of the main effect of the categorical variable would be conducted by examining the change in R^2 when the Dum_1 and Dum_2 variables are entered into the model as a structural set, and the tests of difference among Groups A, B, and C would be conducted as we described above when discussing structural sets. The test of the main effect of the continuous variable would be conducted by examining the change in R^2 when the continuous variable was entered into the model. The test of the interaction between the categorical variable (represented as both Dum_1 and Dum_2) and the continuous variable would be conducted by examining the change in R^2 when the $Dum_1 Con$ and $Dum_2 Con$ variables are entered into the model as a structural set to carry that interaction.

If the interaction were significant,[9] the simple slopes would be tested by calculating the relationships between the continuous and criterion variables for Groups A, B, and C. We begin by solving the regression line equation for the continuous variable's relationship with the criterion. We therefore insert values for the categorical variable into this equation:

$$Y' = (B_3 + B_4 Dum_1 + B_5 Dum_2)Con + (B_1 Dum_1 + B_2 Dum_2 + A)$$

For Group C, which has been assigned values of 0 for both of the dummy variables that combine to represent the categorical variable, the regression equation simplifies as follows:

$$Y' = B_3 Con + A$$

In this equation, the B_3 coefficient is the value of the simple slope representing the relationship between the continuous predictor and the criterion variable for Group C.

To test the simple slope representing the relationship between the continuous predictor and the criterion variable for the other groups, all we have to do is repeat this procedure for each group by using the dummy variables that identify each group as the zero group and recalculating the product term accordingly. Thus, we would test the simple slope for Group A by repeating the procedure above using Dum_2 and Dum_3 to carry the categorical variable's main effect, along with $Dum_2 Con$ and $Dum_3 Con$ to carry

---

[9]As an exercise, consider this question: What do the regression coefficients B_4 and B_5 tell you about the differences in slopes between levels of the categorical variable?

the interaction. Similarly, we would test the simple slope for Group B by repeating the procedure above using Dum_1 and Dum_3 to carry the categorical variable's main effect, along with Dum_1Con and Dum_3Con to carry the interaction.

CATEGORICAL × CATEGORICAL INTERACTIONS: ANOVA VERSUS REGRESSION

Both regression and ANOVA allow us to test the ability of our categorical predictor variables in our research studies to predict the criterion variable, both individually and interactively.

Testing the Interaction

To test the interactions between categorical predictors in estimating a criterion variable, the procedures above again are applied. The predictors are dummy coded, and product terms to carry their interaction(s) are computed. Hierarchical regression is used in which main effects are entered into the predictive model and evaluated prior to the entry of the product term(s). The interaction is tested by examining the ΔR^2 for the step at which the product term(s) are entered into the model. Significant interactions may be probed using procedures to calculate simple slopes by manipulating what the zero values used in the coding of the categorical predictors represent. The results that emerge will approximate the results that would be produced by ANOVA testing the same main effects and interaction(s). Further, as noted above, regression will be less adversely affected by unbalanced designs that produce issues in ANOVA.

Historically, there has been a distinction drawn between ANOVA and regression. ANOVA has often been associated with experimental research, and regression has often been associated with correlational research. Given that many categorical variables are not manipulated, these statements are overgeneralizations of the techniques. Further driving the distinction is the common practice among statistics and social science departments of offering separate courses in ANOVA and regression. What sometimes fails to resonate is that these techniques are both founded in the general linear model, with ANOVA being a simplification of the mathematical operations when all the predictors are categorical.

The Case of the Analysis of Covariance (ANCOVA)

To understand the intersection between the two techniques and thus the artificiality of their distinction, consider the case of **analysis of covariance (ANCOVA)**. Researchers use this technique to remove the predictive ability of one variable (identified as the **covariate**) prior to testing for the main and/or interaction effects of categorical predictors.[10] Interestingly, this covariate may be continuous or categorical, while the predictors tested for main and/or interaction effects may only be categorical. The partialling out of the covariate's ability to account for variance in the criterion variable prior to assessing the effects of the other predictors is essentially the procedure used in hierarchical regression by which predictors are allowed to account for variance in the criterion in a predetermined order. One way to think about this idea is that the ANCOVA is really hierarchical regression masquerading as ANOVA. Recognition of this fact should make the underlying connection of ANOVA techniques to regression techniques more obvious.

Comparing Regression to ANOVA

To illustrate how regression can be used to test interactions between categorical predictors, and to show the similarity of these results to ANOVA techniques, let's revisit the study by Sharp, Sheeley, and Saucier (2004). Recall that they showed White participants one of four statements made by a famous person. They manipulated the race of the person as White or Black and manipulated whether the statement was low or high in prejudice. The dependent measure was the degree of negative self-directed affect (e.g., guilt) the participants reported. In Chapter 14, we analyzed these data using a two-factor ANOVA. We found a main effect of the source's race such that participants reported more negative self-directed affect when they read statements by White (versus Black) sources. We found a main effect of prejudice level such that participants reported more negative self-directed affect when they read high-prejudice (versus low-prejudice) statements. Most importantly, we found that these main effects were qualified by an interaction between the source's race and the prejudice level of the statement. Simple effects showed that participants reported more negative self-directed affect after reading high-prejudice (versus low-prejudice) statements only when the source was White. When the source of the statements was Black, participants' reported levels of negative self-directed affect did not differ.

To analyze the same data using hierarchical regression, we coded the source of the statements as White = 0 and Black = 1, and we coded the prejudice level of the statements as Low = 0 and High = 1. We computed a product term to carry the interaction between the two categorical predictors. We entered the two categorical predictors' individual effects into the first step of a hierarchical regression and entered the product term carrying their interaction into the second step of the regression. The results for this study are summarized in Table 15.2.

---

[10] The appropriate use of ANCOVA requires researchers to verify that the covariate does not interact with any of the predictors in estimating the criterion variable prior to treating the variable as a covariate.

Step	R^2	ΔR^2	B	β
TABLE 15.2 ■ **Summary of the Analysis of the Data in the Sharp et al. (2004) Study**				
Step 1	.29	.29		
Race of the Source			−3.53	−.30
Prejudice Level			5.21	.44
Step 2	.41	.13		
Race × Prejudice			−8.37	−.61

We found that the entry of the categorical predictors' individual effects into the first step of the hierarchical regression accounted for a significant portion of the variance in participants' reported levels of negative self-directed affect, producing an R^2 value of .29 and an adjusted R^2 value of .27. As in the ANOVA, each of the main effects was significant, with the race of the source producing a β of −0.30 and the prejudice level of the statement producing a β of .44. Given the coding of these categorical predictors, these values indicate that participants reported significantly higher levels of negative self-directed affect when the source was White (versus Black) and when the statement was high (versus low) in prejudice. These results mirror the conclusions provided by the ANOVA results from Chapter 14. Further, the entry of the product term carrying the interaction between these categorical predictors significantly improved the regression model, with a ΔR^2 value of .13. This result indicates that the difference in negative self-directed affect reported in response to the high- versus low-prejudice statements depended on the race of the statements' source.

The unstandardized regression equation is as follows:

$$NegAff' = 9.43\,Prej - 0.62\,Race - 8.37\,PrejRace + 4.18$$

Testing the Simple Slopes

To estimate participants' reports of negative self-directed affect as a function of prejudice level, this equation becomes

$$NegAff' = (9.43 - 8.37\,Race)\,Prej + (-0.62\,Race + 4.18)$$

Holding the race of the source constant at White, which we coded as the zero level for the race variable, the equation simplifies to

$$NegAff' = (9.43)\,Prej + 4.18$$

This simple slope, which is significantly different from zero, indicates that there are mean differences between the levels of negative self-directed affect reported by participants in the low- versus high-prejudice conditions when the source of the statement is White. Given the coding of the prejudice variable, the positive slope indicates that significantly more negative self-directed affect is reported in the high-prejudice condition.[11]

To completely probe the interaction, we can recode the race variable as Black = 0 and White = 1, recompute the product term to carry the interaction accordingly, and rerun the hierarchical regression. Doing so produces the following unstandardized regression line equation:

$$NegAff' = 1.06\,Prej - 0.62\,Race + 8.37\,PrejRace + 4.79$$

When we solve this unstandardized regression line equation to estimate participants' reports of negative self-directed affect as a function of prejudice level, the equation becomes

$$NegAff' = (1.06 + 8.37\,Race)\,Prej + (-0.62\,Race + 4.79)$$

We can hold the race of the source constant at Black, which we coded as the zero level for the race variable to test this simple slope. Now the equation simplifies as follows:

$$NegAff' = (1.06)\,Prej + 4.79$$

This simple slope, which is not significantly different from zero, indicates that there are no mean differences between the levels of negative self-directed affect reported by participants in the low- versus high-prejudice conditions when the source of the statement is Black. Together, these simple-slopes analyses mirror the simple-effects analyses we demonstrated in Chapter 14, as do the overall results for the main effects and interaction. See Figure 15.2.

Applying Regression to Test Interactions Between Categorical Predictors in the Barlett (2015) Data

Now let's turn our attention to the Barlett (2015) data that we presented in Chapter 14. In that study, participants reported their levels of hostility after having been exposed to insulting or nice messages online. The issue we raised in Chapter 14 was that the numbers of men and women in the insulting and nice message conditions were unequal, creating an unbalanced design. In fact, the correlation between the participants' sex and the message

---

[11] Notice here that the intercept of the regression line equation indicates the mean of the group assigned zeros for both of the categorical predictors, which in this case is the group who read low-prejudice statements from White sources. By recoding the categorical variables to manipulate which levels of the categorical variables the zeros represent, we can identify the means for all combinations of the categorical variables.

FIGURE 15.2 ■ Simple regression line slopes for the data in the Sharp et al. (2004) study.

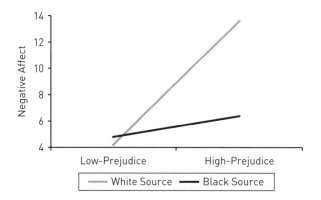

condition assignments was highly significant, $r = -.29$, $p = .003$, with men more likely to be in the nice message condition and women more likely to be in the insulting message condition. This result suggests a violation of ANOVA's assumption that the factors are independent. Thus, using ANOVA to test for the main effects of sex and message content, and for the interaction between sex and message content, is suboptimal. Accordingly, we can test for these effects using hierarchical regression, which handles unbalanced designs more effectively.

We began by dummy coding the sex of participants as Men = 0 and Women = 1 and the message content as Insulting = 0 and Nice = 1. We then computed a product term to carry the interaction between these two categorical predictors. Because of the versatility of regression, we then can decide either to enter the terms for the predictors' individual effects together in the first step of the hierarchical regression or to order the terms for entry. Because there appears to be a logical argument for the temporal precedence of participant sex (as a person variable)[12] over message content (as a manipulated variable), we entered participant sex in the first step of the hierarchical regression, followed by message content in the second step and the product term to carry the interaction between sex and message content in the third step. This analysis is summarized in Table 15.3.

The entry of the main effect for sex in the first step did not account for a significant portion of variance in the participants' levels of hostility, but it was trending toward doing so, producing a ΔR^2 value of .03. The β for the main effect of sex in this step was .17,

---

[12] Temporal precedence refers to when some variable exists prior to another variable. In this situation, the participants' sex exists for them prior to their being exposed to any of the manipulations in this study. It is impossible for a later event to have influence on an earlier event, and logic therefore suggests that events that occur earlier are also entered earlier in hierarchical regression models.

Step	R^2	ΔR^2	B	β
TABLE 15.3 ■ Summary of the Analysis of the Data in the Barlett (2015) Study				
Step 1	.03	.03		
Participant Sex			7.42	.17
Step 2	.06	.03		
Message Content			−7.91	−.19
Step 3	.06	.001		
Sex × Message Content			2.29	.05

indicating the women were marginally higher on hostility than were men. The entry of the main effect for message content in the second step also failed to significantly improve the predictive model above and beyond sex, but it was trending toward doing so, also producing a ΔR^2 value of .03. The β for the main effect of message content was −.19, indicating the mean levels of hostility were higher at marginally significant levels in the insulting message condition than in the nice message condition. The entry of the product term carrying the interaction between sex and message content in the third step did not improve the predictive model significantly above and beyond the main effects of sex and message content, producing a ΔR^2 value of only .001. This result indicates the differences between the levels of hostility reported after receiving insulting versus nice messages were not moderated by the sex of the participants. While we would not always probe a nonsignificant interaction (unless we had very good a priori theoretical reasons to do so), we will do so here to show how the pattern of effects is demonstrated by the simple slopes.

The unstandardized regression equation is as follows:

$$Hostility' = 3.84Sex - 9.32Content + 2.29SexContent + 76.86$$

When we solve to estimate participants' reports of hostility as a function of message content, the equation becomes the following:

$$Hostility' = (-9.32 + 2.29Sex)Content + (3.84Sex + 76.86)$$

We can hold the participants' sex constant at male, which we coded as the zero level for the sex variable. Now the equation simplifies as follows:

$$Hostility' = (-9.32)Content + 76.86$$

This simple slope is not significantly different from zero, indicating that the levels of hostility reported by men following insulting messages are nonsignificantly higher than those reported by men following nice messages. Recall that the size of unstandardized regression coefficients must be interpreted in the context of their measurement scale, and on the scale used in this study for hostility, a difference of 9.32 units is not large enough to be statistically significant.

To completely probe the interaction, we can recode the sex variable as Women = 0 and Men = 1, recompute the product term to carry the interaction accordingly, and rerun the hierarchical regression. Doing so produces the following unstandardized regression line equation:

$$Hostility' = -3.84Sex - 7.03Content - 2.29SexContent + 80.70$$

When we solve to estimate participants' reports of hostility as a function of message content, the equation becomes

$$Hostility' = (-7.03 - 2.29Sex)Content + (-3.84Sex + 80.70)$$

We can hold the participants' sex constant at female, which we coded as the zero level for the sex variable. Now the equation simplifies to

$$Hostility' = (-7.03)Content + 80.70$$

This simple slope is not significantly different from zero, indicating that the levels of hostility reported by women following insulting messages are nonsignificantly higher than those reported by women following nice messages. This result parallels the findings

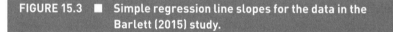

FIGURE 15.3 ■ Simple regression line slopes for the data in the Barlett (2015) study.

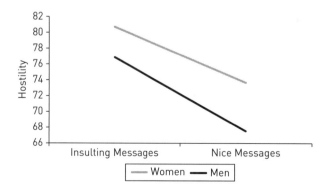

for men. Because the conclusion for the nonsignificant interaction is that the differences in hostility ratings following insulting versus nice messages were not moderated by participants' sex, these simple slopes serve only to verify that conclusion. The pattern of effects is shown in Figure 15.3.

Simply put, while regression analyses testing the main effects of, and interaction effects between, categorical predictors may be a bit more cumbersome, and even alien to some, the results are analogous to those produced by ANOVA for balanced designs, and the analyses themselves circumvent some of the issues that ANOVA fails to resolve in unbalanced designs.

Summary

Our goal in this chapter was to demonstrate the utility of regression to assess the relationships between predictor and criterion variables in many ways. Regression is a fairly universal technique that, based on its foundation in the general linear model, can test the predictive value of one or more predictors individually, in sets, and in interactions. The general linear model consists of a method by which predictive equations are created to examine the relationships among predictor and criterion variable and any number and type. For special cases, the procedure simplifies and creates "different" statistical procedures, such as when ANOVA is used to analyze situations in which the predictors are categorical and a single criterion is continuous. But it is important to remember that these "different" procedures use the same approach and are really not different.

An advantage to regression is that it can use predictors that are either continuous or categorical. ANOVA requires that the predictors be categorical, and researchers may have to artificially create groups to force their continuous predictors into categories, such as by using median splits, resulting in several concerning consequences including potential power loss and increases in type I error rates. Regression allows their predictors to remain on their continuous scales, allowing for more precision in the analysis.

When predictors are naturally categorical, regression analyses may also include these to test for their predictive value. By using methods like dummy coding, the specific categories of the predictor may be represented and tested in the analysis. And when the predictors are categorical, regression provides the results that ANOVA can produce but is less limited by the restrictions inherent in ANOVA, providing a more flexible technique for researchers to use in their pursuit of creative designs as they seek to answer fascinating research questions.

Regression produces line equations to represent the prediction of the criterion by the predictor(s), producing simple regression lines when only one predictor is used to predict the criterion and producing multiple regression lines when more than one predictor is used to predict the criterion. Unstandardized regression line equations report these predictive relationships with the slopes and intercept in the terms of the variables' measurement scaling, while standardized regression line equations report these predictive relationships with the slopes and intercept in the terms of the variables standardized as z-scores. The latter line equations are particularly useful because they better allow for comparisons of the predictive strength of the predictors even when they are measured on different scales.

Several types of multiple regression may be employed. Simultaneous regression is used when all predictors are entered together in one step, and all predictors are assessed for their ability to predict the criterion collectively as well as for their ability to uniquely predict the criterion above and beyond all other predictors in the model. Stepwise regression is used to optimize the empirical fit of a model to a data set by either entering all predictors and then paring it down by deleting unnecessary predictors individually (backward stepwise regression), or by building the model up by entering in necessary predictors individually (forward stepwise regression). Hierarchical regression is used when predictors are entered in some predetermined sequence based on theoretical and logical reasoning. Early steps will have the first opportunities to account for variance in the criterion, with later steps having the opportunity to predict only the variance in the criterion that has not yet been predicted. Variances may be entered and evaluated as individual predictors or as sets. Functional sets consist of predictors that have some theoretical connection or overlap, while structural sets consist of multiple predictors that are required to carry aspects of one predictor, such as when a categorical predictor with three or more levels is dummy coded.

A useful advantage of hierarchical regression is the ability to examine if product terms carrying the interactions among predictors improve the predictive values of the models above and beyond the individual predictors' main effects. Interactions may then be probed by calculating simple slopes that show the relationships between one predictor and the criterion with the levels of the other predictors held constant. These interactions may consist of combinations of continuous X continuous, continuous X categorical, and even categorical X categorical predictors. In the latter case, the regression results will be similar to those produced by ANOVA, except that regression better handles situations that restrict ANOVA such as when researchers use unbalanced designs. Overall, regression provides a useful and universal application of the general linear model for assessing how well our predictors account for variance in outcomes in our research studies.

Conceptual Exercises

1. Describe the overall approach to using the general linear model in data analysis.

2. Why are median splits a bad idea?

3. How do unstandardized and standardized regression lines differ? What is an advantage to using each?

4. How does the regression line equation differ between simple and multiple regression?

5. Imagine that you are conducting a study in which you will use students' attendance, operationalized as the number of classes they attended, to predict their final point total in a research methods course.

   a. Create and describe the components of the simple regression line that would be produced by this study.

   b. If you were to add the students' reported levels of interest in the class as an additional predictor, how would the multiple regression line reflect that addition? Create and describe the components of the multiple regression line that would be produced now. In particular, discuss what the regression coefficients for each of the predictors would represent.

c. What would you expect to happen to the value of the coefficient that represents the relationship between students' attendance and their final point total when the second predictor is added in (b)? Explain your answer.

6. What is likely to be larger: (i) the value of a regression coefficient for a predictor used by itself to predict a criterion variable in a simple regression line or (ii) the value of the regression coefficient for that same predictor when it is used among other predictors to predict the same criterion variable in a multiple regression line? Explain your answer.

7. Explain the differences among the simultaneous, stepwise, and hierarchical regression approaches to handling multiple predictors of a dependent variable.

8. What are the differences between functional and structural sets? Use examples of each to support your answer.

9. Describe the general strategy for testing interactions between any two predictors in regression. Explain how this strategy adapts to accommodate the continuous × continuous, continuous × categorical, and categorical × categorical situations.

10. What are simple slopes? How is the regression line equation that includes two predictors reorganized to test simple slopes?

11. How would you expect ANOVA results to compare to regression results when both of these procedures test interactions between two categorical variables using the same data set?

Student Study Site

Visit the Student Study Site at **https://study.sagepub.com/friemanstats** for a variety of useful tools including data sets, additional exercises, and web resources.

EPILOGUE

Research is an exciting endeavor by which we can collect data to test our hypotheses and document the knowledge we gain. Because research is not conducted in a vacuum, we have provided a context for how we can use statistics to help us understand various aspects of antisocial behavior, such as cyberbullying and intergroup attitudes and behaviors. Let's take a moment to reflect on what we have learned in this textbook.

Based on observations and/or prior research, we can ask questions and frame possible answers to our research questions as a set of mutually exclusive and exhaustive experimental hypotheses. Properly framed hypotheses guide our choices among research designs and the form our data collection should take so that we may decide which hypothesis is supported by our data. Some research questions are best answered by conducting experiments in which we randomly assign participants to different conditions and observe how they behave under those conditions, while other research questions involve observing how individuals who belong to different preexisting groups behave under the same or different conditions. And some research questions can be answered by examining the degree of relationship between or among different measures of behavior. In all of these situations, we collect data and use the quantitative methods described here to help us analyze those data and advance our understanding of behavior.

After collecting our data, the first thing we should do is examine them to decide what statistical models and methods we can use to analyze and present our data to others. Failing to do this can result in our using inadequate methods for analysis that fail to uncover important relationships. Quantile plots, stem-and-leaf displays, box plots, and—with large sets of data—letter-value displays provide us with more information about our data than do conventional histograms and sets of descriptive statistics. Sometimes these data displays can reveal aspects of our data we would miss using more limited methods.

The properties of distributions provide us with the conceptual foundation for the methods of hypothesis testing and estimating parameters we use to analyze our data. These properties include what happens when we add, subtract, multiply, or divide all of the values in a set of numbers by a constant. They also describe what happens when we randomly sample a value from two sets of numbers and either add or subtract these two values to create a new set of values. The effect of performing these operations leads us to the extremely useful standard score transformation and to the central limit theorem, the fundamental theorem in inferential statistics. This theorem provides the basis for constructing confidence intervals for population parameters and constructing hypothesis tests about population means, and it helps us understand the role that sample size plays when we estimate parameters and test hypotheses.

Many of the quantitative methods we use to answer our research questions are based on random sampling from normal distributions, but sometimes our data come from other types of distributions (or the distribution is not known), contain data from more than one source (that is, are contaminated), or contain transcription errors. When this happens, we may observe outliers in our data, and the commonly used sample mean and sample variance will be influenced by those outliers. We can reduce the influence of outliers in our data by using the sample median; trimmed means; Winsorized means; or M-estimators, such as the MOM; for estimates of central tendency and Winsorized variances and the MAD for estimates of spread. Outliers also distort confidence intervals when random sampling from normal distributions is assumed. The bootstrap and its variations provide us with confidence intervals that do not require the more stringent assumptions about the source of our data.

The classical statistical model, which is the basis for many of the hypothesis tests we use, is based on two assumptions: (1) Populations exist with certain parameters, some known and some unknown, and (2) we can estimate the values of the unknown parameters by taking random samples from those populations. However, when we conduct experiments, we do not take random samples—we typically start with a group of participants and randomly assign them to our experimental conditions. Despite that fact, the classical statistical model is the basis for most of the statistical methods we use to analyze our data.

Inferential statistics involve estimating population parameters. Many of the estimators we routinely use were derived by the procedure called maximum likelihood estimation. Estimates derived by this procedure are best estimates in the sense that they are unbiased (or can be easily transformed to unbiased estimators) and are efficient (have low variance).

When testing hypotheses, the classical statistical model requires that we create a set of statistical hypotheses that parallel our experimental hypotheses. Our statistical hypotheses within the classical statistical model are about the unknown parameters of the populations from which we believe our samples were taken. All statistical inference with the classical statistical model involves estimating the parameters of the populations we chose to represent as the source of our data.

With the classical statistical model, we select one of our statistical hypotheses (called the null hypothesis) and calculate the probability of obtaining (in a future research study) our results, or results even more extreme, assuming that the null hypothesis is true. When that probability is below a predetermined level (typically $p < .05$), we reject the hypothesis we are testing and accept the alternative hypothesis. To calculate that probability, we need to know the distribution of the statistic we will use to test the null hypothesis.

We can divide the distribution of our test statistic into two regions. A value of our test statistic in one of these regions (called the critical region or region of rejection) leads us to reject our null hypothesis, because the probability of getting a result in the critical region is judged to be unlikely to have occurred when the null hypothesis is true. The dividing line between these two regions is called the critical value. When the null hypothesis is false, our test statistic does not come from the distribution based on the null hypothesis being true—it comes from another distribution called the non-central distribution.

There are two types of errors we could make when testing statistical hypotheses. One error is to reject the null hypothesis when it is true. Called a type I or alpha error, this indicates that we concluded an effect occurred when it did not. The other type of error is to not reject the null hypothesis when it is false. This error, called a type II or beta error, indicates that we concluded there was no effect when there was. We can only make a type I error when the null hypothesis is true and our test statistic is in the critical region. We can only make a type II error when the null hypothesis is false and our test statistic is not in the critical region.

We want to design our research studies so that the probability of rejecting a false null hypothesis (called the power of our test) is high. Although we cannot calculate the power of our statistical hypothesis test, we know what factors affect the power, and we can use that information to design our experiment to maximize its power. Power functions provide us with a way to decide how large a sample size to use when we design our experiment.

The method for hypothesis testing we use with the classical statistical model is a hybrid of models described by R. A. Fisher and by J. Neyman and E. S. Pearson. Because these two models are incompatible, we need to be careful about how we use concepts like p-value, alpha, and alpha error.

A more realistic model to use to test whether experimental treatments have the same or different effects is called the randomization or permutation model. With this model, we only have to assume that participants are randomly assigned to the different treatments and that participants' behavior reflects the treatment they receive. No assumptions are made about random sampling from populations, and the statistical hypotheses we test here are the same as our experimental hypotheses.

When our research questions are about whether there is a relationship between two variables, we use correlation coefficients to measure the degree of relationship between two variables. We use the Pearson product moment correlation coefficient, r, as a descriptive statistic when both variables are on interval or ratio scales. There are three models for studying these relationships. The randomization/permutation model allows us to test whether there is a relationship without making any assumptions about populations and random sampling. The only assumption we have to make is that when there is *no* relationship between the variables, any value of one variable can occur with equal frequency with any value of the other variable.

We can ask and answer more questions about the relationship between two variables with the other two models, which are based on the classical statistical model. With the bivariate normal distribution model, we assume random sampling from a bivariate normal distribution. Here the Pearson r is the maximum likelihood estimate of the population correlation coefficient. With this model, we can test various hypotheses about the population correlation coefficient and create confidence intervals. There are some robust measures of correlation we can use when we have concerns about whether the assumptions underlying the bivariate normal distribution are met.

The other such model is the linear regression model. Here we use the method of least squares to estimate the slope and intercept of the line that best fits our data (called the sample regression line) and is an estimate for the population regression line. We can use the sample regression line as a basis for predicting performance on one variable from performance on the other. With this model, we can test whether the population correlation = 0.

The linear regression model is a special case of the general linear model. The general linear model is a universal approach that allows us to test hypotheses in many cases. We may have one predictor in a simple regression or more than one predictor in a multiple regression, and we may test interactions among the predictors of any type (for example, categorical and continuous). When these predictors are exclusively categorical, the general linear model provides the basis for this same process in our use of analysis of variance (ANOVA). Overall, the general linear model provides us with a way to estimate the size of treatment effects in our experiments across a wide variety of situations.

Throughout this textbook, we have illustrated the foundations and applications of several statistical techniques. These techniques are related, having common underlying principles, but also allow for appropriate analysis of our data across a variety of situations. We hope that you have learned many useful strategies and practices that you may apply to your own research questions, and we hope that our applications of these statistical methods to research questions related to cyberbullying and prejudice demonstrate the power these techniques have in the pursuit of knowledge to answer fascinating questions across the social sciences.

APPENDIX A
Some Useful Rules of Algebra

Statistics is a branch of mathematics; therefore, it is important for us to be familiar with some of the algebraic operations commonly used in the statistical literature that are the basis for many of the statistical concepts we use. Below are some of the rules for the use of exponents, factors, and fractions in the derivations of the formulas we will use in this book. Although we learned these when we took algebra in high school and college, they are summarized here for easy reference. The best way to learn these rules is to turn them into an English sentence. The letters a, b, c, and d stand for any number.

RULES FOR EXPONENTS

1. The positive exponent of a number tells us how many times that number is multiplied together. In these examples, a is called the base, and the superscripts are the exponents. For example,

$$a^1 = a$$

$$a^2 = a \cdot a$$

$$a^4 = a \cdot a \cdot a \cdot a \quad a \text{ raised to the fourth power is } a^4.$$

2. There is one special case: Anything raised to the 0 power $= 1$; that is,

$$a^0 = 1$$

3. To multiply together the same base with different exponents, we add the exponents:

$$a^b \cdot a^c \cdot a^d = a^{b + c + d}$$

This works in both directions:

$$a^{b+c+d} = a^b \cdot a^c \cdot a^d$$

4. To raise a base already raised to a power to a new power, we multiply the exponents:

$$(a^b)^c = a^{bc}$$

This works in both directions: $a^{bc} = (a^b)^c$

5. A number raised to a negative exponent is 1 divided by that number raised to the positive exponent:

$$a^{-b} = \frac{1}{a^b}$$

This works in both directions:

$$\frac{1}{a^b} = a^{-b}$$

6. Combining rules 3 and 5, we get the following:

$$\frac{a^b}{a^c} = a^{b-c}$$

7. The product of two different bases raised to a power is the product of each base raised to that power:

$$(ab)^c = a^c \cdot b^c$$

CONVERTING EXPONENTS TO RADICALS (ROOTS) AND VICE VERSA

8. We can express values under a radical sign with a fractional exponent:

$$\sqrt{a} = a^{1/2}$$

$$\sqrt[b]{a} = a^{1/b}$$

$$\sqrt[b]{a^c} = a^{c/b}$$

SQUARES AND SQUARE ROOTS OF SUMS AND DIFFERENCES

9. Because exponents tell us how many times something is multiplied together,

$$(a + b)^2 = a^2 + 2ab + b^2$$

$$(a - b)^2 = a^2 - 2ab + b^2$$

The same rules *do not* apply to $\sqrt{a+b}$ and $\sqrt{a+b}$.

SQUARES AND SQUARE ROOTS OF PRODUCTS AND QUOTIENTS

10. All of the following are true . . .

$$\sqrt{ab} = \sqrt{a}\sqrt{b}$$

$$\frac{\sqrt{a}}{\sqrt{b}} = \sqrt{\frac{a}{b}}$$

$$(ab)^2 = a^2 b^2$$

$$\left(ab\right)^2 = \frac{a^2}{b^2}$$

FRACTIONS

11. When the denominators of both fractions are the same,

$$\frac{a}{c} + \frac{b}{c} = \frac{a+b}{c}$$

This goes in both directions.

12. The following equations model how to simplify fractions. The second is a special case of the first.

$$\frac{\dfrac{a}{b}}{\dfrac{c}{d}} = \frac{ad}{bc}$$

$$\frac{1}{\frac{c}{d}} = \frac{d}{c}$$

$$\text{if } \frac{a}{b} = \frac{c}{d}, \text{ then } ad = bc.$$

FACTORS AND FACTORING

13. Factors are numbers that are multiplied together to get another number. Factoring is the process of separating out the factors.

$$ab + ac = a(b + c)$$

$$a^2 + 5a + 6 = (a + 2)(a + 3)$$

$$a^2 - 5a + 6 = (a - 2)(a - 3)$$

$$a^2 + a - 6 = (a - 2)(a + 3)$$

$$a^2 - a - 6 = (a + 2)(a - 3)$$

These go in both directions.

APPENDIX B
Rules of Summation

Because our data consist of numbers, and many of the formulas we use involve adding these numbers together in various ways, we use the summation sign $\left(\sum_{i=1}^{n} X_i \right)$ as a shorthand way to describe adding together n numbers, $X_1, X_2, ..., X_n$, where the values of these numbers can be either the same or different. When the subscript and superscript on the Σ are omitted, it is assumed that the entire set of numbers from 1 to n is being summed. For the following, X_i and Y_i are variables and c is a constant. All of these rules go in both directions.

1. The sum of n numbers, $X_1, X_2, ..., X_n$:

$$\sum_{i=1}^{n} X_i = X_1 + X_2 + \cdots + X_n$$

2. The sum of n numbers *squared*, $: X_1^2, X_2^2, ... , X_n^2$:

$$\sum_{i=1}^{n} X_i^2 = X_1^2 + X_2^2 + \cdots + X_n^2$$

3. Summing n numbers and then squaring that sum:

$$\left(\sum_{i=1}^{n} X_i \right)^2 = (X_1 + X_2 + \cdots + X_n)^2$$

4. The sum of a constant times a variable is the constant times the sum of the variable:

$$\sum_{i=1}^{n} c X_i = c \sum_{i=1}^{n} X_i$$

5. The sum of a constant is the constant times the number of times it occurs. (Note: This is the definition of multiplication—adding the same number repeatedly):

$$\sum_{i=1}^{n} c = nc$$

6. When we have two sets of numbers X_i and Y_i, then when we add the first number in X to the first number in Y $(X_1 + Y_1)$, the second number in X to the second number in Y $(X_2 + Y_2)$, and so forth:

$$\sum_{i=1}^{n} (X_i + Y_i) = \sum_{i=1}^{n} X_i + \sum_{i=1}^{n} Y_i$$

7. WARNING: What works for addition (Rule 6) does not always work for multiplication. The general rule for multiplication is this:

$$\sum_{i=1}^{n} (X_i Y_i) \neq \sum_{i=1}^{n} X_i \sum_{i=1}^{n} Y_i$$

APPENDIX C
Logarithms

Logarithms (and the related concept of exponents) occur frequently in statistics. Here is a brief primer on what logarithms are and the rules of manipulating them.

The **logarithm** of a number (call that number X) is *the exponent of another number (called the base) that produces the first number (X).*

For example, if $X = 1,000$ and the base is 10, then what is the exponent of 10 that yields the value of 1,000? In other words, what is the value of Y so that $10^Y = 1,000$? The answer is 3. We express this as follows:

$$\log_{10} 1,000 = 3$$

Therefore, it follows that

$$\log_{10} 100 = 2$$

$$\log_{10} 10 = 1$$

Rule 2 in Appendix A tells us that anything raised to the 0 power is 1; therefore,

$$\log_{10} 1 = 0$$

The general formula for a logarithm is **$\log_{base} X = Y$**. If a base is not specified, it is assumed to be 10. *Logarithms whose base is 10* are called **common logarithms**. In many applications, the base is the transcendental number e, which equals 2.7182818.... Like π, e does not have any pattern or cycle. *Logarithms with a base of* e are **natural logarithms**, and we use the symbol **ln X** to indicate that the base is e.

RULES OF LOGARITHMS

The following rules are true for all logarithms, no matter what the base:

1. The logarithm of a product is the sum of the individual logarithms:

$$\log XY = \log X + \log Y$$

2. The logarithm of a quotient is the difference between the individual logarithms:

$$\log \frac{X}{Y} \log X - \log Y$$

3. Because $\log 1 = 0$, from rule 2 it follows that

$$\log \frac{1}{X} = - \log X$$

4. Because raising a number to a power is the same as multiplying that number repeatedly (per Rule 1 in Appendix A),

$$\log X^{a} = a \log x$$

APPENDIX D
The Inverse of the Cumulative Normal Distribution

The proportions in the lower tail of a normal distribution are along the left and top of the table, with the first two significant digits in the left column and the third significant digit along the top. The z-scores corresponding to those proportions are on the inside of the table. For example, if $p = .025$, $z = -1.96$.

p	.000	.001	.002	.003	.004	.005	.006	.007	.008	.009
.00		-3.090	-2.878	-2.748	-2.652	-2.576	-2.512	-2.457	-2.409	-2.366
.01	-2.326	-2.290	-2.257	-2.226	-2.197	-2.170	-2.145	-2.120	-2.097	-2.075
.02	-2.054	-2.034	-2.014	-1.995	-1.977	-1.960	-1.943	-1.927	-1.911	-1.896
.03	-1.881	-1.866	-1.852	-1.839	-1.825	-1.812	-1.799	-1.787	-1.774	-1.762
.04	-1.751	-1.739	-1.728	-1.717	-1.706	-1.695	-1.685	-1.675	-1.665	-1.655
.05	-1.645	-1.635	-1.626	-1.617	-1.607	-1.598	-1.589	-1.581	-1.572	-1.563
.06	-1.555	-1.547	-1.538	-1.530	-1.522	-1.514	-1.506	-1.499	-1.491	-1.483
.07	-1.476	-1.468	-1.461	-1.454	-1.447	-1.440	-1.433	-1.426	-1.419	-1.412
.08	-1.405	-1.398	-1.392	-1.385	-1.379	-1.372	-1.366	-1.360	-1.353	-1.347
.09	-1.341	-1.335	-1.329	-1.323	-1.317	-1.311	-1.305	-1.299	-1.293	-1.287
.10	-1.282	-1.276	-1.270	-1.265	-1.259	-1.254	-1.248	-1.243	-1.237	-1.232
.11	-1.227	-1.221	-1.216	-1.211	-1.206	-1.200	-1.195	-1.190	-1.185	-1.180
.12	-1.175	-1.170	-1.165	-1.160	-1.155	-1.150	-1.146	-1.141	-1.136	-1.131
.13	-1.126	-1.122	-1.117	-1.112	-1.108	-1.103	-1.099	-1.094	-1.089	-1.085
.14	-1.080	-1.076	-1.071	-1.067	-1.063	-1.058	-1.054	-1.049	-1.045	-1.041

p	.000	.001	.002	.003	.004	.005	.006	.007	.008	.009
.15	−1.037	−1.032	−1.028	−1.024	−1.020	−1.015	−1.011	−1.007	−1.003	−0.999
.16	−0.995	−0.990	−0.986	−0.982	−0.978	−0.974	−0.970	−0.966	−0.962	−0.958
.17	−0.954	−0.950	−0.946	−0.942	−0.939	−0.935	−0.931	−0.927	−0.923	−0.919
.18	−0.915	−0.912	−0.908	−0.904	−0.900	−0.897	−0.893	−0.889	−0.885	−0.882
.19	−0.878	−0.874	−0.871	−0.867	−0.863	−0.860	−0.856	−0.852	−0.849	−0.845
.20	−0.842	−0.838	−0.835	−0.831	−0.828	−0.824	−0.820	−0.817	−0.813	−0.810
.21	−0.807	−0.803	−0.800	−0.796	−0.793	−0.789	−0.786	−0.782	−0.779	−0.776
.22	−0.772	−0.769	−0.766	−0.762	−0.759	−0.756	−0.752	−0.749	−0.746	−0.742
.23	−0.739	−0.736	−0.732	−0.729	−0.726	−0.723	−0.719	−0.716	−0.713	−0.710
.24	−0.706	−0.703	−0.700	−0.697	−0.694	−0.690	−0.687	−0.684	−0.681	−0.678
.25	−0.675	−0.671	−0.668	−0.665	−0.662	−0.659	−0.656	−0.653	−0.650	−0.647
.26	−0.643	−0.640	−0.637	−0.634	−0.631	−0.628	−0.625	−0.622	−0.619	−0.616
.27	−0.613	−0.610	−0.607	−0.604	−0.601	−0.598	−0.595	−0.592	−0.589	−0.586
.28	−0.583	−0.580	−0.577	−0.574	−0.571	−0.568	−0.565	−0.562	−0.559	−0.556
.29	−0.553	−0.551	−0.548	−0.545	−0.542	−0.539	−0.536	−0.533	−0.530	−0.527
.30	−0.524	−0.522	−0.519	−0.516	−0.513	−0.510	−0.507	−0.504	−0.502	−0.499
.31	−0.496	−0.493	−0.490	−0.487	−0.485	−0.482	−0.479	−0.476	−0.473	−0.471
.32	−0.468	−0.465	−0.462	−0.459	−0.457	−0.454	−0.451	−0.448	−0.445	−0.443
.33	−0.440	−0.437	−0.434	−0.432	−0.429	−0.426	−0.423	−0.421	−0.418	−0.415
.34	−0.412	−0.410	−0.407	−0.404	−0.402	−0.399	−0.396	−0.393	−0.391	−0.388
.35	−0.385	−0.383	−0.380	−0.377	−0.374	−0.372	−0.369	−0.366	−0.364	−0.361
.36	−0.358	−0.356	−0.353	−0.350	−0.348	−0.345	−0.342	−0.340	−0.337	−0.334
.37	−0.332	−0.329	−0.326	−0.324	−0.321	−0.319	−0.316	−0.313	−0.311	−0.308
.38	−0.305	−0.303	−0.300	−0.298	−0.295	−0.292	−0.290	−0.287	−0.284	−0.282
.39	−0.279	−0.277	−0.274	−0.271	−0.269	−0.266	−0.264	−0.261	−0.258	−0.256
.40	−0.253	−0.251	−0.248	−0.245	−0.243	−0.240	−0.238	−0.235	−0.233	−0.230
.41	−0.227	−0.225	−0.222	−0.220	−0.217	−0.215	−0.212	−0.209	−0.207	−0.204
.42	−0.202	−0.199	−0.197	−0.194	−0.192	−0.189	−0.186	−0.184	−0.181	−0.179

(Continued)

(Continued)

p	.000	.001	.002	.003	.004	.005	.006	.007	.008	.009
.43	−0.176	−0.174	−0.171	−0.169	−0.166	−0.164	−0.161	−0.158	−0.156	−0.153
.44	−0.151	−0.148	−0.146	−0.143	−0.141	−0.138	−0.136	−0.133	−0.131	−0.128
.45	−0.126	−0.123	−0.120	−0.118	−0.115	−0.113	−0.110	−0.108	−0.105	−0.103
.46	−0.100	−0.098	−0.095	−0.093	−0.090	−0.088	−0.085	−0.083	−0.080	−0.078
.47	−0.075	−0.073	−0.070	−0.068	−0.065	−0.063	−0.060	−0.058	−0.055	−0.053
.48	−0.050	−0.048	−0.045	−0.043	−0.040	−0.038	−0.035	−0.033	−0.030	−0.028
.49	−0.025	−0.023	−0.020	−0.018	−0.015	−0.013	−0.010	−0.008	−0.005	−0.003
.50	0.000	0.003	0.005	0.008	0.010	0.013	0.015	0.018	0.020	0.023

APPENDIX E
The Unit Normal Distribution

z-Score	Proportion in Tail	Probability Density
0.00	.5000	.3989
0.01	.4960	.3989
0.02	.4920	.3989
0.03	.4880	.3988
0.04	.4840	.3986
0.05	.4801	.3984
0.06	.4761	.3982
0.07	.4721	.3980
0.08	.4681	.3977
0.09	.4641	.3973
0.10	.4602	.3970
0.11	.4562	.3965
0.12	.4522	.3961
0.13	.4483	.3956
0.14	.4443	.3951
0.15	.4404	.3945
0.16	.4364	.3939
0.17	.4325	.3932
0.18	.4286	.3925
0.19	.4247	.3918

(Continued)

(Continued)

z-Score	Proportion in Tail	Probability Density
0.20	.4207	.3910
0.21	.4168	.3902
0.22	.4129	.3894
0.23	.4090	.3885
0.24	.4052	.3876
0.25	.4013	.3867
0.26	.3974	.3857
0.27	.3936	.3847
0.28	.3897	.3836
0.29	.3859	.3825
0.30	.3821	.3814
0.31	.3783	.3802
0.32	.3745	.3790
0.33	.3707	.3778
0.34	.3669	.3765
0.35	.3632	.3752
0.36	.3594	.3739
0.37	.3557	.3725
0.38	.3520	.3712
0.39	.3483	.3697
0.40	.3446	.3683
0.41	.3409	.3668
0.42	.3372	.3653
0.43	.3336	.3637
0.44	.3300	.3621
0.45	.3264	.3605
0.46	.3228	.3589
0.47	.3192	.3572
0.48	.3156	.3555
0.49	.3121	.3538

z-Score	Proportion in Tail	Probability Density
0.50	.3085	.3521
0.51	.3050	.3503
0.52	.3015	.3485
0.53	.2981	.3467
0.54	.2946	.3448
0.55	.2912	.3429
0.56	.2877	.3410
0.57	.2843	.3391
0.58	.2810	.3372
0.59	.2776	.3352
0.60	.2743	.3332
0.61	.2709	.3312
0.62	.2676	.3292
0.63	.2643	.3271
0.64	.2611	.3251
0.65	.2578	.3230
0.66	.2546	.3209
0.67	.2514	.3187
0.68	.2483	.3166
0.69	.2451	.3144
0.70	.2420	.3123
0.71	.2389	.3101
0.72	.2358	.3079
0.73	.2327	.3056
0.74	.2296	.3034
0.75	.2266	.3011
0.76	.2236	.2989
0.77	.2206	.2966
0.78	.2177	.2943

(Continued)

(Continued)

z-Score	Proportion in Tail	Probability Density
0.79	.2148	.2920
0.80	.2119	.2897
0.81	.2090	.2874
0.82	.2061	.2850
0.83	.2033	.2827
0.84	.2005	.2803
0.85	.1977	.2780
0.86	.1949	.2756
0.87	.1922	.2732
0.88	.1894	.2709
0.89	.1867	.2685
0.90	.1841	.2661
0.91	.1814	.2637
0.92	.1788	.2613
0.93	.1762	.2589
0.94	.1736	.2565
0.95	.1711	.2541
0.96	.1685	.2516
0.97	.1660	.2492
0.98	.1635	.2468
0.99	.1611	.2444
1.00	.1587	.2420
1.01	.1562	.2396
1.02	.1539	.2371
1.03	.1515	.2347
1.04	.1492	.2323
1.05	.1469	.2299
1.06	.1446	.2275
1.07	.1423	.2251
1.08	.1401	.2227

z-Score	Proportion in Tail	Probability Density
1.09	.1379	.2203
1.10	.1357	.2179
1.11	.1335	.2155
1.12	.1314	.2131
1.13	.1292	.2107
1.14	.1271	.2083
1.15	.1251	.2059
1.16	.1230	.2036
1.17	.1210	.2012
1.18	.1190	.1989
1.19	.1170	.1965
1.20	.1151	.1942
1.21	.1131	.1919
1.22	.1112	.1895
1.23	.1093	.1872
1.24	.1075	.1849
1.25	.1056	.1826
1.26	.1038	.1804
1.27	.1020	.1781
1.28	.1003	.1758
1.29	.0985	.1736
1.30	.0968	.1714
1.31	.0951	.1691
1.32	.0934	.1669
1.33	.0918	.1647
1.34	.0901	.1626
1.35	.0885	.1604
1.36	.0869	.1582
1.37	.0853	.1561

(Continued)

(Continued)

z-Score	Proportion in Tail	Probability Density
1.38	.0838	.1539
1.39	.0823	.1518
1.40	.0808	.1497
1.41	.0793	.1476
1.42	.0778	.1456
1.43	.0764	.1435
1.44	.0749	.1415
1.45	.0735	.1394
1.46	.0721	.1374
1.47	.0708	.1354
1.48	.0694	.1334
1.49	.0681	.1315
1.50	.0668	.1295
1.51	.0655	.1276
1.52	.0643	.1257
1.53	.0630	.1238
1.54	.0618	.1219
1.55	.0606	.1200
1.56	.0594	.1182
1.57	.0582	.1163
1.58	.0571	.1145
1.59	.0559	.1127
1.60	.0548	.1109
1.61	.0537	.1092
1.62	.0526	.1074
1.63	.0516	.1057
1.64	.0505	.1040
1.65	.0495	.1023
1.66	.0485	.1006
1.67	.0475	.0989

z-Score	Proportion in Tail	Probability Density
1.68	.0465	.0973
1.69	.0455	.0957
1.70	.0446	.0940
1.71	.0436	.0925
1.72	.0427	.0909
1.73	.0418	.0893
1.74	.0409	.0878
1.75	.0401	.0863
1.76	.0392	.0848
1.77	.0384	.0833
1.78	.0375	.0818
1.79	.0367	.0804
1.80	.0359	.0790
1.81	.0351	.0775
1.82	.0344	.0761
1.83	.0336	.0748
1.84	.0329	.0734
1.85	.0322	.0721
1.86	.0314	.0707
1.87	.0307	.0694
1.88	.0301	.0681
1.89	.0294	.0669
1.90	.0287	.0656
1.91	.0281	.0644
1.92	.0274	.0632
1.93	.0268	.0620
1.94	.0262	.0608
1.95	.0256	.0596
1.96	.0250	.0584

(Continued)

(Continued)

z-Score	Proportion in Tail	Probability Density
1.97	.0244	.0573
1.98	.0239	.0562
1.99	.0233	.0551
2.00	.0228	.0540
2.01	.0222	.0529
2.02	.0217	.0519
2.03	.0212	.0508
2.04	.0207	.0498
2.05	.0202	.0488
2.06	.0197	.0478
2.07	.0192	.0468
2.08	.0188	.0459
2.09	.0183	.0449
2.10	.0179	.0440
2.11	.0174	.0431
2.12	.0170	.0422
2.13	.0166	.0413
2.14	.0162	.0404
2.15	.0158	.0396
2.16	.0154	.0387
2.17	.0150	.0379
2.18	.0146	.0371
2.19	.0143	.0363
2.20	.0139	.0355
2.21	.0136	.0347
2.22	.0132	.0339
2.23	.0129	.0332
2.24	.0125	.0325
2.25	.0122	.0317
2.26	.0119	.0310

z-Score	Proportion in Tail	Probability Density
2.27	.0116	.0303
2.28	.0113	.0297
2.29	.0110	.0290
2.30	.0107	.0283
2.31	.0104	.0277
2.32	.0102	.0270
2.33	.0099	.0264
2.34	.0096	.0258
2.35	.0094	.0252
2.36	.0091	.0246
2.37	.0089	.0241
2.38	.0087	.0235
2.39	.0084	.0229
2.40	.0082	.0224
2.41	.0080	.0219
2.42	.0078	.0213
2.43	.0075	.0208
2.44	.0073	.0203
2.45	.0071	.0198
2.46	.0069	.0194
2.47	.0068	.0189
2.48	.0066	.0184
2.49	.0064	.0180
2.50	.0062	.0175
2.51	.0060	.0171
2.52	.0059	.0167
2.53	.0057	.0163
2.54	.0055	.0158
2.55	.0054	.0154

(Continued)

(Continued)

z-Score	Proportion in Tail	Probability Density
2.56	.0052	.0151
2.57	.0051	.0147
2.58	.0049	.0143
2.59	.0048	.0139
2.60	.0047	.0136
2.61	.0045	.0132
2.62	.0044	.0129
2.63	.0043	.0126
2.64	.0041	.0122
2.65	.0040	.0119
2.66	.0039	.0116
2.67	.0038	.0113
2.68	.0037	.0110
2.69	.0036	.0107
2.70	.0035	.0104
2.71	.0034	.0101
2.72	.0033	.0099
2.73	.0032	.0096
2.74	.0031	.0093
2.75	.0030	.0091
2.76	.0029	.0088
2.77	.0028	.0086
2.78	.0027	.0084
2.79	.0026	.0081
2.80	.0026	.0079
2.81	.0025	.0077
2.82	.0024	.0075
2.83	.0023	.0073
2.84	.0023	.0071
2.85	.0022	.0069

z-Score	Proportion in Tail	Probability Density
2.86	.0021	.0067
2.87	.0021	.0065
2.88	.0020	.0063
2.89	.0019	.0061
2.90	.0019	.0060
2.91	.0018	.0058
2.92	.0018	.0056
2.93	.0017	.0055
2.94	.0016	.0053
2.95	.0016	.0051
2.96	.0015	.0050
2.97	.0015	.0048
2.98	.0014	.0047
2.99	.0014	.0046
3.00	.0013	.0044
3.01	.0013	.0043
3.02	.0013	.0042
3.03	.0012	.0040
3.04	.0012	.0039
3.05	.0011	.0038
3.06	.0011	.0037
3.07	.0011	.0036
3.08	.0010	.0035
3.09	.0010	.0034
3.10	.0010	.0033
3.11	.0009	.0032
3.12	.0009	.0031
3.13	.0009	.0030
3.14	.0008	.0029

(Continued)

(Continued)

z-Score	Proportion in Tail	Probability Density
3.15	.0008	.0028
3.16	.0008	.0027
3.17	.0008	.0026
3.18	.0007	.0025
3.19	.0007	.0025
3.20	.0007	.0024
3.21	.0007	.0023
3.22	.0006	.0022
3.23	.0006	.0022
3.24	.0006	.0021
3.25	.0006	.0020
3.26	.0006	.0020
3.27	.0005	.0019
3.28	.0005	.0018
3.29	.0005	.0018
3.30	.0005	.0017
3.31	.0005	.0017
3.32	.0005	.0016
3.33	.0004	.0016
3.34	.0004	.0015
3.35	.0004	.0015
3.36	.0004	.0014
3.37	.0004	.0014
3.38	.0004	.0013
3.39	.0003	.0013
3.40	.0003	.0012
3.41	.0003	.0012
3.42	.0003	.0012
3.43	.0003	.0011
3.44	.0003	.0011

z-Score	Proportion in Tail	Probability Density
3.45	.0003	.0010
3.46	.0003	.0010
3.47	.0003	.0010
3.48	.0003	.0009
3.49	.0002	.0009
3.50	.0002	.0009
3.51	.0002	.0008
3.52	.0002	.0008
3.53	.0002	.0008
3.54	.0002	.0008
3.55	.0002	.0007
3.56	.0002	.0007
3.57	.0002	.0007
3.58	.0002	.0007
3.59	.0002	.0006
3.60	.0002	.0006
3.61	.0002	.0006
3.62	.0001	.0006
3.63	.0001	.0005
3.64	.0001	.0005
3.65	.0001	.0005
3.66	.0001	.0005
3.67	.0001	.0005
3.68	.0001	.0005
3.69	.0001	.0004
3.70	.0001	.0004
3.71	.0001	.0004
3.72	.0001	.0004
3.73	.0001	.0004

(Continued)

(Continued)

z-Score	Proportion in Tail	Probability Density
3.74	.0001	.0004
3.75	.0001	.0004
3.76	.0001	.0003
3.77	.0001	.0003
3.78	.0001	.0003
3.79	.0001	.0003
3.80	.0001	.0003
3.81	.0001	.0003
3.82	.0001	.0003
3.83	.0001	.0003
3.84	.0001	.0003
3.85	.0001	.0002
3.86	.0001	.0002
3.87	.0001	.0002
3.88	.0001	.0002
3.89	.0001	.0002
3.90	.0000	.0002
3.91	.0000	.0002
3.92	.0000	.0002
3.93	.0000	.0002
3.94	.0000	.0002
3.95	.0000	.0002
3.96	.0000	.0002
3.97	.0000	.0002
3.98	.0000	.0001
3.99	.0000	.0001
4.00	.0000	.0001

APPENDIX F
The *t*-Distribution

Degrees of Freedom	Proportion in Two Tails			
	.001	.02	.05	.1
	Proportion in One Tail			
	.005	.01	.025	.05
1	63.657	31.821	12.706	6.314
2	9.925	6.965	4.303	2.920
3	5.841	4.541	3.182	2.353
4	4.604	3.747	2.776	2.132
5	4.032	3.365	2.571	2.015
6	3.707	3.143	2.447	1.943
7	3.499	2.998	2.365	1.895
8	3.355	2.896	2.306	1.860
9	3.250	2.821	2.262	1.833
10	3.169	2.764	2.228	1.812
11	3.106	2.718	2.201	1.796
12	3.055	2.681	2.179	1.782
13	3.012	2.650	2.160	1.771
14	2.977	2.624	2.145	1.761
15	2.947	2.602	2.131	1.753
16	2.921	2.583	2.120	1.746
17	2.898	2.567	2.110	1.740
18	2.878	2.552	2.101	1.734

(Continued)

(Continued)

19	2.861	2.539	2.093	1.729
20	2.845	2.528	2.086	1.725
21	2.831	2.518	2.080	1.721
22	2.819	2.508	2.074	1.717
23	2.807	2.500	2.069	1.714
24	2.797	2.492	2.064	1.711
25	2.787	2.485	2.060	1.708
26	2.779	2.479	2.056	1.706
27	2.771	2.473	2.052	1.703
28	2.763	2.467	2.048	1.701
29	2.756	2.462	2.045	1.699
30	2.750	2.457	2.042	1.697
35	2.724	2.438	2.030	1.690
40	2.704	2.423	2.021	1.684
45	2.690	2.412	2.014	1.679
50	2.678	2.403	2.009	1.676
55	2.668	2.396	2.004	1.673
60	2.660	2.390	2.000	1.671
65	2.654	2.385	1.997	1.669
70	2.648	2.381	1.994	1.667
75	2.643	2.377	1.992	1.665
80	2.639	2.374	1.990	1.664
85	2.635	2.371	1.988	1.663
90	2.632	2.368	1.987	1.662
95	2.629	2.366	1.985	1.661
100	2.626	2.364	1.984	1.660
105	2.623	2.362	1.983	1.659
110	2.621	2.361	1.982	1.659
115	2.619	2.359	1.981	1.658
120	2.617	2.358	1.980	1.658
Infinite	2.576	2.326	1.960	1.645

APPENDIX G
The Fisher r to z_r Transformation

r	z_r		r	z_r
.01	0.010		.22	0.224
.02	0.020		.23	0.234
.03	0.030		.24	0.245
.04	0.040		.25	0.255
.05	0.050		.26	0.266
.06	0.060		.27	0.277
.07	0.070		.28	0.288
.08	0.080		.29	0.299
.09	0.090		.30	0.310
.10	0.100		.31	0.321
.11	0.110		.32	0.332
.12	0.121		.33	0.343
.13	0.131		.34	0.354
.14	0.141		.35	0.365
.15	0.151		.36	0.377
.16	0.161		.37	0.388
.17	0.172		.38	0.400
.18	0.182		.39	0.412
.19	0.192		.40	0.424
.20	0.203		.41	0.436
.21	0.213		.42	0.448

(Continued)

(Continued)

r	z_r	r	z_r
.43	0.460	.72	0.908
.44	0.472	.73	0.929
.45	0.485	.74	0.950
.46	0.497	.75	0.973
.47	0.510	.76	0.996
.48	0.523	.77	1.020
.49	0.536	.78	1.045
.50	0.549	.79	1.071
.51	0.563	.80	1.099
.52	0.576	.81	1.127
.53	0.590	.82	1.157
.54	0.604	.83	1.188
.55	0.618	.84	1.221
.56	0.633	.85	1.256
.57	0.648	.86	1.293
.58	0.662	.87	1.333
.59	0.678	.88	1.376
.60	0.693	.89	1.422
.61	0.709	.90	1.472
.62	0.725	.91	1.528
.63	0.741	.92	1.589
.64	0.758	.93	1.658
.65	0.775	.94	1.738
.66	0.793	.95	1.832
.67	0.811	.96	1.946
.68	0.829	.97	2.092
.69	0.848	.98	2.298
.70	0.867	.99	2.647
.71	0.887		

APPENDIX H
Critical Values for *F* With Alpha = .05

Degrees of Freedom for Denominator	Degrees of Freedom for Numerator											
	1	2	3	4	5	6	7	8	9	10	11	12
1	161.448	199.500	215.707	224.583	230.162	233.986	236.768	238.883	240.543	241.882	242.983	243.906
2	18.513	19.000	19.164	19.247	19.296	19.330	19.353	19.371	19.385	19.396	19.405	19.413
3	10.128	9.552	9.277	9.117	9.013	8.941	8.887	8.845	8.812	8.786	8.763	8.745
4	7.709	6.944	6.591	6.388	6.256	6.163	6.094	6.041	5.999	5.964	5.936	5.912
5	6.608	5.786	5.409	5.192	5.050	4.950	4.876	4.818	4.772	4.735	4.704	4.678
6	5.987	5.143	4.757	4.534	4.387	4.284	4.207	4.147	4.099	4.060	4.027	4.000
7	5.591	4.737	4.347	4.120	3.972	3.866	3.787	3.726	3.677	3.637	3.603	3.575
8	5.318	4.459	4.066	3.838	3.687	3.581	3.500	3.438	3.388	3.347	3.313	3.284
9	5.117	4.256	3.863	3.633	3.482	3.374	3.293	3.230	3.179	3.137	3.102	3.073
10	4.965	4.103	3.708	3.478	3.326	3.217	3.135	3.072	3.020	2.978	2.943	2.913
11	4.844	3.982	3.587	3.357	3.204	3.095	3.012	2.948	2.896	2.854	2.818	2.788

(Continued)

[Continued]

Degrees of Freedom for Denominator	Degrees of Freedom for Numerator											
12	4.747	3.885	3.490	3.259	3.106	2.996	2.913	2.849	2.796	2.753	2.717	2.687
13	4.667	3.806	3.411	3.179	3.025	2.915	2.832	2.767	2.714	2.671	2.635	2.604
14	4.600	3.739	3.344	3.112	2.958	2.848	2.764	2.699	2.646	2.602	2.565	2.534
15	4.543	3.682	3.287	3.056	2.901	2.790	2.707	2.641	2.588	2.544	2.507	2.475
16	4.494	3.634	3.239	3.007	2.852	2.741	2.657	2.591	2.538	2.494	2.456	2.425
17	4.451	3.592	3.197	2.965	2.810	2.699	2.614	2.548	2.494	2.450	2.413	2.381
18	4.414	3.555	3.160	2.928	2.773	2.661	2.577	2.510	2.456	2.412	2.374	2.342
19	4.381	3.522	3.127	2.895	2.740	2.628	2.544	2.477	2.423	2.378	2.340	2.308
20	4.351	3.493	3.098	2.866	2.711	2.599	2.514	2.447	2.393	2.348	2.310	2.278
22	4.301	3.443	3.049	2.817	2.661	2.549	2.464	2.397	2.342	2.297	2.259	2.226
24	4.260	3.403	3.009	2.776	2.621	2.508	2.423	2.355	2.300	2.255	2.216	2.183
26	4.225	3.369	2.975	2.743	2.587	2.474	2.388	2.321	2.265	2.220	2.181	2.148
28	4.196	3.340	2.947	2.714	2.558	2.445	2.359	2.291	2.236	2.190	2.151	2.118
30	4.171	3.316	2.922	2.690	2.534	2.421	2.334	2.266	2.211	2.165	2.126	2.092
40	4.085	3.232	2.839	2.606	2.449	2.336	2.249	2.180	2.124	2.077	2.038	2.003
60	4.001	3.150	2.758	2.525	2.368	2.254	2.167	2.097	2.040	1.993	1.952	1.917
120	3.920	3.072	2.680	2.447	2.290	2.175	2.087	2.016	1.959	1.910	1.869	1.834
200	3.888	3.041	2.650	2.417	2.259	2.144	2.056	1.985	1.927	1.878	1.837	1.801
infinite	3.841	2.996	2.605	2.372	2.214	2.099	2.010	1.938	1.880	1.831	1.789	1.752

APPENDIX I
The Chi Square Distribution

df	.99	.975	.95	.9	.75	.5	.25	.1	.05	.025	.01	.001
						Proportion in Right Tail						
1	0.00016	0.00098	0.004	0.016	0.102	0.455	1.323	2.706	3.841	5.024	6.635	10.828
2	0.020	0.051	0.103	0.211	0.575	1.386	2.773	4.605	5.991	7.378	9.210	13.816
3	0.115	0.216	0.352	0.584	1.213	2.366	4.108	6.251	7.815	9.348	11.345	16.266
4	0.297	0.484	0.711	1.064	1.923	3.357	5.385	7.779	9.488	11.143	13.277	18.467
5	0.554	0.831	1.145	1.610	2.675	4.351	6.626	9.236	11.071	12.833	15.086	20.515
6	0.872	1.237	1.635	2.204	3.455	5.348	7.841	10.645	12.592	14.449	16.812	22.458
7	1.239	1.690	2.167	2.833	4.255	6.346	9.037	12.017	14.067	16.013	18.475	24.322
8	1.646	2.180	2.733	3.490	5.071	7.344	10.219	13.362	15.507	17.535	20.090	26.124
9	2.088	2.700	3.325	4.168	5.899	8.343	11.389	14.684	16.919	19.023	21.666	27.877
10	2.558	3.247	3.940	4.865	6.737	9.342	12.549	15.987	18.307	20.483	23.209	29.588
11	3.053	3.816	4.575	5.578	7.584	10.341	13.701	17.275	19.675	21.920	24.725	31.264
12	3.571	4.404	5.226	6.304	8.438	11.340	14.845	18.549	21.026	23.337	26.217	32.909
13	4.107	5.009	5.892	7.042	9.299	12.340	15.984	19.812	22.362	24.736	27.688	34.528
14	4.660	5.629	6.571	7.790	10.165	13.339	17.117	21.064	23.685	26.119	29.141	36.123

(Continued)

[Continued]

df	Proportion in Right Tail											
	.99	.975	.95	.9	.75	.5	.25	.1	.05	.025	.01	.001
15	5.229	6.262	7.261	8.547	11.037	14.339	18.245	22.307	24.996	27.488	30.578	37.697
16	5.812	6.908	7.962	9.312	11.912	15.339	19.369	23.542	26.296	28.845	32.000	39.252
17	6.408	7.564	8.672	10.085	12.792	16.338	20.489	24.769	27.587	30.191	33.409	40.790
18	7.015	8.231	9.390	10.865	13.675	17.338	21.605	25.989	28.869	31.526	34.805	42.312
19	7.633	8.907	10.117	11.651	14.562	18.338	22.718	27.204	30.144	32.852	36.191	43.820
20	8.260	9.591	10.851	12.443	15.452	19.337	23.828	28.412	31.410	34.170	37.566	45.315
21	8.897	10.283	11.591	13.240	16.344	20.337	24.935	29.615	32.671	35.479	38.932	46.797
22	9.542	10.982	12.338	14.041	17.240	21.337	26.039	30.813	33.924	36.781	40.289	48.268
23	10.196	11.689	13.091	14.848	18.137	22.337	27.141	32.007	35.172	38.076	41.638	49.728
24	10.856	12.401	13.848	15.659	19.037	23.337	28.241	33.196	36.415	39.364	42.980	51.179
25	11.524	13.120	14.611	16.473	19.939	24.337	29.339	34.382	37.652	40.646	44.314	52.620
26	12.198	13.844	15.379	17.292	20.843	25.336	30.435	35.563	38.885	41.923	45.642	54.052
27	12.879	14.573	16.151	18.114	21.749	26.336	31.528	36.741	40.113	43.195	46.963	55.476
28	13.565	15.308	16.928	18.939	22.657	27.336	32.620	37.916	41.337	44.461	48.278	56.892
29	14.256	16.047	17.708	19.768	23.567	28.336	33.711	39.087	42.557	45.722	49.588	58.301
30	14.953	16.791	18.493	20.599	24.478	29.336	34.800	40.256	43.773	46.979	50.892	59.703
40	22.164	24.433	26.509	29.051	33.660	39.335	45.616	51.805	55.758	59.342	63.691	73.402
60	37.485	40.482	43.188	46.459	52.294	59.335	66.981	74.397	79.082	83.298	88.379	99.607
120	86.923	91.573	95.705	100.624	109.220	119.334	130.055	140.233	146.567	152.211	158.950	173.617

REFERENCES

Abelson, R. P. (1985). A variance explanation paradox: When a little is a lot. *Psychological Bulletin, 97*, 129–133.

Algina, J., Keselman, H. J., & Penfield, R. D. (2005). An alternative to Cohen's standardized mean difference effect size: A robust parameter and confidence interval in the two independent groups case. *Psychological Methods, 10*, 317–328.

Anderson, C. A., & Bushman, B. J. (2002). Human aggression. *Annual Review of Psychology, 53*, 27–51.

Anderson, C. A., Deuser, W. E., & DeNeve, K. (1995). Hot temperatures, hostile affect, hostile cognition, and arousal: Tests of a general model of affective aggression. *Personality and Social Psychology Bulletin, 21*, 434–448.

Anderson, C. A., & Huesmann, L. R. (2003). Human aggression: A social-cognitive view. In M. A. Hogg & J. Cooper (Eds.), *The Sage handbook of social psychology* (pp. 296–323). London, UK: SAGE.

Anscombe, F. J. (1973). Graphs in statistical analysis. *The American Statistician, 27*, 17–21.

Antonak, R. F., & Harth, R. (1994). Psychometric analysis and revision of the Mental Retardation Attitude Inventory. *Mental Retardation, 32*, 272–280.

Aquino, K., & Thau, S. (2009). Workplace victimization: Aggression from the target's perspective. *Annual Review of Psychology, 60*, 717–741.

Archer, J., & Coyne, S. M. (2005). An integrated review of indirect, relational, and social aggression. *Personality and Social Psychology Review, 9*, 212–230.

Asch, S. (1951). Effects of group pressure upon the modification and distortion of judgments. In H. Guetzkow (Ed.), *Groups, leadership and men* (pp. 177–190). Pittsburgh, PA: Carnegie Press.

Bakan, D. (1966). The test of significance in psychological research. *Psychological Bulletin, 66*, 423–437.

Barlett, C. P. (2015). Anonymously hurting others online: The effect of anonymity on cyberbullying frequency. *Psychology of Popular Media Culture, 4*, 70–79.

Barlett, C. P., & Gentile, D. A. (2012). Attacking others online: The formation of cyberbullying in late adolescence. *Psychology of Popular Media Culture, 1*, 123–135.

Bettencourt, B., Talley, A., Benjamin, A. J., & Valentine, J. (2006). Personality and aggressive behavior under provoking and neutral conditions: A meta-analytic review. *Psychological Bulletin, 132*, 751–777.

Bravais, A. (1846). Analyse mathématique sur les probabilités des erreurs de situation d'un point [Mathematical analysis on the probability of errors of a point]. *Mémoires présentés par divers savants à l'Académie royale des sciences de l'Institut de France, 9*, 255–332.

Buss, D. M., & Schmitt, D. P. (1993). Sexual strategies theory: An evolutionary perspective on human mating. *Psychological Review, 100*, 204–232.

Carifio, J., & Perla, R. J. (2007). Ten common misunderstandings, misconceptions, persistent myths and urban legends about Likert scales and Likert response formats and their antidotes. *Journal of Social Sciences, 3*, 106–116.

Chambers, J. M., Cleveland, W. S., Kleiner, B., & Tukey, P. A. (1983). *Graphical methods for data analysis*. Boston, MA: Duxbury.

Cochran, W. G. (1954). Some methods for strengthening the common χ^2 tests. *Biometrics, 10*, 417–451.

Cohen, J. (1962). A power primer. *Psychological Bulletin, 112*, 155–159.

Cohen, J. (1969). *Statistical power analysis for the behavioral sciences.* New York, NY: Academic Press.

Cohen, J. (1988). *Statistical power analysis for the behavioral sciences* (2nd ed.). Hillside, NJ: Erlbaum.

Conover, W. J. (1980). *Practical nonparametric statistics* (2nd ed.). New York, NY: Wiley.

Cowles, M. (2001). *Statistics in psychology: An historical perspective* (2nd ed.). Mawwah, NJ: Lawrence Erlbaum Associates.

Cumming, G., & Finch, S. (2005) Inference by eye: Confidence intervals and how to read pictures of data. *American Psychologist, 60*, 170–180.

Cumming, G., & Maillardet, R. (2006). Confidence intervals and replication: Where will the next mean fall? *Psychological Methods, 11*, 217–227.

Cumming, G., Williams, J., & Fidler, F. (2004). Replication, and researchers' understanding of confidence intervals and standard error bars. *Understanding Statistics, 3*, 299–311.

Dodge, K. A., Coie, J. D., & Lynam, D. (2006). Aggression and antisocial behavior in youth. In W. Damon & R. M. Lerner (Eds.), *Handbook of child psychology* (pp. 437–472). Hoboken, NJ: John Wiley & Sons.

Dugard, P., File, P., & Todman, J. (2012). *Single-case and small-n experimental designs: A practical guide to randomization tests* (2nd ed.). New York, NY: Routledge.

Edgington, E. S., & Onghena, P. (2007). *Randomization tests* (4th ed.). Boca Raton, FL: Chapman Hall/CRC.

Efron, B. (1979a). Bootstrap methods: Another look at the jackknife. *Annals of Statistics, 7,* 1–26.

Efron, B. (1979b). Computers and the theory of statistics: Thinking the unthinkable. *Society for Industrial and Applied Mathematics Review, 21,* 460–480.

Efron, B., & Gong, G. (1983). A leisurely look at the bootstrap, the jackknife, and cross-validation. *American Statistician, 37,* 36–48.

Efron, B., & Tibhirani, R. (1986). Bootstrap methods for standard errors, confidence interval, and other measures of statistical accuracy. *Statistical Science, 1,* 54–75.

Emerson, J. D., & Stoto, M. A. (1983). Transforming data. In D. C. Hoaglin, F. Mosteller, & J. W. Tukey (Eds.), *Understanding robust and exploratory data analysis* (pp. 97–128). New York, NY: Wiley.

Estes, W. K. (1977). On the communication of information by displays of standard errors and confidence intervals. *Psychonomic Bulletin & Review, 4,* 330–341.

Fisher, R. A. (1915). Frequency distribution of the values of the correlation coefficient in samples from an indefinitely large population. *Biometrika, 10,* 507–521.

Fisher, R. A. (1925). *Statistical methods for research workers.* Edinburgh, UK: Oliver and Boyd.

Fisher, R. A. (1934). *Statistical methods for research workers* (5th ed.). Edinburgh, UK: Oliver & Boyd.

Fisher, R. A. (1935a). *The design of experiments.* London, UK: Oliver and Boyd.

Fisher, R. A. (1935b). The logic of inductive inference. *Journal of the Royal Statistical Society, 98,* 39–54.

Fisher, R. A. (1956). *Statistical methods and scientific inference.* Edinburgh, UK: Oliver & Boyd.

Forbes, C., Evans, M., Hastings, N., & Peacock, B. (2011). *Statistical distributions* (4th ed.). Hoboken, NJ: Wiley.

Friedmann, H. L. (1968). Magnitude of experimental effect and a table for its rapid estimation. *Psychological Bulletin, 70,* 245–251.

Gaito, J. (1980). Measurement scales and statistics: Resurgence of an old misconception. *Psychological Bulletin, 87,* 564–567.

Galton, F. (1888). Co-relations and their measurement, chiefly from anthropometric data. *Proceedings of the Royal Society, 45,* 135–145.

Gentile, D. A., & Sesma, A. (2003). Developmental approaches to understanding media effects on individuals. In D. A. Gentile (Ed.), *Media violence and children* (pp. 19–37). Westport, CT: Praeger.

Glass, G. V., & Hakstian, R. A. (1969). Measures of association in comparative experiments: Their development and interpretation. *American Educational Research Journal, 6,* 403–414.

Goodall, C. (1983). M-estimators of location: An outline of the theory. In D. C. Hoaglin, F. Mosteller, & J. W. Tukey (Eds.), *Understanding robust and exploratory data analysis* (pp. 339–403). New York, NY: Wiley.

Hampel, F. R. (1973). Robust estimation: A condensed partial survey. *Zeitschrift für Wahrscheinlichkeitstheorie und Verwandte Gebiete, 27,* 87–104.

Harrell, F. E., & Davis, C. E. (1982). A new distribution-free quantile estimator. *Biometrika, 69,* 635–640.

Hays, W. L. (1963). *Statistics for psychologists.* New York, NY: Holt.

Hedges, L. V. (1982). Estimating effect size from a series of independent experiments. *Psychological Bulletin, 92,* 490–499.

Hill, M., & Dixon, W. J. (1982). Robustness in real life: A study of clinical laboratory data. *Biometrics, 38,* 377–396.

Hoaglin, D. C. (1985). Using quantile to study shape. In D. C. Hoaglin, F. Mosteller, & J. W. Tukey (Eds.), *Exploring data tables, trends, and shapes* (pp. 417–460). New York, NY: Wiley.

Hoenig, J. M., & Heisey, D. M. (2001). The abuse of power: The pervasive fallacy of power calculations for data analysis. *The American Statistician, 55,* 19–24.

Hubbard, R. (2004). Alphabet soup. Blurring the distinction between *p*'s and α's in psychological research. *Theory & Psychology, 14,* 295–327.

Hubbard, R., & Bayarri, M. J. (2003). Confusion over measures of evidence (*p*'s) versus errors (α's) in classical statistical testing. *The American Statistician, 57,* 171–178.

Huberty, C. J. (1993). Historical origins of statistical testing practices: The treatment of Fisher versus Neyman–Pearson views in textbooks. *Journal of Experimental Education, 61,* 317–333.

Irwin, J. O. (1935). Tests of significance for differences between percentages based on small numbers, *Metron, 12,* 83–94.

Kagan, J., & Moss, H. A. (1959). Parental correlates of child's IQ and height: A cross-validation of the Berkeley Growth Study results. *Child Development, 30,* 325–332.

Kelley, T. L. (1935). An unbiased correlation ratio measure. *Proceedings of the National Academy of Sciences, 21,* 554–559.

Kerr, N. L. (1998). HARKing: Hypothesizing after the results are known. *Personality and Social Psychology Review, 2,* 196–217.

Krosnick, J. A., Boninger, D. S., Chuang, Y. C., Berent, M. K., & Carnot, C. G. (1993). Attitude strength: One construct or many related constructs? *Journal of Personality and Social Psychology, 65,* 1132–1151.

Lane, D. M., & Sándor, A. (2009). Designing better graphs by including distributional information and integrating words, numbers, and images. *Psychological Methods, 14,* 239–257.

Lehmann, E. L. (1999). *Elements of large-sample theory.* New York, NY: Springer.

Lenth, R. V. (2001). Some practical guidelines for effective sample size determination. *The American Statistician, 55,* 187–193.

Lenth, R. V. (2007). *Post hoc power: Tables and commentary.* Retrieved from https://stat.uiowa.edu/sites/stat.uiowa.edu/files/techrep/tr378.pdf

Lilliefors, H. W. (1967). On the Kolmogorov–Smirnov test for normality with mean and variance unknown. *Journal of the American Statistical Association, 62,* 399–402.

Lord, F. M. (1953). On the statistical treatment of football numbers. *American Psychologist, 8,* 750–751.

Lunneborg, C. E. (1985). Estimating the correlation coefficient: The bootstrap approach. *Psychological Bulletin, 98,* 209–215.

Mayer, G. R. (1995). Preventing antisocial behavior in the schools. *Journal of Applied Behavioral Analysis, 28,* 467–478.

McCullough, M. E., Bellah, C. G., Kilpatrick, S. D., & Johnson, J. L. (2001). Vengefulness: Relationships with forgiveness, rumination, well-being, and the Big Five. *Personality and Social Psychology Bulletin, 27,* 601–610.

McGrath, R. E., & Meyer, G. J. (2006). When effect sizes disagree: The case of *r* and *d. Psychological Methods, 11,* 386–401.

McManus, J. L., Feyes, K. J., & Saucier, D. A. (2011). Knowledge and contact as predictors of attitudes toward individuals with intellectual disabilities. *Journal of Social and Personal Relationships, 28,* 579–590.

Micceri, T. (1989). The unicorn, the normal curve, and other improbable creatures. *Psychological Bulletin, 105,* 156–166.

Miller, S. S., & Saucier, D. A. (2016a). Individual differences in the propensity to make attributions to prejudice. *Group Processes and Intergroup Relations.* Advance online publication. doi: 10.1177/1368430216674342.

Miller, S. S., & Saucier, D. A. (2016b). *Interpreting the meaning of subversive and disparaging racial humor.* Manuscript in preparation.

Neyman, J. (1941). Fiducial argument and the theory of confidence intervals. *Biometrika, 32,* 128–150.

Neyman, J., & Pearson, E. S. (1928a). On the use and interpretation of certain test criteria for purposes of statistical inference. Part I. *Biometrika, 20A,* 175–240.

Neyman, J., & Pearson, E. S. (1928b). On the use and interpretation of certain test criteria for purposes of statistical inference. Part II. *Biometrika, 20A,* 263–294.

Norman, G. (2010). Likert scales, levels of measurement and the "laws" of statistics. *Advances in Health Sciences Education, 15,* 625–632.

O'Dea, C. J., Miller, S. S., & Saucier, D. A. (2016). *"What if they think I'm racist?" Situational factors that affect decisions to discuss diversity initiatives.* Manuscript in preparation.

Olkin, I., & Pratt, J. W. (1958). Unbiased estimation of certain correlation coefficients. *The Annals of Mathematical Statistics, 29,* 201–211.

Pedersen, W. C., Miller, L, C., Putcha-Bhagavatula, A. D., & Yang, Y. (2002). Evolved sex differences in the number of partners desired? The long and the short of it. *Psychological Science, 13*, 157–161.

Pollard, P., & Richardson, J. T. E. (1987). On the probability of making type I errors. *Psychological Bulletin, 102*, 159–163.

Prentice, D. A., & Miller, D. T. (1992). When small effects are impressive. *Psychological Bulletin, 112*, 160–164.

Pritschet, L., Powell, D., & Horne, Z. (2016). Marginally significant effects as evidence for hypotheses: Changing attitudes over four decades. *Psychological Science, 27*, 1036–1042.

Roid, G. H. (2003). *Stanford-Binet Intelligence Scales* (*SB5*; 5th ed.). Itasca, IL: Riverside.

Rosnow, R. L., & Rosenthal, R. (1989). Statistical procedures and the justification of knowledge in psychological science. *American Psychologist, 44*, 1276–1284.

Satterthwaite, F. E. (1946). An approximate distribution of estimates of variance components. *Biometrics Bulletin, 2*, 110–114.

Saucier, D. A., O'Dea, C. J., & Strain, M. L. (2016). The bad, the good, the misunderstood: The social effects of racial humor. *Translational Issues in Psychological Research, 2*, 75–85.

Saucier, D. A., Strain, M. L., Miller, S. S., Till, D. F., & O'Dea, C. J. (2016). *"What do you call a Black guy who flies a plane?" Disparagement and confrontation in the context of racial humor.* Manuscript in preparation.

Saucier, D. A., Webster, R. J., Hoffman, B. H., & Strain, M. L. (2014). Social vigilantism and reported use of strategies to resist persuasion.

Personality and Individual Differences, 70, 120–125.

Senn, S. (2011). Francis Galton and regression to the mean. *Significance, 8*, 124–126.

Shapiro, S. S., & Wilk, M. B. (1965). An analysis of variance test for normality (complete samples). *Biometrika, 52*, 591–611.

Sharp, L. B., Sheeley, W., & Saucier, D. A. (2004, January). *How racism for you makes you feel worse than racism against you: The affective reactions to prejudicial statements made by same versus different race individuals.* Poster presented at the annual meeting of the Society for Personality and Social Psychology, Austin, TX.

Siegel, S., & Castellan, N. J. (1988). *Nonparametric statistics for the behavioral sciences.* New York, NY: McGraw Hill.

Simcha-Fagen, O., Langner, T., Gersten, J., & Eisenberg, J. (1975). *Violent and antisocial behavior: A longitudinal study of urban youth* (OCD-CB-480). Unpublished manuscript. Washington DC: US Office of Child Development.

Smith, M. L., & Glass, G. V. (1977). Meta-analysis of psychotherapy outcome studies. *American Psychologist, 32*, 752–760.

Stevens, S. S. (1946). On the theory of scales of measurement. *Science, 103*, 677–680.

Strain, M. L., Martens, A. L., & Saucier, D. A. (2016). "Rape is the new black": Humor's potential for reinforcing and subverting rape culture. *Translational Issues in Psychological Research, 2*, 86–95.

Stuckless, N. &, Goranson, R. (1992). The Vengeance Scale: Development of a measure of attitudes toward revenge. *Journal of Social Behavior & Personality, 7*, 25–42.

Tajfel, H., Billig, M., Bundy, R., & Flament, C. (1971). Social categorization and intergroup behavior. *European Journal of Social Psychology, 1*, 149–178.

Tate, R. F. (1955). Applications of correlation models for biserial data. *Journal of the American Statistical Association, 50*, 1078–1095.

Thompson, B. (2001). Significance, effect sizes, stepwise methods, and other issues: Strong arguments move the field. *Journal of Experimental Education, 70*, 80–93.

Tokunga, R. S. (2010). Following you home from school: A critical review and synthesis of research on cyberbullying victimization. *Computers in Human Behavior, 26*, 277–287.

Townsend, J. T., & Ashby, F. G. (1984). Measurement scales and statistics: The misconception misconceived. *Psychological Bulletin, 96*, 394–401.

Tukey, J. W. (1960). A survey of sampling from contaminated distributions. In I. Olkin, S. G. Ghurye, W. Hoeffding, W. G. Madow, & H. B. Mann (Eds.), *Contributions to probability and statistics* (pp. 448–485). Stanford, CA: Stanford University Press.

Tukey, J. W. (1977). *Exploratory data analysis.* Reading, MA: Addison-Wesley.

Wechsler, D. (1981). *Wechsler Adult Intelligence Scale–Revised (WAIS-R).* New York, NY: Psychological Corporation.

Welch, B. L. (1947). The generalization of 'Student's' problem when several different population variances are involved. *Biometrika, 34*, 28–35.

Whitley, B. E., Jr., & Kite, M. E. (2010). *The psychology of prejudice and discrimination* (2nd ed.). Belmont, CA: Wadsworth.

Wilcox, R. R. (1998). A note on the Theil–Sen Regression Estimator when the regressor is random and the error term is heteroscedastic. *Biometrical Journal, 40*, 261–268.

Wilcox, R. R. (2003). *Applying contemporary statistical techniques*. San Diego, CA: Academic Press.

Wilcox, R. R. (2010). *Fundamentals of modern statistical methods: Substantially improving power and accuracy* (2nd ed.). New York, NY: Springer.

Wilcox, R. R. (2012). *Introduction to robust estimation and hypothesis testing* (3rd ed.). Amsterdam, The Netherlands: Academic Press.

Willerman, L., Schultz, R., Rutledge, J. N., & Bigler, E. (1991). In vivo brain size and intelligence. *Intelligence, 15*, 223–228.

Yates, F. (1934). Contingency table involving small numbers and the $\chi 2$ test. *Supplement to the Journal of the Royal Statistical Society, 1*, 217–235.

Yuen, K. K. (1974). The two-sample trimmed t for unequal population variances. *Biometrika, 61*, 165–170.

INDEX